Variationist Sociolinguistics

Language in Society

GENERAL EDITOR

Peter Trudgill, Chair of English Linguistics,
University of Fribourg

ADVISORY EDITORS

J. K. Chambers, Professor of Linguistics,
University of Toronto

Ralph Fasold, Professor of Linguistics,
Georgetown University

William Labov, Professor of Linguistics,
University of Pennsylvania

Lesley Milroy, Professor of Linguistics,
University of Michigan, Ann Arbor

Launched in 1980, *Language in Society* is now
established as probably the premiere series in the
broad field of sociolinguistics, dialectology, and
variation studies. The series includes both
textbooks and monographs by Ralph Fasold,
Suzanne Romaine, Peter Trudgill, Lesley Milroy,
Michael Stubbs, and other leading researchers.

Variationist Sociolinguistics

CHANGE, OBSERVATION, INTERPRETATION

Sali A. Tagliamonte

WILEY-BLACKWELL

A John Wiley & Sons, Ltd., Publication

Blackwell Publishing was acquired by John Wiley & Sons in February 2007. Blackwell's publishing program has been merged with Wiley's global Scientific, Technical, and Medical business to form Wiley-Blackwell.

Registered Office
John Wiley & Sons Ltd, The Atrium, Southern Gate, Chichester, West Sussex, PO19 8SQ, UK

Editorial Offices
350 Main Street, Malden, MA 02148-5020, USA
9600 Garsington Road, Oxford, OX4 2DQ, UK
The Atrium, Southern Gate, Chichester, West Sussex, PO19 8SQ, UK

For details of our global editorial offices, for customer services, and for information about how to apply for permission to reuse the copyright material in this book please see our website at www.wiley.com/wiley-blackwell.

The right of Sali A. Tagliamonte to be identified as the author of this work has been asserted in accordance with the UK Copyright, Designs and Patents Act 1988.

Library of Congress Cataloging-in-Publication Data
Tagliamonte, Sali.
Variationist sociolinguistics : change, observation, interpretation / Sali A. Tagliamonte.
    p.   cm.
  Includes bibliographical references and index.
ISBN 978-1-4051-3590-0 (alk. paper) – ISBN 978-1-4051-3591-7 (pbk. : alk. paper)
1. Language and languages–Variation.   2. Sociolinguistics–Research.   I. Title.
  P120.V37T348 2012
  306.44–dc22
                                    2011010578
A catalogue record for this book is available from the British Library.

This book is published in the following electronic formats: ePDFs 9781444344448; Wiley Online Library 9781444344479; ePub 9781444344455; mobi: 9781444344462.

Set in 10/12pt Ehrhardt by SPi Publisher Services, Pondicherry, India
Printed in Malaysia by Ho Printing (M) Sdn Bhd

1   2012

Contents

Acknowledgments

A person only ever stands somewhere along the ladder of life. I am indebted to many great minds and generous spirits who have helped me in my work. My students, my mentors, my colleagues, my friends, they are often the same people with no clear distinction among them. This is one of the truly gratifying aspects of doing sociolinguistics – you become part of a social network, a practice, a community.

My students have always been my best critics. Let them know that each one of them has helped immeasurably with this book. Derek Denis, Bridget Jankowski, Dylan Uscher, and Cathleen Waters: every question we considered over the past few years has made its way into these pages. My students in LIN1256, Advanced Language Variation and Change, January–April 2011 deserve special mention for their critical input to the prepublication version of the manuscript. Marisa Brook, Julian Brooke, Matthew Gardner, Heidi Haefale, Chris Harvey, Madeline Shellgren, and Jim Smith have shown me, yet again, how much teaching embeds learning.

My past has also woven its way through the chapters, as I have returned to my early research to integrate the present state of the field with its foundations. I am blessed by having been mentored by some of the greatest contributors to the field. Shana Poplack, David Sankoff, Jack Chambers, Peter Trudgill, and Jenny Cheshire: this book exists only because I have been able to stand on your shoulders. I am also lucky to have had a knowledgeable and attentive set of critics who scoured the draft manuscript and offered their insights, including four anonymous Wiley-Blackwell reviewers, a savvy team of Wiley editors, my new neighbour Victor Kuperman, my pal Paul Foulkes, and even the General Editor, Peter Trudgill, himself.

No field advances without change. Over the last ten years statistical methods have undergone a veritable renaissance. Chapter 5 evolved over several years of consultation on the state of the art in statistical methods in Variationist Sociolinguistics. I am thankful to Harald Baayen, Daniel Ezra Johnson, and John Paolillo for helping me in my ongoing efforts to model linguistic variation and change in ways that are not only insightful, but also statistically sound.

A sociolinguist is never alone in their research. I am lucky to have had a superb group of lab assistants and project coordinators. The latest, Michael Ritter, has the astonishing ability to manage, organize, interview, transcribe, extract, correct, code, copy, copy-edit, run *Goldvarb, R, and Ant-Conc*, and everything else I need doing.

I am immensely proud of my own academic progeny who have become my friends; Jen Smith and Alex D'Arcy, where would I be without your ongoing collaborations, savvy insights, and unabashed prodding? My wonderful colleagues Elizabeth Cowper, Elaine Gold, Alana Johns, Keren Rice, and Diane Massam: you have been exuberance, friendship, and community to me since I arrived at UofT in 2001. I have found in your model guidance and sanity. My confidant and best drinking buddy Anthony Warner listens and advises and tells me when I am being silly (this is a more important quality than you might think).

Since my last book, three of my children have become teenagers, the youngest one has started primary school, and I have gained a stepson in the early years of his professional life. This is a great learning ground for a sociolinguist. Dazzian, Freya, Shaman, Tara, and Adrian have taught me much of what I know about age grading, innovation, and incrementation. I am so very thankful to be part of the perpetual state of variation and change, love and commotion we live in. And to Duncan, who is the bedrock of my life, I am eternally grateful to have found in one man, husband, lover, gardener, and friend.

Finally, I would like to thank my mom. What I have been able to accomplish in my life was fostered in the love and support and many other intangible gifts she gave me.

Foreword

My grandparents lived in a small town in Southern Ontario. It was a farming hamlet in one of the oldest settled areas of Ontario, Canada, called Maple Station. They owned the general store, gas station, and post office. The store was always filled with locals. When I visited as a child, I would race to the store every time someone came in, trailing behind the adults to eavesdrop on the conversations. In the evenings, my great-aunts and -uncles would visit. Coming from farming stock, the families were huge. My grandfather had eight brothers and sisters and my grandmother had nine. There were people around all the time. They often talked long into the evening, playing Euchre or Crib. I can still hear the lilting cadence of those voices in my mind. This was a world of regularized past participles, double negation, all kinds of variation in vowels and diphthongs, and strange words and expressions. Little did I know of all that then! At the time, I only listened and marveled at how different they sounded.

My mother, who had grown up in that world, became a teacher, a specialist in early childhood education. Yet there were always aspects of her speech that were very different from the Canadian norms in my surroundings. When she talked to my grandparents or my aunts and uncles (her brother and sisters) on the phone, her voice would shift back toward the speech patterns I heard in Maple Station. Sometimes, when telling stories, I would even hear her use the occasional *I says* or *He come*. And when she quoted anyone in her family, her voice always changed.

While I sound just like any other Canadian, there are still parts of my speech that reflect my mother's vernacular, words like "wee" for "small", expressions like "it's a good job" for "it's a good thing". Even today, when my children make fun of some of the words I use and my pronunciations ("tiger" [tægr], "Saturday" [sɛrde:], "southern" [sʌwðrn]) I blame my old-line Southern Ontario roots.

These are the realities of language variation and change. Our life histories are a study of continuities and changes, of ancestry and origins, of time and space, of uncommon similarities across time and remarkable differences across generation gaps. Our heritage follows us wherever we go and throughout our lives. For me, the world came alive when I discovered sociolinguistics because it made my experience make sense. The linguistic difference and variety around me had regularity and meaning, system and explanation. May this book make sociolinguistics – and the world of variation around you – more comprehensible to you.

Sali A. Tagliamonte
Toronto, Ontario

Series Editor's Preface

It is not often that one looks at a book and says "this is *it*." That, however, is precisely what I found myself thinking when I first received the text of Sali Tagliamonte's *Sociolinguistics: Variation, Change and Interpretation*. This *really is it* – this is the book that linguistic variation theory has been waiting for. It has not, however, been waiting too long. Now is exactly the right time for this book to appear; and, I like to think, the Blackwell's *Language in Society* series is exactly the right place for it to appear. The study of "Language Variation and Change" (LVC) has been with us now, as Professor Tagliamonte says, for about 40 years. My own first encounter with the field, at that time still without a name, was at what I believe to be the first ever academic meeting devoted to the topic, the Colloquium on New Ways of Analysing Variation in English held at Georgetown University in the USA in October 1972. This turned out to be the first of a series of annual NWAV conferences which continue to be held to this day – though without the word "English" in the title now – and indeed at the time of this writing, the next meeting is going to be the fortieth. I don't know what Sali was doing in October 1972, but she was certainly not nearly old enough to be at the meeting. In spite of her comparative youth, however, we are very grateful that it has fallen to her to produce in this book a distillation of all the advances that have been made and all the wisdom that has accrued in our now mature field over the last four decades. She is perhaps uniquely qualified – in terms of her erudition, her field-work experience, her analytical innovations, and the large amounts of data and the wide range of language varieties she has worked on – to write the first book which is truly an introduction to LVC, a summary of its main goals and achievements, and a springboard for future progress. She has done this, moreover, in a masterly fashion: not only will the reader of this volume learn how work in LVC is done, they will also learn why we do it, and what the benefits are. All languages are variable – variability is an essential component of human language. But it is only in the last 40 years that we have fully understood the degree to which this is so, have investigated the patterning in which variation is involved, and have developed the concepts and techniques for dealing with it – developments which Sali herself has played a very major role in advancing. As this book shows, any linguistic work which attempts to shed light on the nature of the human language faculty and on the nature of linguistic change, without taking account of language's inherent variability, will inevitably fall short.

Peter Trudgill

Preface

What this Book is About

This is a book about the fascinating, intricate and remarkable relationship between language and society, a field that is typically called sociolinguistics. However, this is not a book about everything in sociolinguistics because sociolinguistics is a very diverse and wide-ranging discipline. Taken broadly, sociolinguistics involves studying the interaction of language, culture, and society. This book cannot do all that. Instead, I focus on the type of sociolinguistics that has come to be known as Variationist Sociolinguistics, or "Language Variation and Change" (LVC). This is the type of sociolinguistics I have been practicing in my own research since 1981. This branch of the sociolinguistics tree is known for its focus on language change as well as its quantitative methods and its concern for accountable methodology. It is the study of linguistic variation and change through observation and interpretation.

Variationist Sociolinguistics deals with systematic and inherent variation in language, both in the present (synchrony) and in the past (diachrony). The goal of LVC studies is to understand the mechanisms which link extra linguistic phenomena (the social and cultural) with patterned linguistic heterogeneity (the internal, variable, system of language) (Sankoff 1988a: 157).

Here is the definition from the leading journal, aptly entitled *Language Variation and Change*:

> *Language Variation and Change* is the only journal dedicated exclusively to the study of linguistic variation and the capacity to deal with systematic and inherent variation in synchronic and diachronic linguistics. Sociolinguistics involves analysing the interaction of language, culture and society; the more specific study of variation is concerned with the impact of this interaction on the structures and processes of traditional linguistics. *Language Variation and Change* concentrates on the details of linguistic structure in actual speech production and processing (or writing), including contemporary or historical sources.

This book is written in this spirit, taking the details of variable linguistic structures of language in use and demonstrating how quantitative analysis can tell us something interesting about what we find, i.e. how variation patterns, why it exists, what explains it.

However, this textbook cannot even cover everything within the quantitative sociolinguistic enterprise. A number of subdisciplines have developed which involve specialized methodological and data-specific practices. Some of these require very specific knowledge that extends beyond what can be covered in a single book. Therefore, I will confine myself to the area of sociolinguistics upon whose foundations these approaches to variation rest and with which I am most familiar. In so doing, I will leave to other experts certain subdisciplines in the field, including sociophonetics with its detailed methods of acoustic measurement and experimentation, discourse analysis with its elaborate qualitative component, aspects of historical linguistics which include variationist techniques, corpus linguistics, and the broad field of sociocultural linguistics. Nevertheless, I hope to demonstrate that variationist sociolinguistic principles and practices, the identification and study of patterns, and all the aspects of the methodology laid out here can be applied in virtually any study of language.

You will find me discussing the same old variable (ing) again. One of my students asked me once in exasperation: *Why do we have to keep talking about variable (ing)?* Why? It provides a familiar model and a good example of how to approach variation, interpret it, and understand it. Besides, there may be some things about variable (ing) we have not discovered yet. I will be sure to find some new variables to talk about too. To support creative thinking I have sprinkled "notes," "tips," and "mini quizzes" throughout the text. Tips provide advice for what the student might encounter in her own research and how to get around it. Notes are elaborations, often my own inner thoughts about research mentioned within the text. Mini quizzes embed learning by questioning the reader on some key point under discussion. I believe that teaching can best be accomplished by "doing." My approach will be to use the findings and observations arising from a series of case studies of "the linguistic variable," the key construct of the discipline, to demonstrate how Variationist Sociolinguistic theory is put into practice. I will embed these studies in the general research trends in the field over the past 40 years. The underlying goal is to show you the links between language and society as they arise from observation and interpretation of variable phenomena.

The book takes as a foundation the major findings of sociolinguistics as put forward in broad-based introductory level textbooks (Wardaugh 2002), with a focus on "Variationist Sociolinguistics" in particular, as synthesized in Chambers (2003). I define "classic" research in sociolinguistics as that conducted by William Labov, Peter Trudgill, Walt Wolfram, Ralph Fasold, and Lesley Milroy. This early research exposed persistent, regular sociolinguistic patterns that have given rise to "sociolinguistic principles." This will be my departure point.

The discoveries of this early body of knowledge is already consolidated in the leading introductory sociolinguistic textbooks in the field. Each chapter ends with a reading list of the major sources I have drawn from. My goal for this book is to put the cumulative findings of the last 30–40 years into context with this foundational work. The findings I will report are meant to broaden and enrich classic sociolinguistic research by bringing the latest evidence to bear on fundamental sociolinguistic observations. Therefore I will focus more on developments to sociolinguistics as put forward in Labov's most recent research as synthesized in his important *Principles of Linguistic Change* volumes (Labov 1994, 2001a, 2010). This work will be brought to the forefront, in the context of, and with reference to, other major research advances in the field, particularly those arising from the journal *Language Variation and Change*. Then, to make practical exactly how this research is done, I will turn to a series of choice linguistic variables. This research encompasses analyses of multiple levels of grammar – phonology, morpho-syntax-semantics, and discourse-pragmatics. Each case study presents findings and observations about how different types of variants are used and how they pattern at the community level and within the systems of grammar of which they are a part. Each case study interprets the findings within the context of sociolinguistic inquiry as I have defined it above.

The textbook is organized as follows. Chapter 1 introduces "sociolinguistic variation theory" (Sankoff 1988a: 140) as Language Variation and Change (LVC). Chapters 2 and 3 synthesize the observations and findings of LVC research that have led to sociolinguistic principles and sociolinguistic theory. These chapters present a synthesis of the pervasive "patterns" both sociolinguistic and linguistic, as, for example, elucidated in Chambers (2003) or Trudgill (2000), from which LVC has developed. Chapter 4 considers issues relating to data collection, field work, and the key methodological issues of how to deal with the effect of individuals and lexical items. Chapter 5 summarizes the state of the art in quantitative methods and statistical practice. Chapter 6 outlines the comparative sociolinguistic approach. Chapters 7–11 present case studies of linguistic variables from phonology to discourse. Each chapter introduces the variable(s), issues arising from studying them, solutions, and findings. Observations are evaluated both from the perspective of sociolinguistic principles as well as in the context of the prevailing knowledge of the variables in the field. Chapter 12 synthesizes the observations so as to provide explanations for both internal and external patterns of language variation and puts them into the perspective of their social and historical context.

Mini Quiz

Q1 Variation Sociolinguistics is the study of systematic and inherent variation in language, past and present.
   (a)   True
   (b)   False
   Answer = TRUE

Figures

Tables

1

Sociolinguistics as Language Variation and Change

Not all variability and heterogeneity in language structure involves change; but all change involves variability and heterogeneity. (Weinreich, Labov, and Herzog 1968: 188)

In this chapter I introduce fundamental concepts and key constructs of the study of Variationist Sociolinguistics that will be detailed in later chapters. Why approach the study of language from this perspective? What can be learned from this method that cannot be learned from other sociolinguistic methods? A major component of this approach to language is that it is linguistic, but also social and statistical. Why is a combined socioquantitative method useful and desirable?

Sociolinguistics

Sociolinguistics has its roots in dialectology, historical linguistics, and language contact with considerable influence from sociology and psychology (Koerner 1991: 65). This is why it has evolved into an exceptionally broad field. An all-encompassing definition would be that the domain of inquiry of sociolinguistics is the interaction between language, culture, and society. Depending on the focus, virtually any study of language implicates a social connection because without this human component language itself would not exist. However, the scope of sociolinguistics in this expansive interpretation is vast. Sociolinguistics has as many different facets as its roots. Some areas of the discipline put more emphasis on one area (culture); some disciplines put more emphasis on another (education). There is no one sociolinguistics other than the overarching unity of language in use. Depending on which aspect of language in use comes to the fore, sociolinguistics diverges into innumerable subdisciplines.

Every day we speak and write and use a complex, structured system to communicate but at the same time that system is evolving. The fundamental LVC (Language Variation and

Variationist Sociolinguistics: Change, Observation, Interpretation, First Edition. Sali A. Tagliamonte.
© 2012 Sali A. Tagliamonte. Published 2012 by Blackwell Publishing Ltd.

Change) question is, *How does this happen?* Weinreich, Labov, and Herzog (1968: 100–101) answered the question by saying, "the key to a rational conception of language change is the possibility of describing orderly differentiation." This order, yet differentiation, as the normal state of affairs (Labov 1982: 17), the idea that variation is an inherent part of language (Labov 1969: 728), is the foundational maxim of the LVC approach. Differentiation, anomalies, and nonstandard features are easy to spot. In fact, just about everyone likes to talk about the wacky, weird, and/or reprehensible bits of language.

> The normal condition of the speech community is a heterogeneous one … Moreover this heterogeneity is an integral part of the linguistic economy of the community, necessary to satisfy the linguistic demands of every-day life. (Weinreich, Labov, and Herzog 1968: 17)

> Variability [is] not.. a nuisance but is a universal and functional design feature of language. (Foulkes, 2006)

Variation in language is most readily observed in the vernacular of everyday life. For example, a teenager says: "that were like sick"; an elderly man recounting a story to his granddaughter says: "you was always workin' in them days." Are these utterances mistakes? Are they slang? Are they instances of dialect? An LVC-oriented sociolinguist views such instances of language in use as an indication of the variable but rule-governed behavior typical of all natural speech varieties. The vernacular was first defined as "the style in which the minimum attention is given to the monitoring of speech" (Labov 1972c: 208). Later discussions affirmed that the ideal target of sociolinguistic investigation is "everyday speech" (Sankoff 1974, 1980b: 54), "real language in use" (Milroy 1992: 66). Variation in language can be observed just about everywhere from a conversation you overhear on the street to a story you read in the newspaper. Sociolinguists notice such variations too. In undertaking sustained analysis, what they discover is that people will use one form and then another for more or less the same meaning all the time the language varies. The harder part is to find the order, or the system, in the variation chaos. The way LVC undertakes this is by means of the "linguistic variable." A linguistic variable is the alternation of forms, or "layering" of forms, in language. A basic definition is "two or more ways of saying the same thing." A more nuanced, early, definition also mentions that linguistic variables should be structural and "integrated into a larger system of functioning units" (Labov 1972: 8).

Linguistic variables in a given speech community, whether morphosyntactic, phonological, lexical, or discursive, do not vary haphazardly, but systematically. Because it is systematic, this behavior can be quantitatively modeled (Labov 1963, 1969). Analyses of heterogeneous structures within the speech community rest on the assumption that whenever a choice exists among two (or more) alternatives in the course of linguistic performance, and where that choice may have been influenced by any number of factors, then it is appropriate to invoke statistical techniques (Sankoff 1988a: 2). The statistical tools used in the study of variation will be discussed in Chapter 5.

The combination of methods employed in Variationist Sociolinguistics forms part of the "descriptive-interpretative" strand of modern linguistic research (Sankoff 1988a: 142–143). Large-scale studies of variation in speech communities from New York to Norwich have produced extensive bodies of data. The descriptive component requires detailed, critical observation of variation and change. The patterns that have emerged from these undertakings have demonstrated that linguistic change is not only the result of universal principles but is also shaped by the social context in which it occurs (Labov 1963: 74). This is where the interpretive component of LVC has proven critical. Descriptions of variation can only be understood in context. While sociolinguistic principles prevail wherever you go, each situation provides a unique interpretation. In the case studies in Chapters 7–11 I will demonstrate how the study of different types of linguistic variables must take into account historical, contemporary, and social facts to explain language use.

The Linguistic Variable

LVC research begins with the observation that language is inherently variable. Speakers make choices when they speak and they alternate among these choices. Take, for example, the use of forms which strikes the ear as nonstandard, unusual, dialectal, or new, as in the examples in Example 1.1.[1]

Example 1.1

    (a)   And then next *mornin'* [In] they were all brought back again. (YRK/002)
    (b)   Our car was *like* seven miles from where the entrance was. (TOR/021)
    (c)   There was a supply boat Ø came down to our cottage everyday. (TOR/036)
    (d)   He was like *so* funny and *so* nice. (TOR/054)

These features can only be fully understood if they are examined alongside the relatively unremarkable alternates with which they vary, as in Example 1.2.

Example 1.2

    (a)   And I started work on an *evening* [ŋ]. (YRK/012)
    (b)   We were oh probably *about* six miles from it. (TOR/054)
    (c)   The people *that* did it were brainwashed. (TOR/069)
    (d)   She's *really* funny, and I think she's *really* pretty too. (TOR/021)

Some variables may even have three or more alternates, as in Example 1.3.

Example 1.3

    (a)   I can't remember what that *building* [in] is called. (TOR/008)
    (b)   I was on vacation for *approximately* six weeks. (TOR/038)
    (c)   I'm only exposed to the people *who* speak the same way that I do. (TOR/016)
    (d)   He's *very* funny; he's *very* generous. (TOR/023)

In other words, speakers may vary among various pronunciations of "ing" at the end of words. They may signal approximation with *like* or *about* or *approximately*. They may choose among relative pronouns *that* or *who* or leave it out entirely. They may select *so* or *really* or *very* to intensify an adjective. These choices are potential "linguistic variables."

> **NOTE** Linguistic variables are typically referred to by inserting the phoneme or morpheme or word that is variable inside parenthesis, i.e. variable (ing), (ly), (that), (so), etc. Phonetic realizations are represented inside square brackets, e.g. [n]. Phonemes are represented inside forward slashes, e.g. /n/.

A linguistic variable in its most basic definition is two or more ways of saying the same thing. An important question is, What does it mean to say two things mean the same thing? One time a student asked this question: what is the difference between a synonym and a linguistic variable? Let us explore this distinction. Synonyms are different lexemes with the same referential meaning as in Example 1.4:

Example 1.4

    (a)   *car, automobile, vehicle, wheels*
    (b)   girl, lass, chick, sheila, babe, doll, skirt

A more restrictive definition of synonymy would require that two synonyms are completely interchangeable in every possible context. In reality, most are not. For example, *lass* is primarily used in Scotland and northern England, *chick* is used in North America, *sheila* in Australia, whereas *girl* is not confined to a particular variety of English. For many practical purposes, such as with the production of dictionaries, it is customary to adopt a looser kind of definition for synonym. Near synonyms are lexemes that share an essential part of their sense, as in Example 1.5:

Example 1.5

    (a)   *interesting, intriguing, fascinating, absorbing, spellbinding, engrossing*
    (b)   *striking, arresting, unusual, out of the ordinary, remarkable, salient*

But this is not the whole story. Linguistic variables must also be alternatives (i.e. options) within the same grammatical system which have the same referential value (meaning) in running discourse (Sankoff 1988a: 142–143). Although some variants may differ subtly in meaning and distribution, if they are part of a linguistic variable they will be members of a structured set in the grammar. Moreover, the choice of one variant or the other must vary in a systematic way – this is what is meant by structured heterogeneity. There is difference, but there is structure to it. Different ways of saying more or less the same thing may occur at every level of grammar in a language, in every variety of a language, in every style, dialect, and register of a language, in every speaker, often even in the same discourse in the same sentence. In fact, variation is everywhere, all the time. This is why it is referred to as "inherent" variation (Labov 1969: 728). Now, consider a more in-depth definition of the linguistic variable:

- two different ways of saying the same thing;
- an abstraction;

- made up of variants;
- comprising a linguistically defined set of some type:
  - a phoneme
  - a lexical item
  - a structural category
  - a natural class of units
  - a syntactic relationship
  - the permutation or placement of items
- although its delineation can be at any level of the grammar, the variants of the variable must have a structurally defined relationship in the grammar;
- they must also co-vary, correlating with patterns of social and/or linguistic phenomena.

Synonyms could be a linguistic variable. However a linguistic variable is more than simply a synonym. Deciding which forms co-vary meaningfully in language is actually a lot trickier than you would think.

Mini Quiz 1.1

Q1 How would a variationist sociolinguist explain the following example?
    "There *was* two of us. Yeah, that's right there *were* two of us."
    (a) Alternation in styles.
    (b) Free variation.
    (c) Linguistic variation.
    (d) Random differentiation.
    (e) Bad grammar.

Q2 Which of the following provides an example of two variants of a linguistic variable?
    (a) And we said, "if you join the club, you must go to church."
    (b) He'd light a furnace for to wash the clothes.
    (c) He was awful homesick, you know, my Uncle Jim.
    (d) To prove I could do it, I had to prove that I could do it.
    (e) There's two girls on my street who have pink hats.

To this point this discussion has focused on the technical description of the linguistic variable. However, there is an entirely different side to linguistic variation that does not come from the mechanics of the linguistic system but involves issues of stigma and salience that come from the external evaluation of language by its users – us humans. There is no reason for a velar sound to be superior to an alveolar sound. There is no reason for a synthetic construction to be better than an analytic one. There is no inherently terrible thing about a double negative. However, there is an absolutely insidious view that certain ways of saying things are better than others. This comes down to the social interpretation of language use.

Most people are convinced that linguistic features are good or bad. For example, here is Sara Kempt, aged 49, in Toronto, Canada (c. 2003), in Example 1.6.

Example 1.6

> … and I think the natural inclination of anybody is to get lazy and sloppy and not think. So I th– there's more and more slang, and people dropping their Gs and things like that, just that … frankly grates on me. I hate it! *Then again, I find myself doing it sometimes.* (TOR/027)

Another fascinating thing about linguistic variables is that people are often completely unaware that they use them, particularly when certain of the variants are not part of the standard language. For example, this is Gabrielle Prusskin, aged 55, in Toronto, Canada (c. 2003). The interviewer has just asked her what she thinks about the word *like*, as in Example 1.7.

Example 1.7

> It's usually young females um when every other word is "like" and it drives me insane. I just *like* I hate it. (TOR/054)

> **TIP**   One way to find a linguistic variable is to look for the words that occur most frequently in data. Are there other ways of saying the same thing? If language is always in flux, then it is just a question of finding out what is on the move in a particular place and time.

Linguistic variables inevitably involve variants that have social meaning. These are typically called "sociolinguistic variables." Sociolinguistic variables are those which can be correlated with "some nonlinguistic variable of the social context: of the speaker, the addressee, the audience, the setting, etc." (Labov 1972c: 237). One variant might have overt social stigma, e.g. "I *ain't* got it", another might entail authority, e.g. "You *must* listen", or prestige, e.g. "I *shall* tell you a story." Yet another variant may be neutral, e.g. "I *have* it." These social evaluations may differ markedly from one community to the next, from one country to the next, from one variety to the next, from one social situation to the next. It may even be the case that one person's admired pronunciation will be another person's loathed one. The patterns of a linguistic variable in the speech community tell the story of how the speech community evaluates the variants of the variable and in so doing this reveals how society is organized and structured. Which groups talk to each other? Which groups do not? How a linguistic feature is socially evaluated often has to do with its history as well. Which groups have been in the community a long time? Which groups are new? Language use is a reflection of the society in which it is embedded and the time period in which it occurs.

> **NOTE**   One time I went to a conference in the United States with my then current group of British graduate students. One of them had a strong accent from a variety of somewhat modest prestige in the United Kingdom. She was shocked to be told, repeatedly, how lovely her accent was. Similarly, I was chagrined to discover that my own middle-class Canadian accent – unremarkable in Canada – was heard as an entirely unbecoming American accent in the United Kingdom.

The primary empirical task of Variationist Sociolinguistics is to correlate linguistic variation as the dependent variable with independent variables (Chambers 2003: 17). The dependent variables are the features of the linguistic system that vary (e.g. the varying pronunciations of the same phoneme, the choice of relative pronoun, the selection of an intensifying adverb). Independent variables are the features associated with the variation. They can be external to the grammar, out in the world, relating to aspects of the social context, situation, community setting, or register. They can also be internal to the grammar, relating to the linguistic environment such as the grammatical category of the word, the type of subject in the clause, or its function.

Patterns in language are observed using a two-part undertaking: (1) find socially and linguistically significant factors that impact variation, and (2) correlate them with general social forces (Labov 1972c: 42). The patterns that arise are used by the analyst to interpret and explain the phenomenon under investigation. The fact that linguistic differentiation in communities has been consistent for different linguistic features and that these patterns repeat themselves across different situations in time and space have given rise to a series of "classic" sociolinguistic patterns from which Variationist Sociolinguistic inquiry has sprung. These patterns provided a baseline for all subsequent research and have informed several new generations of research-based study.

The study of sociolinguistics as LVC is unique in sociolinguistics in two ways: (1) its overriding goal and (2) its methodology. LVC research attempts to solve one of the great paradoxes of language in use – the fact that language is always changing.

The basic LVC procedure is the following:

- Observation – hear and/or see variation in language use;
- Identification – select the linguistic variable for study;
- Reconnaissance – determine if the variation occurs and where;
- Systematic Exploratory Observation:
  o What is the inventory of forms?
  o What are the patterns?
  o When does the variation occur and under what circumstances?
  o Who uses the variation and how?
- Test hypotheses, claims, and observations;
- Interpret and explain the variable patterns, social and linguistic.

To discover the relevant factors (social and linguistic) which give rise to "speakers or writers' sustained and repeated exercise of their linguistic facilities in producing large numbers of sentences" (Sankoff 1988a), the data are analyzed using statistical modeling. This method enables the analyst to ask and answer the following questions:

- Which factors are statistically significant (i.e. not due to chance)?
- What is the relative contribution of the independent factors tested in the model, i.e. which factor group is most significant or least?
- What is the order (from more to less) of factors within the independent factors (predictors), the constraints or constraint hierarchy?
- Does this order reflect the direction predicted by one or the other of the hypotheses being tested?

Notice that Variationist Sociolinguistics has an essentially multiplex nature: on the one hand, empirical and data-based; on the other hand, scientific methods and statistical testing; but there is a third component. Linguistic patterns can only be understood through interpretation. Explanation in sociolinguistics can only happen when statistics are used in conjunction with a strong interpretive component, grounded in real-world language use.

Mini Quiz 1.2

Q1   The primary empirical task of Variationist Sociolinguistics is to:
   (a)   define linguistic variables
   (b)   relate linguistic variables with each other
   (c)   correlate independent variables with each other
   (d)   correlate linguistic variation as the dependent variable with independent variables
   (e)   correlate linguistic variation as the independent variable with dependent variables in society.

Linguistic Change

If I talk to, say, my grandfather, like I talk to one of my friends, he'd just be like, "what?" (TOR/023)

One of the driving forces of Variationist Sociolinguistics is the search for general principles that govern linguistic change. If one form appears to be replacing the other, either in time or along some economic, demographic, or geographic dimension (Sankoff and Thibault 1981: 213) then this may be an indication of language change in progress. Consider the way people talk about the weather. It is often the case that it is either cold or hot outside. When the temperature is extreme in one direction or another people will typically intensify their descriptions. For example, if it is particularly cold a person might say, "It's very cold today!" But would a young person say it the same way? Probably not. A younger person (at least in Canada in the early twenty-first century) is more likely to say: "It's so cold today!" In contrast a middle-aged person is more likely to say: "It's really cold!" If these observations can be substantiated across a wide number of people (e.g. Tagliamonte 2008b) (see Chapter 9), this may be evidence for ongoing evolution of a subsystem of grammar – generational change. This is why linguistic data from different age groups in the same speech community, or different communities in the same country, or even communities in different countries in different circumstances, provide important evidence for understanding how language change may be happening.

All languages change through time. We do not really know why this is, but it is a characteristic of all human languages. They also change in different ways in different places. (Trudgill 2003: 7)

Linguistic change typically proceeds in "an ordered set of shifts in the frequency of application of the rule in each environment" (Labov 1982: 75). What this means is that the rate of use of a particular form, e.g. *very*, *really* or *so*, is not the most important observation. Instead, the contexts in which these forms occur – their patterns of use – is the key element in tapping into linguistic change. For example, *very* and *really* can occur as attributive or predicative intensifiers, as in Example 1.8a, but *so* can only occur as predicative, at least in current prescriptive accounts of English.

Example 1.8

(a) It was a *really* hot day [attributive] and like on the way there I started to feel *really, really* weak [predicative]. (TOR/011)

(b) I was *so* hungry [predicative]. (TOR/013)

These patterns of use are the fundamental units by which linguistic change occur (Labov 1982: 75) (see Chapter 3). Moreover, if the relationship of these environmental contexts can be captured this provides a critical measure for comparison – referred to as a "constraint" on variation. In this case the constraint is the difference between predicative vs. attributive position. Similarities and differences in the significance, strength, and ordering of constraints (the constraint ranking) offer a microscopic view of the grammar from which we can infer the structure (and possible interaction) of different grammars. The various statistical techniques in the LVC toolkit enable the analyst to assess and evaluate the competing influences and in so doing interpret the path of development of language through time and space and social structure (see Chapter 5).

TIP What is the difference between a "variable" and a "factor" or "factor group"? In sociolinguistics "variable" is reserved for the "linguistic variable", the feature that varies and that is under investigation (i.e. the dependent variable). "Factors" are the aspects of the social or linguistic context that influence the variable phenomena (i.e. the independent variables). In statistics these are referred to as "predictors." To avoid confusion I will continue to use the field's current standard term "factor group" or "factor."

LVC analysis asks the question, How can a variable linguistic phenomenon be explained? In this type of analysis the critical component is that the data come from the recurrent choices speakers make in the course of production. In this way, each choice is viewed not simply as an instance or token of use, but as a choice made within the context of the grammar from which it comes. When a large body of repeating tokens is part of the analysis, the choices can be assessed statistically so as to uncover the meaningful patterns of use (Cedergren and Sankoff 1974; Labov 1969; Poplack and Tagliamonte 2001: 89). The choices are taken to represent the (underlying) variable grammar of the speaker as well as the grammar of the speech community to which she belongs (Poplack and Tagliamonte 2001: 94). The goal to investigate language use in the context of language structure is what makes an LVC analysis "accountable."

The Principle of Accountability

A foundational concept in the Variationist Sociolinguistic approach and one that sets it apart from other methods is the "principle of accountability" (Labov 1966: 49; 1969:737–738, fn. 20; 1972c: 72). This is where the analysis begins. Say the analyst is interested in the use of the relative pronoun *who*. The principle of accountability dictates that in addition to examining *who* itself, the analyst must also take into account all the other potential variants within the relative pronoun system. Accountability requires that all the relevant forms in the subsystem of grammar that you have targeted for investigation, not simply the variant of interest, are included in the analysis. The idea is that the analyst cannot gain access to how a variant functions in the grammar without considering it in the context of the subsystem of which it is a part. Then, each use of the variant under investigation can be reported as a proportion of the total number of relevant constructions, i.e. the total number of times the function (i.e. the same meaning) occurred in the data (Wolfram 1993: 206).

Circumscribing the Variable Context

The focus of investigation in LVC is the place in the linguistic system that is variable; in the case of the relative pronoun *who*, it would be the relative pronoun system. However, delimiting a subsystem of grammar is often not an easy task. In many cases, there will be more than one variant (e.g. relative *who*, *that*, etc.). Often one of the variants will be zero which makes spotting these variants particularly difficult. Inevitably, there will be contexts that are ambiguous and cases where the same form can have an entirely different meaning (e.g. in addition to being a relative pronoun, *that* can also be a complementizer, a locative, an expletive pronoun, etc.).

According to the principle of accountability, it is necessary to circumscribe the data to only those contexts that are functionally parallel as well as variable. The task is to determine, sometimes by a lengthy process of trial and error, which tokens are in and which are out.

> The final decision as to what to count is actually the final solution to the problem at hand.
> (Labov 1969: 728)

Perhaps the trickiest problem is to determine which forms mean the same thing. The LVC approach to form/function asymmetry is that distinctions in referential value or grammatical function among different surface forms are often neutralized in discourse (Sankoff 1988a: 153).

> Many "functions" can be carried out by several different "forms" and the question of who, when and why become immediately pertinent in accounting for those actually used. (Sankoff 1988a: 151)

Determining where the linguistic variable varies is called "circumscribing the variable context" (Poplack and Tagliamonte 1989a: 60) or "the envelope of variation" (Milroy and Gordon 2003: 180). This task requires that the analyst identify the total pool of utterances in which the feature varies. In dealing with form/function asymmetry Variationist Sociolinguistics becomes a descriptive-interpretive research enterprise (Sankoff 1988a: 149). In other words, a variationist study has two ways of looking at data: (1) the distribution of forms and (2) the identification of the linguistic function of each form.

Contexts that do not vary but are categorically encoded with one or other variant are not included in the analysis of variation. These are the "don't count" cases (see Blake 1994). This does not mean the categorical contexts are not important. Knowing which areas of the grammar are categorical and which are variable is a critical part of interpreting patterns and explaining linguistic phenomena (see Labov 1972b: 815; Smith 2001); however, categorical contexts cannot be part of an analysis of variation. That would be mixing apples with oranges.

These procedures accentuate that the study of variation is not interested in individual occurrences of linguistic features, but requires systematic study of the recurrent choices an individual makes (Poplack and Tagliamonte 2001: 89). Analysis of these recurrent choices enables the LVC analyst to find the underlying patterns that lead to one choice or the other. A "pattern" is representative. It refers to "a series of parallel occurrences (established according to structural and/or functional criteria) occurring at a non-negligible rate in a corpus of language use" (Poplack and Meechan 1998b: 129).

> The analysis of data can only be as good as the data provided by the extraction process. (Wolfram 1993: 203)

In sum, the LVC approach does not simply study the features of language that are attention-grabbing or unusual all by themselves. It also studies their alternates. This is the real challenge: is there variation? And if so, where exactly does it occur? Where is the variable variable? Labov characterizes this process as a "long series of exploratory manoeuvres" (Labov 1969: 728–729). The case studies in Chapters 7–11 will provide examples of these comprehensive methodological practices.

Along with the key construct of the linguistic variable and the key maxim of the principle of accountability – the next foundational pillar of the LVC approach to sociolinguistics that differentiates it from other methods in sociolinguistics is its quantitative method. Once an adequate number of choices has been taken into account, the patterns of use have been identified and coded, then the analyst can discover the system in the variation using statistical modeling (Cedergren and Sankoff 1974; Labov 1969).

Mini Quiz 1.3

Q1 What is the difference between an occurrence and a pattern?
  (a) A pattern cannot be discerned by systematic and exhaustive quantitative analysis of variability.
  (b) A pattern occurs at a negligible rate in a corpus of language.
  (c) A pattern is a series of heterogeneous occurrences.
  (d) A pattern is representative.
  (e) A pattern cannot reveal the grammatical provenance of forms.

Frequency

How often does a linguistic form occur? The rate of occurrence of a feature is an important first step in understanding variation. The frequency of a feature is dependent on the contexts that are included in the calculation. It is not sufficient to embark upon the counting enterprise by simply counting the number of times a variant of interest occurred in a body of data. Why? First, how often a feature occurs depends on the quantity and nature of the data. Second, the number of occurrences of an item in one body of materials cannot be compared to the number of occurrences in a different body of materials unless there is a way to "normalize" the two data sets. One way to do this is by counting the total number of words in each data set. However, the problem is that data sets can differ markedly in terms of their contents, making overall counts problematic for comparison. For example, if you wanted to study the future in English and you had two interviews of the same individual, but one conversation had focused on upcoming events and the other on past memories you would have a very different tally of future forms per number of words. If you counted how many times a particular future variant occurred out of the total number of times the person used future temporal reference in each data set, proportions of one variant or another would likely be pretty much the same. This is why the frequency of a feature is determined by counting how many times it occurred as a proportion of the number of places where is could have occurred – in other words, a distributional analysis.

The starting point of a variation analysis is a survey of the overall distribution of forms with the same function. The first question to ask is, How many of the variant of interest occur? The second, Out of how many? In other words, How often was there a *possibility* that the variant would occur in the data under investigation? Only with this knowledge can the number of instances of the variant in question become interpretable.

The next step is to determine the independent factors that may influence where the variant under investigation can occur.

Mini Quiz 1.4

Consider the data below and examine the relative pronouns.
(a) And there was a man named Mr Pape who used to come around with fruit and vegetables to the door. (TOR/035)
(b) There was a man that played the piano. (TOR/035)
(c) … she could tell you people who lived here like forty years ago like. (TOR/099)
(d) Then I found out that I had torn the muscle. (TOR/025)
(e) There was a man with a horse and cart that used to deliver them water from the lake for washing. (TOR/035)
(f) You can't really trust a man who doesn't pay child support. (TOR/070)
(g) But there was a man that sat in the middle of the streetcar in a little sort of box. (TOR/049)
(h) There was also a man came up-and-down the street with a small cart and a bell and he sharpened scissors. (TOR/049)

Q1 How many variants are there?
Q2 Which sentence doesn't belong?
Q3 What is the proportion of *who*?

Constraints

> The fundamental unit of change is not the rule but the environmental constraint within the rule. (Labov 1982: 75)

Variationist Sociolinguistics views the behavior of the dependent variable as it distributes across a series of cross-cutting factors, whether external (social) or internal (grammatical). To gain access to this information, it is necessary to determine how the choice of a particular variant is influenced by different aspects of the contexts in which it occurs (Sankoff 1988b: 985).

The frequency of variants will fluctuate considerably from one individual to the next or one situation to the next. A less educated person might use more *got* for stative possession, *You got a pen?* than someone with a college degree, *Have you got a pen?* A person in a conversation with a friend might use it more than with a boss. My children might use it more than I. A person from England might even use a different construction: *Have you a pen?* However, the patterns of variation within the same speech community remain stable (Sankoff 1988a: 153). If *got* is used at all, it tends to be used with second-person subjects. Thus, frequency and pattern are distinct measures of a variable phenomenon. Frequency tends to fluctuate due to external conditions but the tendencies in grammatical patterns stay the same. This finding has been reported and repeated in the literature from the earliest days of quantitative methodology to the most recent. For example, in a study of bare English origin nouns in Spanish, Torres-Cacoullos (2003: 323) concluded "even with typologically similar language, variable rule analysis can reveal details of the grammar that constitute conflict sites, even when rates for variants are similar." Meyerhoff and Walker (2007), studying the varieties of English spoken in Bequia, a small island in the Caribbean, reports that

> raw frequencies of vernacular variants may fluctuate, but language-internal constraints persist. Among the many implications these findings have for the study of linguistic variation and change, perhaps the most crucial is that it affirms "the validity of modeling variable rules in a community grammar, rather than as an aggregation of idiolectal norms." (Meyerhoff and Walker 2007: 346)

What does it mean to count? The sociolinguist tallies each instance of all the variants of the variable then to a consideration of the constraints. The sociolinguist examines how often each variant of the variable occurs in each context. This type of analysis is called a comparison of marginals. It shows the percentages of the different variants in the data (an overall distribution of forms and a factor by factor analysis); for example, in the relative pronoun data above, *who* occurred 3 times out of 7. The overall distribution of *who* is 3/7 or 42.8%. The distribution of relative pronouns could also be examined in terms of animacy of the antecedent. How often does *that* occurs with animate antecedents, *a girl that danced,* as compared to inanimate ones, e.g. *a bar that opened up*. This information would provide a view of how the dependant variable (the choice of relative pronoun) is influence by the animacy of the antecedent (a factor by factor analysis).

Practice LVC

Consider the excerpt in Example 1.9 from an interview with Carla Brennan, age 19, born in Toronto, Canada, c. 1991.

Example 1.9

[107] … but this one- one girl, Sophie, she had like posters, you know. You put stuff- pictures up
in your locker. It's like of a guy or *something*[ŋ], right? She had elephants up in her locker, like …
oh, this is so funny! 'Kay, she had all these elephants. Elephants are cute. She had buttons and
elephant shirts, *everything*[ŋ]. Pure elephants, right. And I go like, "Grow up!" I don't know, she
just took it too far, okay? Anyway, uh one day we were *looking*[n] at *National Geographic* and we
saw, uhm, I don't know, uh, elephants like *being*[n] whatever, stabbed and uh, I don't know what
they were *doing*[n], just *using*[n] their bodies and all this stuff and my friend starts *ripping*[n] out
the pages. She's *laughing*[n], right. And she's *laughing*[n]. I go, "What are you *doing*[n]?" And
then her … this is Sophie's locker right cross an–and then she starts *shoving*[n] the pictures in.
I go, "Andrea, don't, don't!" She's like *laughing*[n] her head off. She put them in and then … this
is like before lunch, like the lunch hour. So, we waited and watched Sophie come to her locker,
open it up and the pictures fall out. She looks at them and she goes, "Oh, uh!" She's just so.
I don't know. She's so like that, just "uh!" And she looks at her friends and she goes, "Who did
this?" And then I'm like … *trying*[n] not to laugh, right? And we're just *watching*[n] this whole
thing[ŋ]. And we're like … And Andrea's *going*[n], "Ha, ha ha!" And I go, "Don't laugh, don't
laugh." And she's like, "Who did this? This isn't very funny guys." And then she goes and
throws them in the garbage. And her friends are like, "We didn't do it Sophia. I don't know what
you're *talking*[n] about." But they were *laughing*[n] too, right? It's terrible (laughing) ….

In this excerpt Carla alternates between the velar nasal with [ŋ] and the alveolar nasal with
[n] in words ending in "ing." The variants of (ing) have been highlighted.

To begin an LVC analysis, start with the principle of accountability. Where does the [ŋ] variant
occur and where could it have occurred, but did not, i.e. [n] occurred instead? To do this count
the realization of the sounds for each word where the ending "ing" occurs. In this way each of
the variants – in this case [ŋ] and [n] – may be examined according to the proportion it represents
of the total number of contexts. What is the overall distribution of [n]? It is 15/18, or 83%.

An LVC analysis proceeds by circumscribing the context of variation. The first step is to
recognize and remove categorical tokens from subsequent analysis. Note, for example, that
there is one token that will never vary between [n] and [ŋ], but only ever occurs as [ŋ]. It is
the lexical item, *thing*. Why is there no variation? Because if *thing* were pronounced as *thin* it
would be a different word entirely. Once a categorical context has been identified, remove it.
In this case, remove all tokens of the word *thing*. This requires an adjustment of the calculation
of variability, namely 14/17. The proportion changes slightly to 82.3%. Had we continued
the analysis to all of Carla's data we would have inevitably found many tokens of the word
"thing." If these were included in the analysis of variable (ing) they would skew the data
toward [ŋ] since none of the tokens would occur as [n]. The second step is to identify contexts
that cannot be unambiguously identified as one variant or the other. In spoken data, not all
variants that qualify as potentially variable can be reliably assessed because they are inaudible,
neutralized, or there is some other cause of indeterminacy. As it happens, another token must
be removed, the lexical item *being*. When speakers pronounce this word there is too much
reduction to distinguish either [n] or [ŋ] for the segment to be assessed. Thus, tokens of *being*
are also set aside. The adjusted variation now has an overall distribution of 13/16. The
proportion changes to 81.2%. As the analyst hones the data like this which forms are in and
which are out becomes an important series of steps in the study.

A critical aspect of circumscribing the variable context is to consistently document the
procedures that were undertaken in extracting the data and deciding which contexts are

included in the analysis. This is the only way that the study can be confidently replicated by the next researcher. The whole comparative sociolinguistic enterprise rests on the consistency of the analyses (see Chapter 6).

An LVC analysis tests for the constraints on variation, whether social or linguistic. As it happens, there is a strong linguistic pattern that underlies the variation between [ŋ] and [n]. Notice that the only tokens which contain the velar variant are the lexical items "something" and "everything", both indefinite pronouns. In contrast, all the other words ending in "ing" are verbs, particularly progressive verbs. I will return to consider this observation further in Chapter 7.

In sum, an LVC approach to sociolinguistics is based on data that is taken to represent the speech community and uses methods that enable the analyst to discover the structure of the variable in the grammar. When you embark on an analysis, you never know what may turn up in the data.

Mini Quiz 1.5

Q1 Take another look at the Carla excerpt. At least one other linguistic variable can be identified. Which of the following is it?
   (a) Variation between *be like* and *go* as quotative verbs.
   (b) Frequent use of discourse marker *like*.
   (c) The tag *right*.
   (d) Use of relative *that* for collective nouns (e.g. There's this recycle club that hangs out).
   (e) All of the above.

TIP People often ask me how I find linguistic variables. If you listen and you look carefully you will find them. Watch for tips throughout the book.

Evolution of the Linguistic Variable

The definition of the linguistic variable in LVC research began with semantic equivalence, i.e. two ways of saying the same thing. At the word level, this definition provides a relatively straightforward case of semantic correspondence since even if pronunciation differs, the word is still the same. However, at other levels of grammar, the axiom of "mean the same thing" becomes more problematic. In morphology, suffixes may be present or not, as with variable (s), e.g. *I say* vs. *I says*, or variable (ly), e.g. *go slow* vs. *go slowly*. Moreover, these differences can have extralinguistic as well as linguistic connotations. The zero variant of variable (ly) is often regarded as American. At the same time presence or absence of the suffix is conditioned by nature of the adverb as abstract vs. concrete (e.g. *go slow* vs. *think slowly*) (see further discussion in Chapter 8). Use of *like* is stigmatized and associated with youth, yet it too has structured patterns of use (see Chapter 9). Use of different intensifiers may seem to have distinct meanings, e.g. *very cold* vs. *really cold*, but the perspective of usage in the speech community reveals that one form is replacing another (see Chapter 11). How can the analyst deal with linguistic variables at all levels of grammar in a systematic manner?

Establishing functional equivalence beyond the level of phonetics-phonology is problematic. Lay people and linguists alike will argue strongly for meaning differences when presented with potential variables, even when they are framed in near identical phrases. Do the two sentences in Example 1.10a–b mean the same thing?

Example 1.10

    (a)   I think she*'ll be* cheeky. (YRK/041)
    (b)   I think she*'s gonna be* pretty cheeky. (YRK/041)

To study this type of variation, the definition of the linguistic variable has come under successive revision. Sankoff (1973) was the vanguard of analyses of variation above the level of phonology. By the early 1980s an extensive debate had arisen (Lavandera 1978; Romaine 1984). Was it appropriate to study syntactic variables or not?

Sankoff and Thibault (1981: 207) laid the groundwork for an accountable approach to this issue by introducing the notion of weak complementarity. This is the idea that linguistic variables can be identified by their distribution across the speech community rather than by the fact that they mean the same thing. They argued that many types of linguistic change do not arise from forms with a common meaning:

> Change does not only occur through drift and perturbation of grammatical systems, gradually proceeding from one closely related form to another. It also occurs by the forcible juxtaposition of grammatically very different constructions whose only underlying property in common is their usage for similar discursive functions. It is this relatively violent type of change, which is probably just as prevalent as the gentle diffusion of rule weightings across time and space, which provides so much difficulty for formal grammatical explanation … (Sankoff and Thibault 1981: 207)

In reality, an LVC analysis begins with the observation that where one variant is used more often another variant is used less. When this observation is made of syntactic, semantic or discourse-pragmatic features, form/function correspondence cannot be sustained because variants involved in the same change may not mean precisely the same thing. However, if they are members of the same structured set in the grammar of the speech community these patterns can be *observed*. The criterion for identifying weak complementarity is a correlation between occurrence rates and some extralinguistic factor of individual speakers such as age, sex, or social index. This is an entirely different measure than is usual in variation analysis, but it can be used as a diagnostic step. It is based on the assumption that certain basic discourse functions will be fulfilled at the same rate from one individual to the next in a given body of data. Take for example the case of auxiliary *avoir* vs. *être* for the verb *tomber*, "to fall" in the Canadian French, *Je suis tombé* vs. *J'ai tombé*. The former is sanctioned by the standard language while the former is nonstandard. Sankoff and Thibault (1981: 211) calculated the rate of use of one variant over the other by line of text and then correlated it with a social index measuring "how important it is to have a mastery of the standard or legitimized variety of the language" on a rising scale of 1–4 (Sankoff and Laberge 1978), as in Figure 1.1.

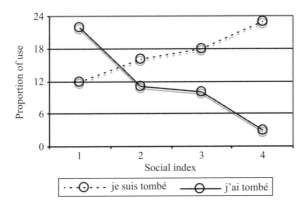

Figure 1.1 Rates of *avoir* and *être* usage with "tomber" per thousand lines of transcription.
Source: Sankoff and Thibault 1981: 211, Figure 1.

Figure 1.1 shows that where one form is used less, the other is used more and vice versa – demonstrating weak complementarity of *avoir* and *être*. The alternation shows meaningful social and linguistic trends in this speech community. The analyst can assume that meaning differences between them have been neutralized and can proceed to analysis of variation.

While debate continues with regard whether or not quantitative methods are appropriate for the analysis of certain types of variation, LVC researchers have carried on much in the same spirit as Rickford (1999):

> The prospects for … carrying the "New Wave"[2] into syntax seem promising but not easy. However, there is no reason to limit our goals and methods to those that require the least effort and/or imagination. This is no way to run a revolution. (Rickford 1999: 32)

One of the expanded notions of equivalence is structural equivalence where two forms are studied in a single variable as long as they are found in the same type of context in the language. General extenders (GEs) are a good example. GEs occur at the end of a sentence, in a specific type of syntactic template and are typically used to generalize to a set, as in Example 1.11. Another important diagnostic is to establish that individuals use alternate forms. The variants in Example 1.11a–c come from the same speaker in the same conversation.

Example 1.11

(a) A lot of the course centers around <u>immunity and inflammation</u> *and stuff like that.* (TOR/135)
(b) I have to focus on my <u>breathing</u> *and stuff.* (TOR/034)
(c) Yeah stuff like that like <u>heparin</u> *and all that stuff.* (TOR/135)

The study of discourse-pragmatic linguistic variables overlaps into conversational analysis and qualitative methods. In this area of research, analysts are primarily focused on the different pragmatic functions of one form or another. Consider the forms *actually*, *really*, and *in fact*, as in Example 1.12 (Waters, in preparation).

Example 1.12

    (a)   [5] Really? [026] Yeah. It was *actually* pretty dry. (TOR/026)
    (b)   [5] You were in high school right? [026] Yeah, I'm *really* pretty much just sick of downtown. (TOR/026)

This type of alternation is at center stage in this controversy. Many researchers believe that these forms mean two entirely different things. In some cases, of course they do, as in Example 1.13a. This example has intensifying function. In other cases there is ambiguity, as in Example 1.13b, where the context could have either intensifying or lexical function. Note that ambiguity is one of the key factors in linguistic change (see Chapter 3).

Example 1.13

    (a)   That's a lot of fun. I *really* enjoyed doing that. (TOR/004)
    (b)   I *really* respected that 'cause most people wouldn't do that. (TOR/004)

The two forms have social value: *really* is casual, vernacular while *actually* is formal, learned. Cathleen Waters recently studied these forms using quantitative methods (Waters, in preparation). Carefully circumscribing the variable context using the principle of accountability and the notion of weak complementary, she demonstrated that in contemporary British and Canadian English *really* is developing and *actually* is fading away. Strong linguistic constraints underlie the use of one or the other: *really* tends to occur in negative contexts and this correlation is becoming stronger in apparent time. This suggests systematic linguistic developments in both of these major varieties of English. Only quantitative methods and diagnostic tests for different processes in linguistic change could have revealed the unique attributes of this system in the grammar of contemporary English.

As LVC research has turned toward linguistic variables that are part of grammaticalizing systems (see Chapter 10), a case can even be made for sometimes including in the analysis contexts that fall *outside* the envelope of variation. Why? Because the phenomenon under investigation may have evolved out of another system. To understand how this has occurred, it becomes necessary to include the broader context of the evolving system in the analysis. Schwenter and Torres-Cacoullos (2008) argue that changing grammatical features make an important contribution to the problem of semantic equivalence. In tense/aspect variables, for example, there is variation across the boundaries of the linguistic variable. Consider the form/function asymmetry of forms used for future temporal reference in English:

- in function, a single form covers a range of meanings
  e.g. *going to* in English; it is a verb of motion and a future marker
  o   He is *going* to the store.
  o   It is *going* to rain.
- in form, different forms serve the same grammatical function
  e.g. *going to* and *will* in English both mark future temporal reference
  o   It is *going* to rain.
  o   It *will* rain.

This means that the variable context cannot be circumscribed by grammatical function because a single form may cover a range of meanings along a developing pathway. Instead the variable context must be extended to include not only all the functions of the extant system (whatever the system under investigation happens to be) but also the array of forms that fulfilled the same function at different stages of the change, as well as meanings that are known to have evolved over the course of the grammatical change (see also Aaron 2010).

There will always be nuances of meaning that are conveyed more by one word, form, or sentence than the other, especially when systems of grammar undergo change. These are the blurry margins of language that must be acknowledged and taken into account. Depending on where you place your analytic lens – syntactic structure vs. speaker agency for example – different aspects of language will come into focus. In the end, the onus is on the analyst to provide defensible arguments to demonstrate relevant social and linguistic correlations. As weak complementarity demonstrates, the proof is in the pudding.

> **NOTE**   What do you think? Analyze my use of *actually* in this book (if the copy-editor leaves them in). Are there any variants? What differentiates the use of *actually* from *really*? Do they really mean different things? Note the following variant from Chapter 9: *only the uses that <u>truly</u> frame constructed dialogue should be included.* Did I really write that? You may also examine the quotes from famous sociolinguists found throughout the book. What do they use?

The Importance of Accountability

An analyst must know what the counts and the calculation of distribution of counts means so that the information can be interpreted in the appropriate way. As I mentioned earlier in this opening chapter, you cannot simply count the number of times something occurs because this does not tell you very much unless you know how many times that something occurs in the body of material. Corpus linguistics typically uses counts per X number of words, e.g. 10 per thousand, 10 per 10 000 etc. However, in LVC research it is critical to know how a variant is influenced by a particular type of context compared to another. This requires knowing the distribution of a feature (variant) out of the total number of contexts where it could have occurred but did not. This is how correlations are established.

What happens if you don't follow the principle of accountability? An early example of how different ways of calculating frequency led to divergent results comes from the study of variable verbal (s), e.g. *He say Ø* vs. *He says*. In a series of narratives told by ex-slaves in the 1940s in the United States, Schneider (1983: 105) reported that the *-s* variant was used most frequently with third person singular at a rate of 72%. Yet a study of exactly the same data reports that third person singular has a rate of 12% (Brewer 1986: 136). How can this discrepancy be explained? Easily. The two researchers used completely different methods for analysis. Brewer counted only the inflected verbs for each grammatical person and then calculated the proportion that each grammatical person represented out of all *-s* inflected verbs. In contrast, Schneider employed accountable methods. He calculated the proportion of *-s* out of all inflected *and* uninflected verbs in each person, i.e. how many third person singular verbs had *-s* out of all third person singular verbs in the data. The counts are simply not comparable. Only Schneider's calculation provides information that can be used to assess the propensity of a grammatical person (i.e. third person singular) to receive an *-s* inflection (see Poplack and Tagliamonte 1989b: 54).

Table 1.1　Count of all quotative types with *be like* as a quotative.

	%	N
Indirect speech	24	186
Direct speech	69	533
Sound/gesture	2.8	22
Hypothetical	3.8	30
Writing	.25	2
Total number of *be like*		773

Table 1.2　Distribution of *be like* according to type of quotative, i.e. viewed as a proportion of the total of each type.

	%	N
Indirect speech	69	186/268
Direct speech	56	533/955
Sound/gesture	55	22/40
Hypothetical	39	30/77
Writing	39	2/17
Total *be like* tokens		773
Total quotative contexts		1357

Another example to illustrate the importance of accountability comes from the use of quotative *be like* (see Chapter 9). One of the main factors influencing the choice of *be like* is the nature of the quotation. How do we establish this? If we count the number of times *be like* is used in a data set and then divide the counts of *be like* according to type of quotative in the data set, we get the results in Table 1.1.

This type of count tells you the number of *be like* tokens for each of the different quotative types. However, it does not tap the patterning of *be like* with regard to quotative type because not all of the quotative types are in the count. To determine how quotative type influences the use of *be like* a different type of count is required. You need to count all the quotative types and then count how often *be like* (as opposed to *say, think, go* or some other quotative) occurred for each type. Table 1.2 shows this result.

The two counts produce diametrically opposed results. Notice that in Table 1.1 it looks as though direct speech is a prime location for the use of *be like*: 69% of *be like* tokens occur with direct speech. However, the explanation for this result is that quotatives that introduce direct speech actually represent the lion's share (70%) of the quotatives in the data, as you can see from the counts in Table 1.2. There are 955 direct quotes in the data out of a total of 1357 quotative frames. However, if we want to know how the type of quotative may influence the selection of *be like* we need to know how often *be like* occurs out of the total number of times each type of quotative occurs. Table 1.2 shows these counts. What you observe is that *be like* is used more with indirect speech than any other type of quotative.

In sum, different ways of counting provide totally different types of information. When counts differ across contexts then simple counts alone will lead analysts to incorrect interpretations. Comparisons of studies based on different ways of counting will lead to faulty interpretations. It is critical for analysts to explain precisely how their data were analyzed so that discrepancies of this type can be revealed. Furthermore, this is the only way to ensure that findings are comparable.

Language Variation and Change and Linguistic Theory

Where is variation in a theory of grammar? Formal theory makes a distinction between I-language and E-language. I-language is the internalized knowledge of an individual speaker whereas any conception of language as something external to the speaker is E-language. Formal theories typically ignore variation, linguistic change, and the transmission of social meaning. As far as Chomsky is concerned, E-language "has no place … in the theory of language" (Chomsky 1986: 26). It would seem then that to implicate variation in a theory of grammar it would be necessary to situate it in I-language. A recent trend in linguistics is to reconsider variation, what has been referred to as "optionality" or as the "probabilistic grammar." Adger and Smith (2005: 149) put it this way: "given widespread, structured variation, how is the mental grammar (I-language) organized so that variation arises?"

Since the early 1990s further developments intent on marrying LVC and theoretical linguistics have emerged (e.g. Cornips and Corrigan 2005; Henry 1998; Meechan and Foley 1994). This enterprise holds promise for the contention that the two frameworks have complementary functions (e.g. Mufwene 1994). The new term of reference is "sociosyntax" (Cornips and Corrigan 2005: 20). Researchers advocate that collaborative research between LVC practitioners and theoretical linguists could herald a paradigm shift, particularly if such joint ventures could lead to uncovering the "E-language forces that are actuating a change and even … possible outcomes" (Fasold 2004: 223).

LVC research confirms that variation is inherent in the individual, the group, the community, and beyond. The best demonstration of inherent variability is alternation of variants in the same individual in the same conversation, as you see in many of the examples in this book. Thus, variation is appropriately situated in the idiolect. But what type of choice mechanism is responsible? In some cases, variation is sensitive to regional distinctions, such as might be subsumed in the notion of competing dialect grammars (Kroch 1989, 2003; Kroch and Taylor 1997). Low-level dialect differences can be quite marked, suggesting a model of competing parameters (Henry 1995). Some variation also has robust supra-local patterns. At the same time general complexity and linear processing effects are apparent. When speakers have a choice between alternative forms they choose the variant which minimizes processing complexity (Grondelaers *et al.* 2009; Hawkins 1994; Jaeger 2008). Thus, some of the regularities and tendencies typical of inherent variability may not necessarily be components of I-language (Sankoff 1978b: 251). On the other hand, while lexical choice can be dialect specific (e.g. *lorry* vs. *truck*), contextual effects (e.g. NP vs. personal pronoun) are more likely to be structural. Speaking for phonological variables, Labov argues that "these variables are in the grammar, they are constrained by the grammar, and they cannot be described apart from the grammar" (Labov 2001a: 84). Variable structures at the morphological and syntactic level are often constrained by semantic distinctions and/or structural configurations whose development can be traced in the history of the language. Incremental differences from one dialect to the next may reflect pathways of change. Thus, some linguistic variables, at least, are heavily embedded in the grammar. Pintzuk (2003: 525) argues that orderly variation in conjunction with the fact that statistical patterns fit formal syntactic models "strongly suggests that a coherent theory relating grammar and usage can and should be formulated." It would seem that Variationist Sociolinguistics can have important insights into which linguistic specifications are the relevant ones. This is one of the challenges of the next 40 years of LVC research – how to make this happen.

Exercises

Exercise 1.1   Spotting linguistic variables ───────────────────────

The sentences in Example 1.14 were extracted from my archive of speech data on UK dialects (Tagliamonte 1996–1998, 1999–2001, 2000–2001, 2001–2003):

Example 1.14

(a)   I've got to cycle all the way back and then this afternoon I'll be cycling back up again! You have to keep those thoughts to yourself.
(b)   She's got a coarse tongue in her.
(c)   I've a feeling that they don't know.
(d)   There's a certain amount of people what just stay but there's people who's out for the bank holiday.
(e)   Youngsters gets far too much.
(f)   Them was built for to feed everything.
(g)   I don't know her; I haven't seen her.
(h)   Eventually she come back and it all got sorted out.
(i)   I went down to the market last Monday.
(j)   I think it's gonna get worse before it'll get better.

Question 1   List three sentences that show alternation of different forms for the same function. Indicate the sentence letter and each of the forms (i.e. variants) below.

(a)   _____

(b)   _____

(c)   _____

Question 2   List three obvious nonstandard features.

(a)   _____

(b)   _____

(c)   _____

Question 3   List three sentences that have only standard features.
Question 4   List a sentence which has three nonstandard features in the same sentence.

Exercise 1.2   The variable context

The complementizer *that* is highly variable in contemporary English, as in Example 1.15 (see also Chapter 5).

Example 1.15

> My grannie says *that* her da was very low, waiting on him, you know. She says Ø the Sunday nicht afore my granda was drowned, she was over at – up at haim, she calls it. (PVG/007)

In order to study this variable it is first necessary to define the variable context.

The parameters in Tagliamonte and Smith (2005: 298) are the following: "All (apparent) matrix + complement constructions where *that* or *zero* were possible, i.e. where the target matrix verb occupied this canonical slot." Such tokens are included as "count" cases. Notice, however, that some of the same matrix verbs may appear in other contexts where they function entirely as "parentheticals." These are constructions that have been bleached "to the point where the phrase acts as an adverbial" because they are "transportable to positions other than that which they could occupy if they were only functioning to introduce a complement" (Thompson and Mulac 1991b: 239–241). Such constructions are not included in the analysis. They are "don't count" cases.

Question 1   Examine the data in Example 1.16. Then decide which contexts are in and which are out.

Example 1.16

> [021] I think he met me, actually, yeah. [Interviewer] Right. How did you come across one another? [021] Well, I was sitting in the – I would be about twenty-five, I think, and I was sitting in the Empire Theatre in Maryport, on my own, watching the picture. (CMK/021)

> [019] I think she won the Waterloo Cup, some big, prestigious thing. I hae nae much an idea about greyhound-racing, but- We called the old boat Silver-Anna, I think. (MPT/019)

> [002] Sure, even the people in the south o this island I think really, if they were getting without being intimidated and all, they would hae went in under the Commonwealth. You-know. I think they would. (PVG/002)

IN:

OUT:

Mini Quiz Answers

1.1   **Q1:** *c*
   Q2: *d complement deletion in first clause; overt complementizer in the second clause.*

1.2 **Q1:** *d*

1.3 **Q1:** *d*

1.4 **Q1:** *3*
      Q2: *d – it is a complement clause*
      Q3: *3/7, 42.8%*

1.5 **Q1:** *c and a*

Notes

1   All the examples used in this book are identified by unique codes identifying the corpus from which
    they come, e.g. TOR = Toronto; in some cases the corpus, the individual speaker, a single digit
    indicator, e.g. "t", and sometimes the age and sex of the speaker. A listing of all the corpus codes can
    be found in Appendix A. All names are pseudonyms.
2   By "new wave" Rickford is referring to the methodology of Variationist Sociolinguistics which is a
    pun on the field's premier conference whose acronym is "NWAV" and stands for "New Ways of
    Analyzing Variation."

Background Reading

Chambers 2003; Fasold 1969, 1971, 1972, 1984; Holmes 1990, 2001; Labov 1963, 1966, 1969; Milroy
    1980, 1981, 1984, 1987; Romaine 1994; Trudgill 1972a,b, 1974a,b, 2000; Wardaugh 2002; Wolfram
    1969, 1974.

2

Social Patterns

It is the mechanisms which link the extra linguistic with patterned linguistic diversity which are the goals of sociolinguistic understanding. (Sankoff 1988a: 157)

This chapter reviews the prevailing social patterns and principles in the LVC framework. A critical vantage point I take in this chapter is retrospective. The LVC approach to analyzing language in use began in the 1960s (Labov 1963). Substantial research has emerged over the intervening decades yet little of these important developments have made their way into sociolinguistic textbooks. To understand these developments it is critical to synthesize the basic principles. LVC studies began with the correlation of linguistic variables with major demographic categories. The regularity of the findings across many different studies and contexts led to the formulation of a number of important generalizations. This chapter consolidates those generalizations.

Social Class

The LVC enterprise began with the correlation of language use and social class. According to Labov (1972c: 212), "the social situation is the most powerful determinant of verbal behaviour." In LVC research social class is meant to model the socioeconomic hierarchy of a community rather than impose "a discrete set of identifiable classes" (Labov 2001a: 113).

Early sociolinguistic research consistently demonstrated the meaningful correlation of linguistic variables by class. Certain variants are used more frequently by the highest status classes and less frequently by the lowest status classes and at intermediate frequencies by the classes in between. The proportion of variants is ordered systematically by social class, often with each class occupying its own "strata" in the community (Labov 1972c: 8). This type of patterning is readily observable in many figures in sociolinguistics textbooks where the lines on the graph representing each social class appear as parallel lines. Labov (2001a: 114) argues that "it is necessary to divide that hierarchy into at least four sections" in order for significant

Variationist Sociolinguistics: Change, Observation, Interpretation, First Edition. Sali A. Tagliamonte.
© 2012 Sali A. Tagliamonte. Published 2012 by Blackwell Publishing Ltd.

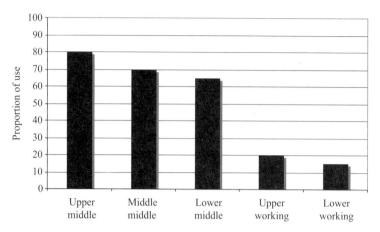

Figure 2.1   Idealized pattern for sharp stratification by social class.

results to emerge. However, many subsequent studies of social class have been successfully carried out with binary divisions, such as middle-class vs. working-class or white-collar vs. blue-collar (e.g. Cravens and Giannelli 1995). This contrast represents a major social divide in the speech communities where most sociolinguistic studies have been carried out (Chambers 2003: 42). Although such divisions are very broad, the fact that the same patterns of behavior have been found across a wide range of studies involving many different varieties and languages increases the confidence that there is a causal link between social status and the use of a given linguistic variable.

In sum, when a linguistic variable has a clear standard vs. nonstandard social evaluation it is sure to be aligned with the prevailing social hierarchy in the community, whatever that might be. Where social class is a relevant social category, linguistic variables will correlate with it. The patterns of the linguistic variable will reflect the social structure.

Sharp Stratification

When there is a wide gap between middle-class and working-class subgroups (e.g. Trudgill 1974b), this pattern is referred to as "sharp" social stratification. The typical pattern of sharp stratification is illustrated in Figure 2.1.

Sharp stratification has been the typical pattern found in the United Kingdom. As Trudgill (1974b) points out, there is often a marked clustering of middle-class and working-class subgroups, but a large expanse between working and middle class. Examples of sharp social stratification for phonological features often come from England where class distinctions (at least up to the 1970s) were quite distinct. Working-class dialects tended to contain features not found in middle-class dialects (e.g. Trudgill 1974b; 1978). In the United Kingdom this pattern is found for both phonological and grammatical variables. In the US, however, this type of stratification is more typically found for grammatical variables. For example, negative concord in Philadelphia exhibited relatively low values for middle-class subgroups, and relatively high values for all working-class subgroups (Labov 1972b). Other examples in the literature include: use of *ain't*, variable use of the copula, leveled past tense forms (e.g. *I seen,*

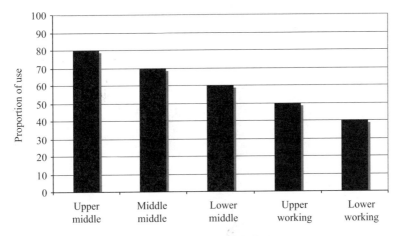

Figure 2.2 Idealized pattern for gradient stratification by social class.

he come), genitive reflexives (e.g. *hisself*), and others. Later studies confirmed the same sharply divided patterns in the social distribution of grammatical variables in other languages. For example, in Canadian French the complementizer *que* ("that") is obligatory in the standard language; however, absence of *que* is widespread among working-class speakers (Sankoff 1974: 348, Table 5), as in Example 2.1.

Example 2.1

C'est la fille Ø j'ai vue.	instead of	C'est la fille *que* j'ai vue.
"That's the girl I saw"	instead of	"That's the girl that I saw"

Gradient Stratification

When there is a continuous stepwise pattern across social groups this correlation is referred to as "gradient" social stratification. The typical pattern of gradient stratification is illustrated in Figure 2.2.

This pattern is also referred to as a "monotonic function" of social class (Labov 1972c: 240; 2001a: Chapter 5). It is easy to see what "monotonic" means by looking at Figure 2.2. There is a regularly decreasing proportion of use from highest to lowest social class.

Linguistic variables that correlate with social class were traditionally divided into three main types: (1) indicators, (2) markers, and (3) stereotypes (Labov 1972c: 237). A key determinant of this typology is the effect of style. Style was originally defined as the amount of attention paid to speech, varying on a scale from casual (vernacular) through to minimal pairs in a wordlist.

Casual style may vary considerably from individual to individual as will the nature of speech in an interview situation. As anyone who has conducted or even listened to a sociolinguistic interview will know, "the degree of spontaneity or warmth in the replies of individuals may vary greatly" (Labov 1972c: 80). In contrast reading, wordlists, and minimal pairs are more constrained and predictable. Despite these differences across style, a key

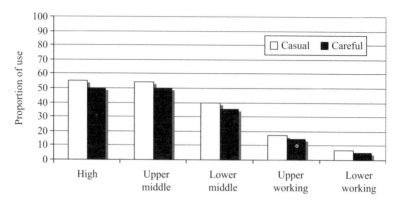

Figure 2.3   Idealized pattern for stratification by social class and style – indicator.

finding for LVC research is that the pattern of variation according casual vs. careful speech will stay constant within a speech community.

The study of how style is produced and organized in speech has developed substantially over the past 30 years, evolving into broader conceptions of style as actively constructed by speakers as part of their personae (Eckert 2000) and according to indexical order (Silverstein 2003). I will focus here only on the basic distinction between casual vs. formal style that can be studied from within a sociolinguistic interview (Labov 2001b: 87). However, there are many ways of pursuing stylistic variation and change and how it relates to speakers, audiences, and identities (for discussion and ideas, see Eckert and Rickford, 2001).

Indicators

A linguistic variable is referred to as an indicator if it correlates with social class, but does not vary by style. Indicators are used in more or less the same way in careful and casual contexts by the individuals that use them. Such variables are typical of regional dialects. A classic example of a sociolinguistic indicator is variable (a:) in Norwich which designates the relative backing of the vowel in words such as *path, bath* (Trudgill 1974b: 98). While the standard variety in England uses a front vowel, in Norwich people use a back vowel and this remains stable across styles. Indicators are not stratified by age so they are not interpreted as change in progress. Figure 2.3 shows an idealized pattern for stratification by social class and style where the linguistic variable is an indicator.

Markers

Linguistic variables are "markers" when they exhibit both class differences and stylistic stratification. Such variables are thought to be "more highly developed" features in the speech community. Speakers are more consciously aware of the variation in the speech community and they represent a more advanced stage in the sociolinguistic diffusion of the linguistic feature (Labov 1969: 237). Figure 2.4 shows an idealized pattern for stratification by social class and style where the linguistic variable is a marker.

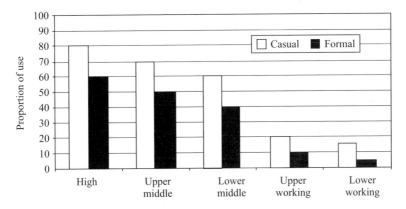

Figure 2.4   Idealized pattern for stratification by social class and style – marker.

The distinction between indicators and markers is particularly relevant in contexts where there are distinct regional dialects (as in England) and where pronunciation varies according to place. Sociolinguistic markers are more prevalent in the LVC literature. There are innumerable cases of clear-cut sociolinguistic markers, including variable (ing), as in Example 2.2a, variable (th), as in Example 2.2b, variable (dh), as in Example 2.2c, negative concord, Example 2.2d–e, etc. (Labov 1972b: 784).

Example 2.2

Variable (ing) – /n/ for /ŋ/
(a)   We used to go *fishin'* [n].

Variable [th] – /d/ for /ð/
(b)   [wIduwt] "without"

Variable [dh] – /t/ for /θ/
(c)   [tIŋk] "think"

Variable (negative concord)
(d)   That ain't *nothing* new.
(e)   I didn't find a proof of the theorem in *none* of these texts.

The association of linguistic variants with social categories is a common result of LVC research; however, the precise nature of the patterns will be locally determined. In one place a variant might be stigmatized; in another place it might be prestigious. Use of an interdental fricative in Louisiana marks Cajun identity (Dubois and Horvath 1998) but in Newfoundland, Newfoundland identity (Clarke 2010). Use of past reference *come* marks rural, uneducated speech in American English (Atwood 1953) but is maintained by young speakers in York, England (see Chapter 11). Use of zero adverbs is typically associated with American English, but is correlated with working-class male speech in York (Tagliamonte and Ito 2002) (see Chapter 8). Unlike early LVC studies, many later projects did not include an independent measure of style as defined by attention paid to speech. Because linguistic markers also correlate with less education or lower socioeconomic scale or occupation these factors have often been taken as a proxy for measuring the formal/casual dimension.

> **NOTE**   Patterns can only be inferred from findings that emerge from analyzed data, typically displayed in figures and/or tables. When you are a sociolinguist you get used to seeing patterns.

Stereotypes

Linguistic stereotypes are linguistic variables that are overtly recognized. They become objects of discussion in the communities in which they are known. Often these features are highly stigmatized. New York City's (r)-lessness is stereotyped in the phrase "toity-toid street" for "thirty-third street" (Labov 1972a). The expression hoi toide for "high tide" in Ocracoke identifies the local accent (Wolfram and Schilling-Estes 1995), while Canadian Raising is stereotyped by "oot" for "out" (Chambers 1991).

In successive stages of a change in progress, a linguistic variable may undergo transition from indicator to marker to stereotype (Labov 1972c):

dialect differentiation → social and stylistic differentiation → metalinguistic commentary
indicator   *marker*   *stereotype*

The correlation of linguistic features with social categories is also found, in part, in the notion of indexicality, the link between a linguistic form and social meaning (Silverstein 2003). Indexicality is complex and has many nuances; however, the core principle is that linguistic behavior has a social interpretation. When a speaker uses *tu* instead of *vous* to address an interlocutor in French these pronouns index a certain power relationship between the two people. Similarly, use of a particular intensifier rather than another can encode certain social characteristics. Use of *so* encodes informality and youth while use of *very* encodes formality and likely an impression of an older or more learned person. Although practitioners working with theories of indexicality and identity in sociolinguistics are focused more on discourse interaction and analysis (e.g. Bucholtz 2005), the central place of linguistic variables and their sociolinguistic correlates is still evident. The nature of the indexing process to involve all levels of linguistic structure, to have regional correlations, developmental phases, and to evolve through time runs parallel to Labov's model of sociolinguistic diffusion. For a good example involving the evolution of variable verbal (s) see Trudgill (1998).

Mini Quiz 2.1

Q1   Consider the following table from Wolfram (1969: 136). What pattern best describes these results?
   (a)   Sharp stratification
   (b)   Gradient stratification
   (c)   Hypercorrection

(d)   The kind of stratification typical of phonological variables

(e)   There is no pattern.

Percentage of [z] absence in third person singular present tense agreement in Detroit black speech according to class.

	Upper middle class	Lower middle class	Upper working class	Lower working class
[z] absence, e.g. he say/ she say	1.4%	9.7	56.9	71.4

Curvilinear Hypothesis

An unexpected finding in LVC research and one that is "difficult for previous theories of language change to account for" (Labov 2001a: xii) is that change tends to be led from centrally located groups as opposed to peripherally located groups (Labov 2001a: 32). In other words, linguistic changes do not originate in the highest or lowest social classes, but in the middle class. This produces an arching pattern by social class and has been called the "curvilinear hypothesis." Figure 2.5 shows an idealized version of this pattern where the distribution of the variable by age is monotonic (not shown) (Labov 2001a: 32) and the individuals in the sample are adults (Labov 2001a: 460).

The higher frequency of the represented linguistic variable among the upper middle and lower middle classes reveals that the change is being led by these social groups. Note that, aside from the higher social class, the main difference is between the middle classes and the working class, a difference that demarcates white-collar professions and blue-collar labor. This binary division has been shown to be the most relevant contrast in contemporary western speech communities (see Cravens and Giannelli 1995). Further distinctions in the social hierarchy,

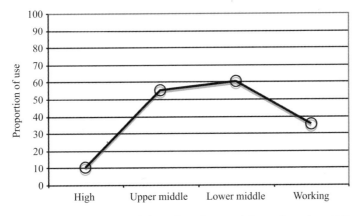

Figure 2.5   Curvilinear pattern for social class when change originates from the middle class.

where possible, can provide additional nuances to a community's social organization and will be better able to measure the details of a change in progress (see Labov 2001a: 31, n. 25).

Sex (or Gender)

Gender is the socially constructed counterpart of biological sex. (Cheshire 2002: 427)

Of all the sociolinguistic principles, the clearest and most consistent one is the contrast between women and men (Labov 1990: 205). This ubiquitous correlation has been stated in many ways. In the following observations, notice how each observation makes a link between women and standard language use.

Females show a greater sensitivity to socially evaluative linguistic forms than do males. (Wolfram 1969: 78)

In careful speech women use fewer stigmatised forms than men, and are more sensitive than men to the prestige pattern. (Labov 1972c: 243)

Females show more more awareness of prestige norms in both their actual speech and attitudes towards speech. (Wolfram and Fasold 1974: 93)

Women, allowing for other variables such as age, education and social class, produce on average linguistic forms which more closely approach those of the standard language or have higher prestige than those produced by men. (Trudgill 1983: 161)

Women on average deviate less from the prestige standard than men. (Cameron and Coates 1988: 13)

Women adopt linguistic features with a relatively wide geographical distribution, the supra-local or national norms. (Cheshire 2002: 430; Milroy *et al.* 1994b; Watt 2002)

The generalization that can be made from these observations is straightforward: women tend to avoid stigmatized forms. This correlation is so strong that Fasold (1990: 92) refers to it as "the sociolinguistic gender pattern" and Chambers calls it "a sociolinguistic verity" (cited in Cheshire 2002: 426, confirmed by Chambers p.c., June 18, 2008).

Figure 2.6 shows an idealized view of what the male–female contrast typically looks like in conjunction with class stratification.

Explanations for the Sex Effect

The big question is why do women and men behave in this way? A number of explanations have been put forward in the literature to explain the sex difference.

1. *Biology.* Women's innate linguistic ability is superior to men's (Chambers 2003: 149–153).
2. *A cultural pattern.* Labov (2001a: 283) argued that "the mechanism of the change crucially involves the initiating role of women at the outset, and the later adoption of the change

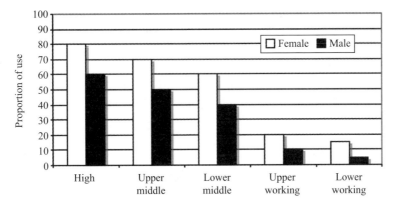

Figure 2.6 Idealized pattern of stratification by sex and social class.

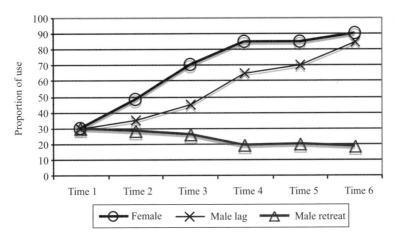

Figure 2.7 Idealized pattern of female-led linguistic change.

by men" typically a generation behind (Labov 2001a: 306). Figure 2.7 includes an idealized view of such a pattern. While the females accelerate in their use of a new form, the males (in the X-marked course) lag behind. If each time interval indicated on the figure is ten years, the male level of use of the innovating form at Time 5 is equal to the female use at Time 3, making the males about a generation behind the females.

3. *Male retreat* from female-dominated change (Kroch 1978). Working-class men, in the face of female-dominated change, march "resolutely in the other direction" (Trudgill 1972b). This hypothetical pattern is also included in Figure 2.7. As the females accelerate a change forward in time, the males (in the triangle-marked course) move in the opposite direction, leading to more extreme differentiation between males and females at Time 6.

4. *Covert prestige*. Men give "covert prestige" to working-class features but women do not (Trudgill 1972b: 182–183). Trudgill elaborates on covert prestige as follows:

covert prestige reflects the value system of our society and of the different sub-cultures within this society, and takes the following form: for male speakers, and for female speakers under 30, non-standard WC [Working Class] speech forms are highly valued, although these values are not usually overtly expressed. These covert values lead to sex-differentiation of linguistic variables of a particular type ... covert prestige also appears to lead to linguistic changes "from below." (Trudgill 1972b: 194)

5. *The social position of women.* Women have less economic power, so rely on symbolic capital – language (Trudgill 1972b: 182–183). In this view, the careful sociolinguistic behavior of women is seen as a reflection of socioeconomic weakness, and of a psychological as well as sociological insecurity (Labov 2001a: 275).
6. *Societal norms and practices.* Differences between men and women relate to the sociolinguistic dynamics of the speech community (Eckert 1989). This involves the linguistic market and how men and women have access to it, the social value and prestige associated with men and women's work, the systems of dominant vs. subordinate groups and other prestige systems in the community (Eckert 2000: 196).

NOTE   The linguistic market refers to how a person's job in the speech community influences language use (Sankoff and Laberge 1978). Compare school teacher to plumber.

Despite the expansive statements about the relationship between language use and female–male differences, it is also critical to remember that they are oversimplifications. Not all women avoid stigmatized forms and not all men embrace nonstigmatized forms. It is obvious from the foregoing statements that the differences between women and men is intricately tied to the social context and social evaluation of the forms in use. Important questions to consider are what makes one form prestigious and another form stigmatized or why women favor certain forms while men prefer others.

In more recent research the focus has shifted perspective so that individual differences within aggregated groups are investigated. Such studies expose individual variations within groups and attempt to interpret and understand the reasons for these differences (Eckert 1988, 1999, 2000). In this research enterprise female–male contrasts are linked to the social evaluation of variants (prestige or stigmatized) as well as to their status in the speech community (i.e. which social groups are using them the most).

> It is only through an analysis of variation that the reality and meaning of a norm can be established at all. (Edward Sapir 1921 – and also Gregory Guy's email signature)

Style and Register

Language variation and change is strongly linked to style or register. Register and style are often used interchangeably in the literature; however, they reflect different perspectives of the same sociolinguistic pattern. The pattern is that people tend to use higher prestige variants more often in more formal styles and lower prestige variants more often in informal styles. Herein lies the difficulty. How is style defined? Is it defined by attention to speech? Is it defined by the audience, e.g. a conversation with a friend vs. a lecture to a group of university students, or is it defined by the nature of the media, e.g. spoken language vs. written language? Perhaps the best way to make this distinction is to say that style refers to the linguistic repertoire of an individual speaker. For example, certain variants have informal connotations, e.g. the [n] variant of variable (ing), as in *workin'* and individuals will exhibit use of this feature in a way that demonstrates style. Register, on the other hand, refers to how an individual performs in particular contexts or social settings. This means that a full exploration of style requires analysis of the range of linguistic variables according to different social purposes, social settings, and media.

A key element of style is that it intersects with sex and social class. The joint mapping of social and stylistic stratification of stable sociolinguistic variables has been replicated in many cities and towns around the world. A prominent finding is that, other things being equal, men style-shift less and women style-shift more (e.g. Eckert 2000: 195). The regularity of these patterns across this wide range of studies attests to the systematic social nature of linguistic variation.

The linguistic marketplace is another way of seeing the relationship between linguistic variables and style and register. This is a concept developed by Sankoff and Laberge (1978). They found that correlations based on social class membership were not very well motivated, since they force the analyst to ignore the fact that people like teachers or receptionists have to conform to "official" speech standards more than do other members of the same socioeconomic strata. With this in mind, a linguistic market index was designed to measure "specifically how speakers' economic activity, taken in its widest sense, requires or is necessarily associated with, competence in the legitimized language" (Sankoff and Laberge 1978: 239). This index was applied to the analysis of several sociolinguistic variables in Montreal French, showing that the higher market index scores correlated with greater use of standard variants. However, it is not clear how the linguistic market should be related to class stratification analysis and social network analysis. Fine-tuning the methodological and analytic relationship between large-scale surveys and other sampling methods and how each reflects language use remains an important issue.

NOTE   Given the prevalence of recording devices today, I am surprised that no one has explored stylistic variation more extensively using LVC metho___ ___hat is required is to record yourself (and willing others) across a wide ran___ ___erent contexts. Which linguistic variables are used differently from one cont___ ___other? How do they shift (frequency or constraints or both)? When do th___ ___? With whom? Under what conditions?

Mobility in Space and Mobility in Class

Language variation and change is also correlated with location, whether defined geographically or socially. The correlation of language use and location is, in essence, dialectology. People tend to sound like where they come from. This led to the well-known dialectological technique of seeking out the most isolated speakers to find the most distinctive regional speech varieties (e.g. Orton 1962: 15–16).

However, people tend to move from one place to another. Traditional dialectological laws attempted to explain mobility vs. isolation, i.e. "mobility causes people to speak and sound more like people from other places" (Chambers 2003: 73). Similarly, when people move from one social class to another, this is reflected in their use of language. The same tendency can be viewed in terms of language contact: "contact breeds imitation and imitation breeds linguistic convergence. Linguistic divergence results from secession, estrangement, loosening of contact" (Weinreich 1953/1968: viii). From this can be formulated yet another sociolinguistic observation, that people adjust their use of certain linguistic variants according to where they live, who they are surrounded by, and who they also wish to emulate. With respect to social mobility, Chambers says it best:

> upwardly mobile individuals adjust the frequency of certain variables in order to sound more like the class they are joining and less like the one they are leaving. (Chambers 2003: 62)

Yet we know that sociolinguistic patterns are not binary. Another aspect of mobility is that it is reflected differently in men and women. Men are typically more oriented to local norms, while women show more extensive usage linguistic features, often incorporating into their repertoire features from outside their local situation, i.e. that are "supralocal" (Milroy, Milroy, and Hartley 1994a). In many cases such features are not necessarily aligned with the standard language. Perhaps the best recent example of this is the repeated finding that women use more quotative *be like* than men (see Chapter 9). In most communities where this feature has been studied, the feature is not local but has been imported from elsewhere. Further, it is a decidedly nonstandard feature. Thus, on two counts, (1) expanded repertoire and (2) expanded orientation, women exhibit their expected tendency.

Social Network, Communities of Practice

In the early days of LVC research, the basic social units for the correlation of linguistic features with extralinguistic phenomena were very broad, with social class being the major unit for aggregating speakers. Recall that the aim was to model the prevailing socioeconomic hierarchy. However, in some cases social class is not the key feature of social organization in a community.

Social groups need not be differentiated by class, but may be grouped according to some other factor. One of the first attempts to explore other dimensions of linguistic variability was Milroy's (1980) study of language use in Belfast, Ireland. Milroy discovered that the linguistic behavior of individuals could not "be accounted for in terms of corporate group membership" (Milroy 1980: 135), but were instead linked to social network. Social networks measured the degree of integration of individuals by measuring an individual's personal network ties with others. These networks could be dense or multiplex. In dense social networks a lot of individuals know each other. In multiplex social networks individuals know each other in more than one capacity, e.g. work together, live in the same neighborhood, and socialize together. Milroy demonstrated that "the closer an individual's network ties are with his local community, the closer his language approximates to localized vernacular norms" (Milroy 1980: 175), i.e. the norms of local, often working-class or rural communities. In essence, the social network functions to maintain norms of communication, what Chambers (2003: 75) refers to as a "norm enforcement mechanism." According to Milroy (1987: 108–109) the network concept has three advantages:

1. it is a useful tool for studying small, self-contained groups;
2. it provides a means to analyze linguistic data in situations where the concept of social class is difficult to apply;
3. it offers a procedure for dealing with variation between speakers at the level of the individual.

Milroy's study brought to the forefront the role of locally defined groups. Focusing in on this type of social categorization schema enables the analyst to examine "the specifics of local practice and local conditions" (Milroy and Gordon 2003: 116).

Mini Quiz 2.2

Q1 The social function of networks is to promote diversity.
   (a) True
   (b) False

This was the beginning of a new direction in the study of language in use. Some researchers started to focus in on the relation between linguistic variation and more narrowly defined social categories. Eckert's (1988) study of a Detroit high school examined divisions within adolescent social networks, i.e. Jocks vs. Burnouts. Many new studies have followed in this tradition by focusing on subgroups within a larger whole, including clan affiliation (Meyerhoff 1997), gang membership (Fought 1999), nerd girls (Bucholtz 1999), and Beijing yuppies (Zhang 2005). In these studies, when linguistic features were found to be used more frequently by one group or the other they were interpreted as identity markers. This research is showing how general patterns of linguistic variation also impact finer-grained differences within the social strata. Speakers can take linguistic variants that have salient social meanings and use them in ways that create new social meanings.

A further development of the trend in the study of linguistic variation and style turns the tables on the object of study and, instead of beginning with the linguistic phenomenon, begins with the behavior of speakers. In this development social meaning is primary and the analysis is focused on any linguistic material that serves a social or stylistic purpose. This development opens up an entirely new area of sociolinguistics in which the operative questions depart substantially from the LVC approach. This area of the field is often referred to as the "third-wave" of sociolinguistics. What are these waves? According to Eckert (2000), this book would be first wave, namely research that studies linguistic variables in community-based corpora using quantitative methods to examine the relation between linguistic variables and social factors such as age, sex, socioeconomic class, occupation, ethnicity, etc. The second wave is distinguished by its ethnographic methodology and its goal is to examine the relation between variation and local, participant-designed categories and configurations. Where linguistic variants were associated with broad categories, these studies would focus in on more fine-grained meaning, e.g. the difference between a linguistic variant associated with say, female, as opposed to female nerd, for example. The third wave focuses in even more on the social meaning of variables. It views styles, rather than variables, as directly associated with identity categories, and explores the contributions of variables to styles. The target of investigation is not only the linguistic variable, but any linguistic material that serves a social/stylistic purpose (Eckert 2008; Podesva 2007; Zhang 2005). A prevailing goal is how speakers construct their personalities using these materials. An idealized overview of the waves can be constructed something like this:

First wave →	Second wave →	Third wave
Social groups	*Social networks*	*Styles*
Sex, age, education	*Communities of practice*	*Identities*
	Jocks, Burnouts	*Individuals*

First-wave studies focus on how, for example, more educated speakers use more consonant cluster simplification. Second-wave studies would focus on how different communities of practice use it, e.g. Jocks vs. Burnouts. Third-wave studies would consider how the same feature is deployed in different styles by the same individual.

Ethnicity and Culture

Another critical influence on variation is ethnicity and cultural orientation. In many countries around the world the populations are made up of people of different backgrounds and ancestries who may not speak the dominant language(s) of the country. For example, English is the dominant language in the United States, Australia, Canada, and the United Kingdom. Yet the peopling of these countries from the time they were settled to the present day has involved a multitude of people with different home languages. For populations whose home language is not English, their use of English may be different from those whose home language is English. Does their use of English model the mainstream speech community? Like linguistic differences across social groups, ethnic background and cultural orientation may act as a barrier to the diffusion of linguistic features in the same way as other social barriers do (Trudgill 2000: 45–46).

What types of patterns are found in the study of variation and change in ethnicity? First, as is well known, certain linguistic features often identify ethnicity. In such cases, an ethnic community will use one word or pronunciation while the mainstream community will use another. Second, certain linguistic variables may be shared, i.e. the variation will exist in both the ethnic community and in the mainstream community; however, the two populations will differ with regard to either the frequency of variants or the patterning of usage of constraints operating on the variation (Fought 2002: 446). A good linguistic variable to consider in this regard is consonant cluster simplification, as in Example 2.3, an omnipresent feature in of all varieties of English.

Example 2.3

These things are going through my head so *fasØ*, going through my head so *fast* (TOR/038)

The frequency of variable (t,d) and the way linguistic constraints operate on it differ across groups. Comparing the well-known constraints on this feature across ethnic varieties reveals subtle differences in the underlying patterns of variation. In the early days of LVC research, Labov (1966), Fasold (1971), and Wolfram (1969) found that people of African

American descent had higher rates of simplification than those of European descent. Further, deletion occurred in more contexts than in European-American dialects, before consonants, pauses, and vowels.

Hazen (2002) demonstrated that three different cultural groups in Warren County, North Carolina (African Americans, European Americans, and Native Americans) showed varying rates of usage of three key linguistic variables: copula absence (Example 2.4a), *was* regulariza-tion (Example 2.4b), and past tense *wont* (Example 2.4c) (Hazen 2002: 240):

Example 2.4

(a) They Ø real nice people.
(b) We *was* going.
(c) We *wont* gonna go.

Much of the early LVC research in the United States suggested that people of African descent (African Americans) and people of Spanish descent (Hispanics) speak differently than European Americans. Further, linguistic changes are not occurring in these groups in the same way as in mainstream populations (Bailey 1987; Labov 1966; Labov 1994: 157). Labov (1966) Fasold (1971), and Wolfram (1969) found that the frequency of variable (t,d) and its linguistic constraints operate differently across groups. For example, African Americans had higher rates of simplification than those of European descent. Further, deletion occurred in more extended contexts, such prevocalic contexts, e.g. *fas'asleep*, whereas it rarely occurs in these contexts in European varieties. However, once a fuller range of variable had been studied it was discovered that African American populations are different from European populations for some features, but not others (Wolfram 2000; Wolfram and Thomas 2002). For example, Mallinson and Wolfram (2002: Table 7) found that three features distinguished Elderly African Americans from Elderly European Americans: variable (s), copula absence with *is*, and variable (t,d) in prevocalic contexts. Other features, however, were entirely the same: variable (s) in third person plural, variable (was), copula absence with *are*. Moreover, the nature, type, and extent of linguistic differences varies across ethnic groups. Wolfram and his associates also studied the Lumbee Indians in North Carolina, United States (Wolfram *et al.* 1997). While they exhibited regularization of the past paradigm of the verb "to be" (Torbert 2001) they also had grammatical markers of Lumbee ethnicity that other varieties in the region did not share, including perfective *I'm* (Wolfram 1996).

Thus, certain types of linguistic variables appear to be diagnostic of ethnic differences generally, e.g. consonant cluster simplification; while others may be unique to one group or another. Attitudinal factors are also implicated in ethnic differences. To what extent does an individual identify with their own, or another, ethnic background? This will always be a matter of degree. Thus, differences in the linguistic behavior of ethnic groups can be due to at least two factors: (1) the continuing effect of the ancestral language spoken by these groups or (2) the effect of identification or alignment with the ethnic group and culture that the individual associates with. For example, non-native pronunciation by first-generation speakers can be inherited by second-generation speakers and developed into a stable dialect with phonological norms of its own.

There can even be influence from a minority ethnic variety onto the surrounding mainstream version of the regional dialect. An early paper by Wolfram (1974) suggested that European Americans in the Southern United States had acquired copula absence from

African Americans. Although the rates of deletion of the copula were considerably less frequent among white Southern Americans than in studies of AAVE in the north (Labov 1969; Wolfram 1969), the constraints underlying the use of the copula were the same. Similarly, Feagin (1997) concluded that r-lessness in White Alabama English was influenced by the speech of African Americans.

NOTE A shibboleth of Italian ethnicity in Canada is the pronunciation of "sandwich" as *sangwich*. My husband, who has ancestors on both sides of his family going back to the Loyalists, calls a "sandwich" a *sangwich*. It is interesting to speculate why he does this. Ethnic markers may emerge in innocuous ways in day-to-day speech.

Notice that interethnic contact and integration in the community as well as an individual's gravitation toward the ethnic community are reflected in patterns of language variation and change. To what extent do ethnic groups within large urban speech communities influence ongoing linguistic change? Horvath's (1985) study of Sydney, Australia revealed that ethnic minority speakers were leading linguistic changes that were affecting the entire speech community. If this is true, then it is likely that a similar trend may be found in other communities, particularly where the ethnic populations are very large in proportion to the locally born residents.

How is the analyst to determine the influence of ethnicity and identity in a speech community or in an individual? Methodologically, it is crucial to be able to separate the frequency of use of a feature, its level of linguistic structure, and its systemic nature in the grammar. Given the appropriate methodology, comparisons across different ethnic groups in the same community can reveal important information about linguistic variation and change.

The focus on frequency of linguistic features in much of the early LVC research has evolved to consider the constraints that underlie them. Santa Ana (1996) found that variable (t,d) in Chicano English, the variety spoken by people of Mexican descent in Los Angeles, United States, was governed by slightly different constraints from those found in dialects spoken by people of British descent. In Toronto, Canada, Walker and Hoffman (2010) studied three ethnic populations across three generations: (1) British origin speakers, (2) first-generation Italians and Chinese, and (3) second- and third-generation Italians and Chinese. Then, they examined two phonological features, one stable feature, variable (t,d) and one change in progress, the lowering and retraction of front lax vowels. They found that the first-generation Italian and Chinese speakers differed in their linguistic conditioning from the second and third generations. The first-generation speakers were not participating in the ongoing change of the Canadian Vowel Shift. However, the second and third generations paralleled the British control group in the operation of constraints. This research shows that by the time individuals are born and raised in the Toronto speech community (second- and third-generation individuals) their internal grammar mirrors the speech community that all the groups share (Walker 2010: 58).

Yet the findings emerging from another major urban center, London, England (c. 2000s) suggest quite a different picture. Kerswill *et al.* (2008) show that ethnic varieties are influencing the language of the whole population. Much of the variation they found in phonological changes originated from the non-Anglo sectors of the population rather than the locals. Cheshire and Fox (2009) report similar findings for variable (was) where well-known constraints on this variable were not operational in London generally. The same trend is emerging in other large European cities where varieties of the host language are spoken by large ethnic minority groups who are immigrants or recent descendants of immigrants. What researchers are demonstrating is that cross-ethnic social contacts allow new forms of speech to diffuse to other speakers and from there enter the old-line populations of the speech community (e.g. Cornips and Nortier 2008; Kotsinas 2001). The effect of ethnicity enables the analyst to understand patterns of convergence or divergence within and across populations of speakers. As large-scale comparative work is undertaken, the understanding of how ethnicity influences language variation and change will increase and provide important windows on global trends and patterns.

The Mass Media

Does television affect the way we speak? Most lay people would say "yes" to this question. Yet a somewhat surprising LVC research says "no" (Trudgill 1986: 40). Linguistic influence must arise through tangible human interaction. Thus, despite the expansion and homogenization of the mass media, linguistic change is proceeding at a rapid rate:

> language is not systematically affected by the mass media, and is influenced primarily in face-to-face interaction with peers. (Labov 2001a: 228)

This finding is based on the numerous studies conducted on American cities (Labov 2001a) and is affirmed in LVC research in many other locations, including Britain, Canada, Australia, and New Zealand. Dialects – particularly urban dialects – are developing and there is ongoing maintenance of local varieties (Chambers 1998b; Milroy and Milroy 1985). Yet new types of communication are developing rapidly. Romaine (1994: 34) cites the example of the word *nerd* emerging in Scandanavia through an American movie and suggests that "the possibilities for change of this type are indeed enormous nowadays, considering how much more mobile most people are, and how much exposure people get to speech norms outside their immediate community through the mass media." The same process is undoubtedly involved in the word *zee* in Canadian English from an American children's song (see below). However, these examples are all lexical items. Borrowing nouns across dialects and languages like this is one of the most pervasive types of language change. What about other levels of grammar?

LVC research on television language presents intriguing new findings. In some cases, media language appears to faithfully reflect ambient community norms. The forms and ranking of intensifiers *very*, *really*, and *so* in the television series *Friends* mirrored reported usage (Tagliamonte and Roberts 2005). However, a study of quotative *be like* in American films found neither sufficient tokens nor the patterns (i.e. constraints) that had been consistently reported in the literature (Dion and Poplack 2007). This suggests that the rapid spread of *be like* in North America was not the result of, nor influenced by, the media. Jane Stuart-Smith recently completed a large-scale analysis of media influence in Glasgow, Scotland (Stuart-Smith 2010). The data come from a working-class community and comprise 36 adolescents from 10–15 years of age and 12 adults. Four phonological changes diffusing from southern England were targeted for investigation, including TH-fronting, the use of [f] for [T], DH-fronting, the use of [v] for [D], T-glottaling, the use of [ʔ] for [t], and L-vocalization. The claim is that these forms are increasing in Glasgow due to the influence of the television show *EastEnders*, one of the most watched shows in the United Kingdom. Yet the findings from the study reveal that actual contact with Londoners is a better predictor than is exposure to television in the appropriation of incoming variants. Simple exposure to television or to *EastEnders* in particular was not significant. Yet measures of "engagement with television" were highly significant for all four phonological changes, suggesting that television does play some role. The results from these studies are puzzlingly equivocal, perhaps because the precise nature of media influence is difficult to define or measure. This is a tantalizing new horizon for development in future research. Further, it remains to be discovered what type of linguistic feature – lexical, morphology, syntax, pragmatic – can arise from contact with the media. Moreover, what will be the effect of the different *types* of new media? Television and print media are being swamped by the Internet, android phones, and new vistas of communication media (see Chapter 11).

Mini Quiz 2.3

This example comes from a study of a single individual (Mike) who is attempting to sound like an African American rather than his own ethnic background, European American (Cutler 1999: 433). Figure 2.8 shows the results of Cutler's distributional analysis of three phonological variables and an idealized display of her anecdotal report of grammatical features in Mike's speech compared to those of African Americans and European Americans.

1. Schwa pronunciations of "th," as in "the other side" = "duh oda side"
2. r-lessness, "her" = "ha"
3. TH-stopping of voiced dental fricatives in word initial position, "the" = "duh"

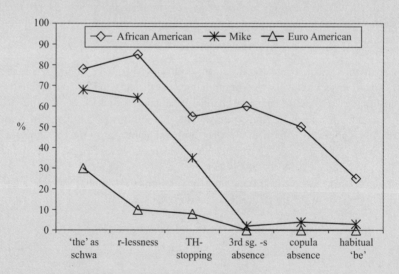

Figure 2.8   Frequency of phonological and grammatical variables.
Source: Cutler 1999: 433, Figure 1.

4. third singular –s absence, "he say"
5. copula absence, "what up?"
6. habitual "be," "I be talking"

Q1 What overall finding does the figure reveal?
Q2 What does this tell us about Mike's linguistic ability to "align" with AAVE vernacular norms?
Q3 What do these results suggest?

An important question for future research is to explore the impact that ethnic groups may have within large urban speech communities. Can ethnic groups influence ongoing linguistic change? If so, why and how? What are the implications for language change? When generation, ethnic, and other standard social factors are also brought into the analysis, what will this reveal?

If teenagers spoke only to octogenarians, there might indeed be a breakdown in intelligibility. (Chambers 2002b: 365)

Age

Language use is intrinsically correlated with speaker age. Everyone notices that older people and younger people do not sound the same. A person who was born in 1900 will not speak the same variety of English as a person born in 2000. The question is why? Is it due to linguistic change? Or is there some other explanation? To figure this out, sociolinguists have utilized two important kinds of analyses. The most obvious one is the analysis of linguistic features in chronological time. However, an even more important perspective comes from the construct of apparent time, an important and useful analytical tool for the analysis of variation (Bailey *et al.* 1991b). In an apparent time study, generational differences are compared at a single point and are used to make inferences about how a change may have taken place in the (recent) past. Age differences are assumed to be temporal analogues, reflecting historical stages in the progress of the change. The technique has been in use since the early 1900s (e.g. Gauchat 1905; Hermann 1929) and has become a keystone of Variationist Sociolinguistics (Bailey 2002; Bailey *et al.* 1991b; Labov 1963, 1966). A gradually increasing or decreasing frequency in the use of a linguistic feature when that feature is viewed according to speaker age can be interpreted as change in progress (Sankoff 2006). This pattern has provided the basis for a synchronic approach to language change. Analytically, apparent time functions as a surrogate for chronological (or real) time, enabling the history of a linguistic process to be viewed from the perspective of the present. However patterns of linguistic features correlated with speaker age can also identify other types of change in the speech community. Sometimes there is ongoing linguistic change in the underlying grammatical system. Sometimes speakers change the way they speak at different ages. Sometimes the whole community is changing the way they speak. Sometimes both types of change happen at the same time. The only way to tell is to uncover the patterns and interpret them.

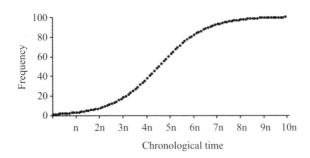

Figure 2.9   S-curve of linguistic change.

Generational Change

Linguistic change (generational change) is one of the cornerstones of sociolinguistics. The fact that linguistic change exists is not in question. All languages change over time. Models of linguistic change from historical linguistics (diachrony) have provided the basic model of how change happens. Innovations initially spread slowly as new forms gradually replace older ones. As this happens, there is acceleration with a maximum rate at mid-course. Then at the end of the period of change, the increase of new forms slows down and the older forms remain rare until they disappear or get left behind in specific contexts. Typical contexts in which linguistic features get "left behind" are formulaic utterances, sayings, songs, and poetry, as in Example 2.5.

Example 2.5

(a)   My friend, who *shall* remain nameless … (TOR/034)
(b)   I was going "Oh no, *shall I, shan't I?*" (YRK/049)
(c)   Auld Lang Syne "old long time" "The good old days"
(d)   The north wind *doth* blow …

When a change has reached this point it is considered complete (Altmann *et al.* 1983; Bailey 1973; Kroch 1989; Labov 1994: 65–67; Labov 2001a; Weinreich *et al.* 1968).

> **NOTE**   Diachrony is the development of a linguistic system (language) over a period of time in the past. Synchrony is the development of a linguistic system (language) in the present time.

The progress of linguistic change has been enshrined in the form of the now familiar S-curve, as in Figure 2.9, which was generated using the values given by Labov (2001a: 452, Table 14.1; Tagliamonte and D'Arcy 2009: 58).

A critical contribution of Variationist Sociolinguistics is the ability to identify and study this type of linguistic change in present-day speech communities. According to Labov (1994: 84) the classic pattern of linguistic change in progress when viewed in apparent time is a monotonic slope by age (Labov 2001a: 171), as in Figure 2.10.

Figure 2.10 shows a steady increase in the proportion of use of a linguistic feature from one age cohort to the next. Note the stepwise pattern. This is referred to in the literature

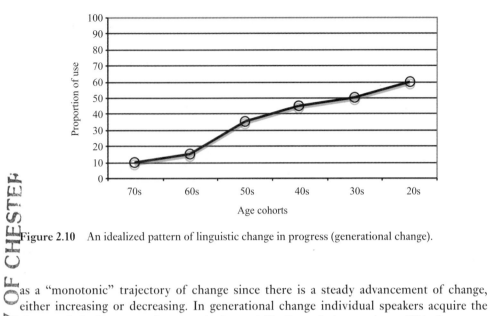

Figure 2.10 An idealized pattern of linguistic change in progress (generational change).

as a "monotonic" trajectory of change since there is a steady advancement of change, either increasing or decreasing. In generational change individual speakers acquire the characteristic frequency for a particular variable from their caregivers. This frequency may increase in adolescence and even undergo reorganization (see below), a typical characteristic of change in progress. However, by late adolescence (approximately age 17) an individual's linguistic system is thought to stabilize and from that point onwards is maintained for the rest of his or her life. In this way regular increases in the values adopted by individuals from one generation to the next lead to linguistic change for the community (Labov 1994: 84).

Mini Quiz 2.4

This figure plots the development of quotatives across the current youth population in Toronto (Tagliamonte and D'Arcy 2004a). Note that since the view is with regard to a developing system from young to old, the view shows increasing age from left to right.

Q1 Which of the following observations is consistent with Figure 2.11?
  (a) The frequency of *be like* rises incrementally across speakers.
  (b) The frequency of *say* falls from youngest to oldest speakers.
  (c) The frequency of *be like* rises sharply, then remains high.
  (d) The frequency of *think* shows rapid change.
  (e) The frequency of *go* is stable.

Q2 Which individual quotative is the most stable in apparent time?
  (a) *be like*
  (b) *think*
  (c) *go*
  (d) zero
  (e) other

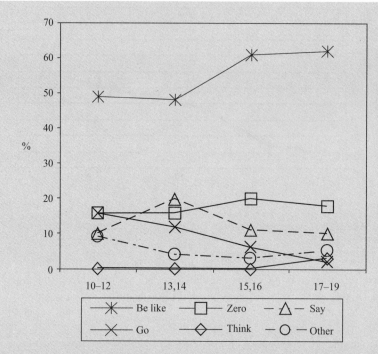

Figure 2.11 Overall distribution of quotatives by age in Toronto English, c. 2002–2004. *Source*: Tagliamonte and D'Arcy, 2004a.

Q3 Which quotative declines in apparent time?
  (a) *be like*
  (b) *think*
  (c) *go*
  (d) zero
  (e) other

Q4 Of the sociolinguistic observations that could be made about Figure 2.11, which is the most dramatic?
  (a) Canadian Youth use a lot of different quotatives.
  (b) Canadian Youth use the *say*, *go*, and *think* as quotatives.
  (c) Use of quotatives is important to Canadian Youth.
  (d) Canadian Youth use *say* more in some age groups than others.
  (e) Canadian Youth use *be like* more than any other quotative.

Age Grading

When linguistic features are viewed in apparent time and exhibit age differences as in Figure 2.10 this is not necessarily evidence of generational change in progress. The same pattern could potentially reflect another phenomenon – age grading.

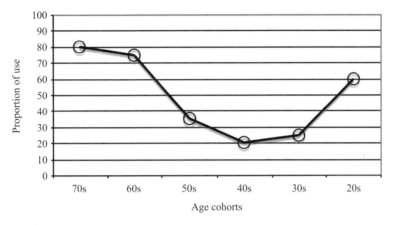

Figure 2.12   An idealized pattern of age-graded change.

Age grading is when people of different ages use language differently simply because they are at different stages in their life. They use "speech appropriate to their age group" (Wardaugh 2002: 194). Labov's definition of age grading is:

> If individuals change their linguistic behaviour throughout their lifetimes, but the community as a whole does not change, the pattern can be characterized as one of age grading. (Labov 1994: 84)

Age grading accounts for the fact that as people age their use of certain features may wane or vanish altogether. Alternatively, certain features may emerge as a person gets older. Note that there is no ongoing linguistic change of the grammar of the language, but rather change is localized to the behavior of a certain age group.

The classic pattern of age grading is a u- or v-shaped curve (Downes 1984: 191). (Of course, the inverse can also be true, i.e. a curve with a hump or point in the middle.) Figure 2.12 presents an idealized pattern of an age-graded change.

Figure 2.12 depicts the expected pattern for a nonprestigious linguistic feature that is age graded. When such features are not part of the standard language, they tend to peak during adolescence "when peer group pressure not to conform to society's norms is greatest" (Holmes 1992: 184). In middle age when societal pressure, job advancement, and child rearing come to the fore people tend to become more conservative. According to Holmes (1992: 186) "in their 'middle-years' people are most likely to recognize the society's speech norms and use the fewest vernacular forms." The use of standard or prestige forms peaks between the ages of 30 and 55 when people experience maximum social pressure to conform to the norms of the standard language. Then in old age, "when social pressures reduce as people move out of the workforce and into a more relaxed phase of their life," the non-prestigious forms may resurface (Cheshire 2005: 1555; Downes 1998: 24; Labov 1994: 73).

Age-graded change typically involves linguistic features that: (1) have a high degree of social awareness (Labov 1994: 111–112), or (2) "have a rapid life-cycle" (Wolfram and Fasold 1974: 90). This is why features that become age-graded are those that are more able to be consciously controlled. The typical example used in the literature is the adolescent to adulthood transition. Adolescents use more slang terms (whatever they may be at a given time), more swear words, etc. (see Holmes 1992: 183) but as they get older and enter the workforce their use of these features is thought to recede. This process is called "sociolectal retrenchment" (Chambers 2003: 95). Adolescent lexical items are typically cited as examples of age-graded phenomenon. For example, Wolfram and Fasold's (1974) description of age grading refers to pre-adolescents as "teeny-boppers" and adolescents are cited as using slang expression such as *heavy* for "nice." Today (c. 2010) pre-adolescents would not know what *either* of these words mean. Both these words have already come and gone.

An example of stable age grading is the pronunciation of the alphabet letter "Z" (Chambers 2003). In most places in the world, including Canada, the pronunciation of the letter is [zɛd]. In contrast, the US the pronunciation is [zi]. This creates a dilemma for Canadian children who watch American television shows and learn their alphabet by singing a popular American song that pronounces the last letter of the alphabet as [zi]. The children acquire this pronunciation but as they get older they change over to [zɛd] to align themselves with the adult population. However, what scenario can account for the upswing of the pattern shown in Figure 2.12? It is doubtful whether the middle-aged Canadian adults will change back to pronouncing [zi] in their old age. But then, who knows? When they sing that alphabet song to their grandchildren, what pronunciation will they use? To my knowledge, no one has checked (see also Boberg 2004: 259–260).

> **NOTE**   I am Canadian and my youngest son happens to have a name that has two zeds, *Dazzian*. One time he was hospitalized in a US hospital. On several occasions the hospital's personnel asked me to spell his name. I replied, "D, A, zed, zed, I, A N." Different people kept coming back to ask me the same question. Eventually someone asked me directly, "What is 'zed'? Is it a nickname?" It finally dawned on me that they were having trouble establishing the correct spelling of Dazzian's name. So, I spelled it out again "properly" "D, A, zee, zee, I, A N."

The Adolescent Peak

In early sociolinguistic research it was assumed that the step-by-step, monotonic pattern of linguistic change visible in Figure 2.2 would simply extend into the younger age groups, i.e. those under 20 (Labov 2001a: 454). However, when a number of early studies began to include preadolescents and adolescents in their analyses (e.g. Ash 1982; Cedergren 1973, 1988) a crest in the curve of change appeared in the late teenage years. This pattern is shown in Figure 2.13.

Figure 2.13 shows that the frequency of the incoming form is highest among 15–17 year olds. In fact, evidence from many studies has revealed that pre-adolescents use incoming forms less frequently, not more frequently, than their immediate elders. Postadolescents use the same forms less frequently. The difference in usage between these critical age groups creates a peak in the apparent time trajectory.

The discovery of a peak in apparent time marked "an idiosyncratic or at least unexpected feature" (Chambers 2003: 223) in the progress of change. Ash (1982) suggested that the peak might indicate that the change was receding. Cedergren (1988: 53) alluded to the social

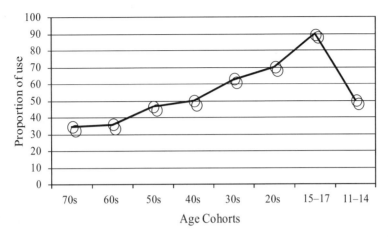

Figure 2.13   An idealized pattern of the adolescent peak

importance of the incoming form in the "linguistic marketplace" (Bourdieu and Boltanski 1975), suggesting that there was pressure from the community to use the feature. Chambers (2003: 195) argued that the dip in frequency after adolescence could also be explained as a return to adult norms following the adolescent years, i.e. sociolectal retrenchment. In this latter view, the peak simply reflects age grading because it is associated with a particular phase in life. Others suggested that the incoming forms had reached their limit and were receding (Labov 2001a: 454–455). However, the recurrence of a pattern with a peak within similar age cohorts across a variety of different linguistic variables in numerous localities suggested a more principled explanation (Labov 2001a: 454–455; see also Tagliamonte and D'Arcy 2009: 59).

Labov (2001a: 458) offered the findings from nine ongoing female-dominated sound changes in Philadelphia to provide empirical support for a model of linguistic change that incorporates this peak. Among women a peak was visible for every variable, eight among 13–16 year olds and one among 17–29 year olds. Labov (2001a) argued that the peak is created by the logistic incrementation of linguistic change. Remember that the view of the data is from the perspective of apparent time – a snapshot in time. Not real time. In this frozen moment, the peak is the crest of an advancing wave of change. The drop-off above the maximum is due to the fact that the older speakers stabilized at an earlier point in the advancing change when the incoming form was that much less frequent. The drop-off below the maximum, among the younger speakers, is due to the shorter time period of time they have been participating in the change. They simply have not yet amassed the increments that the next oldest adolescents have.

> **NOTE**   Incrementation refers to an increase in the frequency of an incoming linguistic change. A peak in the incrementation process is simply an artifact of the apparent time construct. It is really the leading edge of a change in progress.

Vernacular Reorganization

How does the vernacular form and develop? A strong and recurrent finding from LVC research is that children acquire the vernacular of their primary caretaker, typically their mother (Kerswill 1996a; Kerswill and Williams 2000; Labov 2001a). This basic fact coupled with the pervasive finding in LVC research of gender asymmetry suggests a further gender difference. Which vernacular are children going to acquire? Undoubtedly, it will be the language of their caretakers. If women are the caretakers and women are ahead in the progression of linguistic change, then children will get an enhanced step forward on this cline from their mothers. A question that arises is, Are there differences between young male and female children in the adoption of their mother's vernacular? Further, it is quite obvious that children must at some point come to speak differently from their caretakers otherwise change would never happen. This means that at some point children adopt a norm that is different from the one they have acquired. This changing of the vernacular is known as vernacular reorganization and it occurs in the preadolescent and adolescent years (Labov 2001a: 415). Vernacular reorganization is necessary for linguistic change to advance.

Evidence for vernacular reorganization comes from several sources. Payne's (1980) research in Philadelphia showed that the children of out-of-state parents were able to acquire ongoing language changes in the local community that their parents did not use. Kerswill and associates (Kerswill 1994, 1995, 1996a, 1996b; Kerswill and Williams 2000) studied the ideal laboratory for examining this process. Milton Keynes in England was created in the early 1970s by the immigration of people from many dialect areas. When the community was studied in the early 1990s the youngest children used the dialect of their caretakers; however, the 8-year olds exhibited departures from the parental pattern and the 12-year olds even more so. Such findings reveal that vernacular reorganization is already underway by age 8 and continues to advance into adolescence. LVC research in the late 1990s and early 2000s continues to demonstrate that the age span between approximately 8 years of age and the 20s is a key timeframe for studying the advancement of linguistic change in progress (e.g. D'Arcy 2004; Tagliamonte and D'Arcy 2007a; Tagliamonte and D'Arcy 2009).

Mini Quiz 2.5

Figure 2.14 shows some of the results from two surveys of Panama City, Panama, one in 1969 and one in 1982–84 (Cedergren 1973; 1988). The years on the x-axis are birth dates of the speakers in the sample. The figure shows the percentage of ch-lenition. The phoneme /tʃ/ has the standard variant [tʃ], a voiceless palatal affricate. The lenited variant is [ʃ], a voiceless palatal fricative. Lenition is regarded as a process of weakening because the stop articulation is lost to aspiration.

Q1   What is the most obvious sociolinguistic pattern in Figure 2.14?
  (a)   The stability of the linguistic change.
  (b)   A steep peak in the use of the lenited variant among the second youngest group.
  (c)   Greater use of the lenited variant among the youngest Panamanians.

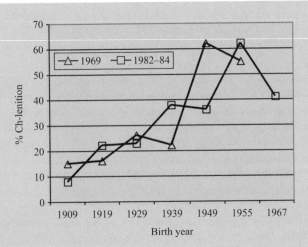

Figure 2.14 Ch-lenition in Panama c. 1969 and 1982–84.
Source: Cedergren, 1988: 53, Figure 4.

    (d)   Greater use of the lenited variant among older Panamanians.
    (e)   Age grading.

Q2   The pattern in Figure 2.14 can be interpreted as:
    (a)   Change in progress.
    (b)   Stylistic variation.
    (c)   Stable stratification.
    (d)   Age grading.
    (e)   Social stratification.

Q3   What aspect of this study provides the strongest possible test for the apparent time hypothesis?
    (a)   The sample of members across age groups.
    (b)   The second survey on the same random sample of all age groups, with the addition of a new group born in 1967–77.
    (c)   The use of survey techniques.
    (d)   The study of a linguistic variable undergoing change.
    (e)   The study of the city of Panama where changes were occurring very quickly.

Q4   Given the results in the figure when do Panamanians acquire the accelerated rates of ch-lenition?
    (a)   Before they are 3 years old.
    (b)   In adolescence.
    (c)   In their twenties.
    (d)   In their forties.
    (e)   Not until they are over 40.

Q5   What could explain the peak for the second-youngest age group in both surveys?
    (a)   Age grading.
    (b)   Statistical hypercorrection.

(c)   The postadolescents are on the leading edge of change.
(d)   ch-lenition is a stigmatized variant.
(e)   ch-lenition is a stylistic marker in the speech community.

Q6   By the time of the second study in 1988 ch-lenition had become the object of social awareness and overt social commentary, something that had not been the case at the time of the first study. When linguistic features reach this stage, what are they called?

Social Change

Age differences within a speech community may not be the result of ongoing generational change or age grading. Instead, a u-shaped pattern in apparent time may indicate socio-cultural changes and speakers' different responses to that change. Consider the case of Cajun English in Louisiana. Dubois and Horvath (1998) found a u-shaped pattern by speaker age for the use of stopped variant, [d], of the interdental fricatives [T] and [D], as in Example 2.6.

Example 2.6

(a)   variable (th)   "this" →   [dIs]
(b)   variable (dh)   "that" →   [dæt]

The middle-aged speakers had a dip in apparent time, just as in Figure 2.12. The older and younger generations had heightened use of the vernacular forms; their use of the [d] variant was as high as their grandparents. In explaining this u-shaped pattern in apparent time, Dubois and Horvath (1998: 257) did not appeal to age grading as an explanation, but instead linked it to the sociocultural situation. Over the period represented by the data there had been a decline in positive evaluation for Cajun identity followed by a Cajun renaissance. They argue that the resurgence of older Cajun features among the younger generation of speakers is due to the positive evaluation of Cajun identity. The linguistic variables involved, variable (th) and (dh), were not changing incrementally over time, as in generational change, nor were stable among for people of a particular age. Instead, there was recycling from one generation to the next of specific variables with socially correlated meaning. The social meaning of the variables had changed so that they could be used again.

How can the analyst assess whether an apparent-time correlation between the use of a linguistic feature and speaker age is generational change, age grading, recycling, or some other type of change? The best way to tell is to have a real-time perspective – ideally a comparison with data from two points in time. Unfortunately, the vast majority of sociolinguistic data in the literature comes from apparent time. The easiest way to remedy the apparent-time–real-time problem is to conduct an apparent-time study but then compare the findings with an earlier study of the same community. Labov's (1963) study of Martha's Vineyard, for example, was supported with dialect data that had been collected in the *Linguistic Atlas of New England* (Kurath 1939). The problem was that studies from the early nineteenth century or earlier were not conducted with the same methods nor with the detail of later studies. This means that the data are often quite different, making comparisons at best suggestive.

The issue of disentangling linguistic change from age grading is of such great consequence that in the 1980s and 1990s resurveys of classic sociolinguistic study sites emerged. Cedergren (1988) and Trudgill (1988) led the way with their resurvey of Panama City and Norwich. In the 2000s came resurveys of Martha's Vineyard (Blake and Josey 2003; Pope, Meyerhoff, and Ladd 2007). Other communities that have been resurveyed include Montreal, Canada (Blondeau 2001; Sankoff and Blondeau 2007; Sankoff, Blondeau, and Charity 2001), and various locales in Finland (Nahkola and Saanilahti 2004; Nordberg 1975; Nordberg and Sundgren 1998; Paunenen 1996). These are trend studies. Trend studies involve resampling the same age range of speakers with similar social attributes in the same speech community at different points in time (Bailey 2002; Sankoff 2006).

Trend studies have consistently established an increase in the frequency of incoming forms, affirming the validity of the apparent time construct. Cedergren (1988) reported that in the 13 years intervening between her initial and follow-up investigations in Panama, the frequency of ch-lenition had increased among speakers between the ages of 40 to 70 years (see Figure 2.14). Tagliamonte and D'Arcy (2007a) demonstrated that in a period of just seven years, young people in Ontario, Canada had substantially increased their use of quotative *be like*. Sankoff (2006) summarizes research testing the apparent time construct by saying:

> Together, trend and panel studies of the past decade have confirmed the validity and usefulness of apparent time as a powerful conceptual tool for the identification of language change in progress.

Nevertheless, there have been clear indications from trend studies that individuals may be able to shift the frequency of linguistic features well into adulthood. It seems, therefore, that the assumption of postadolescent linguistic stability that underlies much sociolinguistic research may not reflect the actual situation as accurately as initially believed (see also Labov 2001a: 446–447). Recall that the apparent time construct relies on the assumption that individuals' grammars stabilize in late adolescence. But what if they do not? There is yet another type of change to consider – change through the lifespan.

Lifespan Change

> Age-graded diversity ... demonstrates that the ontogeny of language must continue through a speaker's lifetime. (Guy and Boyd 1990: 16)

Community change is when "all members of the community alter their frequencies together or acquire new forms simultaneously" (Labov 1994: 84). In this type of change "individual speakers change over their lifespans in the direction of a change in progress in the rest of the community" (Sankoff 2005: 1011). This type of change has come to be referred to as "longitudinal change" (Sankoff 2005: 1011) or lifespan change (Sankoff and Blondeau 2007: 562).

The ideal way to test for linguistic change across the lifespan is through a panel study. In panel studies the same individuals are followed for an extended period of time. Unfortunately, this type of study is rare. Most panel studies are small (e.g. Brink and Lund 1979; Nahkola and Saanilahti 2004; Palander 2005; Robson 1975; Tagliamonte 2007); however, there are at least two large-scale studies, such as in Finland (e.g. Sundgren 2009) and Denmark (e.g. Gregersen, Maegaard, and Pharao 2009). Some show that individuals change the frequency

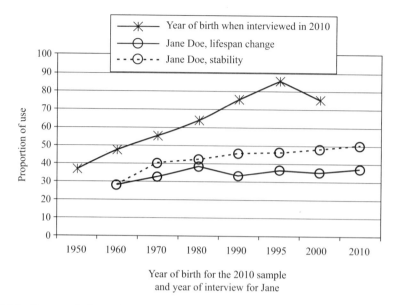

Figure 2.15   Pattern of a feature increasing in use over 60 years in real time for Jane Doe and apparent time for the speech community.

of features involved in change. Sankoff (2004) performed a case study of two of the boys involved in the British documentary series *Seven Up*, filmed in seven-year increments from 1963 when the children were seven years old. She found that both boys had made "some significant phonetic [...] alterations to their speech after adolescence" (Sankoff 2004: 136).

Montreal French is unique in having been sampled in 1971, 1984, and 1994 (e.g. Blondeau 2001; Sankoff and Blondeau 2007; Sankoff and Cedergren 1973; Thibault 1986; Thibault and Daveluy 1989). This is a unique window on linguistic change in real time. Blondeau discovered an increase in the use of simple personal pronouns (*on, tu, vous*) and Sankoff and Blondeau (2007) found that use of posterior [R], an incoming change from above, was also more advanced. Thus, in both cases, the older speakers had moved along with the change in progress. The Swedish town of Eskilstuna was sampled in 1967–1968 (Nordberg 1975) and again in 1996 (Nordberg and Sundgren 1998; Sundgren 2009). The frequency of changes in progress in the late 1960s had increased in 1996. Given the results of these studies, apparent time actually underestimates the rate of change (see also Boberg 2004; Sankoff and Blondeau 2007).

An idealized picture of apparent time compared to real time can illustrate the difference between lifespan change vs. stability. This is shown in Figure 2.15. Suppose there was a sociolinguistic study that followed a single individual through her lifetime – *Jane Doe* – born in the year 1950. The study interviews *Jane* every year from the time she is a pre-adolescent in 1960 until 2010 when she is 70 (the circled line). In 2010 a study is undertaken of the same speech community with representation from individuals in their 70s (the same age as *Jane*) down to the pre-adolescents born in 2000. Two plausible lifespan trajectories are shown for *Jane*. The solid line models the hypothesis of incrementation to a peak in late adolescence followed by stability. The dashed line models the hypothesis of modest lifespan change. An incoming linguistic change in progress is at an early stage of development in 1960. In 2010 an apparent time sample shows that the incoming form has increased in frequency across the members of the speech community. The younger the individual the more they use the incoming form, particularly the adolescents born in 1995 who are on the leading edge of the change and exhibit the expected peak in apparent time. Compare the cohort of 70 year olds in 2010 with *Jane* who is also 70 in 2010. They have more or less the same rate of use of the incoming form in 2010; however, the precise frequency of use among these speakers would depend on the extent of lifespan change. This is something that will, I hope, be made more precise in future studies.

This same linguistic question can be tackled in historical data by utilizing data from the past over lengthy periods of time. In this case, researchers rely on written documents in the historical record produced by the same individual over their lifetime (e.g. Nevalainen and Raumolin-Brunberg 2003: 83–109; Raumolin-Brunberg 2005; 2009). One can imagine all manner of different corpora from the past that might be used to make observations about linguistic change: print media, literary works, radio broadcasts, etc. The more difficult part is to find the data, devise a sample, and construct the appropriate data set.

Distinguishing generational change from lifespan change from community change from age grading is one of the big issues in contemporary LVC research (Labov 1994: 46)

TIP Any claim for linguistic change requires evidence from two points in time. Apparent time is good. But real time is better. If you can, find a real-time point of comparison for your study.

Stability

Despite all this discussion of change, at any given point in time, the vast majority of the grammar is stable and categorical. However, there are also many features that are variable but not changing. This demonstrates that variability is inherent to language rather than simply a transition from one state of a linguistic system to another (Labov 2001a: 75). Features that are variable but stable include those that correlate with social factors and/or differentiate styles, e.g. variable (ing), (t,d) (see Chapter 7), as well as those that cue levels of formality or processing effects, e.g. variable use of the complementizer *that* (see Chapter 5). Stability is easily recognizable by a flat pattern when a linguistic feature is viewed according to speaker age, such as in Figure 2.16.

Figure 2.16 shows that the frequency of a form remains stable across the adult community. Substantial research has demonstrated that certain linguistic variables exhibit stable variation of this type. In fact, some linguistic variables have been like this for centuries, e.g. variable (ing), (th], (dh), and negative concord (Labov 2001a: 85–92) cites.

The stability of these features confirms that linguistic variability is not simply a conduit for linguistic change, but also pervades the speech community as an inherent part of the linguistic system.

If variation is nothing but a transitional phenomenon, a way-station between two invariant stages of the language, it can have only a limited role in our view of the human language faculty. Inherent variation would then be only an accident of history, a product of the unsurprising finding that human beings cannot abandon one form and adopt another instantaneously. (Labov 2001a: 85)

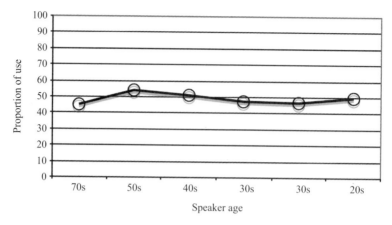

Figure 2.16   An idealized pattern of a stable linguistic variable.

Types of Change

> Not all variability and heterogeneity in language structure involves change; but all change
> involves variability and heterogeneity. (Weinreich *et al.* 1968: 188)

Linguistics has a long history of attempting to explain language change. When it comes to
the quantitative study of linguistic variation and change, the prevailing question is how did
this variation come to be? An important part of explaining change requires in-depth
knowledge of where the change originated, its underlying mechanisms, and its stage of
development.

Trees and Waves

The earliest model of linguistic change was the family tree model which is based on the
notion of linguistic descent, the idea of one language being a later stage of another according
to mother, daughter, sister relationships (Bloomfield 1933: 316 ff; Hoenigswald 1960; Labov
2007). In this view languages and their linguistic features descend from earlier stages of the
same language over time, such as the development of the Romance languages, Italian, French,
and Spanish, from Latin, e.g. Latin *annus* (year) became Italian *anno*, Spanish *año*, French
année, with the English derivative *annual*. The underlying assumption is that this history is a
progression from generation to generation that is regular and without exception. The same
pattern is repeated in synchronic change as a monotonic pattern in apparent time as we saw
earlier in Figure 2.2. However, in actuality languages are influenced by a host of other factors.
Another model, the wave model (Bailey 1973), is the idea that new features of a language
spread from a central point outwards like waves just as when a stone is thrown into a body of
water. This allows for more than simply change by descent. In this model dialects that are
closely associated with each other in ways other than genetics – socially, economically,
culturally – will influence each other in such a way that changes can arise *across* the branches
of a linguistic family tree. For example, the Norman invasion of England in 1066 led to

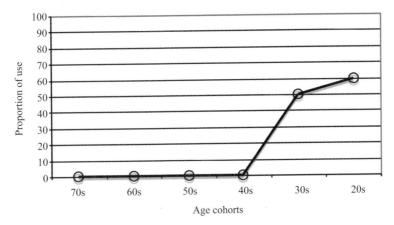

Figure 2.17   An idealized pattern of linguistic change from across the branches of the family tree, i.e. from outside the community.

heavy borrowing from French which led to innumerable vocabulary and spelling changes in English. Even today, in England the pronunciation of the borrowed French word "restaurant" may have a final nasal vowel (as in French) rather than some kind of final consonant. According to recent research both family tree models and wave models are needed to account for the history and relatedness of language families (Labov 2007: 382).

The dichotomy between linguistic change that is inherited from within the family tree vs. linguistic change that comes from external sources is an important distinction for interpreting patterns of LVC at any given point in time.

What kind of sociolinguistic pattern would be expected from a borrowed change as opposed to a change in progress? Such a change would not show a regular monotonic shift from one generation to the next. Instead, a change would happen abruptly in response to some external influence. Figure 2.17 provides an idealized view of what such a change might look like. Watch out for it!

Above and Below

In traditional sociolinguistic studies the nature of change was also described in terms of (1) change from below and (2) change from above (Labov 1994: 78). Change from below is "the normal type of linguistic change." It is a development that comes from within the system itself (Labov 2007: 346) (Figures 2.2 and 2.9). Such changes include processes such as generalization, extension, analogy, and the like (see Chapter 3). Change from above on the other hand is "the importation of elements from other systems" (Labov 2007: 346). It is important to keep in mind that the term "above" is not meant to imply that the changes are higher on the socioeconomic scale. The critical dimension is the place of origin of the linguistic feature. While these may often be prestigious features, they need not be. For example, in early sociolinguistic research Trudgill (1974b) showed that nonstandard features from London were spreading to other British cities. These were changes from above since they were imported from elsewhere. The change idealized in Figure 2.17 above is this type of change.

Change from above has these identifying characteristics:

- imported from outside the speech community;
- speakers are aware of it;
- socially motivated;
- may involve a reversal of the trajectory of change.

Change from below has these identifying characteristics:

- develops spontaneously within the speech community;
- speakers are not consciously aware of it, at least in the initial stages;
- linguistically motivated, but may be driven by social motivations.

Drift vs. Contact

> Every word, every grammatical element, every locution, every sound and accent is a slowly changing configuration, moulded by the invisible and impersonal drift that is the life of language. (Sapir 1921: 149)

The same dichotomy has been referred to in another way, namely whether the change in question has arisen (1) naturally from within the system itself, or (2) through contact. Natural changes can be considered the traditional type of change which is thought to be phonetically gradual, exceptionless, and every token of a phoneme in a phonological context is affected (Kerswill 1996a: 178). This type of change is often called drift as in the quote above. Contact-induced change comes from any factor of the external world which causes languages to change. While geographic factors may facilitate or impede development, society and culture provide innumerable influences on change as well.

Leveling

Another way of looking at these processes is through the lens of dialect leveling, a phenomenon that has been most extensively studied in the United Kingdom and in Europe where longitudinal jockeying among many different dialects, dialect regions, and countries (e.g. Scotland, England, Northern Ireland, Ireland, and Wales) has been going on for centuries. Peter Trudgill (1986: 98) has been at the forefront of research on dialect leveling, which he defines as a process which leads to "the reduction or attrition of marked variants," where "marked" refers to forms that are "unusual or in a minority" (Trudgill 1986: 98). Dialect leveling involves two different processes: (1) leveling across geographic space – geographical diffusion, and (2) leveling of linguistic forms as an outcome of accommodation (mutual convergence) between speakers of difference dialects. Such processes are not straightforward, however, as linguistic change progresses quite distinctly in different types of communities (e.g. Kerswill 2003, 2009a,b). In the United Kingdom the typical situation is a largely monolingual base and people move from one dialect region to another. UK researchers report that mobility has increased dramatically over the past 50 years leading to disruption in traditional community norms. As Kerswill points out, a high degree of mobility leads to the weakening of group-internal linguistic norms. The population, in turn, becomes more receptive to linguistic innovation, taking up diffusing change more readily and thus change proceeds more rapidly (Kerswill 2003: 224). This is why research in the United Kingdom has been dominated by studies that share a concern with the spread of features in geographic and social space (e.g. Foulkes and Docherty 1999) and several large-scale research projects have arisen which track these changes in apparent time (e.g. Kerswill 1996b, 2003, 2009a,b; Kerswill and Williams 2000; Kerswill *et al.* 2008). One of the major trends is that regional dialect speakers are eschewing linguistic features which are "particularly indicative of their local roots while at the same time adopting some features which are perceived to be non-local" (Kerswill 2003: 225). The pattern for dialect leveling at the community level would be consistent with Figure 2.17 with the added proviso that the frequency and use of the feature used by the under 30 year olds is a supralocal norm and potentially a more common variant in the larger pool.

In some cases, very high-contact communities with large populations of adults not only from different dialect areas but also from different countries speaking different languages (e.g. London) might be expected to lead to imperfect learning, and thus simplification and rapid change of the host dialect. It is difficult to conceive how these different processes could be disentangled in practice. Ethnic influences must be distinguished from differences relating to social class, education, age of arrival, social networks, identity, allegiance, and potentially many other factors.

Transmission vs. Diffusion

In the United States linguistic change across communities is viewed somewhat differently. The two leading questions are as follows: Has the change evolved within the speech community through transmission, i.e. descent from earlier version of the same language, i.e. tree model? Has the change evolved through diffusion from one community to the next, i.e. wave model? Transmission involves change from below. It is "the unbroken sequence of native-language acquisition by children" which results in "the continuity of dialects and languages across time" (Labov 2007: 346). Transmission emerges in the context of change internal to the speech community (Figure 2.10). Children advance a linguistic change to a level beyond that of their caretakers in the same direction over successive generations (Labov 1994: Chapter 14). This is said to produce a "faithful reproduction" (Labov 2007: 345) of existing patterns. Incrementation is the increase in frequency from childhood to the age of stabilization (somewhere around age 17). Diffusion involves change from above. It is change that originates from outside (Figure 2.17). This typically arises in the context of "contact between speech communities" and the "transfer of features from one to the other" (Labov 2007: 347). In the situation of change from above where change is diffusing from one place to another, the original patterns weaken and there is loss of structural features. This crucially implicates the constraints on variation as key indicators of the mechanisms of change.

Given the essential differences between these types of change as well as the overlaps between them it is critical for the analyst to observe and interpret both the pattern and its social and linguistic correlates. The nature of linguistic patterns in the speech community will provide clues as to the origins of a particular linguistic phenomenon. When children participate in a linguistic change we can expect an increase in the frequency of incoming forms and a faithful replica of the extant patterns. However, in diffusion there will be changes in the "extent, scope, or specificity of a variable" (Labov 2007: 346). The question is how to identify these processes. What does a process of weakening look like? What does it mean to lose structural features?

Table 2.1 Difficulty of acquisition of linguistic variables.

Rank	Linguistic feature	Age of acquisition
1 (most difficult)	i. lexically unpredictable phonological rules	By 3 (?)
	ii. new phonological oppositions	By 3–13
	iii. grammatical change; parameters	By 8 (?)
2	iv. prosodic systems	
3	v. grammatical change	Adolescence? Lifespan?
4	vi. morphologically conditioned changes	Not before 4–7; then lifespan
5	vii. reassignment of words or lexical sets to other morphological classes	Lifespan
6	viii. mergers	Lifespan
7	ix. neogrammarian changes	Lifespan
8	x. lexical diffusion of phonological changes	Lifespan
	xi. borrowing, new lexical forms of old words; new phonetic forms of existing morphological categories	
9	Borrowing, vocabulary	Lifespan

Source: Kerswill 1996a: 200, Table 4.

Levels of Grammar

Transmission of linguistic features from all levels of grammar is not in question in the case of linguistic descent. Children learning their native language are able to acquire the grammar of their parents regardless of whether it is a unique pronunciation or a pragmatic nuance. However, when linguistic features are imported from one speech community to the next (diffusion), the level of grammar becomes critical. Are all features perfectly replicated linguistically and socially? It is well known that people of different ages have different abilities in acquiring language. Kerswill (1995) argues that the age of the transmitters of linguistic change is a critical factor in diffusion. Children are capable of learning new linguistic forms, their frequency, and their underlying linguistic patterns. Adults, on the other hand, may be able to learn a new form and use it to a certain degree, but they are unable to acquire the structural detail of underlying linguistic patterns. According to Labov (2007: 371), "an unbroken sequence of parent-to-child transmission is required to maintain complex patterns of phonetic, grammatical, and lexical specification." In essence, there are tangible and complex contrasts between transmission by children and diffusion by adults. Moreover, according to research by Kerswill (1995) and Labov (2007: 371) the nature of linguistic change found under different sociolinguistic conditions can be predicted and identified according to patterns of the variation. Kerswill (1996a: 200, Table 4) proposed a difficulty hierarchy for linguistic variables, as in Table 2.1. Such a hierarchy along with a consideration of the origins and nature of a linguistic change in a given community can provide analysts with a new way of explaining linguistic variables and the mechanisms of change that underlie them.

As changes propagate across the landscape from urban centers to smaller cities to outlying communities, how are the changes evolving? Do they maintain the underlying constraints and patterns found at the source? Or are they modified, extended, simplified, or otherwise? Kerswill's model can be used to interpret change within and across communities. It can determine whether a change has been transmitted or diffused, or whether it is the result of some other process. Examination of the details of variation from a cross-community perspective, as detailed by Kerswill (1996a) and Labov (2007), will enable scholars to provide a rich interpretation of the patterns of variation they find in their data.

> **TIP**   Notice that Kerswill puts a question mark on grammatical change. Given the widespread grammatical changes going on in English over the past 100 years, exploring cross-dialectal patterns of grammatical change stands out as a promising new research agenda.

Phase of Development

Another important dimension to interpreting patterns of linguistic variation in time is to consider the change in terms of its stage of development, i.e. how long has it been going on? Where is it on the S-curve (see Figure 2.9)? A linguistic change can be (1) nearly completed, (2) mid-range, (3) new and vigorous, or (4) incipient (Labov 1994: 67, 79–83). Nevalainen and Raumolin-Brunberg (1996: 55) apply the following classification in their research on incoming forms they studied in the history of English between 1410 and 1681.

Each phase in the history of a change is thought to have a particular social nature. When a change is incipient it may not have strong social correlates. However, when the change starts up the middle section of the S-shaped curve (Figure 2.9), social factors become significant. By the time changes reach the middle range their association with particular age cohorts and/or social characteristics weakens. Then, as changes near completion, social differences level out and there tend to be fewer distinctions across the socioeconomic hierarchy. Such a progression might be mapped onto the frequency metric proposed by Nevalainen and Raumolin-Brunberg (1996: 55), as in Example 2.7.

Example 2.7

Incipient	≤15%	no age or social correlates
New and vigorous	15–35%	social factors become significant
Mid-range	36–65%	social factors weaken
Nearing completion	65–85%	social differences level out
Completed	≥85%	

This model presents a testable hypothesis for the examination of data. In a series of articles Tagliamonte and D'Arcy (Tagliamonte and D'Arcy 2004a,b, 2007a) set out to explore these phases in an linguistic change in progress as well as nature of incrementation, vernacular reorganization and lifespan change. We discovered that the male/female contrast was developmental in the rise of use of *be like*. The frequency of the incoming form incremented through adulthood; however, the grammar underlying the change did not change (see Chapter 9). These findings require corroboration from other speech communities and across communities.

In sum, the key to understanding linguistic variation and change is to be able to interpret sociolinguistic patterns. The rich body of research that sociolinguistic studies has provided over the past 40 years or more has substantiated that sociolinguistic patterns are fundamental – generational change, age grading, lifespan change – each leave different "tracks" in the speech community. The next phase in sociolinguistic research will be to determine whether the same patterns are relevant for all types of variables and to determine to what extent these patterns are applicable to diverse sociocultural contexts, both local and supralocal, on the world stage.

NOTE   Watch a senior sociolinguist at a conference talk. He or she might be staring at the handout, scribbling on the figure or table that depicts the study's findings. Why? Because sociolinguists know that the key to explaining linguistic variables lies in interpreting the patterns. Once you understand the patterns, you will understand the variable.

Principles of Linguistic Change

Due to the overwhelming consistency of patterns of linguistic change and their associated social correlates, Labov (1990) first formulated two principles of linguistic change. The original principles were Principle I: In stable sociolinguistic stratification, men use a higher frequency of nonstandard forms than women; and Principle II: In the majority of linguistic changes, women use a higher frequency of the incoming forms than men. These were revised to four principles of linguistic change (Labov 1994, 2001a).[1]

Principle 1 (change from below)
"Linguistic change from below originates in a central social group, located in the interior of the socioeconomic hierarchy" (Labov 2001a: 188). This principle emerges from findings that exhibit the curvilinear pattern shown earlier in Figure 2.5. The so-called "interior" social classes (lower middle and upper middle class) lead linguistic change. They have a higher frequency of incoming forms.

Principle 2 (stability)
For stable sociolinguistic variables, women show a lower rate of stigmatized variants and a higher rate of prestige variants than men (Labov 2001a: 266). Principle 2 strongly implicates women's social role in the speech community. This situation is exemplified in Figure 2.6 where women consistently have higher frequencies than men.

Principle 3 (change from above)
In linguistic change from above, women adopt diffusing forms at a higher rate than men (Labov 2001a: 274). Principle 3 suggests that one of the identifying features of change from above would be the greater use by women of diffusing forms and a greater use by men of local and/or dialectal variants.

Table 2.2   The gender paradox.

Women	Men
Conform to sociolinguistic norms that are overtly prescribed, i.e. stable stylistic variables, variable *(who)*	Conform less to overt prescription
Conform to innovations from within the speech community (transmitted changes)	Conform less to innovations regardless of origin
Conform to diffusing innovations even when they are not overtly prescribed, e.g. variable *(be like)*	

Principle 4 (change from below)

In linguistic change from below, women use higher frequencies of innovative forms than men do (Labov 2001a: 275, 292–293). Principle 4 suggests that an identifying feature of change from below would be the greater use by women of innovative forms.

Notice that there is an essential paradox in male–female behavior, the gender paradox, as in Table 2.2. Labov repeats the gender paradox: "While women consistently conform more closely than men to variants that are overtly proscribed, they conform less than men to variants that are not overtly prescribed (change from below), but which are innovative." His explanation continues:

> both conservative and innovative behaviours reflect women's superior sensitivity to the social evaluation of language. In stable situations women perceive and react to prestige or stigma more strongly than men do, and when change begins, women are quicker and more forceful to employing the new social symbolism, whatever it might be. (Labov 2001a: 291)

Eckert explains it another way:

> Generalizations about the use of standard language can be linked to generalizations about women's position in society … women have to do much more than men simply to maintain their place in the standard language market … women may have to use linguistic extremes in order to solidify their place, wherever it may be … (Eckert 2000: 192)

Why do women lead in 90% of the innovations of language wherever they originate? After all, the behavior of men and women in one community may not be identical to another and what is considered prestigious may also vary and change over time. Glottalization was once a lower-class dialect feature in England. Trudgill's (1972b) study of Norwich showed that the men were using t-glottaling the most. Ten years later the use of t-glottaling was accelerating among young women in Wales (Mees 1987). Another 10 years later it had spread north to Newcastle (Milroy *et al.* 1994b) and York (see Chapter 7). The use of this feature by woman was apparently instrumental in reversing the traditional stigma that this feature once had.

> The explanation that is suggested by the diffusion of the glottal stop in England "is not that females favour prestige forms … but that they create them." (Milroy *et al.* 1994b: 351)

So, is the evaluation of diffusing changes as "prestigious" an artifact of their use by women? A larger question that is of pressing concern is to understand the social and cultural mechanisms that lead to the diffusion of linguistic change. All this emphasizes how critical it is to take a broad and in-depth perspective of the context in the study of variation and change. The interaction of multiplex social factors and also the nature of the linguistic change itself must be considered.

Mini Quiz 2.6

Q1 What type of linguistic variants are favored by women in change from above?
   (a) In any type of change women favor the standard forms.
   (b) The conservative variants.
   (c) The nonstandard variants.
   (d) The local variants.
   (e) The incoming prestige variants.

Q2 In stable sociolinguistic stratification:
   (a) Women lag behind men.
   (b) Men use a higher frequency of nonstandard forms than women.
   (c) Men and woman behave the same.
   (d) The incoming prestige form is subject to overt criticism.
   (e) Women favor the incoming prestige forms more than men.

Sex vs. Gender

The sociolinguistic literature alternates between sex and gender as terms for describing male/female differences. Straightforwardly, "sex" refers to the physiological distinction between males and female. "Gender" on the other hand refers to the social and cultural roles that individuals appropriate depending on their opportunities, expectations, and life experiences. A complicating factor is whether a person's innate sex influences their use of language or whether it has more to do with how a person is socialized. Some researchers have argued that the social construct of gender provides a more accountable explanation of linguistic variation than a binary contrast between male and female (e.g. Eckert 1989, 1999, 2000, 2008; Eckert and Rickford 2001). Considerable research from the late 1980s onwards has uncovered this pattern in the behavior of men and women in different speech communities. In an American high school in Detroit, Eckert (1988, 1989, 2000) demonstrated that there were greater differences between different groups of girls and boys (Jocks vs. Burnouts) than between girls and boys generally. Subsequent research focusing on "micro" groups, i.e. subgroups within the broad social categories of age, sex, education, etc., has proven to be highly insightful for understanding the dynamics of sociolinguistic variation.

These studies emphasize how important it is to check individuals' patterns within the broad categories of sex, social class, and education to determine if, and where, parallels exist across individuals. Of course, any one researcher cannot do everything, so individuals tend to focus in on aspects of linguistic variation and change that most interest them.

Sociolinguistic Diffusion

Labov's (2001a) model of the diffusion of linguistic change within the speech community evolves by stages:

Stage 0: Stability.

Stage 1: Association of a variant with a reference group. This association occurs near the bottom of the S-shaped curve; the change begins to be accelerated within the reference group, and to a lesser extent, with those who interact most frequently with members of the group.

Stage 2: Gender specialization. The sound change becomes associated with one or the other gender.

Stage 3: Gender split. Males in the lower social classes show a consistent pattern of retreating from or resisting a female-dominated change.

Stage 4: First generation acceleration. When the children of the young women of Stage 2 enter the speech community, males show a sharp step upward.

Stage 5: Second generation acceleration.

Stage 6: "Third generation approximation. As changes near completion, the difference between men and women becomes smaller. If the variable becomes a social marker or stereotype, a linear alignment with social class develops, along with the interaction between social class and gender ... If the change is generally adopted in the community, gender differences will disappear" (Labov 2001a: 308–9).

The changing temper of the period in which we live is reflected in a changing language. (McKnight 1925: 16)

Summary

Patterns in language data can implicate language external influences or language internal processes or both. The frequency of linguistic variants examined accountably with careful circumscription of the variable context and arrayed according to the age of the individual can reveal much about the nature of the linguistic variable. Is the pattern of distribution of a feature flat, sloping, peaking, or otherwise? This will inform the interpretation of language usage in the community. What type of linguistic change is in evidence? The patterns provide an important clue. The study of linguistic change in progress has repeatedly demonstrated that several key characteristics of the social context are crucial to understanding language change. Three features pointing to the social nature of linguistic change are the following (from Labov 2001a: 75): (1) the unpredictability of change, (2) the unrestricted directionality of change, and (3) the existence of stable variation.

The classic sociolinguistic patterns are based on independent variables which were defined according to major sociological categories such as class, education, style, and sex. When sociolinguistic surveys are based on large-scale samples such as the city studies of the 1960s and 1970s, speakers were categorized based on these gross social categories. There are, of course, innumerable (if not infinite) ways of delineating groups in society. Other correlates that have also been considered include ethnicity, race, mobility, network, register, interactional context, attribute of the interlocutor, and group affiliation, among many others. At the same time it has become increasingly obvious that speakers utilize the variation within their linguistic repertoires to accomplish plenty of other social meanings (e.g. Eckert 2000). All of these external, socially defined, characteristics may influence the choices people make when speaking or writing.

Yet the structure of the variable grammar is also a critical facet of structured heterogeneity. The explanation for any array of data does not arise from overall frequencies alone, nor from an apparent time display of those frequencies. The analyst must consider the constraints that underlie the frequency of linguistic features, whether these relate to the nature of the grammatical structure, the relationships among syntactic categories, etc.

In sum, the study of LVC requires reference to external conditions and internal conditions to explain variation. The level of grammar of a feature is important and so are its geographic origin and social evaluation, and these different facets all contribute to understanding the whole. A grammatical pattern may be the key to determining where a linguistic feature came from. A feature's history in a community may explain its social value. The type of social correlates a variant has may reveal its evolution. The development of a linguistic feature reflects social and economic change.

NOTE   A common problem in LVC presentations is that researchers show a lot of output from statistical modeling (numbers, probabilities, coefficients, etc.) and then go on to expound an interpretation that cannot be found in the analysis. Make the link between evidence and explanation!

Exercises

Exercise 2.1   Tips on interpreting sociolinguistic patterns

In LVC research patterns in language are usually presented in a table or a figure. These display the story of the linguistic variable under investigation. It is critical to know how to present data informatively and how to interpret what you see.

When you read a table or a figure, make note of the following:

- What variant is being charted? If the measure is of [n], do not interpret it as [ŋ].
- You cannot make claims about things that are *not* shown.

Exercise 2.2   Identifying sociolinguistic patterns

Figure 2.18 shows the distribution of variable (h) in York, United Kingdom, c. 1997, as in Example 2.8.

Example 2.8

(a)   I'm *'anding my* notice in tomorrow. (YRK/090)
(b)   Why are you *hasslin'* now? (YRK/090)

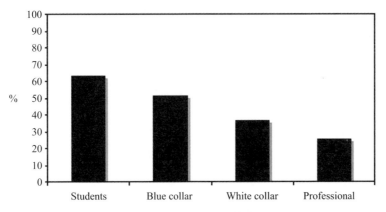

Figure 2.18 Distribution of variable (h), York English, c. 1997.

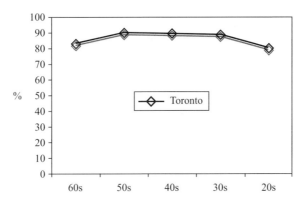

Figure 2.19 Distribution of variable (that), Toronto, c. 2003–2004.

Question 1 What type of stratification is evident?
Figure 2.19 shows the distribution of variable (that) in Toronto, Canada, as in Example 2.9.

Example 2.9

I don't think *that* that's a matter of choice. I think Ø it's a matter of helping our system out. (TOR/127)

Question 2 What type of linguistic situation is evident?
Figure 2.20 shows the distribution of [f], [t], and Ø variants as opposed to [θ] (Wolfram 1969: 92). Answer the questions below.

Question 3 What is this variable a clear example of?
(a) hypercorrection
(b) free variation
(c) a gender indicator
(d) a social class indicator.
(e) a social class indicator and a gender indicator.

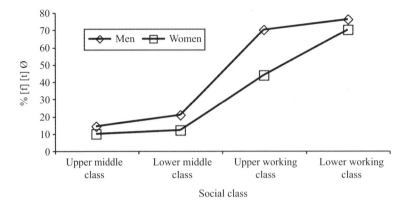

Figure 2.20   Distribution of [f], [t], and Ø variants as opposed to [θ].
Source: Wolfram, W. (1969) *A Sociolinguistic Description of Detroit Negro Speech*. Washington, DC: Center for Applied Linguistics (CAL), p. 92, Figure 21; reproduced by kind permission of CAL.

Question 4   What does this figure also reveal?
(a)   The gender groups in each social class are consistently stratified, with women scoring lower than the men.
(b)   The gender groups in each social class are not consistently stratified.
(c)   The gender groups are highly variable and there is no consistent pattern.
(d)   The gender groups in each social class are consistently stratified, with men scoring lower than the women.
(e)   The relevant gender pattern is obscured by social class.

Question 5   What is the main cause of sex and gender differences in language use?
(a)   ability
(b)   education
(c)   mobility and social contacts
(d)   women like the standard language more
(e)   men are not as innovative as women.

Exercise 2.3   Interpreting sociolinguistic patterns

Figure 2.21 presents data from Trudgill's study of Norwich, England (Trudgill 2000: 37). It shows the distribution of local Norwich forms, which Trudgill refers to as "non-RP." The three linguistic variables are (i) variable (ing), (ii) variable (t), and (iii) variable (h), as in Example 2.10.

Example 2.10

(a)   *dancin'* for "dancing"
(b)   *be[ʔ]r* for "better"
(c)   *'anding* for "handing"

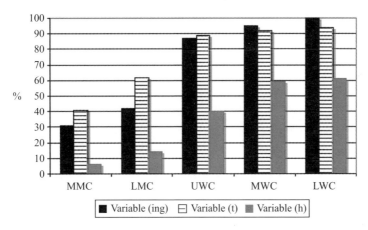

Figure 2.21 Distribution of non-RP variants for three linguistic variables in Norwich English, c. 1972. *Source:* Trudgill 2000: 37, Table 5.

NOTE The term "RP" refers to the most prestigious upper-class pronunciation of British English. Why "received"? In Victorian English "received" meant "socially acceptable."

The data are presented as overall proportions according to six socioeconomic classes: Lower Working Class (LWC), Middle Working Class (MWC), Upper Working Class (UWC), Lower Middle Class (LMC), Middle Middle Class (MMC) and Upper Middle Class (UMC).

Figure 2.21 reveals several important sociolinguistic patterns. What can you say about the linguistic behavior of members of each of the socioeconomic groups? What differences in behavior between the various groups can you observe? Can you be more confident of some observations than of others?

First, the social classes clearly differ. This can be confidently stated because of the parallel results for three different variables. However, there is less confidence in the details of these patterns and on their interpretation, e.g. the extent of differences between MC and WC, without further information about how the data were collected and analyzed.

Question 1 How important are the various differences among the various working classes between UWC, MWC, and LWC?

Question 2 How important are the various differences between MMC and LMC?

Question 3 How important are the various differences between the middle classes as a whole and the working classes as a whole?

Question 4 How important are the various differences between LMC and UWC?

Question 5 How does performance on the (h) variable appear to be different from performance on the (ing) and (t) variables in all social classes?

Question 6 Is there any difference in performance in variable (ing) and (t)?

Question 7 What other information would you require to strengthen any conclusions you would wish to draw?

Mini Quiz Answers

2.1   Q1: *a*

2.2   Q1: *False*

2.3   Q1: *Mike's speech follows that of African Americans more closely than northern whites across phonological variables, but patterns with European Americans with grammatical features.*
      Q2: *While he was able to acquire features of phonology, prosody, and lexis, he did not acquire grammatical patterns.*
      Q3: *A conflict between wanting to participate in urban black male youth culture and the reality of being apart from this social sphere.*

2.4   Q1: *c*
      Q2: *d*
      Q3: *c*
      Q4: *e*

2.5   Q1: *b*
      Q2: *a*
      Q3: *b*
      Q4: *b*
      Q5: *c*
      Q6: *Stereotypes. Ch-lenition had made the transition from marker to stereotype.*

2.6   Q1: *e*
      Q2: *b*

Note

1   Current Principle 2 used to be Principle 1; Current Principles 3 and 4 used to be Principle 2.

Background Reading

Gregersen *et al.* 2009; Labov 1963, 1966, 1969, 1971, 1972a,b, 2001a,b; Macaulay and Trevelyan 1977; Ochs 1992; Silverstein 1976, 1979, 1985; Trudgill 1974a,b; Wolfram 1969, 1971, 1974.

3

Linguistic Patterns

In the case of languages, observation will show, not only how they function today, but also how the ever changing and conflicting needs of their users are permanently at work silently shaping, out of the language of today, the language of tomorrow. (Martinet 1952: 125)

This chapter reviews the linguistic patterns that underlie variation. Such patterns reflect the omnipresent internal mechanisms operating on linguistic systems. Much of this chapter is based on developments in historical linguistics, where the mechanisms of linguistic change are a primary focus. I have relied heavily on the work of Hock (1991), Hock and Joseph (1996), and Joseph and Janda (2003a) which describe in great detail the different processes and tendencies in linguistic change.

To situate the study of linguistic patterns within the LVC enterprise, let us begin considering Weinreich, Labov, and Herzog's (1968) five problems in the study of linguistic change.

1. Constraints   What are the constraints on change?
2. Transition   How does language change?
3. Embedding   How is a given language change embedded in social and linguistic systems?
4. Evaluation   How do members of a speech community evaluate a given change and what is the effect of this evaluation on the change?
5. Actuation   Why did a given linguistic change occur at a particular time and place that it did?

In the first two decades of LVC research, most studies focused on the embedding problem, the search for how observed linguistic changes are embedded "in the matrix of linguistic and extra linguistic concomitants of the forms in question" (Weinreich *et al.* 1968: 101). Note however that the formulation of the embedding problem subsumes not only social facts about the speech community, but also pressures from within the linguistic system. The emphasis in most sociolinguistic textbooks, however, is on the social side of analysis. Yet few textbooks discuss in any detail the internal constraints on linguistic variation (but see Walker 2010). In the early

Variationist Sociolinguistics: Change, Observation, Interpretation, First Edition. Sali A. Tagliamonte.
© 2012 Sali A. Tagliamonte. Published 2012 by Blackwell Publishing Ltd.

days of sociolinguistic inquiry, perhaps this was due to the more pressing need to establish that linguistic change could be observed in progress by studying its social context. However, innumerable research studies subsequently have established the importance of linguistic patterns. Linguistic patterns give us a window into the variable grammar and the omnipresent mechanisms in the linguistic system.

Let us review Labov's (1963) classic study of phonological change on Martha's Vineyard, Massachusetts in this light. The target variable was the raising of the nucleus in the diphthongs /ay/ and /aw/. The diphthong /ay/ was raised first; later, [aw] began to be raised as well, partly under pressure from the former change. Furthermore, both changes were favored when the diphthong was followed by a voiceless obstruent. These patterns were intricately connected with social forces. Raising of /ay/ began in a particular social subgroup, the Yankee descendants of the island's original settlers. As Martha's Vineyard became an increasingly popular holiday spot, the Yankee natives developed an unconscious need to distinguish themselves from the visitors. Raising in /ay/ began to take on this social meaning. It then spread from /ay/ to /aw/ and to less favored phonological environments, as well as to new generations and to different ethnic subgroups on Martha's. In this way, the sound change was "embedded" in the phonological system and the social milieu, a classic example of variability without linguistic change. Notice the extent to which the variable had well-defined linguistic patterning at the outset – favored when followed by a voiceless obstruent. Moreover, as the change spread in the speech community the variable underwent certain linguistically defined changes: extension from one sound, /ay/, to another sound, /aw/, and use of the favored pre-voiceless-obstruent environment to other phonological environments. These shifts pinpoint the critical linguistic patterns that underlie the variation.

Thus, the question that an analyst should be keenly interested in when studying a linguistic feature is what are the linguistic patterns that are relevant to the variation? How are these patterns reflected in the social structure of the community? What do they mean?

> **NOTE**   There are now two updates to the Martha's Vineyard story (Blake and Josey 2003; Pope *et al.* 2007). Check out what happened.

In the broader field of linguistics, identification of patterns in language data is key to understanding linguistic mechanisms. At least as far as formal theories of grammar are concerned, these mechanisms are categorical. Where there is an environment for linguistic rules to apply, they do. Where the environment does not exist, they do not. No variation. The revolutionary idea in Labov's model of sociolinguistics was his discovery that language change had critical social dimensions and that alternations (patterns of variation) in the data were the key to understanding how change was taking place. Variation was an inherent part of the system. As the review of Labov's Martha's Vineyard study shows, Variationist Sociolinguistic studies have paid attention to the linguistic patterns underlying variable phenomena from the early days. Labov's later study of the copula in New York City (Labov 1969) showed that there were regular and predictable phonological and syntactic constraints on variable copula absence in some varieties (e.g. AAVE), that could be directly related to copula contraction in other varieties (e.g. mainstream North American English). Where mainstream North American English could contract the copula, as in Example 3.1a, AAVE could delete it, as in Example 3.1b.

Example 3.1

    (a)   He'*s going to* try to get up.
    (b)   He Ø *gon'* try to get up. (12. T-Bird, 451) (Labov 1969: 717)

Moreover, there were regular linguistic patterns influencing the variation as well. Copula deletion was favored with pronoun subjects and with following progressive verbs, as in Example 3.2 (Labov 1969: 717).

Example 3.2

    (a)   *He* fast in everything he do. (16, Jets, 560)
    (b)   Boot always *comin'* over to my house to eat … (10, T-Birds, 451)

Subsequent study of linguistic variables from all levels of grammar has demonstrated this type of conditioning. The frequency of use of one variant or another is fundamentally linked to the linguistic contexts in which they occur whether at the level of phonology, morphology, syntax, semantics, or even pragmatics. Developments in testing for and explaining these effects have gradually become a driving forces in LVC studies. Innumerable underlying contextual patterns have been found for virtually every linguistic variable studied. Moreover, the same patterns also repeat themselves across different situations in time and space. The fact that linguistic principles guide language change has been well known in historical linguistics since the early 1800s. As investigations of linguistic variation and change developed in the 1970s and 1980s the importance of linguistic patterns has come more and more to the forefront. At the same time, it has become increasingly obvious that both social and linguistic factors are involved in language variation and change. One of the prevailing conclusions of research in LVC from the 1990s into the 2000s has been the affirmation that variables are sensitive to both linguistic and social factors:

> although this linguistic conditioning factor [merging low back vowels] may set the stage for vowel change, we would claim that language-external, that is, social, factors are also critical. (Clarke, Elms, and Youssef 1995: 224)

> null subject variation in the Spanish of Mexican-descent children in California significantly affected by a rich array of linguistic and nonlinguistic factors. (Bayley and Pease-Alvarez 1997: 368)

> *was/were* variation … is a complex phenomenon, subject to a range of external and internal constraints. (Cheshire and Fox 2009: 34)

> the interweaving of sociophonetic and linguistic information in speech is so complete that no natural human utterance offers linguistic information without simultaneously indexing some social factor. (Foulkes and Docherty 2006: 419)

It is not sufficient simply to report that social and linguistic patterns are relevant to a linguistic variable. It is also necessary to understand why. The phenomenon must be explained. So, the question for us at this point is, When you observe variation, what is the linguistic mechanism that underlies it? How do linguistic patterns operate at different levels of grammar to impact linguistic variation and change? For this exploration we must turn to traditional historical linguistics where sound change, analogy, reanalysis, and metaphorical extension are fundamental (see Joseph 2004: 61).

Sound Change

Perhaps the obvious place to start exploring linguistic patterns is the place where LVC studies started, namely with variation at the level of phonology. The fact that there are different pronunciations for the same word is a straightforward observation. At earlier times this variation was considered decay or laziness. However, in actuality there are mechanical processes underlying these alternations. In fact, sounds are shifting and changing in the language all the time. Some of the sounds are in the process of change and some of the sounds are variable due simply to mechanistic reasons, such as rate of speech, but there is always a process that underlies them. When someone "drops their g's," as in *I'm goin' shoppin'*, what is the linguistic mechanism? When someone deletes their *t*'s or *d*'s what is the underlying process? A number of general mechanisms operate in all languages all over the world. They are persistent, pervasive phonological processes. The most common of them are changes that make pronunciations simpler (Hock 1991: 127).

Assimilation, Weakening, Loss

Many types of sound change involve simplification and are regularly conditioned sound changes. Perhaps the most widespread is assimilation. This is a process in which sounds within words are influenced by other sounds that surround it. This has the effect of simplifying the pronunciation of the word because it streamlines the articulatory gestures required of the tongue in the mouth. The sound that triggers assimilation is usually an immediately preceding or following sound. A simple and straightforward example is English plural formation. Although the plural suffix is always written as -*s*, it is pronounced as [s] or [z] depending on the nature of the preceding sound. If the preceding sound is voiceless, the suffix is pronounced [s], a voiceless sound. However, if the preceding sound is voiced, the suffix is pronounced [z], a voiced sound, as in Example 3.3.

Example 3.3

    (a)   *cat* → [kæts]
    (b)   *dog* → [dɔgz]

Note that this alternation is categorical in English. It applies across the board in all environments which have the appropriate sound. Assimilation processes are rampant in language and comprise processes that assimilate voice, place, and virtually any other phonological grouping. Some commonly recognized assimilatory processes are umlaut, vowel harmony, and palatalization. Two common processes in speech are considered assimilation – contraction and word final devoicing (Hock 1986).

    Another simplification mechanism is weakening or lenition. This is a process which involves a relaxation, reduction, or even total omission of sounds. It often occurs in the middle of words and in voiced sounds, especially in rapid speech. Hock (1986: 83, Figure 5.1)

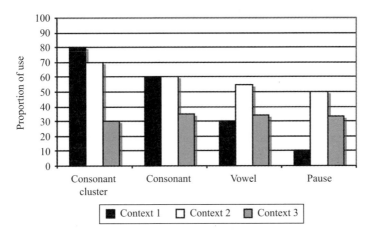

Figure 3.1   Idealized pattern for sound change via weakening.

presents a hierarchy of weakening defined along a continuum of increased voicing and sonority. Geminate "t" and "d" weaken to [t] and [d]. Then [d] can weak to [r, l, ð], then further to [y] and to [h]. Similarly, [t] can weaken to [ɵ, ʔ] and then to [h]. In English this process can be observed in the use of the voiceless dental stop [t]. The weakening of word medial [t] distinguishes North American and British English. Consider the common word "butter." In many forms of British English the word-internal stop is pronounced as a voiceless alveolar stop, [t], in standard North American English /t/ is pronounced as a flap, [D]. However, in contemporary British dialects, the glottal stop pronunciation, i.e. [bʌʔr], is sweeping the country (e.g. Fabricius 2002; Mees 1987; Milroy *et al.* 1994a; Stuart-Smith 1999b). However, the meaning of "butter" never changes. You still put it on your toast.

One of the important uses of linguistic patterns is to show that contexts in the grammar may be conditioned differently and thus have unique explanation (e.g. Raymond, Dautricourt, and Hume 2006). Figure 3.1 shows an idealized pattern for a linguistic feature conditioned by the phonological context. Context 1 is conditioned strongly by weakening, context 2 only weakly, and context 3 not at all. These kinds of comparisons enhance the facility of linguistic constraints to explain variable phenomena.

The most extreme case of simplification is the loss of a speech sound. Loss is often a result of an earlier weakening. The ends of words are especially prone to loss. For example, "spaghetti" pronounced without the final vowel among people of Italian descent or "Santa Claus" pronounced without the final [z] among African Nova Scotians. However, simplification is not limited to such previously weakened contexts. Loss can also happen of its own accord. Some of the reasons given in the literature for this are that "our voice often trails off" at the end of utterances, both in intonation (which goes down to a fairly low pitch) and in the precise articulation of speech sounds (Hock and Joseph 1996: 130). The principle of least effort has long been regarded as one of the major motivations for language change (Labov 2001a: 16). Although processes of simplification are prevalent in language, other competing processes work against this tendency (Labov 2010: 7). Of course, it cannot be possible that all change is explained by this principle or else there would be little left of language. Instead, language change is the result of balancing forces, one tending toward simplification, the other toward differentiation (Hock 1991: 235–236; Labov 2010: 371–372).

Morphological Change

Changes in morphology are also due to a number of pervasive processes. When someone attaches a novel suffix to a word or deletes an affix, what is the linguistic mechanism?

Analogy

> Humans are simply analogical animals. Language structure and language use are also predominantly analogical, and this is why analogy is the backbone of universal grammar. (Anttila 2003: 438–439)

Analogy is one of the core areas of cognition (Gentner, Holyoak, and Kokinov 2001) and under-lies virtually all linguistic processes. Analogy in language works by association and similarity and can be viewed in historical data as well as in the language we hear every day. Most often, irregu-lar forms are remade into the shape of more common, systematically generated, forms. Common standard suffixes are added to the two mass nouns in Example 3.4a–b and a novel verb in (4c). Regular forms may also become irregular, based on an existing pattern, as in Example 3.4d where the irregular verb *caught* (already with preterite marking) is found with the common past tense suffix. Analogy is involved in the creation of new words, which are often generated on the model of already existing words, as in the addition of *–licious* to the word *mint* on the model of *delicious* as in Example 3.4e. Notice that the examples come from different levels of grammar; Example 3.4a–c implicate morphological processes, both nominal and verbal while Example 3.4d–e is morphological and Example 3.4e is morphological, lexical, and perhaps semantic.

Example 3.4

(a)   They have tables outside and everything, and they're serving teas and *coffees* and sandwiches. (TOR/038)
(b)   We had some *beers* at this guy's house. (TOR/021)
(c)   Well, the oil prices *nose-dived* so there was no work for them. (TOR/087)
(d)   *Interviewer:* What's the biggest fish he could have caught? Like that? [06] That he's *caughten? Interviewer:* Yeah. (TOR/006)
(e)   *Mintilicious* (advert for cool summer drink, Toronto, summer 2010)

There are two main types of analogy, (1) leveling and (2) four-part analogy. Leveling involves paradigms, while four-part analogy does not.

Leveling

Leveling is "the complete or partial elimination of morphophonemic alternations within paradigms" (Hock and Joseph 1996: 155). A paradigm is a set of inflected forms of a given word or a subset of such forms. The best contemporary English example of leveling occurs in the past tense paradigm for the verb "to be," variable (was), as in Table 3.1.

Here you can see that the standard forms *you were* and *they were* have been eliminated and the past tense morphological form has become identical for all grammatical persons. In dialects that have this paradigm there is a single form, i.e. *was*, for past tense "be."

Table 3.1   Leveled paradigm for past tense "to be."

	Singular	Plural
First person	I was	We was
Second person	You was	You was
Third person	(S)He was	They was

The direction of leveling is unpredictable across languages or dialects (Hock and Joseph 1996: 156). Although research has shown that leveling to *was* is the more common pattern across dialects, in some places the paradigm levels to *were*, as in Example 3.5.

Example 3.5

(a)   It *weren't* us with a funny accent. (Schilling-Estes and Wolfram 1994: 298)
(b)   Everything *were* going great. (YRK/004)
(c)   He *were* a bus conductor or something. (CLB/061)

Four-part Analogy
Four-part analogy is identified as "the remaking of a morphologically derived formation on the model of another, generally more productive pattern" (Hock and Joseph 1996: 160). The reason for the term "four-part" is due to the four-step pattern in Example 3.6.

Example 3.6

(a)   1   2   3   4
(b)   a is to   a   as   b is to   x
(c)   *cat* is to   *cats*   as   *coffee* is to *coffees*

A straightforward example is the plural suffix -*s*, which is the most common way to make a noun plural in English, as in Example 3.7.

Example 3.7

hat: *hats*
coffee: *coffees* (see Example 3.6c above)

Four-part analogy operates on forms that are morphologically related. In most cases the pattern being modeled is productive in the language, as in the -*s* suffix in Example 3.7 above, although analogical trends can also be based on less productive patterns, as in the –*en* suffix of past participles in Example 3.8.

Example 3.8

take: *taken*
caught: *caughten* (see also Example 3.4d above)

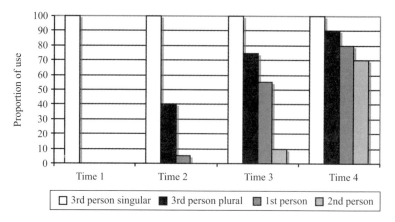

Figure 3.2   Idealized pattern for morphological change via analogical extension – leveling.

This shows us that analogy can operate in predictable ways (toward the more common pattern) and also in unpredictable ways (toward a rarer pattern). For further discussion and examples, see Hock and Joseph (1996: 160–164).

> **NOTE**   Consider the second person "you": *you was/are (singular)* vs. *you was/are (plural)*. Analogical leveling has made them indistinguishable. Yet in many dialects of English around the world distinct second person plural pronouns abound: *you lot, you guys, yins, yous, ya'll*, etc. (see Labov 2010: 372).

Figure 3.2 shows an idealized pattern for morphological change via analogical extension. A linguistic change must start somewhere. We can imagine a time of stasis when a phenomenon is categorical, as in Time 1. Gradually a context that shares some quality of similarity or parallelism starts behaving like the other, as in Time 2. At Time 3, another context with yet another common overarching characteristic follows suit. At Time 4 all the same contexts in the grammar pattern together. We might imagine that as this hypothetical change takes hold, it accelerates. Notice that the imaginary second-person context in Figure 3.1 changes quickly to be like the rest. The main pattern is the gradual convergence of like forms. Note too that because this change involves a grammatical paradigm, it would be considered a case of leveling. We might speculate on the possibility that the *–en* participle in English might gradually spread to become the favored marker of past time in English in this way.

Extension, Generalization

Extension or generalization is the most common pattern underlying linguistic change and the underlying mechanism is inevitably analogical. This refers to a change in the use of a linguistic feature such that it comes to be used in a new context, i.e. extension. According to Harris and Campbell (1995) "extension changes the use of a linguistic expression by adding one (or more) contexts in which that expression can be used." Under this definition both types of analogy are also generalizations of one type or another. Examples 3.7 and 3.8 above are extensions since they represent the use of plural *-s* and *–en* in words that are not normally expected to take these inflections. Knowing the pervasive underlying mechanism of extension shows you how and why forms such as *they was* and *coffees* are created. The first is extension via analogical leveling, the second is extension via four-part analogy.

Mini Quiz 3.1

Q1 What process underlies the following examples:
  (a) The pronunciation of the [t] as [D] in the word "butter."
  (b) The pronunciation of "button" as [bʌDn] or "Tim Horton's" as [tIm hordənz] where I would pronounce the word-internal stops as [ʔ].
  (c) The plural "shrimps" as in the following examples:
      7 Yeah and then you have to give them *shrimps*, the shrimps are not as big as those we eat. They are also micro *shrimps*. (TOR/011)
        Boats from far and wide came to Maryport to fish *shrimps*. (MPT/015)

  (d) The use of "was" in the following construction:

    If it *was* someone else, then yeah I would go. (TOR/140)

Clipping

Clipping is a type of morphological change where a fragment comes to be used rather than the original word. Either the second part of the word is clipped, as in Example 3.9a, or the first part of the word is clipped, as in Example 3.9b. It is also possible that there is variation in the choice of clipped variants (Example 3.9a–b). In recent years the shortening of words has come to the forefront of attention due to the rise of new media and computer-mediated communication where such phenomena are thought to be rampant. Also notice that clippings can go in two directions, sometimes toward shorter forms; sometimes back to longer ones, as you can see in Example 3.9c–d.

Example 3.9

  (a) chemistry → chem; mushrooms → mushys (see Chapter 11, Example 11.17)
  (b) mushrooms → *shrooms*; kayak → *yak*
  (c) okay → *ok, k, kk, okie dokie* (check Chapter 11, Example 11.24)
  (d) good bye → *bye, bye bye*

Example 3.10

  (a) I have a philosophy test Wednesday, *chem* test Thursday. (TOR/030)
  (b) [8] I've really gotta study now. [043] *Okie dokie*. (CMC/8&043)
  (c) [6] So, you're not into pyromania? [023] Hell, no! *Pyros* are weird. (TOR/023)

A quick check of the TEA enabled me to provide the examples in Example 3.10, but clippings are difficult to find because you need to know what you are looking for. These two examples happen to come from teenagers but this phenomenon is pervasive. See if you can spot clippings. Check advertisements or signs. Check your latest text message or Facebook post.

Syntactic Change

Syntactic change involves the arrangement of words in sentences. This can involve a wide range of different phenomena from the omission of one or more words, such as subject dropping, as in Example 3.11, variable *do*, as in Example 3.12, or any phenomena that involve the alternate placement of words in sentences.

Example 3.11

    (a) No, Ø haven't done that actually. (YRK/018)
    (b) Ø Just vanished haven't they? (YRK/081)
    (c) I think I have it in my purse. … Ø hope I can find it. (TOR/064)
    (d) Yeah, but I remember the islands, yeah. Ø used to have a lot of fun. (TOR/113)

Example 3.12

    (a) I *dinna* mine fa taen it. (BCK/001) "I don't remember who took it."
    (b) I *o na* mine fa come in. (BCK/001) "I don't remember who came in." (Smith 2001: 232)

An apt contemporary example is Example 3.13. The original phrase is Shakespeare's, but it turns up in a recent live stage show as well as the name of a popular nail polish. Interestingly, the phrase is often misquoted as Example 3.13b. It appears that commentators cannot quite get the word order right because English does not place adverbials in preverbal position anymore. Note too the use of the present *comes* where contemporary varieties would use the present progressive (see Rissanen 1999: 216, 201).

Example 3.13

    (a) By the pricking of my thumbs, something wicked *this way* comes. (Shakespeare, *Macbeth*, IV, i)
    (b) Something wicked comes *this way*.

These variations in word order often lead to reanalysis and impact sentence structure. For example, forms that become clitics can evolve into affixes. Adverbs often evolve into pragmatic markers (Brinton 1996), as with *hopefully* in Example 3.14. In this case the original lexical meaning of being in a "hopeful" state has bleached. There is not a single token in either the Toronto or York data; yet this function can be easily found in stage directions, as in Example 3.14e from the *Friends* data.

Example 3.14

    (a) *Hopefully*, I'll be a top line hair stylist. (TOR/096)
    (b) I'll be *hopefully* going international. (TOR/096)

(c) I'm going to *hopefully* go to the Aveda Hair Institute in Toronto. (TOR/096)
(d) He's coming back this year, *hopefully*. (BCK/002)
(e) Rachel: Is– is he coming? (Looks *hopefully* out the door.) Tom: Umm, no.

Such markers can, in turn, set the patterns of variation for the rest of the grammar. The suite of internal linguistic factors constraining the zero option in complement clauses in English were found to mirror the collocation patterns of the epistemic marker *I think* (Tagliamonte and Smith 2005) (see also Chapter 5). Further, some structures may be more prone to change than others. For example, main clauses are thought to undergo change more easily than dependent clauses (Hock 1986: 332). These observations provide the analyst with ways of interpreting patterns in data.

Reanalysis

One of the most pervasive mechanisms in syntactic change is reanalysis. Reanalysis is often made possible by ambiguity, the case of more than one interpretation for the same construction (e.g. Campbell 1998: 283; Timberlake 1977: 168). Ambiguity may cause a new marker to develop to distinguish one function from the other (see variable (ly) in Chapter 8) or some contexts may be reanalyzed as having a different structure and meaning (see variable (going to) in Chapter 10). Reanalysis may occur earlier in contexts that are unmarked or more natural with respect to the change.

Ambiguous contexts are often found. For example, in Example 3.15a "going to" could be a present gerund or a future marker. In Example 3.15b "so" could be an intensifier or a comparative. In Example 3.15c "have got" could be dynamic or stative. Many cases of ambiguity pass unnoticed because there is no uncertainty of meaning in context. For others it may be quite difficult if not impossible to distinguish one meaning from another. At earlier stages of a change, ambiguity might be expected to be more prevalent than at later stages (Traugott 2010).

Example 3.15

(a) I'm *going to* buy them a second-hand video. (YRK/044)
(b) They were *so* frozen that he couldn't take them off. (TOR/104)
(c) He*'s got* a lot of respect in the world for his playing. (TOR/048)

Reanalysis may be based on constituent structure, hierarchical structure, category labels, grammatical relations, or the degree of cohesiveness between constituents. According to Hopper and Traugott (1993: 235) "every new analogy is a minor reanalysis." Notice the direct parallel with what variationists refer to as form/function asymmetry (Poplack and Tagliamonte 2001: 4). This is the critical departure point for a variation analysis which bases its evidence on the patterned organization of unstable forms and functions in discourse which arise from systematic examination.

A long time ago the way to say *I don't know* in English was *I know not*. This is perhaps the most heavily studied syntactic change in LVC research and involves the order of tense and negation markers in a sentence. As the word *do* underwent longitudinal grammaticalization from a verb of causation to a support for tense, negative declarative sentences alternated between *know not* and *do not know*. Between 1500 and 1800 the constructions with *do* gradually took over. Check the splendid figure in Kroch (1989: 223), based on Ellegård (1953). A number of scholars have studied this development demonstrating that linguistic and social factors were implicated (Nurmi 1999; Stein 1990; Warner 2004, 2005) although there are conflicting interpretations that have yet to be resolved. Since this change took several hundred years and the data comprises writing from people who advanced in age over time, the study of *do* offers analysts the ideal testing ground for the examination of age grading, generational change, and lifespan change. Authors in the history of English (Warner 2004) use more *do* as they get older, including Shakespeare (Stein 1991), as in Example 3.16a–b.

Example 3.16

    (a)   Part Fooles, put up your Swords, you *know not* what you do. (Shakespeare, *Romeo and Juliet*, I, i, c. 1591–95)
    (b)   I *do not know* One of my sex; no woman's face remember. (Shakespeare, *The Tempest*, III, i, c. 1610–11)

Another well-studied syntactic variable is the change from so-called verb second order (V2) where the verb comes second after some other element in the sentence. This was the norm in Old English; however, there was extensive variation in Middle English, as in Example 3.17a–b (Warner 2007) and in contemporary English the same types of constructions are mostly subject–verb order.

Example 3.17

    (a)   And pen *seid pe deuelles* to him
          And then said the devils to him
    (b)   And pen *pe deuelles seiden* to ham
          And then the devils said to them

The selection of different orders is sensitive to many different factors and there are innumerable interactions between pragmatics and syntax with additional implications of dialectal variation and language contact (e.g. Kemenade 1997; Kroch and Taylor 1997; Pintzuk 1993, 1996; Pintzuk and Taylor 2006). More recently researchers have begun to explore the influences of information structure as well making this variable another important feature for further investigation.

A few studies have been able to use real-time data to conduct both an apparent time study of a single point in time alongside a lifespan study. It appears that both types of change operate in tandem (e.g. Jensen 2009; Sankoff and Blondeau 2007). This might lead you to think that, for example, no one says *I know not* anymore. However, in some dialects the change toward *do* support is still going on (see Example 3.12b). Moreover my students and colleagues report that they have heard and/or read examples of *I know not* recently. This is one of the fascinating things about variation and change. The traces of it are left behind. It is interesting to speculate why *I know not* and any other archaism turns up from time to time. What is yet to be developed is more nuanced understanding of the relationship between the different types of change. Are the processes similar or different and how are they interrelated?

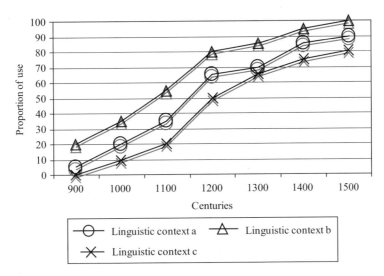

Figure 3.3 Idealized change in progress that exhibits the Constant Rate Effect.

Do some types of linguistic variables continue to change across the lifespan and others not? Studies that can disentangle these issues will undoubtedly be at the forefront of LVC research in the twenty-first century.

The Constant Rate Effect

Because syntactic change operates on the patterning of sentences (Hock and Joseph 1996: 203), it affects a large part of the grammar simultaneously and involves abstract patterns and knowledge of syntactic structure. A whole area of LVC research is devoted to the analysis of these types of changes (see discussion in Pintzuk 2003). Among the many important findings from this area of the field is the discovery of the Constant Rate Effect (Kroch 1989).

The Constant Rate Effect (CRE) was originally a hypothesis about the nature of syntactic change (Kroch 1989). According to this hypothesis "the frequency of use of competing linguistic forms may differ across contexts at each point in time during the course of the change, [but] the rate of change for each context is the same" (Pintzuk 2003: 513–514). The S-shape pattern of linguistic change remains the same (see above, Figure 2.9): the "constant" is the fact that the pattern of change is the same across linguistic contexts. The reason for this is due to the fact that the contexts "are merely surface manifestations of a single underlying change in grammar" (Kroch 1989: 199).

Figure 3.3 shows that the change follows the same path across linguistic contexts. A "linguistic context" could be the difference between different types of sentences, e.g. declarative vs. interrogative, different types of clauses, e.g. main vs. subordinate clauses, different types of subjects, e.g. NP vs. pronoun, or any other grammatical contrast. Subsequent to Kroch's original research, this pattern has been found in the history of many different languages (English, French, Greek, Portuguese, and Yiddish) (for a summary see Kroch 2003). Given the general application of the constant rate hypothesis, it was renamed the Constant Rate Effect.

The CRE holds "only for contexts in which the surface forms are reflexes of the same underlying grammatical alternation" (Pintzuk 2003: 515). The claim concerns the frequency of the incoming form only and does not consider the multiple constraints that may be operating on the variation. In essence, the display shown here provides a diachronic perspective on the constraint ranking of a single linguistic pattern (linguistic contexts a, b, and c) over time. The CRE and related research in historical syntax is the most comprehensive integration of LVC research and syntactic theory.

The study of syntactic variation of this magnitude requires large historical corpora that represent hundreds of years of data in real time. Early corpora of this type include the Helsinki Corpus and the Corpus of Early English Correspondence. The Research Unit for Language Variation and Change at the University of Helsinki in Finland provides a Corpora Resource Database (CoRD) which lists a remarkable array of corpora.[1] More recently, large multi-university projects have developed which aim to produce syntactically annotated corpora for all stages of the history of English.[2] As we move into the future the study of change over time will become more possible.

Mini Quiz 3.2

Q1   The *constant rate effect* refers to:
   (a)   An effect which measures the frequency of a given variable in historical context.
   (b)   The process by which the frequency of linguistic variables is measured.
   (c)   The idea that language is constantly changing.
   (d)   The idea that linguistic change happens at the same rate across different constructions.
   (e)   The idea that linguistic change happens at different rates across different constructions.

Semantic Change

Semantic change shifts the meaning of words so that they acquire "new or broader meanings" (Hock and Joseph 1996: 228). A number of different mechanisms underlie semantic change. The foremost of these are metaphor and metonymy.

Metaphorical and Metonymic Extension

Metaphor involves similarity across domains whereas metonymy involves shifts within the same domain (Traugott and Dasher 2002: 78). In metaphorical extension words shift from one domain to another based on similarity – *a calm lake* → *lake as calm as glass*. In metonymic extension one word is used for another within the same domain based on some relationship or association between them – *the crown of a queen* → crown = queen. These are typical examples found in textbooks; in real life mundane examples are everywhere. Consider the metaphors in Example 3.18a or the metonymy in Example 3.18b (see also Chapter 1,

Example 1.4). There are various other processes: litotes change words from stronger to weaker meaning (*brutal* = bad); see Chapter 4 and also Example 3.18c; hyperbole changes words from weaker to stronger meaning (see variable (intensifiers) in Chapter 11); degeneration makes words into something less than they were before (*kill* = *get upset with*); and elevation makes them into something more (*hit* = *kill*). Once you start looking for metaphors, you will find them everywhere.

Example 3.18

(a) life as a ladder (see Preface), bleaching of meaning, grammaticalization pathway, etc. (see below)
(b) white cake = a person of Caucasian ethnicity
(c) fucking → freaking, fricking etc.

Words may become narrower or broader. Moreover, words may cycle from one metaphoric shift to the next, as in Example 3.19. Note the extension by color up to the late 1700s and a shift to a verb while retaining the sense of importance or seriousness in the 2000s.

Example 3.19

(a) *cardinal*, c. 1225: one of the 70 ecclesiastical princes who constitute the pope's council whose typical apparel was a scarlet cloak.
(b) *cardinal*, c. 1756: a scarlet colored bird.
(c) *cardinal*, c. 1775: a short cloak worn by ladies, originally of scarlet cloth with a hood.
(d) *cardinals*, c. 1960: an American baseball team, St Louis Cardinals.
(e) *cardinals*, c. 2006: to fail by mythic proportions, to choke,[3] e.g. He *cardinals* every time he's in the spotlight.

These developments are not the typical types of change tapped by LVC research. Semantic variation has been studied successfully using variationist methods (see e.g. Thibault, 1991). Among many semantic developments in English is the use of "hot," which has various meanings within the same individual in the same conversation, as in Example 3.20. The use of "awesome" to mean "great" (see Chapter 11, Examples 11.11b and 11.17) is another good example that has recently extended from an earlier use (c. 1598), "full of reverential fear." This type of variation could be tapped in apparent time and tested for linguistic and social factors.

Example 3.20

(a) The first thing they think about a girl is whether they are *hot* or not. (TOR/013)
(b) They have home cooked meals, like *hot* meals. (TOR/013)

Check out the Historical Thesaurus of the Oxford English Dictionary to explore the lexical history of a concept or meaning in the history of English.[4] At the time of writing, the OED acknowledges the use of "hot" in Example 3.20a in the US since 1926, giving the example "Aphrodite ... was the hot momma of goddesses." However, the specifically contemporary meaning of "hot" in the example (which at least in the UK is sometimes interchangeable with "fit" (meaning both good-looking and sexually attractive) has still not made it into this dictionary.

> **NOTE**   Think of the words that are currently being used around you. What has caused them to change from their original meaning and how has this happened? *Sick = good*; *lame = boring*; *epic = awesome*; *jokes = funny*.

Other Tendencies and Hypotheses about Linguistic Change

Functional or Counter-functional

The functionalist hypothesis argues that one of the overarching tendencies in language change is to avoid losing information that is semantically relevant. This tendency has often been advocated, particularly in reference to English-based creoles, where preceding overt markers of tense or aspect and/or disambiguating temporal adverb or conjunction lead to unmarked forms, as in Example 3.21. The overt suppletive mark on *ben* disambiguates the temporal reference time and the overt marker *a* disambiguates aspect. The unmarked verb *kom* is interpretable due to this disambiguation from context and thus does not need to be marked itself, i.e. it is not semantically necessary.

Example 3.21

Jien	*ben* (de)	*a* taak wen dem	*kom*
	[overt tense]	[overt aspect]	[unmarked verb]
Jane	was	talking when they	came (Mufwene 1984: 216)

Yet antifunctionalist patterns have also been reported. Instead of overt marks leading to non-overt marking, overt marks may lead to more overt marks. Similarly, zero forms may lead to more zero forms. In fact, this pattern has been reported for nouns and verbs (Poplack 1979; 1980b; 1981; Scherre and Naro 1991; Scherre and Naro 1992), as in Example 3.22. In Example 3.22a the overt inflection -*ed* is followed by another overtly marked verb while in Example 3.22b a bare verb, *look*, is followed by two additional unmarked verbs. This phenomenon has been referred to as "discourse parellelism" or "parallel processing."

Example 3.22

(a)   Bunch of us *walked* up the stairs and sat down and Caroline *looked* up.
(b)   When I *look* in like that and I *look* in that door and I *look* back in the corner … (Poplack and Tagliamonte 1991a: 324)

Consider the idealized Figure 3.4, which shows the frequency of overt morphology on verbs according to the nature of preceding disambiguating information. This is compared across two varieties, variety 1 and 2. In variety 1 a preceding overt marker, whether inflection, suppletion, adverbial, conjunctive, or otherwise often leads to a bare verb form, as in Example 3.23a–d. In

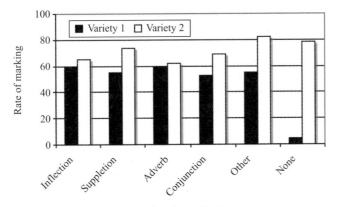

Figure 3.4 Idealized functional effect.

variety 2 there is no effect. Whether there is a preceding mark or not does not influence the appearance of bare verbs.

Example 3.23

    (a) Jane look<u>ed</u> up. She *see* the bird.
    (b) Jane <u>heard</u> a sound. She *see* the bird.
    (c) <u>Yesterday</u>, she *see* the bird.
    (d) <u>After</u> she *see* the bird.

The two patterns are distinct and would require different explanations. Only one variety shows evidence of functional disambiguation (variety 1).

These antithetic tendencies can be probed by further examination of the effect of various types of disambiguating information. There may be nuances across types (e.g. Poplack 1980a,b) and there may be entirely counter tendencies. The analyst's interpretation must rest on an assessment of the patterns.

Grammaticalization

The decisive factors for the triggering and continuation of a grammaticalization process are not to be found exclusively in the grammaticalizing items themselves, but also in changes in related linguistic categories and subsystems. (Diewald 2002: 117)

In the study of linguistic variables above the level of phonology a particular type of language change comes to the forefront – *grammaticalization*. Grammaticalization is the evolution of lexical items into grammatical forms (Meillet 1912: 131). It happens in long series of transitions that may be conceived as a path, or trajectory, over time (Hopper and Traugott 1993: 3) as content words evolve into the functional apparatus of the grammar: tense/aspect markers, pronouns, adverbs, etc. Grammaticalization is subject to certain general processes and mechanisms of change (Traugott and Heine 1991a: 3) and can be identified by various diagnostics (Fischer and Rosenbach 2000: 8–9). The following well-known cline of grammaticalization is found in Hopper and Traugott (1993: 3), as in Example 3.24a. Example 3.24b provides a somewhat idealized example using the contemporary English use of *going to* for future temporal reference, which in contemporary North American English at least is beginning to coalesce with the commonly occurring grammatical subject, "I." Because grammaticalization may go on for centuries at any given stage of the change, forms with different functions are present in the linguistic system. For example, all the forms in Example 3.24b coexist in some contemporary varieties of English, even alongside the older form *will*, as in Example 3.24c. Notice the parallels with the variationist notion of inherent variation (Chapter 1).

Example 3.24

   (a)   content word   > grammatical word   > clitic   > inflectional affix
   (b)   *go*   > *gonna*   > *I'm onna*   > *I'm a*
   (c)   *I'm a* be up in the club/Doin' whatever I like/*I'm a* be poppin' that bubbly/Cool and livin' that good life/Oh let's make this last forever/Party and we*'ll* chill together. (Black Eyed Peas, "Imma Be," *The E.N.D.*, 2010)

Grammaticalization has now been studied in a wide variety of languages. The history of English has been extensively examined from this perspective, beginning with early studies by Traugott (1989) to later compendiums (Traugott and Heine 1991a,b) and overviews (Hopper and Traugott 1993). Although the notion of grammaticalization is controversial (e.g. Joseph 2001, 2004), the diagnostics of grammaticalization are particularly useful for interpreting linguistic patterns in language variation and change.

According to Heine (1991), grammaticalization involves four interrelated mechanisms which relate to different levels of grammar: (1) semantics, (2) pragmatics, (3), morphosyntax, and (4) phonetics:

1. *desemanticization* – loss of semantic content or "bleaching" of meaning;
2. *extension* – generalization of forms to new contexts;
3. *decategorialization* – morphological reduction or loss in morphosyntactic properties characteristic of the source forms, e.g. cliticization, affixation;
4. *erosion* – phonetic reduction, e.g. loss of phonetic segments, suprasegmental features, phonetic autonomy, adaption to adjacent units, simplification.

These mechanisms of grammaticalization offer diagnostics for interpreting trends in the evolution of forms. The type of large-scale survey data that is often used by sociolinguists – representative community-based samples of spoken vernacular language data – can provide a picture of varying stages in the grammaticalization process if the data come from a broad enough age sample (say 9–90, i.e. 80 years) and providing that whatever change is under investigation is happening in such a way as to be captured by this time span. Sociolinguistic corpora often come from nonstandard dialects or local vernaculars and so may shed light not only on community-based, regional norms, but also situate linguistic change at a particular point in its evolution.

Hopper and Traugott (1991: 22–31) put forward a number of diagnostics which identify stages from less to more grammaticalized:

1. layering
2. specialization
3. persistence
4. linguistic correlations.

Grammaticalization is characterized by substantial variation due to the fact that emerging forms coexist with an already existing layer of functionally equivalent ones (Hopper and Traugott 1993: 22). This is the principle of layering. The variability that exists in layering can provide a dynamic representation of the degrees of grammaticalization attained by different forms. As grammaticalization proceeds, the number of choices gets smaller and the survivors take on more general grammatical meanings. This is identified as "specialization." The meaning and function of a grammatical form is also linked to its lexical past. Traces of the original meaning tend to persist (Hopper and Traugott 1993: 28). At any stage of grammaticalization linguistic patterns (e.g. semantic associations, collocations, the effect of one linguistic context or another, etc.) can be correlated with the evolving grammatical morphemes. These provide crucial keys to viewing the diachronic process of grammaticalization in synchronic data (Traugott and Heine 1991a: 6). When internal linguistic constraints (or correlations) on variable forms can be traced to those attested in the historical record, they can be interpreted as persistence. Such information can then provide insights into what earlier points in the development of these areas of grammar may have been like. Similarly, as forms take on new grammatical functions, shifts and reweighting of contextual effects may be observed.

These changes are best viewed with diachronic data and real time; however, LVC researchers have also discovered that the same patterns can be observed in synchronic data in apparent time as well. A further discovery is that varieties may represent different stages of a change.

Figure 3.5 stylizes a change in progress that exhibits grammaticalization. In this case we observe a gradual weakening of an early association with a particular linguistic context (linguistic context b), which gradually shifts to equal occurrence in linguistic contexts a and b, i.e. the constraint levels over time. This linguistic context might, for example, be an association of a particular intensifier with predicative contexts (linguistic context b) in the year 900. Then the intensifier gradually spreads incrementally to attributive contexts (linguistic context a) to the point where in 1500 it is used equally in both contexts.

The grammatical function(s) of forms and their status in the community can be evaluated in a number of ways. First, assess the frequency of an incoming variant. Examine how it correlates with speaker age. The level of use can be used to interpret a change as an early, mid or late stage in the history of the change. Compare the frequency of the incoming features across communities. A community with a low rate of an incoming form might be interpreted as lagging behind in the course of change if a comparable mainstream/urban variety has a significantly higher frequency. Second, examine the linguistic features associated with the linguistic change to determine if attested constraints exist. If so, examine the direction of effect and assess its strength. For example, a linguistic feature in one community might pattern strongly according to a constraint that was attested in the early stages of a change. In another community this constraint may have no effect, i.e. it has leveled. This would suggest

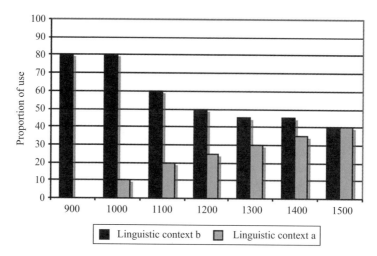

Figure 3.5   Idealized pattern of a grammaticalizing feature according to a relevant linguistic context.

a later stage in the course of change and thus that the change in the second community has progressed further on the grammaticalization path. Contextual factors can be correlated with the different variants in the data using quantitative techniques such as distributional analysis to assess their patterning. Further analysis using statistical modeling can assess the significance of these patterns and their relative importance when all factors are considered simultaneously. The comparative method (see Chapter 6) is then used to assess similarities and differences across age groups in a community or across related communities.

When sociolinguists have tested the diagnostics of grammaticalization in inter- and intracommunity studies the frequencies and patterns of linguistic features have exposed the tracks of a grammaticalizing change.

> The key to understanding language change is not to look at elements atomistically, but to see them in connection with other elements in actual use. (Joseph 2004: 62)

Contact languages such as pidgin and creole languages are ideal for the study of grammaticalization processes (Baker and Syea 1996; Mufwene 1996a; Sankoff 1990). Pidgins and creoles typically develop under extreme sociohistorical circumstances. Linguistic restructuring which is normally gradual takes place over a shorter time period, providing telescoped diachronic evidence. At the same time, the contact languages contributing to the formation of the pidgin or creole (lexifier, substrate) often continue to coexist, offering valuable comparative evidence for the behavior of the forms in question. For example, Sankoff and Brown (1976) studied the development of the relative clause marker *ia*, in Tok Pisin. This form was originally a place adverb, as in Example 3.25a, which extended its use and became a deictic or demonstrative, as in Example 3.25b. Then it further extended to highlight embedded noun phrases as a general bracketing device; see Example 3.25c. Finally, it became a full-fledged relative clause maker, as in Example 3.25d.

Example 3.25

(a)   Tu stap *ia*. "You stay here."
(b)   Disfela *ia*, ol ikosim em haumas? "This one, how much do they charge for it?"

(c)   Na em, man *ia* [lapun man *ia*] stap autsaid ia. "And this man, [this old man], stayed outside."
(d)   Na pik *ia* [ol ikilim bipo *ia*] bai ikamap olsem draipela ston. "And this pig [they had killed before] would turn into a huge stone."

The precise role of grammaticalization in creolization remains controversial as ongoing research suggests that pidgin and creole contact situations give rise to a number of different types of change, some of which are apparent, rather than authentic, cases of grammaticalization (Bruyn 1995). It then becomes critical to assess the extent to which the linguistic processes observed in pidgin and creole language situations mirror ordinary diachronic developments.

A variationist approach tests for the progress of grammaticalization from lexical to grammatical meaning using the following steps:

- Gather information about the lexical source and early usage patterns.
- Project the development pathway from early to later stages e.g. going to: human → animate → inanimate.
- Operationalize factor groups historically implicated in the change.
- Include each factor group in a statistical analysis.
- Partition the data to reflect early to later stages of development based on external (sociogeographic or socioeconomic ecology) e.g. conservative dialect/variety → innovative dialect/variety. Compare and contrast across partitions using comparative sociolinguistic methods.

Lexical Effects

Best practice demands that certain independent factors are part of a variation analysis, namely "individual, lexical or other idiosyncratic patterning" (Poplack and Tagliamonte 2001: 104). Of these, lexical effects in particular have been a fundamental concern (e.g. Guy 1980) because any lexical item of sufficient frequency may skew the overall distributions in a data set. Coding for lexical item enables you to assess the contributions of each word (see Milroy 1987: 133; Tagliamonte 2006a: 121–123; Winford 1992: 352 n. 6; Wolfram 1993: 213–214). Where such influences are discovered, it is critical to assess their effect for whether or not they skew the results, parallel the overall system, or exhibit an advanced state of the system.

Let us take the case study of variable (ed) (Poplack and Tagliamonte 2001) to illustrate.

Past Temporal Reference
Many studies have tackled the variation between marked and unmarked verbs with past temporal reference, variable (ed). Among the many factors that have been found to influence this alternation is the widely cited claim that stative verbs favor overt marking of tense in English-based creoles (Bickerton 1975, 1981), as in Example 3.26.

Example 3.26

(a)   Cause the Mayfish *was* anchored there; a terrible dreadnought, she *was*. (SAM/001)
(b)   They *had* all a good time. (SAM/001)

Table 3.2   Distribution of zero marking of tense on stative verbs across varieties.

| | Early African American English | | | | | | | | |
| | Samaná | | Ex slaves | | North Preston | | Guysborough Enclave | | Guysborough Village | |
	%	N	%	N	%	N	%	N	%	N
have	1	715	4	158	not tabulated					
be	1	1497	3	400						
know	9	98	19	16	50	16	39	56	2	51
like	5	10	100	1	38	8	50	2	0	3
want	31	58	50	8	71	24	15	26	56	18
love	50	2	100	1	0	3	100	2	0	1
own	–	0	–	0	–	0	50	2	0	2
stay	4	54	12	17	45	11	25	24	7	14
live	16	57	30	10	7	15	53	19	5	20
hear	16	19	–	–	–	0	–	0	–	0
see	30	53	33	6	5	20	–	0	0	8
think	9	11	17	6	0	10	0	8	0	11
TOTAL STATIVES	24	470	27	105	26	117	37	125	7	102

Source: Poplack and Tagliamonte (2001: 142, Table 6.9).

Consider the analysis in Table 3.2.

There is a wide range of frequencies of unmarked variants across verbs; however a central divide is apparent. *Have* and *be* comprise hundreds of tokens and are virtually always marked. In contrast, other verbs have much higher rates of zero marking. If *have* and *be* are treated together compared to the rest, the difference is dramatic: 3% vs. 15.8%. This means that any claim about stative verbs must control for the effect of *have* and *be* otherwise the data will be greatly skewed toward these two specific verbs rather than the group of all stative verbs.

Another claim in the literature is that verbs with the same form in present and past participle are more likely to be unmarked in the preterite than other strong verbs, as in Example 3.27:

Example 3.27

(a)   He kicked it over the full back's head, *run* round the full back and caught it. (YRK/002)

(b)   And from there we fell down and *come* round so. (SAM/002)

Consider the data in Table 3.3.

Class I verbs are highly restricted. There is only one that has high rates of unmarking – the verb *come*, which also happens to be extremely frequent. The claim about Class I verbs is

Table 3.3   Frequency of unmarked verbs in Class I across varieties.

	Samaná	Ex slaves	North Preston	Guysborough Enclave	Guysborough Village
Class I verbs					
come	412	57	49	80	47
run	11	8	6	9	3
become	8	–	1	–	–
Total class I	431	65	56	89	50
Proportion class I represented by *come*	96%	88%	88%	90%	94%
% zero on *come*	37%	95%	76%	50%	38%
% zero on remainder of strong verbs	22%	21%	17%	23%	3%

Source: Adapted from Poplack and Tagliamonte (2001: 135, Table 6.5).

really a claim about one verb. Moreover, notice that all the varieties share this lexical tendency. A check of the literature reveals that preterite *come* is attested in North America, England, Scotland, and Ireland. This means that high rates of unmarked *come* is a common feature of English dialects (see Chapter 11). The unique patterning of certain verbs such as *be, have,* and *come* is a large part of the explanation for the occurrence of unmarked verbs. This argues against a systemic effect of aspect or verb type as had been argued in earlier research (Poplack and Tagliamonte 2001: 141).

Whether or not the presence of a particular lexical item skews the results or is simply part of the natural distribution of the data can only be determined by analysis. Identify the frequent lexical items or larger collocations and code them independently.

- How to find frequent lexical items:
  - Run your data through a concordance program and produce a wordlist
  - Check frequency dictionaries
  - Check electronic resources

> **TIP**   People of different ages use different adjectives. I might say "that's intriguing," but my students are more likely to say "that's sick." When I lived in England (1995–2001) everyone said "that's brilliant." In Toronto (2001–2007) "that's awesome" was extremely common. I have often thought that adjectives would be a good choice for quantitative investigation. Adjectives do not, of course "mean the same thing," but they are structurally equivalent categories in the grammar and I will bet they also co-vary with patterns of social and linguistic phenomena. Listen for how the people around you talk about things that are good or bad.

Exemplar Theory

The frequency of words and collocations of words is becoming recognized as a key part of linguistic competence, variable grammars and linguistic change. A recent proposal for modeling these influences is exemplar theory, the idea "the cognitive representation of a word can be made up of the set of exemplars that have been experienced by the speaker/ hearer" (Bybee 2002: 271). Exemplar theory is a model of perception and categorization that is based in psychology. It comes into LVC studies from research on speech perception (e.g. Pierrehumbert 2001; 2002; 2003) but it is beginning to be taken up as a viable explanation by more and more researchers studying variation of all kinds.

Exemplar theory provides a natural means of testing and interpreting frequency effects. It holds that information from language experience is processed by the listener and becomes part of the stored representation of the language. Lexical items are considered to be distributions of remembered exemplars stored in the mind complete with all their acoustic, social, and contextual information intact. A term used to describe this is the "exemplar cloud." This conception of language diverges dramatically from the idea that lexical representations are stored in some abstract or invariant form. Instead, remarkably detailed linguistic cues are stored and activated every time individuals experience language. People match the acoustic signal to the stored distribution it most resembles, while the task of speech production involves averaging over a relevant part of the distribution. The information that remains in memory is thought to be quite abstract since speakers are known to be sensitive to repeated occurrences of all kinds of linguistic variables, including patterns of agreement (Poplack 1980b, 1981; Scherre and Naro 1991), tense (Tagliamonte and Poplack 1993), syntactic structure (Weiner and Labov 1983) etc. At the same time, exemplars decay. This means that more recently encountered utterances are stored with higher activation levels than older utterances, and socially and contextually relevant exemplars may receive more activation than less relevant exemplars. One of the attractions of exemplar theory is that linguistic and nonlinguistic indexical information can be attached to lexical items. In phonology, factors such as frequency of outcomes, prosodic and segmental configurations, and representation of words across categories are all relevant. The same is true of the experience people have with different populations or social groups. Exemplar theory is particularly useful for acquisition where children do not immediately know whether phonological variants are allophonic/ phonological or sociolinguistic or both (Foulkes and Docherty 2006). Exemplar models provide "the tools" to explore how all these many factors are handled by the linguistic system (Pierrehumbert 2006: 528). Exemplar theory is experiential and compelling with commonalities to the interpretation of human experience in other fields and practices.

Bybee (2002) documents the influence of frequency on a number of what she refers to as "reductive changes": variable (t,d), variable (th) in Spanish, vowel shifts, the reduction of vowels to schwa, and the deletion of schwa in American English, e.g. "camera" → [kQmr´]. All such changes are influenced by word frequency – high frequency words tend to change before low frequency words. However, "articulatory reduction cannot run rampant, but may be constrained by predictability in discourse" (Bybee 2002: 269). There is also a collocation effect such that not simply frequent words, but frequent collocations will exhibit reduction processes more than infrequent ones: compare *grand piano* vs. *grand piazza*. However a paradox in lexical diffusion is that sound changes affect high frequency words first, but analogical changes affect low frequency words first. For example, low frequency verbs such as *weep/wept, leaped/lept, creep/crept* are said to be regularizing to *weeped, leaped* and *creeped*, yet more frequent verbs with the same pattern, e.g. *keep/kept, sleep/slept, leave/ left*, are not. This means that the predictability of a collocation will influence whether it will be reduced.

NOTE   There is a single token of *crept* in both the York Corpus and the TEA: (i) I *crept* down the ladders and went home (YRK/017/72/M) and (ii) There are other words that have crept into ... (TOR/113/M/85), both from elderly men. In contrast, the equally rare tokens of *creeped*: (ii) I'd laugh so hard if I got it though. And then be *creeped* out (CMC/034) and (iii) It was old and missing fur, and really twitchy and strange. Kind of *creeped* me out (TOR/012), are both are from adolescent females. Also note the expression-like usages, namely "to be creeped out." Do these suggestive tokens support the hypothesis that low frequency words regularize?

Studies of sociophonetic variation are particularly suited to interpretation using the exemplar model. The research of Docherty, Foulkes, and associates (2000, 2002, 2005) has argued that the cognitive representations of words are not limited to their frequency, but combine linguistic and sociolinguistic information. Both types of information are present from the first stages of acquisition (Smith, Durham, and Fortune 2009). Moreover, this influence continues through the lifespan (Foulkes and Docherty 2006: 432). The "sociolinguistic monitor ... observes, processes and stores social information" (Foulkes and Docherty 2006: 512). In Foulkes and Docherty's words,

> sociophonetic variability is strongly governed by the individual's exposure to the statistical properties of ambient sound patterning and also by how the individual interprets and manipulates his/her social context. (Foulkes and Docherty 2006: 433)

Exemplar theory has also been applied to grammatical variation (Bresnan *et al.* 2007; Bresnan and Hay 2008; Hay 2006b; Hay, Nolan, and Drager 2006). In syntax, as with phonology, the grammar is assumed to be quantitative and learned from exposure to other speakers. Depending on the nature of the exemplars that successive generations are exposed to, there will be subtle differences in the variable grammar. It seems that exemplar theory is a quantitatively viable means to test the effects of our experience with language. According to Mufwene (2001: 22) "linguistic features in a system also constitute part of the ecology for one another. Removal, insertion, or modification (of the role) of a variant affects the distribution of other variants in a subsystem, thus yielding a different kind of system overall."

These differences are captured by examination of the patterns that underlie a variable process, in the constraint ranking of factors and in their relative strength. As argued by Bresnan and Hay, "The grammar arises as a set of analogical generalizations over stored chunks of previously experienced language – lexicalized phrases or constructions – which are used to build new expressions analogically" (Bresnan and Hay 2008: 256). The linguistic variable they target for investigating these effects is variation between two different dative constructions in the verb *give* in New Zealand and American English, as in Example 3.28.

Table 3.4 Bybee's model for types of change underlying lexical diffusion.

Reductive change	Analogical change
Affects high frequency words and phrases earlier	Affects low frequency words earlier
Affects high frequency words and phrases to a greater extent	No effect of high frequency words and phrases
Automation of production	Words confirm to the stronger pattern of the language

Source: Bybee 2002: 270–271.

Example 3.28

(a) He would *give* [everyone] [a copy of the DVD]. (TOR/008) double object construction
(b) It would *give* [an outward sign] <u>to</u> everyone around you. (TOR/102) prepositional dative construction

The constituents of the construction comprise the recipient, *everyone,* and the theme, *a copy of the DVD/an outward sign.* A set of linguistic factors constrains the choice of construction, including log length of recipient, log length of theme, type of recipient, type of theme, givenness of recipient, givenness of the theme, semantic class of the verb, *give,* animacy of the theme and recipient. Testing these effects in a statistical model showed that while many of the factor groups were parallel between the United States and New Zealand, others varied. For example nonanimate recipients are more likely to be used in the double object construction in New Zealand than in the United States. In addition, in New Zealand the age of individuals (with birthdates that spanned 1850–2000) was significant. This shows that varieties of English differ quantitatively in the syntax of *give,* providing evidence that grammar is quantitative and learned from exposure to other speakers. They refer to this as "gradient grammar." This is basically the same as what variationists have called "variable grammar." Note too that the point by point comparison between the two major varieties of English using statistical modeling mirrors comparative sociolinguistics (see Chapter 6).

In sum, early LVC research noted that lexical effects were important; however, the method for dealing with these effects was to remove them from the data by employing type/token ratios. With the advent of exemplar theory, frequency has become an important part of the analysis. Frequency effects can be used as a diagnostic for identifying the cause of linguistic change (Bybee 2002: 270) because the nature of a change determines how frequency effects will operate. Bybee's model for identifying the mechanism of lexical diffusion is shown in Table 3.4.

A recent contribution to this issue comes from Erker and Guy (2010) who studied the variable presence of subject pronouns in Spanish, as in Example 3.29:

Example 3.29

(a) Tú tienes razón. "You're right"
(b) Ø tienes razón.

Subjecting nearly 5000 contexts to analysis of an array of conditioning factors, they discovered that frequency effects are subject to a threshold. All the constraints were weaker

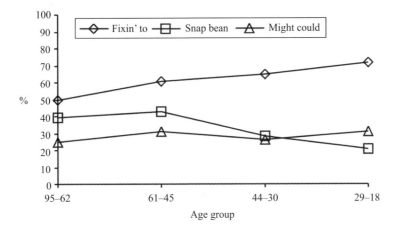

Figure 3.6 Three variants in apparent time in Texas, USA, c. 1980s.
Source: Bailey 1991: 258, Figure 13.

and less predictive of subject pronoun absence among the low frequency verbs and stronger and more predictive in high frequency verbs. This result demonstrates that abstract conditioning factors are mediated by individual lexical items and the levels of frequency matter. Speakers must employ/encounter a lexical item at some minimal frequency in order to process information about collocations and other features. Beyond that level, items may be differentiated by many constraints, but below that level, speakers have too few tokens to assess specific information about a word's patterns of occurrence.

Linguistic patterns embody the variable grammar. Different types of linguistic change – phonological, morphological, syntactic, semantic, pragmatic – predict different trajectories of change. This is because different underlying mechanisms are involved. Phonological change may involve weakening while a morphological change may involve leveling or analogy. The different patterns that can be expected are graphically illustrated in the contrasts among Figures 3.1–3.5. At the same time the effect of individuals, groups, lexical items, and types need to be disentangled. By paying attention to linguistic patterns the analyst can infer what type of change is underway in the language.

Exercises

Exercise 3.1 Identifying linguistic patterns

Figure 3.6 shows the distribution of three linguistic variants across four age groups in Texas, US in the 1980s: the double modal *might could*, the future construction *fixin' to*, the lexical item *snap bean* (for *green bean*) (adapted from Bailey *et al.* 1991b).

Question 1 This graph illustrates sociolinguistic patterning:
(a) in real time.
(b) in apparent time.

(c)   without respect to time.
(d)   there is insufficient data to judge.

Question 2   Which variant is most stigmatized?
(a)   fixin' to.
(b)   snap bean.
(c)   might could.
(d)   there is insufficient data to judge.

Question 3   Given the pathway of change evident in Figure 3.4, which variant would you
            least expect a teenager to use?
(a)   fixin' to.
(b)   might could.
(c)   snap bean.
(d)   there is insufficient data to judge.

Question 4   The data suggest that *fixin' to* is:
(a)   an expanding innovation.
(b)   a relatively stable lexical form.
(c)   a declining lexical feature.
(d)   there is insufficient data to judge.

Question 5   Which linguistic form would be a good target for an investigation of gram-
            maticalization? Why?

Exercise 3.2   Interpreting linguistic patterns   ————————————————

Figure 3.7 shows the increasing use of stative possessive *have got* with different types of
complement in English from 1750 to 1995 (adapted from Kroch 1989: 209).

Question 1   What well-known linguistic patterns does Figure 3.7 exhibit:
(a)   in terms of frequency?
(b)   in terms of the linguistic constraint abstract vs. concrete?

Figure 3.8 shows the use of deontic *have to* by type of verb (adapted from Tagliamonte 2004a:
48, Table 7).

Question 2   What linguistic patterns does Figure 3.8 exhibit:
(a)   in terms of frequency?
(b)   in terms of the linguistic constraint stative vs. punctual?

Mini Quiz Answers

3.1   **Q1**: *weakening*
      Q2: *weakening. Extension of the intervocalic flap, [D], found in other intervocalic word medial contexts
      in Canadian English, e.g. "ladder" or "latter" as [læDr].*

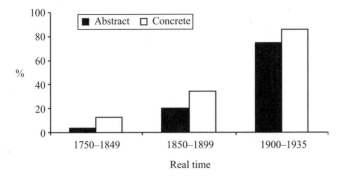

Figure 3.7 Frequency of *have got* for possession by nature of the complement in real time.
Source: Kroch 1989: 209, Table 2.

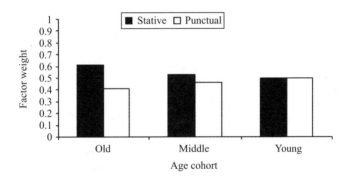

Figure 3.8 Frequency of *have to* for deontic modality by verb type in apparent time in York English.
Source: Tagliamonte 2004: 48, Table 7.

Q3: *extension via four-part analogy*
Q4: *extension via leveling of subjunctive "it were" to the more common collocation "it was"*

3.2 **Q1**: *d*

Notes

1   http://www.helsinki.fi/varieng/CoRD/corpora/index.html (accessed December 27, 2010).
2   http://www-users.york.ac.uk/~lang18/pcorpus.html (accessed December 27, 2010).
3   http://www.urbandictionary.com/define.php?term=cardinal (accessed August 5, 2010).
4   http://www.oed.com/thesaurus.

Background Reading

Anttila 1989; Campbell 1998; Hock 1986, 1991; Hock and Joseph 1996; Joseph and Janda 2003a,b; Lehmann 1973; Visser 1963–73, 1970.

4

Data and Method

A speech community cannot be conceived as a group of speakers who all use the same forms; it is best defined as a group who share the same norms in regard to language. (Labov 1972c: 158)

the individual is very difficult to understand; even the small group is very hard to understand unless you know something about the community or group they're coming from, because the individual's behavior is determined by the social forces that intersect with their individual lives. (Labov 7.19.2006, quoted in Gordon, 2006: 348)

Sociolinguistic data is unique in that it attempts to tap the norms of the speech community under investigation. LVC methods are unique in that they attempt to explain the nature of socially embedded linguistic phenomena. In this chapter I discuss the types of data and methods that are used for studying language in social context. In particular, I discuss and give examples from my own fieldwork and corpus construction projects. I will also discuss a key issue in the analysis of linguistic variation and change in the speech community: how to deal with individuals and with lexical items.

The Speech Community

The speech community has three main dimensions: (1) well-defined limits; (2) a common structural base; and (3) a unified set of sociolinguistic norms (Labov 2007: 347).

The classic sociolinguistic studies were based on large-scale, random sampling of urban speech communities, e.g. the corpora collected by Labov in New York City, Wolfram in Detroit, and Fasold in Washington. These studies were followed soon after by a plethora of others that expanded the sociolinguistic data collection enterprise to different parts of the world and initiated new sampling methodologies. Sankoff and Cedergren's survey of

Variationist Sociolinguistics: Change, Observation, Interpretation, First Edition. Sali A. Tagliamonte.
© 2012 Sali A. Tagliamonte. Published 2012 by Blackwell Publishing Ltd.

Montreal required modifications to the random sampling methods to find the francophones. Milroy's sample from Northern Ireland followed social networks. Poplack's study of Ottawa focused on five neighborhoods where francophones represented a large proportion of the population. Later studies modified the original random sampling method even more. These developments were motivated by the different research questions the researchers had in conducting the study. There were undoubtedly other motivations, including reduced funding, the need to prioritize, and undoubtedly other mundane reasons. Unfortunately, the world has changed considerably since the 1960s. Where once it was possible, both practically and monetarily, to collect a (modified) random sample, by the 2000s large-scale surveys have become incredibly difficult. A request for an interview is looked upon not just suspiciously but as a nefarious activity. The end result is that samples are smaller, more socially oriented, and often focused on specific individuals or groups. In some cases, the samples are relatively large, but not entirely random. The result is perhaps not ideal; Labov (2001a) refers to these developments as "truncated methodology," and believes they are limited in their utility for the study of language change within the speech community. Nevertheless, as we shall see, new findings are arising every day with fresh insights into the study of language variation and change.

Corpus Building

the most exciting aspect of corpus work: the opportunity it affords to serendipitously discover what one wasn't looking for, to characterize the patterned nature of linguistic heterogeneity, and in particular to hidden, unsuspected or "irrational" constraints that are simply inaccessible to introspection or casual perusal. (Poplack 2007)

Much has been written about corpus building in the last ten years. The early variationist work set the foundation for a groundswell of corpora from New York City to Panama and Buenos Aires, from Norwich and Reading to Saudi Arabia and South Africa. Poplack's early paper on constructing mega-corpora (Poplack 1989) set a new standard for computerized data sets. Beal, Corrigan, and Moisl (2007) and Beal *et al.* (2007) take stock of the many differences in methods and projected end-users of corpora and a documentation of best practices in corpus construction and preservation. As we move forward into the twenty-first century, advances in hardware, in annotation systems, in digitization, in computerized corpus work – all these are making the work of sociolinguists exponentially greater and easier. Nevertheless, as Poplack (1989) points out, sociolinguists must not lose sight of the goal – to produce a corpus of "interest, value and current relevance." To do so requires that researchers step back from the hardware, the computer programming, and the million-word repositories and remember the fundamental questions that a corpus is meant to answer. It is tough to create a sociolinguistic corpus. There will be considerable water under the bridge between the time of the slammed doors and tense stories to the time when a savvy website sports the fancy graphs and tables. When you are face to face with someone you have never seen before and you have to talk to them for at least an hour, you need to have a question that will rouse a story. When confronted with the data, you have to know what to do with it, how, and why.

Creating Sociolinguistic Corpora

LVC research is known for its preoccupation with corpora whether written or spoken. Written corpora come from collections of materials from the past whether correspondence or literary work. Spoken corpora are typically built from conversations with real people in real communities. Sociolinguists often know more about the people in their corpora than anyone realizes. This is perhaps the thing that most sets apart this area of linguistics – its grassroots. Depending on the nature of their data, variationist sociolinguists have tended to be the linguist in the archive tracking down old letters, learning Old English, or compiling historical repositories. Alternatively, they are in the street, on the island, out in the field, in the pubs and coffeehouses and porches, wherever they need to be. In fact, sociolinguists are pretty much always at work wherever they are.

Throughout this book I use examples from various corpora I have collected over the years or that have been collected by my students and collaborators.[1] Most of the examples will come from the two larger corpora: the York English Corpus and the Toronto English Archive of Spoken Materials. Appendix A provides a listing of all the corpus codes so that each example in the book can be tracked back to its source, its time of collection and its location in the world. Every example can be traced back to the original conversation and to the person who uttered it.

NOTE   7-13-10. I am on the bus going home from work. Two young guys are talking to each other. They are relatively well educated – secondary school graduates. One works at a liquor store, the other for a transit company. Both are native speakers of English. They are guys, but their use of *like* is very frequent. Then, I hear a bare past participle, *I seen the movie*. There is no adverbial, something that favors this feature earlier in the history of English (see Chapter 10). Is this feature becoming more frequent in Canadian English?

The York English Corpus

In 1997 I collected the York English Corpus (Tagliamonte 1996–1998). My goal was to obtain a representative sample of the vernacular of the city of York in England. Individuals were chosen strictly on the basis of their native status in the community. Each speaker was required to meet the sampling criteria of having been born and raised in York. Following the techniques developed by Milroy (1980; 1987), we entered the community through three independent social networks: (1) acquaintances in the university service personnel; (2) neighbors and friends of the interviewers; and (3) a community church. Because one of the main goals of the project was to track linguistic change in the community, we made every effort to stratify the sample by age and sex. Due to the three-pronged network strategy the speakers represent the range of occupations and education levels typical of the city.

The sample shown in Table 4.1 is made up of 92 individuals, ranging in age from 15 to 91 years of age and divided among 40 men and 52 women. All had been educated at least to the

Table 4.1　York English Corpus (c. 1997).

Age	Male	Female	Total
17–34	11	12	23
35–65	13	22	35
66+	13	20	33
Total	37	54	91

age of 14. Of the speakers educated beyond the age of 16, there is a range from technical college to university, although those in the latter category are a minority.

The interviews are similar to those obtained in many other sociolinguistic projects of this kind. Each one contains some or all of the elements of informal discourse – personal reminiscences, narratives of personal experience, group interactions, folk stories, and many vibrant characterizations of the city of York today and in the past.

The Toronto Corpora

From 2003 to 2006 I collected the Toronto English Corpus (Tagliamonte 2003–2006). My goal was to collect a socially stratified sample of Toronto English as spoken by people born and raised in the city. I anticipated that this would provide a baseline of Canadian English as spoken in Toronto at the turn of the twenty-first century. The goals of the study were: (1) to investigate changing features in the speech community, their history in the English language and their current state of development in Toronto; and (2) to contribute new insights into the social and linguistic motivations of language change.

At the outset, I thought I could simply apply the tried-and-true methods outlined in Labov's early work in New York City (Labov 1972a) or Poplack's Ottawa-Hull Corpus (Poplack 1989), i.e. random sampling by going door-to-door to find willing participants with the appropriate sampling criteria. Unfortunately, this procedure was an abysmal failure. The problem is that half the people who lived in Toronto in 2003–2004 were not born and raised in Toronto, nor even in Canada. In fact, 49% of the population of Toronto in the early 2000s were not born in Canada. Some neighborhoods, I discovered, were 90% immigrants! The solution to this problem was to use the most recent census data to target neighborhoods in the city with the lowest proportion of speakers born outside Canada. We ended up with seven neighborhoods with between 25–44% immigrants. Then, we proceeded with a quota-based sample, in which we aimed to achieve a minimum stratified sample for each of the seven neighborhoods, as in Table 4.2.

This procedure was also not entirely successful. Over 69% of the people were not at home. A still worrying proportion of people we met at their doorsteps, 19%, were not born and raised in Toronto, even within our selected neighborhoods. Our success rate in obtaining a sociolinguistic interview was very low (2.4%). We had to find another solution. We enhanced our chances of obtaining an interview using the social network and friend-of-a-friend techniques developed by Milroy (1980; 1987). We went to neighborhoods and knocked on doors to get initial interviews. Upon completion of the interview, we attempted to network for additional speakers in the same neighborhood. The strategy of combining modified

Table 4.2   Sampling strategy for Toronto neighborhoods.

Age	Male	Female	Total
20–39	2	2	4
40–59	2	2	4
60+	2	2	4
TOTAL	6	6	12

random sampling with social networking led to about a 50–50 balance between interviews collected using random sampling and those collected using social networking.

Another important goal of the fieldwork in Toronto was to achieve socioeconomic stratification. This presented another tricky problem. In Canadian society in the late twentieth century most people who are born and raised in Toronto are middle class. Moreover, most people with time (and interest!) to talk to an interviewer for an hour or more are typically middle class and relatively well educated. Our solution to this dilemma was to scout out the neighborhoods before entering them. We selected streets that best represented each neighborhood's socioeconomic situation and to whatever extent possible we established and developed ethnographic links with the neighborhood. Nevertheless, socioeconomic stratification in Toronto of people born and raised in Toronto is biased toward the middle class. This is simply the way it is in Toronto. The corpus reflects the norm of the speech community.

From 2002 to 2006 a series of smaller corpora were collected within a course I taught through the Research Opportunities Program (ROP) at the University of Toronto. The course was set up as a mini-project to tap into linguistic innovations in the pre-adolescent and adolescent population of Toronto. Students in the ROP course[2] interviewed members of their own social and familial networks between the ages of 10–20 (e.g. their sisters, mothers, cousins, neighbors, friends, etc.). The interviewers, aged 20–22, are not simply participant observers but actual members of the same community. This makes this corpus one of the few data sets collected by in-group members of the youth culture of the community. The "interviews" focus on informal topics such as school activities, hobbies, sports, friends, and lots of commiseration about problems with their parents, boyfriends and girlfriends, etc.

Together these corpora make up the Toronto English Archive (TEA) of spoken materials. The sample as of the summer of 2010, shown in Table 4.3, consists of 267 individuals, ranging in age from 9 years of age to 92 and divided among 123 men and 144 women.

Types of Corpora

In the many sociolinguistics laboratories all over the world: "Instead of handling beakers and chemicals, … technicians and students are transcribing and analyzing tapes containing hundreds of hours of people speaking." (Poplack 2010)[3]

Over the last 40 years there has been a growing number of data sets from many varied situations, some of them pivotal for the evolution of LVC studies. Bailey's discovery of the Ex-Slave Recordings in the Rare Book Room of the Library of Congress (Bailey, Maynor, and Cukor-Avila 1991a); Elizabeth Gordon's discovery of the Mobile Unit recordings of

Table 4.3 Toronto English Archive of Spoken Materials (c. 2003–2010).

Date of birth	Speaker age	M	F	Total
1991–1993	10–12	8	7	15
1990–1989	13–14	7	6	13
1987–1988	15–16	8	6	14
1984–1986	17–19	20	28	48
1979–1983	20–24	14	17	31
1974–1978	25–29	10	8	18
1964–1973	30–39	10	17	27
1954–1963	40–49	17	14	31
1944–1953	50–59	8	21	29
1934–1943	60–69	9	5	14
1924–1933	70–79	4	10	14
1914–1923	80–89	7	5	12
pre-1913	90+	1	0	1
TOTAL		123	144	267

New Zealand English which led to the Origins of New Zealand English project (ONZE)[4] (Gordon 2004; 2008); and Popack and Sankoff's serendipitous trip to Samaná in the Dominican Republic (Poplack and Sankoff 1987) – all these have led to far-reaching developments for LVC studies. Other corpora from fieldwork on the far north shore of Scotland (Smith and Tagliamonte 1998), Tristan da Cunha (Schreier 2002) and innumerable far-flung locales are bringing unprecedented new insights into the research arena. Novel corpora are emerging as well. Sankoff's (2004) study of the 7 UP film series in the UK enabled her to study change in real time. My own study of the television series *Friends* based on the transcripts of the show from the Internet provided a view of how media language reflects contemporary norms (Tagliamonte and Roberts 2005).

Corpus-building in the late twentieth century must deal with extreme multi-ethnic urban centers. Labov (1966) once characterized the speech community as a group of speakers who share a set of evaluative norms governing social and stylistic variation. However, the complexity of modern cities such as New York, London, or Toronto does not lend itself to this conception of the speech community. Can we say of any of these cities today the same thing that Labov said of New York City in 1966 (Labov 1966: 186), namely "New York City is a single speech community"? Supportive to Labov's original conception, my research on Toronto has shown tremendous consistency across neighborhoods and ethnic groups. The major social and stylistic differences across these groups remain rooted in the level of education and occupation type – at least among those who were born and raised in Toronto, which is the current composition of the corpus. Yet research on London, UK, is uncovering a different situation. In an analysis of the highly ubiquitous variable (*was*), Cheshire and Fox (2009: 34) found that none of the known constraints on its patterning operated consistently across groups. They conclude that

The challenge for future studies of language variation and change in our large multicultural urban cities is how best to incorporate linguistic diversity into a coherent account of language use that takes full account of the different language histories, language ecologies, and social dynamics of urban speakers.

The differences between Toronto and London may be due to the nature of the populations that were sampled. They may be due to differences in the social structure in Canada and the UK. Exploring these possibilities will inform the next generation of studies of the world's cities.

> **NOTE**   In Toronto, where 49% of the population were not born in Canada, let alone Toronto, it is difficult to imagine the type of cohesive speech community that Labov envisaged. Yet, everyone who is born and raised in Toronto knows that you pronounce Toronto as [trɒnə] not [tɒrɒnto]. There is no second [t] in "Toronto." Moreover, "Scarborough," one of the eastern suburbs of the city, is pronounced [skɑrbəro] not [skɒrbrə], as is a place of the same name in Yorkshire, England. These are indications of overarching community-wide norms.

New Data Sources

The media and the Internet are presenting sociolinguists with a mind-boggling array of new and interesting corpora, making large-scale studies easier than ever. The possibilities for answering key sociolinguistic questions seem to be at our fingertips. The history of development of a linguistic feature can be tracked in immense, tagged, corpora from the history of the English language. Register variation can be studied by comparing online magazines, newspapers, government records, news casts, pod casts, blogs, and vlogs. Change in real time can be tracked in the same way. Where once students had to "hit the streets" to collect sociolinguistic interviews, in the past ten years my students have collected data from online books, personal ads, television shows, songs, text messages, Facebook sites, etc. The possibilities are endless. Yet the gold standard of Variationist Sociolinguistics remains the rich vernacular corpora where people live and breathe and talk to each other, where they can see, hear, and reach out and touch them. The analyst has the ability to tap into language variation and change in the fluid, online buzzing choir of the speech community.

> The speech community is an overarching social reality. The notion of a social fact – that language exists in the community exterior to the individual – is our central theme. The way in which this social pattern is grasped by the individual speaker and the way it changes over time is our central problem. (Labov 7-19-2006, quoted in Gordon 2006: 350)

A basic challenge for all fieldwork in the speech community is tapping into this vernacular register. The problem is, as it has always been in fieldwork, combating the observer's paradox. A complete stranger arouses the level of attention paid to speech. This is exacerbated by an audiorecording device and microphone, the key tools of sociolinguistic fieldwork, which introduce formality and induce self-monitoring. Moreover, the link to an academic institution (about which we are required to be transparent due to modern ethics clearance practices) enhances people's expectation for standard speech. The solution to this problem is still the many tried and true Labovian techniques for tapping the vernacular (e.g. Tagliamonte 2006a: Chapter 3). The following are particularly germane:

- place recording device out of sight
- no paper, clipboards, or nametags
- let the informant lead the topic of discussion
- use your own best vernacular
- display a relaxed demeanor
- enjoy the conversation.

Sociolinguistic interviews are fluid, meandering conversations that are underlain by the intense drive of all good interviewers to get the story. Sometimes this requires perseverance, as in Example 4.1a. Sometimes it requires restraint, as in Example 4.1b. Most times, however, a sociolinguistic interview becomes an utterly fresh and remarkable recounting of life stories that really need to be told, as in Example 4.1c. In my view, it is a privilege and an honor to be a part of this amazing human process.

Example 4.1

 (a) [Interviewer] We want to hear all about your life story and what you get up to on the side. [Interviewee] What life story? I ain't got a life story! (laughter) [Interviewer] So how long have you lived down this end then? (YRK/066)

 (b) [Interviewer] No, tell me, tell me. [Interviewee] No! Wait, Let me finish! So then– [Interviewer] No, tell me that story you were gonna tell me yesterday. [Interviewee] What story? I don't remember a story. I'm in the middle of story already. Let me finish! (TOR/001)

 (c) Oh my God I have a story to tell you! (TOR/999)

Back to Brass Tacks

Studies of language in the speech community require you to knock on doors and pound the pavement. Here are some tips from my Toronto interviewers Sonja Molfenter and Matt King:

- Work in pairs, approach streets together, one on each side.
- Two-way radios are a great security tool. Having them allows you to tell your partner when you are entering someone's house, what address you are at, how long you will be, etc. They are also much cheaper and more efficient than mobile phones.
- Interviewers must communicate often. This helps keep sense of humor when a door is slammed in your face. This also allows interviewers to use their time effectively by switching streets when no one is home, not from the city, not interested etc.
- Knock *and* ring the doorbell. Doorbells don't always work!
- If possible do the interview immediately. If you can't, try to set it up right away. If that does not work try to get the potential informant's phone number. Do not simply give them yours. They won't call back.
- Communicate clearly and simply about what the study is about, do not try to "sell" what you are doing (puts you in the "pushy, annoying canvasser" category) or be too vague (puts you in the "criminal, home intruder" category – especially for young males).

- Be very aware during the interview. Listen intently while also planning a new question. If the informant stops talking and you don't have a new question, the conversation abruptly stops and it suddenly becomes an interview again.
- Emphasize the people's history part of the study. People love to tell you about their history. Researching the neighborhood's history can provide a goldmine. People enjoy "teaching" you about their area's history. For example, in the 1950s "Hurricane Hazel" swept through neighborhoods in Toronto's west end. Older people told great stories about this event.
- Remember that certain events beyond your control will affect the way the community responds to you. Some of the events that affected us adversely included:
  o   long weekends and rainy days;
  o   a rash of hate crimes in a Jewish community made people less willing to participate;
  o   after the Greeks won the Euro Cup Soccer finals in 2004 no one in the target neighborhood, which happened to have Greek roots, would answer the door the following day.

The Individual and the Group

Throughout the early days of Variationist Sociolinguistics, study after study demonstrated that although every person has his or her own idiolect, individuals in large part mirror the group(s) to which they belong or affiliate themselves (Guy 1980). Labov (2001a) observes that deviations from the mean are "not normally large enough to disturb the regularity of the patterns when 5–10 speakers are included in each group."

Whether corpora are large or small, the analyst should always check both group and individual patterns. Let us see what a difference this can make. Consider the use of intensifying adverbs, as in Example 4.2.

Example 4.2

(a)   I wish I had a British accent, British accents are *so cool*. (TOR/001)
(b)   Well, you're a *very hot* nerd. (CMC/014)
(c)   Like I'm *really lucky* that someone like my two *really good* friends like live five minutes walking distance from me. (TOR/004)

The data come from teenagers between 16 and 19, born and raised in the city of Toronto. Their ethnic backgrounds are widely divergent. Figure 4.1 shows the proportion of intensifiers out of the total number of intensifiable adjectives.

With the exception of *pretty*, females use a little more of each of the most popular intensifiers. However, the broader result is that the males and females pattern similarly. The same hierarchy of intensifiers – *so* > *really* > *very* – is found for males and females. The question is, does this reflect consistent behavior across all individuals? Or does grouping the males and females together mask individual differences? Figures 4.2 and 4.3 separate out each of the speakers, first males, then females.

Observe the extreme uses by particular individuals at both ends of the variation spectrum. This reveals how the practice of aggregating speakers will homogenize a broad range of uses (Eckert 1999: 194). As predicted, the males are more conservative than the females.

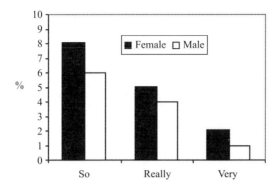

Figure 4.1 Distribution of intensifiers by speaker sex, Toronto, c. 2003–2004.

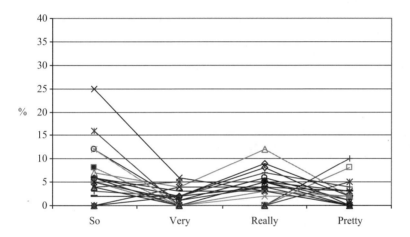

Figure 4.2 Distribution of intensifiers by individual males in Toronto, c. 2003–2004.

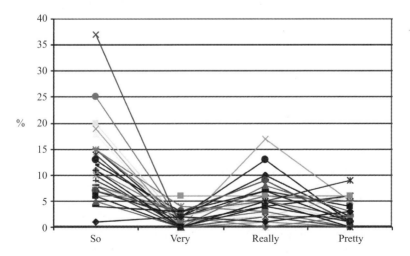

Figure 4.3 Distribution of intensifiers by individual females in Toronto, c. 2003–2004.

But the two figures also reveal a community trend that is remarkably similar in both aggregates. While the individual *rates* of use of particular intensifiers differ, their *pattern* within the system tends to have the same contour as the grouped pattern. This key point was illustrated in the early 1980s by Guy (1980) who showed convincingly that the individual mirrors the norms of his/her community. The demonstration in Figures 4.2 and 4.3 shows comparable results, and for a variable that is nonphonological (as Guy's was) and embodies a change in progress (rise of intensifier *so*). It also provides corroborating evidence of Labov's (2001) observation that the great cities of North America are remarkably homogeneous.

> **NOTE**   It is interesting to speculate about the highest frequency users of *so*. As it happens, the highest male user at 25% is a 19-year-old guy who was working in a hair salon at the time of his interview while the highest female user, 36%, is a 16-year-old girl. Further, in-depth analysis of these speakers would undoubtedly reveal a whole other nuance to the intensifier study.

Analysts may focus on the general pattern or the individual pattern or both in interpreting the observed variation; however, the existence of community norms even in large, complex speech communities is a key underpinning of sociolinguistics. Of course, it still remains for us to answer the mysterious question of "how the great cities achieve relative geographic uniformity" (Labov 2001: 232).

Mini Quiz 4.1

Q1   What other sociolinguistic pattern do you observe when you compare the male and female findings in Figures 4.2 and 4.3?

Constructing an LVC Study

One time I went to a conference talk and the presenter reviewed a series of factor groups that were being tested in the statistical model. In the question period I got up and said, "Could you please tell us *why* you are testing for those factors?" The person did not know. An LVC study has to have a point. Whatever the study is about, there must be a reason for embarking upon it in the first place. Make sure you know which sociolinguistic issue you are tackling. The point of the study should be straightforwardly stated as well as the reasons for undertaking it. In what follows, I provide some requisite points of departure for an LVC study.

Scientific Report or Literary Essay?

Think of your research as a scientific report, not a literary essay. What I often see in papers is a lot of what I refer to as "blah blah." A long-winded discussion is not as important as thoroughly backed up facts, rigorously situated within the research literature. Research papers should contain clear coherent language and a logical step-by-step argumentation.

Data

Ask yourself why your feature occurs where it does and why it doesn't occur where it could have. Formulate hypotheses in a testable way and start coding your data in such a way as to test these hypotheses. All too often analysts will have great ideas but they will avoid confronting the data. The only way to find out if your idea will work out is to find out. If you do, you will discover pretty quickly whether or not your idea is feasible. If you do not have enough data, leave open the possibility of collecting more. Establish early on how many tokens of your variable you get in a certain easily measured amount of data. If there are not enough to warrant a study, stop and find another linguistic feature. You do not want to get to the end of your data and find out there is not enough to warrant an analysis.

> **TIP**   Once my students have embarked on a research project, they know that the first question I am going to ask them is "What is your overall distribution?" If they don't know the answer, they aren't doing the work.

Variation, Super Tokens and Suggestive Tokens

Liberally sprinkle your paper with examples that cogently illustrate the linguistic variable. The best examples are super tokens, as in Example 4.3 from Smith (2009: 70), namely variant forms from the same speaker in the same stretch of discourse, and if possible with the same lexical items or in parallel constructions (see discussion, Tagliamonte 2006a 96–97). If not, find a context that is parallel. Show at least two variants. Show enough context to establish common function across variants. This especially important with discourse-pragmatic features, where variant functions prevail.

Example 4.3

(a)   It's not time for *breakfast*[Ø] yet. It's not time for *breakfas*[t] yet.
(b)   Ma trousers *is* fa'in doon … they'*re* too big.

The next best examples are suggestive tokens. This is when a variant appears in a specific location providing a tantalizing indication that a known variable may be present in some unexplored data set. Suggestive tokens are ones that warrant further investigation. They are a sign to the analyst that she should go on a reconnaissance mission into the data. Consider these Facebook updates from some of my Canadian friends from 2010, as in Example 4.4.[5]

Example 4.4

(a) Feel for u big time – my turn is going to come on Wednesday or Thursday!!! Big game tonight for Canadian juniors – r u following them? (10.5.2010)
(b) Yeah Leafs won – didn't see the game, but am happy with the end result!!! (10.13.2010)
(c) Have a extra ticket in 200 level suite for Habs-Sens game tonight if anyone interested. (9.25.2010)

These posts exhibit a well-known Canadian penchant for ice hockey with considerable discussion of games, tickets, and names of favorite teams. The posts also provide glimpses into several linguistic variables: (1) the use of *have* for stative possessive meaning, e.g. *have an extra ticket*; (2) the use of *going to* for future temporal reference, e.g. *my turn is going to come*. Previous research has established the trajectory of these changes in Toronto (Tagliamonte and D'Arcy 2009). Another aspect of these posts is that they come from individuals who live hundreds of kilometers north of Toronto, suggesting parallel developments elsewhere in the country. This hypothesis is currently under investigation (Tagliamonte 2010–2013). There is evidence for other linguistic variables that may be particular to this type of discourse; (3) the use of zero subjects, e.g. *am happy*; and (4) copula absence, e.g. *if anyone interested*.

Mini Quiz 4.2

Take another look at the excerpts in Example 4.4.

Q1 Spot a feature that suggests that some of the individuals are from the younger generation.
Q2 Spot other potential variables.
Q3 Calculate the overall distribution of zero subjects by clause.
  (a) Ø Feel for u big time –
  (b) my turn is going to come on Wednesday or Thursday!!!
  (c) Ø Big game tonight for Canadian juniors –
  (d) r u following them?
  (e) Yeah Leafs won –
  (f) Ø didn't see the game,
  (g) but Ø am happy with the end result!!!
  (h) Ø Have a extra ticket in 200 level suite for Habs-Sens game tonight if anyone interested.

Know Your Variable

Be sure you have understood what your variable is. For example (t,d) deletion involves underlying consonant clusters, as in Example 4.5.

Example 4.5

The governme[nt] agency lea[rnd] a lot after hurricane Gilbe[rt].

Which *t*'s and *d*'s are part of the variable context? Which are not? For example, flapping involves alternation between [t] and [d], but not in every context, as in Example 4.6.

Example 4.6

(a)   the pool noo[d]le ... No one ever says nootle
(b)   spider ... spi[t]er ... No one ever says spiter.

> **NOTE**   One time in England my daughter, Freya, who was about 5 at the time, referred to a "spider" as a [spaytr]. I corrected her pronunciation, "Freya, it's a *spider* not a *spiter*." Freya replied. "We are in England mommy, we say *spiter* here!" Of course, you will recognize this as a consummate case of overgeneralization on Freya's part.

Phonological variables often present neutralized contexts where the sound under investigation is masked by the following segment, as in Example 4.7.

Example 4.7

Variable (t,d) exclude:
(a)   aroun[d] [t]en ...

Variable verbal (s) exclude:
(b)   You get[s] [s]ick of them if you had too many (DVN/001)

Circumscribing the Variable Context

Circumscribing the variable context is the most challenging part of conducting a sociolinguistic study. Follow the tried and true rules:

> **TIP**   Cardinal Rules for Circumscribing the Variable Context:
>
> 1.   Include all applications and nonapplications – remember the "principle of accountability."
> 2.   Include only those forms with the same function (or make an argument for an alternative strategy).
> 3.   Exclusions and inclusions should be made on the basis of your own data.

Methodological Advice

If you are listening to audiorecorded data to extract tokens, plan to go through your data only once. Code for everything you need from the sound recording into your token file on this pass. You do not want to have to go back and do it again. It takes too much time.

Ensure that everything you put into your writing is relevant to your study. Establish the connections and make them explicit. If there is no connection; do not put it in.

When providing examples from corpora, ensure that you are able to put the relevant example into the context of its occurrence. Consider the examples in Example 4.8. The meaning of the word "got" is ambiguous. When the context is included in Example 4.9a–b, you can easily infer that Example 4.8a is the active meaning, "to acquire," while Example 4.8b is the stative possessive meaning.

Example 4.8

(a)   They *got* the money. (TOR/045)
(b)   They *got* basketball. (TOR/003)

Example 4.9

(a)   They got a committee together. They *got* the money, they put together bake sales and stuff like that, got money, bought the equipment and had the city put it in. (TOR/045)
(b)   Fair Havens is really fun because they have all the sports up there. They have beach volleyball. They *got* basketball. They *got* tennis. They *got* fishing. (TOR/003)

If the feature under investigation has a conversational use, the interactional context may be required to disambiguate function. Consider the uses of Canadian *eh* which is reported to span 10 different types (Gold 2005: Table 2) including statements (Example 4.10a), questions (Example 4.10b), and storytelling (see Chapter 10, Example 10.30). Of the 273 tokens in the TEA, however, the vast majority were fixed expressions from our Canadian-born interviewers, as in Example 4.10c–e.

Example 4.10[6]

(a)   [2] What do you think about premarital sex? [005] Um I agree– like I don't disagree with it. Everyone has sex *eh*. (TOR/005)
(b)   [054] I guess you have to get to class *eh*? [5] Yup.
(c)   [076] The main part of our business was homes. [5] Was it *eh*.
(d)   [084] I got one for nine ninety nine at Bluenotes. [7] Bluenotes *eh*.
(e)   Yeah, so it was like a year later. [2] Really eh. Holy shit.

When embarking on a study of a linguistic variable that has been studied before, follow previous methodology so that your work is comparable and improve upon it where this is warranted. Document the points of difference. Build the possibility of falsification into your analysis so that you can come back to it and update it in the future.

Extract from the literature the bits that will enable you to support your hypothesis. It is not sufficient to simply cite a source because it discusses the same variable or the same issues. You should cite the exact part of the argumentation or analysis that is relevant, with a page number. Keep adding to your reference list. Remember sociolinguistic theory and principles. Situate your work in previous research. Everything that we may find today or in the future has probably been found before. Find out who has made those discoveries and interpretations and make the link between that study and your own.

Provide a detailed plan for testing the claims in the literature and how you will interpret results of one type or another. Illustrate with examples from the corpus. Remember that some claims are not testable. Your task is to figure out which ones are, formulate ways of testing them, and then do it. Where possible, include hypotheses that are provocative. There is no point in attempting to prove that some feature is what everyone already thinks it is, or proving that some feature functions just like everyone says it does.

Think about the difference between a claim, an observation, a suggestion, a hypothesis. You should not say a researcher "claimed" this, that, or the other, if he or she has simply made an observation. Moreover, it is important to keep in mind that the evidence to support each of these is qualitatively different, or it should be.

Evaluating a finding as "interesting" is not sufficient. You should substantiate why. It is important to be able to identify relevant issues in the literature you are reading. An issue can be a controversy or a question that arises from earlier work. An issue is what makes a feature worthy of investigation. Do not use adjectives such as *most, many, a lot, some, anywhere, quite frequently* in your analysis unless you can say exactly how many.

So what? Make sure no one can say this about your research. State the broader relevance of your research clearly.

> **NOTE**   Compare the argumentation of scholars in different fields arguing for more or less the same thing based on the same kind of data with no knowledge of each other's work: (1) Jones and Schieffelin (2009) and Tagliamonte and Denis (2008b); (2) Tagliamonte and Smith (2005) and Torres-Cacoullos and Walker (2009a,b).

Research Ethics

Sociolinguistic corpora are by their nature extremely personal. A sociolinguistic "interview" is really not an interview at all, but a conversation between two people. Depending on the personality and skill of the interviewer and/or the personality and demeanor of the individual being interviewed, the conversation can be simply casual, riotous, or intensely personal. When individuals agree to have a conversation with a sociolinguist, they are usually told that no one but the researchers will ever have access to their interview and they are guaranteed complete anonymity. Sociolinguists go to great lengths to ensure that this confidentiality is maintained. This is why sociolinguistic corpora are usually private. Access is restricted depending on what the original ethics agreement stipulated.

For most sociolinguists the privilege of having such material is a debt on the part of the analyst. Rickford suggests that "an investigator who has obtained linguistic data from members of a speech community has an obligation to use the knowledge based on that data for the benefit of the community, when it has need of it" (Rickford 1997). Practices vary across sociolinguists in terms of their ongoing relationship with the communities they study. Some researchers continue to do fieldwork in the same community for many years: Springville (e.g. Cukor-Avila 1995) and Ocracoke (Wolfram and Schilling-Estes 1995) among others. There is a long history of sociolinguists doing research in their home towns and so the analysts are always linked to their fieldwork sites, e.g. Norwich (Trudgill 1972a),

Buckie (e.g. Smith *et al.* 2009; Smith and Tagliamonte 1998). Family, friends, children, and spouses of sociolinguists are often in the data too, and obviously – although this is rarely noted – so are the sociolinguists.

The Gold – Your Data

Nothing is more thrilling than to dip into a corpus and go exploring. If I want to give myself a really good day, I drop everything and scrutinize my data. You never know what you will find. You never know what people will say or how they will say it.

In the summer of 2004 when I was collecting the Toronto English Corpus, the entire East Coast of North America had an electrical failure. Labov has always talked about the "danger of death" story as eliciting the best narratives; however, for us it was, *Where were you when the lights went out?* Here are some excerpts from some of the blackout stories.

MARY BUICK, age 60 (TOR) – East York
Oh it was a hoot. It was just so much fun. … it was wonderful 'cause everybody was sitting outside and they were talking to each other and the kids were playing. It was really interesting. Very, very nice. … They should do it a couple of times a year, just to get everybody together, because it really brought people together.

KEVIN CONFLITTI, age 25 (TOR) – Scarborough
Actually, I– I was in a parking lot waiting to pick up some weed and the guy never showed up and I kept wondering why my cell phone wasn't working. was trying to call this guy back for hours and I was like "What the fuck is this guy doing?" And I was like "Why the hell am I– why is my cell phone not working?" So after two hours of waiting in that one spot– … I was desperate 'cause there was– at this time there was a– there was a big drought, no we— no– no weed to find so I– I had to do what I had to do. But anyways I took off from a parking-spot and I noticed all the lights were out and I– I never clicked in that it was like some massive power-outage but I don't know. I– I got to a gas station, started asking questions and some– some lady just told me whatever and after that, um, I was just kind of shocked 'cause I had no weed.

ALISTAIR MAKSIMOWSKI, age 25 (TOR/071) – West End
Oh yeah! I was making cookies and the oven went off. I didn't even notice, like they– like, "Why aren't they baking?" (laughs) Like 'cause the oven doesn't have a light, so I can't even– I couldn't even tell. I kept opening it, closing it. "No, not ready yet." … it was pretty funny.

CANDICE YURANYI, age 40 (TOR/040) – The Annex
Yeah, we were home. I was crossing the street when the lights went off– ah the power went out, and I could– I knew it happened, because the high school there has their own generator and that shut down, so usually there's a hum, and suddenly there was no hum, so I knew something happened, and then of course all the Italians like run out of their homes, "Ah, no power, no power!" So, we knew something happened, and then um, but I didn't– I had no idea how bad it was. And when I found out how bad it was I started panicking I mean I thought, "Oh my god."

GABRIELLE PRUSSKIN, age 55 (TOR/078) – Eglinton/Lawrence
No. I was like miserable. It was so hot. It was so brutally hot and I'm nuts when it's that hot. You know what I mean? I c— I'll live without you know lights, you know, without dishwashers or washing machines. I'll live without anything but the fact that it w—that– I couldn't breathe. It was just like– it was just so brutal. So I never– I mean we didn't go out and– I mean I think it's

great that that happened all over the city and people were meeting their neighbors for the first time. I, however, did not get into that activity.

Mini Quiz 4.3

Q1   How many linguistic variables can you find in the data? (You can use different speakers.)
Q2   How many super tokens are there in the Blackout data?
Q3   How many suggestive tokens are there?
Q4   Consider the following words in these data. What do they tell you about the location, the age of the speakers, the nature of the discourse, etc.? Do any other words or expressions stand out?
     hoot
     cell phone
     weed
     gas station

The Real World

Nothing can be more frustrating than the ups and downs of fieldwork and data collection. Sociolinguistic research is always a real-life undertaking just as much as it is a scientific endeavor. There has never been a fieldwork expedition without a story to tell. There has never been a study or a project or a paper that has not had some kind of adventure or calamity attached to it. Let me provide two illustrations:

1. I was in my first course in Variationist Sociolinguistics. We students were charged with finding a neighborhood and conducting sociolinguistic interviews with residents. Despite my feelings of trepidation at the reality of "entering the community" and "tapping the vernacular," my partner and I headed out. We had read all the course readings, we had duly listened to our professor's advice, we followed all the instructions. On the streets of one of the outlying communities in Ottawa in 1981 we talked to people on the street and people talked to us. As our fieldwork project progressed according to plan (or so we thought), we asked for an interview. Not long afterwards, two police cruisers suddenly charged down the street with sirens blaring and red lights flashing. They screeched to a halt in front of us. Two policemen jumped out and we were asked for identification. Our contacts on the street thought we were petty thieves trying to case the neighborhood houses for subsequent robbery. It was a traumatizing experience. Needless to say, that particular neighborhood remains unstudied.
2. Consider a much later experience. Like many children of sociolinguists, mine have been subjected to scientific scrutiny from birth. In one study of these corpora I had hoped to model the linguistic mechanisms underlying copula acquisition. Figure 4.4 shows the distribution in real time of the acquisition of the copula by my son, Shaman.

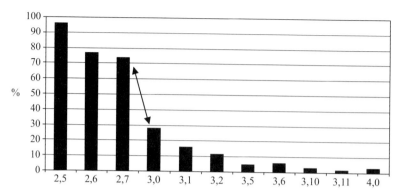

Figure 4.4   Distribution of zero copula in real time by year and month – Shaman.

The data comprise thousands of tokens of the copula covering the period between 2.5 years of age through to four years of age – a singular and important data set. However, note the dramatic difference between time 2,7 and 3,0 indicated by the arrow. By 3.0 Shaman had pretty much acquired the copula. Then notice that there is a four-month hiatus in real time precisely at this juncture, unlike at any other point. Why? That was the four-month period just after the family moved to England. It took me four months to regroup and start recording the children after the big move. Can you believe it? In that mundane and unavoidable life situation – and unknown to me at the time – I had missed the acquisition of the copula!

These are (some of) the joys and sorrows of doing sociolinguistic fieldwork.

Mini Quiz Answers

4.1   **Q1**: *The women appear to have a broader range of frequency of use of the variants than the men. This can be confirmed by comparing the standard deviation between females and males, e.g. "so" female 7.27 vs. male 6.14.*

4.2   **Q1**: *Use of "r u" for "are you," a well-attested feature of computer mediated communication (Baron 2003a).*
   Q2: *"a̲ extra ticket" instead of "an̲ extra ticket"; lack of definite articles, e.g. "Leafs," "Canadian Juniors"; "anyone" instead of "anybody."*
   Q3: *5/8, 50%*

4.3   **Q1**: *There are at least three.*
   (a) Intensifiers, so, very, really, pretty
   (b) Complementizers
   (c) Quotatives, I thought … zero… be like

   Q2: *Gabrielle: I was like Ø miserable; It was so hot; it was just so brutal*
   Mary: It was really interesting. Very, very nice. …

   Q3: *There are at least three. Find some more.*
   (a) Stative possessive, e.g. I have no idea
   (b) Past perfect, had vs. preterite, e.g. I knew something happened
   (c) Future, e.g. I'll live without …

Q4: *hoot = slang for "fun"; middle-aged?;*
    cell phone = North America;
    weed = marijuana; middle aged?;
    gas station = North America

Notes

1 I thank the following people for their various contributions: interviews, transcriptions, data extraction and coding, and all kinds of stuff like that! Elise Ashcroft, Martin Bailes, Clarissa Clemente, Alex D'Arcy, Jonille De Los Santos, Derek Denis, Mercedes Durham, Elizabeth Godfrey, Michael Hepworth, Manami Hirayama, Rachel Hudson, Rika Ito, Bridget Jankowski, Megan Jones, Helen Lawrence, Danielle Martin, Christopher Roberts, Jennifer Smith, Dylan Uscher, and Cathleen Waters.

2 Special thanks to the undergraduate students who participated in my ROP 299Y1 courses from 2002–2006: Stephanie Cali, Jonille Clemente, Sidonia Couto, Derek Denis, Glenna Fraumeni, Jada Fung, Marion Hau, Madeleine Macdonald, Carol Tse, Dylan Uscher, Muhammad Velji, Jessica Wertman, Eric Woo.

3 http://www.trudeaufoundation.ca/program/fellowships/current/2007/shanapoplack (accessed August 12, 2010).

4 http://www.lacl.canterbury.ac.nz/onze/ (accessed June 12, 2011).

5 Sports teams are often referred to by their nicknames: Leafs, Habs, and Sens are short forms for the Canadian hockey teams: Toronto Maple Leafs, Montreal Canadians, and Ottawa Senators respectively. The Canadian Juniors is the name of another Canadian hockey team.

6 The numbers in square brackets here are speaker numbers. Single digit numbers are the interviewers. Triple digit numbers are subjects.

Background Reading

Fasold 1969; Labov 1966, 1972a, 1990, 2001a; Milroy 1980; Poplack 1989; Sankoff and Cedergren 1973; Wolfram 1969.

5

Quantitative Analysis

Quantitative work is not a substitute for but rather an adjunct to linguistic analysis. Varbrul only performs mathematical manipulations on a set of data. It does not tell us what the numbers mean, let alone do linguistics for us. If we are asking: "what is a good linguistic generationalization?" the answer comes from our linguistic theory, not from a statistics program. (Guy 1988: 133)

This chapter focuses on the quantitative methods of LVC research. I begin with a brief review of the standard tool, logistic regression using the *Varb* family of programs and their interpretation. I assume intermediate knowledge of the use and functions of the variable rule program. Useful descriptions of how to use the variable rule program are plentiful in the existing literature. References can be found in the reading list at the end of the chapter along with information about how to download the program and manual from the Internet. Here, I focus instead on several new tools on the market, mixed effects models, random forests, and condition inference trees. The discussion and implementation of mixed effects modeling relies heavily on Baayen (2008), Gries (2009b), and Johnson (2009).

All the analyses in this chapter were conducted on a data set comprising variable (that) in York English. This file can be downloaded from www.wiley.com/go/tagliamonte or my own website.[1] My goal is to provide you with a transparent step-by-step procedure that you can follow along with either in theory or in practice. In other words, if you download the data and work your way through the text you will be able to do the analyses yourself.

The Quantitative Paradigm

The quantitative methods of LVC research developed in the early 1970s and have continued to develop and evolve ever since. Much of this practice is founded in basic variationist tenets, assumptions, and principles (see Chapter 1); the rest is set down in the precedents of 40 years of statistical experience with analyzing variation using statistical modeling.

Variationist Sociolinguistics: Change, Observation, Interpretation, First Edition. Sali A. Tagliamonte.
© 2012 Sali A. Tagliamonte. Published 2012 by Blackwell Publishing Ltd.

The essential goal of variation analysis is to understand the behavior of the dependent variable according to a series of factors, either external (social) or internal (grammatical), namely the multidimensional contexts in which it occurs (Sankoff 1988b: 985).

> **TIP** In the LVC literature the term "factor" can refer to the entire factor group being tested, e.g. *following phonological segment,* or it can refer to one of the individual factors within a factor group, e.g. *pause, consonant, vowel.* Watch out for this!

Distributional Analysis

The first step in a quantitative analysis is to know how often the variants of a variable occur in a given body of data. The second step is to assess the distribution of variants across the full range of factors that are thought to condition them – a comparison of marginals (Rand and Sankoff 1990: 4). This comprises the frequencies and counts of each variant of the dependent variable in the data, either alone (an overall distribution of forms), or according to independent variables (a factor by factor analysis). A key component of a distributional analysis is to examine the cross-tabulation of factors in order to assess how different factors intersect with one another. The results from these analyses are typically displayed in 2- or 3-way tables or figures, such as in Chapters 2–4.

> It is ... useful to alternate between cross-tabulations and multivariate analysis whenever we are dealing with social factors. While cross-tabulations display the existence of interaction, multivariate analysis can measure the size of the effect. (Labov 2001a: 85)

Once the analyst has examined the frequency and distribution of the linguistic variable and has explored and assessed the impact of their intersection, it is appropriate to turn to statistical modeling.

Statistical Modeling

Statistical modeling provides a formal mathematical assessment of the relationship between the dependent variable and the independent variables. The tool that variationists tend to use is logistic regression and the software package variationists tend to use is called the variable rule program, a.k.a *Varbrul* (Cedergren and Sankoff 1974), *Goldvarb 2.0* (Rand and Sankoff 1990), or *Goldvarb X* (Sankoff 1988b: 6; Sankoff, Tagliamonte, and Smith 2005).

The variable rule program is what statisticians refer to as a generalized linear model. This means it is capable of modeling binary variables with multiple factors influencing them (Sankoff 1988b: 2). The particular software referred to as the "variable rule program" was developed in the early 1960s by David Sankoff, a mathematician. His social network included some of the most prominent sociolinguists of the time, making him uniquely positioned to understand the enterprise of studying language in use and to apply statistical modeling to its analysis. Perhaps due to this fortuitous social fact, sociolinguistics was one of the first subfields of linguistics to embrace the use of this statistical tool.

> **NOTE** The term "independent variable" does not mean that all the independent variables are statistically independent of each other. That is up to the analyst to figure out.

In order for a generalized linear model to be appropriate for an analysis, the dependent variable must have certain characteristics: (1) it must consist of a choice between two or more specified sounds, words, or structures during performance; (2) the choice may seem chaotic or unsystematic when examined cursorily; and iii) the choice must recur repeatedly in discourse. Given these conditions statistical inference can be invoked (Sankoff 1988b: 2). Variable rules are "the probabilistic modeling and the statistical treatment of discrete choices and their conditioning" (Sankoff 1988b: 2). This type of analysis is ideal for sociolinguistic data where a myriad of factors influence the choice of one variant or another.

Notice that none of the figures or tables in Chapters 2–4 has any measure of statistical significance. They are just pictures of patterns. How can we determine if the patterns are statistically significant or just a fluke? The variable rule program enables the analyst to determine whether or not any of the factors considered exert a genuine effect (i.e. are statistically significant) or are due to chance (i.e. not statistically significant). Moreover, it can assess the effect of numerous factor groups at the same time. This is critical because 2-way comparisons do not reveal the other potential factors that impact on variable phenomena. For example, a distributional analysis that displays the effect of age and sex will be blind to grammatical person or temporal reference or any other factor that has the potential to influence the variation.

Mini Quiz 5.1

Q1 Variable rules demonstrate important linguistic relationships.
  (a) True
  (b) False

The Three Lines of Evidence

The variable rule program offers the analyst a number of different results that can be used to understand variable phenomena and to build an effective argument to explain it. They are referred to as "the three lines of evidence" (Poplack and Tagliamonte 2001: 92; Tagliamonte 2002: 731): (1) statistical significance, i.e. which factors are statistically significant at the $p = 0.05$ level and which are not; (2) effect magnitude (strength of factors), i.e. which factor group is most significant (largest range) or least (smallest range); and (3) constraint hierarchy or direction of effects, i.e. what is the order (from more to less) of factors within a linguistic feature. This evidence permits comparisons between analyses, contexts, and groups, depending on how the data is partitioned.

Statistical Significance

The variable rule program assesses which factors are statistically significant (at the 0.05 level) and which are not. Both significant factors as well as nonsignificant factors are important for interpreting the results. Significance of one or a set of specific factor groups may lead to one interpretation. Significance of another factor group (or set) may lead to another.

> **NOTE**   What does $p < 0.05$ mean? This is the default significance threshold in the variable rule program. Given the many diverse cross-cutting factors in a sociolinguistic study this p-value is considered an appropriate threshold for significance.

Constraints

The variable rule program assigns factor weights or probabilities to each category of the factor groups included in the analysis using what is called "contrast coding." Contrast coding compares the mean of the dependent variable for a given factor within a factor group to the overall mean of the dependent variable. A value is provided for each factor in a group. The factor groups are essentially tests of independent variables that are thought to influence the choice of one variant over another. This provides a measure of each of the factors' contribution to the dependent variable as well as an assessment of the factors' relationships to each other. Constraint ranking is the hierarchy from more to less of the factor weights of categories within a factor group. In essence this is the grammar underlying the variation – the variable grammar (Poplack and Tagliamonte 2001: 94).

Strength

A nonstatistical interpretation of the relative strength of each factor group can be assessed by considering: (1) the range in each factor group; and (2) the order of selection of factors in the regression analysis. While these are not always meaningful, they are generally helpful to interpretation, especially when there is little interaction in the factor effects. The range is determined by subtracting the lowest factor weight from the highest factor weight in the factor group. When these numbers are compared for each of the factor groups in an analysis, the one with the highest number (i.e. range) typically identifies the strongest constraint. The lowest number identifies the weakest constraint, and so forth. The order of selection of factors can be viewed by scrutinizing the progress of the regression in the output of the variable rule program. The factor group that is selected first, second, and so forth unfolds as the step-up procedure of the regression progresses. The order of selection of factor groups typically mirrors the order of strength of factors as assessed by the range. This may not always be the case. For example, it is possible that within a factor group a particular environment, represented by a very small number of tokens, might have a near-categorical effect, while the other environments, represented by much larger numbers of tokens, might be much closer. In this case, the range for that factor group might be greater than it would be for another factor group that has more effect. This means that if there is conflict between the range and the order of selection of factor groups, it will be necessary to seek other evidence to argue for which factor group is in fact the strongest.

> **TIP**   What is the difference between interaction and collinearity? Collinearity is the case of correlation between two or more factor groups, e.g. first person subjects are always pronouns. Interaction is the case of one factor depending on another, e.g. as formality increases, the use of certain linguistic variables increases.

The three lines of evidence combine to arrive at an interpretation. One line of evidence is not usually enough to make a strong argument or may provide only partial confirmation of a hypothesis. A good argument arises only after a course of many different analyses and comparisons performed on the same data set. A good argument uses the total amount of consistent supportive evidence in the analysis to interpret the findings.

Finally, the interpretative component must be brought into the analysis. Does this order reflect the direction predicted by one or the other of the hypotheses being tested? Each of these bits of information can, and should, be used to build the argumentation about the linguistic variable. Similarities and differences in the significance, ordering of constraints, and strength of contextual factors provide a microscopic view of the grammar of the data under investigation, from which the analyst may infer the structure of the grammar. The results are interpreted using all the information taken together (see discussion: Tagliamonte, 2007: 204).

In the next section, I will make these relatively abstract descriptions practical by conducting a series of quantitative analyses of a well-studied and pervasive linguistic variable. Furthermore, I will embark on a systematic comparison of various statistical tools on the market by presenting a rudimentary, but consistent, analysis of the same data set. For an additional perspective using a similar approach and a more detailed discussion of statistical practice, see Tagliamonte and Baayen (2011).

> **NOTE**   The term "variable rule analysis" has evolved as the most popular term for a logistic regression analysis performed by the variable rule program. Sometimes researchers use the term "multivariate analysis," referring to the multiple variables (or factor groups) that are modeled simultaneously in the analysis (see the quotation from Labov on p. 121). However, the statistical model is always the same – logistic regression. Someone could do a study on this variation. The choice of alternate would likely correlate with real time.

The Case Study – Variable (that)

Variable (that) is the alternation between an overt complementizer, *that*, and its omission, as in Example 5.1.

Table 5.1   Explanations for *that*/Ø variability.

Grammaticalizaton of epistemic phrases (Thompson and Mulac 1991)	Complexity principle (Rhodenburg 1998)
Factors favoring zero: Epistemic matrix verb First/second person pronouns Present tense Additional elements in matrix verb phrase Pronominal subject in complement clause	Factors favoring zero: Intervening material Additional elements in matrix verb phrase Pronominal subject in complement clause

Example 5.1

(a)   My mother, at the end of the meal, suddenly decided Ø she'd go to … town. (YRK/r)
(b)   In the– about 1926 or so, my mother decided *that* she'd have a … new house. (YRK/r)

Complementizer *that* is considered optional (Haegeman and Guéron 1999: 100, 173). There are two prevailing explanations. The variation is the result of: (1) the grammaticalization of epistemic phrases; and (2) an overriding complexity principle. Thompson and Mulac (1991a,b) predict more *zero* with epistemic verbs, e.g. *think*, first person subjects, present tense, simple matrix verb phrases (i.e. no additional elements), and when the subject of the complement clause is a pronoun. This is because constructions with these characteristics, as in Example 5.2a–b), are developing their own pragmatic functions and have stopped functioning as complementizers.

Example 5.2

(a)   That was the Rock and Roll era that *I mean* we'd never heard of Rock and Roll. (YRK/e)
(b)   It's just a sign of the times *I think* you could call it evolution. (YRK/e)
(c)   We thought we were– *you know* we'd got the earth with thirty bob. (YRK/e)

Rohdenburg (1998) predicts more *zero* with pronominal complement subjects and when there is no intervening material between matrix and complement clause. This is because the overt complementizer only appears when the phrase structure is complex. These two hypotheses are summarized in Table 5.1.

While both theories predict more overt *that* in certain conditions (e.g. pronominal subjects in the complement clause), only the grammaticalization hypothesis predicts more zero with epistemic verbs. These competing theories can be put to the test using statistical modeling.

Further details of background, methodology, and analysis of variable (*that*) in the United Kingdom can be found in Tagliamonte and Smith (2005). There are also many other studies of this feature (e.g. Rissanen 1991; Finegan 1995; Elsness 1984; Lopez Couso 1996; Cheshire 1996), whether using LVC methods (Torres-Cacoullos and Walker 2009a,b) and or psycholinguistic methods (Jaeger 2005, 2010).

Table 5.2　Logistic regression of the linguistic factors conditioning *zero* complementizers in York English.

Input	0.877		
Total N	1932		

	FW	%	N
Lexical verb in matrix clause			
Think [t]	0.72	95.5	873
Say [S]	0.50	75.4	240
Know [K]	0.29	67.4	141
Other [O]	0.26	61.7	678
Range	*46*		
Matrix subject			
First person singular [I]	0.62	90.1	1248
NP [O]	0.33	58.7	424
Other pronoun [P]	0.29	59.2	260
Range	*33*		
Additional elements in matrix verb phrase			
Nothing [N]	0.56	83.4	1454
Something [A]	0.37	65.9	478
Range	*19*		
Complement clause subject			
Personal pronoun [P]	0.54	74.6	493
Other [O]	0.40	80.6	1439
Range	*14*		
Intervening material			
None [N]	0.54	83.2	1527
Some [Y]	0.36	63.7	405
Range	*17*		
Verb tense			
Present [R]	0.56	80.4	573
Past [A]	0.37	78.1	1359
Range	*19*		

Goldvarb Logistic Regression

Table 5.2 displays the results of a *Goldvarb X* logistic regression analysis of the contribution of factors selected as significant to the probability of a zero complementizer in York English. All tokens with tense/aspect morphology other than simple past or present were removed from the data set to facilitate direct comparison across platforms. The characters in square brackets reflect the mnemonic codes used for data analysis in *Goldvarb* and which will reappear later in the chapter in other analyses.

This is a typical *Goldvarb* analysis table. The information represented in the table is assembled from different places in the *Goldvarb* output (see Tagliamonte 2006a: Chapters 9–10).

The table shows the total number of tokens considered (Total N), the proportion of the application value (%), in this case *zero*, and the number of tokens per cell (N). All of this information is found in the comparison of marginals output. The input value or corrected mean (Input) and the factor weights or probabilities (FW) come from the output of either a one-step regression or a step-up/step-down regression. The factor weights selected for presentation of the results come from the best stepping down iteration of the logistic regression.

The following information is needed to interpret variable rule analysis results:

- title of table, with the application value clearly stated;
- all the factor groups that have been run in the analysis, those selected as significant, and those not selected as significant with both of these indicated;
- total number of tokens in the analysis (Total N);
- corrected mean/input;
- listing of each factor, with factor weight (probability) to at least two decimal points;
- listing of each factor's proportion and number in cell (Ns);
- range for each significant factor group.

The "application value" is the variant the analysis is focused on, here the zero variant. The "input" indicates the overall tendency of the dependent variable to surface in the data, i.e. 0.877. The "total N" records the total number of contexts treated in the analysis, N=1932. The N records the number of tokens in each cell, e.g. 873 tokens of the matrix verb *think*. The factor groups that have been considered in the analysis are listed with the results for each factor. Point-form numbers are "factor weights." These indicate the probability of the dependent variable to occur in that context. The closer these numbers are to 1, the more highly favoring the effect is; the closer they are to zero the more disfavoring the effect is. The range provides a non-inferential measure of the relative strength of the factor. The higher this number is, the greater the contribution of that factor to the probability of the form. Good practice also requires the analyst to report the factor groups selected as significant and those *not* selected as statistically significant. This is because nonsignificant factors are also an important part of the interpretation.

> **NOTE** The "range" is a nonstatistical measure of relative strength of the factor. It is just a number, not a factor weight (i.e. no decimals).

The results show that that the overall probability of a zero complementizer is 0.877 (the Input or Corrected Mean), a fairly high value. Given that this is a binary variable (i.e. *that* vs. Ø) a disfavoring effect can be interpreted as favoring the alternate variant, i.e. overt *that*. The total number of tokens considered in the analysis is 1932 (Total N). This is quite a lot of data for a syntactic linguistic feature and sufficient to be relatively confident in the results even though six factor groups are in the model. Note that the Ns/cell are robust in all cases (the lowest is N=141 for the verb *know*). The logistic regression has determined that six factor groups are statistically significant in both the stepping up and stepping down procedure: lexical verb, matrix subject, additional elements in the matrix verb phrase, complement clause subject, intervening material, and verb tense.

The constraint rankings expose the underlying patterns or constraints on *that*/Ø alternation. This is a key element in understanding the variable grammar (Poplack and Tagliamonte 2001: Chapter 5). The statistical model was constructed so that individual verbs that have always had highly differentiated patterns across a long history of change – *think, say, know,* and *tell* – were treated separately in comparison to all others. The table shows this effect is strongest, with a range of 46. Note that the verb *think* highly favors zero with a factor weight of 0.70. This finding has been replicated in virtually every study of this linguistic variable: British dialects (Tagliamonte and Smith 2005), American dialects (Thompson and Mulac 1991a), and Canadian dialects (Torres-Cacoullos and Walker 2009b: 22, Table 3). The results for matrix subject test for grammaticalization. According to Thompson and Mulac's hypothesis, first person singular pronouns should favor *zero*. In this data, grammatical person stands out well ahead of the rest, favoring zero at 0.62. Note too that this is the second strongest effect, with a range of 33. The remaining four factors are also statistically significant, but are much weaker. They all exert approximately the same strength. Remarkably, these results replicate almost to a tee the results obtained for other British dialects (Tagliamonte and Smith 2005: 301, Table 6). This is an important benefit of having a common statistical tool in the field. Results can be directly compared across studies. Such triangulation of findings adds additional support to the solidity of the results.

In sum, the constraint ranking for each effect mirrors the predictions made by the hypotheses of grammaticalization and complexity. First person singular subjects favor zero at 0.62. A sentence with no additional elements in the matrix verb phrase favors zero at 0.56. Personal pronouns favor at 0.54. A sentence with no intervening material favors at 0.54. Finally, present tense contexts favor at 0.56. Thus, both explanations can account for the observed variability. However, the two most important constraints – matrix verb and type of matrix subject – suggest that linguistic factors, and in this case grammaticalization, are the driving force underlying the variation in this system.

It is widely claimed that *that* is a stylistic option that is deleted in informal contexts (e.g. Huddleston and Pullum 2002: 953; Leech and Svartvik 1975: 249; Quirk *et al.* 1972: 317; Zandvoort 1969). In contrast, the overt form *that* is considered formal: "less personal, less familiar, less warm, less friendly, less emotive. It is objective, factual, formal, official, sometimes tending to hostility" (Storms 1966: 262). Such observations suggest that variable (*that*) may have sociolinguistic correlates. Given Principle 2 which holds that for stable sociolinguistic variables, women show a higher rate of prestige variants than men (see Chapter 2), we might expect women to use more of the more formal variant (i.e. overt *that*) than men. We can also use occupation and education as a proxy for social and stylistic patterns. More educated individuals tend to have greater sensitivity to standard or prestige forms in language use. Individuals in white-collar jobs will have greater need of formal language in their everyday experience.

Let us conduct another analysis, this time including the standard sociolinguistic factors that are often found in many LVC studies – age, sex, education, and occupation. Table 5.3 shows the results.

The results show that age and occupation exert statistically significant effects on the variation. First, there is a regular progression from oldest to youngest speakers such that the zero complementizer becomes more frequent as the individuals get younger. Second, blue-collar workers have a greater tendency to use the zero complementizer than white-collar workers. However, neither speaker sex nor education is significant, as indicated by the square brackets. Given that a sex difference is expected for linguistic change (Principle 3 or 4) (see Chapter 2) and occupation, not education, is the distinction of relevance, variable (that) may be interpreted as a stylistic option rather than a social marker or a change in progress. Exposure to formal language through occupation exerts the strongest influence on the use of an overt complementizer.[2]

Table 5.3   Logistic regression of the social factors conditioning *zero* in York English.

	FW	%	N
Input	0.877		
Total N	1932		

	FW	%	N
Age			
Younger (under 35) [Y]	0.56	82.6	759
Middle (36–65) [M]	0.51	79.5	737
Older (66 and older) [O]	0.40	72.2	436
Range	*16*		
Occupation			
Blue-collar [B]	0.62	87.4	420
White-collar [W]	0.47	76.8	1512
	15		
Sex			
Male [M]	[0.51]	80.4	842
Female [F]	[0.49]	78.1	1090
Education			
Up to minimum age [−]	[0.52]	81.0	1036
More than minimum age [+]	[0.48]	76.9	896

You will notice that Tables 5.2 and 5.3 present the results of linguistic and social factors separately. This is standard practice in LVC research due to the fact that linguistic and social factors have complex interactions that inevitably lead to inaccurate results. I will return to this problem below.

The findings to this point seem sensible, relatively unproblematic, and straightforward to interpret to arrive at an explanation for variable (that) in York. It is a highly structured variable with strong linguistic constraints that mirror previous findings. The statistical significant of factors and their direction of effects supports both complexity and grammaticalization as explanatory of the variation. There is some indication of social evaluation and possible change, but these effects are minor and open to question. Can any of the new statistical tools on the market elucidate the analysis? Let us now turn to a consideration of the contemporary controversy over the choice of statistical method.

Challenging the Variable Rule Program

In the early 2000s there has been increasing skepticism about whether or not the variable rule program continues to be the most appropriate statistical tool for LVC research. The criticisms center on (1) the type of statistical model, namely logistic regression; and (2) variationist methodology in general. These criticisms tend to come from outside the variationist sphere, from researchers who may not be as well informed themselves about the history, development, and practice of variationist methods. The evolution of methodology (both statistical and otherwise) in Variationist Sociolinguistics from the 1970s is often unfamiliar to incoming generations of researchers. Researchers across the subfields of linguistics often do not share the same background or the same vocabulary. This is exacerbated by the fact that the methodological practices of Variationist Sociolinguistics are largely unknown outside this specialist field. Further, the variable rule program is a custom design with idiosyncratic displays that are never seen in any other disciplines (e.g. factor weights), which make the results of variable rule analysis suspicious to other practitioners.

Developments in statistics over the past thirty years have introduced new tools, in particular generalized mixed-effects models, and there is a growing literature advocating these models. A generalized mixed effects model incorporates two types of effects: mixed effects and random effects, hence the name "mixed effects model," or more simply a mixed model (Bates 2005a: 27). Mixed effects models have recently come into LVC studies through packages such as *Rbrul* (Johnson 2009; R Team 2007). Seasoned researchers and students alike are under increasing pressure to appropriate the newer tools and techniques. However, at the point of writing many researchers do not know the differences between these statistical packages and their different tools, nor do they have the background to make informed decisions about how to use them most effectively.

I will review the similarities and differences among these statistical tools and their advantages and disadvantages. Each toolkit offers different strategies for dealing with common data problems, e.g. interaction, collinearity. First, let us review a number of thorny issues that have provoked the debate over statistical tools.

> **TIP** What is the difference between a statistical tool and a toolkit? The tool is the type of statistical model, e.g. logistic regression, mixed effects, random forest. The toolkit is the software package, e.g. *Goldvarb, Rbrul, R.*

The Effect of the Individual

In LVC studies observations of the same speaker are grouped together and examined across other individuals. Not having the individual in an analysis while at the same time grouping individuals into one external factor or another (e.g. age, social group, education) may create inappropriate aggregations, especially with unbalanced numbers of tokens across individuals (as is typically the case) (see Paolillo 2009). Variationists have long been aware of this problem; however, it is still often raised as a neglected issue in the literature (see e.g. van de Velde and van Hout 1998). The effect of the individual is an obvious and unavoidable dilemma for studies of real people in real speech communities. There will always be some degree of overlap or redundancy across factors. Older speakers tend to be less educated than younger speakers. A disproportionate number of males (rather than females) tend to work in blue-collar jobs. Education level is highly correlated with job type. In statistics this is referred to as collinearity; when factors are correlated with other factors. One of the problems with putting many such factors into a statistical model is that one factor or another may be found to be statistically significant when actually it is not. This is referred to as a Type I error. As is well known in LVC research, the analyst must always entertain the possibility that this type of error may occur, especially in models of the speech community where social factors are inevitably interrelated. (This is why social and linguistic factors are only included together in a variable rule analysis when they have previously been run separately and the results are the same.) For example, a model might return a result that sex is statistically significant with females favoring a standard variant. The analyst might interpret this to mean that females in the population at large demonstrate a statistically significant effect over males. However, it could also be that a particular group of females in the data set have rates of the favored variant well out of step with their group (for a recent demonstration see D'Arcy and Tagliamonte 2008b).

While it is true that LVC studies often do not report the effect of individuals this should not necessarily be taken as an indication that the analyst has not considered individual behavior. A typical LVC study comprises a relatively large number of tokens from a small number of individuals. This is why a key step in the research process is to conduct cross-tabulations of the individuals in the sample by all the factor groups that have been coded into the data. An analyst must establish whether the individuals pattern similarly or not; whether they pattern similarly for each internal factor; whether or not the internal or external factors are overlapping and, if so, how. When the individual is not included in an analysis, it should be due to the fact that analyst has simply chosen not to include individual in the statistical model. This presumes, of course, that the analyst has previously checked the individual patterns and discovered that the individual actually does not matter (see for example Tagliamonte and D'Arcy 2009: 93, n. 28). Why would a sociolinguist treat the individual as if he did not matter?

LVC studies have consistently discovered that individuals tend to behave alike with respect to the underlying grammatical patterns of linguistic features as members of a cohesive speech community (see Chapter 2). Labov's (1972a) early work was groundbreaking in the discovery that the individual's grammar was a reflection of a community-wide grammar and his later work continues to affirm this:

> environmental constraints … give us a characteristic profile for the application of [a] rule to any given individual, group, or speech community. It is an extraordinary result that these profiles are essentially the same for all the peer groups studied – that is, the rule is a part of a single grammar which we can construct for this speech community. (Labov 1972a: 89)

> We're not studying social variation; we're studying the structural basis for it. (Labov 7.19.2006, quoted in Gordon 2006: 350)

A notable demonstration of this phenomenon is Guy's (1980) study comparing individual and group behavior (see also Wolfram and Beckett 2000). Guy showed that although individuals exhibit different frequencies of particular variables, the patterns of use in the individual tend to remain constant across the speech community (given sufficient numbers). This critical relationship between the individual and the group has been addressed in LVC research throughout its evolution (e.g. Poplack and Meechan 1998b; Poplack and Tagliamonte 2001; Sankoff 1978a; Sankoff 1974; Sankoff *et al.* 2001). In later research this phenomenon has been tested in contexts of second language acquisition (Bayley and Langman 2004), the acquisition of sociolinguistic competence (Bayley and Regan 2004), and in creole continua (Meyerhoff and Walker 2007) all with the same result – group data are reliably and regularly repeated for each individual.

Of course it is not always the case that individuals share the same norms as the group to which they belong. In fact, some individuals decidedly do not. These are the individuals that help to interpret and explain the variation in the first place.

> insiders skew our sociolinguistic data by exaggerating its main trends, by running ahead of their cohort … oddballs, whether outsiders, aspirers, or interlopers, skew it by running against the main trends. (Chambers 2003: 114)

In sum, the question of the individual in a statistical model of a variable phenomenon is underlain by an understanding of the speech community not recognized in other social sciences. LVC studies are founded on the notion of community grammars where the individuals in the sample are believed to be a representation of the community as a whole (Labov 1966). This is one of the foundational constructs of the field. Analysts have not yet fully explored the precise nature of individual vs. community variation across linguistic variables (phonetics to pragmatics) or according to different types of factors (assimilation, reanalysis, etc.).

Independence of Observations

Are the factor groups being considered in an analysis independent or nonindependent? There are two ways of thinking about this question. We can consider: (1) the number of tokens for each individual; and (2) the relationship among the factor groups in the analysis. The first issue is moot. We need as many observations per individual as is possible and logical for our analysis. However, the second issue is murkier. Observations that are causally connected in some way can be expected to share some aspect of their variation. This makes them nonindependent. These overlaps and interactions are problematic for logistic regression because the nature of the statistical model requires that the factors being tested are orthogonal – that they are independent. The problem is that nonindependence is the norm for language. Guy (1988) specifically addressed the issue of how far a statistical model can be pushed with respect to nonorthogonal factor groups and individual speakers:

> Having understood the problem that non-orthogonality presents, we should consider how to find it when it occurs, and how to resolve it. The simplest way to find it is of course to carefully examine any coding scheme one has established before attempting a *Varbrul* analysis. But if one's self-vigilance fails on some occasion, or if the non-orthogonality arises from an unnoticed change or maldistribution of the data, then the problem will manifest itself in the *Varbrul* out put as (1) meaningless results, and/or (2) non-convergence.[3] When either of these occurs, they should be taken as a warning to check for non-orthogonal factor groups. (Guy 1988: 128).

Guy (1988: 128) considered an extreme example – individual and sex in the same statistical model. Given a data set of 6 individuals, 3 male and 3 female, this would, of course, lead to the following highly non-independent data, as in Table 5.4.

Of course, a severely problematic case such as this would be easy enough for the smart analyst to avoid. In a real data set, however, the connections between factor groups may not be so transparent. In many cases, you may not even know what interactions exist until you go looking for them.

Table 5.4 Non-orthogonal factor groups. Worst case scenario.

Individual	1	2	3	4	5	6
Male	✓	✓	✓			
Female				✓	✓	✓

Source: Guy 1988: 128, Table 3.

Table 5.5 Non-orthogonal factor groups. Likely case scenario.

Type of modality	First person	Second person		Third person	
		Definite	Generic	Definite	Generic
Generic	0	0	433	0	61
Objective	146	28	0	290	0
Subjective	157	52	0	12	0

> **NOTE**   Independence of factor groups means that a given constraint has the same force, regardless of what other constraints might be in the same environment. Interaction of factor groups means that a given constraint has a different force, depending on the effect of factor groups.

Consider the case of deontic modality where different forms are thought to encode variant nuances of authority: Objective, the authority originates from some external source, as in Example 5.3a; Subjective, the authority comes from the speaker herself, as in Example 5.3b; and Generic, the authority comes from outside, but it is framed with a generic pronoun, as in Example 5.3c.

Example 5.3

(a)   Why do we *have to* be so dominated by these typical names? (TOR/007)
(b)   I *got to* start eating better, and like exercising. (TOR/020)
(c)   All you *have to* do is like get the stupid rhythm right. (TOR/123)

The literature claims that second person subjects have a "stronger" force than those with first person subjects and first person subjects are stronger than those with third person subjects (Coates 1983: 37). When you examine the different types of modality according to grammatical person and these nuances of meaning you find a system that is heavily skewed, as in Table 5.5.

First person subjects are never generic, second person subjects are mostly generic (84%, 433/513) and third person subjects are mostly objective (70%, 290/363). If the grammatical person is put into the model and is selected as statistically significant there is no way to tell if this is the result of second person generics or the nature of the modality. If type of modality

Table 5.6   Idealized logistic regression showing nonindependence of factor groups.

	FW		%	N
Input	0.60			
Total N	700			
Age				
Younger (under 35) [Y]	0.80	╲	65	100
Middle (36-65) [M]	0.60	╳	32	200
Older (66 and older) [O]	0.40	╱	70	200
Range	*40*			
Sex				
Male [M]	0.50		80	350
Female [F]	0.43		50	350
Range	*7*			
Education				
Up to minimum age [−]	0.90		75	350
More than minimum age [+]	0.30		55	350
Range	*70*			

is put into the model, the same is true. If both are put into the model, the model will be compromised because the two factor groups are not independent. So, the analyst must decide how this problem is to be solved.

The variable rule program assumes that the factor groups in the analysis are independent (e.g. Guy 1988: 126–127). Therefore the analyst must ensure independence of factors *prior to* modeling the data. As Labov points out, "vigorous efforts must be made to locate interaction wherever one suspect it is to be found" (Labov 1990: 221, n. 16).

> **TIP**   When a cross-tabulation of two factors results in a cell that is greater than 95% of the data or less than 5% of the data, apply Greg Guy's (1988: 132) rule: "don't push it past 95%."

How to Find Interaction in a Variable Rule Analysis
Indications of interaction between factor groups can be found in the results of a variable rule analysis in a number of ways (see Tagliamonte 2006a: 229–233). One way is to examine the relationships between factor weights and percentages for each factor group. If there is interaction in the model, these two measures will not line up, i.e. the ranking of the factor weights will not match the ranking of proportions, as in Table 5.6.

If such mismatches are found, as with age group in Table 5.6, it would indicate that the age factor group interacts with some other factor group in the model. Were this to appear in a conference talk or a publication, it would also indicate that the analyst had not done her work properly.

Standard variationist practice recommends comprehensive cross-tabulation of factor groups to obviate this problem (e.g. Tagliamonte 2001a: 49):

Varbrul differs from some types of multivariate analysis in that it assumes that the various factor groups have independent effects. But users should clearly understand that THEY are not required to assume independence. On the contrary, one should be aware of the problems posed by interaction, how to detect it when it occurs, and know what to do about it. (Guy 1988: 134; upper case in original)

The solution to problems of interaction in a variable rule analysis is not black and white. It depends on what the interaction is and why it exists. A common solution to this problem is to create a new factor group that accounts for the intersection of the two. This is referred to as an "interaction factor group." Constructing such a factor group from the data in Table 5.5 would produce the factors in Example 5.4.

Example 5.4

(a) Generic (including second and third person subjects)
(b) Objective (including first, second, and third person)
(c) Subjective (including first and second person)

Another way to deal with interaction is to use dummy recoding, a technique described by Paolillo (2002: 89–92). This procedure involves creating an interaction factor group for each set of factor groups thought to interact in a statistical model. If the main effect for any constraint and for any of the dummy interaction factor groups for that constraint are selected as significant in the analysis, then there is a significant difference between them. For example, suppose you wanted to test whether the patterning of type of modality between British and Canadian English was significantly different from each other. You would need to create a model in which type of modality and variety were run as main effects along with a so-called "dummy interaction" factor group, as in Example 5.5.[4]

Example 5.5

Type of modality (Generic, Subjective, Objective)
Variety (British, Canadian)
Dummy interactions (Generic British, elsewhere: Generic Canadian, elsewhere; Subjective British, elsewhere; Subjective Canadian, elsewhere; Objective British, elsewhere; Objective Canadian, elsewhere)

Although it is a relatively complex procedure, it has been used effectively to study phonological variables in New Zealand English (Sigley 2003) and to compare the global diffusion of *be like* across dialects of English (Buchstaller and D'Arcy 2009).

There are several other prevailing issues that come to the fore in criticisms of statistical methodology. They are not entirely statistical in orientation, but relate to research design and implementation.

The Kitchen Sink

A common problem is that statistical models will not produce optimal results if they contain too many factor groups and too many factors. There is an obvious and straightforward reason for this: multiple factor groups, many factors, complex interactions, and unbalanced data sets increase the challenge for any statistical model. Inexperienced researchers will often throw everything into a variable rule analysis (hence the "everything but the kitchen sink" analogy that David Sankoff used to describe to me), often with very few tokens in some cells. Even before statistical analysis begins, the study is severely compromised. The means to solving this problem depends on the statistical tool employed. Using the variable rule program, it is ill advised to run more than about six factor groups in a model. This also depends on how much data you have in your analysis. Too few tokens may not be sufficient for statistical significance (Poplack and Tagliamonte 2001). Newer tools offer greater flexibility; however, even mixed effects models cannot handle highly complex interactions effectively (Tagliamonte and Baayen 2011). This issue remains regardless of the statistical tool – do not overtax your model.

Tokens per Individual

The number of tokens each individual will render for analysis is unpredictable and highly varied. If one individual happens to contribute 100 tokens but another individual contributes only 10, this may have a significant impact on the results. Many studies apply a limit on the number of tokens per individual. Note, however, that this practice was developed for frequently occurring phonological variables and was conceived as a means to limit the amount of data per speaker as well as to obviate the disproportionate contribution of lexical items. Yet in more recent developments in the field this is the very thing analysts want to study. Exemplar based hypotheses, for example, require knowing the effect of frequent lexical items on variable processes; however, having a restriction on tokens per speaker removes the possibility for testing the difference between frequent and nonfrequent words. As increasingly more variationist work has turned to morphological and syntactic variables, the issue of how many tokens per speaker has taken a different turn. Given a rarely occurring feature, it becomes necessary to conduct an exhaustive search by an individual for as many tokens as possible.

Tokens per Cell

The number of tokens in an LVC study can range from hundreds to thousands. How many tokens is enough is not a straightforward question. A generally accepted number of tokens per cell in order for the selection of one variant or another to be modeled statistically is in the range of 30 tokens (see Cedergren and Sankoff 1974; Guy 1980, 1993; Labov 1969). The figure of 30 is a reasonable objective for statistical testing (see also Baayen 2008: 215), though with morphological and syntactic variables, which occur less frequently than do phonological ones, it is not always attainable. General statistical laws dictate that with fewer than 10 tokens there is a high likelihood of random fluctuation, but with numbers greater than 10 there is 90% conformity with the predicted norm, rising to 100% with 35 tokens (see Guy 1980: 20). As such, if 30 tokens per environment cannot be attained, any number in excess of 10 is preferable.

Type / Token Ratio

The ratio of token types per individual is an important consideration. A disproportional amount of one type of token for some individuals, but not others may also skew the data. For example, a large number of monomorphemes (*mist*) over past tense forms (*missed*) across individuals (imagine interviews conducted in a very foggy location) might skew analysis of variable (t,d). An individual who talks at length to her young children during an informal interview (e.g. *Freya, you must get off the computer this minute*) might skew an analysis toward the use of deontic *must*. Wolfram (1993) recommends no more than three tokens of a given word per speaker. Standard practice advises establishing a type/token ratio depending on the size and/or nature of the data set. It is also possible that a type/token ratio is not advisable, especially if frequency is part of the research question. Whatever methodology you use must be linguistically justified.

The Pre-statistical Toolkit

The well trodden methodological practices I have outlined here were designed to ensure that at the point of statistical modeling the factor groups in a variation analysis are independent, the effect of the individual has been ruled out, the effect of lexical item has been controlled, and the problem of small numbers has been dealt with as far as possible..

In sum, variationist methodology incorporates as standard practice techniques of research design that obviate many potential statistical pitfalls that can arise in an analysis *before* statistical modeling takes place. These practices are the foundation of LVC methodology (for detailed discussion see Guy 1988, 1993; Tagliamonte 2006a; Young and Bayley 1996).

Drawbacks to the Variable Rule Program

As a statistical tool the variable rule program has several major drawbacks. For a pointed discussion of problems, consult Johnson (2009). Simply stated, the variable rule program is a single statistical tool – logistic regression – that can model discrete, fixed effects only. Fixed effects are factors with a limited number of possible factors (or levels, in statistics). Such factors have a restricted set of categories (e.g. male vs. female, pronoun vs. full noun phrase, etc.) and are replicable across different data sets, at different times in different places. The problem is that two key elements of a typical LVC study are not fixed, but random: (1) the individuals that make up the sample; and (2) the words they use. Take, for example, the complementizer data analyzed in Tables 5.2 and 5.3. It comprises 1932 tokens from 33 individuals and is made up of 69 different matrix verbs. How likely is it that these individuals and the matrix verbs they use precisely represent the community from which they are drawn, the city of York?

While the fixed effects, speaker sex (male vs. female) can be replicated across communities (there will always be males and females in every community), the exact distribution of individuals and words cannot. Statisticians argue that there must be statistical validation that the factor groups in an analysis are statistically significant over and above the effect of the individuals that happen to be in the sample and the words they happen to use. If widely diverging individuals are nested in fixed effects such as sex, education, social class, and age, then social effects may appear to be significant, when in fact they are not.

Another problem with the variable rule program is that it cannot model continuous factor groups such as age. This is why LVC research groups speakers into age cohorts such as <35, 36–65, and 66+ in Tables 5.2 and 5.3. The variable rule program also cannot handle continuous variables so phonetic variables are best analyzed by other tools. Finally, the variable rule program does not provide a simple means of dealing with interaction (see discussion in Tagliamonte 2006a: 229–233). It can be done, but the procedures can be onerous.

Mini Quiz 5.2

Q1   Which of the following capabilities does the variable rule program have?
   (a)   Supports continuous responses.
   (b)   Supports continuous variables.
   (c)   Estimates between group effects.
   (d)   Takes into account by-speaker and by-item correlations.
   (e)   Estimates fixed effects.

New Toolkits for Variationist Sociolinguistics

In the last 10 years or so there have been important new developments in statistical techniques for analyzing complex linguistic systems. Two new toolkits are particularly suited for the variationist enterprise. They are *Rbrul,* a new version of the classic variable rule program (Johnson 2009) and *R*, a widely used and multi-faceted open source statistical package (Team 2007). Both *Rbrul* and *R* can perform logistic regression just like the variable rule program; however, they also offer additional tools for data analysis that *Goldvarb* is either unable to do or is able to do only with considerable effort and manipulation (Johnson 2009). Perhaps the most important new tool is mixed effects modeling (Bates 2005a,b; Pinheiro and Bates 2000).

Mixed effects models can take into account by-speaker and by-item correlations. They estimate between-group effects (like gender) at the same time as within-group effects (like individual speaker). They support continuous factor groups like age or lexical item as well as continuous responses (dependent variables) like vowel formant measurements. This means you can include all kinds of different factors in the same model.

In the next section, I will make these relatively abstract descriptions practical by conducting a series of quantitative analyses of a well-studied and pervasive linguistic variable. Furthermore, I will embark on a systematic comparison of various statistical tools on the market by presenting a rudimentary, but consistent, analysis of the same data set.

You should be able to work your way through the analyses in this chapter on your own. Download the data file (YRK_COMP_Tagliamonte.txt) from www.wiley.com/go/tagliamonte or my own web page, load the data into the *R* console, and follow along with the text. Do not be concerned if there are slight differences between what you produce and what you see in the textbook. Minor elements may have changed in the transition.

Rbrul

The advantage of using *Rbrul* (Johnson 2009: 376) is that it has familiar variationist traits as well as the ability to conduct mixed effects models. It will read *Goldvarb* token files; it will return results in *Goldvarb* factor weights; it has a user interface that steps the researcher through the process in a series of easy steps; and it employs a step–up/step–down procedure for logistic regression. The *Rbrul* step–up/step–down model, when run as a set of fixed effects, should be virtually identical to the *Goldvarb* step–up/step–down analysis (Johnson 2009). If needed, *Rbrul* also reports results in log odds typical of other disciplines. In sum, *Rbrul* offers variationist sociolinguists a bridge between the variable rule program and standard statistical packages.

Basic Rbrul Steps

To start using *Rbrul* you must install *R* first. Then go to the *Rbrul* website and download *Rbrul*. In *R* issue the command in Example 5.5a which will provide the prompt in Example 5.5b.

Example 5.5

  (a) Rbrul()
  (b) MAIN MENU
       1-load/save data
       9-reset 0-exit
       1: 1

Simply follow the series of *Rbrul* prompts. Table 5.7 shows you the actual steps to running a step–up/step–down logistic regression of variable (*that*) in York English, as indicated in the bolded responses. Note that in this model the zero complementizer is coded as "Z".

Note that the analyst can choose from different types of models (one-level, step-up, etc.) and different types of responses, and can pick and choose among the factor groups. In this example, I have chosen the six linguistic factor groups 4, 5, 6, 7, 8, and 9, which correspond to Verbs.1, Matrix.subj, Add.elm, Sub.subj, Int.mat, and Tense. The labels for each factor group as the headers in the Excel file that contains the data. The statistical model that would be produced by the sequence of commands in Table 5.2 is the same as that shown in the same table. *Rbrul* also offers the choice of running factor groups as random or continuous and it can assess interaction directly. The analyst simply selects which two factor groups should be tested for interaction in the model.

Mini Quiz 5.3

Q1 Using *Rbrul* replicate the analyses shown in Tables 5.2 and 5.3. Is the analysis the same or different?

Mixed Effects Modeling

The very nature of sociolinguistic data, drawn always from the production of individuals, inevitably from less than ideally distributed data sets, and with innumerable cross-cutting social and linguistic factors, is the epitome of the type of data that mixed models are designed

Table 5.7   *Rbrul* modeling menu.

```
MODELING MENU
1-choose variables 2-one-level 3-step-up 4-step-down 5-step-up/
step-down
8-settings 9-main menu 0-exit
10-chi-square test
1: 1
Choose response (dependent variable) by number, or Enter to keep
  Dep.var (1-Dep.var 2-Main.subj 3-Verbs.3 4-Verbs.1 5-Matrix.subj
  6-Add.elm 7-Sub.subj 8-Int.mat 9-Tense 10-Indiv 11-Sex 12-Age
  13-Occ 14-Edu 15-Context)
1: 1
Type of response? (1-continuous Enter-binary)
1:
Choose application value(s) by number? (1-T 2-Z)
1: 2
Choose predictors (independent variables) by number, or Enter to
  keep Main.subj & Verbs.1 & Matrix.subj & Add.elm & Sub.subj &
  Int.mat & Tense (2-Main.subj 3-Verbs.3 4-Verbs.1 5-Matrix.subj
  6-Add.elm 7-Sub.subj 8-Int.mat 9-Tense 10-Indiv 11-Sex 12-Age
  13-Occ 14-Edu 15-Context)
1: 4
2: 5
3: 6
4: 7
5: 8
6: 9
7:
Are any predictors continuous? (4-Verbs.1 5-Matrix.subj 6-Add.elm
  7-Sub.subj 8-Int.mat 9-Tense Enter-none)
1:
Any grouping factors (random effects)? (4-Verbs.1 5-Matrix.subj
  6-Add.elm 7-Sub.subj 8-Int.mat 9-Tense Enter-none)
1:
Consider an(other) pairwise interaction between predictors? Choose
  two at a time. (4-Verbs.1 5-Matrix.subj 6-Add.elm 7-Sub.subj
  8-Int.mat 9-Tense Enter-done)
1:

Current variables are:
response.binary: Dep.var (Z vs. T)
fixed.factor: Verbs.1 Matrix.subj Add.elm Sub.subj Int.mat Tense

MODELING MENU
1-choose variables 2-one-level 3-step-up 4-step-down 5-step-up/
  step-down
8-settings 9-main menu 0-exit
10-chi-square test
1: 5
```

to handle. Mixed effects models are claimed to be an ideal tool for exploring this type of data because they handle different types of factor groups (fixed and random) easily and effectively while at the same time permitting the analyst to compare and contrast factor groups using interaction terms within the same model.

Importantly, mixed effects models enable the analyst to run the individual as a random effect. As I mentioned earlier, fixed effect models may overestimate the statistical significance of social factors (creating the possibility of Type I errors); a mixed effects model is more conservative. In *Rbrul* factor groups are selected as statistically significant only "when they are strong enough to rise above the inter-speaker variation" (Johnson 2009: 365). The tradeoff is that *Rbrul* is more likely than *Goldvarb* to fail to identify an effect that really does exist (creating the possibility of Type II errors) (Johnson 2009: 365). Furthermore, we can run age as a continuous effect, obviating the need to model the data using age groupings. This means that we do not have to decide on where to draw the line across the population. The model will let us know if age is significant or not. The downside of running age as continuous is that it does not permit the analyst to see an adolescent peak or U-shaped curve of age grading as described in Chapter 2. This must be explored using some other statistical means (see e.g. Tagliamonte and D'Arcy 2009).

TIP   A Type I error is when a factor group is selected as significant, but it is actually not significant. A Type II error is when a factor group is not selected as significant, but it actually is significant.

Table 5.8 shows a mixed effects model. The factors groups entered into the model are the same fixed effects as previously. The difference is that this time the individual is run as a random effect and age is run as a continuous effect.

Unlike the familiar variable rule analysis tables typical of LVC publications, what you see here is the actual output of *Rbrul*'s best stepping-up run copied and pasted from the computer screen. Here, as with *Goldvarb* output, we find a variety of different important bits of information. Each factor group in the model is preceded by a "$" and is followed by its name.[5] The results for each factor are listed by row, first with the log odds values, or coefficients. The log odds values are followed by the number of tokens per cell followed by the proportion of the dependent variable. The last column shows the centered factor weights (as in *Goldvarb*).[6] The information under "$misc" provides the deviance, degrees of freedom of the analysis, "df", the intercept, grand mean, and centered input probability.

Goldvarb factor weights range between 0 and 1, while log-odds can take on any positive or negative value from negative infinity to positive infinity and are anchored around zero. The coefficients are similar to the factor weights – they tell us the degree of contrast among factors and hierarchical organization of their effect. The intercept is similar to the "input" in *Goldvarb* – it provides a baseline from which the model predictions are built. The intercept of the model in Table 5.8 is positive, 1.967 in log-odds units, indicating a strong tendency toward zero. In *Goldvarb* neutral is a factor weight of 0.5. For log odds units, zero is neutral. A positive value is a favoring effect; a negative value is a disfavoring

Table 5.8　*Rbrul*, mixed effects model, individual random, age continuous.

```
BEST STEP-UP MODEL WAS WITH Indiv (random) + Verbs.1 (1.16e-65) +
Matrix.subj (1.23e-31) + Int.mat (2.24e-09) + Add.elm (5.26e-07) +
Tense (3.7e-06) + Sub.subj (0.000353) + Age (0.00571) + Occ
(0.00804) [A]

STEP-UP AND STEP-DOWN MATCH!

STEPPING DOWN:

LEXICAL VERB IN MATRIX CLAUSE
$Verbs.1
 factor logodds tokens Z/Z+T centered factor weight
  Think  1.196   873 0.955   0.768
    Say  0.252   240 0.754   0.563
  Know  -0.687   141 0.674   0.335
  OTHER -0.762   678 0.617   0.318

MATRIX SUBJECT
$Matrix.subj
 factor logodds tokens Z/Z+T centered factor weight
   I  0.965  1248 0.901   0.724
   O -0.416   260 0.592   0.397
   P -0.549   424 0.587   0.366

ADDITIONAL ELEMENTS IN MATRIX VERB PHRASE
$Add.elm
 factor logodds tokens Z/Z+T centered factor weight
    N  0.429  1454 0.834   0.606
    A -0.429   478 0.659   0.394

COMPLEMENT CLAUSE SUBJECT
$Sub.subj
 factor logodds tokens Z/Z+T centered factor weight
    P  0.267  1439 0.806   0.566
    O -0.267   493 0.746   0.434

INTERVENING MATERIAL
$Int.mat
 factor logodds tokens Z/Z+T centered factor weight
    N  0.466  1527 0.832   0.614
    Y -0.466   405 0.637   0.386

TENSE
$Tense
 factor logodds tokens Z/Z+T centered factor weight
    R  0.371  1359 0.864   0.592
    A -0.371   573 0.618   0.408
```

Table 5.8   *(Cont'd)*

```
OCCUPATION
$Occ
 factor logodds tokens Z/Z+T centered factor weight
   B  0.457    420  0.874  0.612
   W -0.457   1512  0.768  0.388

AGE
$Age
 continuous logodds
    +1 -0.019

$misc
 deviance df intercept grand mean
  1360.226  13  1.967  0.791

Current variables are:
response.binary: Dep.var (Z vs. T)
fixed.factor: Verbs.1 Matrix.subj Add.elm Sub.subj Int.mat Tense Occ Edu
fixed.continuous: Age
random.intercept: Indiv
```

effect. The "deviance" is a measure of how well the model fits the data, or how much the actual data deviate from the predictions of the model. The larger the deviance, the worse the fit. When the model has many factors, this number increases. The df (degrees of freedom) here is the number of parameters in the model, a measure of model complexity. The indication [A] after a model summary means that the p-values are those associated with adding those variables, sequentially, to the model. The indication [D] (not shown) means that the p-values are those associated with subtracting those variables, sequentially, from the model.

The results in Table 5.8 largely replicate the fixed effect models in Tables 5.2 and 5.3. Adding individual as a random effect and age as a continuous effect provides statistical validation that the linguistic factors are significant over and above the effect of individual. We can also be more confident in the statistical significance of age and occupation. Unfortunately, the mixed effects model as shown does not tell us very much about why, or how, age is significant. I will return to this issue below. Moreover, a big question still remains: why does variable (*that*), a highly conditioned morphosyntacitc variable with constraints that are cognitive/pragmatic in orientation, have social correlates at all? There is actually some debate about this in the literature. While some researchers report social effects on variable (that) (e.g. Fries 1940), others have found none (e.g. Cofer 1975; Jaeger 2005). This is an interesting controversy that may be particularly well suited for testing with different statistical tools. Let us now turn to *R* and see if its tools offer us any further insight.

NOTE There have been innumerable studies of the intensifier system using quantitative methods; however, no study so far has taken into account the effect of lexical adjective. Yet adjectives vary from one locality to the next, from one generation to the next, and from male to female – a classic random effect. How might treating individual and adjective as random effects in a statistical model of intensifier use impact the interpretation of variation and change in the contemporary English intensifier system?

R

R is an exponentially more powerful tool for statistical analysis than *Goldvarb* or *Rbrul*. Further, it can be used for a multitude of different functions and applications, including graphics, corpus mining (Gries, 2009a), and untold other uses. In linguistics, *R* has mostly been used for analyzing the type of experimental data obtained in psycholinguistic experiments (e.g. Baayen, Davidson, and Bates 2008; Jaeger 2008); however, more recently it has started being used for the analysis of linguistic variation and change (Bresnan and Hay 2008, Bresnan and Ford 2010; Jaeger 2005; Tagliamonte, submitted; Hay 2006a).

As with any statistical package there is a steep learning curve; however, with *R* the learning curve is precipitous in part because the capabilities of the tool are that much more sophisticated but also because there is no user-friendly interface. Its command-line operations can be intimidating to many users. My aims here are as follows: (1) to demonstrate how straightforward statistical modeling is within the *R* environment (really, it is!); (2) to offer some basic know-how to get you going; and finally, (3) to show you some cool new tools and how they augment and enrich the LVC analyst's toolkit as well as offer fresh insights into the interpretation of variable (that).

An advantage of using *R* is that it has a consistent uniform syntax for specifying statistical models no matter which type of model is being fitted (Baayen 2008: viii). The analyst can switch fluidly from standard logistic regression modeling (as with *Goldvarb*) to mixed effects modeling (as in *Rbrul*) to random forest analysis, to condition inference trees (*R only*) and many other techniques.

Basic R Steps

Enter *R* and load all the libraries you will require, as in Example 5.6a–d. Having saved your data as a tab-delimited or csv Excel file, e.g. YRK_COMP.txt, call it into the *R* console window, by giving it the name "that" and specifying its type. For a tab-delimited file on a MAC, use Example 5.6b; for Windows, Example 5.6c:

Example 5.6

```
(a)  library(languageR)
(b)  library(Design)
(c)  that <- read.delim(file.choose())
(d)  that <- read.delim(choose.files())
```

To begin, there are various ways to review what is contained in your data file (or data frame as *R* aficionados refer to them), which is always a good idea. Start by listing the header names of each column (your factor groups) with the command in Example 5.7a. These are the labels you must use when you instruct *R* to run one statistical model or another. You can also check the factors with the command in Example 5.7b. The command in Example 5.7c produces the output in Example 5.7d.

Example 5.7

(a) `> names(that)`
    `[1] "Dep.var" "Main.subj" "Verbs.3" "Verbs.1" "Matrix.subj"`
    `"Add.elm" "Sub.subj"`
    `[8] "Int.mat" "Tense" "Indiv" "Sex" "Age.3way" "Age" "Occ"`
    `[15] "Edu" "Context"`

(b) `>str(that)`
(c) `>summary(that)`
(d)

```
Dep.var  Main.subj          Verbs.3       Verbs.1    Matrix.subj Add.elm Sub.subj Int.mat
 O:1528 1        :1248 Think      :873 Know   :141 I:1248    A: 478  O: 493  N:1527
 T: 404 3        : 148 Say        :240 OTHER  :678 O: 260    N:1454  P:1439  Y: 405
        6        : 109 Know       :141 Say    :240 P: 424
        2        : 103 Suppose    : 94 Think  :873
        i        :  62 Be & adjective: 88
        z        :  60 Complex verbs : 48
        (Other) : 202 (Other)        :448
Tense        Indiv      Sex    Age.3way      Age          Occ      Edu
A: 573  nbond    : 167 F:1090  M:768    Min.    :19.00 B: 420  -:1036
R:1359  dburns   : 148 M: 842  O:463    1st Qu. :34.00 W:1512  +:896
        echapman : 134         Y:701    Median  :48.00
        rcotton  : 123                  Mean    :48.75
        sevans   : 107                  3rd Qu. :62.00
        kyoung   : 100                  Max.    :95.00
        (Other)  :1153
```

The headers, in Example 5.7d, including Dep.var, Main.sub etc., are the labels for each of the columns (factor groups) in the data file and are the same as the labels in the *Rbrul* output since, of course, the same data file was used. In this analysis the dependent variable is coded as T = *that*; O = zero complementizer. The numbers are the total number of tokens (counts) for each variant. The factor group "Age" is the actual age, numerically, of each individual. *R* automatically calculates the minimum, median, mean, maximum, etc. Here the oldest person is 95 and the youngest is 19.

Distributional Analysis
To view a distributional analysis (comparison of marginals) of the dependent variable you must issue a command that will transform the column with your dependent variable codes (T and O) into numeric values. The command in Example 5.8a–b permits the analyst to view

the distribution of the zero complementizer by the six main internal factor groups modeled in the earlier analyses, here labeled Verbs.1, Matrix.subj, Add.elm, Sub.Subj, Int.mat, and Tense.

> **NOTE** You can name your columns (factor groups) anything you like; however, long names are difficult to type out in the R command line every time you want to do something. Make them short and/or copy and paste them from another file or from an earlier point in the R console file.

Example 5.8

(a) `that$is.O <- as.numeric(that$Dep.var=="O")`
(b) `summary(isO ~ Verbs.1 + Matrix.subj + Add.elm + Sub.Subj +`
    `Int.mat + Tense, data = that)`

This produces Table 5.9, like the comparison of marginals in *Goldvarb* although somewhat less informative. The names of the factor groups are the same as in the earlier *Rbrul* and *Goldvarb* analyses. The single digit codes in the second column are listed earlier in Tables 5.2–5.3.

Table 5.9 *R*, comparison of marginals for the zero complementizer.

```
is.O      N=1932
+-----------+-----+----+-----------+
|           |     | N  |   is.O    |
+-----------+-----+----+-----------+
|Verbs.1    |Know | 141|  0.6737589|
|           |OTHER| 678|  0.6165192|
|           |Say  | 240|  0.7541667|
|           |Think| 873|  0.9553265|
+-----------+-----+----+-----------+
|Matrix.subj|I    |1248|  0.9014423|
|           |O    | 260|  0.5923077|
|           |P    | 424|  0.5872642|
+-----------+-----+----+-----------+
|Add.elm    |A    | 478|  0.6589958|
|           |N    |1454|  0.8342503|
+-----------+-----+----+-----------+
|Sub.subj   |O    | 493|  0.7464503|
|           |P    |1439|  0.8061154|
+-----------+-----+----+-----------+
|Int.mat    |N    |1527|  0.8316961|
|           |Y    | 405|  0.6370370|
+-----------+-----+----+-----------+
|Tense      |A    | 573|  0.6178010|
|           |R    |1359|  0.8638705|
+-----------+-----+----+-----------+
|Overall    |     |1932|  0.7908903|
+-----------+-----+----+-----------+
```

Table 5.10   *R*, mixed effects model, individual random, age as continuous.

```
Generalized linear mixed model fit by the Laplace approximation
Formula: Dep.var ~ Matrix.subj + Verbs.1 + Add.elm + Sub.subj +
Int.mat + Tense + Age + Sex + Edu + Occ + (1 | Indiv)
   Data: that
  AIC   BIC  logLik  deviance
  1389  1472  -679.3    1359
Random effects:
 Groups  Name          Variance   Std.Dev.
 Indiv   (Intercept)   0.41134    0.64136
Number of obs: 1932, groups: Indiv, 33
Fixed effects:
                Estimate  Std. Error  z value  Pr(>|z|)
(Intercept)     2.041509  0.559568    3.648    0.000264***
Matrix.subjO   -1.391238  0.192261   -7.236    4.62e-13***
Matrix.subjP   -1.519005  0.171171   -8.874    < 2e-16***
Verbs.1OTHER   -0.072345  0.236323   -0.306    0.759508
Verbs.1Say      0.935660  0.276523    3.384    0.000715***
Verbs.1Think    1.894484  0.277216    6.834    8.26e-12***
Add.elmN        0.844323  0.159095    5.307    1.11e-07***
Sub.subjP       0.534426  0.159133    3.358    0.000784***
Int.matY       -0.927123  0.168948   -5.488    4.07e-08***
TenseR          0.739611  0.152387    4.854    1.21e-06***
Age            -0.021039  0.006807   -3.091    0.001997**
SexM            0.233471  0.300102    0.778    0.436586
Edu+           -0.414057  0.340109   -1.217    0.223443
OccW           -0.650085  0.375800   -1.730    0.083653.
----
Signif. codes: 0 '***' 0.001 '**' 0.01 '*' 0.05 '.' 0.1 ' ' 1
```

Mixed Effects – R

Table 5.10 shows a generalized linear mixed model *(lmer)* (Bates 2005a). The *R* code that produced it is shown in Example 5.9. As with the previous model in Table 5.9, Individual ("Indiv") is included as a random effect. Using *R*, the random effect is entered into the model by adding "|" which means "given" or "conditional on" (Bates 2005a: 27). I have selected the Factor Group "Age," which lists the age of each individual in the sample.[7] This means that R will treat Age as continuous. I leave the matrix verb as a 4-way categorical variable ("Matrix.subj") to facilitate a direct comparison with the earlier *Goldvarb* analysis in Table 5.2; however, it could as easily be modeled as a random effect itself by using "Verbs.3" which lists each verb individually.

Example 5.9

```
(a) that1.lmer = lmer(Dep.var ~ Verbs.1 + Matrix.subj + Add.elm
    + Sub.subj + Int.mat + Tense + Age + Sex + Edu + Occ +
    (1|Indiv), data = that, family = binomial)
(b) that1.lmer
```

At the outset, it is important to mention that unlike *Goldvarb, R* uses "treatment" coding for the assessment of factor groups. In treatment coding one of the factors in each factor group is selected as the baseline or reference level. This means that a value is provided only for the factors that are not the reference level; the values reflect the contrast between the reference level and other levels. As a default, *R* will select the factor whose label comes first alphabetically as the reference level. In this case, it is "O" for the zero complementizer. *R* tells us that the total number of observations (i.e. tokens), "Number of obs," is 1932 and that there are 33 individuals, "Indiv", in the sample. (Had we run verb as a random effect, "Verbs.1", we would have discovered that there are 69 different verbs coded in the data.) The fixed effects in the model are listed in the order they appeared in the formula. The reference level for matrix subject is "N" or noun phrase; for lexical verb, it is the verb "know"; for tense, past tense, "A"; for Sex, female "F"; for Education, less educated represented by "–"; and for occupation "B", blue-collar. We are provided with the estimated coefficients "Estimate" in log-odds, the standard errors, "Std. Error", z values and p values.

How is the analyst to interpret this output? The list in Example 5.10 provides a basic guide (see Hay 2011); however, we will focus our attention on the "traditional" three lines of evidence of LVC practice: (1) statistical significance; (2) relative strength of factors, as measured here in the significance codes; and (3) constraint ranking, as measured here in the relative coefficient values.

Example 5.10

- Intercept
  - The baseline of the model
  - It is the log odds of the dependent variable being one factor rather than the other
    - 2.041509
    - this positive value shows the model estimates the likelihood of zero as very high
- Estimated coefficients in log odds
  - Comparable to *Goldvarb's* factor weights
  - A positive value is a favoring effect of zero complementizer; a negative value is a disfavoring effect
  - 0 is neutral (in *Goldvarb* 0.5 is neutral)
    - for SexM = 0.233471
    - this positive value shows a somewhat higher likelihood of zero for males opposed to females, here the default
- Deviance
  - Comparable to *Goldvarb's* log likelihood
  - A measure of how well the model fits the data
  - The larger the deviance, the worse the fit
  - The more factor groups, the higher the number
- Degrees of freedom
  - A measure of the number of parameters in the model or model complexity
  - The greater the number, the more complex the model
  - Use in comparison of models
- Standard error
  - Sampling fluctuation
- Z value
  - The divergence in the results
- P values "Pr(>|z|)"

o   How much evidence is there against the null hypothesis
o   Level of significance
o   *R* provides an easily interpreted measure of the relative strength of each factor in a factor group

This model shows the relative influence of the social and linguistic factors. The linguistic factors are all highly significant and at relatively high levels, as indicated by the three stars. The p values are extremely low, well below the 0.05 threshold of significance. The social values are mostly not significant. Only Age and, at a marginally significant level, Occupation exert statistically significant effects.

This model shows which factors are statistically significant and at what level of significance. Unlike *Goldvarb* we can see immediately the statistical evaluation of the relative strength of each one. The linguistic factors are all strongly significant, as indicated by the p values, which are extremely low, and the three stars, '***'. Of the social factors only Age at $p < 0.01$, '**', and Occupation, $p < 0.05$, '·', exert statistically significant effects. The constraint ranking of factors is inferred from the difference between the reference level at 0 and the estimated coefficients. For example, for the matrix subject, "I" is the reference level, while other personal pronouns "P" and other pronouns "O" have negative coefficients in comparison, −1.52 and −1.39 respectively, both highly significant from "I", as indicated by the p values, $p < 0.001$, and the stars, '***'.

NOTE   A question that arises is are "O" and "P" significantly different from each other? You can easily reorder the factors in *R* making either "O" or "P" the reference level, i.e. that `$Matrix.subj <- factor(that$Matrix.subj, level=c("O",` `"I", "P"))`. When you do, *R* quickly returns the following result, revealing that "I" is significantly different from "O" at $p < .001$, but not significantly different from "P".

```
Matrix.subjI -1.394958 0.192211 -7.257 3.94e-13 ***
Matrix.subjP 0.126476 0.193643 0.653 0.513665
```

Baayen (2008: 305) recommends calculating the goodness of fit of the model using Somers2 Dxy, which is a rank correlation between predicted probabilities and observed responses (Baayen 2008: 224), as in Example 5.11, where the C value 0.879 indicates a high level of fit.

Example 5.11   Somers2 Table 5.9

```
> probs = 1/(1+exp(-fitted(that1.lmer)))
> somers2(probs, as.numeric(that$Dep.var)-1)
    C       Dxy     n      Missing

0.8794783  0.7589566   1932.0000000 0.0000000
```

We could take the analysis another step forward by running the matrix verbs as random rather than as a 4-way categorical group (not shown here). Instead, I will simply compute the Somers2 Dxy assessment of goodness of fit of the model, as in Example 5.12.

Example 5.12   Somers2, *R*, Generalized Linear Mixed Model, Individual and Verb as random effects, Age as continuous

```
> probs = 1/(1+exp(-fitted(that2.lmer)))
> somers2(probs, as.numeric(that$Dep.var)-1)
      C        Dxy        n       Missing
0.9048026  0.8096052    1932.0000000  0.0000000
```

This exercise reveals that when the verbs are included in the model as random effects the fit of the model to the data is slightly better – compare Somers2 0.879 in Example 5.12 for the model in Table 5.9 (individual as random) vs. the model not shown (with individual *and* verb as random) Somers2 0.905. The very high C value provides yet another statistical confirmation that this is a highly structured variable.

Checking for Interaction – R

R (like *Rbrul*) also provides the analyst with a simple and straightforward means to check for interactions. This is a relatively onerous process with *Goldvarb*; however, in *Rbrul* and *R* it is simple. In *R* simply add a star (or variations thereof; see Baayen 2008: 185) to the same formula, as in Example 5.13. For example, let us check for a potential interaction between education and occupation, as in Table 5.11.

Example 5.13

(a) `that1.lmer = lmer(Dep.var ~ Verbs.1 + Matrix.subj + Add.elm`
`+ Sub.subj + Int.mat + Tense + Age + Sex + Edu * Occ +`
`(1|Indiv), data = that, family = binomial)`
(b) `that1.lmer`

The assessment of interaction is shown by the colon, i.e. "Edu+:OccW", bolded. The results show straightforwardly that there is no interaction between sex and education, p = 0.986.

The process of fitting different models, collapsing factor groups, testing for interactions, refitting etc. should continue until the analyst has found the model or models that best account for the variation. Then, the analyst is left to make use of all the bits of evidence to interpret and explain the results in the context of the speech community and in time and space.

> **TIP** As I tell my students, model fitting involves running the data "every which way but loose." If you haven't checked every plausible possibility, you have not taken it far enough.

An important methodological point to highlight at this juncture is that the primary goal of sociolinguistic research is not to find the simplest model that accounts for most of the variation as in experimental research, but rather to find the combination of factor groups that best elucidates the behavior of the variable in the data under investigation. In particular, sociolinguists need to be able to assess the consistency of factors across social groups and between internal factor groups. Further, comparison across constraint hierarchies and the relative strength of factors is critical to address questions relating to language change, grammaticalization, acquisition, contact, ancestry, etc. Sometimes low frequency factors will be key indicators of restructuring. Nonsignificant factors will provide insights into leveling. Factors not significantly

Table 5.11 Test of interaction between education and occupation.

```
Generalized linear mixed model fit by the Laplace approximation

Formula: Dep.var ~ Verbs.1 + Matrix.subj + Add.elm + Sub.subj +
         Int.mat + Tense + Age + Sex + Edu * Occ + (1 | Indiv)

  Data: that

  AIC   BIC   logLik  deviance
  1388  1477  -678.1  1356

Random effects:
 Groups Name            Variance  Std.Dev.
 Indiv  (Intercept)     0.39844   0.63122

Number of obs: 1932, groups: Indiv, 33

Fixed effects:
                  Estimate Std. Error z value Pr(>|z|)
```

	Estimate	Std. Error	z value	Pr(>|z|)
(Intercept)	-1.876441	0.568064	-3.303	0.000956***
Verbs.1OTHER	0.068893	0.236555	0.291	0.770871
Verbs.1Say	-0.940434	0.276738	-3.398	0.000678***
Verbs.1Think	-1.901034	0.277359	-6.854	7.18e-12***
Matrix.subjO	1.389089	0.192070	7.232	4.75e-13***
Matrix.subjP	1.523593	0.171280	8.895	< 2e-16***
Add.elmN	-0.836869	0.159105	-5.260	1.44e-07***
Sub.subjP	-0.530651	0.158990	-3.338	0.000845***
Int.matY	0.917904	0.168802	5.438	5.40e-08***
TenseR	-0.737690	0.152363	-4.842	1.29e-06***
Age	0.020228	0.006753	2.996	0.002738**
SexM	-0.313190	0.302868	-1.034	0.301099
Edu+	-13.390279	811.021183	-0.017	0.986827
OccW	0.502504	0.389378	1.291	0.196867
Edu+:OccW	**13.911891**	**811.021267**	**0.017**	**0.986314**

different from each other will elucidate parallels or shifting constraints, and so on. This is why model parsimony is not as important in sociolinguistics as it is in other fields and should not overtake the central goal of explaining and interpreting the patterns of variation.

Comparison across Tools

Table 5.12 directly compares the results across the analyses for the key factor group Lexical Verb in the Matrix Clause where *think, say, tell, know*, and "other" were tested as a categorical factor group. Note the difference between sum coding in *Goldvarb* and *Rbrul* compared to the treatment coding in *R*.[8]

This overview shows the different ways of calculating the results and how they were displayed across models. The results are consistent in that *think* and *say* highly favor the zero complementizer while the others are much more likely to appear with the overt complementizer.

Table 5.12 Comparison of calculations for matrix verb as a 4-way categorical factor group.

	Goldvarb FW	*Rbrul* FW	*Rbrul* LogOdds (sum coding)	*R* Log Odds (treatment coding)	*R* P value	Count
Think [t]	0.72	0.768	1.196	1.89448	8.26e–12***	873
Say [S]	0.50	0.563	0.252	0.93566	0.000715***	240
Know [K]	0.29	0.335	–0.687	default	default	141
Other [O]	0.26	0.318	–0.762	–0.07235	0.759493	678

Further, the distinct pattern of *think* over *say* is clear across the board. Note that the treatment coding in *R* clearly shows that the category "Other", which is a mixed bag of over 60 additional, low frequency, verbs is not significantly different from *know* (the reference level). This suggests that *know* could be grouped with "other". Otherwise, there is not a lot of difference among these analyses. The consistent ranking among these verbal categories is apparent in each one.

> **TIP**   Note that for factor groups with more than two factors, it is important to set the "default" category (level) appropriately so that you can assess the significance of the most relevant contrasts (Drager and Hay 2010).

Random Forests and Condition Inference Trees

I now turn to two other techniques embodied in *R* that are ideal for exploring the combined effect of multiple factors in complex data sets. They are random forests and conditional inference trees. For a more detailed discussion of the utility of these tools for analyzing variation see Baayen (2009) and Tagliamonte and Baayen (forthcoming).

Random forests are able to take a set of factor groups and determine which of the variants is most probable (Breiman 2001). They work through a data set by trial and error to establish whether a factor group is a useful predictor of variant choice or not. In so doing, they construct a large number of conditional inference trees, the random forest. The advantage of the random forest is that the model works with samples of factor groups, which obviates one of the most problematic methodological issues in LVC research. Earlier I said that inexperienced researchers often throw too many factors into the same analysis. With a random forest this does not matter. Similar factor groups can be run in the same analysis. The analyst can easily view which ones are more important than others.

To use these models, install the Party package and dependencies in *R*, as in Example 5.14.

Example 5.14

library(party)

Like the *lm()* and *lmer()* functions, the way to conduct a random forest analysis is to use the function *cforest()* followed by the specification of the factor groups you want in the

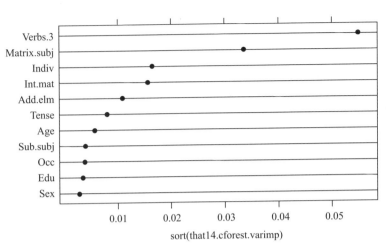

Figure 5.1   R, random forest, linguistic, and social factors, all verbs.

model. Let us run a statistical model that includes all the social and linguistic factors, with Age as the actual age of the informants (continuous), verbs as all the individual verbs and individuals as all the individuals separately, as in Example 5.15. The results are plotted with the *dotplot* command, as in Example 5.15b, and the factor groups are ordered according to variable importance (varimp).

Example 5.15

```
(a)  that14.cforest = cforest(Dep.var ~ Matrix.subj + Add.elm +
     Sub.subj + Int.mat + Tense + Sex + Age + Occ + Edu + Indiv +
     Verbs.3, data=that)
(b)  that14.cforest.varimp = varimp(that14.cforest)
(c)  dotplot(sort(that14.cforest.varimp))
```

Figure 5.1 illustrates the relative importance of each factor group. Lexical verb is by far the most important factor group, followed by the matrix subject, the individual, intervening material, additional elements, tense, and age, followed by much less important factors: the subordinate subject, followed by occupation, education, and sex. This type of analysis is excellent for exposing the relative contribution (i.e. strength) of each factor group on the variable under investigation. The disadvantage of the random forest analysis is that it does not show us how the factors work together, namely the constraint ranking of factors within each factor group. This is a critical aspect to any analysis of variation and change. The advantage of the conditional inference tree is that it is able to depict the subtle interactions in the data using a hierarchical display.

In a classification tree each factor group is assigned a p-value indicating the level of significance as well as its relationship to other factor groups in the model. In this case, when all the factors were included in the analysis the tree was so complex it became cumbersome and unhelpful (not shown; it would not have fit on the page). Instead, let us focus on the factors that are most contentious in the literature on the borderline of significance in the statistical models – sex, age (as continuous), occupation, and education. The R code to produce this model is shown in the command line in Example 5.16. The tree is shown in Figure 5.2.

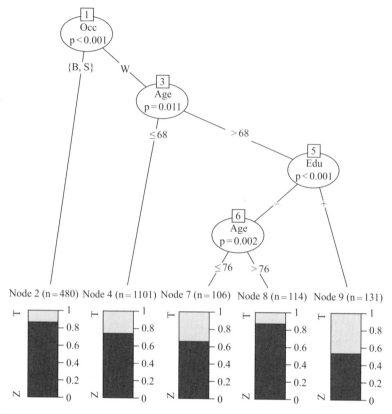

Figure 5.2   *R*, conditional inference tree, social factors.

Example 5.16

(a)   `that14.ctree = ctree(Dep.var ~ Sex + Age + Occ + Edu, data=that)`
(b)   `plot(that14.ctree)`

TIP   Try constructing different conditional inference trees using combinations of different social and linguistic factors. All it takes is adding or subtracting what goes into the basic formula,

e.g. `that1.ctree = ctree(Dep.var ~ Matrix.subj + Verbs.1`
         `+ Add.elm + Sub.subj + Int.mat + Tense, data=that)`
e.g. `that2.ctree = ctree(Dep.var ~ Matrix.subj + Sub.`
         `subj, data=that)`
e.g. `that3.ctree = ctree(Dep.var ~ Add.elm + Int.mat +`
         `Verbs.1, data=that)`

Isolating the social factors in this way provides a visually dramatic portrait of the social nature of variable (that) in York. What does this view tell us? First, occupation at the top of the tree is the most important social factor conditioning complementizer choice. Recall that Occupation was selected as significant in the *Goldvarb* logistic regression (white-collar workers, +edu, favored the zero variant) and was marginally significant in the *R* mixed effects model in Table 5.10, p = < 0.1. In the random forest it is much lower down in importance than Age. Second, students, "S," behave as blue-collar workers "B", a result that was also visible in one way or another in previous results. However, at this point the results get interesting, at least from a sociolinguistic perspective. The York speech community is highly differentiated based on speaker age. Recall that age has been selected as significant by all the analyses regardless of whether age was run as a continuous or a categorical factor group. The conditional inference tree shows us how age intersects with the other social factors. A white-collar worker aged ≤68 uses the most zero complementizers. Individuals over 68 use zero complementizers as well, but more so if they are less educated and especially if they are less than 76. In other words, education is a greater predictor of complementizer use among the older people in the community. In contrast, among the younger individuals occupation is the greater predictor of usage. Why would there be a split between the generation over 76 and those under 68? Recall that these data were collected in 1997. Anyone aged 68 in 1997 was 16 in 1945. Therefore the people under 68 are precisely the generations of the post-World War II era. Taken together with earlier historical research on York (Finnegan 1982), the split in the population at age 68 suggests that the zero complementizer was a social indicator for this generation. How does it contribute the explanation for variable (that) in York? The results in Figure 5.2 suggest that it has undergone a social reanalysis in the last 50 years or so. Where once it marked social groups (as reflected in education level), it has come to be a stylistic option (as reflected in the use of the standard language in one's job type).

Mini Quiz 5.4

Construct a conditional inference tree to view the relationship between type of matrix subject and matrix verb. e.g. `that1.ctree = ctree (Dep. var ~ Matrix.subj + Verbs.1, data = that)`. Which combination of subject and verb is *least* likely to have the zero complementizer? Notice how the results across analyses converge in their display of these results.

It is still not clear how this plays into the strong linguistic factor groups and the course of change toward more zero complementizers in the history of English. I have purposefully used a linguistic variable in this chapter that I have not fully analyzed, interpreted, presented, or published. The puzzle is only half done. There may be several different – statistically valid, linguistically justified, socially compelling – interpretations of this variable in York. Pursuit of such findings may well make contributions to areas as diverse as grammaticalization, the influence of social factors on morpho–syntactic variables, the difference between written and spoken language, and the utility of mixed effects models to language variation and change among others.

Practical Advice

My recommendation for what statistical tool to use for variation analysis is to set up the possibility to analyze your data with an expansive toolkit and a set of handpicked tools. Construct an Excel file with all the different types of factor groups you will need to conduct analyses in *Goldvarb*, *Rbrul*, and *R*. Call it your "root" file. In order to make this data file usable across platforms, duplication of factors groups is necessary. For example, if you coded for individual in *Goldvarb*, you would have been restricted to single character codes. This requires using most of the characters in the courier keyboard. The weirder ones are not readable by *Rbrul/R*, so this factor group must be recoded or removed from analysis. It is simple enough to code each speaker as their actual name (see listing in Example 5.7d under the column "Indiv"); however, then this factor group cannot be read in *Goldvarb*. Similarly, a *Goldvarb* token file may contain many tokens with a slash somewhere in the string (due to one factor or another being unknown or missing). These tokens can be analyzed in *Goldvarb*, but not in *Rbrul* or *R*.[9] Using Excel they can be sorted and deleted for analysis in *Rbrul* and *R*. This is why you need multiple configurations for the same factor groups if you want to be able to use all the toolkits. From my perspective at the point of writing, distributional analyses along with cross-tabulations are simplest in *Goldvarb*. Basic fixed effect runs seem to hold up reasonably well to the powerful mixed models I have tested here (see Table 5.12) at least with linguistic features such as variable (that) where the community and individual grammars are parallel and the explanatory factors are consistent and strong. However, the ability to provide statistical validation of this fact using mixed models is satisfying and may prove decisive with other types of linguistic variables. *Rbrul* provides factor weights for all factors in a factor group (sum contrasts). This makes comparative studies simpler because it is possible to compare each factor's level and effect across data sets from earlier points in LVC research history. *R* is ideal for complex models and assessing the levels of significance of factor groups. Interactions can be tested easily either in *Rbrul* or *R* but I still like to see the *Goldvarb* cross-tabulations first in order to see (and understand) what is going on inside each cell. Random forests are particularly fitting for data exploration and can be used as another prequel for informing logistic regression modeling, whether fixed or mixed. Finally, the condition inference tree in Figure 5.2 revealed unforeseen patterns of variable (that) in the York speech community. This is compelling testimony for its potential to provide a more nuanced understanding of other variables, contexts, and situations. To date only *R* will allow you to use random forests and conditional inference trees. *R* is also a cornucopia for plotting and displaying data. But that is another story.

Summary

The horizon for the study of language variation and change is bright and exciting. The difficult part will be to find the best way to use all these new tools effectively and to marshall their full potential for interpreting and explaining linguistic variation and change. As a new body of findings builds over the next generations, analysts will be ideally armed to tackle the big questions of the field.

I have not pursued the many looming questions in the ongoing debate on statistical tools. Among these are how to deal with small data sets, what to do with missing information that the variable rule program easily handles with a slash function in the LISP syntax, and what to do about categorical speakers (e.g. Tagliamonte and Baayen forthcoming). More pressing challenges are whether or not mixed effects models are actually appropriate for sociolinguistic data where the data are highly unbalanced, and which of the many other statistical tools might be (more) appropriate (see e.g. Roy submitted). Among the most important questions on the horizon is one that William Labov recently put to me (November 4, 2010): *What is the cognitive validity of the statistical models that we are fitting to our data?* Only with the judicious use of the full range of statistical methods available alongside careful, indeed acute, sociolinguistic interpretation as well as reaching out to joint socio–psycho–linguistic enterprise will we be able to fully explore the answer to this question. We are going to be living in interesting statistical times in LVC research in the years to come.

In my explorations of different tools and practices for quantitative analysis, I have found that the most important thing of all is to understand your data, to be accountable to your data, and to make every effort to explain the data. The statistical models are tools. They enable the analyst to accomplish all these goals more effectively. It is up to the analyst to ask the most telling questions, to wisely interpret the patterns, and to craft the best explanations.

I would like to end this chapter with the best advice I have received so far when it comes to which statistical tool to use in the analysis of language variation and change:

> I do not believe that it makes any difference what methods are used as long as they are used correctly and sometimes ingeniously. (David Sankoff, p.c. May 21, 2009)

Exercises

Exercise 5.1   Interpreting variable rule analysis tables   ——————————

Table 5.13 displays the results for variation in strong verb morphology, as in Example 5.17, in four varieties of Early African American English: Samaná English, SE; the Ex-Slave Recordings, ESR; North Preston, NPR; and Guysborough Enclave, GYE (Poplack and Tagliamonte 2001: Table 6.3).

Example 5.17

   (a)   She *take* the train yesterday.
   (b)   She *took* the train yesterday.

Work through the questions to understand the table. The same basic procedures are relevant for the interpretation of *any* variable rule analysis table.

Question 1   What is the dependent variable?

Question 2   Which of the two variants involved is the application value being considered in the analysis presented in the table? In other words, the probability of which variant are we looking at? This means, what variant of the two that are possible (marked vs. not-marked) is represented by the factor weights (a.k.a. probabilities – the two digit, point form numbers)?

Question 3   What is the overall propensity of the stem form to occur in each variety? In other words, generally speaking without consideration of any conditioning effects, how likely is the stem form to occur in each variety?

Quantitative Analysis

Table 5.13 Five logistic regression analyses of the contribution of factors selected as significant to the probability that strong verbs will surface as stems (all factor groups selected as significant).

	Early African American English										
	SE			ESR			NPR			GYE		
Corrected mean:	.21			.29			.15			.22		
Total N:	2488			537			535			574		
	FW	%	N	FW	%	N	FW	%	N	FW	%	N
VERB CLASS												
I Verb stem = participle (e.g., *come/came/come*)	0.72	39	431	0.97	90	69	0.96	75	56	0.91	53	89
II Verb stem ≠ preterite ≠ particple (e.g., *take/took/taken*)	0.27	10	832	0.42	23	223	0.33	13	239	0.40	23	235
III Preterite = particple (e.g., *say/said/said*)	0.59	30	1225	0.35	20	245	0.50	20	240	0.39	22	246
Range	*45*			*62*			*63*			*52*		
Temporal disambiguation												
Preceding verb unmarked	0.72	47	472	0.75	51	75	0.87	53	98	0.81	57	63
Preceding verb marked	0.44	20	1741	0.45	28	428	0.38	14	378	0.45	24	433
Range	*28*			*30*			*49*			*36*		
VERBAL ASPECT												
Habitual	0.66	35	193	0.67	40	161	0.76	38	132	0.73	37	292
Punctual	0.18	25	2005	0.41	26	321	0.40	17	349	0.23	15	241
Range	*17*			*26*			*36*			*50*		

Source: Poplack and Tagliamonte 2001: 133, Table 6.3.

Note that the corrected mean hovers around 0.20 for all the Early AAE varieties. Critical evidence for inferring the underlying grammar is to interpret the patterns in the data. Examine the linguistic tendencies that lead to the use of the unmarked form across varieties and compare how these are the same or different.

Question 4 What factor(s) are statistically significant?

Question 5 What factor group contributes the greatest effect on the occurrence of the stem form of strong verbs, i.e. *the* strongest constraint?

Question 6 What is the constraint hierarchy for the strongest factor influencing strong verb morphology?

> **NOTE** Anything over 0.5 is said to "*favor*" the variant under investigation. Anything below 0.5 is said to *dis*favor. However, a more refined way to look at this is the *pattern* among the factor weights. Which ones are higher and which ones are lower? And how do they group together?

Table 5.14 Wald statistics for prepositional dative of the verb "give" – New Zealand English.

	x^2	d.f.	P
Log length of recipient	11.95	1	0.0005
Log length of theme	7.76	1	0.0053
Pronominal recipient	26.42	1	<0.0001
Pronominal theme	37.94	1	<0.0001
Givenness of recipient	2.81	1	0.0935
Givenness of theme (factor + higher order factors)	24.87	3	<0.0001
All interactions	14.82	2	0.0006
Animacy of recipient	12.60	1	0.0004
Semantic class (factor + higher order factors)	20.53	4	0.0004
Age	6.16	1	0.0460
Nonlinear	5.67	2	0.0172
Givenness of theme × semantic class (factor + higher order factors)	18.58	3	0.0006
Total nonlinear + interaction	18.48	3	0.0003
Total	110.32	13	<0.0001

Source: Bresnan and Hay 2008: 251, Table 1.

Question 7 Are the constraints the same or different across varieties?

Exercise 5.2   Mixed effects models

The analysis in Table 5.14 comes from Bresnan and Hay's (2008) study of the dative alternation in the verb *give*, as in Example 5.18:

Example 5.18

(a) "You don't know how difficult it is to find something which will please everybody, especially the men. Why not just *give them cheques*?" I asked.

(b) You can't *give cheques to people*. It would be insulting.

Question 1 Which three factors contribute the most to the variation?
Question 2 Which factor group is not significant?
Question 3 Which factor group has the greatest degrees of freedom?

Mini Quiz Answers

5.1   Q1: *True*

5.2   Q1: *e*

5.3   Q1: *The same factor groups are statistically significant (or not). The factor groups have the same constraint ranking and the relative strength of factors stays the same. Of course! The statistical tool is the same – fixed effects logistic regression.*

5.4   Q1: *OTHER matrix subject; verb "say"*

Notes

1   http://individual.utoronto.ca/tagliamonte/.
2   A third category in the "Occupation" Factor Group is "Student", with the label "S" in subsequent analyses. In these models I have collapsed this category with the category "B", blue-collar workers because the distributional analyses had shown them to be patterning similarly. Remember this when we consider other analyses.
3   Nonconvergence arises in variable rule analysis when there is collinearity or interaction among factor groups in the model. In the variable rule program this is signaled directly by a warning of "No convergence at iteration X" in the output (for further discussion see Tagliamonte 2006a: 153–155).
4   Here is a model for this dummy recoding using Goldvarb's LISP syntax (Paolillo 2002):

```
( (1) (2)
(0 (G (COL 3 B) ) (x (ELSEWHERE) ) )
(0 (G (COL 3 C) ) (x (ELSEWHERE) ) )
(0 (S (COL 3 B) ) (x (ELSEWHERE) ) )
(0 (S (COL 3 C) ) (x (ELSEWHERE) ) )
(0 (O (COL 3 B) ) (x (ELSEWHERE) ) )
(0 (O (COL 3 B) ) (x (ELSEWHERE) ) ) )
```

5   The name is whatever label has been given to the column in an Excel file.
6   Both *Goldvarb* and *Rbrul* are able to report factor weights as centered or uncentered; however, users are advised to conduct analyses with the setting "centered" (Johnson, p.c. March 17, 2010).
7   *R* interprets numbers in a factor group as continuous. There are ways around this. Consult the *R* literature.
8   *R* uses treatment coding as a default, but sum coding can be specified using `(contr.sum())`.
9   Analysts who use *Goldvarb* are accustomed to the utility of the slash function, "/", which enables a particular factor in a particular factor group to be ignored from consideration from the analysis of that factor group. The reason for the slash is because interruptions, noise, and other types of interference are the norm in sociolinguistic data sets. This means that incomprehensible or missing pieces of information are frequent. Further, there will also be individuals for whom various social facts are absent; for example, an individual who refuses to divulge his or her age or birthdate or an individual whose education is unknown. Since every token is precious, it is important to be able to use these tokens in the analysis even if some information is missing. So far, I do not know the solution to this problem for using *Rbul* or *R*.

Background Reading

Baayen 2008; Bayley 2002; Bayley and Young forthcoming; Blake 1997; Cedergren and Sankoff 1974; Drager and Hay 2010; Gries 2010; Guy 1988, 1993; Hay 2006a; Jaeger 2008; Johnson 2009; Paolillo 2002; Rand and Sankoff 1990; Rickford 1991; Rousseau and Sankoff 1978a,b; Sankoff 1988a,c; Sankoff and Labov 1979; Sankoff and Rousseau 1979; Sankoff *et al.* 2005; Tagliamonte 2006a; Young and Bayley 1996.

Downloads and Internet Addresses

Download the Goldvarb manual at http://courses.essex.ac.uk/lg/lg654/GoldVarb2001forPC manual.htm.

Download the variable rule program at: *Goldvarb 2.1*, a system 9 application for Macintosh, can be downloaded at http://albuquerque.bioinformatics.uottawa.ca/GoldVarb/GoldVarb.html.

Goldvarb X, an application for system 10, either Macintosh or Windows, can be downloaded at http://individual.utoronto.ca/tagliamonte/goldvarb.htm.

Rbrul, along with a manual for its use, is available for free download at http://www.danielezrajohnson.com/Rbrul.R.

The Rbrul list is at rbrul.list@gmail.com.

R is available for free download at http://www.r-project.org/.

6

Comparative Sociolinguistics

We cannot argue from silence … Things we consider quaint when we hear them on the Cape or in the Blue Ridge may be found in the back streets of Boston or Raleigh, where academics from Harvard or Duke rarely venture. (McDavid 1985: 16)

In this chapter, I explore the insights that can be gleaned from comparing and contrasting the results of statistical models of linguistic variables. Comparison, especially based on the different types of evidence available from statistical modeling, as well as triangulation, will often uncover remarkable subtleties about the nature of linguistic features.

Comparison

The study of language behavior across data sets is called "comparative sociolinguistics" (Poplack and Tagliamonte 2001; Tagliamonte 2002). Comparative sociolinguistics concerns the connection (i.e. relationship) of linguistic variation in one body of materials to another. For example, a common observation of vernacular dialects of English is the use of *was* for third person plural. The examples in Example 6.1a–b come from Ireland, Scotland, and Canada. Does the form pattern according to the same grammar across all these dialects? Systematic comparison across the varieties is necessary to figure this out. Where are the similarities? Where are the differences?

Example 6.1

(a)   The dry-irons *was* hard to work with. (CLB/012)
(b)   My prayers *was* always answered. (GYV/001)
(c)   War time wedding *was* all called fae. (BCK/002)

Variationist Sociolinguistics: Change, Observation, Interpretation, First Edition. Sali A. Tagliamonte.
© 2012 Sali A. Tagliamonte. Published 2012 by Blackwell Publishing Ltd.

The answers to these questions require a twofold approach. First, the methodology of Variationist Sociolinguistics enables different influences on linguistic features to be disentangled through systematic examination of their behavior. Second, an approach that compares these findings across related data sets (dialects, social groups) permits inter- and intra-corpora similarities and differences to be interpreted. This methodology builds directly from three strands of linguistics – dialectology, sociolinguistics, and historical linguistics.

Comparison requires contentualization. Perhaps two bodies of material are being compared to show difference, perhaps to show similarity, perhaps to gauge both difference *and* similarity. The relationship between the entities being compared must be made clear. They may match by social criterion such as social class, age, level of education, or alternatively be differentiated by some key contrast (Bailey and Maynor 1989: 23).

The Comparative Method

The research program exploring underlying grammatical relationships between dialects, particularly that between British and American English, is nearly a century old. This research began with standard dialectological methods. In the absence of suitable corpora, principled data collection, formulation, and operationalization of hypotheses, and an accountable statistical analysis, most studies were at most suggestive. As LVC research has evolved into the twenty-first century the standards for comparison in this enterprise have received increasing attention as researchers have renewed their efforts to establish linguistic links across the globe (e.g. Clarke 1997b; Harris 1986; Rickford 1986b).

Ideally, as Schneider (2004: 263) observes, to establish trans-Atlantic connections we should aim for:

> evidence of historical connections, functional identities, or similar effects … – it is only parallels of such a subtle nature or the joint weight of several sets of data that should allow us to assume direct transmission in select instances.

In historical linguistics it is widely held that earlier stages in the history of a language can be observed through comparative analysis of cognate forms (sets of reflexes) in later, sister varieties (Hoenigswald 1960: 119; Meillet 1967). The comparative method is "the procedure whereby morphs of two or more sister languages are matched to reconstruct the ancestor language" (Hoenigswald 1960: 119). The comparative method in historical linguistics is based on comparative reconstruction, which has as its basis shared correspondences of linguistics features (Hoenigswald 1960; Meillet 1967). The application of these methods to sociolinguistics began with Weinreich *et al.*'s (1968) introduction of the notion of "structured heterogeneity" in the speech community which was later developed further by Labov (1982). This work laid the foundations of the quantitative variationist approach (Labov 1966, 1970, 1972c; Labov *et al.* 1968) which elaborated a method of analysis founded on assumptions of accountability, testing hypotheses systematically against data, and building generalizations on well-formed comparative studies. The methods of Variationist Sociolinguistics make it particularly useful for conducting comparisons, where the focus of the comparison is on the patterning of linguistic variables. In particular, constraints on linguistic features are held to be a reflection of diachronic patterns even after centuries of geographic separation

(Labov 1980a: xvii). Information arising from the lines of evidence from variation analysis is the key to determining similarities and/or differences (Poplack and Tagliamonte 2001).

Comparative sociolinguistic research developed initially from issues surrounding the origins and development of AAVE. This long-term debate provides a conundrum for the comparative sociolinguistic endeavor as researchers from all areas of the field attempted to reconstruct the likely characteristics of the ancestor of AAVE. In comparative sociolinguistics, the means by which the sister varieties are compared is the set of correspondences provided by the results of the statistical modeling, what Labov (1982: 75) referred to as "finely articulated structures." In fact, the quantitative paradigm provides the kind of "precise information on the states of the language" called for by Meillet (1967: 138).

This is accomplished by comparing the patterning of variability in each possible source. If the conditioning effects on the variable linguistic features show patterns approximating those found in a putative source, we can conclude that they represent structures drawn from that source (e.g. Poplack and Tagliamonte 1999b; 2001: Chapter 5). On the other hand, where dissimilarities are found, we have grounds for concluding that the phenomena in question belong to different linguistic systems (e.g. Tagliamonte 1998a; Tagliamonte, Poplack, and Eze 1997).

A key notion in a comparative sociolinguistic approach is the notion of a "conflict site." This is defined as a form or class of forms that differs functionally and/or structurally and/or quantitatively across the varieties in question (Poplack and Meechan 1998b: 132). By quantitatively analyzing patterns of distribution at grammatical sites where varieties are held to be distinct, the precise nature of similarities and differences across data sets can be pinpointed. If the results match the observations made in the literature for the putative source varieties, then we appeal to this similarity to posit a link between the two. On the other hand, dissimilarities require the analyst to contextualize and evaluate the differences in the context of linguistic developments in all the varieties under investigation. If the variability in the data is part of ongoing linguistic change, then it must be analyzed in terms of where it came from and its stage of development in the grammar, consistent with Jespersen's suggestion that "to understand a linguistic system, we must know how it came to be" (Jespersen 1924).

Comparative LVC studies typically focus on data sets that share characteristics, e.g. the contrast between real and apparent time, for tracing the roots of extraterritorial varieties of English, for isolating systems in language contact. This methodology has also been implicitly or explicitly adopted by numerous scholars in a wide range of applications, including comparisons of English, Spanish, and French dialects and comparisons across villages, age groups, and social networks.

Mini Quiz 6.1

Q1   The class of form which differs functionally and/or structurally and/or quantitatively across varieties is referred to as:
(a)   A test site.
(b)   A deviant constraint.
(c)   A conflict site.
(d)   A linguistic variable.
(e)   A vernacular anomaly.

Comparison in Origins

One of the most compelling motivations for comparative sociolinguistic analysis is to ascertain the history and origins of a variety, in particular the drive to establish connections between old and new world roots. The most contentious of these endeavors is the disputed ancestry of AAVE. Two geographic locales that were major contributors to early US population movements are the UK and West Africa. Do the linguistic features of US varieties whose speakers have African ancestry continue to have patterns that can be traced back to languages in Africa or have alternative influences overshadowed these roots? Either way, the contemporary features will have arisen through processes of linguistic change, but from one source, or the other, or both?

By necessity much of the linguistic evidence brought to bear on this issue has focused on features which are either frequent or widely attested in AAVE or which pattern contrastively in that variety compared to mainstream American English. Some notable contributions have included variable (s) (see Chapter 8), variable (was) (Wolfram and Thomas 2002, Tagliamonte 2000), variable (copula) (Rickford 1996; 1998; Walker 2000) and variable relative pronouns (e.g. Tottie and Harvie 2000). The problem is that these linguistic variables appear in so many varieties they could be subject to universal constraints. This makes comparison a self-defeating circle. For example, the Type of Subject constraint on variable (s) is present in many UK dialects, leading some analysts to hypothesize that varieties that exhibit this constraint have UK roots. However, if the constraint is, in fact, universal, then variable (s) is not an ideal test for trans-Atlantic connections and the ancestry of dialects.

In the pantheon of linguistic features that have been considered in this research endeavor, nonstandard habitual forms and their associated functions present a particularly good case. The aspectual meaning of "habitual" is said to be grammaticalized across all the putative sources for Atlantic contact vernaculars – Irish English, British dialects, and West African languages (e.g. Harris 1986; Hopkins 1994; Rickford 1986b). Most, if not all, of the research that discusses these features is based on present temporal reference forms, whether *do be*, *do + V*, verbal *-s*, *do +V +ing*, *do + be +V + ing* or various combinations thereof, as in Example 6.2.

Example 6.2

(a) I would say, "oh, *do be* careful!" (SMT/024)
(b) [1] Have you seen Curly? [025] Yeah, he *do come* in sometimes. (SMT/025)
(c) She likes all the soaps. But I *likes* quizzes. (DVN/003)

The distribution patterns of these features as well as their diachronic and synchronic development is discussed extensively in the literature. However, the criss-crossing of origins (Northern vs. Southern Ireland vs. southwest British) coupled with postmigration dialect contact in the US leaves little room for unambiguous interpretations of the dialect contact situation (McDavid 1985: 19–20; Montgomery 2001). Even in the rare case when sociohistorical links can be firmly traced back in time, as in the case of Vernacular Newfoundland English (Clarke 1997b, 2010), the sheer lack of the feature in question in the transported variety presents the ultimate paradox for the comparative endeavor. Unstressed periphrastic *do*, as in *I do think*, *I do go*, etc. should have been part of the dialects of the founding populations of Newfoundland, yet it does not exist in contemporary Newfoundland

English, not even in the most conservative varieties. Clarke (1997c: 338) concludes that "there may never be final answers to the mysteries of dialect and language mixing." In sum, the trick of the comparative endeavor is to find just the right diagnostic – ideally a variable that is restricted to the data sets under investigation and has more or less the same function (Wolfram 2000: 47).

A "diagnostic" is a feature that can establish correspondences between varieties because it reveals the underlying mechanism of the grammar. An ideal diagnostic is one that functions in a nontrivial way in one variety while simultaneously functioning in a different nontrivial way in another variety.

> **NOTE** Was unstressed periphrastic *do* ever a part of Newfoundland English? See Wagner (2007) for another perspective.

Comparison in Language Contact

The comparative sociolinguistic framework is also useful for the study of language contact. In this situation the relationship between varieties is slightly different. Often one variety is an indigenous language, sometimes referred to as a substrate language. The other variety is the contact variety, often a pidgin or creole, e.g. the relationship between Guyanese Creole and English (Bickerton 1975), Nigerian Pidgin English and the indigenous languages of Nigeria (Tagliamonte 1997).

Meyerhoff (2009: 311) introduces the following principles for interpreting the results of comparative sociolinguistic analysis in the context of language contact, each based on one of the lines of evidence:

1. *Statistical significance.* Where the same factor groups are significant constraints on a variable in the statistical model and in the contact variety, this is interpreted as weak transfer or replication.
2. *Relative strength of factors.* Where the same factor groups are significant in both model and replica, and the ordering of these factor groups is the same in both model and replica, this is interpreted as (strong) transfer.
3. *Constraint ranking.* Where the same factor groups are significant in both model and contact variety, and the ordering of factors with groups (the constraint hierarchy) has the same ranking in model and contact variety, this is interpreted as calquing, a literal translation from one variety to the other.

In sum, comparative sociolinguistic methods can be applied to any situation where the analyst aims to understand the linguistic relationship between two varieties. The two varieties must be related (at least putatively) across some external set of criteria according to which they can be assumed to have sociocultural links. Then, by utilizing the lines of evidence made available by variationist statistical techniques, the interpretation of results can proceed according to the following procedure.

Compare and contrast factor groups in a statistical model according to:

- statistical significance
- relative strength
- constraint hierarchy.

> **NOTE**   It is interesting to speculate which line of evidence is the strongest indicator of similarity across varieties, the relative strength of the factor or the constraint ranking of the factor? Note that Meyerhoff's (2009) model suggests the former whereas Poplack and Tagliamonte's (2001) discussions of method suggest the latter. This is open for empirical investigation.

Standards for Comparison

Standards for comparison in comparative sociolinguistics are summarized in Table 6.1. These were explicitly laid out in Montgomery (1989: 240). Poplack and Tagliamonte (2001) formulated the auxiliary principle of finding an appropriate conflict site and added the three lines of evidence from variationist methodology – statistical significance, constraint hierarchies, and the relative strength of factors.

Not all linguistic features are useful in establishing correspondences. While cross-variety comparison is most revealing when the element compared entertains a *unique* association with a source variety it is often difficult, if not impossible, to find such a feature. Thus, the

Table 6.1   Standards for comparison.

(a)   Full, explicit descriptions of the grammatical features within each variety, on a quantitative basis, and according to the principles of accountability:
    i.   attend to form and function
    ii.   specify the linguistic environments of occurrence
    iii.   tabulate the frequency
    iv.   interrelationship with other features of grammar
       • *Statistical significance*
       • *Constraints and constraint ranking*
       • *Relative strength of constraints*
(b)   The existence of the grammatical features in question should be as closely limited to the varieties (registers) concerned as possible.
    • *sufficient quantities of valid data*
    • *characterize its style and sociolinguistic features*
    • *are the target forms screened out of the data?*
(c)   Demographic information from the documentary record demonstrates a historical connection between the groups speaking the varieties concerned.

Source: Montgomery, 1989: 240.

most common circumstance is to find comparative studies of features that do not differ across varieties. This may lead to the invocation of coincidental, superficial, or universal similarities. However, the diagnosticity of a variable can be enhanced by statistical modeling where the statistical signficance of constraints, the hierarchy of constraints, and their relative strength can be mathematically verified.

Constructing a research project in which all these standards of comparison are appropriately met is tough, and to some extent dependent on coincidence. Any project that specifically addresses as many of the external criteria as possible and that fully complies with methodological considerations can contribute strong empirically based observations. These, in turn, can be used to inform future work. Let us consider a case study as an example.

> we must attribute to language-users an internalized comparative method. (Bailey 1973: 17)

Variable (did)

When I moved to England in 1995, one of my most thrilling discoveries was the existence of a dialect in rural Somerset where the verb *do* is used periphrastically in the affirmative, as in Example 6.3.

Example 6.3

(a)   That's where I *did* get my chicken manure from. (SMT/007)
(b)   Well, this one in particular I *did like*. He was a nice chap. (SMT/004)

The reason this was so exciting to me was that fresh in my mind was the doctoral research I had conducted on the variety of English spoken in a remote community in the Dominican Republic, Samaná (Poplack and Tagliamonte 1991b; Tagliamonte 1991). Samaná English is spoken by the descendants of American ex-slaves who migrated to the Dominican Republic from the American South in the 1820s (Poplack and Sankoff 1987: 291). In this variety the very same construction is found (Tagliamonte 1991), as in Example 6.4.

Example 6.4

(a)   They had a little road way out there what they *did go* over. (SAM/002)
(b)   I *did like* to eat the sugar. I used to like to eat the sugar. (SAM/017)

Moreover the two varieties – Samaná and Somerset – appeared to use variable (did) in the same way – alternating with *used to*, *would*, and the preterite and encoding for past habitual meaning.

Taken together these facts sparked my curiosity. First, the feature itself is about as highly circumscribed as a contemporary linguistic feature can be. In the United Kingdom it is localized to the southwest. In the United States it is circumscribed to the south. Second, dialects in the southwest of England were among the input varieties in the southern United States in the seventeenth century (Le Page and Tabouret-Keller 1985; Rickford 1986b: 260, 265). Such sociohistorical links can be corroborated by the fact that variable (*did*) is attested with similar distributional patterns in the Ex-Slave Recordings (Tagliamonte 1991), the

Ex Slave Narratives (Schneider 1989: 138–139), and Gullah (Pargman 2000). This means that variable (*did*) must have been a feature of earlier varieties of AAVE (which arose in the American South) that in turn could have been transported to Samaná during the African American Diaspora. Here then is the plausible link between Somerset and Samaná.

Of course, discovering that a linguistic feature exists in a particular locale and actually finding sufficient authentic data that documents its vernacular use is an entirely different task. In 1997, by lucky coincidence a student arrived at the University of York whose hometown was Wincantin, in rural Somerset, Megan Jones. It was not long before Megan was out in the field interviewing friends and family. Although variable (*did*) was rare in the data she collected, we embarked upon a study anyway, knowing that it might be the last chance to document this obsolescent feature. It also provided an unprecedented opportunity for tracking the diffusion of linguistic features from the United Kingdom to the United States. As far as I am aware these are the only two contemporary varieties in which variable (*did*) exists with the same circumscribed function (habitual past). Consequently, comparative sociolinguistic analysis of this feature in Somerset and Samaná is a showcase for the requirement proposed by Montgomery (1989: 240) that comparative features be as closely limited to the varieties concerned as possible.

A thorough examination of the literature revealed that variable (*did*) was reported in the United Kingdom until roughly 1800. By the late twentieth century it was moribund. However, the southwest has long been a stronghold for older dialect features (Chambers and Trudgill 1980) and this is why Megan's elderly relatives were still using it. The time period through which variable (*did*) was reported in both standard and dialectal usage in the United Kingdom corresponds with migrations from Britain to North America. Moreover, Rissanen's (1985) research confirms that the form was in use in seventeenth-century American English. Further, LePage and Tabouret-Keller (1985: 38–39) point out that working-class migrants from Bristol and Somerset in particular, and southwest England more generally, went to the American plantations in the seventeenth century as indentured laborers and servants. Thus variable (*did*) was undoubtedly a productive part of the vernacular. If so, then the language of American residents in the early colonization period likely embodied some if not all of the conditioning factors that operated on variable (*did*) at earlier stages in the history of the English language.

Many linguistic constraints can be salvaged from the historical literature describing variable (*did*), including the favoring effect of a preceding *did* (Example 6.5a), a preverbal adverb (Example 6.5b), or the tendency of the form to occur in a subordinate clause (Example 6.5c). For full discussion of these (and other) constraints see Jones and Tagliamonte (2004).

Example 6.5

(a) They had a little road way out there, a small road what they <u>*did*</u> go over there. The people <u>*did*</u> come. (SAM/002)
(b) 'Course we <u>always</u> *did drink* the home-made wine, didn't we? (SMT/020)
(c) I wasn't never a cider drinker. I'm afraid it *did* <u>do</u> funny things to me. (SMT/007)

At least one constraint is documented from the literature on creoles (e.g. Patrick 1999: 203). Overt, typically preverbal, markers are expected for past actions where the order of verbs in the discourse is inverted from the actual order of events as they took place in the past. This is clearly evident in Example 6.6a where the action of "blowing out" holes in the hills of Somerset would surely have come *before* the holes themselves. Note that this is a context where the standard English past perfect could be used. The other context where overt markers are expected in creoles is with stative verbs with past temporal reference, as in Example 6.6b–c (Bickerton 1975: 70). In reality, nonstative temporally anterior verbs are extremely rare – notice that the best example I could find in the Somerset data is not even rendered with a preverbal *did*, but a preterite. Past reference statives occur more frequently.

Example 6.6

(a)   Used to come down over the hill, you-see and they could fire back into the hill. Made lots of holes with their mortars. Holes, you-know, where they *blew out.* (SMT/002)
(b)   Nobody *did know* how to look after that proper. (SMT/002)
(c)   Rabbit stew *did have* the dough-boys and all in, lovely. (SMT/013)

We can quantitatively model the behavior of *did* testing specifically for the contribution of all these constraints. Then, using the method of comparative sociolinguistics, we can assess the statistical significance, constraint hierarchy, and relative strength of factors in each analysis. Interpreting these results from a historical and comparative perspective will provide evidence for how the variation can explained.

Table 6.2 shows two logistic regression analyses testing these linguistic constraints differentiated by source (English vs. Creole) to the probability of *did* in past habitual contexts in Somerset and Samaná (abstracted from Jones and Tagliamonte 2004: 112, Table 1).

Answers to the following questions provide the evidence for assessing the similarities and differences in the grammar of variable (*did*) in these varieties:

• Which of the factors is statistically significant?
• What is the relative contribution of the linguistic features selected? Is it strong or weak?
• What is the constraint ranking of the categories within each factor?
• Finally, does this order reflect the direction reported in the literature?

Parallels will provide evidence that variable (*did*) is operating with the same systemic organization. These correspondences are taken to infer that these two data sets have inherited the patterns from a common source. When such parallels multiply across factors, each measure bolsters the evidence pointing toward a shared grammar. If the evidence is not parallel on a number of points then this mitigates the interpretation of shared correspondences. If there is are no parallels, then the analyst must seek other explanations. Interpretation must be tempered by the nature and depth of the correspondences. Table 6.3 summarizes the findings.

Of the constraints reported in the historical record on English dialects, Samaná and Somerset share not only the constraint ranking, but also statistical significance for three of them – parallel processing, adverb position, and clause type (indicated by ✓). Somerset and Samaná also share the direction of effect and statistical significance of the anteriority effect reported for creoles, but not their stativity.

Could these systematic patterns in the use of variable (*did*) have arisen independently in each of these locales? Preverbal tense, mood, and aspect markers may be indicative of universal and/or prototypical features of human language (Bickerton 1981). If so, then the parallels, however convergent, may simply reflect these pervasive mechanisms. Yet the subtle

Table 6.2 Logistic regression of internal factors contributing to the probability of *did* in past habitual contexts in Somerset and Samaná.

Historical constraints	Somerset Input 0.064 Total N = 3388			Samaná Input 0.062 Total N = 1047		
	FW	%	N	FW	%	N
Parallel processing						
Preceding *did*	0.85	27	222	0.80	25	24
Preceding other	0.47	6	3166	0.49	7	1019
Range	*38*			*31*		
Adverb position						
Preverbal	0.79	23	56	0.87	33	9
Other/none	0.49	7	3332	0.50	7	1034
Range	*30*			*37*		
Clause type						
Subordinate	0.60	10	513	0.68	16	139
Other	0.48	6	2875	0.47	6	904
Range	*12*			*21*		
Creole constraint						
Stativity/anteriority						
−Stative, +anterior	0.72	17	119	0.90	38	24
−stative, −anterior	0.55	8	1921	0.54	8	593
+stative, −anterior	0.40	4	1285	0.41	5	406
Range	*32*			*49*		

Source: Adapted from Jones and Tagliamonte 2004: 112, Table 1.

Table 6.3 Comparison of similarities and differences in internal linguistic features in Samaná and Somerset.

Variety	Historical			Creole	
	Parallel Processing	Adverb Position	Clause Type	Stativity	Anteriority
Somerset	✓	✓	✓	✗	✓
Samaná	✓	✓	✓	✗	✓

nature of the correspondences, in terms of distributional frequency, statistical significance, ranking of constraints, and relative strength of factors all point to the fact that the two varieties have the same grammar for affirmative periphrastic *did*. There is no documentation of the effects of adverb position and clause type observed here except in earlier varieties of English. Morever, they are dialect specific to the southwest. This supports the hypothesis that the patterns have English ancestry and the convergence of evidence argues further in favor of this interpretation.

Could the patterns be universal? With respect to parallel processing the two varieties are congruent. The fact that the same effects are reported both for many other varieties and for other linguistic features supports a universal explanation (see Scherre and Naro 1991). Another possible factor for universal status is the creole stativity/anteriority constraint. Neither Samaná nor Somerset pattern in the same way as predicted for English-based creoles with respect to the effect of stativity. Instead, they pattern along with English dialects, and both varieties share precisely the same constraint hierarchy. Thus, the available evidence suggests that this aspect of the constraint is not universal. The effect of anteriority however is shared – variable *(did)* is favored in [+anterior] contexts in Somerset and Samaná just as it is in Mesolectal Jamaican Creole (Patrick 1991). Is this universal? Since creoles exhibit this pattern and creoles have been argued to pattern with universals, such a result is suggestive. However, this possibility cannot be conclusively determined without further evidence.

Is there evidence for restructuring of the original patterns of variable *(did)*? Since the form is not reported outside the British Isles, there is no evidence to suggest it was inherited from some other source. While it is true that the Samaná speakers might have acquired this feature from the surrounding Caribbean creoles, none of the evidence unambiguously points in this direction either. Supporting this is the fact that research on other tense/aspect features in Samaná English has consistently demonstrated patterns distinct from creoles (e.g. Poplack 2000; Poplack and Tagliamonte 2001). Of course, such evidence alone is insufficient to discount diffusion from Caribbean creoles for the anteriority effect. However, the key fact that obviates this is the correspondence with Somerset. Even if the Samanese speakers had acquired this from surrounding English-based creoles, the fact that the same patterns are found in Somerset makes a strictly creole connection implausible. In sum, all of the evidence points to the observation that the use of variable *(did)* in Somerset and Samaná is the result of historical continuity and could only have arisen through community-internal transmission.

Taken together, these results also highlight that while the ranking of constraints may sometimes be universal (Wolfram 2000), linguistic features such as variable *(did)*, that involve different levels of grammar and multiple constraints, are complex enough to have embedded within them the tracks of dialect specific tendencies. Only attention to the multiplex of factors and the details of their operation can disentangle the nature and origin of each linguistic pattern. The results from this study corroborate Poplack and Tagliamonte (2001) in advocating the rigorous standards for cross-variety comparison outlined in Table 6.1.

The lines of evidence converge in demonstrating both the steadfast retention and systemic nature of periphrastic *did* in Somerset and Samaná. It is also important to note that even on the verge of extinction this dialect feature has retained complex diachronic patterns and systematic linguistic conditioning.

> Studies of actively changing grammatical features of the English language applied to enclave situations such as these underline the interplay between obsolescence, linguistic variation and language change and highlight the role of social isolation and community identity to understanding the complexities of the processes involved. (Tagliamonte 1997: 62)

Notice how much the shared retention of features is critical for establishing common ancestry. It is only when linguistic data of the appropriate nature exist that analysis can be performed that can determine the character of the diagnostic forms and functions. Because the sociohistorical record is often fraught with ambiguous interpretations it is often impossible to disentangle population mixes, proportions of different dialect speakers, and the myriad of different social influences of the time. Consequently a rigorous methodology and linguistic evidence is critical.

> **NOTE** What happens to constraint on variation in obsolescence? Some research suggests that variables at the end point of change will exhibit upheaval in the "natural ordering of constraint effects" (Wolfram and Schilling-Estes 1995: 711). Yet in Somerset and Samaná variable (*did*) continues to maintain a complex set of constraints and patterns of constraints that can be traced in the history of English even when the obsolescent variant, i.e. *did* + verb, has nearly disappeared from the grammar. Here is an opportunity for future research to weigh in on conflicting results.

Exercises

The following two exercises use the comparative method for diverse data sets for the purposes of answering distinct questions. Note the broad applicability of the method and the utility of logistic regression "to find basic similarities of grammatical systems and constraints on variation that may be masked by differences in frequency" (Cameron 1992: 315, 327; Tables 4 and 5).

Exercise 6.1   Interpreting comparative analyses across data sets

Code-switching vs. borrowing
The following data come from a study on language contact. This study was innovative in applying a comparative sociolinguistic analysis to the problem of distinguishing code-switching from borrowing (Budzhak-Jones and Poplack 1997). In this case the data have been partitioned into two types of nouns used by the same speakers, Ukrainian nouns and English-origin nouns. The dependent variable is nominal inflection (gender, number, and case), which is obligatorily expressed in large part by a single surface form, as in the inflection on *car* in Example 6.7:

Example 6.7

(a)	do	**cary,**	zastartuje	**car<u>u</u>**	ïde	dodomu
	to	car-<u>F.sg.Gen</u>,	starts	car-<u>F.sg.Acc</u>,	drives	home

"… goes to the car, starts the car and drives home"

The question is, do the nouns in these two data sets pattern the same or differently? Poplack and Budzhak-Jones hypothesize that if the English-origin nouns pattern like the Ukrainian nouns then they are patterning along with the recipient language and must be borrowed. If they pattern differently, then they must be code-switches.

Table 6.4 displays the results of two independent variable rule analyses of the contribution of factors to the probability of nonstandard inflection in monolingual Ukrainian nouns and English-origin singleton nouns in Ukrainian-English bilinguals' discourse. Square brackets indicate nonsignificance. Also note the lack of metalinguistic speech (e.g. audible pauses, false starts, commentary, etc.) with the Ukrainian nouns.

Table 6.4   Logistic regression analyses of nonstandard marking on Ukrainian and English origin nouns in monolingual Ukrainian conversations.

	Nouns	
	Ukrainian	English–origin
Corrected mean	0.075	0.186
Total N	261	239
Factor groups considered in the analysis:		
Number		
Plural	[ ]	[ ]
Singular	[ ]	[ ]
Gender		
[Masculine (M) required, M modifier]	0.60	0.64
[Non-M required, non-M modifier]	0.57	0.60
[M required, no modifier]	0.32	0.37
[Non-M required, no modifier]	0.14	0.17
Range	*46*	*47*
Case		
[Non-nominative (N) required, no modifier]	0.88	0.77
[N required, no modifier]	0.64	0.60
[Non-N required, non-N modifier	0.37	0.35
[N required, N modifier]	0.33	0.28
Range	*55*	*49*
Flagging		
Metalinguistic speech	–	0.79
Pause/False start	0.72	0.70
Demonstrative pronoun	0.50	0.72
No flag	0.48	0.36
Range	*24*	*43*

Source: Budzhak-Jones and Poplack 1997: 248, Table 12.

Question 1   The results reveal that variability in inflectional marking on Ukrainian nouns is conditioned by:
(a)   Number, case, gender, and flagging.
(b)   Case only.
(c)   Gender, case, and flagging.
(d)   Gender and case.

Question 2   Comparing Ukrainian nouns to English-origin nouns in Ukrainian discourse demonstrates that the strongest effect on nonprescriptive marking in both cases is:
(a)   Number.
(b)   Gender.
(c)   Flagging.
(d)   Case.

Question 3 For gender, which factors favor nonprescriptive marking across the two analyses?

(a) [Masculine (M) required, M modifier] and [Non-M required, non-M modifier]

(b) [M required, no modifier] and [Non-M required, no modifier].

(c) [Non-M required, non-M modifier] and [Non-M required, no modifier].

(d) [Masculine (M) required, M modifier] and [M required, no modifier].

Question 4 Examining the *hierarchy of constraints* for case:

(a) Modified nouns in non-nominative case show the greatest effect.

(b) Prescriptive case assignment is favored overall, with nominative cases contributing the least effect.

(c) Modified nouns show the greatest effect, while unmodified nouns show the least.

(d) Nonprescriptive case assignment is favored overall, with non-nominative cases contributing the greatest effect.

Question 5 Comparing the overall results for the Ukrainian-origin and English-origin nouns, what observation best describes the patterning?

(a) The *patterns* of variability in native Ukrainian and singleton nouns are different.

(b) The *patterns* of variability in native Ukrainian and singleton nouns are the same.

(c) The *patterns* of variability for gender and case are similar, but different for all other factors.

(d) The *lack* of patterning indicates that the two categories are different.

Exercise 6.2   Strong transfer, weak transfer or calquing

The following results were abstracted from a study on language contact in the South Pacific. This study was innovative in applying a comparative sociolinguistic analysis to the problem of how to track the emergence of structure in creole languages (Meyerhoff 2009: 310, Table 4).

The dependent variable is the realization of subjects and objects as overt or non-overt (absence). Note the alternation between the subject *they* and the object *Rambo* and the subsquent null realizations, as in Example 6.8.

Example 6.8

> Afta Ø oli karemaot Rambo long prisin Ø i kam kilim Ø, Ø I ded
> then Ø AGR take.out Rambo from prisin Ø AGR come kill Ø, Ø AGR dead
> "So (they) get Rambo out of prison, (and) (he) comes kill (him), (and then) (he) is dead."

In this case the data compare two different languages: Bislama, the creole, and Tamambo, the indigenous language. The question is whether there has been language transfer from Tamambo to Bislama. Let us focus on the realization of objects to consider this question.

Table 6.5 displays the results of two independent variable rule analyses of the contribution of factors to the probability of nonprescriptive inflection Tamambo and Bislama.

Table 6.5   Comparison of constraints on absence of free N/pronoun objects in Tamambo and Bislama.

	Tamambo			Bislama		
	Input.40 Total N = 147			Input.14 Total N = 869		
	FW	%	N	FW	%	N
Role of referent in preceding clause						
Subject	0.89	77	22	0.82	37	93
Direct object	0.87	81	37	0.90	62	217
Other argument	0.35	30	10	0.70	28	195
Not present	0.20	17	78	0.11	2	364
Range	*69*			*79*		
Type of possession						
Inalienable	0.71	54	39	0.35	21	134
Alienable	0.42	38	106	0.53	27	735
Range	*29*			*18*		

Source: Meyerhoff 2009: 310, Table 4.

Comparing the two analysis using the three lines of evidence answer the following questions:

Question 1   What is the difference between Tamambo and Bislama with regard to the effect of a referent in the preceding clause?

Question 2   What is the nature of the effect of type of possession?

Question 3   Which factor group has the strongest effect?

Question 4   Given Meyerhoff's criteria for interpreting language contact phenomena as weak transfer, strong transfer, or calquing, what type of language contact phenomenon is this?

Question 5   What conclusion do you hypothesize Poplack and Budzhak-Jones argued for in their paper?

Mini Quiz Answer

6.1   Q1: *c*

Background Reading

Bailey and Maynor 1985, 1989; Cameron 1992; Cukor-Avila 1997, 1999; Dubois and Horvath 2007; Fasold 1972; Hickey 2004; Holm 1975/1984; Horvath and Horvath 2003; Kurath 1928, 1939, 1949, 1964; Labov *et al.* 1968; McDavid 1985; Meyerhoff and Walker 2007; Montgomery 1989, 1997, 2001; Montgomery and Chapman 1992; Mufwene 1996b, 2000, 2001a,b; Mufwene *et al.* 1998; Otheguy, Zentella, and Livert 2007; Poplack 2000; Poplack and Meechan 1995, 1998a; Poplack and Tagliamonte 1999b; Rickford 1986a, 1990a,b, 1991, 1998, 1999; Rickford and Blake 1990; Singler 1991; Winford 1997, 1998; Wolfram 1969, 1999, 2000; Wolfram and Schilling-Estes 2004; Wolfram and Sellers 1999; Wolfram, Thomas, and Green 1997.

7

Phonological Variables

In this chapter, I consider how sociolinguistic patterns are reflected in phonological variation. Phonological variables are straightforward in the sense that they are obvious functional equivalents. When the context of the variation is a word, e.g. "asked" [æskt] and it alternates between one pronunciation and another, say [æks] vs. [æsk] vs. [æskt], there is little to dispute that the function is the same. While phonological variables can often be easy to circumscribe, e.g. variable (h) in English, others, such as variable (t) in British English, are influenced by so many factors that defining the envelop of variation can be quite tricky.

Variationist sociolinguistics was built on the study of phonological variation. The study of sound change, particularly vowels, mergers, and chain shifts, is the most well studied area of the field from Labov (1963) to Labov (1994, 2001a, 2010). I will not replicate the massive coverage of these phenomena in these (and other works) but focus in on two well studied and easy to analyze phonological variables – variable (t,d) and (ing). Phonological variation is highly sensitive to social influences, including social class, social network, education, and sex.

Phonological variation is featured in the famous song "Let's Call the Whole Thing Off" written by the Gershwins in 1937, which compares various regional dialects, as in Example 7.1.

Example 7.1

> You say *eether* and I say *eyether*. You say *neether* and I say *nyther*; Eether, eyether, neether, nyther. Let's call the whole thing off! You like *potato* and I like *potahto*. You like *tomato* and I like *tomahto*; *Potato, potahto, tomato, tomahto*! … Let's call the whole thing off!

The song highlights varying pronunciations of the vowel sounds [i], as in "neether" vs. [ay], as in orthographic "nyther," and [e] as in "tomato" vs. [ɑ:] as in "tomahto," represented here in "eye dialect," the representation of dialectal speech in nonstandard spellings (see Preston 1985). Vowels are one of the most highly variable aspects of English and are widely recognized as the prime means for differentiating dialects from one another (Wells 1982:

Variationist Sociolinguistics: Change, Observation, Interpretation, First Edition. Sali A. Tagliamonte.
© 2012 Sali A. Tagliamonte. Published 2012 by Blackwell Publishing Ltd.

178). Not surprisingly, the vast majority of studies of variation are based on vowels. Labov's research in particular has unearthed large-scale changes involving the vowel systems of the regional dialects of North American English (Labov 1991, 1994; Labov, Yaeger, and Steiner 1972). He has referred to these changes as "chain shifts," in which a group of related sounds changes at the same time. A key factor in Labov's chain shift hypotheses is the drive to maintain contrasts. As one sounds replaces another, the displaced sound shifts position to replace another sound and that sound shifts to replace another, and so forth. Labov divides contemporary North American English into three dialect regions based on this rotation of vowel sounds marking dialect differences that are the "most important feature on the landscape of American English" (Labov 1991).[1] The focus on vowel systems in North America differs from the situation in the UK, where there is a long history dialect of differentiation and a wider range of phonological, phonetic, and suprasegmental variables have been studied. In other languages with important dialect differentiation more work is also done by consonants, e.g. Arabic's variable (q) (e.g. El Salman 2003) and variable (θ) (e.g. Nahar Al-Ali and Mahmoud Arafa 2010). These differences across languages suggest that the type of variation that can manifest from one context to the next may also vary in systematic ways.

Foulkes and Docherty (2006: 410–419) provide an inventory of different types of phonological and phonetic variables. In each case the variation also has complex social correlates.

- variation in the composition of the phoneme inventory
  - Scots dialects have rare phonemes /x/ and /ʍ/ which now alternate with the standard English variants (see Lawson and Stuart-Smith 1999; Stuart-Smith 1999a)
- variation in the phonotactic distribution of phonemes
  - *r*-ful (rhotic) vs. *r*-less (nonrhotic) dialects
- lexical distribution of phonemes
  - North vs. south in England is marked by many of these contrasts, e.g. the pronunciation of /a/ and /ɑ:/ in words like *path, bath, class* (note the variation in Example 7. above) (see Boberg 2009)
- allophonic variation (the most common type of phonetic variables)
  - in Newcastle, UK, stops are variably realized as plain oral plosives but can also be largynealized and glottal (e.g. Milroy *et al.* 1994; Stuart-Smith 1999a)
  - in varieties around the world /l/ has vocalized to various degrees (see Horvath and Horvath 2003).

Research on /p,t,k/ in northern English varieties (Derby and Newcastle) has demonstrated some voiced variants and higher rates of glottalization among young people as new variants diffuse across Britain. Moreover, acoustic analysis shows that there is systematic variation in the speech community of a spectrum of other variants each with their own sociolinguistic profile, for example the voiced variants are correlated with older men while the pre-aspirated type are strongly associated with young women. It appears that everyone marks their place in the social hierarchy in phonetically distinguishable ways in the United Kingdom. Foulkes, Docherty, and their associates have conducted numerous studies of this and other phonological variables, all with rich data, analyses, and interpretation.

Variable (t,d)

In 1999, my colleague Ros Temple and I embarked upon a study of variable (t,d) in York English (Tagliamonte 2005). We anticipated that we would find all the widely attested constraints on this variable but we were in for a surprise. Variable (t,d) has been one of the most frequently studied variables in Variationist Sociolinguistics. It has been variously referred to as: *-t,-d* deletion, coronal stop deletion, consonant cluster simplification, past inflection, and probably a few others. It refers to the deletion of coronal stops from word-final consonant clusters, as in Example 7.2.

Example 7.2

(a) We was walking down Micklegate and we grabbed him and *grabØ* this lad as well. (YRK/079)
(b) When I changed it, I *dropØ* the other. (YRK/044)
(c) During the *weekenØ* we'll usually go into town. During the week, we'll stay around here. (YRK/093)
(d) It's a good job I hung *arounØ* 'cos I was destined to take him. He was destined for me to take him around. (YRK/027)
(e) I did a college course when I *lefØ* school actually, but I left it because it was business studies. (YRK/008)
(f) I was told afterwards. No, I was just *tolØ*. (YRK/057)

The earliest examinations of this linguistic variable date back to studies of AAVE in the 1960s, but variable (-t,d) is not restricted to this variety. It occurs in virtually every variety of English ever studied. Although it is variable across varieties of English, the variability is not solely attributable to universal phonetic factors but has consistently been shown to be a function of higher levels of linguistic organization, specifically the morphophonology. This makes it an ideal testing ground for exploring phonological and morphological processes in lexical phonology (Guy 1991b) or syllabification (Santa Ana 1996).

> **NOTE** Lexical phonology is an approach to phonology in which the lexicon is conceived as a series of ordered levels. Each level is the domain for certain phonological or morphological processes. The interaction between phonology and morphology is accounted for by word building processes. Syllabification refers to how words are separated into syllables. This differs across dialects and across languages and also differs depending on morphological separation or phonological separation, e.g. "learning" as "learn-ing" vs. "lear-ning."

Research suggests that there is considerable uniformity to the patterns underlying this variable. According to Guy's Lexical Phonology-based explanation (Guy 1991a) all varieties of English should behave the same with respect to morphologically conditioned variability. However, many of the varieties that have been studied have a strong American urban bias with some rare exceptions, e.g. Sydney, Australia. A few studies are based on specific ethnic groups, some of them second-language or first-generation L1 speakers of English. This means that we still do not have a broad understanding of variable (t,d) in the global community.

The studies to date show that variable (t,d) is a stable, sociolinguistic variable, i.e. it is not in the process of change. It qualifies as a linguistic marker because it correlates with style or formality, but not socioeconomic class or apparent time. The linguistic patterns underlying variable (t,d) are its major "claim to fame," and it is apparent that variable (t,d) has been present in the language for some time (see Poplack and Tagliamonte 2001: 110–114). The complexity and internal systematicity to these patterns has been one of the best demonstrations in the literature of the intricate link between variation and morpho-phonological processes in language.

Linguistic Patterns

Variable (t,d) is conditioned by three linguistic factors: (1) the preceding and (2) following phonological contexts, and (3) the morphological structure of the word.

Following Phonological Context
The nature of the phonological segment which follows the final /t,d/ is consistently the strongest linguistic constraint. Obstruents (and nasals) trigger the most deletion, followed by liquids, then glides, and finally following vowels or pauses (the latter two contexts varying in order between dialects). Thus, there will be more simplified clusters in contexts such as Example 7.3, below, than in Example 7.4.

Example 7.3

    (a)   I was so *shockØ* by it. (YRK/049)
    (b)   We *handcuffØ* somebody to somebody in a pub in York once and dropØ t'key down t'drain. (YRK/079)
    (c)   How my *husbanØ* came to drive the cattle lorry. (YRK/002)

Example 7.4

    (a)   I've been *bombed*, I've been *shelled*, I've been *torpedoed*. (YRK/076)
    (b)   We *lost* all our youth to the war. (YRK/086)
    (c)   He *laughed*. (YRK/076)
    (d)   Because two wheels had *popped*. (YRK/095)

Guy (1991a) found a similar order but with /l/ and /r/ behaving differently: specifically /l/ patterned with the obstruents in triggering high rates of deletion. This prompted him to suggest that the effect of the constraint is largely due to whether or not the consonant in question can resyllabify onto the following syllable: /tr-/ and /dr-/ are acceptable syllable onsets in English, which means, for example, that the final /t/ of went can resyllabify onto the onset of the first syllable of *round*, and is therefore less likely to be deleted than when followed by *lame*, where resyllabification is blocked by the nonacceptability of */tl-/ onset clusters. However, Labov (1997) demonstrates that a resyllabification analysis is not consistent with the constraint ranking within the following context or the phonetic quality of the output. For example, in his data nondeleted tokens of pre-vocalic /d/ were not produced with the same release as word-initial prevocalic /d/ and nondeleted tokens of /t/ followed by /r/ were never produced in the same way as the clusters which occur in words like train (i.e. with devoiced, "aspirated" /r/). Moreover, as he points out, glottal reflexes of /t, d/ frequently occur in word-final position, including in possible clusters. Most data that have been analyzed exhibit the overall stop/nasal > glide > vowel/pause hierarchy. However, the relative positions of /r/ and /l/ can be used to provide empirical support to either Guy's resyllabification account or Labov's refutation of it.

Preceding Phonological Context

The influence of preceding phonological context has been found to be weak in some varieties and strong in others; but it always appears to be involved in the variation. Labov (1989) found it to be a relatively weak linguistic constraint in AAVE, yet studies of Hispanic varieties find it to be strong. Santa Ana (1996) reports factor weights with a range as great as morphological class and greater than following segment for Chicano English (US citizens of Mexican descent) and Bayley found it to be the strongest constraint among Tejano speakers (Texans of Mexican or Latin American descent) (Bayley 1994: 314). Whatever the strength of the effect, the most common finding is that variable (t,d) varies roughly in proportion to the sonority of the preceding segment: less sonorous segments (stops and fricatives) tend to favor deletion while more sonorous segments disfavor it, which means that there will be more deletion in contexts such as in Example 7.5 below than those in Example 7.6, although exceptions to the hierarchy also occur. For example, /s/ consistently behaves differently from other fricatives, yielding the following pan-dialectal generalization: /s/ > stops > nasals > other fricatives > liquids (Labov 1989).

Example 7.5

(a) We'd have either beans on *toas* or toasted teacake. (YRK/001)
(b) They *stop* making bricks. (YRK/087)
(c) My *husban* came to drive the cattle lorry. (YRK/002)

Example 7.6

(a) We *handcuff* somebody to somebody in a pub in York once. (YRK/079)
(b) We got *involv* with a big exhibition. (YRK/087)
(c) I went to a school *call* Park Grove. (YRK/086)

Morphological Category

In addition to the phonological constraints, there is systematic variation according to the morphological identity of the word. Uninflected or monomorphemic words, such as in Example 7.7, undergo deletion at the highest rate and regular weak past tense forms, as in Example 7.8, at lesser rates.

Example 7.7

(a) He came for a *weeken* 'cos he'd had a fall. (YRK/007)
(b) I was earning eight *pound* a week. (YRK/007)

MONOMORPHEMES
mist, pact

PAST TENSE VERBS — semi weak
lost, left, told
PAST TENSE VERBS — regular weak
missed, packed

Figure 7.1   Constraint ranking of morphological categories on variable (t,d).
Source: Tagliamonte and Temple 2005: 285, Figure 1.

Example 7.8

(a)   They *knocked* it down. (YRK/007)
(b)   If the door *open* she saw me. (YRK/044)

Verbs which have stem vowel alternation in addition to a coronal stop past-tense suffix, as in Example 7.9, are referred to as "ambiguous verbs" by some and as "semi-weak" verbs by others. These unique verbs pattern in between. They have more deletion than regular past tense forms but less deletion than monomorphemes.

Example 7.9

(a)   But we still *kep* corresponding all the time. (YRK/080)
(b)   He *left* home early. (YRK/020)

Past participles, as in Example 7.10, are treated separately in some analyses; however, they tend to pattern with regular weak verbs.

Example 7.10

(a)   I've *work* for Laing's. (YRK/045)
(b)   I'd only *booked* in for forty-eight hours. (YRK/036)

The constraint ranking across these morphological types is as illustrated in Figure 7.1. The highest cluster simplification rate is found for monomorphemes, then an intermediate effect for semi-weak verbs, and the lowest rates are found for regular weak verbs.

The most extensive research on variable (t,d) has been conducted by Guy (1980, 1991a,b, 1997; Guy and Boberg 1997, 1989). A key contribution was his explanation of variable (t,d) within the framework of Lexical Phonology (e.g. Mohanan 1986). This went beyond the descriptive adequacy achieved by the standard Generative Phonology by offering an explanatory rationale for the interaction of morphological and phonological structure. I will not reproduce the detail of his functional/semantic argument. Basically, he argues that the /t,d/ suffix in past tense forms has a greater functional load than in a monomorpheme. Based on lexical phonology, different morphological categories are exposed to the variable deletion rule at two different levels. Monomorphemes enter the lexical phonological component with their final consonant clusters already formed, whereas the clusters in semi-weak forms are derived at level 1 and regular past tense forms at level 2. The monomorphemes are thus potentially exposed to the deletion rule three times, whereas the regular past tense forms can only be exposed to it once. This implies that there will be an exponential relationship between deletion rates in the two categories, with three times as much deletion in monomorphemes as in the regular inflected forms, and twice as much in the irregular forms. The strong prediction of such a model is that, if the morphological structure of word classes is the same across varieties, then the same patterning for *t,d* deletion should hold across varieties, at least for native speakers.

Guy's model was subsequently tested by Santa Ana (1996: 275) on Chicano English and received "solid, independent confirmation." Guy and Boyd (1990) found differences between Philadelphia speakers of different ages in the patterning of *-t,d* deletion in the semi-weak class, which they took to indicate that their younger speakers were analyzing them as monomorphemes, whereas the older speakers had a bimorphemic analysis. It is not inconceivable that the morphology of the past-tense forms in this limited, unproductive verb class should be treated differently in different dialects as well as differing across age groups, but there is less reason to assume cross-dialectal differences in the regular past-tense forms. Thus the prediction that arises from research on variable (t,d) is that there will be a robust difference between rates of deletion in regular past-tense versus monomorphemic forms, with semi-weak forms patterning either with the monomorphemes or intermediately between the other two classes.

Summary, Variable (t,d)

Given the consistency of early research findings on variable (t,d) we can make informed hypotheses that predict how variable (t,d) will pattern in new data. First, since variable (t,d) seems to exist in a staste of stable variation in English, one would expect this stability to persist. A large corpus representing a speech community should exhibit a horizontal line if variable (t,d) is plotted by frequency in apparent time. Second, variable (t,d) is a known linguistic marker. Therefore, males can be predicted to have a higher frequency of simplified clusters than females (the gender effect) and lower status groups will have a high frequency than high status groups (the class effect). Third, the well-known linguistic constraints which underlie variable (t,d) can be predicted to obtain across varieties and potentially within sub-groups of the same community. However, there are two phonological constraints and one grammatical constraint. Will all three endure across varieties?

How might these hypotheses be tested? Take a corpus representing a speech community. Examine the use of variable (t,d) according to speaker age (apparent time). What can you expect to find? Figure 7.2 plots the overall distribution of simplified clusters in two large-scale samples taken from two cities, York, England (c. 1997) and Toronto, Canada (c. 2003–2004).

The first prediction for variable (t,d) is confirmed. The pattern in apparent time is relatively level in both communities.

Next, we might predict that variable (t,d) in Toronto would also exhibit the well-known sociolinguistic correlates, including a gender effect and an effect of formality. Figure 7.3 shows the distribution of simplified clusters in Toronto, but now separates the male and female speakers.

Figure 7.4. shows the same analysis of the York data.

While the Toronto data exhibit no sex effect in any age group, the York data reveal an interaction between speaker age and sex. Among the middle-aged York speakers there is a visible sex effect such that males tend to use simplified clusters more than females. The same

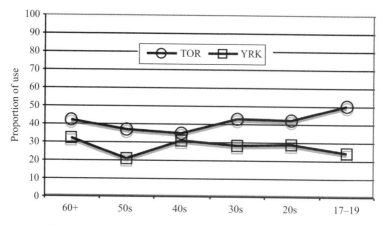

Figure 7.2 Overall distribution of simplified clusters of variable (t,d) in York, UK (c. 1997) and Toronto, Canada (c. 2003–2004).

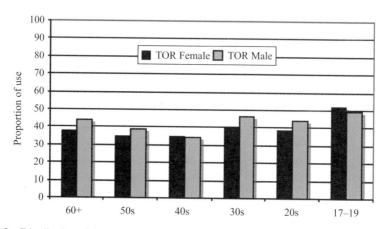

Figure 7.3 Distribution of simplified clusters for variable (t,d) by gender and age in Toronto, Canada.

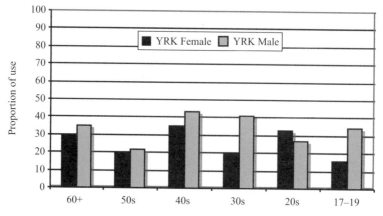

Figure 7.4 Distribution of simplified clusters for variable (t,d) by gender and age in York, UK.

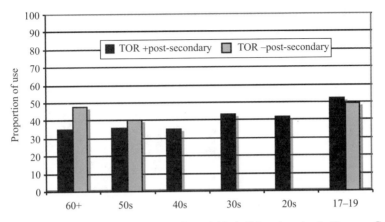

Figure 7.5 Distribution of simplified clusters for variable (t,d) by education in Toronto, Canada.

is true among the late adolescents (the 17–19 year olds). However the 20 year olds and the older generations (50+) have no sex effect. These findings reveal that variable (t,d) is not doing much social work in Toronto, but it has some kind of social value in York.

Mini Quiz 7.1

Q1 Which of the following are characteristics of male speech?
  (a) Males show a greater sensitivity to socially evaluative linguistic forms.
  (b) In careful speech men use fewer stigmatized forms than females.
  (c) Males are more sensitive than females to the prestige pattern.
  (d) Men are sensitive to covert prestige norms.
  (e) Males show more awareness of prestige norms in their attitudes toward speech.

Of course, these displays do not reveal the effect of the standard language which can, in part, be measured by education level. Figures 7.5. and 7.6 plot the distribution of variable (t, d) by education level in each community.

Figures 7.5 and 7.6 expose a marked difference in the social fabric of Toronto and York respectively. Notice that some bars are missing. This is due to the fact that in York many speakers have no post-secondary education and in Toronto individuals without post-secondary education exist only among the 17–19 years olds and among the 50+ year olds. Interestingly, the two extremes of the age spectrum show both similarity and difference. In York and Toronto the oldest generations are parallel in exhibiting an education effect for variable (t,d): simplified clusters occur most often among less educated speakers. However, among the youngest generation (17–19 year olds) there is a contrast. In York, simplified clusters are the mark of education, while in Toronto there is no education effect.

Phonological Variables

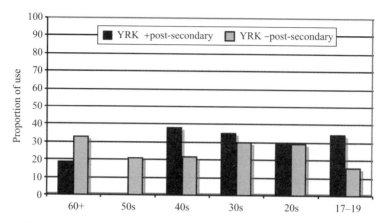

Figure 7.6 Distribution of simplified clusters for variable (t,d) by education in York, UK.

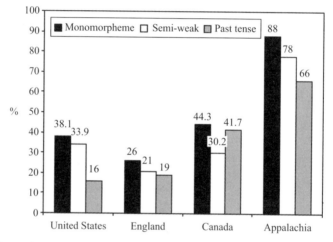

Figure 7.7 Comparison of frequency of simplified clusters by grammatical category across communities.

Both distribution by sex and education reveal marked social differences across communities, but will the strong underlying linguistic patterns of North American studies prevail? Recent work on variable (t,d) in British English has shown differences of consequence between North American and British varieties of English. While the effects of preceding and following phonological segment are parallel, the pattern according to morphological category is contrastive. Figure 7.7 shows a comparison of simplified clusters in past tense verbs, semi-weak verbs, and monomorphemes in the United States (Guy 1991b), Appalachia (Hazen 2002), and England (Tagliamonte and Temple 2005).

Figure 7.7 shows that the pattern of variation for variable (t,d) is somewhat different across communities. In the United States past tense forms are reduced least often while monomorphemes and semi-weak verbs have similarly high rates. However, in northern England monomorphemes have the highest rates, but there is nothing to differentiate semi-weak verbs and past tense verbs. In Canada monomorphemes are also high for simplified clusters, but regular verbs seem strangely elevated. This may be due to the higher education level of the speakers, as we saw earlier in Figure 7.5, or it may indicate a dialect difference. A study of Appalachian English (Hazen 2002) reveals that the frequency of simplified consonants is far higher than in the earlier research on North American varieties. While the strong effect of monomorphemes seems to hold in this variety, here too verbal elements are less distinct than in the early studies of variable (t,d). If these differences are real, then it seems likely that other varieties of English will provide important new insights into variable (t,d) in the future.

> **NOTE** In northern varieties of British English forms such as *telt* for "told" and *selt* for "sold" are common, e.g. Tom Winter *telt* us that (MPT/032). How might this impact the grammatical category effect on variable (t,d)?

Variable (ing)

The first studied and perhaps most famous linguistic variable in the quantitative study of linguistic variation and change is variable (ing) in English, and its alternation among variants for orthographic "ing," excluding monomorphemes, e.g. *thing*, as in Example 7.11.

Example 7.11

(a) We were *having* [ŋ] a good time out in what we were *doin'* [n]. (YRK/031)
(b) I've said there'd be *somethin'* [n] on her desk by nine o'clock tomorrow *morning* [ŋ]. (YRK/041)
(c) I'm just *startin*[n] at the *beginning*[ŋ] of this episode. (YRK/080)
(d) So they're *investigating*[ŋ] ways of *puttin*[n] up a fire-wall. (YRK/040)

The standard variant is a velar nasal [ŋ]; however, at least two variants involve the alveolar nasal, but use different vowels, i.e. [In] and [in] as well as variants with a velar stop, [iŋk] and [iŋg].

Variable (ing) was the first linguistic variable to be studied quantitatively. The first quantitative study of this variation was conducted in the United States in the late 1950s (Fisher 1958). This was followed quickly by a series of early studies of the (ing) variable in the United States (Labov 1966; Wald and Shopen 1981), Australia (Horvath 1985; Shnukal 1978; Shopen 1978), and Britain (Labov 1989; Ramisch 1989; Trudgill 1972b). It is said to occur in virtually all varieties of English and it has become one of the most widely studied features of the English-speaking world (Chambers 2002a: 120; Petyt 1985: 174).

Variable (ing), like variable (t,d), is considered a stable sociolinguistic variable. This means that the feature is not undergoing linguistic change and therefore a correlation with age is not expected. Yet Horvath's (1985: 97) study in Australia demonstrated that [n] was a feature correlated with teenagers. Similarly, Labov's work in New York City found that [ŋ] is sensitive to age. Such findings hint at one of the other well-known sociolinguistic patterns, age grading. Yet, like variable (t,d), there is more to variable (ing) than sociolinguistic correlations..

Historical Perspective

The suffix *–ing* evolved during the Middle English period from the coalescence of at least two different grammatical forms – a present participle and a verbal noun (Visser 1963–1973: 1081).

> **NOTE**   Do you know when "Middle English" was? How about "Old English"? What time period is represented by Shakespeare's language? Dickens' language? See Appendix B to put the historical periods of English in perspective.

Present Participle
Prior to Middle English, the Old English form of the present participle was *-ende*. During the Middle English period there is a gradual disappearance of this form and its variants as they were gradually replaced by [n]. This came about through a series of weakening processes, beginning with the vowels in /ende/ and /inede/ reducing to schwa, then loss of the final schwa, then simplification of the final *–nd* cluster in unstressed syllables to arrive at [n].

Evolution of the present participle ending: Middle English

- /ende/ /inede/   reduction of /e/ to schwa   [əndə]
- loss of final schwa   [ənd]
- simplification of [nd] cluster   [nd]

Thus, there is actually "no dropping of 'g'" in present participles, as this variation is often conceived to be. The form [n] is the relic, an old form of the present participle.

Verbal Noun
In Old English there was a verbal noun which was formed with the ending *–ung* (Labov 1989: 87). In Middle English it began to be spelled *-ing* or *-ynge*.

Evolution of the verbal noun ending: Middle English

/ung/   becomes /ing/ in Middle English
[ŋ] becomes [n]

Whether this form of the verbal noun's suffix was a direct descendant of the Old English verbal noun or was formed on analogy with it, the capacity of this *–ing* suffix to operate in all nouns with similar configurations continued. Simultaneously, from the same time period, there has also been an independent tendency for the velar nasal [ŋ] to be pronounced with its alveolar relative [n] (Visser 1963–1973: 1083).

The Expansion of the –ing Form
The two independent origins of the *–ing* form converged with the concomitant expansion of the use of the *–ing* ending which displaced all the other endings that had been there before. These developments result in what Visser (1963–1973: 1097) describes as "an extraordinary expansion of the function range of the form in *–ing*." The changes had a distinct pattern of diffusion in Britain. For example, the metamorphosis of the present participle ending *–ind* into *–ing* originated in southern Britain (Visser 1963–1973: 1096). It took some time for the

ending *–ing* to spread north into the Midlands where *-end* was in used, and then further north where *–and* was the usual spelling. This long process of diffusion led to a proliferation of different renditions of the suffix during the Middle English period. As Visser (1963–1973) describes it, there was: "A bewildering medley of different spellings all over the country."

Development of Social Evaluation

By the eighteenth century, substitution of [n] for *–ing* was very common but it was not highly regarded. For example Rice (1765) refers to the [n] variant as "a vicious and indistinct Method of Pronunciation, and ought to be avoided" (Jespersen 1961a: 356). Despite such admonishments, [n] also had a certain degree of prestige. Jespersen, for example, refers to it as "fashionable" (Jespersen 1961: 356). Rhymes from various authors, as in Example 7.12 and Example 7.13, support this interpretation.

Example 7.12

(a) Garrick, 1777, *flirt:n'* rhymed with *curtain*; *willing* rhymed with *villain*
(b) Byron, early 1800s, *children: bewildering*
(c) Shelley, early 1800s, *pursuing: ruin* (Jespersen 1961a: 356)

Example 7.13

(a) For who wou'd grudge to spend his *Blood in* /His honour's Cause? Quoth she, A *Pudding*. (1663 Butler, *Hudibras*, I, iii, 219) (Visser 1966: 1085)
(b) The first maxim a couple of lines may be *said in*,/ if you are in a passion, don't swear at a *wedding*. (1840 R.H. Barham, *Ingoldsby Legends* (World's Classics) p. 405) (Visser 1966: 1085)

According to Jespersen (1961a: 356) "The aristocracy, and 'horsy' people generally, are said to favour [n]." He adds, however, that it, "is certainly less frequent among ladies." In such statements, we see the beginning of observations suggesting that variable *–ing* was socially conditioned. In Early Modern English variable (ing) was geographically split in the UK – [ŋ] predominated in the south and [n] in the north (Labov 1989: 88), with the [n] form used "especially in Scotch and Irish English" (Visser 1966: 1084).

Sociolinguistic Patterns

In modern studies the sociolinguistic patterns of variable (ing) are famous, particularly its correlation with sex and social class. Consistent findings for variable (ing) are that females favor [ŋ] while males favor [n]. The [ŋ] variant is correlated with formality in speaking: in careful styles in perhaps all standard accents of English, this suffix is pronounced [ŋ], that is with the velar nasal consonant (Chambers 2003: 121–126). In contrast, [n] is associated with working class and less education. For example, Fischer (1958) suggests that [ŋ] "symbolizes female speakers and [n] symbolizes males." Labov's (1972c: 243) study in New York City and Trudgill's (1974a) study in Norwich (England) were foundational for documenting the social patterns of linguistic variables in the speech community. Labov observed that the use of [ŋ] demonstrates that women are "being more sensitive than men to overt sociolinguistic values." The famous figures illustrating the structured layering of variable (ing) by speech style and social class should by now be enshrined in the LVC hall of fame (see Labov 1966: 259, Figure 10.7; Trudgill 1974: 92, Figure 14). Remarkably, Trudgill found precisely the same type of structure and social layering in England. There was an increase in [ŋ] forms from everyday speech to more formal styles, suggesting that the *-ing* variable "is a very good indicator of social context" (Trudgill 1974a: 92). Further, stylistic variation was found to be greatest in the case of the Upper Working Class (Trudgill 1974a: 92). Trudgill argues that this is due to the linguistic insecurity of this sector of the population. This interpretation is echoed in Trudgill's association of [ŋ] with female speech, which has evolved into an association of the variants with particular sociosymbolic value – [ŋ] is prestigious; while [n] holds covert prestige. Even into the 2000s sociolinguists report that in careful styles, in perhaps all standard accents of English, this suffix is pronounced [ŋ] (Chambers 2003: 122). This is antithetic with the association of [n] with the aristocracy in the eighteenth century, which suggests that the social value of variants may change from one time to the next. This is the type of indexing of linguistic variants that third wave sociolinguists are interested in (e.g. Campbell-Kibler 2009) (see also Chapter 2).

> **NOTE**   The sociolinguistic value of a variant is its correlation with social meaning. Social meaning can vary due to any number of broad sociocultural factors (sex, education) or specific local attributes (nerds, geeks), or both.

Given the contemporary social class associations for variable (ing) it is reasonable to expect that education would influence the variation between [n] and [ŋ] as well – those speakers with more education would be expected to use more of the velar variant and those with less education, more of the apical variant. Variable (ing) is considered a stable sociolinguistic variable. This means that a correlation with age is not expected – and, in fact, correlation with speaker age is rare. Such findings hint at other types of linguistic change that may be lurking in the distribution and conditioning of variable (ing).

Linguistic Patterns
In addition to the frequently attested sociolinguistic patterns associated with variable (ing), more recent studies cast a different light on variable (ing). A host of linguistic constraints also underlie this variation, including the effect of preceding and following phonological context, number of syllables in the word, type of word, etc. I will focus here on only one – the grammatical category of the word containing *–ing*. Houston's (1985: 110) research on cities across Britain found that when the *–ing* suffix occurred in nominal categories (e.g. nouns and adjectives) the [ŋ] suffix was more frequent, while less nominal categories (e.g. progressives and gerunds) had more of the apical [n] suffix. Houston explained this result with reference to the historical facts about variable (ing). She argued that "the modern *–ing*/*-in* alternation had a continuous history originating in the Old English verbal noun and participle" (cited in Labov 1989: 88–89). The conditioning of the alternation between [n] and [ŋ] could thus be traced back to the origins of the *–ing* suffix in the English language. In fact, the variability could be explained as a continuation of alternations from older stages in the history of the language, which over the centuries had been transformed into social and stylistic variation (Labov 1989: 87).

The interplay between social and linguistic factors on variable (ing) may prove definitive in interpreting and explaining this frequent and ubiquitous linguistic variable. Which factors are the explanatory ones in which community, and under which conditions? As with variable

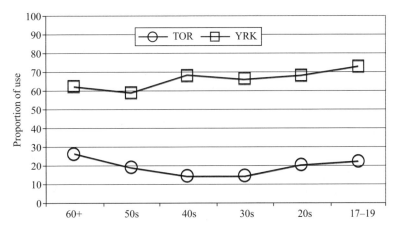

Figure 7.8 Overall distribution of alveolar variants of variable (ing) in York, UK (c. 1997) and Toronto, Canada (c. 2003–2004).

(t,d) the grammatical conditioning is assumed to operate similarly across varieties (Labov 1989: 87). However, despite the large number of studies on variable (ing), even in the early 2000s this information remains geographically and socially circumscribed with an over-representation of varieties in the United States, in Australia, and in Britain. (This is also true of variable (t,d).) Even in these countries, the data come from a small number of regions and with the exception of Trudgill's (1974b) study these have all been based on relatively standard varieties. Trudgill's (1974b) study targeted Norwich while Houston's targeted only six speakers per locale across a wide range of British cities (Houston 1985). Early quantitative studies of variable (ing) tested sociolinguistic constraints, but not linguistic ones. Houston (1985) and Labov (1989) focused on internal grammatical constraints, but not social ones.

Analysts have still not answered all the questions that remain about variable (ing). Variable (ing) is a sociostylistic variable in North America, but it is grammatically constrained in the United Kingdom. It will be interesting to discover what its characteristics are in locations and speech communities *other* than those that have already been studied.

Summary, Variable (ing)

Given the consistency of early research findings on variable (ing) we can predict (or at least make reasonable hypotheses about) how variable (ing) will pattern in new data. First, like variable (t,d) it is one of the prototypical stable sociolinguistic markers of English. It should exhibit a monotonic pattern in apparent time. Further, males can be predicted to have a higher frequency of [n] than females (Principle 2). Second, given the findings in New York and Norwich, lower social status groups, i.e. the working class or less educated speakers, can be predicted to have a higher rate of [n] (the class effect). Third, underlying the sociolinguistic patterns there is a longitudinal history of weakening and regional variation that might be expected to influence variation as well.

This hypothesis can be tested by examining the distribution of variant forms in a representative corpus from a speech community. This should reveal a stable frequency of variants in apparent time. Figure 7.8 plots the overall distribution of the alveolar variant in York (c. 1997) and Toronto (c. 2003–2004).

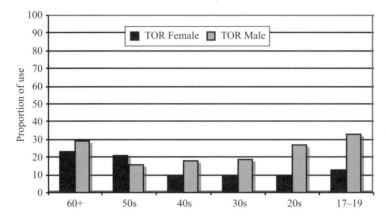

Figure 7.9   Distribution of alveolar variants for variable (ing) by gender and age in Toronto, Canada.

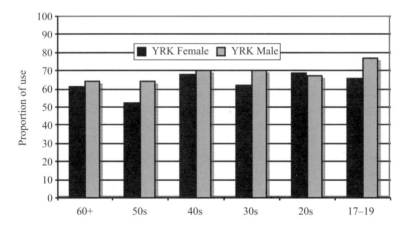

Figure 7.10   Distribution of alveolar variants for variable (ing) by gender and age in York, UK.

The prediction for variable (ing) is confirmed. As with variable (t,d), the pattern in apparent time is level in both communities. It is immediately apparent however that the overall rate of [n] is much higher in York than in Toronto. This distinguishes variable (ing) from (t,d). What explains this difference?

Given the highly divergent frequencies of variable (ing) in these communities, we might wonder if the same sociolinguistic patterns would obtain, namely a gender effect and an effect of formality. Figure 7.9 shows the distribution of the alveolar variant in Toronto, but now separates the male and female speakers. Figure 7.10 shows the same analysis of the York data.

In Toronto there is a notable correlation among the younger end of the age spectrum: males use the nonstandard variant more frequently. However, in York there is little of this effect overall. These results reveal that variable (ing) is a sociolinguistic variable in Toronto – at least among the people under 50 years of age – but not in York.

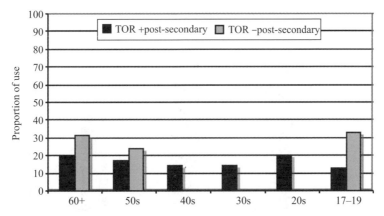

Figure 7.11 Distribution of alveolar variants for variable (t,d) by education in Toronto, Canada.

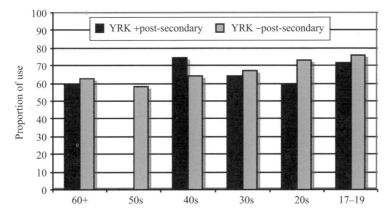

Figure 7.12 Distribution of alveolar variants for variable (ing) by education in York, UK.

Let us consider the effect of the standard language by measuring the use of the alveolar variant by education level. Figures 7.11 and 7.12 plot the distribution of variable (ing) by education level in each community.

Figures 7.11 and 7.12 corroborate the difference in social structure that was evident for variable (t,d). In Toronto, where one's education level is correlated with age, the alveolar variant occurs more frequently among those with no post–secondary education. In York, the alveolar variants do not seem to be influenced by education.

It now becomes a critical (and interesting) question to test the effect of grammatical category which taps into a longitudinal historical pattern from hundreds of years ago in the history of English. Will the historical linguistic patterns prevail?

In York the underlying grammatical constraints are so strongly implicated in variable (ing) that they override the social factors (Tagliamonte 2004b: 399). But what will the Toronto data show? Figure 7.13 presents a comparison across communities of the effect of nominal vs. verbal categories.

Figure 7.13 shows that, despite the widely divergent frequencies of the nonstandard variant, variable (ing) patterns similarly across communities. However, this view presents

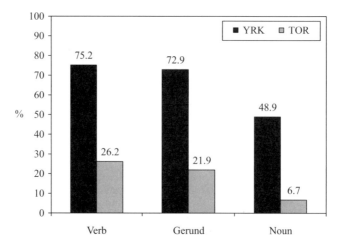

Figure 7.13   Comparison of frequency of alveolar variants of variable (ing) by grammatical category across communities.

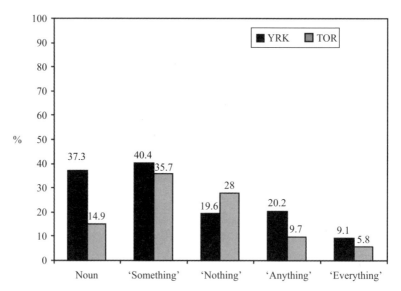

Figure 7.14   Pattern of alveolar variants of variable (ing) among nouns compared with indefinite pronouns in York and Toronto.

only the major categories – verbal elements, gerunds, and full nouns. If we now examine frequently occurring pronouns such as, *anything, everything, nothing,* and *something,* as in Figure 7.14, a contrasting pattern emerges.

Something and *nothing* have higher rates of the alveolar variant in Toronto than full noun phrases. In York *something* and full noun phrases behave the same way, in contrast to the others.

Whether these differences are social or linguistic remain in question; however, this demonstrates how important it is to code for these frequent nominal types separately. One wonders what may underlie the general noun vs. verb distinction in other places.

In sum, these two well-studied, stable linguistic variables reveal that inherent variability is pervasive in the communities studied. However, the constraints on the variables – their variable grammar – differ in subtle ways. Moreover, there are pointed differences in the social embedding in the speech community. Thus, while there is confirmation of the principles of linguistic change in large part, there are also distinct local differences. As with variable (t,d), it will be interesting to compare and contrast community-based patterns of variability in British and North American varieties of English and in contexts near and far-flung from the original source of the variation (i.e. northern England). How long do the grammatical constraints last in transplanted varieties? What does it take for an essentially linguistic pattern to become a feature for social stereotyping? How might the American vs. British contrast in perception lead to mistaken identity? These questions remain for future studies.

The consensus in early sociolinguistic research was that phonological variables, particularly those with stable patterns, exhibit established sociolinguistic and linguistic patterns. However, as we have seen, there is reason to believe that variables (t,d) and (ing) have much to offer in the differences that might be found across communities and contexts, and even within the speech communities in which they are found.

Tips for Studying Phonological Variables

Phonological variables can be among the simplest linguistic variables to study depending on which one you choose. They are more accessible. They are often abundant. They are found anywhere in the English-speaking world. Phonological variables have often been well studied in the past so there is extensive existing information to inform new research. However, because they are frequent they provide far more data than is possible to handle in a typical study. This means it is necessary to have a plan for exactly how to deal with the deluge of data. How many tokens will be extracted from each speaker? What procedure will be implemented so as to ensure adequate representation across types? Since phonological variables are so sensitive to formality, it may be necessary to extract from a certain part of an interview, say the second half, so that the data are less formal. Perhaps a study of a certain sector of the population is in order; if so, which one and why? How many tokens of each word will be included? Will it be important to restrict the number of tokens or is inclusion of every instance critical? (see Chapter 4). Each decision that is made must be weighed against the goals of the study. If the goal is to study the effect of lexical items on a variable process, it will be critical to include every instance of even the most frequent words in your analysis. However, this will exponentially increase the expenditure of energy in extracting and coding these items. The investment in effort depends on what the questions are and how the data is to be analyzed.

NOTE   Some phonological variables are quite rare. For example, Foulkes (1998) found only 82 tokens of intrusive [r] in 13 hours of material from 32 speakers (2.6 per speaker on average) with only 7 tokens of [r]. Intrusive [r] is the result of an overgeneralization. [r] is inserted when words that end in certain vowels are followed by another word beginning in a vowel, e.g. "law and order" becomes "lawr and order."

Ambiguity

A frequent problem that arises in the study of phonological variables is when the sound under investigation is obscured by a similar sound occurring in an adjacent context, either preceding or following. These are contexts where it is impossible to discern one variant or the other because the following consonant assimilates to the preceding one. For variable (t,d) these are contexts where the final alveolar occurs immediately before another alveolar, as in Example 7.14a–b. For variable (ing) these are contexts where (ing) occurs immediately before another velar, [g] or [k], as in Example 7.14c–d.

Example 7.14

> Variable (*-t,d*)
> (a) I can remember as a child um we seem<u>ed</u> [t]o have a lot more snow in those days. (YRK/031)
> (b) I peak<u>ed</u> [t]oo early. (TOR/010)
>
> Variable (*-ing*)
> (c) On your way out there, you're gett<u>ing</u> [g]igs consistently. (TOR/026)
> (d) They're in Wellington boots and garden<u>ing</u> [g]ear. (YRK/017)

These contexts are typically excluded in a variation study. Of course, they could be potentially very interesting for an acoustic study since a more meticulous analysis could tease apart the different types of assimilation and other phenomena that could arise under these circumstances.

Another problem is when independent phonological processes may also obscure the feature under investigation. For example, in narration in particular the simple past or simple present may be used, but with regular weak verbs in third person singular these are indistinguishable if consonant cluster simplification has occurred, as in Example 7.15.

Example 7.15

> So, your daddy came out. He *tapØ* the car ...[*taps* or *tapped?*] (YRK/040)

Were the analyst to include uninflected present-tense verbs, which may have arisen from past-tense verbs with phonologically deleted markers, this would distort the proportion of *-s* occurrence on the verb, in this case *turn*. However, it is also important to keep track of how often this situation arises. If hundreds of cases such as this were found in a data set this would be cause for pursuing an explanation.

Yet another potential case of ambiguity may arise in the case of elision, something that is prevalent in some varieties. For example, modals such as *would* may be elided in AAVE and in Caribbean and Guyanese creole, as in Example 7.16a. Thus, when contexts such as in Example 7.16b are found in your data, they should be excluded too.

Example 7.16

> (a) And he would come home late in the night, and when he Ø *come* home late in the night, he'd go and urine just by the post here. (Guyanese Creole) (Rickford 1987: 388)
> (b) I suppose you Ø *call* Hannah married, but she's not. (DVN/003)

Exceptional Distributions

In quantitative variation studies exceptional distributions are contexts which, by some quality of their nature (lexical type, phonological configuration, or participation in higher level variation), do not follow the regular trends of the linguistic variable under study.

In phonological variables exceptional distributions can involve haplology, where there is loss of one of two phonetically similar syllables in a sequence. Such contexts can also be reasonably excluded on the same grounds. This includes contexts where variable (ing) is added onto a verb as a suffix that ends in unstressed *-en*. In these cases, "the *-in* pronunciation causes it to end in two identical syllables," as in Example 7.17. Excluding such contexts ensures that each token in the analysis is a true suffix on the verb, not influenced at all by the base form of the verb (Wolfram and Fasold 1974: 143).

Example 7.17

    (a)   I went to the ope<u>nin'</u> night of that. (YRK/089)
    (b)   I'm frightened to death of thunder and light<u>nin'</u>. (YRK/011)

Tokens involving direct speech, as in Example 7.18, or metalinguistic commentary, as in Example 7.19, are often excluded from analyses of variation as well as impersonations, songs, or sayings that may have been learned by rote.

Example 7.18

    (a)   She was like, "we're *going* at the end of October and that's that." (YRK/289)
    (b)   And that Tracey from Coronation Street, she was always "*going playing* her tapes." (YRK/231)

Example 7.19

So she sang, "Three Blind Mice," you know the one… "and she cut off their tails with a *carving* knife." (YRK/200)

It may also be the case that certain forms are so phonologically reduced that the final syllable has coalesced with the stem. Those implicated in variable (ing) include contexts such as "going" which reduces to [gənə] or [gən], as in Example 7.20a, and "trying" which reduces to [traynə], as in Example 7.20b.

Example 7.20

    (a)   It's quite scary thinking he's *gonna* be a doctor. (YRK/250)
    (b)   I'm round the ship *tryna* to find him. (YRK/296)

These contexts are likely to be under the influence of independent processes of gram-maticalization (see Chapter 10).

Lexical Effects

Another source of exceptional distributions is lexical. One of the well-known practices in quantitative studies for the treatment of potential lexical effects is to have a type/token

Table 7.1   Distribution of simplified clusters for *just* in comparison with grammatical categories in York, UK and Toronto, Canada.

	York, England		Toronto, Canada	
	%	N	%	N
just	53	76	79	153
Monomorpheme	32	663	42	2794
Past tense	25	439	42	2560
Ambiguous	17	281	30	726

strategy in place to deal with lexical items that are much more frequent than others (Wolfram 1969: 58; 1993: 214). Among the advantages of this practice is the fact that it ensures an adequate distribution of types. A typical way to impose a control for lexical effects is to include only a certain number of tokens of a given lexical item per speaker. The limit has more to do with the demands of the research situation than with any principled number. For example, in my study of variable (t,d) in York English, when there were five tokens of any one lexical item from a single speaker, we did not extract anymore.

Perhaps the best example of an exceptional lexical distribution in a phonological variable is the word "and" in the study of variable (t,d). Most analysts exclude it. It is not difficult to understand why. Imagine the effort required to extract and code all the instances of "and" in a data set only to find that 99.9% of them are pronounced [æn], effectively skewing the data so that they must be removed from the analysis! This is why you must always be sensitive to what is in the data. Lexical items can skew the distribution in one way or another for any number of reasons. Of course, those lexical exceptions are interesting in and of themselves since they are likely behaving idiosyncratically for a reason, e.g. grammaticalization. The analyst should pay judicious attention to what arises from the data to spot such phenomena.

Consider the word *just* – a frequent lexical item that has a consonant cluster and is one of the members of the monomorpheme category typically studied in variable (-t,d). Does it skew the data? First, if there has been a type/token strategy in place, the number of tokens of *just* will not overwhelm the data set, but it will still likely be one of the more frequent lexical items in the data set. Coding for individual lexical items enables you to consider the behavior of *just* independent of its category. Consider the distributions in Table 7.1, where the frequency of t,d deletion for *just* [st] is compared to other monomorphemes and the other grammatical categories (past tense, e.g. *entered* [rd] and ambiguous verbs, e.g. *left* [ft]).

Table 7.1 shows that *just* has relatively high rates of t,d deletion compared to the other categories, even the other monomorphemes. Second, and most importantly, does the heightened rate of simplified clusters for *just* skew the data? This is a trickier question. The only way to find out is to examine the social and linguistic patterning of *just* and compare it to the rest of its cohort. If it behaves the same, albeit at heightened rates, then it does not skew the overall result. If it exhibits patterning distinct from other monomorphemes, then clearly something else is going on. Let's first consider the important effect of preceding phonological segment. *Just* is obviously a favorable context for deletion because the preceding sound is [s] and we know that [s] favors deletion the most. Is this due to the effect of *just* or

Table 7.2   Distribution of simplified clusters in *just* and other preceding [s] words.

	%	N
Preceding [s]	58.8	1295
Just	79	154

Table 7.3   Distribution of simplified clusters in *just* compared to all other contexts for following phonological context.

	Consonant		Vowel		Pause	
	%	N	%	N	%	N
All other contexts	58	2759	24.5	2245	26.8	926
just	91	107	50	34	62	13

to the effect of a preceding [s]? One way to answer this question is to assess how the frequency of deletion for *just* compares to the other words that have a preceding [s].

Table 7.2 shows that *just* has a simplified cluster 79% of the time, a relatively high rate compared to the overall distribution of 41.5%, but then preceding [s] contexts in general have high rates of simplified clusters, nearly 60%. Next, consider the effect of following phonological context in Table 7.3.

Table 7.3 and Figure 7.15 show that *just* patterns the same as all the other tokens. So far, it appears that despite its high deletion rates and frequent occurrence, *just* is patterning along with all the other tokens. Another clue is to plot the distribution of *just* by age of the speakers. Is the frequency of deletion stable over time just as it is with the other categories?

Figure 7.16 shows that simplified clusters with *just* are stable in apparent time parallel to simplified clusters overall. All these findings point to the fact that *just* is *not* swaying the overall effects of variable (t,d) in the grammar and that it behaves just like any other mono-morpheme in the variable context. Nevertheless, the high rates of deletion are intriguing, especially given the fact that this study imposed a type/token ratio on all lexical items.

> **TIP**   What are the implications of imposing a type/token restriction on words such as *just* in a study of variable (t,d)? A study using *all* the tokens of (-t,d) and exemplar theory to interpret the results may prove quite interesting.

In sum, exceptional distributions involving lexical effects are a key issue in the study of language variation and change, and they are particularly germane to the study of phonological variables due to the fact that individual words comprise the sample for study. They are also

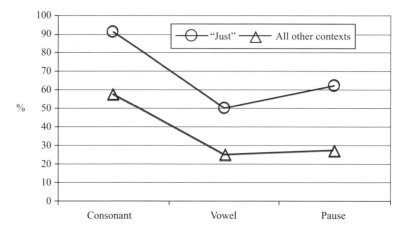

Figure 7.15   Distribution of simplified clusters for *just* and all other contexts by following phonological segment.

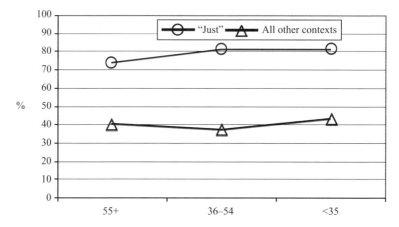

Figure 7.16   Distribution of simplified clusters in apparent time in Toronto English.

heavily implicated in exemplar theory. Lexical effects have been found in many levels of grammar. Research on the variable use of subjunctive morphology in Canadian French shows that a single verb, *falloir* "to have to," is the strongest predictor that prescriptive subjunctive verb morphology will appear instead of indicative morphology in contexts of subjunctive mood (Poplack 1992). Similarly, coding for lexical adverb in the study of variable (ly) revealed an important contrast between the adverb *really* and all other adverb types (Tagliamonte and Ito 2002). Coding for lexical adjective in a study of intensifiers enabled us to chart the grammaticalization of the incoming intensifier *so* (Ito and Tagliamonte 2003). In studies of variable (that) as a complementizer, the collocation of certain verbs and the null variant was critical for explaining the variation (Tagliamonte and Smith 2005; Torres, Cacoullos, and Walker 2009a,b) (see also Chapter 5). Knowing the distribution of your linguistic variable by lexical item enriches your research. If the lexical item is coded, then when you analyze your data, you can include or exclude certain lexical items depending on their impact on the overall distribution of variants. Alternatively, you can test for the effect of a lexical item by putting it in as a random effect in a mixed effects statistical model. The lexical item may contribute key information for interpreting and explaining linguistic features.

Selected Extraction

In some cases, extracting tokens of a linguistic variable requires a selective extraction process. In the study of variable (t,d) adequate representation of morphological classes was critical for the statistical analysis. Ideally, a healthy proportion of past tense forms, semi-weak verbs, and monomorphemes is required to uncover the differences among them. However, this presents a methodological problem. Monomorphemes with final clusters are extremely frequent. Past tense forms are also relatively frequent. However, semi-weak verbs that have a consonant cluster are relatively rare. Unless there is some way to restrict the number of monomorphemes and past tense forms generally and get an adequate number of semi-weak verbs a strategy is required. One way to deal with this methodological issue is to implement a strict protocol in which, for example, the first 20 tokens (or as many as exist) in each class are extracted for each speaker. In the case of variable (t,d) extracting from all available data is necessary to adequately represent the ambiguous verb category. Past participles with underlying consonant clusters can also be included in this procedure to assess whether they behave similarly or differently from regular past tense forms.

Phonetic Realization

In coding phonological variables using impressionist techniques there is always the question of how precisely to categorize the sounds. This is always a matter of degree since, of course, the speech signal is incredibly complex and nuanced. In fact, whether variable (t,d) is actually a case of deletion of segments or some other phonetic process is yet unknown. The analyst must make a choice of how to categorize variants, and further, this choice must be transparent so that future research may replicate it. In my own study of variable (t,d) in York English, we classified the tokens as zero realization or as one of nine different phonetic types. For the purpose of the analysis of t,d deletion, however (and consistent with previous studies), we considered any phonetic reflex of underlying /t,d/ to be a realization, and therefore a non-application of the deletion rule. A later study of variable (t,d) in Toronto English we simply coded for realization or not. This greatly simplified the coding process and enabled us to extract a far greater number of tokens.

Another issue in the study of phonological variables is whether to code for the underlying phonological context or the surface phonetic environment. In the York study, we did both. In coding the phonetic environment we took into account the full range of phonetic detail available from the audio recordings, including voicing, degree of closure, and whether or not preceding/following stops were released. However, since -t,-d deletion is a phonological rule operating on underlying forms, we assumed that the conditioning environments are the underlying segments preceding and following the target /t,d/, whatever their surface realization.

Elaborated vs. Simplified Coding

The analyst is always struggling between precision and efficiency. However, it is usually the case that more detail is better because you cannot go back and do things over again without taking a great deal of time (Tagliamonte 2006a: 101).

For example, in coding morphological category for variable (t,d) we discovered that there were considerably more categories in the data than had been reported in the literature. We differentiated between the major categories, true monomorphemes (e.g. *mist*), past tense forms of semiweak verbs (e.g. *kept, left*), and past tense forms of regular verbs (e.g. *missed*). However, we also coded separately for suppletive forms such as *found*, replacive forms such as *sent*, and preterite *went*. Past participles were also coded uniquely. In coding the category in this elaborate way, we were able to analyze the data with past participles as a separate category as well as included with other past tense forms. In this case, we were able to establish that they patterned similarly to the regular past tense forms so the decision was to treat them with past tense forms in the final analysis.

Research Questions Arising

Variable (ing) and variable (t,d) are the most widely studied linguistic variables in the world. Given this fact, you might think that sociolinguists know everything there is to know about them; however, certain important issues have arisen over the years that remain to be worked out.

The sociolinguistic and linguistic patterns underlying variable (t,d) and (ing) are well known but only in a limited number of varieties of English and under certain conditions. The vast majority of studies are based on American English, with only a few studies on other major varieties of English (e.g. in Australia, the United Kingdom, Canada), and a smattering of research on anything other than standard varieties (e.g. African American and Hispanic varieties in the United States, Jamaican Creole). What insights might arise from the study of variable (t,d) in more exotic varieties, in indigenized Englishes, in ethnic varieties within complex urban speech communities (see Walker and Hoffman 2010)? What is the social meaning of variable (-t,d)? How do individuals manipulate these variables as they move from one social context to another? Since we know a good deal about how these features pattern in broad surveys of speech communities, how might this assist future researchers in studying smaller groups within those same speech communities?

Frequently occurring phonological variables are also ideal features for the study of lexical effects and the testing of theories that argue for exemplar-based learning (e.g. Bybee 2002; Hay 2006a). For new students of sociolinguistics, variable (-t, d) and (ing) are excellent choices. They are found easily, are frequent, and require minimal amounts of data to do a viable study. They have a long history of study in the literature, making replication straightforward, both with respect to methodology and the testing of hypotheses. The only problem is that because of the foregoing issues they are relatively mundane as far as new discoveries are concerned. Still, new twists can be found. For example, variable (t,d) was a key variable for the study of local vs. universal factors in child language acquisition in northern Scotland (Smith, Durham, and Fortune 2007). Variable (ing) has recently been used to study how linguistic variation carries social meaning. Listening to American voices with varying frequencies of variable (ing), listeners judged the voices as less educated and less intelligent when they used [In] rather than [ŋ]. Further, these judgments came from the fact that the speakers were heard as having regional accents (Campbell-Kibler 2009). Another interesting aspect of variable (ing) is that its linguistic patterns link its history to the United Kingdom (see Tagliamonte 2004b). How might this be used to study the history of varieties whose ancestry is disputed?

> **NOTE**   Tackling a controversy is the best way to have fun while doing sociolinguistic research. Notice an issue? Identify a feature that will elucidate it. If an underlying linguistic pattern for variable (ing) marks it as northern British, then varieties with this origin can be predicted to retain this pattern, and varieties that do not should differ. Weigh in. Watch the sparks fly.

Exercises

Variable (ʔ) in York English

Glottal replacement of [t] by a glottal stop in words such as *butter, letter* has been reported in British English since the 1970s; however, by the early 1990s it was spreading very rapidly, not only in urban areas but also into regional dialects in the north of England (Milroy *et al.* 1994b).

In the city of York in 1997 younger speakers in the community were also using the glottal stop; however, there was considerable variation, as in Example 7.21, suggesting that there might be more to this variation than simply social influence.

Example 7.21

(a)   This holiday was better [ʔ] that I just had, and the one before that was better [t] than that one. (YRK/004)

(b)   I'm always shouting [ʔ] at drivers, calling them all names under sun you know. Most of them aren't repeatable [t] in polite c– um company. (YRK/025)

The data in Example 7.22 list a representative sample from two individuals.

Example 7.22

(a)
Nancy Heath, 004, Female, 20
[ʔ] he STARTED dancing with me
[t] the UNIVERSITY of Durham apparently
[t] I was a bit PATRIOTIC towards them
[ʔ] he was GETTING a bit funny
[t] One of them like he was DEVOTED to sport
[ʔ] I don't NOTICE the difference really
[ʔ] I think it'll be PRETTY good
[ʔ] a bit EXCITED about that
[t] knowing they'll all be EIGHTEEN
[t] There's a Ritzy in every major CITY isn't there?

(b)
Paul Gregory, 025, Male 23
[t] Black with red LETTERING

[ʔ] Um,PUTTING quick release alloy wheels on it
[ʔ] The small ring's got FORTY teeth on it
[ʔ] the big ones got FORTY-eight teeth on it
[ʔ] I've got another one that's a FORTY-two
[ʔ] Cyclo COMPUTERS yeah
[ʔ] He had like cyclo-COMPUTER on his bike
[t] It was probably actually SUPPORTING me behind us
[t] We end up going about EIGHTEEN
[ʔ] but it's a bit LIGHTER than mine

Exercise 7.1   Identifying phonological variables

Question 1   What possible trends do you notice in the data that might lead you to posit testable hypotheses for analysis?

(a) _____

(b) _____

(c) _____

Exercise 7.2   Interpreting phonological variables

A logistic regression analysis of age, sex, and social class for variable (ʔ) in York English is shown in Table 7.4.

Question 1   What is the strongest constraint on variable (ʔ)?

_____

Question 2   What does the constraint ranking for age show?

_____

Question 3   Which type of words are resisting the incoming variant [ʔ]?

_____

Mini Quiz Answer

7.1   Q1: *d*

Note

1   Quoted from http://www.ling.upenn.edu/phono_atlas/ICSLP4.html (accessed April 1, 2011).

Table 7.4 Logistic regression analyses of the
contribution of social factors selected as significant to the
probability of [ʔ].

	Factor weight	Total N
Corrected mean:	0.47	
Total N:	1017	

	Factor weight	Total N
Age		
<30	0.58	866
30–50	0.15	151
Range	*43*	
Sex		
Male	0.56	511
Female	0.44	506
Range	*12*	
Syllables		
Two	0.58	641
Three	0.42	230
Four	0.29	146
Range	*27*	
Education		
Less educated	[0.53]	509
More educated	[0.47]	508

Background Reading

Bayley 1991; Docherty and Foulkes 1999, 2000, 2005; Docherty *et al.* 1997, 2002; Fasold 1972; Foulkes 2006; Foulkes and Docherty 2000, 2006; Foulkes, Docherty, and Watt 1999, 2005; Guy 1980, 1991b; Guy and Boyd 1990; Labov 1989; Labov *et al.* 1968; Milroy *et al.* 1994a, 1994b; Neu 1980; Santa Ana 1996; Tagliamonte and Temple 2005; Wolfram 1969.

8

Morpho–Syntactic Variables

The extension of probabilistic considerations from phonology to syntax is not a conceptually difficult jump … underlying probabilities are consistently and systematically patterned according to internal (linguistic) and external social and stylistic constraints. There is no reason not to expect similar patterning elsewhere in the grammar. (Sankoff 1973: 58)

In this chapter, I consider how sociolinguistic patterns are reflected in morpho–syntactic variation. Although early variationist research focused on phonological variables, the study of alternations in morphology and syntactic–semantic options has risen to become a major component of LVC studies.

There are fundamental differences between phonological variables and all other levels of grammar (Sankoff 1988a: 153). Variation between two pronunciations within the same word does not entail a change in referent or syntactic function – "envelope" is the same item regardless of whether it is pronounced [ɔnvəlop] or [ɛnvəlop]. In contrast, variation between two different lexical items, structures, or tense forms "can almost always have some usages or contexts in which they have different meanings or functions" (Sankoff 1988a: 153). For example, some people might argue that when "vase" is pronounced [veiz] the vase in question is plain and unremarkable, but when it is pronounced [vɒz] it is expensive and made of crystal. Even more might argue that *I shall go* means something entirely different from *I'm gonna go*. Still greater dissent might emerge if I argued that *He has done the work* means the same as *He did the work*. As we will see, the study of linguistic variables above the level of phonology requires critical and informed attention to the form/function dichotomy by meticulous circumscription of the variable context and other well-documented methodological practices.

Morpho–syntactic variables, or grammatical variables, have traditionally been viewed as features which mark social differences more dramatically than phonological ones (e.g. Chambers 2003: 57). However, when these variables are viewed in terms of their socio-historical context they often tell an additional story. Sometimes stigmatized features are in reality older forms that have been preserved in certain sectors of the population, whether

Variationist Sociolinguistics: Change, Observation, Interpretation, First Edition. Sali A. Tagliamonte.
© 2012 Sali A. Tagliamonte. Published 2012 by Blackwell Publishing Ltd.

regionally or socially or ethnically defined (e.g. preterite *come*). Sometimes changes from above have still not penetrated the vernacular grammar (e.g. relative *who*).

A critical point in my own academic thinking came when I realized that the differences I was finding across varieties could be viewed from an entirely different angle – grammaticalization. Grammaticalization is the process by which lexical forms develop grammatical meanings, e.g. the verb "go" comes to mark future time, "I'm going to go." This type of change provides terrific data for the study of linguistic variation and change because it embodies both variation *and* grammatical change. The study of grammaticalizing changes also reflects the particular stage or level of participation of a community in ongoing language developments because grammaticalization may take place at different rates depending on the location or nature of the community. In many cases, synchronic variation is the symptom of longitudinal changes that have been going on in the language for a long time. In this way, different patterns across communities may mirror stages in the evolution of forms.

The study of grammatical variation is a little lopsided as most of the research is on morphology, not syntax. Why is this? In part, it is simply the natural evolution of a field which started out studying sound change and has since been broadening to investigate other areas of the grammar. In part, it has to do with the types of changes that are going on in contemporary varieties. It also has to do with how long it takes for certain changes to evolve. Syntactic changes typically involve phenomena that distinguish languages from each other, particularly the ordering relationships between verbs and their complements, but also the behavior of clitics, agreement patterns, etc. (Pintzuk 2003: 511). These types of changes often take centuries to go from one state to another. It is not surprising that researchers who study syntactic change typically examine historical corpora that span many hundreds of years. This type of research was spear-headed by Kroch (1989) and has been developed and extended by numerous others (e.g. Pintzuk 1993, 1995; Santorini 1993; Taylor 1994), across a range of languages (English, French, Greek, Portuguese, Yiddish). This research has consistently demonstrated the systematicity of linguistic features undergoing change as well as the "close fit between statistical patterns of usage and formal syntactic analysis" (Pintzuk 2003: 525). More recently, there has been a resurgence of new interest in applying probabilistic models of syntax to linguistic features above the level of phonology (Bresnan *et al.* 2007; Bresnan and Ford 2010; Bresnan and Hay 2008).

I will focus on several morpho-syntactic variables. The first, verbal -*s*, is a tried and true morphological feature which has been extensively studied. It provides both a retrospective on language variation and change studies as well as some provocative cross-linguistic insights using the comparative method (Chapter 6). The second, adverbial -*ly*, requires looking into the history of English for an explanation. The third, the deontic modal system, implicates not only morphology, but also syntax and semantics. Here too you will see how the present and the past are intertwined and the pervasive interface between the social and the linguistic.

Verbal (s)

Variable verbal (s) involves the variable absence of the -*s* suffix in third person singular contexts (where Standard English has categorical -*s*), as in Example 8.1, and the variable presence of an -*s* suffix in persons other than the third singular (where Standard English has none), as in Example 8.2.

Example 8.1   Third person singular

  (a)   She always *phones* me here and *reverse∅* the charges to me. (GYV/006)
  (b)   He *comes* every three times a week he *come∅*. (DVN/001)

Example 8.2   Third person plural

  (a)   Well, dreams *comes* true. Lots of dreams *comes* true. (GYE/063)
  (b)   'Cos then people *come∅* along and they *comes* in with the kiddies. (DVN/009)

Like many morphological variables, variable (s) has a standard and nonstandard form, depending on the linguistic context: an -*s* is standard in third person singular and nonstandard everywhere else. Yet in many varieties there is variation in both contexts. How can this variation be explained?

African American Vernacular English

When variable (s) was first studied from a quantitative perspective it formed part of a larger set of linguistic variables conscripted for the study of AAVE in the United States (other -*s*'s were possessive -*s* and plural -*s*); however, variable (s) was soon subject to scrutiny with respect to English-based creoles in Central America and the Caribbean as well (e.g. Bickerton 1975). Verbal -*s* (or *hyper* -*s* as it was sometimes called (Bickerton 1975: 134)) was originally considered an unsystematic importation into the AAVE grammar on the basis of three types of evidence: (1) it was rarely found in the third person singular; (2) it was not subject to style-shifting; and (3) it did not exhibit regular phonological conditioning. Therefore verbal -*s* was deemed "irregular and unsystematic" (Labov *et al.* 1968: 167), as a case of free variation.

Consistent with this interpretation, verbal -*s* in AAVE was highly variable across individuals and strongly conditioned by extralinguistic factors, i.e. it was not found in formal styles or in middle-class adult speech. Analyses of possible linguistic constraints on verbal -*s* in AAVE such as collective vs. noncollective subject, also showed no significant effects. The only constraint to emerge was one promoting absence of -*s* on the second member of a conjoined verb phrase (Fasold 1972; Myhill and Harris 1986: 28) which was attributed to the "rapid onset of a fatigue factor" (Fasold 1972: 130). Some researchers even suggested that it should be interpreted as a purely stylistic accommodative device African Americans used to render their speech more suitable for interaction with speakers of Standard English (Myhill and Harris 1986: 31). These results were entirely unlike other linguistic variables that had been studied in AAVE (e.g. the copula and past tense), both of which had regular linguistic and social patterns.

> **NOTE**   Given the central role that the absence of -*s* (plural, possessive, and verbal) has played in the study of AAVE, it is not surprising that a speaker of Samaná English made the following observation about the speech of European Americans: "They talks with -*s*."

At the same time, another body of research evolved suggesting that verbal -*s* was neither random nor the result of "unstable acquisition" of Standard English present-tense marking but was instead an aspectual feature, marking durative (Brewer 1986; Jeremiah 1977; Pitts 1981), or habitual (Pitts 1986; Roberts 1976) or [-punctual] aspect (Bickerton 1975). All these studies appealed to a non-English origin for verbal -*s*, suggesting that in AAVE it represented "the adoption of a Standard English form without the Standard English grammatical component" (Pitts 1986: 304). They generally suggested that verbal -*s* in AAVE was derived from its creole roots. While the *form* is an English suffix, the *function* was not English, but a creole aspect marker indicating habitual or durative. Take, for example the -*s*'s in Example 8.3. They certainly look like they are encoding repeating action, don't they?

Example 8.3

And when you win, they *comes* on your street and *tells* you. (Pitts 1986: 79)

This was perhaps the first time such a mismatch in form and function had been identified. It meant that features could exist in the grammar of a variety that looked like one thing (English inflection), but behaved like another (Creole aspect). However, the only way to conclusively identify such a phenomenon is to take a quantitative approach and analyze the underlying details of distribution and patterning. Put in larger context, can an interpretation of aspect be sustained? Take for example the -*s*'s and lack thereof in the sentence in Example 8.4. Notice that the uninflected verbs, e.g. *get* and *say*, also encode habitual meaning.

Example 8.4

When things *gets* bad, the lieutenant get wind of something: he *get* mad and *say*, "there's gonna be no more numbers." (Pitts 1986: 79)

> **NOTE** The study of verbal (s) is a good example of how a researcher's assumptions can sometimes impair her ability to interpret sociolinguistic patterns. It is the age-old phenomenon of seeing what you know and not seeing what you don't know.

Yet there was another interpretation of verbal -*s* in AAVE on the horizon. This body of research suggested that variation in the occurrence of verbal -*s* in AAVE was neither a creole feature nor a case of hypercorrection but simply a continuation of the tendency prevalent throughout the history of English to mark (or fail to mark) -*s* across the verbal paradigm. Evidence from a compilation of folk narratives recorded from elderly African Americans in the 1940s data was particularly telling (Federal Writers' Project 1941). Based on earlier research, Schneider (1983: 104) reasoned that if the occurrence of verbal -*s* in contemporary AAVE had derived from an originally suffixless system then an earlier stage in its history would reveal *less* verbal -*s*. However, he found the opposite result; 72% of the third person singular subjects in the folk narratives had a verbal -*s* suffix. Thus, they could not be interpreted as hypercorrection. Further, he found that verbal -*s* occurred more than half the time in the first person and in the second person plural. As it happens, British dialects are also known to have this type of variation. In northern Britain the present tense paradigm had -*s* in all grammatical persons; in southern Britain, a zero variant in third person singular was prevalent in some dialects. Schneider reasoned that the verbal -*s* variability in early AAVE had originated from contact with British settlers who had immigrated to the southern United States from these different dialect areas in the United Kingdom. Further, he argued that mixing of British settlers from these different locales in the Southern United States had produced an agreement system with variable but frequent use of verbal -*s* among the African Americans (Schneider 1989: 104). Support to this interpretation came from the fact that the narrative data showed regional differences according to the origin of the British settlers in those locales.

Another account of verbal -*s* in AAVE came from the study of a dialect spoken in Philadelphia. Myhill and Harris (1986: 27) discovered that -*s* tended to occur in narrative clauses regardless of person and number of the subject but was virtually absent from present reference contexts. Their response to this pattern was to suggest that verbal -*s* had been a grammatically empty inflection in AAVE, but was reinterpreted as a marker of historical present in storytelling. In this view, verbal -*s* was an innovation made possible by the existence of an inflection with no clear grammatical function.

> **NOTE**   Variable (s) has undergone recycling of its social function in other communities as well (see Trudgill 1998).

Notice that many different explanations are offered for the same linguistic feature and some are entirely contradictory to one another. This type of situation is exciting for the sociolinguistic enterprise because it raises many questions: What is the origin of verbal -*s* in AAVE? What is its function in the grammar? Note too how much of the research on verbal -*s* was fixated on a particular variety of English – AAVE – and its origins. This demonstrates how intimately sociolinguistic studies are linked with political considerations and their social and cultural implications. Linguistic controversy is compelling. Which explanation is the correct one?

Sociolinguistic methods can help to mediate between competing explanations for linguistic behavior. Unfortunately, deciding between competing explanations for sociolinguistic patterns is not as easy as you might think. In this case, not only are there sociocultural underpinnings that embroil the analyst in all manner of debate, but critical methodological problems require a more satisfactory resolution. The approaches different researchers take to the data, the corpora under investigation, and the methodologies used in the analyses differ considerably. This made it difficult to draw definitive conclusions from early research on variable (s). As researchers continued to examine this feature in new data and from new perspectives, the focus turned to the underlying constraints and the relative strength of factors.

The Ex-Slave Recordings and Samaná English

The emergence of two corpora in the early 1980s, the Ex-Slave Recordings and the Samaná English corpus, led to another chapter in the verbal -*s* story. The Ex-Slave Recordings are a series of recordings of African American ex-slaves from the 1940s (Bailey *et al.* 1991a). This unique corpus provided a real-time perspective on AAVE. Samaná English provided another perspective. This is a variety of AAVE that was spoken in Samaná in the Dominican Republic until the early 1990s. Poplack and Sankoff (1987) collected interviews from the last generation of native speakers of English from this small village. Many of the residents could trace their ancestry to African American slaves who had immigrated there in the 1860s. They spoke English, often monolingually, despite the fact that the Dominican Republic is a Spanish-speaking country. Poplack and Sankoff (1987) reasoned that, due to the social and geographic isolation of the community since the time of immigration, the English they spoke might give insight into an earlier stage in the development of AAVE. Shana Poplack and I undertook a study on verbal *-s* in these two data sets. As Schneider (1983) had shown for the WPA Slave narratives from the United States, verbal *-s* was prevalent. Where Schneider had found 72% *-s* in third person singular, the Ex-Slave Recordings had 71% and Samaná English had 56%. Moreover, there was plenty of *-s* in other grammatical persons as well. We showed that there was a complex set of phonological and grammatical constraints underlying variable (s) (Poplack and Tagliamonte 1989a, 1991a). More importantly, we discovered that Samaná English had constraints on variable (s) usage similar to those reported in the history of English: *-s* was more frequent with nouns than with pronouns. This is the classic pattern of the Northern Subject Rule that can be traced back to Northumbria in the ninth century – what is now northern England and Scotland. A famous quote by Murray, a Scottish dialectologist writing in the late 1800s, describes the Northern Subject Rule as follows (Murray 1873: 211):

> When the subject is a noun, adjective, interrogative or relative pronoun, or when the verb and subject are separated by a clause, the verb takes the termination -s in all persons.

The effect is very straightforward. If it applies, then variable (s) should correlate with full noun phrase subjects as opposed to pronouns. Interpreted quantitatively, *-s* can be expected to be more frequent after a noun phrase (e.g. *the cattle*) than after pronouns (e.g. *they*), as in Example 8.5.

Example 8.5

The cattle all *goes* to, to the big markets, these days … they *go* straight to the slaughterhouse. (DVN/008)

When Poplack and Tagliamonte (1989a) found the contrast between full noun phrases and personal pronouns to be statistically significant in Samaná English, they interpreted it to be a synchronic reflex of this old Northern Subject Rule. Several years later, they found the same constraint in the varieties of English spoken in two comparable communities in Nova Scotia, Canada (see also Poplack and Tagliamonte 2001: 188–189). This provided corroborating evidence to suggest that the English spoken in these relic communities, all populated by the descendants of African Americans, could be traced back to British dialects. This interpretation was even more compelling since the same constraint was found in the English spoken in a neighboring Nova Scotia community, Guysborough Village, which was populated by the descendants of British settlers. Figure 8.1 shows the constraint ranking for the subject type constraint in each of these varieties.

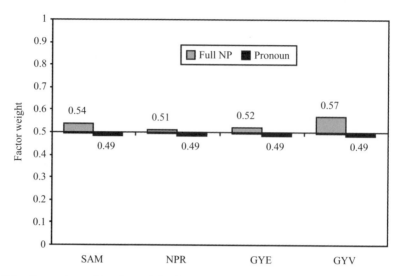

Figure 8.1   Constraint ranking for verbal -s in pronouns vs. NP contexts.

The figure shows that the subject type constraint operates in the same way across varieties. Noun phrases favor verbal -s while personal pronouns disfavor it. Moreover, the strength of this constraint is more or less parallel across the board.

Expanding Studies of Verbal -s

By the early 2000s – some 10 years later – dozens of studies of variable (s) from many regions emerged: Newfoundland, Appalachia, Liberia, England, the southern United States, Ireland, northern Britain, etc. Montgomery (1997: 137) tracked the patterns and constraints on variable (s) across more than four centuries and two continents in the evolution of Scottish English into Scots-Irish English into Appalachian English. In addition, a number of studies of historical corpora were conducted. Variable (s) continues to be a litmus test for historical origins.

Most researchers find that noun phrase subjects correlate with -s's while the third person pronoun *they* does not. This constraint operates to a greater or lesser degree depending on the community. These growing findings across many studies have highlighted yet another dimension to variable (s) variability – the relative strength of the type of subject constraint varies.

Wolfram (2000) presented two arguments to explain these differences in North America. First, he argued for two versions of the subject type constraint: a "European-American version that shows a strong subject constraint, where -s is favored for noun phrases over pronouns," and an "African American Vernacular English version of the rule in which the noun phrase constraint is 'relaxed'." By this he means that it appears with third person pronouns. Second, he argues that third singular -s absence is found in African American communities, but not in the founder English dialects in southwest England (Wolfram 2000: 55).

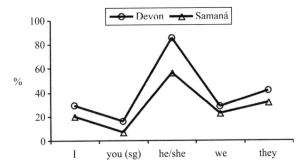

Figure 8.2 Distribution of variable (s) by grammatical person, Devon and Samaná.
Source: Poplack 2004: 213, Figure 7.1.

British Dialects

Elizabeth Godfrey and I conducted a study of variable (s) in southwest England, Tiverton, Devon (Godfrey and Tagliamonte 1999) which provided an additional piece to the verbal -s story. Here, as in the early AAVE studies, there was variation across the verbal paradigm and lots of -s's. When Poplack and Tagliamonte conducted a direct comparison of the Devon data to the Samaná data they found a near-perfect match in terms of relative frequency of verbal -s across the verbal paradigm (Poplack and Tagliamonte 2005). Figure 8.2 shows the comparison of the frequency of variable (s) by grammatical person in Tiverton and Samaná.

Figure 8.2 shows that third singular -s absence *is* part of the traditional grammar of Devon. The distributions of -s are in fact higher in Devon, not only in third singular, but in all grammatical persons. The relative rate across the other grammatical persons is remarkably parallel between the two varieties. While this comparison is revealing, recall that frequency is not definitive for the comparative enterprise. Further evidence comes from a comparison of the constraints.

The most relevant one is, of course, the type of subject diagnostic. Figure 8.3 shows a comparison of the factor weights for noun phrases and pronouns between the North American varieties studied earlier (Samaná, North Preston, Guysborough Enclave, and Guysborough Village) and Tiverton (TIV), in Devon.

There is a parallel pattern in every variety such that full noun phrase subjects favor the -s variant while personal pronominal subjects disfavor its use. The consistency of the constraint ranking for type of subject across varieties provides strong evidence to suggest a common grammar among them. Despite the differences in rates of verbal -s across varieties (not shown here), this factor applies in the same way and is statistically significant across the board. All these varieties share the African American version of the rule, regardless of whether the speakers have African ancestry or not.

Further research on other British dialects from northern Scotland, northeast England, and Northern Ireland – the regions where the Northern Subject Rule originated – uncovered yet another nuance. Figure 8.4 shows an intervariety comparison for the type of subject constraint now adding in data from two communities in Scotland, Buckie (BCK) and Cumnock (CMK), from northern England, Wheatley Hill (WHL), and one from Northern Ireland, Cullybackey (CLB).

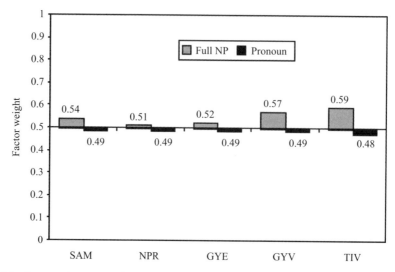

Figure 8.3   Inter-variety comparison of the type of subject constraint.

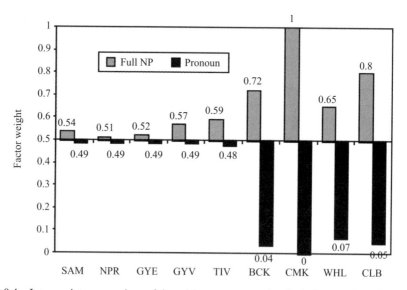

Figure 8.4   Inter-variety comparison of the subject type constraint, including northern Englishes.

Just as Wolfram argued, there appear to be two versions of the rule; some varieties show robust variability; some are near categorical. However the contrast is not exactly as he predicted. Wolfram (2000: 55) argued that African American dialects exhibit a type of overgeneralization that is typical of the kind of linguistic change that takes place in language contact. Here you can see that the "generalized" version of the rule is not only found in communities populated by the descendants of African Americans, but also in communities populated by the descendants of British settlers, namely Guysborough Village in Canada and

Tiverton in Devon. In other words, there are clear parallels in both constraint ranking and strength of the noun phrase/pronoun contrast between communities that do not share geographic proximity or ethnic identity.

What is the explanation for the observed patterns? Recall the transmission/diffusion dichotomy discussed in Chapter 3 where one of the results of a diffusing change is a loss of structural detail or reorganization of constraints. When people move from one place to another patterns of language use (i.e. constraints) are likely to restructure or reorganize. Thus, an original pattern may morph into something quite different from what it started out as when it is transported from one place to another. At the source (northern English), plural personal pronouns had no -s inflection. In the other communities, both in the UK and in North America -s extended into pronominal contexts. While the original pattern is preserved in the constraint ranking – full noun phrases have more -s than personal pronouns – it is not preserved in quality. There has been overgeneralization. This type of restructuring is, after all, one of the main mechanisms of linguistic change (Chapter 3). It should not necessarily distinguish varieties based on ethnicity. Instead, the underlying explanation is more likely to be that all these varieties represent regions to which variable (s) was transported. The cross-variety patterns have the hallmarks of diffusion.

Even at the turn of the twenty-first century, variable (s) is still encountered in vernacular dialects of English (see Preface). Can it be used as a diagnostic tool for understanding the history and development of a variety where it occurs? The constraint differentiating noun phrases and pronouns is so widespread (despite having varying strengths) among the varieties in which it has been examined is evidence that it is suspiciously universal rather than circumscribed. Yet languages that distinguish pronoun and other subjects with inflection on the verb are rare (Börgars and Chapman 1998: 92). This means that as far as typology is concerned, the nature of the subject type constraint has the right qualities of a good diagnostic for making comparisons. I suggest that the evidence in Figure 8.4 is the kicker. The only place where the constraint is structurally sound is where it originated – the regions where variable (s) is the result of transmission. This begs the question of whether ancestral lineage always leads to the preservation of constraints, especially after generations of other influences.

There is another nuance to the Northern Subject Rules that remains elusive – the effect of adjacency. According to historical reports, verbs nonadjacent to their subjects are marked with -s regardless of the nature of the subject. Thus, the best test of the Northern Subject Rule would be to distinguish all four contexts: noun phrases and pronouns in both adjacent and nonadjacent conditions. The key context is the case of a nonadjacent pronoun without an -s, as in Example 8.6. The prediction is that they should exhibit an -s ending or at least have -s more often than the adjacent contexts.

Example 8.6

third plural:
(a)   They [only] *comes* there every so often. (DVN/001)
(b)   They [usually] *turn* round and say, "well, don't expect much from him." (DVN/002)

third singular:
(c)   He [still] *dos* the Tiverton Harriers now, don't 'em. (DVN/002)
(d)   He [still] *do* all this bacon and eggs and stuff. (DVN/004)

Table 8.1 shows a four-way test of the Northern Subject Rule in both third singular and third plural contexts in Tiverton (Godfrey and Tagliamonte 1999: Table 3).

Table 8.1   Variable -*s* in Tiverton, southwest England.

Type of subject	Third singular	Third plural
NP – nonadjacent	[0.42]	0.84
NP – adjacent	[0.43]	0.64
Pronoun – nonadjacent	[0.73]	0.43
Pronoun – adjacent	[0.52]	0.42

Source: Godfrey and Tagliamonte 1999: 106, Table 3.

Table 8.1 reveals that the adjacency effect of the Northern Subject Rule is preserved for noun phrase subjects in third personal plural: compare 0.84 > 0.64 – but it does not operate for pronoun: compare 0.43 and 0.42. This can be explained by the fact that the pronoun context is an extended context and so despite the fact that -*s* appears here, the constraint has lost structural detail in its use in the extended context. But something strange is going on with respect to third person singular. These pronouns show a clear ranking with nonadjacent pronouns favoring -*s* at 0.73 and adjacent ones at 0.52. Without comparative studies these results are difficult to interpret; however, they show that if variable (s) is an inheritance from northern Britain, the adjacency constraint has been restructured, but in a different way than the subject constraint. This is why it would be interesting to compare these multiple constraints in other varieties.

Two varieties with abundant verbal -*s* stand out as exceptions to the Northern Subject Rule: Newfoundland English (Clarke 1997a) and Southern American English (Cukor-Avila 1997). These differences may be the result of varying founder populations, to the nature of the linguistic change, to a break in transmission, or to local conditions. These mysteries remain to be solved.

New research emerging from studies of other regions in the UK (McCafferty 2003, 2004; Pietsch 2005), in North America (José 2007), and other varieties (e.g. Van Herk and Walker 2000) is adding important comparative elements to the ongoing story of variable (s). Discovering which constraints are preserved and how will enable analysts to explain whether variable (s) is the result of transmission or diffusion.

Mini Quiz 8.1

Q1   Take a look at Example 10.30 in Chapter 10. There are (at least) three suggestive morpho-syntactic variables. What are they? HINT: look at the realization of subjects.

Q2   Conduct a study of variable indefinite pronouns (*anyone, everyone, nonone, someone* vs. *anybody, everybody, nobody, somebody*) in this book. What is the main point of differentiation that determines where -*one* variants occur over -*body* variants?

Adverb (*ly*)

Another variable feature of morphology in contemporary varieties of English is the formation of adverbs. Adverbs are usually recognizable by their *-ly* suffix, e.g. *slowly, happily, tremendously*. However, it has long been recognized that there is variation here – sometimes adverbs are marked by *-ly* but sometimes they are not. In some varieties alternation between these two variants can be found. As ever, the best demonstration of inherent variability is alternation in the speech of the same individual in the same conversation, as in Example 8.7.

Example 8.7

(a) I mean I was *real* small and everything you-know *really* tiny built and I was small in stature as well. (YRK/041)

(b) I mean, you go to Leeds and Castleford, they take it so much more *seriously* … They really are, they take it so *serious*. (YRK/046)

(c) We get our pension on a Monday and pension day comes around so *quickly* doesn't it? … It does come round *quick*, you-know, you can't believe it. (YRK/031)

Given the widespread reports of contemporary and historical variation in the language, and the readily found examples of alternation, this feature fits all the qualifications of a linguistic variable.

To gain a full picture of variation, a good place to start is always the historical record. In this case, the variability is the result of longitudinal change. Zero is the earlier form while *-ly* is the newcomer which has gradually been replacing it. Let us try to figure out how this has come about.

English adverbs were originally formed from adjectives by adding *-e*, as in Example 8.8 (Mustanoja 1960: 314; Robertson 1954: 134).

Example 8.8

(a) *georn* "eager" → *georne* "eagerly"
(b) *wid* "wide" → *wide* "widely"

These variants were very common in Old English and Middle English, as in Example 8.9 (Wyld 1927: 253).

Example 8.9

Wel coude he sitte on hors and *faire* ryde. (Chaucer, c. 1343–1400)

However, if the adjective had already ended in *-e*, this created a situation where there was no formal distinction between adjective and adverb, as in Example 8.10.

Example 8.10

(a) *blide* = "joyful" or "joyfully"
(b) *clæne* = "clean" or "cleanly"

Adjectives that ended in *-lic* also existed and these too underwent *-e* suffixation, as in Example 8.11.

Example 8.11

(a) *freondlic* "friendly" (adj.)   =   `freondlice* "friendly" (adv.)
(b) *earmlic* "wretched"(adj.)   =   *earmlice* "wretchedly" (adv.)

Adverbs such as "boldly," "sweetly," or "earnestly" (see Onions 1966) could also have alternative adverbial forms, as in Example 8.12.

Example 8.12

eornoste "earnest"   →   *eornostlice* or *eornoste* "earnestly"

This means that ambiguity between adverb and adjective function has existed from this early stage onwards.

Between the Old English and Middle English period final unstressed *-e* ceased to be pronounced in English. This means that any of the words that had previously taken the *-e* suffix lost the distinction between adjective and adverb, as in Example 8.13.

Example 8.13

(a) OE: *heard* (adj.), *hearde* (adv.)   →   ME: *heard* (adj. and adv.) "hard = difficult"

Old English *heard* in adjectival function and *hearde* in adverbial function became *heard* ("difficult"). Here, the adverb has a zero mark. The fact that the same form had two functions led to the term "dual form adverb," although it seems that "dual function" might have been more appropriate.

It has been argued that the ambiguity between adjectival and adverbial function is what promoted the use of the suffix *-lice* (and its descendent *-ly*) since it resolved the ambiguity (Mustanoja 1960: 314; Robertson, 1954: 134–135). This led to *-lice* and later *-ly* becoming "the real indication of adverbial function" and it was thereafter used "to an ever increasing degree" (Jespersen 1964: 408).

Yet the zero forms prevailed. They are said to have been "common" throughout the Elizabethan period (1558–1603), in Shakespeare in particular, as in Example 8.14 (Abbott 1879; Emma 1964).

Example 8.14

(a) Which the false man do's *easie*. (*Macbeth*, II, iii.156)
(b) 'Tis *noble* spoken. (*Antony and Cleopatra*, II, ii.99)

They can also be found in Milton (1608–1674), as in Example 8.15 (Emma 1964: 115).

Example 8.15

(a) … and to the'Eastern Gate/ Led them *direct*. (*Paradise Lost*, 12, 638–640)
(b) And sits as *safe* as in a senate house. (*Comus*, I, 99)

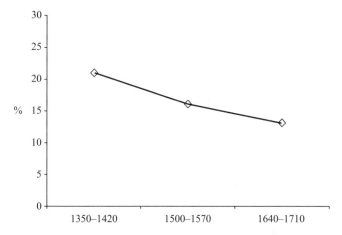

Figure 8.5 Overall distribution of -*Ø* adverbs in the history of English.
Source: Nevalainen 1997: 161, Table 3.

Lowth's influential grammar book (Lowth 1762/1775: 125) quotes Swift (c. 1667–1745), as saying "Adjectives are sometimes employed as adverbs, improperly, and not agreeably to the Genius of the English language," e.g. *extreme elaborate*, *marvellous graceful*, etc. Yet Jespersen (1961b: 371–2) reports the following examples from Swift himself, as in Example 8.16.

Example 8.16

'tis *terrible* cold … it has snowed *terribly* all night. (Swift, *Journal to Stella*, 132)

According to Van Draat (1910: 97), use of the zero form is "of the most frequent occurrence in the eighteenth [century]." Such statements are supported by Nevalainen (1994a,b, 1997) where variation between the new adverbial suffix -*ly* and the older form is analyzed in texts from Late Middle and Early Modern English in the Helsinki corpus. Her examination of all dual form adverbs in these materials reveals that the "zero-forms lose ground in the Early Modern English period" (Nevalainen 1994b: 142). In a later analysis (Nevalainen 1997) based on the five Late Middle and Early Modern English subperiods in the Helsinki corpus this can be graphically illustrated, as shown in Figure 8.5.

In 1350–1420 zero forms represented 21% of the adverbs whereas in the later period they represent only 13%. The distributional differences over the three periods are statistically significant (p < 0.05) and the difference between the Late Middle and the latter part of Early Modern English period is highly significant (p < 0.01) although the differences between adjacent periods are not. Nevalainen interprets this as an indication of the gradual "demise of zero derivation as a regular process of adverbialization in Standard English" (Nevalainen 1997: 183).

Thus, there is gradual loss of the zero adverb in Early Modern English with many adverbs shifting to suffixed forms with -*ly* by the eighteenth century (Nevalainen 1994b: 141). In the nineteenth century, under the influence of an expanding educational system and the development of strong prescriptive norms, the zero form became overtly stigmatized (Van Draat 1910: 97), at least in the United Kingdom. In contrast, by the turn of the same century in North America, Noah Webster (c. 1758–1843) was sanctioning the zero variant (Mencken 1962: 389). According to some American commentators the zero adverbs are "an ancient and dignified part of our language, and the pedantry which discountenances them is not to be encouraged" (Greenough and Kittredge 1901). By the end of the nineteenth century in the United States the zero form of the adverbs was treated as being "etymologically sound" and was reported to be "constantly heard in the professional and social conversation of cultured people" (Mencken 1962).

Given this historical perspective it becomes an interesting sociolinguistic question to ask What is the nature and character of variation and change in -*ly* and zero adverbs in contemporary varieties?

Synchronic Perspective

Despite the sanctions against the use of the zero adverb by prescriptive grammarians in the United Kingdom, variation between -*ly* and zero forms is reported in virtually all nonstandard dialects. Some examples from Reading in the south (Cheshire, 1982: 80–81) and Wheatley Hill in the north are shown in Examples 8.17–8.18 (Tagliamonte, forthcoming).

Example 8.17

> Reading English, Southern England:
> (a)   We had it on fire one night, *honest*.
> (b)   He writes really *quick*.

Example 8.18

> Wheatley Hill English, Northern England:
> (a)   It was all carpeted *beautiful*. (WHL/004)
> (b)   He's a *real* good gardener; he's a *real* good grower. (WHL/023)

Despite the fact that zero forms can be easily found, they are still associated with nonstandard (Quirk *et al.* 1985) or colloquial language (Poutsma 1926: 634) and are typically considered features "of the illiterate" (Poutsma 1926; Pulgram 1968) and even considered "vulgar" by some (Van Draat 1910: 97). Zero adverbs are also associated with certain genres. Alford (1864: 203) for example, suggests that "this adverbial use of adjectives is entirely poetical and not ever to be allowed in prose." Similarly, Poutsma (1926: 632) observes that zero forms are used when accommodating metre or rhythm in poetry, but "literary English would hardly tolerate [them]" (Poutsma 1926: 385).

The zero adverb has also been associated with pidgins and/or creoles, presumably due to the fact that pidgins at least are known to have reduced inflectional and derivational morphology as compared to the source languages (Arends 1995: 31). According to Crystal (1995) in creoles "adjectives are routinely used in adverbial function." Yet, Crystal (1995: 327) also lists the zero adverb as a characteristic of "Estuary English," a variety of British English held responsible for ongoing dialect leveling throughout the United Kingdom.

In the United States the zero adverb is also widely reported (Mencken 1961; Pooley 1933; Ross 1984). According to Wolfram and Schilling-Estes (2006: 378) variation between -*ly* and –*Ø* is found in informal contexts with "a range of adverbs and contexts" in contemporary vernacular dialects. Earlier research had suggested it is geographically and socially diffused in the US (Mencken 1961: 388); however, it is attested most often in southern dialects of American English, particularly Appalachian and Ozark English (Christian, Wolfram, and Dube 1988: 168–169; Wolfram and Schilling-Estes 2006: 378), as in Example 8.19, and Alabama English as in Example 8.20 (Feagin 1979: 331).

Example 8.19   Appalachian and Ozark English, US

(a)   I come from Virginia *original*. (AE/96: [26])
(b)   It *certain* was some reason. (AE/37: [321])
(c)   People do it *different*. (OE/34: 4)
(d)   ...*spotless* clean (OE/38: 2)

Example 8.20   Alabama English, Southern US

(a)   Lots of times in hospitals, people have s-people [sic] that's *real* sick.
(b)   ... and two boys come around right *quick* and run right into the front of the bus.

It is also easily found in Canadian varieties, such as Vernacular Nova Scotian English in Canada, in Example 8.21.

Example 8.21   Nova Scotian English, Guysborough Village, Nova Scotia, Canada

(a)   They'd feel *awful* depressed. (GYV/109)
(b)   They had two or three *real* heavy gales. (GYV/103)

There is also evidence for zero adverbs in widely separated locales elsewhere in the world, Tristan da Cunha, as in Example 8.22 (Zettersten 1969: 80) and in the Channel Islands, as in Example 8.23 (Ramisch 1989: 161). No doubt other examples can easily be found in other published papers, just as I found most of these.

Example 8.22

(a)   "Fred!" I say, "Fred! Jump up *quick*!"
(b)   Every thing is coming on *nice* ...

Example 8.23

(a)   You get wherever you're going pretty *quick*. (37.180)
(b)   I can't tell you *exact*, but say about 3 pound fifty. (18.345)

Most of these studies, if they comment on the appearance of zero adverbs at all (most do not), suggest that it is a characteristic of colloquial, informal, or dialectal speech (Christian *et al.* 1988; Zettersten 1969). This is echoed in most descriptions of this variation in contemporary grammar books (Leech and Svartvik 1975; Quirk *et al.* 1985: 404). The standard/nonstandard dichotomy is also said to be an important factor (Hughes and Trudgill 1987; Trudgill 1990). Supportive evidence for this can be found in Macaulay's (1995) research on a Scottish dialect (Ayrshire), where the most important factor in the choice between *-ly* and zero was socioeconomic class.

In sum, variation between *-ly* and zero adverbs presents an interesting linguistic phenomenon for quantitative study. It is a clear grammatical change, namely adverbialization via the suffix *-ly*, that can be placed in time and space. It has resulted in longitudinal variation (or layering) between an older form – "suffixless or flat adverbs" (Mencken 1961: 390) – and a newer form marked by an *-ly* suffix. The current situation is succinctly stated by Schibsbye (1965: 151):

> A development is taking place in the direction of *-ly* as the general adverbial ending; most adverbs have reached this final stage, but a number have not yet acquired the suffix, and a group is still at some point of the development, so that some adverbs occur both with and without the suffix.

This variability must have begun at least by the Middle English period, nearly 700 years ago. Moreover, as readily observable from Nevalainen's research, there is a gradual change toward the increasing use of *-ly* in the Early Modern English period. The persistence of this variation shows that the change is still not yet resolved, in Britain or in North America, nor in locales far flung from these major varieties. This provides analysts with the opportunity to track a linguistic variable at an advanced point along the S-curve of linguistic change.

In addition, underlying the variation between *-ly* and *–Ø* are at least two internal constraints involving the semantics of the manner adverb and the different types of adverb.

Semantics of Manner Adverb

The foremost linguistic constraint associated with the use of *-ly* and zero is the difference between abstract and concrete meaning. Jespersen (1961b: 38) reports that *-ly* is used for describing "manner, and often in a figurative sense." Similarly, in his grammar book, Schibsbye (1965: 152) suggests that literal usage promotes the zero adverb, while figurative or metaphorical uses tend to be marked with the suffix. Thus, *his hands were stuck _deep_ into his pockets* but, *solidarity represents a real and _deeply_ felt article of trade union faith.* Evidence for the existence of such a constraint comes from Donner's (1991: 4) quantitative study on Middle English where he found that the zero form is preferred in contexts with concrete meaning, as in Example 8.24, whereas *-ly* suffixation was preferred in contexts with abstract meaning, as in Example 8.25. Note Examples 8.24c and 8.25c from Toronto.

Example 8.24   *Concrete*

(a) I've walked upstairs dead *quick*. (YRK/019)
(b) I put winch-rope round on the back of t'axle and back t'trailer to pull it forward as *tight* as I could. (YRK/013)
(c) She sank her teeth in *deep* enough to get to muscle. (TOR/066)

Example 8.25 *Abstract*

   (a)   Thursday was meat and potato pie, if I remember *rightly*. (YRK/044)
   (b)   They take it so much more *seriously*. (YRK/046)
   (c)   I scanned it, I don't really have a reason to study it *deeply*. (CMC/5)

Function of the Adverbs

Another factor, reported as far back as Early Modern English, is the effect of adverb function. At earlier stages of English, the intensifier function of adverbs (i.e. adverbs which modify either adjectives or adverbs) tended to be zero marked, as in Example 8.26.

Example 8.26 *Intensifiers*

   (a)   And then he had an *awful* big sheep. (YRK/066)
   (b)   If you do *absolute* perfect, you might get a C. (YRK/089)
   (c)   My first set of skids I used were *real* strong ones. (YRK/013)

    This is repeated in (Poutsma 1926: 634–635) with the added observation that the zero form is especially frequent with adverbs of degree and intensifiers. In contrast, adverbs that modify verbs (i.e. manner adverbs), as in Example 8.27, are thought to be *-ly* marked (Nevalainen 1997: 169; Peters 1994: 284). However, as Example 8.28 shows, the zero form is possible here too. Opdahl (2000a; 2000b: 32) states that alternation between *-Ø* and *-ly* will generally not exist except with manner adverbs in contemporary English.

Example 8.27 *Manner adverbs*

   (a)   He was talking *nice* and *sensible* to them like. (YRK/015)
   (b)   I mean you look at life *different*. (YRK/063)
   (c)   Couldn't get rid of me *quick* enough. (YRK/076)

    No studies – to my knowledge – report on the zero form with sentence adverbs, as Rika Ito and I found in York English, as in Example 8.28a–c (Tagliamonte and Ito 2002). On inspecting various dialect studies, however, I found the text in Example 8.28d in examples from the Guernsey/Channel Islands (Ramisch 1989: 161) and, reporting on vernacular dialects in the United States, Wolfram and Schilling-Estes (2006: 338) note the example in Example 8.28e. This suggests that the zero form in sentence adverbs may be more extended in regional dialects than previously thought.

Example 8.28 *Sentence adverbs*

   (a)   And she usually baby-sits once a week. *Definite*. (YRK/041)
   (b)   *Funny* enough we had a telephone call. (YRK/063)
   (c)   *Honest* they did. (YRK/070)
   (d)   Golly, I've never thought about it like that. *Honest*, I haven't. (35.36)
   (e)   I come from Virginia *original*.

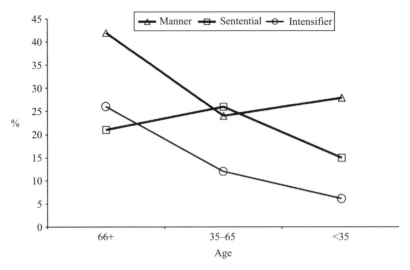

Figure 8.6   Distribution of zero adverbs in York English by age.

This scenario of long-term variation and change in English adverb formation presents an interesting area for study. First, if the trend between 1350 and 1710 reported by Nevalainen (1994a,b, 1997) has continued, we might expect an even lower frequency of –Ø adverb forms in contemporary varieties of English. Second, the relatively gradual rate of change and the fact that the zero adverb is still in use suggests that the patterning of -*ly* and –Ø in contemporary varieties may reflect ongoing developments in the morphological derivation processes. Taken in context with reports from the historical record, it should be possible to track the underlying mechanisms or constraints by which this change has spread or is spreading through the linguistic system. On the other hand, reports on the same variability in the US but with much higher frequencies of the zero form point to the fact that this historical trend may be reversing; that is, toward a situation with *more* zero adverbs. Further evidence about the direction of change, even in one variety, will shed light on this mystery. Third, the grammaticalization of -*ly* has been highly sensitive to external (social) factors, at least in the last century. Moreover, it appears to have been subject to more overt social stigma in Britain than in North America. These differing sociocultural contexts (ecologies) for the development of the -*ly* suffix may shed light on the interrelationship between grammatical and social factors in language change.

When Rika and I examined variable (ly) in York English, we uncovered a number of social and linguistic patterns. First of all, the different types of adverbs operated differently. Figure 8.6 shows the distribution of zero adverbs in apparent time for the three adverb types: intensifying, manner, and sentential.

Intensifying adverbs are evidently moving incrementally toward more -*ly* variants. However, intensifiers have a unique history, which I will discuss in detail in Chapter 11. The steep decline in the zero form for this type of adverb is actually due to the development of *really* as the preferred intensifier in York. The use of the zero variant for sentence adverbs is also declining, especially among the younger speakers. As for manner adverbs, the surprising finding is that although they have declined since the oldest generation of speakers, they are quite a stable component of the contemporary vernacular (c. 1997) with

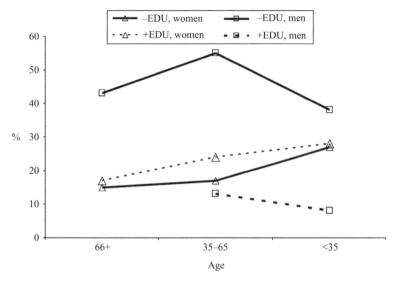

Figure 8.7 Distribution of zero adverbs in York English by age, sex, and education.
Source: Tagliamonte and Ito 2002: 253, Figure 5.

a frequency of 28% among the youngest generation. Why does the zero adverb prevail under adverse social stigma?

In Tagliamonte and Ito (2002), we argued that the zero adverb had developed a distinct sociolinguistic profile in York. It was highly correlated with a particular social group – less educated men, nearly all of whom worked in blue-collar jobs. Figure 8.7 shows the distribution of zero adverbs by age, sex, and education in York English.

Figure 8.7 shows that regardless of age, the less educated men stand out. They use the zero variant at the highest frequencies, well above those of the others. (Note: there are no educated men in the oldest age group.) The women on the other hand are moderate users of the zero form, there is little differentiation by education level, and the use of zero is increasing.

Mini Quiz 8.2

Q1 How might the results in Figure 8.7 be interpreted in terms of the principles of linguistic change?

At the same time, we discovered that there was more to the variation between *-ly* and zero than simply social meaning. Underlying these sociolinguistic patterns was a strong propensity for *-ly* to occur with abstract meanings and zero with concrete meanings. In fact, this constraint was the most significant factor constraining variation in adverb formation in York in the late 1990s, just as it was in the early days of the variable adverb suffixes in the fourteenth century. Figure 8.8 shows the distribution of manner adverbs according to adverb meaning by age.

Figure 8.8 shows that concrete adverbs have more zero forms in all age groups. In contrast, abstract adverbs rarely occur with anything but the *-ly* suffix among the older speakers, and not at all among the younger speakers.

Morpho-Syntactic Variables

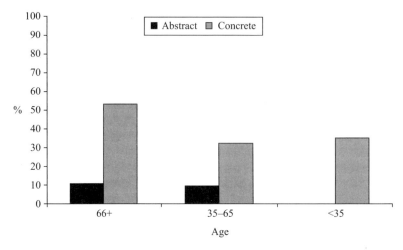

Figure 8.8 Distribution of zero variants by adverb semantics and age in York English.

It appears that the zero adverb is retained in York English as a sociolinguistic resource, particularly for encoding less educated male speech. However, it also encodes a specific type of adverb – concrete manner adverbs – a tendency that can be traced back at least 650 years. The zero adverb is not being used in a new way, but in the same old way – a reflection of the inherent and structured variation of centuries. The sociolinguistic value of the zero variant is built out of the extant grammatical constraints and patterns. Not everyone uses it, but if they do the long-time grammatical patterns prevail. Given this perspective, the longitudinal continuity of the zero adverb, at least in this variety, cannot be attributed to illiteracy, informality, creolization, or dialect leveling. Instead, it persists as a healthy variant, particularly among certain sectors of the population, and in all speakers in certain specialized contexts. Once again, remember Trudgill's observations about men and covert prestige. If it continues to hold a social value that is desirable, its continuity is assured.

The linguistic and social profile for the zero adverb in York in Northern England must be contextualized. These facts may only hold true in the north of England where the York data originate. As Trudgill (1990: 65–78) and others have argued, northern British dialects are generally more conservative than the southern ones. In this case, the use of the zero adverb in York according to constraints which can be traced to earlier stages in the language may be dependent on conservatism, i.e. the variety is lagging behind in the change. It may be that northern British dialects in general provide an important historical perspective on linguistic variables of English that have been undergoing grammatical change over the last few centuries. Of course, the only way to find out is to compare the York results with other varieties.

NOTE Linguistic variables can sometimes be simultaneously favored by older uneducated males and younger educated females in a speech community, e.g. glottal stops (e.g. Milroy *et al.* 1994); definite article reduction (Tagliamonte and Roeder 2009); and perhaps others. It is interesting to speculate how these findings can be reconciled with the four existing principles of linguistic change.

In fact, the findings from the York English study provoked speculations about the contrast between British and American English. Recall that zero adverbs were at their height of usage in British English in the eighteenth century (Partridge 1969: 214; Van Draat 1910: 97). Given that this corresponds to the time period of massive migration from Britain into North America (Bailyn 1986; Bailyn and DeWolfe 1986; Fischer 1989), North American English was likely predisposed by its founders to develop from a stage when the zero adverb was prevalant. Frequent citations of the zero adverbs *quick* and/or *slow* in American dialects, as in Example 8.29 (Rice 1927), along with easily found eighteenth-century examples of these forms, as in Example 8.30, underscores this connection.

Example 8.29

(a) They need it *quick* and they don't care how. (American English, written, *New York Times*)
(b) We'll come back *quick*. (American English, spoken)
(c) No matter how fast or *slow* an observer moves ... (American English, written) (Liddle 1999: 14–15, 22)
(d) He's got to thaw *slow*. (American English, written, Brown K24: 182) (Opdahl 2000a: 464)
(e) ... and two boys come around right *quick* and run right into the front of the bus. (Southern American English, Alabama) (Feagin 1979: 331)
(f) The widow said I was coming along *slow* but sure, and doing very satisfactory. (*Huckleberry Finn*, Ch. 4)
(g) But I slid out of the jacket *quick* as lightning, and saved myself. (*Huckleberry Finn*, Ch. 6)

Example 8.30

(a) It grew so *slow*, as provoked him to take it up. (W. Ellis, Chiltern and Vale Farm, 109, c. 1773) OED IX, p. 240
(b) I am told you speak very *quick*. (Earl of Chesterfield, *Letters to His Son*, II, 25 c. 1748) OED VIII, p. 53
(c) ... you place your Churn in a paile of cold water as deep as your Creame riseth in the Churne; and in the churning thereof let your stroakes goe *slow* and be sure that your churne be cold when you put in your creame. (Early Modern English, Markham, 112) (Nevalainen 1994a: 250)

In the UK the rise of prescriptive norms in the nineteenth century heavily stigmatized the zero form (Lowth 1762/1967: 126; Poutsma 1926) and it came to be restricted to highly informal styles, "colloquial usage" (Partridge 1969: 14), and "familiar speech." In contrast, in the United States the zero adverb developed in a context where it was championed by the prevailing prescriptivests, e.g. Noah Webster (Mencken 1962: 389). This may be why zero adverbs in the United States, and perhaps elsewhere in North America, have endured longer than in the United Kingdom. It did not have the same sociolinguistic stigma. But this does not necessarily mean that zero adverbs are increasing in frequency in contemporary North American English. They may, as in York, simply be circumscribed to similar sectors of the population, specialized for particular types of modification and maintained this way across generations. Of course, such speculation requires further study, particularly with studies in apparent time that would confirm or mitigate claims for the putative increase in the frequency of the zero adverb in contemporary North American dialects (Wolfram and Schilling-Estes 1998: 338). It would also be instructive to know which of the adverbs in the "range of adverbs and contexts" (Wolfram and Schilling-Estes 2006: 378) are actually found in contemporary vernacular dialects of North America.

Given the potential of this particular linguistic feature to uncover historical, social, and linguistic patterns of variation I am surprised that variable (-ly) has not been the subject of more research in North American dialects up to now.

Modal (have to)

Another variable that involves morphology, syntax, and semantics is the deontic modality system. Here too contemporary varieties are positioned at varying stages along the pathway of change. This is not surprising. The modals have been in constant flux since the Old English period (e.g. Denison 1993; Lightfoot 1979). This is why studying the modal system in contemporary English is an ideal test site for the investigation of linguistic variation involving grammatical change. Recent evidence suggests the emergence of a new category, the semi-modals, within in the deontic modal system (see Bybee, Perkins, and Pagliuca 1994; Krug 2000). When new categories in grammar develop, they originate in already existing lexical words or phrases. So the question is, what words are undergoing grammatical change in this system and how?

The deontic modals encode meanings of obligation or necessity. We use them when we want to exert pressure on ourselves or on someone else to do things. The layering of forms in this system is multiplex, involving *must*, *have (got) to*, and *got to*, as in Examples 8.31 (British English and 8.32 from Canadian English (other variants might also be considered, e.g. *need to*, *should* but were not considered in this study).

Example 8.31

   (a)   Next time I'm in the doctor's I *must* ask to see the physio. (TIV/004)
   (b)   They *have to* keep up with the Jones' now. (MPT/026)
   (c)   You*'ve got to* have a vice of some kind. (CMK/022)

Example 8.32

   (a)   I said, "You *have to* come up." I said, "You *must* come up." And to the person on the phone, I said, "I*'ve gotta* go." (TOR/075)
   (b)   Do what you *gotta* do in class. It's not like you enjoy doing it but you have to do it if you want to go anywhere, so. (TOR/010)
   (c)   We're like, "Somebody's *got to* shut this off." (TOR/012)

An interesting aspect of this system (and as we shall see the same holds true of other systems) is that each variant represents a successive stage in the longitudinal evolution of the system. As outlined in Table 8.2, *must* is the oldest, dating back to the Old English period (Traugott 1999; Warner 1993). Most scholars trace deontic *have to* to Middle English. The construction *have got to* evolved much later, in the nineteenth century. Most recently, *got to* and *gotta* emerged.

This scenario of long-term evolution of forms for the same function, with their contrasting morphosyntactic categories (modal, periphrasis, phonetic coalescence) makes for an interesting

Table 8.2 Outline of the development of deontic modality variants.

Old English	Middle English	Early Modern English	Nineteenth century	Twentieth century
mot: permission or possibility	*mot → must:* deontic and epistemic develop permission reading lost	*must*	*must*	*must:* "old, established"
	have to first attestations	*have to* fully established	*have to*	*have to*
			have got to *got to* first attestations colloquial	*have got to* *got to* colloquial
				gotta vulgar

case study. First, because the major variants (*must→ have to → have got to → got to*) entered the language at different points in time, their distribution across dialects may shed light on the stages of development of the deontic modality system itself. The forms also embody varying degrees of auxiliary-hood. While *must* is a full-fledged modal, the other contenders are only modal-like by degree and this is undoubtedly a result of ongoing development. Tracking the synchronic status of this system – form and function – across dialects should enhance the existing knowledge of this system. This, in turn, should inform us of the nature of this area of English grammar as well as its status in the larger history of its development.

British English, c. 1997–2001

I first started looking at this area of the grammar in the York English Corpus (Tagliamonte 2004a). By then, Jennifer Smith and I had begun an ambitious new project aiming to unearth the roots of English (Tagliamonte 2001–2003; Tagliamonte forthcoming). The new corpora we were collecting originated in key regions of southwest Scotland, northeast England and Northern Ireland. In addition, my concurrent project on vernacular dialects in the UK generally (Tagliamonte 2000–2001) meant that we had at our disposal a range of corpora from highly isolated and conservative communities to relatively urban ones proximate to the mainstream. It was an ideal opportunity to tackle the question of the grammaticalization of the deontic modal system (Tagliamonte and Smith 2006). This continuum of dialects permitted us to explore reported changes in the deontic modality system. We speculated that the cross-dialectal perspective would encompass some of the later recorded steps in the historical changes that had been reported for the deontic modals. In essence we hypothesized that deontic modality in these synchronic dialects would show us a window on diachrony.

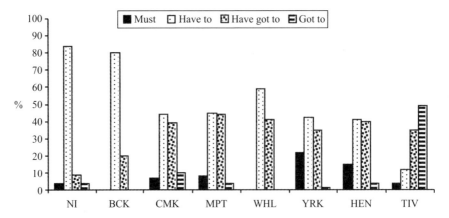

Figure 8.9 Overall distribution of deontic modal forms across dialects.

Figure 8.9 shows the distribution of forms used for deontic modality across dialects. The more northerly dialects, including Northern Ireland (NI) and Buckie (BCK), are on the left. The more southerly dialects, including Henfield (HEN) in Sussex and Tiverton (TIV) in Devon, are on the right.

Must, indicated by the black columns, is particularly rare in Northern Ireland (NI) and Northern Scotland (BCK), leading us to suggest that deontic *must* may never have been present in these dialects. In contrast, notice the high rate of *have to*, the bars with the dots, in Northern Ireland and Buckie. *Have to* competes with *have got to* in the series of communities from Cumnock to Henfield. This continuum can be interpreted as a reflection of ongoing retention of an older layer in the development of forms. The variation itself provides an indication of the state of development of the grammatical system. Where *have to* is more frequent it can be taken as evidence that the variety is more conservative. The two most remote communities exhibit the most *have to* – Northern Ireland and Buckie. In contrast, where *have got to* is more frequent, it can be taken as evidence that the new layer has made inroads into the system. In other words, we had caught the system in flux.

Jen and I argued that the different frequencies of forms provided a mirror of the varying effects of social context and geographic location across these eight different communities. We also suggested that the contrast between the proportion of older and newer forms provides a particularly interesting mirror of the pathways of change. The dialect data reveal that: (1) *must* may never have been firmly established in some dialects; and (2) whether *must* was present in all the dialects or not, it is clearly obsolescent now. Why is deontic *must* in decline? Some researchers argue that it may be the loss of the particular stylistic register associated with *must* (e.g. Biber *et al.* 1999) – in Conradie's (1987: 179) terms "an anti-authoritarian development" which also jibes with Mair's idea of increasing "colloquialization" (Mair 1997a; see also Hundt and Mair 1999), particularly of American English (see also Leech 2003: 236–237), as well as Myhill's (1995) notion of "democratization." It might also have been due to the general loss of grammatical subject-oriented uses (Warner 1993). Whatever the reason, it seems clear that such developments must be rooted in changes external to the system, perhaps in distinctions of style, genre, or register (see also Facchinetti, Krug, and Palmer 2003).

> **NOTE** When was the last time you heard deontic *must*? Check the signs in the local swimming pool – *swimmers <u>must</u> take a shower before entering the pool*. When these types of signs change, we'll know that language change has reached the next phase.

The next step was to tap into the underlying patterns, weights, and strengths of contextual factors in order find out what explains the differences. While much of the earlier work on obligation/necessity had concentrated on nuances of semantic function of each variant, an alternative approach is to test for objective correlates of variant distribution and patterning; in other words, constraints on the variation reported in the literature. Unfortunately, the main internal constraints operating on the deontic modality system were not independent (see Table 5.5). To handle this interaction, the data were partitioned according to a three-way interaction factor group that contrasted the type of reference of the subject with the source of the authority.

When the type of reference of the grammatical subject is definite, there are two different types of authority. Objective readings are those where the authority comes from a source other than the speaker, as in Example 8.33.

Example 8.33 *Objective readings, definite subjects*

(a) You know, why do we *have to* be so dominated by these typical names? (TOR/007)
(b) Aye, when I go and visit him I *have to* go outside. (CMK/027)

Subjective readings are those contexts where the authority comes from the speaker herself, as in Example 8.34, regardless of the grammatical subject.

Example 8.34 *Subjective readings, definite subjects*

(a) I just feel like total crap about myself and it's like, "*I got to* start eating better, and like exercising." (TOR/009)
(b) We told her owner "You*'ve got to* get control of that dog. You*'ve got to* get a license." (TOR/031)
(c) Oh you *must* get it. She borrowed it from someone else. (YRK/006)

When the type of reference of the subject is generic – when the authority comes from outside – the reading is always objective, as in Example 8.35:

Example 8.35 *Generic readings*

(a) But you *have to* wear shoes in the river. 'Cause of all those … crabby clam things and all the rocks and stuff. (TOR/005)
(b) You*'ve got to* take the blood when the fever is on. (MPT/029)

The spoken dialect data in the UK consistently demonstrated that *have to* was favored for objective readings in clauses with definite subject readings, while deontic *must* had retreated to the core of deontic meaning – in contexts of subjective obligation. The large, cross-generation York English Corpus provides the best illustration, as in Figure 8.10.

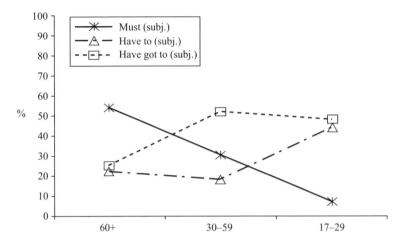

Figure 8.10 Distribution forms for deontic modality in contexts of subjective obligation by generation in York.
Source: Tagliamonte and Smith 2006: 374, Figure 9.

Figure 8.10 shows restructuring of the core contexts of deontic modality – subjective obligation meaning, as in Example 8.34. While *must* drops steadily for this function, *have to* has only begun to supplant *have got to* among the youngest generation. As *must* recedes, *have to* is steadily taking its place. Supportive to the idea of ongoing retreat of *must* is the fact that it is often found in formulaic utterances (Example 8.36) and in communities that have the most middle class speakers (York; Henfield).

Example 8.36

   (a) I haven't watched it a lot *I must admit*. (YRK/006)
   (b) I had agorophobia, *I must tell you*. I couldn't go on holidays. (YRK/003)

Thus, where Standard English prescribes *must* for obligation/necessity, these spoken synchronic dialects show us that its use is highly restricted. Instead, robust use of *have to* and *have got to* and their vigorous jockeying for this function reveal that deontic modality is among the "modals on the move" in contemporary English (see Leech 2003).

   Why did *have to* come back? Linguistic and social factors must have intervened to favor the return of *have to*. In the case of *have to* and *have got to*, the former is often considered monoclausal (e.g. Heine 1993; Krug 2000; van Gelderen 2004), while the latter is considered biclausal. These structural differences might explain why there is a visible resurgence of the simpler *have to* form – it more readily fits into the modal auxiliary slot. If purely linguistic factors were involved, *got to* should have easily won out. Yet, this form has only made inroads in one community (Tiverton). Social factors must surely be at play: (1) there is a pivotal point in the progress of change among the youngest generation (20–40 year olds); and (2) female speakers are leading this development. This suggests that the social evaluation of forms overrides the classic profile of change from below. Instead, this is change from above, from outside the community. Labov also suggests that women tend to advance change at about a generation ahead of men (Labov 2001a). This fits the pattern of change uncovered here. With

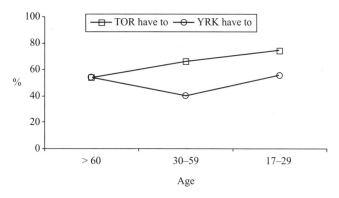

Figure 8.11   Distribution of deontic *have to* in Toronto, Canada and York, UK in apparent time.

must in decline, *have got to* imbued with the social value of "informal" and *got* vulgar, the women began to favor the already grammaticalizing *have to*. In the late 1990s in York, they were leading the way in its increasing use as the favored deontic modal in the United Kingdom. However, at the time it was still not clear how this change was diffusing elsewhere in the world.

Toronto, c. 2004

My move to Toronto in the midst of this study and the compilation of the Toronto English Corpus gave me the opportunity to extend the study even further. Alex D'Arcy and I conducted a study of deontic modality in Toronto English (Tagliamonte and D'Arcy 2007b), which provided us with a broader perspective. Figure 8.11 provides a comparative apparent time perspective on *have to*, comparing British and Canadian varieties of English.

Have to starts out fairly robust among the older speakers in York, but dips in the middle and then resurges among the youngest generation (the "twist of fate" identified in the earlier study). In Toronto, on the other hand, there is a monotonic increase of *have to* from oldest to youngest speakers. This finding led us to ask a number of pointed questions: Are the two varieties operating on their own accord, reflecting independent developments, dialectal divergence, or what? What is the underlying mechanism that may be guiding the ongoing course of change? Is the same process of grammaticalization happening in both varieties?

Using the underlying semantic distinctions as a main predictor of variant choice, Figure 8.12 shows the distribution of *have to* in three of the UK varieties studied earlier (York, Buckie, and Wheatley Hill) in comparison with Toronto English.

In the British varieties *have to* is consistently favored with objective readings in clauses with definite subjects, while subjective and generic subjects pattern together, disfavoring *have to*. In contrast, Toronto English distinguishes itself with a unique profile. *Have to* has specialized for objective readings in clauses with definite subject readings, just as in British English, but in Toronto it has also spread into generic contexts. Both of these favor *have to*.

In sum, in Toronto people use *have to* with generic statements as in Example 8.37a, whereas in British English *have got to* is used, as in Example 8.37b.

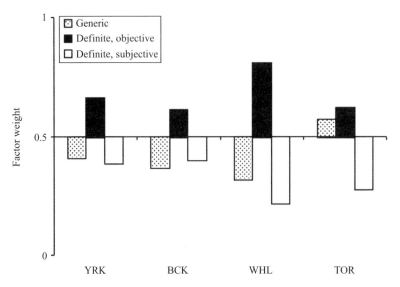

Figure 8.12   Factor weights for the probability of deontic *have to* by type of modality across varieties, York, Buckie, Wheatley Hill, and Toronto.
Source: York, Buckie, Wheatley Hill: Tagliamonte and Smith 2006: 368, Table 4.
Toronto, Tagliamonte and D'Arcy 2007a: 205, Figure 2.

Example 8.37

    (a)   ... you *have to* be very aggressive... to win. (TOR/015)
    (b)   ... you'*ve got to* be amazingly talented ... to win. (YRK/034)

All the major varieties of English are said to exhibit structured heterogeneity (layering) for expressing deontic modality. Each of these dialects does too. However, among the youngest generation in both locales there is a move toward *have to*. The interesting thing is that despite this parallelism in the course of change, the underlying organization of the system is different. Moreover, it looks like the Canadian system is in advance of the United Kingdom.

What will happen next? Will British dialects continue their present course toward increasing use of *have to*? Will *have to* become more auxiliary-like as time goes on, and show more signs of advanced grammaticalization? Will the sociolinguistic correlations persist? And if so, how will they figure in the ensuing steps of this historical process? I have not forgotten *need to*. This form was not included in the original UK study; it is present in that data only at low levels of frequency. According to Leech (2003: 229) *need to* is the fastest growing form in both British and American English from 1961 and 1999 and it appears to be a major player in British English (Nokkonen 2006). In contrast, in Toronto it is a minority variant that is stable in apparent time (Tagliamonte and D'Arcy 2007b: 71, Figure 4). The explanation for this contrast has still not been explained.

Another curiosity is the building evidence that the middle-aged generation in the United Kingdom in the late twentieth century is the locus of a pivotal change. This result must be situated in the context of other studies in which this particular generation has been identified as a watershed of linguistic change more generally (e.g. Chambers 2002b, 2004; Hay and Schreier 2004; Tagliamonte 2006b). Broader study of deontic modality (and other systems of grammar) across other varieties of English will present us with an opportunity to further expose similarities and divergences between contemporary varieties and enrich our understanding of grammatical change.

Studying Morpho-Syntactic Variables

Morpho-syntactic-semantic variables present the sociolinguist with rich linguistic features to investigate. Strictly morphological variables include the variable presence of suffixal endings, as with variables -*s* and -*ly*. Strictly syntactic variation includes the study of movement and word order in historical syntax (e.g. Pintzuk 1993, 1995; Pintzuk and Kroch 1989). A variable such as *have to* crosscuts morphology, syntax, and semantics. When dealing with variables above the level of phonology variables tend to be multifaceted with implications for several areas of the grammar. This is, in fact, what makes them so interesting. The analyst can discover the operation of both potential universal constraints (e.g. the subject type constraint on verbal -*s*) and local deviations (e.g. in some varieties variable -*s* in both locations, in others variable -*s* with noun phrases only). What is the reason for these divergent patterns? It is incumbent on the analyst to sift through the synchronic and diachronic record and determine which explanation best fits the facts.

Tips for Studying Morpho-Syntactic Variables

The biggest hurdle for the study of morpho-syntactic variables is circumscribing the variable context. This process ensures that the contexts that go into the analysis are: (1) semantically, functionally, or structurally equivalent (depending on the nature of the feature), and (2) actually variable. In this process, the first step is to determine which contexts are variable and which are not. This is often not possible a priori, but requires considerable experience with the data. The analyst must always be wary of the function of each form and the range of contexts in which it occurs. The possibility of categoricity is always present.

A key consideration is what to include in the study. In the analysis of morphological variables such as verbal (-s), (-ly), and deontic modality only those contexts that can alternate with the same meaning are included in the analysis. Consider the variable (ly), which has the variants -*ly* and zero. When embarking on a study of this variable, you will immediately notice that many adverbs cannot take one or the other of these forms. First, some adverbs are always zero, including *early*, *late*, *long*, and *high* (Leech and Svartvik 1975: 195). Since none of these adverbs takes -*ly*, they are excluded from the variable context. Second, many adverbs have a zero variant that is not semantically related to the -*ly* variant, i.e. not functionally equivalent, including *lately*, *hardly*, *directly*, *shortly*, etc. For example, *direct* as in Example 8.38a is excluded because it means "immediately" in this context. Yet the token in Example 8.38b is included because *direct* in this context can alternate with *directly* meaning "in a direct way without deviation."

Example 8.38

(a) He drove home *directly* after arriving (= "immediately"). (Leech and Svartvik 1975: 195)
(b) 'Cos in those days as well you used to get er milk *direct* from a- a dairy on a morning. (YRK/071)

Third, in preverbal contexts the zero form also does not occur. Thus, *gently* in Example 8.39, which cannot alternate with *gentle*, is excluded. However, *slowly* in the same example is included.

Example 8.39

> They were just *gently* moved up and down, very *slowly*. (YRK/005)

By the same reasoning *really* as intensifier in Example 8.40a is included, but not where *really* is used to emphasize the speaker's belief, as in Example 8.40b, where it has a different function.

Example 8.40

> (a) So I was *really* bummed out, but um, you know. (YRK/049)
> (b) She *really* is butch. (YRK/030)

Fourth, verbs of perception such as *smell, feel, look,* and *sound* as in Example 8.41 also should be excluded since this context is said to be only marginally acceptable with the *-ly* form, as indicated by the question mark in Example 8.41a. However, note the presence of such forms in the Toronto Corpus (8.41b) (Quirk *et al.* 1985: 407; Thorndike 1943).

Example 8.41

> (a) ?The flowers smell *sweetly*. (Quirk *et al.* 1985: 407)
> (b) So everybody looks *stupid*. (TOR/026)

The same is true of comparatives and superlatives with suffixes (*-er* and *-est*) as in Example 8.42.

Example 8.42

> If I do that they get over it much *quicker* than if I interfere. (YRK/041)

NOTE   Determining which contexts are variable and which are not involves a two-pronged approach: (1) scour the literature for observations, and (2) scrutinize the data.

In the study of deontic modal variation, only contexts which have the meaning *"it is necessary that…"* are included. This variable presents a host of challenging issues. First, the analyst will immediately discover that many uses of *have to* are invariant. For example, contexts involving past or future markers, as in Example 8.43, only ever occur with *have to* or *need to*. On grounds of invariance these are excluded from a variationist analysis.

Example 8.43

> (a) I was so glad that I <u>didn't</u> *have to* have anything amputated. (YRK/049)
> (b) I think <u>I'll</u> *have to* do some shopping this afternoon. (YRK/039)
> (c) I <u>used to</u> *have to* get club cheques out to clothe the lads. (YRK/003)

Second, many tokens of one of the prime variants, i.e. *must*, will not have deontic meaning. As it happens, *must* is most often used for epistemic meaning. Epistemic modality affirms a speaker's evaluation, belief, or knowledge of a proposition. In contexts such as Example 8.44, where the present perfect is used, *must* was found to occur categorically.

Example 8.44

(a) It *must have been* when York races were on. (YRK/068)
(b) In my teens in York there *must've been* nine cinemas. (YRK/001)

On the basis of functional equivalence such uses are excluded from the analysis of deontic modal variation. Yet some contexts of epistemic meaning, as in Example 8.45, admitted a small amount of variation.

Example 8.45

(a) It *must* be something to do with kangaroos or something. (YRK/053)
(b) Our Paul's twenty oh, oh good grief, he *must* be twenty-four. (YRK/019)
(c) You *must* know where that is. (YRK/020)
(d) They*'ve got to* be a lot more intelligent than us haven't they? (YRK/078)

Similarly, *must* is often used in formulaic expressions, as in Example 8.46; however, here too there was a certain amount of variation, as in Example 8.46d.

Example 8.46

(a) You *must be* joking. (YRK/049)
(b) I feel really bitter about it, *I must admit*. (YRK/044)
(c) *I must confess*, I've known Maurice er, nearly forty years. (YRK/071)
(d) *I have to say*, one of my favourite bits of music … is Vivaldi's Gloria. (YRK/034)

What is the analyst to do with these varying degrees of variation across these non-deontic contexts? In this case, it is worthwhile to extract the epistemic contexts and code them independently for type. In this way the frequency and distribution of *must* can be determined for different semantic functions. Categorical and near-categorical contexts can easily be excluded or included for the actual variationist analysis later on. Moreover, having extracted all the *musts* means that the range of different levels of variability across contexts is known, thus providing important clues as to the explanation of variation (and change) in the modality system generally. As researchers have begun to discover, extending variation analysis to related parts of the grammar that are *not* part of the variable context are also important for LVC research (see Aaron 2010).

In sum, the interpretive component of Variationist Sociolinguistics comes to the fore in the analysis of linguistic variables above and beyond phonology. The analyst must be very exacting in examining the data and including only the appropriate contexts in the analysis of variation. However, the categorical and near-categorical contexts can also prove valuable in better understanding your variable.

How to Determine What Is Variable and What Is Not?

A good strategy to adopt when studying morpho-syntactic features is, at the outset, to let the data provide the evidence of variability. This is because the literature and one's own intuitions often fail to make the best judgment about the propensity for variation. The best test is to include all the potential contexts, and then examine them later. If the contexts display categoricity, exclude them from your variation analysis; if they are variable, include them.

A good example comes from the study of variable (ly). Sentence adverbs as in Examples 8.47a–b and 8.48a–b were found to be variable. However, when such adverbs were uttered as a single response accompanied by expressions such as *oh, yes*, and *yeah*, as in Examples 8.47c and 8.48c, they turned out to be categorically marked *-ly*. Thus, the former contexts were included in the study and the latter contexts were excluded.

Example 8.47

    (a)   I was an angel. *Absolute*. (YRK/025)
    (b)   And I had years of utter misery. *Absolutely*. (YRK/003)
    (c)   [078] Oh yeah but it'd mount up in two years wouldn't it? [078] Oh *absolutely* yeah. (YRK/078)

Example 8.48

    (a)   And she usually babysits once a week. *Definite*. (YRK/041)
    (b)   But she's number one. *Definitely*. (YRK/041)
    (c)   [Interviewer] Would you ever move from York? [008] Yeah, *definitely*. (YRK/008)

Challenges and Solutions

Many of the challenges that arise in the study of morpho-syntactic variation are quite different from those that emerge in the study of phonological variation. Most of them are related to the fact that semantic differences in morphology and syntax across forms are quite subtle. Grammatical variation is often quite difficult to spot:

> An initial difficulty in the analysis of syntactic variation lies in deciding what to analyse, as grammatical variant often evade the conscious awareness of speakers and listeners. (Cheshire 2003: 246)

Ambiguity

Another problem that can arise is ambiguity. Already you have seen examples of forms that do not have the same meaning (which are excluded) and examples of forms which have the same meaning but which are clearly categorical (which are excluded). However, what happens if you simply cannot tell if the form has the same meaning or not because of two or more possible readings?

This case arises in the study of deontic modality where – at least in some corpora – there is structural ambiguity between the obligation/necessity reading and the older but still possible meaning of possession for the verb *have*, as in Example 8.49. Both examples come from American plays circa 1900 (Jankowski 2004: 91).

Example 8.49

    (a)   This treatment is the strongest one we *have to* offer you. (Wit/11,8, c. 1995/1998)

    (b)   It's simply a chance that one *has to* take. (CsW/373, 1, 41–42, c. 1925)

The solution to this problem is not entirely worked out in the field so far. Although standard practice is that such tokens should be removed from consideration, more recent studies have argued that contexts that are ambiguous are a vital part of the explanation (Schwenter and Torres-Cacoullos 2008; Traugott 2010). Such tokens should thus be coded separately since only further analysis and interpretation will provide the answer to whether and how they should be included or not and what part they may play in the analysis of variation.

Exceptional Distributions

As discussed earlier, exceptional distributions are cases that are outside of the regular systematic behavior of the system. This anomalous behavior can be due to a number of circumstances. In morpho-syntactic variables exceptional patterns tend to involve sequences that have become conventionalized. For example, there may be cases where the individual lexical items have become part of a larger chunk or prefab (a sequence of words that has become conventionalized). Take for example phrases such as *I mean, you know*, and *I see*. In studies of verbal *-s* they are excluded (e.g. Godfrey and Tagliamonte 1999: 99–100) because these items are functioning as discourse markers, not verbs, as in Example 8.50.

Example 8.50

    (a)   We'd seen the roses, *you see*. (YRK/004)

    (b)   Should have made it a bigger thing, *I think*. (YRK/004)

Discourse markers are very frequent in contemporary spoken data, as we will discover in Chapter 9. Many conventionalized utterances do not retain their lexical meanings. For example, in a study of past tense *be* (variable *was/were*), constructions such as in Example 8.51a are excluded (Cheshire and Fox 2009: 12; Tagliamonte and Smith 2000: 160). In a study of deontic modals, constructions such as in Example 8.51b were excluded.

Example 8.51

    (a)   So, I had friends, *as it were*, from my own environment. (YRK/008)

    (b)   I haven't watched a lot, *I must admit*. (CMK/015)

The asymptomatic patterns of these constructions are typically identified by categorical or near categorical usage of one variant or the other.

NOTE   When Rika Ito and I submitted the York adverb paper to the *Journal of Sociolinguistics* one of the reviewers commented that the zero adverb was not possible for sentential adverbs and that we had made a mistake in including them. The data contradicted this assumption. This is why I always say, "let the data be your guide."

How Research Develops

The investigation of variable (s) provides a good illustration of the ongoing evolution and development of sociolinguistic analysis. In 1989 and 1991 Poplack and Tagliamonte (1989a, 1991a) conducted studies of the variation between *-s* and Ø in Samaná English and African Nova Scotian English. The prevailing literature contained a wealth of different and conflicting explanations for the function and origin of *-s* in contexts other than third person singular. This is why Poplack and Tagliamonte based their analysis on the premise that verbal *-s* in all contexts other than third singular was insertion and grouped all non-third singular contexts together for analysis. As it turns out, in so doing, they lumped together two environments that should not have been collapsed together.

Several years later, Montgomery *et al.* (1993) conducted a study of verbal *-s* on a corpus of letters written by nineteenth-century African Americans. In these data they discovered that only one context was variable – third person plural – and within it the subject type constraint was operational (see also van Herk and Walker 2005). Moreover, another linguistic pattern was found to be in the mix: the proximity to subject constraint. In this pattern, any verb not adjacent to its subject will take *-s*. Because this constraint is a well-known pattern in northern British English (see example in Exercise 8.2), Montgomery *et al.* (1993) argued that the linguistic patterning found in the letters could be traced back to northern British English varieties and argued for a shared origin of white and black varieties of English in the southern United States (Montgomery *et al.* 1993: 349).

Montgomery *et al.* (1993) also made a critical methodological observation. They noted that their data could not be compared directly with either Schneider's (1983) WPA Ex-Slave Narratives or Poplack and Tagliamonte's (1989a) analysis of Samaná and the Ex-Slave Recordings. These studies had not separated out the third person plural contexts from the general non-third person singular contexts. They were right. The relevant context was buried inside the data.

I can recall Professor Montgomery gently suggesting to me that maybe I should have separated out the third plural contexts. We had, in fact, coded these contexts, but had never run the third person plural contexts separately. I went back to the data and redid the comparison of marginals. This led to another series of papers, but this time the critical division of the data was made so that the important constraint, the well-documented Northern Subject Rule, could be revealed.

NOTE   Never underestimate the wisdom of a sociolinguist who has coded thousands of tokens of a linguistic variable. They usually know what they're talking about.

The moral of the story is threefold. First, as a general point it is always better to make as many distinctions in your data as you can. Being able to separate out one context from the next might prove pivotal at a later time; in the case of verbal *-s*, it was the ability to simply rerun the data and focus in on third person plurals. Second, it is important to scour the literature for reported patterns of variation. The reports of type of subject and proximity to subject patterns were readily apparent in the literature. Although I had coded these distinctions in the data files I had not noticed that they should have been disentangled (and, of course, I should have). Third, notice what an impact a researcher's premises have on how the data for investigation are divided and interpreted. The early research on verbal *-s* had thought it was simply a grammatical mistake. Only after dozens of studies can we now reasonably say that variable (s) – at least in some dialects – is an inheritance from early patterns that can be traced back to northern Britain. It is still not clear why this variation is so widely diffused across the world's Englishes. As more consistent cross-variety comparisons are conducted, we will get closer to understanding this phenomenon. Given the relatively low frequencies of verbal *-s* outside of third person singular contexts, this may take place before the feature has disappeared altogether.

Research Questions Arising

Variable (s), (ly), and deontic modality each present the analyst with opportunities to explore key elements of language variation and change research – origins, diffusion, grammatical change, and social correlates. Despite extensive study, there are still many varieties where these features have not yet been studied. For example, given the historical trajectory of change it would be interesting to know how variable (ly) has evolved in varieties of English outside of the UK. While there is at least one large-scale study (e.g. Opdahl 2000a), it is still not clear what is going on in communities across North America. Reports in the literature suggest that the zero suffix is still around. If so, historical constraints such as the contrast between concrete vs. abstract meaning may be preserved (similar to the NP vs. pronoun) constraint with variable (s). Another potentially rich area of study would be to consider deontic modality. The interplay between *must, have to,* and *gotta* presents a layered cohort of variants that spans the spectrum of formality. This makes it an excellent choice for a study of style or register variation.

> **TIP**   One of my students (Michael Ritter) studied *Craigslist* personal ads across Canada and discovered that despite the fact that deontic *must* was rare in spoken corpora, it appeared in 48% of all deontic modality contexts in the personal ads, e.g. *Must love dogs, Must be easygoing*, etc. It is important to think creatively when tackling a linguistic variable. Where is a good place to find it?

Thinking about morpho-syntactic variation more broadly, it is worthwhile to consider whether there are changes in the morphology of a language at a given point in time. For example, over the last 1500 years English has changed from being a mainly synthetic language to a mainly analytic language. This means it has changed from being a language with many endings to one with fewer endings. It is probably worthwhile for future studies of morphological variation to consider how variation in morphology relates to this longitudinal change.

Exercises

Exercise 8.1   Identifying morpho-syntactic variation

The excerpt in Example 8.52 comes from the TEA. The speaker is Lorne Hyland, speaker [069], a male aged 27 born and raised in Toronto. The interviewer is [7]. Answer the questions based on this data.

Example 8.52

[069] Oh okay, so you'll notice on the four-hundred when you're driving North, there are subdivisions from- you-know it's a half-hour drive and- or forty-five minutes and it- there's forty-five minutes of houses. And when I was a kid going up there when I was ten, it was forest. All of it. Farms and forest. [7] So it's just boomed. [069] It's just oh, it's completely changed. ... Oh yeah, I mean the development in this city is- in the city it's- itself yeah, big- big time development. Like I saw the, the Bata Shoe Museum go up. I mean, there's like a condo, at least like- I don't know, thirty condos every year go up. All the- around the Skydome, I saw the Skydome go up. The- the exhibition stadium get knocked down. Like yeah it's- there's a lot of things- and it's weird because you actually like forget. "Oh what was that building that was there? I have no idea." And you just sort-of ... [7] You accept the changes. [069] Oh you have to, yeah. And you know lots of buildings- and it's sad because there's a lot of beautiful buildings that get torn down, which are really- and this is- I guess when- I guess people- what people don't realize about the city is that it is a very liv– living- like people live here, it's a very suburban city in a way.

Question 1   At least one morpho-syntactic variable can be authenticated from this sample of data, i.e. you will observe two different forms used for the same function. Name the variable and list the tokens (examples) below. HINT: It involves the verb "to be."

The variable is: _____

The tokens are: _____

(a) _____

(b) _____

(c) _____

(d) _____

Question 2   Calculate the overall distribution of the nonstandard variant.

Question 3   At least one other nonstandard feature stands out as frequent and multi-functional. Identify it and list the context in which it occurs.

The variable is: _____

_____

_____

_____

Exercise 8.2   Spotting linguistic variables

The following story comes from a narrative told by Laura Sturgess, aged 67 in Durham County, England (c. late 1990s). Laura's speech reveals many potential linguistic variables for research.

Like when I put mi foot in the fire- eh. I went the bingo. Mi husband doesn't like bingo you know. And we went to the prize bingo. There was our Sharon, our Helen, Elizabeth and me. And it was what used to be the Globe in Durham. I mean, I'm going back a few year. Gets in. Playing bingo. Won. We all won. Got all these things, great. And I looked at mi watch. I says, "God we'll have to get that five-to-five bus. He'll kill us." It was a Saturday. Run out. They all was getting on the bus. Mi foot went in the fire-bucket. And I'm running over the road. And mi foot was trapped in the fire-bucket. We didn't get on the bus. Everybody was laughing. Got mi foot out the fire-bucket. They had to take the fire-bucket back into the bingo. The embarrassment! Got a taxi home at the finish. We were too embarrassed to get on the bus. Ee god! Ee I have no money, pet, but I've got an interesting life.

Question 1   There is one syntactic variant in this excerpt whose nonstandard variant is quite frequent (N = 7). In the space below, list the tokens of the nonstandard variant.

Here are your hints: (i) it is a syntactic variable; (ii) the variants you must list are the nonstandard ones only; (iii) the nonstandard variants occur precisely 7 times in the excerpt.

Token (a) _____

Token (b) _____

Token (c) _____

Token (d) _____

Token (e) _____

Token (f) _____

Token (g) _____

Question 2   What varies? [name the feature of language involved in the co-variation]

_____

Question 3   There is at least one other variable (hint: morpho-syntactic) that can be *authenticated* in the excerpt above, i.e. both variants for the same meaning are present. Which variable is it? List the two contexts.

Hint: (i) it is a morpho-syntactic variable; (ii) the two variants occur in the very same sentence!

(a) _____

(b) _____

Question 4   In the same excerpt above you will see numerous *other* nonstandard forms, indicating potential linguistic variables in the data. List four. None of the four should come from the discourse/pragmatic level of grammar!

(a) _____

(b) _____

Table 8.3 Logistic regression analysis for nonstandard "be" (*is/was*) in nonexistentials in Early New Zealand English.

Factor group	Factors	%	FW	N
Gender/birth date	Male pre-1870	23	0.861	238
	Male post-1870	4	0.401	355
	Female pre-1870	3	0.389	192
	Female post-1870	3	0.324	279
Tense	Past	9	0.545	952
	Present	2	0.175	112
Subject type	Regular plural	14	0.721	252
	Conjoined	8	0.719	36
	third p. pronoun	7	0.444	589
	first p. pronoun	5	0.370	132
	Irregular plural	1	0.183	51
Input = 0.041				

Source: Hay and Schreier 2004.

(c) _____

(d) _____

Exercise 8.3   Interpreting morpho-syntactic variables

The results presented in Table 8.3 come from a study of subject–verb agreement in nonexistential contexts in New Zealand English (Hay and Schreier 2004). The linguistic variable is the alternation between different morphological forms of the verb "be" in the present, i.e. *is/are* or past tense, i.e. *was/were*, as in Example 8.53.

Example 8.53

(a) Present: The volunteers *is* there resting vs. The volunteers *are* resting.
(b) Past: The volunteers *was* there resting vs. The volunteeres *were* resting.

Question 1   The results reveal that singular concord is favored in which linguistic contexts?

(a) Past tense.
(b) Regular and conjoined plurals.
(c) Third person pronouns.
(d) First person pronouns.

Question 2   What category contains the most data?

(a) Males.
(b) Females.

(c) Past tense.
(d) Pronouns.

Question 3 Examining the proportions, distribution, and hierarchy of constraints for singular concord reveals that *is/was* can be best explained by:

(a) Time period.
(b) Type of subject.
(c) Older males talking with past temporal reference using nonpronominal subjects.
(d) Older women talking with past temporal reference using nonpronominal subjects.

Question 4 Which of Labov's (2001) principles explains the 1870 situation?

(a) Principle 1.
(b) Principle 2.
(c) Principle 3.
(d) Principle 4.

Question 5 Given these results, which of the following examples would be most likely to occur with singular concord?

(a) The men *was* armed.
(b) He and the photographer *was* upstairs.
(c) They *was* glassed over.
(d) We *was* always good friends.

Mini Quiz Answers

8.1 Q1: *The use of zero subjects in lines o, q; reduplicated subject in line n; definite article absence in line r; use of "anyways"(as opposed to "anyway"); indefinite pronouns "everybody" and "anybody."*

Q2: *In the examples there is variation between* –**one** *and* –**body** *for every form except "nobody," which is always "nobody". In contrast every use of an indefinite pronoun in the text is rendered as* –**one**!

8.2 *On one hand, the pattern reflects Principle 2, stability: the men have a higher rate of zero adverbs than the women. However, this is true only of the educated men. On the other hand, there are patterns that reflect Principle 3, change from above: the women use more zero adverbs than the educated men. Moreover, the educated middle-aged women use more of them and the use of the zero adverb by women is increasing.*

Background Reading

Studies of verbal (s)

Clarke 1997a; Cukor-Avila 1997; Feagin 1979; Godfrey and Tagliamonte 1999; McDavid 1969, 1977; McDavid and Davis 1972; Montgomery and Fuller 1996; Montgomery *et al.* 1993; Nevalainen and Raumolin-Brunberg 2003; Nevalainen, Raumolin-Brunberg, and Trudgill 2001; Poplack and Tagliamonte 2004; Schneider 1983, 1989; Singler 1997; Wright 2001, 2002, 2004.

Studies of adverb (ly)

Cheshire 1982: 80–81; Edwards and Weltens 1984: 113; Hedevind 1967; Hughes and Trudgill 1987: 20; Leeds 1974; Matthews 1938: 214; Tagliamonte, forthcoming; Tidholm 1979; Trudgill 1990: 80; Wright 1898–1905.

Studies of modal (have to)

Collins 2005; Corrigan 2000; Dollinger 2008; Facchinetti *et al.* 2003; Jankowski 2004; Krug 1998; Leech 2003: 236–237; Myhill 1995; Palmer 1979; Shepherd 1983; Tagliamonte and D'Arcy 2007b; Tagliamonte and Smith 2006; Wilson 2005.

9

Discourse/Pragmatic Features

It is precisely at the blurred margin between the syntactic and the extrasyntactic that the study of syntactic variation is particularly revealing and has the most to contribute. (Sankoff 1988a: 156)

In this chapter, I consider how sociolinguistic patterns are reflected in discourse-pragmatic features. These features straddle the boundaries of syntax and pragmatics.

There has been a groundswell of interest in discourse-pragmatic features over the last fifteen years in sociolinguistics. However, discourse-pragmatic features present particularly thorny problems for quantitative analysis. The vast majority of research on these types of variables has been qualitative. Why is this the case? What can a quantitative approach contribute to our knowledge of these features?

Discourse-pragmatic features are currently undergoing proliferation and expansion in contemporary English, some at a particularly fast rate. Linguistic change can be tapped within a condensed time frame. Recall that one of the major issues in contemporary sociolinguistics is the separation of patterns of linguistic change from patterns of age grading, lifespan change, and bona fide change in progress in the speech community. The best way to do this is through real-time studies. However, linguistic change typically takes place too slowly for analysts to be able to catch it in action. Because discourse-pragmatic changes seem to be happening quickly in the late twentieth and early twenty-first centuries, they allow for linguistic change, age grading, and lifespan change to be studied together.

Quotative (*be like*)

Beginning sometime in the early 1980s the North American quotative system began to reorganize. A new variant, quotative *be like*, as in Example 9.1, entered the system and started competing with the existing forms such as *said, asked, thought*, etc.

Variationist Sociolinguistics: Change, Observation, Interpretation, First Edition. Sali A. Tagliamonte.
© 2012 Sali A. Tagliamonte. Published 2012 by Blackwell Publishing Ltd.

Example 9.1

So then, she *was like*, "Oh, it's okay. Just remember to count to five and everything's okay." And I *was like*, "Oh, that's- that's that's okay." So then um, today she *asked* me again, "How are you juggling everything. I hope everything's going okay." And I *said*, "Well not really this week. This week is really stressful." (TOR/030)

The rise of *be like* is possibly the most vigorous and widespread change in the history of human language. Among Canadians in their twenties *be like* rose from constituting a mere 13% of the quotative system in 1995 to dominating the system seven years later in 2002. What type of change is this? Is it the result of regular processes of linguistic change? Or is it a classic case of age grading?

Due to the rapid expansion of *be like* it is possible to address the interface between real and apparent time and, in particular, determine whether age grading is involved. The rapid expansion of *be like* can tell us how changes diffuse globally and whether or not they increment in the same way across the different regions to which they are transplanted. Research on the quotative system from the mid-1990s onwards has begun exploring these questions. Early research on this feature focused on its use among young people and how people perceived it. However, only a corpus providing a cross-section of speakers from pre-adolescence to young adulthood, covering the time period in which age grading is supposed to occur, can address the question of linguistic change or age grading (Chambers 2003: 206–211).

The linguistic patterns underlying the use of *be like* can tell us much about its origin, development, and function in the grammar. Three main patterns have been studied in the literature.

Type of Quote

The first pattern relates to the type of quote. Researchers believe that *be like* was first used to introduce hypothetical speech (Romaine and Lange 1991: 262), but has gradually expanded to introduce all types of quoted dialogue, even direct speech, a classic case of extension. To test whether this is true and exactly what type of pattern exists, the analyst must categorize quotations into different types. If the quoted material is contained in a sequence of interchanges that advance the storyline or was part of an utterance to which the protagonists responded, it can be considered direct speech. However, if the quoted material is a report of an attitude or a general feeling of the narrator or group of people, it is considered hypothetical speech. For example, in Example 9.2 and Example 9.3, the final occurrence of the *be like* quotative introduces hypothetical speech. Contrast this with the preceding quotative verbs. These introduce direct speech.

Example 9.2

(a)   She's *like* "Right, you know, we're taking you out."
(b)   I *was like* "Ah I don't want to go out. Please no."
(c)   And they *'re like* "Come on, go and get dressed."
(d)   And Sue Parker– Sue Parker's dad makes home brew wine and it's so strong it's absolutely lethal.

(e) So she brought a bottle of that round and we drank that.

(f) I *was like* "O.K. I want to go out!" (UK/j)

Example 9.3

(a) We're walking around and Season *goes*, "Oh my God! There he is!"

(b) I'*m like*, "There who is?"

(c) "Well, there's Luigi."

(d) I'*m like*, "Luigi? The guy in the picture, Luigi?"

(e) And she'*s like*, "Yeah!"

(f) And I jumped behind her and I'm looking over her shoulder.

(g) "See right over there." [She points]

(h) She's pointing him out and everything and he seemed to be coming over this way.

(i) And I'*m like*, "Oh my God! Oh my God! Oh my God!"

(j) I was having a heart attack. (CDA/a)

Grammatical Person

The second pattern relates to the grammatical person of the subject. The use of *say* and *go* is reported to be favored for third person subjects, as in Examples 9.2a, 9.3c, and 9.3e, while *be like* was restricted to first person, as in Examples 9.2b, 9.2f, 9.3b, 9.3d, and 9.3i. However, Ferrara and Bell (1995: 279) claimed that *be like* underwent an expansion in function in the early 1990s in the United States. In their most advanced corpus (c. 1994), a change from the previous samples was found: nearly half of all tokens of *be like* were being used with third person subjects. However, to actually test this effect in data, the analyst must categorize each quotative verb according to the grammatical person of all the subjects in the data: first, second, or third.

Sex of the Speaker

The third pattern relates to the sex of the speaker. According to the literature *be like* is used more by females than by males. This difference is also one of the most well-known diagnostics of linguistic change in progress. According to some researchers the sex effect is predicted to be developmental, arising as the course of change accelerates. Yet Ferrara and Bell (1995: 277) argued that as the frequency of *be like* increased and expanded into a broader range of contexts it gradually lost its association with female speakers and spread to males as well.

Why does *be like* pattern in these ways? Ferrara and Bell (1995) argued that the patterns underlying the use of *be like* are indications of its ongoing grammaticalization. As discussed in Chapter 3, grammaticalization refers to the process by which words become part of the grammar of a language. When this happens the original meaning of the word tends to be lost (i.e. semantic bleaching) allowing it to generalize to more and more contexts in the grammar (i.e. expansion) and spread across the speech community and outwards into other communities. Females are traditionally regarded as being at the forefront of linguistic change (see Chapter 2), whether change from above or below. Thus, it was logical to expect that

Table 9.1   Predictions for increasing grammaticalization of *be like*.

Measure	Initial stage	Later stage
Sex	Females use more than males	Neutralization of sex difference
Grammatical person	Encode first person	Expansion into third person
Quote type	Used for internal dialogue	Expansion into direct speech

Source: Tagliamonte and Hudson, 1999: 159, Figure 1, extrapolated from Ferrara and Bell 1995.

females would have a higher frequency of *be like* generally, but how the sex effect is reflected developmentally remained in question.

Table 9.1 presents a summary of Ferrara and Bell's (1995) predictions. These can be used to interpret the linguistic patterns underlying the use of *be like* as it develops.

According to this model if an analyst finds that *be like* s found with third person subjects and is used with direct speech, then we may interpret this as an indication that the variety has reached a later stage in the development of *be like*. Further, if *be like* is found to be used as often by males as females, this too indicates a later development. In this way, patterns of use can be used as measures of developmental change of a linguistic feature within and across varieties.

The case studies that follow track the development of *be like* from 1995 to 2006. The analyses examine *be like* using the principle of accountability and test the effect of the following contextual constraints across time and space: (1) first person grammatical subjects, (2) the type of quoted material, and (3) the speaker's sex.

Be Like c. 1995–1996

In 1995 and 1996 students in my undergraduate sociolinguistics course at the University of Ottawa in Ottawa, Canada and the University of York in York, England collected narratives of personal experience from their peers, students between 18 and 28 years of age. Rachel Hudson and I analyzed the quotative system in these data (Tagliamonte and Hudson 1999). Table 9.2 shows the overall distribution of forms.

As noted by all scholars who had examined the quotative system up to that point, *say* was the most frequent form, representing approximately one-third of all quotatives in each variety: 31% in British English and 36% in Canadian English. This is consistent with its status as the standard form as well as its general semantic function. On the other hand, the distribution of the other forms is quite different between the two corpora. In British English *go*, *be like*, and *think* are equally represented (18%), with the zero quotative making most of the remainder (10%). In Canada however, *go* and the zero quotative are robust, 22% and 20% respectively, while *think* is negligible (4%). *Be like* represents 18% of the total number of all quotatives in British English and 13% in Canadian English.

As I have discussed previously, distributions such as those reported in Table 9.2 are informative; however, they do not reveal the patterns that may underlie the use of these forms, nor the relative strength of the impact of these patterns on variant choice when all potential effects are considered simultaneously. Both these perspectives will provide

Table 9.2   Overall distribution of quotative verbs, university students.

Quotatives	British English, 1997		Canadian English, 1995	
	%	N	%	N
say	31	209	36	219
go	18	120	22	135
be like	18	120	13	79
think	18	123	4	27
zero	10	66	20	123
Other	4	24	5	29
Total		665		612

Source: Tagliamonte and Hudson 1999: 158, Table 2.

important clues as to the competition and reorganization that may be taking place within the quotative system and lead to an explanation.

To tap these deeper trends, we performed a logistic regression analysis of the contribution of a set of social and linguistic factors, including speaker sex, grammatical person, and content of the quote to the probability that *be like* will be used as a quotative verb in these data. The results are shown in Table 9.3.

In British English *be like* is favored by females, at 0.67. In Canadian English the same constraint hierarchy is observed for *be like*, i.e. females favor it, but here the effect is not statistically significant.

Mini Quiz 9.1

Q1   What principle of linguistic change is observable in Table 9.3?

The next step is to observe the internal linguistic conditioning of the quotatives. The results for grammatical person reveal that *be like* is favored in first person contexts in both British English, 0.56, and Canadian English, 0.60, and in both cases it is statistically significant. Similarly, as far as the type of quote is concerned, *be like* is favored for nonlexicalized sound and internal dialogue and disfavored for direct speech, at 0.45 and 0.47 in both varieties.

This evidence from the overall frequency of forms suggests that we have caught these two varieties at an early stage in the development of *be like*. In both locales the innovative form represents less than 15% of the system. Nevertheless, *be like* has systematic and parallel linguistic patterning in both varieties, which also mirrors patterns of use reported in the United States. Only the sex effect shows a discrepancy across varieties. It could be that the low threshold of *be like* use in Canada prevents this factor from being selected as statistically significant. In this case, we can resort to the constraint hierarchy for evidence (Poplack and

Table 9.3   Logistic regression of the contribution of internal and external factors to the probability of *be like* vs. all other quotative verbs. Factor weights not selected as significant in square brackets.

	British English		Canadian English	
	FW	N	FW	N
Quote type				
Nonlexicalized sound	0.67	39	0.64	17
Internal dialogue	0.57	194	0.69	75
Direct speech	0.45	427	0.47	517
Range	*22*		*22*	
Grammatical person				
First	0.56	272	0.60	245
Third	0.43	251	0.41	232
Range	*13*		*19*	
Sex				
Female	0.67	298	[0.54]	382
Male	0.36	367	[0.44]	230
Range	*31*			

Source: Tagliamonte and Hudson 1999: 160–163, Tables 3–5.

Tagliamonte 2001). Females show a preference for *be like* in both locations. This is bolstered by independent evidence that *be like* is a female feature in Canadian and British English (Buchstaller 2006; Dailey-O'Cain 2000). Based on Labov's (2001a: 418) description: "when a change from below is detected or suspected in a city, it has been found that the most advanced speakers can regularly be located among young women, 20 to 30 years old, … [and] upwardly mobile," Rachel and I argued that *be like* is a change at an early stage of development. But what type of change?

> **TIP**   Tagliamonte and Hudson (1999: 166) noted that their British narratives had more introspection and less action than their Canadian narratives. Perhaps this is one of the reasons why *be like* has made such rapid in roads into British English. To date no one has taken up their call for more research on narrative style across different varieties of English, style, or other social factors (but see Johnstone 1990).

Be Like, c. 2002–2003

Let us now move forward in time to 2002–2003. Students in one of my undergraduate research courses at the University of Toronto, in Canada, interviewed members of their own families and social networks, mostly brothers, sisters, and close friends. These materials

Table 9.4 Overall distribution of quotative verbs, Canadian youth, 9–19 years of age, c. 2002–2003.

Quotative verb	%	N
be like	58	1198
zero	18	362
say	11	227
go	7	136
think	2	34
other	5	101
Total		2058

Source: Tagliamonte and D'Arcy 2004a: 501, Table 2.

were comparable to the earlier Canadian and British data in terms of speaker age and socioeconomic class as well as providing a partial real-time perspective. More important to the building information on *be like* is the fact that this sample includes speakers from the ages of 9–19. This age span comprises distinct education levels within the Canadian educational system (primary school, middle school, high school, and first-year university). Thus this sample comprises the age groups who are actively engaged in the vernacular reorganization and incrementation of *be like*. This permitted Alex D'Arcy and me to tackle the question of how *be like* was changing in apparent time (Tagliamonte and D'Arcy 2004a). Table 9.4 displays the overall distribution of forms among the pre-adolescent and adolescent speakers.

Focusing first on the inventory of forms, this variety comprises the same four major quotatives – *say, go, think, be like* – and zero as found previously. However, by this point in time (2002–2003), *be like* represents a full 58% of the quotative system, dwarfing both of the traditional forms *say* and *think*. *Think* is particularly scant, accounting for a mere 2% of the data. *Go* is also rare at 7%. All other quotatives combined represent only 5% of the data. *Be like* has virtually taken over the system in Toronto English.

Figure 9.1 displays a comparison of the overall distribution of quotatives in Canadian English in 1995 and the current data set from 2002 to 2003.

The perspective of real time provides a stunning display of rapid linguistic change. In 1995, the frequency of *be like* was only 13% among Canadian 18–28 year olds. In the more recent materials the overall frequency is 58%. A direct comparison with the 17–19-year-old speakers in the TEA (not shown) (see Tagliamonte and D'Arcy 2004a) reveals an even higher overall frequency, with *be like* representing 62% of quotative usage. The proportion of *be like* increased by more than four and a half times in seven years! In contrast, *say, go,* and *think* all dropped in frequency. Where once scholars consistently reported *say* to be the most frequent form (representing approximately one-third of the quotative system) (Blyth, Recktenwald, and Wang 1990; Ferrara and Bell 1995; Tagliamonte and Hudson 1999), it is no longer, now accounting for just 11% of quotative verbs overall. This suggests that *be like* has now moved in on the territory once held by *go, think,* and *say* in Canadian English, not simply *go* and *think*, as reported in Tagliamonte and Hudson (1999: 167). Yet the proportion of zero and other forms remains constant, suggesting that at least some parts of the system remain unaffected by the encroachment of *be like*.

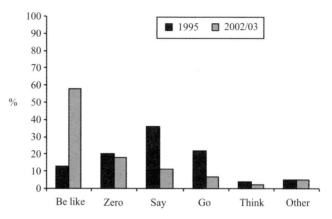

Figure 9.1 Distribution of quotatives in Canadian English, c. 1995 and c. 2002–2003.
Source: Tagliamonte and D'Arcy 2004: 502, Figure 1.

> **NOTE** Quotative *be like* is not the only new quotative at the turn of the twenty-first century. In California, *be all* is reported (Rickford *et al.* 2007; Waksler 2001), but so far it has not come to Toronto. Apparently, *be all* is one of those short-lived innovations and this is perhaps why it has not diffused. In London, *this is* has come into the vernacular (Fox and Cheshire 2009). What's next?

Be Like across the Speech Community

The next step was to consider *be like* from the perspective of the whole speech community by analyzing this feature in the full TEA. Using these materials Alex D'Arcy and I once again analyzed *be like*, this time by tracking its progression within the entire speech community (Tagliamonte and D'Arcy 2007a).

Figure 9.2 displays the frequency of each of the main quotatives according to speaker age.

This graphic representation of the Toronto speech community reveals a significant watershed in the population. Among speakers under age 30 *be like* overshadows all other forms. Conversely, *say* is by far the front-runner among those over 40. In the middle, among the 30 year olds, we find a generation in flux where the frequency of *be like* is virtually equal to that of *say*.

Our goal was to find out whether these Torontonians share the same (variable) grammar for *be like*. We tested for the operation of the constraints discussed earlier. Table 9.5 provides the same statistical model for each age group for whom *be like* is robust: the 9–14 year olds, the 15–16 year olds, the 17–19 year olds, the 20–29 year olds, and the 30–39 year olds.

Let us work through the three lines of evidence in variation analysis. First, all the constraints are statistically significant for all age groups that use *be like*. The second line of evidence is constraint ranking. Here, the hierarchies are entirely as predicted. Internal

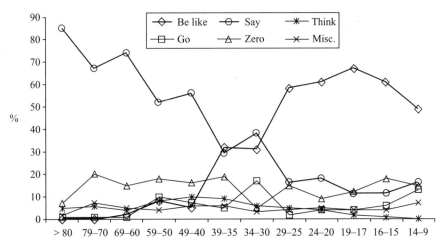

Figure 9.2 Overall distribution of quotatives across the generations in Toronto English.
Source: Tagliamonte and D'Arcy 2007a: 205, Figure 2.

Table 9.5 Logistic regression of the contribution of internal and external factors to the probability of *be like*, Canadian English, Toronto, Canada, 2003–2004, 9–39 years of age.

	9–14 years		15–16 years		17–19 years		20–29 years		30–39 years	
Input	0.63		0.85		0.82		0.72		0.31	
total N	600		505		1992		1138		524	
	FW	N	FW	N	FW	N	FW	N	FW	N
Quote type										
Thought	0.70	50	0.73	87	0.54	408	0.55	265	0.70	138
Direct speech	0.48	479	0.44	351	0.49	144	0.48	775	0.41	327
Range	*22*		*29*		*5*		*7*		*29*	
Grammatical person										
First	0.56	170	0.55	163	0.55	804	0.56	460	0.51	232
Third	0.47	316	0.46	230	0.45	905	0.44	499	0.49	191
Range	*9*		*9*		*10*		*12*		*2*	
Sex										
Female	0.53	423	0.55	340	0.56	1518	0.52	732	0.48	346
Male	0.44	177	0.41	165	0.33	473	0.47	406	0.53	178
Range	*9*		*14*		*23*		*5*		*5*	

Source: Tagliamonte and D'Arcy 2007a: 206, Table 2.

dialogue consistently favors *be like* over direct speech. The grammatical person constraint is stable with first-person subjects favoring *be like* and third persons disfavoring. Finally, females favor *be like* over males, except among the 30 year olds, where males slightly favor.

The consistency in statistical significance of factors, as well as in the constraint hierarchies for each age group, shows remarkable stability across the population of *be like* users, suggesting that it is firmly entrenched in their community grammar. Moreover, observe also that this form is used well into the adult population (the 30 year olds), although Figure 9.2 clearly corroborates earlier research heralding this as an under-40s phenomenon (Ferrara and Bell 1995: 286).

The third line of evidence is strength. Notice that the strength of quotative type differs depending on speaker age. It stands as a clear second-ranked constraint for the 9–14 and 15–16 years olds, with ranges of 22 and 29, respectively. It is also one of the top-ranked constraints among the 30 year olds. But, among the 17–19 year olds and the 20–29 year olds it is very weak. There is little to add about the first versus third person constraint, except to note that it is also quite weak, particularly among the 30 year olds. Finally, the sex effect peaks in strength among the 17–19 year olds. Interestingly, among the 30–39 year olds, it operates in the opposite direction, albeit weakly; males, not females, favor *be like*. In sum, despite the apparent stability of *be like* in terms of the significance of factors, the detailed evidence from the constraint rankings and their relative strength shows us subtle changes going on in the system.

The next step is to model what the underlying mechanisms driving this system might be. The 30 year olds are likely to have been the first generation of *be like* users. If so, then the speakers in their 20s represent the second generation. These age groups can be positioned in the model as Stage 1 and Stage 2. Labov's (1994; 2001a: 447) account of sound change sets the age of stabilization for phonological features at about 17. In these data, not only do the 17–19 year olds have the highest frequency for *be like*, but they are also the group where the sex effect is strongest. We therefore take them to represent Stage 3.

Table 9.6 reconfigures the results from Table 9.5, grouping the data into the three age groups that are on the advancing edge of change. The pathway of change can be deduced from an examination of the evidence.

At Stage 1, *be like* favors inner thought. In fact, most studies concur that *be like* entered the quotative system carrying with it this pragmatic correlation. Further evidence to support this comes from the fact that the effect of content of the quote is strongest among the 30 year olds, the early adopters of *be like* in the 1980s. If so, then we would expect the pragmatic constraint to be most salient for them, and it is.

A favoring effect of *be like* with first person has been reported in the literature from the inception of *be like* use, thus it must have been an early correlation as well. The evidence in support of this position is that the grammatical person constraint reaches statistical significance for every age group. It too is present from the beginning, although somewhat stronger at Stage 2 and beyond. In sum, the evidence from studies suggest that *be like* has reached what I will refer to as Stage 3 in its evolution, at least in Canadian English as spoken in Toronto: it is being used for direct speech as much as internal dialogue, however it continues to be favored with first person subjects and has developed a strong female lead.

Putting the research on *be like* in perspective reveals that it has quickly made inroads into the quotative system of contemporary English over the past 20 years or so. The fact that *be like* was actually more frequent in British English (18%) than Canadian English (14%) in 1995–1996 highlights the fact that the spread of this linguistic features does not follow geographic lines of diffusion (since, of course, Canada is much closer to the US where *be like* is thought to have originated). Yet the same internal linguistic factors seem to be pervasive, suggesting transmission. In the earliest stages, *be like* in both British and Canadian English was highly localized, used for nonlexicalized sound or internal dialogue and for first person

Table 9.6 Contribution of external and internal factors on the use of *be like* in Toronto English, 17–39 years of age, 2003–2004 reordered.

	Stage 1	Stage 2	Stage 3
	30–39 years	*20–29 years*	*17–19 years*
Corrected mean	0.32	0.71	0.81
Total N	453	1137	1842
	FW	FW	FW
Quote type			
Thought	0.74	0.55	0.54
Direct speech	0.41	0.48	0.49
Range	*33*	*7*	*5*
Grammatical person			
First	0.52	0.56	0.55
Third	0.48	0.45	0.45
Range	*4*	*11*	*10*
Sex			
Female	0.49	0.52	0.55
Male	0.52	0.48	0.35
Range	*3*	*4*	*20*

Source: Tagliamonte and D'Arcy 2007a: 208, Table 3.

subjects. These were the very same linguistic patterns as had earlier been reported in American English.

By 2003–2004, just seven years later, *be like* had risen to be the majority form for all speakers between the ages of 9 and 19 in Canada. The same internal constraints on *be like* continue to be operational. As in earlier studies, *be like* is favored in first person contexts, a constraint that is maintained in apparent time. The consistency of this effect across major varieties of English Canadian and British English (Tagliamonte and Hudson 1999) and American English (Blyth *et al.* 1990; Ferrara and Bell 1995), and in real time among African Americans in the rural south (Cukor-Avila 2002), suggests that it is a defining feature of *be like*. Similarly, the effect of content of the quote was also operative. However, with this constraint comes evidence for ongoing grammaticalization. Where once *be like* was almost always used for inner dialogue or thought – and this is the strongest constraint reported by those who have tested for it (e.g. Cukor-Avila 2002; Tagliamonte and Hudson 1999) – by the early 2000s there is evidence of *be like* expanding into direct speech (see also D'Arcy 2004). The 17–19 year olds in Toronto in 2003–2004 use more *be like* to represent direct speech than any other form. With increasing frequency, speaker sex had become significant, at least for the most advanced speakers. The correlation between frequency and sex was confirmed by apparent-time data: the more frequent *be like*, the stronger the effect of sex, corroborating the conjecture that the further *be like* diffuses, "the more likely it is to differentiate male and female speech" (Tagliamonte and Hudson 1999: 167). Thus, rather than neutralizing, the external constraint of speaker sex becomes more marked, increasing in strength as *be like* specializes further into the quotative system.

When did the sex effect develop? Early studies were inconsistent in their findings for sex (Blyth *et al.* 1990; Dailey-O'Cain 2000; Ferrara and Bell 1995; Tagliamonte and Hudson 1999). According to Ferrara and Bell's model, the sex effect is there from the beginning, and gradually neutralized as *be like* expanded in function and diffused in the speech community. Yet in the studies I have reported on here, *be like* appears to do the opposite. It develops a correlation with female speakers as it rises in frequency, until this becomes one of the strongest constraints on its use. This is precisely what would be predicted if, as Labov (2001a: 308) suggested, sociolinguistic variation develops subsequent to linguistic variation (see Chapter 2).

It will be interesting to see what the next step in this process will be. Where in the grammar will *be like* expand to next? Which direction will it go? How far and wide into other speech communities around the world? Will all varieties change at the same rate and in the same way? When will another new quotative surface?

New research by Buchtaller and D'Arcy (2009) has begun to answer these questions. Examination of the diffusion of *be like* across Canadian, British, and New Zealand English using comparative sociolinguistic methods reveals that some constraints (e.g. grammatical person, content of the quote) are constant; however, the constraint ranking of factors and their relative strength differs. In contrast, the sociolinguistic conditioning is unique in each locale. Therefore, it appears that when a change diffuses from one major variety of English to another it does so by restructuring part of the variable grammar as the change embeds itself in the locale (pre-existing) system. This process does not appear to be distinct from the diffusion of linguistic change *within* dialect areas. As Labov (2007) demonstrates, weakening of patterns and structural loss is typical of diffusion. The question now becomes how to distinguish between dialect leveling and geographic diffusion (see Kerswill 2003) and then to factor in the potentially simultaneous mechanisms of grammaticalization (Tagliamonte and Denis 2008a).

Another question for future research is whether the adolescents and young adults who are using *be like* nearly categorically today will continue to do so as they grow older (see Tagliamonte 2008a).

Mini Quiz 9.2

Q1　Take a look at Example 10.30 in Chapter 10. There are (at least) three suggestive discourse-pragmatic variables that are frequent in the example and warrant investigation. What are they? HINTS: (i) they both occur in a specific location in the sentence structure; (ii) they appear to be sprinkled through the narrative.

General Extenders

General extenders (GEs) are features of English that occur at the ends of sentences, have a relatively structured configuration, and typically serve to "evoke some larger set" (Dubois 1992: 198) by generalizing from a preceding referent to the larger class of items to which that referent belongs. Example 9.4 illustrates. In Example 9.4a, *or something like that* refers to other types of fruit that are like mangos. In Example 9.4b, *or something* alludes to means of transportation aside from buses. In Example 9.4c, *and things like that* calls attention to all the detritus that one might find outside on the ground.

Example 9.4

    (a)   So then I asked for like, mango *or something like that.* (TOR/020)
    (b)   I'll walk, or I'll take the bus *or something.* (TOR/002)
    (c)   I tried to cover it up by kicking a bunch of dirt and sawdust *and things like that.* (TOR/053)
    (d)   Then you'd do your scales *and all that stuff.* (TOR/016)
    (e)   They used to grow tomatoes *and stuff like that.* (TOR/042)
    (f)   Yeah, lots of towels, and sinks *and stuff.* (TOR/017)

In addition to these typical GE combinations a number of idiosyncratic forms can sometimes share a similar function. These include *and so on* (Example 9.5a) and *or whatever* (Example 9.5b), among others.

Example 9.5

    (a)   Then of course the wagons came along with uh, the bread, and the milk, *and so on.* (TOR/060)
    (b)   So if you opened their cab door for them, and you stuck out your hand, you'd get a quarter or a nickel *or whatever.* (TOR/111)

The inclusion of these forms in a study of GEs is debatable (see Cheshire 2007); however, we will include them in the discussion as members of a general set of utterances that occur in sentence final position.

Historical Perspective

Table 9.7 shows that GEs can be traced back to the fourteenth century (Poutsma 1926: 914).

The earliest forms appear to have been the fixed expression types, such as *and such, and so forth,* and *et cetera.* A set extending use of *and things* can be found in Shakespeare (c. 1596), (Example 9.6a); however, the same type of reading for *and stuff* is more difficult to substantiate at this early period. Example 9.6b is perhaps the earliest example in the OED.

Example 9.6

    (a)   We will haue rings, *and things,* and fine array. (*The Taming of the Shrew*)
    (b)   Lewis, I find you pretend to give the Duke notions of the mathematics, *and stuff.* (J. Lewis, *Mem. Dk. Glocester,* c. 1697)

The disjunctive forms with *or* (*or something; or whatever*) appear to be later developments, only turning up in the nineteenth century. This timeline is important, as we shall see, because it is critical for understanding and interpreting variation and/or change in the GE system.

GEs are reported in contemporary Germanic, Romance, and other language families, suggesting that they are not unique to English but occur across a wide range of related languages.

Table 9.7   Timeline of earliest attestation of general extenders (OED).

Middle English	Early Modern				Modern			
	14th	*15th*	*16th*	*17th*	*18th*	*19th*	*20th*	*21st*
and such	(1400–1450) --							
and so forth	(1574) ---							
and things	(1596) --							
et cetera	(1640) ---							
and stuff	(1697) ---							
and that	(1702) --							
or something	(1814) ---------------------------------							
or whatever	(1905) -------------------							
and crap	(1951) -------------							
and shit	(1957) -----------							

Source: Tagliamonte and Denis 2010: 340, Figure 1.

Previous Research

By the early 2000s there were numerous studies of GEs, each attempting in its own way to explain how social, grammatical, and discourse-pragmatic factors condition GE usage and realization.

Social Factors

The frequency and type of GE is intimately linked to the social context. The foremost of these is the correlation of GE use with particular socioeconomic groups. Higher use of GEs is associated with working-class speech and certain GEs in particular, e.g. *and that* (e.g. Cheshire 2007: 165). Other GEs such as *and stuff* and *and things* are associated with middle-class speakers. GEs are typically associated with youth speech. Dubois found that age was the strongest factor influencing GE use in Montreal French in corpora from 1971 and 1984, suggesting that GE usage is age-graded (Dubois 1992: 185). In New Zealand the highest frequency users were the young middle-class females and young working-class males (Stubbe and Holmes 1995: 77). Stubbe and Holmes (1995: 83) attribute the accelerated frequency of GE use by young middle-class females as a change from below, with this group leading the change.

GE use is also associated with the interactional context, with respect to both in-group affiliation and informal registers. In Stubbe and Holmes' (1995: 79) data, *and so on* and *or so* were used only in formal interviews, never in conversations, suggesting that they are prestige variants. A similar finding is reported for American English (Overstreet and Yule 1997: 252) where *and so on* and *et cetera* are more frequent in formal discourse, and that *and everything, and stuff, or something, or anything,* and *or whatever* are features of informal speech suggesting that some forms convey formality and others, informality.

Discourse-Pragmatic Factors

Besides functioning as markers of a general set, GEs have been associated with a wide range of discourse-pragmatic functions, identified as participation, interaction, and identification. *Participation* involves ideas of politeness and shared assumptions where the speaker uses GEs to make a connection with their interlocutor through shared knowledge about the topic under discussion (Overstreet 1999: 98). Note that in Example 9.7, the interviewer apparently uses the GEs to claim knowledge of the yacht club scene to ask a question about the interviewee's experience.

Example 9.7

> [7] Right, right. Um, the– is it a tight community at those– at the yacht-clubs and *things-like-that?* Like is– are there lots of functions *and things?* (TOR/044)

The *interaction* function of GEs involves turntaking and conversation organization where the use of GEs marks transitions in discourse, such as questions, as in Example 9.8, or a topic shift, as in Example 9.9.

Example 9.8

> But they would have all kinds of bands. Like every Sunday in the park, they would have like jazz bands *and things*. But what I was always fascinated with was when the bagpipers came down in their beautiful regalia and I just was fascinated with the ones that would play those big drums, 'cause they would swing around their– their mallets and– *and stuff*. (TOR/051)

Identification functions associate GEs with particular social identities such as youth speech or male/female distinctions.

Linguistic Factors

An intriquing fact about GEs is that the generic element and referent do not always match. Consider the GE *or something* in Example 9.9. It may refer to a list of things that a deity might leave for a nonbeliever or to the various actions that might be offered as a sign of a deity's existence.

Example 9.9

> (a) If there's really a god leave a sign *or something.* (TOR/016)
> (b) If there's really a god leave a sign or a sheep or a book ...
> (c) If there's really a god leave a sign or a send a storm or slam a door ...

Thus, while GEs have a primary discourse function of generalizing to a set (Aijmer 1985), there is evidence of extension. What does this type of development tell us?

> **NOTE**   If GEs are strongly associated with group affiliation, one hypothesis that can be made is that they should be more prevalent among people who share common characteristics. If this is so, then a potentially rich study design would be to conduct matching interviews with old friends compared to strangers. What will happen to the use of general extenders?

Grammaticalization
Recent studies have analyzed the GE system of contemporary English in terms of grammaticalization. Cheshire (2007) specifically tests the hypothesis that GEs are undergoing grammaticalization by analyzing GE use among young people aged 14–15 in three towns in England in the late 1990s: Reading, Milton Keynes, and Hull. The argument for the grammaticalization of GEs comes from linguistic patterns that can be explained using the three mechanisms of grammaticalization: decategorialization phonetic reduction, and bleaching.

Decategorialization   Decategorialization involves the loss of semantic and syntactic properties characteristic of the original lexical category of a form. How can this be tested for GEs? The assumption is that when GEs first entered the language they generalized to a set based on their referent. Thus, their semantic and syntactic properties matched the referent: *stuff* for mass nouns; *things* for count nouns, etc. However, in American English *and stuff* and *or something* both occurred in contexts where there was no discernable set extending function and in British English *or something* had extended beyond set-marking. Thus, it appeared that GEs could become bleached of their previous morphosyntactic properties so that they no longer matched the features of their referent. The expectation, therefore, is that GE forms on the forefront of grammaticalization will be found in positions where their morphosyntactic are discordant with their morphosyntatic referents.

Phonetic reduction   Cheshire, following Aijmer (2002: 227), Erman (1995: 145), and others tested for the effect of short vs. long GEs. She discovered that the shorter variants – *and stuff* (vs. *and stuff like that*), *and things* (vs. *and things like that*) – exhibited greater decategorialization (Cheshire 2007: 169). Under the hypothesis that the shorter GE forms result from the erosion of the longer ones, this trend identifies another diagnostic of grammaticalization (Cheshire 2007: 167).

Bleaching   The original function of GEs was to signal that their referent was a member of a general set of related elements; however, many researchers observed that this set is often difficult to reconstruct (e.g. Winter and Norrby 2000: 4). This is especially true of the short forms where the general set is not easily projected, again supporting a grammaticalization explanation. Cheshire (2007: 179) finds that GEs function in the communicative domains of information management, textual organization, speech management, turntaking, and the interpersonal relationship between speakers. Many individual tokens were found to be multifunctional, conveying several pragmatic meanings. This plurality of meanings is emblematic of restructuring leading to grammatical change. Grammatical change can be identified in other ways as well. For example, GEs observed to be most advanced along the cline of grammaticalization (*and that, and everything,* and *or something*) co-occur the least often with other discourse markers. Cheshire (2007: 185) argues that as the GEs develop new pragmatic functions, they no longer need the support of other discourse markers. In this way, absence of collocation with discourse markers would be another disgnostic of grammaticalization.
    These results set the scene for a replication study in another variety of North American English.

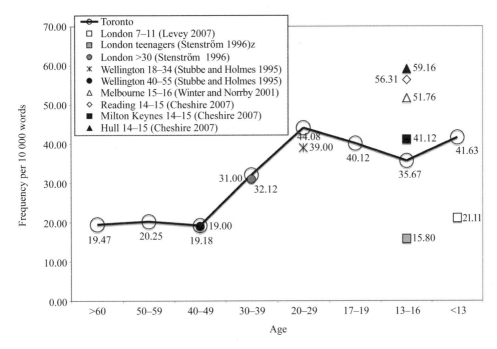

Figure 9.3 Cross-study comparison of GE frequency per 10 000 words.
Source: Tagliamonte and Denis 2010: 349, Figure 2.

Toronto English, c. 2004

In 2007, Derek Denis and I conducted a quantitative analysis of the GE system in the TEA (Tagliamonte and Denis 2010). Because of the broad age range of the speakers (aged 9–92) we were able to directly address the claims of grammaticalization by using the apparent time construct. Further, we utilized the comparative sociolinguistic method to analyze the nature of this discourse-pragmatic system more generally. We began with a simple comparison of the frequency of GEs per 10 000 words, a measure that enables us to compare across most of the earlier studies.

Figure 9.3 plots frequency per 10 000 words by speaker age (see also Cheshire 2007: 162, Table 2). Age is shown across the x-axis, from oldest to youngest such that adolescents and pre-adolescents are on the right. The comparison includes the adolescents in the three English towns studied by Cheshire (2007), Winter and Norrby's (2000) study of Melbourne Australia, Stenström et al.'s (2002) study of the COLT corpus which comprises London adolescents in 1996, Stubbe and Holmes (1995) analysis of Wellington, New Zealand, and Levey's examination of pre-adolescents in London (Levey 2007).

The frequency of GEs in the Toronto data by age group is shown by the joined lines with the large circles while other studies are indicated by smaller designators. The older populations exhibit a remarkable correspondence across studies. The data from the earlier studies on 20–29 year olds, 30–39 year olds and among the 40–49 year old match the Toronto speakers nearly identically. This finding lends support to the idea that these features are a relatively stable feature of English, linked to age, at least in terms of overall frequency. In contrast, notice that the comparisons for young people in the different communities have quite *different* rates of GEs. There are six studies of 13–16 year olds and three studies of <13 year olds. The highest frequency is 59.16 in Hull in the late 1990s and the lowest is 15.8 in London in 1996. This might be due to the fact that GEs have been increasing over time. However, the Toronto adolescents are the most recent data and they fit somewhere in the middle, more like Milton Keynes than either London or Hull or Reading in England or Melbourne in Australia. Nevertheless, the cross-variety perspective reveals that GEs are overall more frequent among the young than those over 30. The crux of the issue is whether the high rates of GEs among this sector of the population are the result of age grading, as Dubois (1992) suggests for the GEs in her Canadian French data from Montreal, or whether they can they be explained by ongoing change (Cheshire 2007), or both. The first hypothesis predicts that speakers simply use more GEs during their adolescent years then their use declines as they become adults, retreating perhaps to a nominal frequency that is sociolinguistically correlated – age grading. The second hypothesis predicts a system in which ongoing developments among GEs are shifting their grammatical function – namely grammaticalization. Without further analysis there is no way to solve this question.

Let's begin the analysis of the Toronto GE system by taking an inventory of forms. This is shown in Table 9.8.

> **NOTE**   Table 9.8 constitues the full inventory of forms in Toronto, c. 2004. What general extenders are found in your variety? How do they compare to the ones found in Toronto?

The Toronto data are consistent with previous research in that the speech community exhibits a rich variation of forms. However, several main variants predominate: *and stuff* and *or something* are the most common. This is consistent with Overstreet and Yule's (1997) study of American English where these were also the top-ranked forms. Similarly, *and stuff* is one of the most frequent variants in England, particularly in Hull (Cheshire 2007: Table 5). In contrast, Australian English (Dines 1980: 20) had only two *stuff* forms, compared to eighteen *thing* forms and 1.7% of all adjunctive forms in the London-Lund Corpus were *stuff* forms (Aijmer 2002: 221). Thus, salient contrasts in frequency are evident. This is especially true of the GE variant containing *and stuff*, which seems to be frequent in some locales, but not in others. The same is true of the GE *and that*. Although widely cited as a marker of working-class speech in Australia, Scotland, and figuring prominently in Cheshire's British towns, particularly the working class (Cheshire 2007), *and that* rarely occurs in Toronto (only 2% of all GEs). A number of pointed similarities and differences exist across varieties. Nevertheless, if younger people are changing the way GEs are used in recent times, then we need an analysis that compares these forms consistently across varieties according to age, sex, and occupation. Further, examination of the diagnostics of grammaticalization can establish the state of grammatical development of forms.

Building on the argumentation put forward by Cheshire for British English we replicated each of the tests she designed as follows (Tagliamonte and Denis 2010):

(1) Loss of lexical material
    (a)   e.g. *and stuff like that* → *and stuff*
    (b)   e.g. *and everything like that* → *and everything*, etc.

Table 9.8 Overall distribution of GEs and fixed expressions in Toronto, c. 2003–2004.

General extender	N	%
Forms with stuff		
and stuff	381	17
and stuff like that	218	10
other long *stuff* forms	74	3
	673	
Forms with *things*		
and things	44	2
and things like that	93	4
other long *thing* forms	82	4
	219	
Forms with −*thing* +quantifier		
or something	347	16
or something like that	146	7
	493	
and everything	146	7
and everything like that	27	1
	173	
or anything	87	4
or anything like that	42	2
	129	
or nothing	4	1
Fixed expressions		
or/and/but/so/like whatever	307	14
and all that	73	3
and that	41	2
and so on	36	2
and whatnot	22	1
other fixed expressions	30	1
TOTAL	2200	100

(2) Decategorialization
   (a) e.g. *stuff* with mass nouns→ with count nouns → with other phrases
   (b) e.g. *things* with count nouns→ with mass nouns → with other phrases, etc.
(3) Semantic change
   (a) Set marking → no set marking
(4) Pragmatic shift
   (a) Occurrence with discourse markers → lessening or lack of co–occurrence.

If grammaticalization is still in progress, then we would expect a shift in patterning from the oldest to youngest speakers according to these measures. If grammaticalization has already occurred, the more advanced pattern should prevail across the speech community.

Table 9.9 summarizes the results of this series of tests for the most frequent of the GE variants (Tagliamonte and Denis 2010: Figures 4–7).

Table 9.9 Summary of findings for distributional tests of grammaticalization.

General extender	(1) Loss of lexical material	(2) Decategorialization	(3) Semantic change	(4) Pragmatic shift
and things	X	X	X	✓
and things like that	–	X	X	✓
and stuff	X	X	X	X
and stuff like that	–	X	X	X
or something	✓			
or something like that	–			

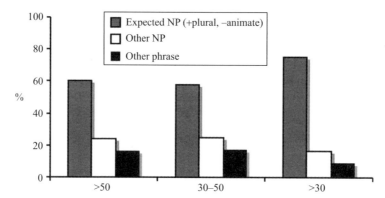

Figure 9.4 Test of decategorization of *and things like that*.
Source: Tagliamonte and Denis 2010: 355, Figure 6.

The Xs represent the case of no change in apparent time while the checks indicate that the development was visible in apparent time. As an exemplar of the many distributional analyses that went into this series of tests, Figure 9.4 shows the test for diagnostic (2) for the form *and things*.

Where long *thing* forms would be expected (i.e. for count nouns) this is where they occur *least* frequently, and for each age group. The extended contexts, other types of NPs and phrases, are the most frequent across the board. This is the profile we would anticipate for an advanced grammatical profile, the opposite result to the expectation for a long GE form. Moreover, the fact that the same ranking of these internal linguistic contexts is parallel in each age group means that a later stage of grammaticalization is represented by the entire community. This means that *and things like that* is decategorized and has been for some time, at least since the oldest people in Toronto acquired their variety of English. Yet the same tests showed an advanced grammaticalization profile in England. This means that the GE system in British and Canadian English is actually quite divergent with respect to grammaticalization. Unlike many other studies, in this case British English appears to be ahead of North American English.

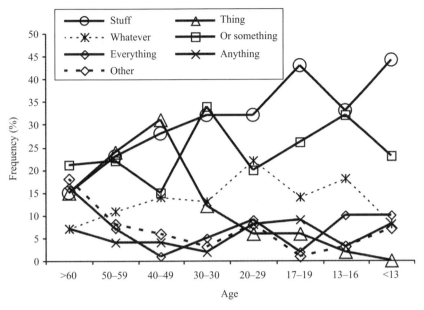

Figure 9.5   Distribution of GE types in apparent time.
Source: Tagliamonte and Denis 2010: 358, Figures 7–8.

> **NOTE**   Did GEs develop from long forms to short forms? We do not yet have a study of an earlier point in time to establish this. It may be the case that features from different levels of grammar undergo different types of reduction in linguistic change.

This is not to say that there is no change in progress in Canadian English. Recall from Table 9.7 that there are considerable frequency differences across GE types. If the differences are not to do with grammaticalization *within* each cohort of related forms, then perhaps there is another way of looking at the system. We reconfigured the data so as to group the GEs according to quantifier and/or generic so as to view their trajectory in apparent time: forms with *stuff, things, something, everything, anything*, and a group of other forms with a wide variety of types, including *and shit like that, and so on*, and *and what not*.

Figure 9.5 shows the distribution of these types in apparent time.

This perspective provides an informative view of the developments within the GE system in Toronto. Among the oldest speakers, there was a mixed system of forms with a wider variety of types, particularly the over 50-year-olds. However, as the individuals get younger, the system is becoming incrementally more dominated by *stuff* forms. So, underlying all this variability there is a dramatic changeover taking place. Note, however, that one type, those with *whatever*, remain relatively stable (the dotted lines).

Logistic Regression

Let us now subject the four most frequent GE types (*stuff, things, something,* and *whatever*) to logistic regression to evaluate the simultaneous influence of these effects and their statistical significance in Table 9.10. In this analysis of the GE system each type (e.g. *stuff, thing,*

Table 9.10 Four independent logistic regression analyses of the main GEs in Toronto English.

	Stuff		Thing		Something		Whatever	
Input	0.30		0.07		0.13		0.23	
N	668		198		297		495	
Total N	2134							
Factors	FW	%	FW	%	FW	%	FW	%
Age								
<30	0.57	37	0.36	4	[0.50]	23	0.56	17
30–50	0.50	30	0.70	16	[0.52]	25	0.48	13
>50	0.33	17	0.77	21	[0.49]	22	0.35	8
Range	*24*		*41*				*21*	
Sex								
Male	0.53	34	0.43	7	[0.50]	23	[0.52]	15
Female	0.47	28	0.58	12	[0.50]	23	[0.47]	13
Range	*6*		*15*					
Education								
College and above	[0.50]	31	0.42	11	[0.48]	22	0.55	16
Less than college	[0.50]	32	0.55	7	[0.53]	25	0.42	10
Range			*13*				*13*	
Category of referent								
Mass noun	0.36	20	[0.47]	8	0.67	38	[0.50]	14
Count noun	0.52	32	[0.53]	10	0.51	24	[0.51]	14
Other phrase	0.52	33	[0.50]	9	0.46	20	[0.50]	14
Range	*16*				*21*			

Note: Factors in square brackets were not selected as statistically significant.
Source: Tagliamonte and Denis 2010: 360, Table 9.

something, or whatever) is run as a group of like items (including long and short forms and variants thereof) as opposed to all other contexts.

Table 9.10 shows that for two out of the three main GE types the most important constraint on variation is the effect of speaker age: the range values are 24 for *stuff*, 41 for *thing*. These results confirm that *thing* variants are declining, while *stuff* is increasing. In contrast, *or something* variants are stable (despite the peaks and valleys in the distributional results in Figure 9.5). The effects of sex and education differ depending on the GE type; however, their effects are much weaker than age. Notice that *stuff* is favored by males (0.53), whereas the receding generic *thing* is favored by females (0.58). Why is this typical? Most of the time, it is females who lead a linguistic change in progress. Education plays a minor role, but only for *thing* – not for *stuff* and or *something*.

One measure of grammaticalization visible in this model is the category of "referent" which measures decategorialization of the GE constructions. Unlike the distributional analyses based on contrasts *within* each GE type (i.e. the difference between *things* vs. *and things like that*, etc.), we can interpret the results derived from the logistic regression of the entire GE system as an indication of each GE type's overall stature in Toronto. Here, the factor weights reveal that *stuff* variants are favored in the unexpected contexts (count nouns and other phrases). In contrast, *something* variants are favored for mass nouns (an extension context) but not for the even more extended, non-noun, phrases. *Thing* forms do not exhibit this effect. The *thing* variants are low in frequency in each referent context, and the factor weights reveal no significant patterning across them. This suggests that GE forms with *thing* are fully decategorized. Moreover, the leveled factor weights for the category of reference (0.47, 0.53, 0.50) show that as it recedes it does so consistently across contexts.

In sum, these results corroborate previous research in highlighting the complex social correlates of GE use; however, unlike the case of New Zealand and England, there does not appear to be the same degree of socioeconomic differentiation. Instead, indicators of change dominate Toronto's GE profile yet there is little evidence for ongoing grammaticalization. So, evidently there is a change in progress, but what kind of change is it?

Recall that *stuff* variants – whether long or short – are by far the most frequent GEs overall (31%; see Table 9.7). Moreover, this is a new development that has occurred among those under 30. In contrast, GEs with *things* are infrequent and currently being swamped by the surging use of a form that is rising incrementally through the generations. Thus, Derek and I argued that this is a case of lexical replacement – *stuff* is taking over as the adjunctive generic in the GE template in Toronto.

TIP These days it seems that the word *stuff* is increasing for more than just general extenders. In Toronto it is among the top 100 words in the TEA (95th). I wonder if this is in comparison to other varieties, and whether this frequency has changed in apparent time and if so how? Like the adverb study in York, this GE study may be providing a hint of a change in progress elsewhere in the grammar.

Studying the Discourse/Pragmatic Variable

Studying discourse-pragmatic variables means applying the quantitative paradigm to above the level of the sentence and into discourse level phenomena and pragmatics. From the beginning this has been a rocky undertaking. The first and perhaps foremost challenge to be confronted is determining whether the variants mean the same thing. Quantitatively inclined researchers will argue for sufficient similarity in usage for statistical analysis. Qualitatively inclined researchers will say that such an approach "misunderstands" the phenomenon. Such criticisms are really the result of different research orientations: (1) discourse analysts focus on the divergent pragmatic functions of forms in the context of talk; and (2) variationists focus on the social and linguistic patterns of forms that have common functions. There is no resolution to this issue in sight. Researchers may take one position or the other depending on their orientation and will be subjected to criticism by the other. Papers are rejected from journals because a reviewer of an opposing methodological philosophy has reviewed the paper. In some cases, entire papers have been written about why you cannot study discourse-pragmatic features quantitatively (e.g. Singler 2001), and yet there has been a groundswell of research contributions that have done just that (see Chapter 9).

At the crux of this conflict is, once again, the definition of the linguistic variable. If variationists adhere to the most rudimentary notion of the linguistic variable, namely that variants must mean exactly the same thing (see Chapter 1), discourse-pragmatic features cannot be studied quantitatively. This is the source of the objections to such studies. However, there are many different types of meaning and appropriate quantitative means to approach variation. Features of language that do discourse-pragmatic work are often not just multifunctional in nature, but downright "squishy." The word *like* in contemporary English is a good example. It can function as a verb, noun, adjective, comparative, adverb, etc., as in Example 9.10.

Example 9.10

   (a) I *like* pizza.
   (b) There's nothing *like* pizza.
   (c) I feel *like* pizza.
   (d) Pizza is *like* awesome.
   (e) Pizza is *like* my favorite.

Tips for Studying Discourse/Pragmatic Variables

The challenge for the analyst who tackles an investigation of a form that is imbued with different pragmatic nuances is to isolate uses that are relevant to the function under investigation. For example, *like* has been attributed with a number of different pragmatic meanings: a marker of focus or new information (Underhill 1988), a discourse marker or discourse particle (D'Arcy 2005a), an adverb of approximation (D'Arcy 2006). The challenge is to circumscribe the variable context to one of these functions. An analysis of the approximating adverb *like*, as in Example 9.11a, will be quite different from the variable context for quotative *like*, as in Example 9.11b.

Example 9.11

   (a) There are *like* a dozen pizzas on the table.
   (b) My mom's *like*, "Here's your pizza," and I'm *like*, "Thanks!"

Let us take quotative *like* as an example. To conduct a variation analysis, only the uses that truly frame constructed dialogue should be included. This is the tricky part. How do you pick out of the data the cases of quotative use? In Example 9.12, the first use of *like* does not function as an introducer to dialogue and should not be included. The second use of *like* precedes a clause of constructed dialogue, therefore functioning as part of the quotation frame (Romaine and Lange 1991: 261). The analyst must systematically cull the data so that only the quotative uses are retained.

Example 9.12

And there was *like* this bloke that jogged past the window and so we *were like*, "Ooh a boy!" (UK/b)

This example might seem straightforward; however, other cases are trickier. Consider the examples in Example 9.13.

Example 9.13

    (a)   He just went, "Oh yeah *like* yeah really." (UK/b)
    (b)   So my friends said *like* to go away but not very politely *like* "Fuck off, go away." (UK/x)

Although it might look like these uses of *like* are quotative, they are not. Instead, these uses of *like* encode the meaning "for example/such as/in other words/as if to say" and should be excluded from the analysis of quotative verbs.

The data may present even more problems for the analyst to resolve. For example, in many cases direct speech is reported with no quotative verb nor an attributed speaker, namely a "zero" quotative (Mathis and Yule 1994). However, if there is no quotative verb, how is the analyst to decide whether it is a quotative frame or not? Clues from context become critical. For example, if there is a change in person or number, as in Example 9.14, these contexts can be independently verified as instances of a "zero quotative." However, in the absence of a change in the person of the verb, the entire complex was interpreted as one quotative context. For example, in Example 9.15 there is only one quotative context introduced by the verb *go*:

Example 9.14

    (a)   Three people phoned me one night, Ø "You're being an idiot."
    (b)   Ø "What?"
    (c)   Ø "You're being an idiot."
    (d)   Three people. I *was like,* "I better stop being an idiot." (TOR/003)

Example 9.15

    And so we *were like– going* "Oh wow, you know, you've got to come to this party." (UK/b)

Another issue that arises is that Example 9.15 has two quotative verbs *like* and *go*. What to do? Best practice dictates that you make a decision about how to handle such cases and then treat them all the same. Additionally, ensure that they can be retrieved independently if further analysis is required at a later point. In this case, my own studies adopted the procedure of coding the second quotative, in this case *go*.

It may also arise that certain examples cannot be coded for one or another of the factors in the analysis. In the study of quotative *be like*, grammatical person and the nature of the speech the quotative verb was introducing were both critical. Cases where grammatical person could not be unambiguously determined, as in the second quotative in Example 9.16, should also be excluded from the analysis of variation.

Example 9.16

    (a)   And I was *like,* "What the hell happened there?"
    (b)   *Was like,* "That was June Devlin." (UK/j)

If the quote formed part of an "*I said, she said*" sequence or advanced the storyline, as in Examples 9.17a–b and 9.18a–b, then it can be treated as direct speech. If, on the other hand, it encoded an attitude or a general feeling of the narrator or a group of people, as in Examples 9.17c or 9.18c, then it can be considered internal dialogue.

Example 9.17

   (a)   It could be twenty-five degrees outside and they'*re like*, "Where's your sweater?"
   (b)   I'*m like*, "Sir, I'm dying as it is."
   (c)   It'*s like*, "I'm not going– you want to get my sweater?" (TOR/003)

Example 9.18

   (a)   And then they were *saying* like, "Oh, um, so you're doing like, the grade twelve, um, calcu-lus? So isn't that like O.A.C?"
   (b)   And then I'*m like*, "Sort of."
   (c)   But like they were just being so like stupid. Not stupid, but just like ignorant, and like they think that they know everything. So I *was like*, "Whatever." (TOR/001)

Incomplete or incomprehensible tokens, as in Example 9.19, where it is impossible to ascertain what type of speech the quotative verb is introducing, should be excluded from consideration in the analysis of *content of the quote*.

Example 9.19

   (a)   It *was like*, "(incomprehensible)." (UK/v)
   (b)   Like, for example *like*, Ø "(nonsensical mumbles)." (TOR/001)

In many cases, it is difficult to assess the function of linguistic features based on occur-rence alone. Yet how do you study a linguistic feature whose function is indeterminate? Weak complementarity (see Chapter 1) provides an independent validation. Dines (1980) used this method to show that certain GEs fulfilled the same discourse function for working-class speech. In so doing Dines was able to identify other constructions and devices with the same function in middle-class speech. These methodological innovations enabled discourse-pragmatic features such as GEs to be studied accountably using quantitative methodology.

The results of applying quantitative methods to the analysis of discourse-pragmatic features speak for themselves. Research on quotatives (Buchstaller and D'Arcy 2009), GEs (Cheshire 2007), discourse *like* (e.g. Andersen 2001), negative expressions (Pichler 2009), etc. are contributing useful and insightful LVC research even though the variants under investigation do not mean precisely the same thing.

Another methodological challenge that is particularly difficult for the quantitative study of discourse-pragmatic features is figuring out where the feature did not occur (see earlier discussion of accountability more generally in Chapter 1).

Consider the use of so-called discourse *like*, another nonstandard feature that appears to be rapidly evolving in contemporary English. The excerpt in Example 9.20 comes from a young woman, aged 16, born and raised in Toronto, Canada.

Example 9.20

(a) [01] He has a problem with reading in front of a large group of people and people he's not comfortable with. So either *like* speeds up or *like* mumbles or um he says something wrong and then he *like* stops and he *like* makes these weird noises. 'Cause *like* in grade eight we were doing *like* the Passion play over the P-A and then he made *like* this *like* (noise). It's so funny and *like* everyone ... everyone remembers and we always make fun of him. So then when he had the speech he had *like* everything on *like* paper and then *like* he came to a sentence and he's like "Ah ... ah oh wait ah" and then he started the sentence again and then he got stuck again. He's like "Oh ... never-mind." And everybody's like "Yeah!"

It is very easy to spot where *like* occurs, but it is an entirely different task to identify where *like* does not occur. You might notice however that *like* is frequent in certain contexts such as before noun phrases, e.g. *like everyone, like paper, like he*.

You could then make the decision to focus on this one specific location for *like*, namely pre-DP position. This would provide a common denominator from which to gain an accountable perspective on the frequency and distributional patterns of *like*. One of the first questions that would arise might be whether to include personal pronouns in the count, as well as whether to restrict the analysis to certain functions (subject vs. object). However, you would be embarking on an analysis that would tap the usage patterns of *like* in a way that could be assessed as a component of the grammar and could be compared and replicated across studies. An alternative analysis might examine the preverb phrase position, as in *like stops* vs. *Ø came*. Such an approach can systematically circumscribe the nonapplication sites. Then you could proceed with the task of deciding which of these to count in and which to leave aside, what types of contexts to treat as categorical, exceptional, or indeterminate. You could even tackle all the potential syntactic positions, as did Alex D'Arcy (2005a). By doing so, you would be able to assess variation and change for discourse *like* in the grammar as a whole.

To embark on an accountable study of discourse-pragmatic features in this way requires tremendous time and expenditure. Imagine how long it takes to find all the cases where *like* did not occur. However, tapping into the underlying mechanisms of discourse *like* by contemporary teenagers provides researchers with an unprecedented opportunity to examine some of the most important issues in the study of linguistic variation and change.

> [The word *like* is] "very much used in colloquial and vulgar language to modify the whole of one's statement, a word or phrase modestly indicating that one's choice of words was not, perhaps, quite felicitous. It is generally used by inferiors addressing superiors" (Jespersen 1940: 417–418). [*Note the date!*]

Let us consider how critical it is to take an accountable approach to discourse-pragmatic features. Consider Figure 9.6 from D'Arcy (2005b).

Figure 9.6 contrasts occurrences of *like* counted by two different methods. On the left, it charts the raw number of *likes* in two different types of verb strings (simple finite verbs vs. auxiliary constructions), and on the right it shows the results achieved through accountable methods. When instances of *like* are simply counted, 92 precede a finite verb, as in Example 9.21a. In contrast, there are only 75 in auxiliary constructions, as in Example 9.21b.

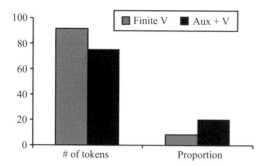

Figure 9.6 Comparison of token count and proportion count for *like*.
Source: D'Arcy, Alexandra (2005b) Tracking the development of discourse "like" in contemporary (Canadian) English. Doctoral thesis proposal. Toronto, Canada, March 16, 2005. Reproduced by kind permission of the author.

Example 9.21

(a) I *like* went to camp.
(b) I was *like* going to camp.

Based on the counting model, finite verbs present a preferred location for *be like*. However, there are more than 1100 finite verbs in these materials, but just 372 auxiliary constructions. When the raw numbers are compared to the proportional analysis, there is a dramatic difference between these two perspectives. Preceding a finite verb is, in actuality, an infrequent position for *like*. Because finite verbs are so frequent in general, it *seems* as though *like* occurs with them often; however, this is incorrect. Instead, *like* occurs two and a half times more frequently with an auxiliary. This result highlights the importance of accountable methods in explanations for all variable linguistic phenomena, including discourse-level features.

Age Grading vs. Linguistic Change
The question of age grading vs. linguistic change is a key question that has arisen many times in the analysis of language variation and change. How do we know that apparent time is a viable proxy for real time? Without real-time evidence, it is only a hypothesis, albeit a highly substantiated one (see Sankoff 2006). The problem is that real-time data are very difficult to come by.

In 2002, one of my students, Jonille Clemente, interviewed her 16-year-old sister for a research project I was conducting on teenagers in Toronto (see Chapter 4, n. 2). She conceived a plan to do an interview every year in September from then on. True to her word she has been conducting an interview with her sister every since. These are the joys that come from inspiring students to understand language variation! I have able to construct a small but vital panel study spanning eight years of a single speaker from the age of 16–23 in the years 2002–2010 (Tagliamonte 2008a).

One of the first features I have undertaken of these materials is the use of *like*. Figure 9.7 shows a real-time comparison of the use of quotative *like*, as in Example 9.22a, and discourse marker *like*, as in Example 9.22b, by Clara.

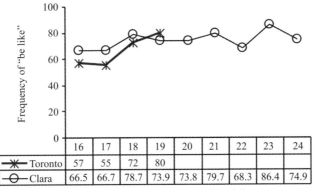

Figure 9.7   Distribution of quotative *like* in real time (Clara) and in apparent time (all 9–19 year olds in Toronto).

Example 9.22

(a)   So then, she *was like*, "Oh, it's okay. Just remember to count to five and everything's okay." And I *was like*, "Oh, that's, that's okay." (TOR/001)

(b)   … But it was okay. It was kind of whatever *like* not really boring, but just *like*, "Okay. So when you guys going-to leave?" (TOR/001)

One of the questions we asked a 20-year old Clara in 2007 was whether she thought her language had changed since she was 16. Her reply is shown in Example 9.23.

Example 9.23

Oh yeah sometimes I really wonder if my vocabulary has improved. 'Cause really I don't think it has. Maybe. But I don't think so. I still have the same things like I start my sentences with "ands" and then I end with like "so yeah!" I still do that. But I can't help it. (TOR/140)

Clara claims her language has not changed and that she cannot help how she sounds. What do you hypothesized has happened to her use of quotative *be like*?

Figure 9.7 shows the snapshot of individuals between 9 and 19 in 2002–2003 (Tagliamonte and D'Arcy 2004a) compared with Clara's ongoing use of *be like* from age 16–20 (between 2002 and 2006).

When she was 16, Clara had rates of *be like* slightly higher than the group of other 16 year olds in Toronto. Since then she has graduated from high school, gone to university, entered the faculty of nursing at a local university, and started working at the cardiac unit of a major Toronto hospital where she works to this day. In the context of this life history, notice that her rate of *be like* rises until she is 18, at which point the advancing trend recedes just a little, back to the level she was at when she was 16. You can imagine what I was thinking about how to interpret the data that year. However, notice what has happened since then. Clara's use of *be like* remains relatively stable, sometimes falling; sometimes rising; however, these differences are not statistically significant. This finding provides real-time support for Labov's (2001a) hypothesis that after a period of incrementation an individual's use of an incoming form will stabilize in late adolescence. Compare Figure 9.7 with Labov's linear model of incrementation for a single female speaker, Figure 14.1 (Labov 2001a: 448, Figure 14.1).

With all this in mind, the data from Clara must be put in context. She's a member of the age sector of the speech community who is most likely to be advancing change. She is young, female, middle-class, upwardly mobile and, by age 20, in her second year at a professional university program. The findings from the analysis show that *be like* is strongly conditioning by tense and temporal reference; it maintains the grammatical person constraint but the pragmatic condition is weak. All this points to the fact that Clara is at the forefront of change. What will happen as she gets older, becomes more established in her career, marries her long-term boyfriend, and possibly has children?

Research Questions Arising

Discourse pragmatic features raise clear and important issues germane to the variationist enterprise: the nature of the linguistic change, its mechanisms, and stages of development. For example, the recent, rapid rise of *be like* means that we can catch change as it is happening. The antithetic claims for change in progress vs. age grading in the context of apparent grammaticalization mean that there is the possibility of disentangling these issues as well.

Other smaller points of method and practice remain to be fleshed out. For example, there has been perhaps an overly stringent focus on the same main constraints on *be like* – first person vs. third person, two types of quotation (direct speech and inner thought), etc. Little is known of the patterns for first person plural/third person plural. Additional quotation content types are present in contemporary data, such as *be like* used for quotes of written language, e.g. *The tours were like "Come on the boat; swim with the fish"* (TOR/a), which refers to a sign. Use of *be like* with tense/aspect constructions other than historical present, present, and simple past are evolving. Many other linguistic patterns remain to be uncovered and explored. As far as the GE system is concerned, many questions have arisen out of the recent research. Syntagmatic length is debated as a diagnostic of grammaticalization of discourse-pragmatic variables. While Cheshire (2007) and Tagliamonte and Denis (2010) took up the challenge of testing earlier claims that this might be the case, the results arising from their own investigations have cast considerable doubt on this measure. It remains controversial whether the short forms such as *and stuff* and *and things* derived from the longer forms *and stuff like that, and things like that*, etc. Loss of lexical material (somewhat akin to clipping) and phonetic reduction (e.g. *gonna* evolving from *going to*) may reflect different phenomena. Givon's (1990) quantity principle, which argues that more grammaticalized forms will be shorter than less grammaticalized forms, may serve as an additional line of argumentation. Regardless of such principles, it does not look as if GEs could have undergone this type of development. Work on grammaticalization suggests that newer variants in a grammaticalizing system do not necessarily have the least developed profile, as might be expected. For example, Torres-Cacoullos and Walker (2009b: 43) report that *going to*, the newer variant in the future temporal reference system of English, has less semantic retention and more semantic bleaching than *will* – the opposite of what is predicted. What implications does this have for the study of the GE system in particular and for grammaticalizing change in the discourse-pragmatic level of grammar more generally? Perhaps the known measures of grammaticalization are not as staunch as once thought.

To stretch the possibilities for new research into the broader spectrum, note that quotatives and GEs have so far been studied in (mostly) mainstream populations. It will be critical to discover how and if different social groups within the same community are participating in variation and/or change in either of these systems. Given that there is so much evidence to suggest that minority groups are not participating in the large-scale phonological changes that are going on in the United States, it is likely that discourse-pragmatic features do not either.

Quotative *be like* is also a good candidate to explore the difference between diffusion and transmission. In the United States, the pronunciation of the so-called "short-a" vowel (e.g. *badge*) is influenced by a complicated array of linguistic factors that have persisted in the transmission of the system from generation to generation in and around New York City. However, the same linguistic factors are regularly weakened or lost during the transplantation of the system to other cities such as Cincinnati or New Orleans (Labov 2007). Do the constraints on *be like* change in the same way as it spreads to new communities (see Tagliamonte and Denis 2008a)? There is also the compelling question of lifespan change. Are the young people who grew up with *be like*, *and stuff*, discourse *like*, and any of the other frequent discourse markers of contemporary English going to keep using them as they get older? Will they stop using them when they enter the work force? When they have children? Will any or all of these forms evolve? And if so, how? Or will they disappear?

NOTE   Is *be like* the result of geographic diffusion or transmission? On the one hand it is a supralocal change that must surely be the result of endogamous change, i.e. diffusion. Yet the constraints on *be like* appear to be preserved across the major varieties of English (which is unexpected for change via diffusion). Also antithetic to prediction is the fact that constraints and weights are <u>not</u> preserved across generations in the same community where incrementation and ongoing restructuring is evident. Yet this is where preservation of constraints is expected. What's going on?

Exercises

Exercise 9.1   Identifying discourse pragmatic variables ————————————

Question 1   Consider the eight tokens in Example 9. 24 from a study of discourse *like* in York, England. What simple and straightforward hypothesis might you formulate with regard to the placement of *like* in a sentence?

Example 9.24

Like it takes you- takes you ten minutes to go.
Never thought no more about it *like*.
Like everything still went back.
So… didn't stop her going out drinking *like*.
…and it took her *like* four attempts.
All this time you're *like* keeled over.
That was *like* two years ago.
There was *like* nothing.

Table 9.11   Variable rule analysis of the contribution of speaker sex to the probability of different quotatives.

	say	*go*	*be+like*	*think*	Zero	N
British English						
Sex						
Female	0.41	[0.46]	0.67	0.49	[0.47]	298
Male	0.57	[0.53]	0.36	0.51	[0.53]	367
Canadian English						
Sex						
Female	0.62	0.35	[0.54]	0.55	[0.50]	382
Male	0.31	0.73	[0.44]	0.42	[0.50]	230

Source: Tagliamonte and Hudson 1999: 160, Table 3.

Exercise 9.2   Interpreting discourse pragmatic variables

Table 9.11 shows the effect of speaker sex on the probability of use of four different quotatives (*say, go, be+like,* and *think*) in two contexts – British English and Canadian English.

Question 1   What quotative(s) do females favor in British English?
Question 2   What quotative(s) do females favor in Canadian English?
Question 3   What quotative(s) do males favor in British English?
Question 4   What quotative(s) do males favor in Canadian English?
Question 5   What is the biggest difference between British and Canadian English with respect to quotative use and speaker sex?

Mini Quiz Answers

9.1   Q1: *This is a trick question. The more relevant question is what kind of change is "be like"? If it is change from below (from inside the community) it is Principle 4. However, if it is change from above (from outside the community) it is Principle 3. In both cases, women lead. We need more information to formulate a definitive answer.*

9.2   Q1: *The use of "so" at the beginning of lines d, f, h, j, k, n, t, x, and bb; the use of "eh" at the end of lines d, f, i, k, n, y, and bb; the use of "right" in lines b, e, m, and u.*

Background Reading

Studies on general extenders
Aijmer 1985, 2002; Brinton 1996; Cheshire 2007; Dines 1980; Dubois 1992; Erman 1995; Overstreet 1999; Stubbe and Holmes 1995; Tagliamonte and Denis 2010; Winter and Norrby 2000; Youssef 1993.

Studies of quotative *be like*
Blyth *et al.* 1990; Buchstaller 2001a,b, 2002, 2006; Buchstaller and D'Arcy 2009; D'Arcy 2004; Dailey-O'Cain 2000; Ferrara and Bell 1995; Mathis and Yule 1994; Romaine and Lange 1991; Singler 2001; Tagliamonte 2009; Tagliamonte and D'Arcy 2004a,b, 2005; Tagliamonte and Hudson 1999; Winter 2002.

10

Tense / Aspect Variables

Grammatical marking by its very nature results from the whittling away of once more semantically meaningful and pragmatically powerful morphemes. Such whittling away is not likely to happen in the space of a generation. (Sankoff 1990: 310)

In this chapter, I turn to a discussion of a particular type of variable – those that involve the tense/aspect system.

Tense/aspect variables are very difficult to study for a number of reasons: (1) there are often more than two variants; (2) the variable context is never clear cut, and (3) there is inevitably more than one defensible method for analyzing them. The literature abounds with studies of tense/aspect features; however, most studies are descriptive, targeting one variety or another that exhibits a strange or unusual or nonstandard verbal feature. In the history of Variationist Sociolinguistics much of the early work focused on the unique tense/aspect features of AAVE invariant *be* (Bailey and Maynor 1985; Brewer 1974, 1979; Myhill 1988; Viereck 1988), *steady* (Baugh 1984), *done* (Feagin 1991), etc. Because tense/aspect features tend to be salient they often provide good evidence for exploring social factors in a given speech community. Because they are often rare they may provide solid evidence for tracking the origins of dialect features. Where do all these strange verb forms come from? Why do they exist? What types of patterns underlie them?

One of the most interesting facets of tense/aspect variables is that they tend to be a prime context for grammaticalization, a type of language change whereby lexical forms develop grammatical meaning (see Chapter 3). This enables us to study language change in a core area of grammar in a context where both linguistic phenomena and social factors combine in the course of change. Due to their facility in tapping into diachronic change they are critical variables for tracking the origins and development of varieties of English. Not surprisingly then, such features have figured prominently in the sociolinguistic literature, particularly in the notorious debate over the origins of AAVE. Two case studies will be used to delve into this topic. The first, *going to* for future temporal reference is a well-documented longitudinal

Variationist Sociolinguistics: Change, Observation, Interpretation, First Edition. Sali A. Tagliamonte.
© 2012 Sali A. Tagliamonte. Published 2012 by Blackwell Publishing Ltd.

change. This is perhaps why it is the most heavily studied and pervasive tense/aspect variable in the literature. The second, variation in the *perfect*, is also widespread across varieties of English, but it is perhaps the thorniest tense/aspect variable ever studied. Nevertheless its unique characteristics offer many important insights for interpreting linguistic variation in social and historical context. It will demonstrate the challenge of extreme form–function asymmetry and the necessity of appropriate methodology. As with the morpho-syntactic features in Chapter 8, the indomitable relationships between society and grammar across time and space will be exposed.

Grammaticalization and Tense/Aspect Variables

Changes associated with grammaticalization ordinarily do not come about abruptly but continue over a long period, often centuries, as forms pass through a series of stages from lexical to grammatical (Hopper and Traugott 1993: 3). The development of tense/aspect features is perhaps the best studied of all grammaticalization processes. This is likely due to the fact that the pathway of change is so protracted that layering of forms and constructions can be observed at any given point in time (Hopper, 1991: 3).

Grammatical change in synchronic data can be identified by layering and form/function asymmetry (Bybee *et al.* 1994; Kurylowicz 1965). Patterns of variability reported in the historical record and in the literature on the particular grammatical process under investigation are used as diagnostics of the state of development of the system. For example, the original lexical associations of a developing grammatical morpheme often strongly condition its later distribution patterns (Bybee and Pagliuca 1987). Research suggests that early associations may persist indefinitely, shaping the nature of the grammatical system (Torres-Cacoullos and Walker 2009b). Crucially, assessment of the linguistic patterns conditioning the choice between competing forms can be used to determine the underlying system that produced it and, in so doing, the stage of development of the grammatical change (e.g. Traugott and Heine 1991a,b).

A variationist's approach to studying a grammaticalizing feature involves extracting each token within the relevant system. Each token is coded for the independent linguistic features implicated in the change that can be extrapolated from the literature. Then, these features are operationalized as factors in a statistical model and tested for significance, constraint ranking, and strength of the effect. The resulting findings are then used to draw comparisons with the relevant varieties under investigation while at the same time casting the analysis into the larger context of linguistic change. As the study of grammaticalization using LVC methods has evolved, researchers have begun to realize that studying grammaticalizing systems requires the development of LVC methodology. For example, frequently occurring contexts that fall outside the envelope of variation (but which are related to the variation under investigation) can provide valuable explanatory insight regarding the diachronic shifts within the variable context (Aaron 2010).

In the study of grammaticalizing systems both frequency of the incoming marker and its patterns of use become critical bits of evidence for assessing the stage of development of the change. Frequency provides a measure of the form's infiltration of the system; however, it does not provide information about the underlying mechanism that produced it. The explanation for the variation in the system does not lie in the overall rate of occurrence of forms in a given context but in the precise configuration of their characteristics of participation in the system of which they are a part.

The methodological steps for studying tense/aspect features in terms of grammaticalization can be summarized as follows:

1. Find an area of the grammar that is undergoing grammatical change. Isolate the place in the grammar where this is occurring. Where are the contexts that encode the relevant meaning? Which forms are used in these contexts?
2. Consult the literature for descriptive and analytic research on the system. What was the grammaticalizing form's original category? What is it turning into? How did it begin to change? How did it evolve? What are the related system(s) – forms and functions?
3. Identify the relevant constraints on the grammaticalization process and operationalize these in a series of tests.
4. Perform an analysis that can assess the statistical significance, strength, and patterning of the relevant constraints.
5. Interpret the findings against the historical and social context.

This is the methodology I will illustrate in the following case studies.

Future (going to)

Perhaps one of the best examples of tense/aspect variation and change in English is in the future reference system where *will* and its contracted variant *'ll* alternate with various phonologically reduced variants of *going to*, as in Example 10.1. In each case the speaker is making a prediction about an event that is yet to occur, a defining property of future meaning (Bybee and Pagliuca 1987):

Example 10.1

(a) Music's *gonna* evolve and change, so language *will* evolve and change too. (TOR/045)
(b) You and I *are going to* be as smart as we've ever been and we *'ll* march down to the back gate. (YRK/017)

Without further analysis the nature of this variation is impossible to assess. The first step is to consider the historical record.

Historical Perspective

In early Old English, future time was expressed by the simple nonpast with some kind of adverbial specification, as is still found today, as in Example 10.2.

Example 10.2

(a) The wee one *comes* <u>tomorrow</u>. (AYR/039)
(b) School *starts* <u>next week</u>. (TOR/039)

Motion	Movement toward a	Prediction
-------------------->	figurative goal	
movement toward a	-------------------->	-------------------->
goal involving	(loss of spatial	Non-human subject
change in location.	meaning)	non-1st person
intention	intention	
human subject	human subject	
1st p subject	1st p subject	

Figure 10.1   Pathway for grammaticization of *going to*.

In this early period, two verbs *sceal* (*sihall*) and *wille* (*will*) expressed present obligation and volition/willingness respectively. Gradually they both began to lose their intrinsic meaning (Traugott 1972; Visser 1963–1973: 677) and entered into a long phase of variabilility. The two markers alternated according to the illocutionary act performed and the grammatical person of the subject noun (Lowth 1762/1775; Taglicht 1970; Zandvoort 1969). They shared the future temporal reference system in English for centuries.

However, around the end of the fifteenth century the construction *going to* emerged. The earliest unambiguous use as a future marker is thought to be from 1482, as in Example 10.3.

Example 10.3

Therefore while this onhappy sowle by the vyctoryse pojmpys of her enmyes *was going to be* broughte into helle for thesynne and onleful lustys of her body (*The Revelation to the Monk of Evesham*) (Danchev and Kytö 1994: 69)

By the seventeenth century *going to* is reported with a wide array of lexical verbs while still retaining strong associations with its literal meaning of "intention" and "movement" (Danchev and Kytö 1994). *Going to* has been encroaching into the future temporal reference system ever since, particularly over the twentieth century.

Considerable study has been devoted to the study of how future markers develop and so-called *go* futures (a.k.a. andative futures) grammaticalize according to a common path. They begin as lexical verbs of motion, then they come to express movement toward a figurative goal and subsequently begin to mark intention. Eventually they express prediction. Of course, at any one time future markers may have all these meanings.

Figure 10.1 sketches a developmental trajectory for the grammatical development of *going to*.

The change toward increasing use of *going to* is not only well documented, but a multitude of internal linguistic factors are implicated in its grammaticalization as a marker of future reference. *Shall* and *will*, and now *will* and *going to* are widely agreed to be semantically distinct. However, *shall* is generally receding from contemporary varieties of English and *going to* is interchangeable with *will* in many contexts.

Analysts have still not sufficiently addressed how this longitudinal change is playing out in contemporary varieties of English.

Change across Varieties

In the early 1990s Shana Poplack and I embarked on a project that focused on the origins and development of African Nova Scotian English in Nova Scotia, Canada. Inspired by research on grammaticalization in creole languages (Sankoff 1977, 1979), we began with one of the most extensively studied gramaticalization pathways – the evolution of the *go* future.

Characteristics of the African Nova Scotian communities along with other coexisting varieties in Canada permitted several dimensions of comparison: (1) regionality – urban vs. rural; (2) degree of integration – enclave vs. mainstream; and (3) ethnicity – African vs. British. Residents of two enclave communities inhabited by the descendants of African Americans in Nova Scotia (North Preston and Guysborough) were assumed to have minimal contact with mainstream developments and thus conservative with respect to grammatical change. In contrast, residents of urban Ottawa (the capital city of Canada) were assumed to have had maximal contact and thus a more advanced profile. In Guysborough, however, two ethnic groups, one African and one British, had coexisted in the same general demographic location for a century or more, but within separate neighborhoods and entirely independent social networks. The predominantly British-origin group were considered to represent an intermediate position among the group, not mainstream, but not as conservative as the enclaves. Thus the continuum of varieties was hypothesized to be arrayed from most conservative to most advanced as follows:

North Preston   →   Guysborough Enclave   →   Guysborough Village   →   Ottawa

How would the two major future variants – *will* and *going to* – pattern? We hypothesized that the use of *going to* in these varieties would reveal the grammaticalization of *going to* as a marker of future reference because they could be arrayed so as to reflect different points in the course of change. Our hypothesis was that the most conservative varieties would have the least *going to* while the more advanced ones would have more.

Figure 10.2 shows the distribution of the major future variants in each of the communities (Poplack and Tagliamonte 1999b).

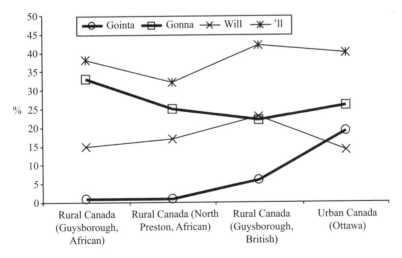

Figure 10.2   Distribution of the major future variants in each of the communities.
Source: Poplack and Tagliamonte 1999: 328, Figure 1.

First, note that the future temporal reference systems across all communities have vigorous variation between *gonna*, *will*, and *'ll*. The majority form in the future temporal reference system for all communities is *'ll*, demonstrating that phonological coalescence for the *will* future is well advanced in all. Notice however that the variety that stands apart from the rest is Ottawa; both *gonna* and *gointa* (the variant that preserves [t]) are frequent and if combined would vie for the most frequent form. This supports the hypothesis that the urban community is more advanced in terms of grammaticization of the *go* future. We hypothesized that rural Canada would be more conservative with regard to ongoing grammaticization of *going to* than urban Canada. Constant with this hypothesis, Guysborough Village has the most *will* and less frequent use of both *going to* variants. Notice too that the three rural varieties are much closer in patterning to each other than might have been expected. The crossover pattern is due to urban Ottawa where the *going to* variants are in the majority. The context for the most frequent use of *gonna*, the anticipated advanced variant (on grounds of advanced phonetic reduction), is most frequent in North Preston, the most conservative variety – a result which runs counter to expectation. However, frequency is only one facet of the grammaticalization process. We need to be able to assess the state of the grammatical system in each variety.

Operationalizing Constraints on Grammaticalization

Factors contributing to the patterning of forms used to express future temporal reference included connotations of modality, degree of volition, certainty or prediction, intentionality, point of view, speaker attitude, probability or imminence of the event taking place, etc. Unfortunately, these gradated semantic distinctions are very difficult to test directly; however, they are captured in the more mechanical subsystems of the grammar. Many syntactic and lexical features are claimed to affect future expression (in general) throughout the history of English (see discussion in Poplack and Tagliamonte 1999b).

At least six (testable) constraints can be found in the literature. *Going to* was originally associated with future-in-the-past contexts and this reportedly continues in its contemporary distribution patterns. It is used more frequently from the perspective of time passed (Example 10.4a–b) than from the point of view of the present, as in Example 10.4c-d.

Example 10.4   Point of reference

Past:
(a)   I foolishly thought I' *d get* one at hospital, but I didn't. (YRK/009)
(b)   I was sure that she just *wasn't gonna* turn up. (YRK/004)

Speech time:
(c)   Look I '*ll* relieve you of your embarassment. (YRK/087)
(d)   I was like, "Oh I'*m gonna* have scars!" (YRK/049)

Another factor implicated in this grammatical change is the person and number of the subject. Readings of volition or control are associated with *will*. First person subjects, as in Example 10.5a and 10.6a–b, tend to exercise these more, and so are predicted to occur more with *will*.

Example 10.5   Grammatical person

First:
(a)   I haven't got hold of him yet, but I '*ll* kill him when I do. (YRK/076)
(b)   We'*ll* not go any further into that. (YRK/030)

Going to has been associated with immediacy as in Example 10.9a–d rather than distant future as in Example 10.9e–h.

Example 10.6   Proximity in the future

Immediate:
(a)   I knew I *was gonna* be finishing like within the hour. (YRK/034)
(b)   It'*s gointa* rain today, I thought. (YRK/007)
(c)   Oh yes he '*ll* come in and stop in now if you like. (YRK/076)
(d)   Don't bother sitting down, it '*ll* ring again in a minute. (YRK/030)

Nonimmediate:
(e)   Yes, you can often spot the ones that you feel will always be a reserved type of person. (YRK/006)
(f)   He's *gonna* be like that for the rest of his life. (YRK/052)
(g)   By the end of this century there'*s gonna* be a change in the staffing of the Churches. (YRK/063)
(h)   Yeah. I '*ll* be flying out there next week on a visit you-know 'cos you've got to haven't you. (YRK/040)

The inherent lexical nature of the verb is another factor implicated in the grammaticalization of a form. Increased use of *going to*, originally a verb of motion, with another verb of motion, such as *go* as in Example 10.7a–c, or *come*, as in Example 10.7d–f, implies semantic bleaching, or the loss of the original semantic content. Thus, a tendency toward such collocations is consistent with further grammaticalization.

Example 10.7   Lexical verb

Go:
(a)   Now we'*ll go* back to where we were before. (YRK/002)
(b)   He's *gonna go* over there and there 's gonna be no piano there. (YRK/079)
(c)   We're going to get the bus and we'*re gointa go* in to see my Mam. (YRK/083)

Come:
(d)   Oh, great, there's surely somebody *gonna come* past. (YRK/013)
(e)   He's *gonna come* round here when I buy this house. (YRK/079)
(f)   I wonder how many'*ll come* back. (YRK/019)

Subordinate clauses, as in Example 10.8a–b, rather than main clauses in Example 10.8c–d, are often discussed as being a favorable location for *going to*. Perhaps this is because future in the past readings tend to be in subordinate clauses.

Example 10.8   Type of clause

Subordinate:
(a)   And I was stuck to the back wondering what I *would do*. (YRK/024)
(b)   I don't know whether she's *gointa* teach the sheep yoga or what! (YRK/020)

Main:
(a)   It's gonna chase the wire now. (YRK/058)
(b)   In York everyone will always know it as Rowntree. (YRK/067)

In the beginning, *going to* was restricted to human subjects undergoing movement (Example 10.9a–c). Then it presumably generalized to nonmovement readings (Example 10.9d). As its meaning generalized from movement/intention to prediction, it began to appear with nonhuman subjects (Example 10.9e–f) and with existentials. Subjects are no longer confined to animates capable of movement. This kind of lapse in restriction on the type of subject collocated with a grammaticalizing form is a common feature of grammaticalization, and develops as the item is generalizing in meaning. This means that if *going to* is favored with nonhuman and existential subjects (Example 10.9g) it can be taken as a sign of relatively advanced grammaticalization.

Example 10.9   Animacy

Human:
(a)   I'*m going to* be a policeman. (YRK/011)
(b)   That child *isn't going to* have a very fair crack of the whip. (YRK/083)
(c)   The man is an idiot. He'*ll* destroy everything. (YRK/087)

Nonhuman:
(e)   I don't think *the world* will ever be rid of war. (YRK/067)
(f)   The lock *will* cost like so much money. (YRK/049)
(g)   I think *it*'ll be pretty good. (YRK/004)

Existential:
(h)   *There* won't be any problems after that. (YRK/014)

These multiple observations from the literature provide testable hypotheses about the development of *going to*, which in turn provide diagnostics. The next step is to apply them in a relevant context. Given the linguistic pathways of this grammatical change, consistent comparison of the forms used for future reference across varieties may provide a view of the development of *going to*. Such information can then be used to situate varieties vis-à-vis each other as well as to reveal important insights into the details of the mechanism of linguistic change. We can test these constraints from the historical record as factors in a logistic regression analysis. Let us see how these constraints operate by examining the cross-variety comparison of the five communities as in Table 10.1 (Poplack and Tagliamonte 1999b: 333, Table 3).

In order to interpret these results we will make full use of the three lines of evidence. First, which factors are statistically significant and which are not? Second, what are the underlying patterns – the constraint hierarchies of each of the effects, i.e. the ordering of factors within a linguistic factor group? Third, does this order reflect the direction predicted by the hypotheses

Table 10.1 Logistic regression analysis of *going to* in five North American varieties. Factor groups not significant in square brackets.

	Enclaves			Rural	Urban
	SAM c. 1981–83	NPR c. 1991	GYE c. 1991	GYV c. 1991	OTT c. 1990–91
Overall tendency:	0.59	0.55	0.50	0.31	0.48
Total N:	396	723	994	199	302
Point of reference					
Past	0.85	0.86	0.86	0.67	0.92
Speech time	0.44	0.40	0.43	0.45	0.40
Range	*41*	*46*	*43*	*22*	*52*
Grammatical person					
Second, third person pronouns and third person NPs	[0.50]	[0.51]	0.57	[0.54]	0.61
First person	[0.50]	[0.49]	0.42	[0.46]	0.38
Range			*15*	*8*	*23*
Proximity in the future					
Immediate	[0.47]	[0.49]	[0.53]	0.66	[0.59]
Non-immediate	[0.51]	[0.52]	[0.48]	0.35	[0.43]
Range				*21*	*16*
Lexical content					
Verb of motion	0.34	0.33	0.35	0.32	[0.51]
Other verb	0.56	0.54	0.54	0.61	[0.50]
Range	*22*	*21*	*19*	*29*	
Type of clause					
Subordinate	[0.58]	0.68	0.69	[0.59]	[0.55]
Main	[0.48]	0.46	0.45	[0.47]	[0.48]
Range		*22*	*24*	*12*	
Animacy of subject					
Human	[0.50]	[0.50]	[0.50]	[0.50]	[0.48]
Nonhuman	[0.49]	[0.52]	[0.53]	[0.48]	[0.59]

Source: Poplack and Tagliamonte 1999: 333, Table 3.

in the literature? Putting all these results together, these findings can be interpreted based on the predicted temporal and grammatical development of the *going to* future.

Constraint Ranking

The relation of more to less in each factor group (the constraint hierarchy) for each variety is virtually identical. The six varieties are different in only two contexts. The first is the effect of proximity in the future. Here, the five varieties partition into two groups, with the dividing line being between the three enclave varieties and the others. *Going to* is clearly favored for immediate future reference (consistent with prescriptive characterizations) in Guysborough Village and Ottawa; but there is no effect of temporal specialization in any of the enclaves. The second feature is the effect of animacy. Only in Ottawa is *going to* favored for inanimate subjects, a context which is claimed to represent the most generalized and hence the most grammaticalized for *going to* (Bybee *et al.* 1994: 5).

Relative Strength of Factors

The strength of these constraints differs markedly across varieties, as measured by the range values. Point of reference is one of the strongest constraints operating on the variation across all the varieties, while the effects of other factors shift in systematic ways. *Going to* rarely occurs with a verb of motion. This avoidance of *going to* with a verb of motion verb (an early stage correlation) is only evident in the enclave/rural communities. It has been neutralized in Ottawa. In contrast, Ottawa has innovated favoring *going to* with nonhuman subjects (0.59) that is not present in any of the other varieties. These differences suggest that *going to* is more advanced in Ottawa and less advanced in the rural communities and support the idea that the varieties are located at different points on the continuum of the grammaticalization of *going to*.

The position of Guysborough Village is pivotal. It is remote and relatively isolated like the neighboring Guysborough Enclave (as well as the other enclaves), but shares ethnic, racial, and other attendant characteristics with urban Ottawa. Interestingly, however, in its progress along the line of grammaticalization, as measured by the range, Nova Scotian Vernacular English spoken in Guysborough Village appears to be more closely aligned with the African-origin enclaves: the effects of clause type and lexical content remain greater in these varieties when compared with Ottawa, while the effects of animacy and grammatical person of the subject have neutralized or are in the process thereof. On a fifth measure, point of reference, Guysborough Village has a much lower range than any of the others. Only on one measure, proximity in the future, is Guysborough Village aligned with urban Ottawa, i.e. along racial and ethnic lines. Thus, another implication of these findings suggests that the language spoken by isolated speakers, whether of African or British origin, has the constraints that were operative at an earlier stage of the English language, and which are now receding from mainstream varieties.

Does this type of analysis provide conclusive evidence? These findings are based on separate varieties of English spoken in different communities. These were in turn taken to reflect different points along the grammatical development of *going to* as a marker of future reference in the history of the English language. But how do we know that these intervariety differences are actually the result of language change happening at different rates? Recall that North Preston had the most advanced profile of phonetic reduction of *going to* to *gonna*. So, there is at least some indication that the enclaves are different. The differences across varieties could be the result of spontaneous parallel development. However, some other factor could be implicated. The interpretation of grammaticalization for cross-community differences could be corroborated by evidence from intracommunity differences, namely change in apparent time. They could also be explored more fully by testing the same conditioning factors reported in a North American context elsewhere.

Language Change in Apparent Time

When I moved to England in 1995 one of the first things I noticed was that my own variety of English was different from that of the people around me in many ways. Obviously, there were dramatic phonological differences. However having recently conducted the analyses of future

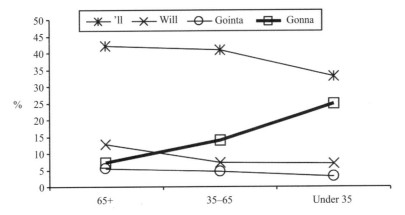

Figure 10.3   Distribution of future variants in York, UK, c. 1997 by generation.

temporal reference in the North American varieties, I was primed to hear variants of the future. One salient feature of my own speech was a highly frequent use of *gonna* to mark the future in comparison to everyone around me. As Bybee *et al.* (1994: 297) suggest, it is necessary to conduct analyses of grammaticalizing features as "these changes are taking place." In due course, I embarked upon a study of future temporal reference in the newly collected York English Corpus (Tagliamonte 1996–1998). My goal was to test the possibility that my North American grammar was more advanced in the grammaticalization of *going to* than British English.

The York English Corpus, with individuals between the ages of 17–92, represents approximately 100 years of apparent time. If *going to* was in the process of grammaticalizing in this speech community, I predicted that its patterns of use in each generation would show evidence of grammatical development. First, let us determine how the future variants are distributed.

Not surprisingly, as in the North American varieties studied earlier (Table 10.1), there is variation among future variants, even in the same stretch of discourse by the same speaker, as in Example 10.10:

Example 10.10

(a)   If anything*'s gonna* go wrong, it*'s gonna* go wrong that first night. There *won't* be any problems after that. (YRK/014)

(b)   Who knows what the next century*'ll* bring? It*'s gonna* be quite interesting! (YRK/067)

Figure 10.3 shows the generational differences across the major future variants in York English. It shows that the future forms *will* and *'ll* are decreasing in frequency. On the contrary, *gonna* does just the opposite. It increases from oldest to youngest speakers in a stepwise progression. What explains this change in apparent time? I immediately suspected grammaticalization; however, frequencies of forms alone do not provide us with sufficient information about the pathways of change. The next step is to test for the well-known hallmarks of grammaticalization underlying these frequencies.

Table 10.2 shows a logistic regression analysis of virtually the same set of constraints as tested in Table 10.1.

Table 10.2   Logistic regression analysis of *going to* in York English. Factor groups not significant in square brackets.

Age group	Older	Middle	Younger
Corrected mean:	0.24	0.32	0.40
Total N:	409	390	539
Point of reference			
Past	0.81	0.65	0.84
Speech time	0.44	0.48	0.45
Range	*37*	*17*	*39*
Grammatical person			
Second, third person pronoun	[0.51]	0.60	0.62
First person pronoun	[0.47]	0.40	0.40
Full NP	[0.67]	0.47	0.32
Range		*20*	*30*
Proximity			
Immediate	[0.47]	[0.49]	0.57
Non–immediate	[0.52]	[0.50]	0.47
Range			*10*
Education			
Beyond 16 years	0.63	0.56	[0.48]
To 16 years	0.45	0.44	[0.53]
Range	*18*	*12*	
Lexical content			
Other verb	[0.51]	[0.52]	[0.50]
go	[0.52]	[0.33]	[0.54]
come	[0.22]	[0.31]	[0.22]
Type of clause			
Subordinate	[0.55]	[0.53]	[0.55]
Main	[0.49]	[0.49]	[0.49]
Animacy of subject			
Human	[0.51]	[0.49]	[0.50]
Nonhuman	[0.36]	[0.62]	[0.48]

Source: Tagliamonte 2002: 75, Table 28.8.

Before I discuss the findings in Table 10.2, try this quiz.

Mini Quiz 10.1: *Interpreting results*

Q1   Which factor contributes a statistically significant effect to the probability of "be going to" in all age groups?
   (a)   Grammatical person.
   (b)   Type of clause.
   (c)   Point of reference.
   (d)   Animacy.

Q2 Which age group(s) have the highest probability of "be going to"?
(a) Younger speakers.
(b) Older speakers.
(c) Middle-aged speakers.
(d) Both older and middle-aged speakers.

Q3 What is the total number of contexts considered in this study?
(a) 539.
(b) 409.
(c) 1500.
(d) 1338.

Q4 Which factor(s) consistently disfavor "be going to" across generations?
(a) Speech time, the lexical verb "come," and main clauses.
(b) Speech time, full NPs, and the lexical verb "come."
(c) Speech time, human subjects, and female speakers.
(d) Speech time, more educated speakers, and main clauses.

Q5 Examination of the hierarchy of constraints for grammatical person reveals that:
(a) All the generations are different.
(b) All the generations are the same.
(c) There is a dramatic shift in usage, in which "be going to" has become the marker for full NPs as opposed to all other subject types.
(d) There is a dramatic shift in usage, in which "be going to" has expanded into third person subjects and full NPs disfavor it.

Q6 Examination of the hierarchy of constraints for animacy reveals that
(a) In the oldest generation "be going to" was restricted to human subjects, but in the youngest generation animacy of the subject has no effect on the choice of "be going to."
(b) In the oldest generation animacy of the subject has no effect on the choice of "be going to," but in the youngest generation it does.
(c) Human subjects consistently favor "be going to."
(d) Nonhuman subjects consistently favor "be going to."

Q7 Examination of the hierarchy of constraints for type of clause reveals that:
(a) All the generations are different.
(b) All the generations are the same.
(c) There is a shift in usage, in which "be going to" has become constrained by the subordinate clause.
(d) There is a shift in usage, in which "be going to" has become constrained by the main clause.

Q8 Overall, the most significant factor contributing to the use of *going to* across the sample is:
(a) Grammatical person.
(b) Proximity in the future.
(c) Point of reference.
(d) Lexical verb.

Q9   Which factor sets the younger speakers apart from all others?
     (a)   Grammatical person.
     (b)   Proximity in the future.
     (c)   Point of reference.
     (d)   Lexical verb.

Q10 Comparing the overall results across generations, what observation best
     describes the patterning?
     (a)   Longitudinal stability in the linguistic system.
     (b)   Decreasing use of "be going to" over time.
     (c)   Increasing use of "be going to" over time and significant reorganization of
           its capacity to mark FUTURE temporal reference.
     (d)   Increasing use of "be going to" over time but no significant reorganization
           of its capacity to mark FUTURE temporal reference.

The constraints are shifting in ranking, strength, and significance across age groups. As reported in the historical record and in contemporary studies *going to* is used more frequently as the future of time passed than as the future from the point of view of the present. The same is true of the North American varieties in Table 10.1 as well as in York English. Note that point of reference is one of the strongest, if not the strongest, constraints on the realization of *going to* and this is true for each age group. I said earlier that *going to* likely entered the future reference system via future-in-the-past contexts. These results show that it continues to dominate the future temporal reference system in this context.

Earlier in the history of English *will* alternated with *shall* and *shall* had well-known correlates with first person. Grammaticalization predicts that *going to* will be used with first person subjects capable of motion. Yet as you see here, consistent with Table 10.1, non-first person subjects favor *going to*. First person subjects have a consistent disfavoring effect for *going to*, indicating the strong presence of *will/'ll* in these contexts. This demonstrates that the strong association of first person subjects with the original sense of desire of *will* persists very late in its grammaticization, even to the point where *going to* does not extend to this context. Notice, however, the shift in usage, when the factor weight for first person subjects is compared with that of other personal pronouns across age groups. In the oldest generation there is little to distinguish first person from second or third person with respect to propensity of *going to*, but NP subject highly favor *going to*. However, in both the middle and younger generation *going to* has clearly expanded into third person subjects and full NPs disfavor. Thus, the oldest generation is unique on two counts: (1) there is no difference in their use of *going to* with first person; and (2) *going to* is favored in full NP contexts only. Neither of the other two generations exhibits either of these trends.

Going to is traditionally associated with immediacy and this reading was present from the early eighteenth century. Here, however, the middle-aged and older speakers show no difference between immediate and non-immediate contexts. In direct contrast, the younger speakers exhibit a statistically significant propensity for *going to* for immediate future reference. In the North American study this trend was found for the most mainstream urban variety (Ottawa).

Increased use of *going to* with a verb of motion implies desemanticization or the loss of its original lexical meaning. None of the age groups in York shows a significant effect of lexical verb, and the same as was found for Ottawa.

There is no effect of subordinate as opposed to main clauses for *going to* in York, suggesting that this earlier pattern has leveled. Recall that this effect was statistically significant in the enclaves in North America but not in the more mainstream variety. So, once again York parallels Ottawa.

As discussed earlier, *going to* is said to have started out with animate subjects (usually human) but gradually generalized. However, this effect is not significant in any age group. Nevertheless, the patterns of the constraint ranking are revealing. In the oldest generation *going to* rarely occurs in nonhuman subjects, with a probability of only 0.36. In contrast, in the youngest generation animacy of the subject has no effect on the choice of *going to*. The middle-aged speakers actually favor *going to* with nonhuman subjects. This suggests that the use of *going to* may have evolved further along the path of grammaticization on this measure relatively recently since the tracks of this development are visible in apparent time.

In sum, the variant inventories and constraints conditioning the variants of *going to* are distinct across age groups in the city of York, as follows:

1. Phonological reduction of *going to* increases incrementally from oldest to youngest speakers.
2. Restriction of *going to* to animate nouns in the oldest generation disappears in the younger generations; this is apparent in the lower factor weights for nonhuman subjects in the oldest generations, which are neutralized in the youngest generation.
3. The neutrality between first vs. other grammatical subjects in the oldest generation shifts to a statistically significant favoring effect of *going to* with first person subjects in the two younger generations.
4. Specialization of *going to* in full NP subjects in the older generation changes to a significant increase in use with third person pronouns in the younger generations.
5. Allocation of *going to* to immediate future reference is exhibited in the youngest speakers only.

These incremental alternations in apparent time are consistent with progressive grammatical change and reflect an ordered series of shifts in factor weights of the type noted by Labov (1982: 76). These tendencies can be directly related to the principles of grammaticalization. The historical pathway of *going to* is visible, in the behavior of each measure, to a greater or lesser degree, depending on the measure, and on the generation.

Comparison between Inter-variety and Intra-variety

Let us now compare the results from the North American (Table 10.1) and British (Table 10.2) data and focus on the factors most heavily implicated in grammatical change. Consider the factor weights for grammatical person. The patterning for the middle and youngest generations in York is similar to the elderly speakers in Ottawa and Guysborough Village in Canada. Next, consider the oldest age group in York. Their patterning of constraints is quite distinct from the middle and younger age groups in the same community in that there is no effect. But notice how similar the overall pattern here is to North Preston and perhaps most surprisingly Samaná. With respect to the measure of proximity in the future, here, the youngest speakers in York are also not patterning with their elders. There is a distinct favoring effect of proximate future reference in the youngest generations, but not in the middle or oldest generation. Once again, the youngest generation in York is patterning like the elderly speakers from Ottawa and Guysborough Village, the two varieties representing a further advanced step along the grammaticalization cline for *going to*. Thus, with respect to the two constraints that appear to be implicated in the ongoing grammaticalization of *going to*, we can now make the observation that the youngest generation in Britain looks like the oldest generation in Canada. Further, the oldest generation in Britain looks much like the African American enclaves in North America.

The two analyses in conjunction with one another provide corroborating evidence for a number of overarching hypotheses. They demonstrate that grammatical change can be viewed in synchronic data. Further, the details of the grammaticalizing form appear to be reflected in variable constraints on its grammatical distribution. This may be viewed across sister varieties, as well as across different generations of the same community. The differences and similarities across the varieties can be attributed to the fact that they reflect different points in the pathway of change of *going to* as a marker of future reference in English. This also lends support to the hypothesis that the relative degree of grammaticalization across communities may be related to the different ecological circumstances of their sociocultural history (see also Tagliamonte and Smith 2000).

Finally, the comparative perspective has revealed an additional and broader dimension. Not only are there consistent parallels in the constraint ranking of factors across age groups, they are nearly identical to the hierarchy of constraints found for the North American varieties in Table 10.1. Moreover, these results are consistent with the grammaticalization of *going to*. The same path is visible in the behavior of each measure of grammatical change in apparent time just as it was visible across varieties. This further validates the idea that the effects are typical of English and part of the broader grammatical changes underway in the future reference system. Grammaticalization of *going to* has progressed more quickly in North America than in Britain so there may be a case for external influence in York especially since there seems to have been an acceleration of this change in the last 50–60 years. Further comparative research will fill in more of this emerging picture.

Summary

What has studying *going to* shown us? Evidently, tense/aspect features are excellent channels by which to study grammatical change. We have also discovered that grammatical change can be analyzed in contemporary sociolinguistic data sets that include a representative sample of speakers by age. Moreover, the details of the lexical history of a grammaticizing form may be tracked in the variable constraints on its grammatical distribution across different dialects as well as across generations of the same community. In conjunction with the earlier research on *going to* what is compelling is the extent to which a cross-variety perspective leads to a greater understanding of the diachronic pathways of change. With this bird's eye view, the differences and similarities seen across the generations in York and across varieties in North America can be attributed to the fact that they reflect different points in the pathway of change of *going to* as a marker of future reference in English.

Yet many questions remain. It is undoubtedly the case that this change is evolving in other varieties of English. The different measures of grammaticalization could be compared and contrasted in profitable ways. For example, analysts could assess whether North American varieties grammaticalized faster than British varieties. We could discover if it is possible for different varieties to select their own set of forms. One variety might select one phonetically reduced variant and a second variety another. What aspects of grammaticalization are universal across varieties? what aspects are idiosyncratic? Do the diagnostics of grammaticalization outlined by Bybee and Pagluica (1987) always apply? The profile of an early stage in grammaticalization predicts retention of lexical meaning while at a later stage forms will be more bleached. Yet Torres-Cacoullos and Walker (2009b) found that *going to* (the newer layer in the system) is actually *less* bleached than *will* (the older form) in Quebec City, Canada. There is also the question of whether phonetic coalescence happens early or late. Recall that the evidence from GEs (Chapter 9) hints that longer variants (*and things like that*) are just as decategorized as shorter variants (*and things*).

Further, Torres-Cacoullos and Walker (2009b) suggest that the internal measures of grammaticalization reviewed here are not the only means by which *going to* develops. Instead, they suggest that each form, *will/'ll* and the variants of *going to* also have particular collocation patterns that, in part, determine their linguistic patterns. Those relevant to Quebec City are listed in Example 10.11:

Example 10.11

(a) *I'll..*
(b) *I'll never ...*
(c) *What am I going to do?*
(d) *Is there gonna be ... ?*

The argument is that these collocations underlie the linguistic patterns uncovered in the logistic regression analysis:

1. The favoring effect of first person singular for *will* is attributed to the collocation *I'll*.
2. The favoring effect for *will* of indefinite adverbs is attributed to the use of *never* which makes up one third of the indefinite adverbs and the collocation *I'll never, we'll never, she'll never,* etc.
3. The favoring effect of questions for *going to* is attributed (Example 10.12c–d)
4. The favoring effect of third person questions is attributed (Example 10.12d)

The question is whether these collocation patterns are particular to the place and time – Quebec City, Canada in the late twentieth century – or if they are a part of the grammatical pathway of the *going to* future more generally. Equally important will be to explore statistical methods of determining whether such collocations exert a significant effect on the overall system and to what extent (as we tested for *just* in Chapter 2). The building findings show us that there is much work remaining in understanding how *going to* is developing in the English future temporal reference system, and more generally how grammatical change operates across linguistic systems. Cross-variety comparisons of how the future is evolving also promise to expand our knowledge of grammaticalization (see e.g. Wagner and Sankoff forthcoming). The impact of frequent collocations on other types of linguistic variables may be far-reaching.

NOTE   How might collocations have influenced the development of other grammaticalization pathways? A check of *quick* reveals a disproportionate number of expressions of the type: *as quick as*, e.g. *as quick as a flash / as quick as that / as quick as [we] can*. Can this explain why *quick* is one of the foremost adverbs cited as having the zero form?

Perfect (have)

The present perfect in English is an ideal place to analyze tense/aspect variation, to explore longitudinal change, and to test for similarities and differences across varieties. Why? First, this area of the grammar stands out for the sheer number of different surface forms (layering) and second, it is in the process of ongoing change that has still not been resolved in contemporary English.

The Standard English perfect construction is made up of two parts: an auxiliary *have/ has* + a past participle, as in Example 10.12.

Example 10.12   Auxiliary have + past participle

    (a)   I *have sold* two bale of yams for three dollars. … I'*ve sold* seven grain for a cent. (SAM/021)
    (b)   There were one or two bigger shops in York which *have gone*. (YRK/006)
    (c)   Well, there's always *been* change … ever since man *has been* there's always *been* change. (GYV/111)

There is reasonable consensus on three basic semantic/pragmatic functions of the present perfect (or perfect as it is often called): continuative, experiential, and resultative. The continuative perfect makes reference to a time span throughout which an event or situation obtained, as in Example 10.13a. The experiential perfect refers to a situation which has occurred once or repeatedly before the present, as in Example 10.13b. The resultative perfect refers to a past situation that has led to some present result or state but does not involve a time span, as in Example 10.13c.

Example 10.13

    (a)   Continuative
         I'*ve* always *been* involved in St George's Church. (YRK/048)
    (b)   Experiential
         We'*ve danced* in Durham and London and Lichfield and Scarborough. (YRK/087)
    (c)   Resultative
         She'*s* just *started* with us. (YRK/044)

The implicit view of the perfect is that the auxiliary *have* maps directly onto its respective functions in the discourse. In reality, however, these contexts are often not marked by the expected *have* + past participle, but by many other forms and constructions.

Synchronic Patterns

In my 1991 dissertation, I identified seven different constructions in Samaná English which could occur across the semantic/pragmatic functions of the perfect (Tagliamonte 1991; 1996: 352–355): standard preterite forms, as in Example 10.14a, lone past participles ("lone" due to the fact that there is no auxiliary in the surface string), as in Example 10.14b; pre verbal *been*, as in Example 10.14c, pre verbal *done*, as in Example 10.14d, auxiliary *be* (instead of *have*), as in Example 10.14e, verb stems, as in Example 10.14f, preverbal *ain't*, as in Example 10.14g, and a construction with three verbs, as in Example 10.14h–i. No other bundle of meanings within the tense/aspect system has so many different variants.

Example 10.14

Preterite:
(a)   They all *died* out already. (SAM/013)
Lone past participle:
(b)   She never *been* a person to walk. (SAM/002)
Preverbal been:
(c)   They *been* fixing the road. (SAM/015)
Preverbal done:
(d)   I *done* bought your land … (SAM/010)
Auxiliary be + verb:
(e)   I'*m* pass a lot of trouble. (SAM/002)
Verb stems:
(f)   I never *like* the city. (SAM/013)
Ain't + past participle/past tense:
(g)   He *ain't* wrote yet. (SAM/019)
Three verb cluster with auxiliary be:
(h)   I'*m done been* over there plenty, but I don't like it. (SAM/005)
Three verb cluster with auxiliary *have*:
(i)   He *had done been* to Saint Thomas and place. (SAM/001)

No other bundle of meanings within the tense/aspect system has so many different variants.

Explanations for Variability in the Perfect

There are a number of explanations for why perfect meaning is so highly variable. One hypothesis is that lone past participles, i.e. constructions with an unambiguous past participle with no preceding auxiliary, such as those in Example 10.15, are simply preterites. In many English dialects *seen* is the preterite of *see*; *done* is the preterite of *do*, etc. These examples come from small villages in Northern Ireland (Tagliamonte, to appear) and in Canada.

Example 10.15

Preterite
(a)   I didn't say I could either. I just went along and *done* the work. (GYV/107)
(b)   I *done* that job for the next ten years 'til I was sixty. (MPT/014)

298 *Tense/Aspect Variables*

(c)   He come in and looked in – he *seen* the deer. (GYE/045)
(d)   I *seen* a thing in the paper the other day. (CLB/013)

Yet not all lone past participles occur in contexts that equate with the preterite. In some cases the forms might also be the result of auxiliary deletion since they occur in contexts that would also permit the present perfect, as in Example 10.16. In this case the surface forms – with and without *have* – fulfill the same function: *I seen, he done, I been* mean the same as *I have seen, he has done, I have been*. These types are also attested across a wide range of English dialects (Barber 1964; Wright 1898–1905).

Example 10.16

(a)   I *seen* the tractor-marks, they're right up to the windowsill, like. (PVG/006)
(b)   So really and truly he *done* very well. (SMT/005)
(c)   I *been* in milk all my life. (SMT/015)

Given the fact that the lone past participle can be used to mean simple past, past perfect, or present perfect, another hypothesis is that the lone past participle is an innovation, a generalized past time marker.

NOTE   The idea that the lone past participle is an innovation is a strange hypothesis, since the same verb form for use in preterite and present perfect contexts is actually a historical pattern that has existed for hundreds of years. Other linguistic features have also been regarded as innovative when they are actually quite old, e.g. the zero adverb, discourse *like*, etc. Make sure you check the history books before you decide if something is old or new.

An extension of the generalized past marker hypothesis predicts that the use of a lone past participle is the first stage in a process which will lead to the eventual loss of the perfect tense in English. This conclusion is not without precedent. The position of the perfect in the history of many languages is notoriously unstable, having been alternatively lost and reintroduced at various times in languages such as High German, French, Russian, Swedish, and some Slavic languages (Scur 1974: 22; Vanneck 1955). In French, the gradual relaxation of the degree of recentness or current relevance required for use of the perfect enabled its form to supplant the simple past while losing its original meaning. Under this hypothesis we could predict extension of past participles into preterite contexts. For some varieties, constructions with no tense marking may by be explained by distinct origins. AAVE and English-based creoles present a strong case for this type of argumentation (Rickford 1977, 1986b). For example, in Guyanese Creole the perfect tense does not exist. Instead, free morphemes in preverbal position encode aspectual rather than tense, distinctions such as remote past, completive, or anterior. When *have* occurs, it patterns according to the Guyanese Creole grammar even though the forms are English in origin (see Bickerton 1975: 129). Two frequently occurring forms in perfect contexts are *done* and *been*, as in Examples 10.17 and 10.18 (as well as in Example 10.16).

Example 10.17   *done*

   (a)   I never *done* nothing to him. (NPR/024)
   (b)   We never *done* did very much in the salt water. (GYE/063)
   (c)   Leo *done* stoled your codfish down the road. (NPR/024)
   (d)   I *done* alright then. (YRK/075)

Example 10.18   *been*

   (a)   Her wedding was better than some of these wedding ... I *been* seeing. (NPR/016)
   (b)   I *been* in three accidents; never got a blemish. (NPR/016)
   (c)   I *been* had my deed ever since. (NPR/030)
   (d)   Then I came back – I *been* back since nineteen-sixty-seven. (YRK/006)

The auxiliary-deletion hypothesis would explain these constructions as variants of the perfect in which an underlying auxiliary *have* is deleted. However, the same surface form also fulfills the classic description of creole verb patterns in which free morphemes encoding tense/aspect functions are inserted between subject and predicate. On closer inspection, some of them do not correspond to the English perfect tense because they are not always directly translatable into standard English via *have* deletion. Notice for example that the sentences in Examples 10.18b–c and 10.19c do not provide a reading consistent with the removal of (standard) English *have*. This is taken as evidence that the forms cannot be equated with an English function (Bickerton 1975; Mufwene 1984). Such examples are rare and reports of similar form/function asymmetries can be found in nonstandard varieties of English, as in Example 10.19a–b (Feagin 1979: 255–256).

Example 10.19   Alabama English

   (a)   I *been knowin'* your granddaddy for forty years.
   (b)   Well, I chewed tobacco some, and then I started smokin' – started smokin' cigarettes. Course I – I *been quit* about 15 years since I smoked.

While Alabama English may have had influence from AAVE, Newfoundland English has not, and yet constructions such as in Example 10.20 are known to occur (Noseworthy 1972: 22).

Example 10.20   Newfoundland

   I *been* cut more wood than you.

Moreover, traditional descriptions of these varieties have equated these forms with functions approximating those claimed for creoles. *Done* has been referred to as a completive/emphatic marker while *been* is said to have connotations of remoteness (Feagin 1991; Noseworthy 1972).

Another rare perfect construction is the "three verb cluster" which comprises an auxiliary + *done* + past participle (either inflected or not). Some examples from Appalachia (Christian *et al.* 1988: 33), Alabama (Feagin 1979: 122), the United States, and Canada are shown in Example 10.21.

Example 10.21

Ozark English:
(a)   Them old half gentle ones *has* all *done disappeared*.
Appalachian English:
(b)   … because the one that was in there *had done rotted*.
Annistan, Alabama English:
(c)   You buy you a little milk and bread and you*'ve done spent* your five dollars!
Nova Scotia:
(d)   I think I*'m done give* you enough now. (NPR/038)

Additionally, attestations of *be* as an auxiliary in perfect contexts instead of *have* are also found, as in Example 10.22a–b, Alabama (Feagin 1979: 127), and also in Canada.

Example 10.22   Auxiliary *be* + verb

(a)   Some of the unions *is done gone* too far.
(b)   It was so quiet I thought everybody *was done gone* to bed.
Nova Scotia:
(c)   If a child *is taken* measles, and you don't know … you get that and steep it and give them that the next morning (GYE/045)
(d)   The older ones that I knew, a lot of them *is passed* away. (GYV/107)

Finally, prescriptive grammars widely acknowledge that, even in Standard English, many perfect contexts readily admit preterite morphology (Leech 1987: 43), as in Example 10.23.

Example 10.23   Preterite in present perfect

(a)   I never *saw* a moose for forty years. (GYV/108)
(b)   I don't know how many quilts I *made* in my life. (GYE/045)
(c)   She's been here all the time; we hardly ever *saw* her. (YRK/004)
(d)   You said you *looked* into some other research. (TOR/005)
(e)   Jenn relentlessly *made* fun of me for it. (TOR/008)

It is puzzling that such a narrowly circumscribed area of the grammar would have so many different variants. What could be going on? As it happens, when the perfect tense in the English is put into historical perspective we find that it is a relatively new development that has evolved considerably over the past few hundred years (e.g. Curme 1977; Traugott 1972; Visser 1963–1973). In fact, the long and complex history of the development of the perfect in English provides an eye-opening backdrop for interpreting these synchronic patterns of variation.

NOTE   Spanish is another language where the development of tense/aspect systems in contemporary varieties presents ideal opportunities for the study of grammaticalization, e.g. perfect (Schwenter 1994a,b; Schwenter and Torres Cacoullos 2008); future (Aaron 2010; Torres 1989; Torres-Cacoullos 1999).

Historical perspective

In Old English there were only two tenses: past and nonpast. The past covered not only what is represented by the simple past of today, but also durative past time (what is now covered in part by the past progressive), as well as the present perfect and past perfect of the contemporary system (Strang 1970: 311). This can be seen in Example 10.24, where the simple past tense inflection marks a context that today would be expressed as *have* + past participle.

Example 10.24

Fæder min,	se	tima	*com*
Father mine,	that	time	came.

Father, the time has come. (Traugott 1972: 183)

Many researchers acknowledge that the simple past and present perfect were once interchangeable, including those where either one or the other alone would be required in contemporary usage. Denison (1993: 352) cites examples where he says the present perfect "appears to be commuting with a simple past." He bases this observation on two facts: (1) parallelism with preterite usage; and (2) parallel adverbial collocation patterns. During the change from Old to Middle English this two-tense (past vs. nonpast) inflectional verb system underwent substantial elaboration (Strang 1970: 98) and the most prominent expansion was the development of the present perfect and past perfect.

A general overview of the history of the present perfect can be summarized in five main points:

1. The present perfect has been realized variably by preterite and perfect surface forms in English for centuries.
2. Variability in these forms was far more extensive during the Middle English period than in the contemporary standard system.
3. Competition among auxiliaries *be*, *have*, and *done* to signal present perfect meaning was common in the early stages of the development of the present perfect. This variability still persists in nonstandard varieties of contemporary English in North America, the Caribbean, and in the UK.
4. Lone past participles, specifically the three verbs *been*, *done*, and *seen*, have been attested, particularly since the early nineteenth century, but may have originated much earlier.
5. Inflection on the main verb was variable in Middle English.

NOTE Surprisingly, the past perfect has rarely been studied (see Cukor-Avila 1995) yet it is more frequent than the present perfect and is in hearty competition with the preterite, e.g. *After I threw him out, I kept hearing he was outside the house* (YRK/003/line 3396) vs. *It was six weeks I think after I'd thrown him out* (YRK/003/line 3465). It promises to offer additional insights into the grammaticalization of tense/aspect systems.

The Perfect in Samaná English

In the early 1990s, I completed my PhD dissertation on the past temporal reference system in Samaná English. The characteristics of this unique community offered an important perspective on an earlier stage in the history of AAVE. A major goal of my study was to examine the different tense/aspect features, including the present perfect (Tagliamonte 1996, 2000; Tagliamonte and Poplack 1995).

As a first step in the analysis, I considered the evolution of the perfect in the history of English. The *have/has* + past participle construction developed in the Middle English period and gradually spread "into more and more linguistic environments" (Harris 1984: 322). The contemporary system evolved over the following centuries (see e.g. Elsness 1997), although not necessarily to the same extent in all varieties of English. Observations regarding the details of this development offered a number of testable constraints.

Among the most prominent linguistic patterns in the development of the perfect was a competition across verb types. At first, *have* and *be* competed as auxiliaries (Denison 1993: 358; Fridén 1948; Strang 1970), as in Example 10.25a. Compare the example from Samaná English in Example 10.25b.

Example 10.25

  (a)   He took his wyf to kepe whan he *is gon* vs. and also to *han gon* to solitarie exil. (Brunner 1963: 87)
  (b)   I'*m never been* in prison. Never in my life, *I've been* in prison. (SAM/021)

The two auxiliaries were favored for different types of verb: *have* occurred with transitive verbs and *be* with certain intransitive verbs denoting the idea of becoming or turning or being transformed into something (also referred to as "mutative"), as in Example 10.26a. Denison (1993: 344) describes the history of perfect *be* in English as a "continuous retreat in the face of the advancing *have* perfect." *Have* gradually generalized to more and more verbs and eventually ousted *be* (Curme 1977: 359). Compare the example in Example 10.26b from Samaná English.

Example 10.26

  (a)   These days *are* now *chaunged*. (OED, Spenser, *Faerie Queene* 4.4.I.3)
  (b)   The town *is changed*. The town Samaná is not Samaná no more. (SAM/003)

During the Middle English period a "three-verb structure" (Visser 1963–1973: 2209) also developed, as in Example 10.29. Similar examples have been reported from Older Scots (Craigie *et al.* 1937–; Curme 1931: 23) where these forms were literary. Traugott (1972: 146) also notes that the main verb in the three-verb cluster may be bare (i.e. uninflected). Note the example from Samaná in Example 10.27b.

Example 10.27

  (a)   And many other false abusion. The Paip (= Pope) *hes done invent*. (Traugott 1972: 146)
  (b)   And he told me that he *had done pass* through them English books. (SAM/006)

Table 10.3 Overall distribution of surface forms in past temporal reference in Samaná English.

	%	N
Preterite (*-ed* or strong)	62	4997
Verb stem	17	1374
Habitual, progressive etc.[a]	15	971
was/got passive	2	150
had + past participle	1.5	120
have + past participle[b]	1	86
Lone past participle (*seen, been, done*)	0.7	58
Unambiguous present tense morphology, e.g. *-s*	0.6	27
be + verb	0.5	39
ain't + verb	0.5	36
done + verb	0.1	10
had + *done* + verb	0.07	6
be + *done* + verb	0.05	4
TOTAL N		7878

[a] This category consists of habitual forms such as *used to*, *would* + verb and variants of the progressive, e.g. *was going*, which are not the focus of this investigation.
[b] This includes *have/has/'s*, as well as a following verb form which could include unmarked weak verbs and strong verbs with preterite morphology, in addition to standard English past participles.
Source: Tagliamonte, 1997: 46, Table 1.

By the mid-nineteenth century attestations of lone past participles in present perfect contexts, as in Example 10.28, becomes prevalent (Visser 1963–1973: 1298). Visser (1970: 1298) suggests they may be forerunners of the contemporary constructions which are frequently reported in early-twentieth-century English dialects, both American (Atwood 1953: 43), and British (Wright 1898–1905: 298). Compare the Samaná examples in Example 10.28b.

Example 10.28

(a) I *seen* um both a-hanging in chains by Wisbeach river. (OED, Charles Kingsley, *Alton Locke*, c. 1870)
(b) I never *seen* him. (SAM/001)

In sum, many of the same constructions reported for the perfect in the history of English, in English-based creoles, and in contemporary English dialects existed in the data. However, an inventory of forms does not provide an evaluation of the function they fulfill. The question was whether Samaná English was patterning like English or some other grammar.

Conducting a variation analysis of the perfect presented a methodological challenge. How is the analyst to study this linguistic feature accountably? Based on the historical fact that the perfect arose from a more general past tense, I began the analysis by counting the overall frequency and distribution of surface morphological forms within the past temporal reference system as a whole, as in Table 10.3.

Table 10.4   Overall distribution of surface forms in present
perfect contexts in Samaná English.

	%	N
Surface morphology:		
Preterite[a]	25	96
have + verb[b]	22	82
ain't + verb	7	26
Verb stem	17	64
Lone past participle (*seen, been, done*)	11	31
be + verb	10	37
done + verb	2	8
been + verb	2	9
had + verb	1	4
Three verb cluster with *be*		4
Three verb cluster with *have*		1
Present	0.5	2
TOTAL N		364

[a] Includes *got* passives, modals with past morphology, and *do*-support.
[b] Includes *have, has,* and *'s* as well as *haven't, hasn't*.
Source: Tagliamonte 1997: 47, Table 2.

This approach provides an overview of the entire past temporal reference system in the variety. Note that the majority tense/aspect form is the preterite (whether weak verbs with an *-ed* suffix or strong verbs), a total of 4997 contexts – 62%. In contrast, there are only 86 tokens of *have* + past participle. This reveals that the perfect is generally rare when viewed against the backdrop of past time generally, but it does not tell us where it is variable with the preterite.

> **NOTE**   A default form typically makes up the majority of the tense/aspect system (see Patrick 1999; Poplack and Tagliamonte 1999a; Sankoff 1990; Tagliamonte 1998a). Extracting *all* past temporal reference tokens is a huge investment in time to study something that represents only 1% of the data.

In the second analysis, I tabulated the overall frequency and distribution of perfect forms in contexts that fulfilled the semantic function of the present perfect (continuative, experiential, or resultative) what I referred to as "present perfect contexts" (Tagliamonte 1996: 354). This restricted the analysis to only those contexts where the standard present perfect construction *could have* occurred but other constructions could occur as well. Table 10.4 shows the results.

Once the data are partitioned into the relevant semantic context, notice that the proportion of the perfect auxiliary rises markedly. In present perfect contexts, *have* + verb occurs 22% of the time. Still, preterite morphology (either inflected with *-ed* or a strong verb)

Table 10.5 Overall distribution of surface forms found in present perfect contexts across corpora.

	SAM		NPR		GYE		GYV		OTT	
	%	N	%	N	%	N	%	N	%	N
Surface morphology:										
Preterite[a]	25	96	45	233	50	365	45	174	23	138
have + verb[b]	22	82	6	31	21	152	37	143	70	423
ain't + verb	7	26	6	29	2	17	–	0	–	0
Verb stem	17	64	9	47	5	33	7	2	1	7
Lone past participle	11	31	18	93	18	133	5	21	3	17
be + verb	10	37		3	1	7		2		2
done + verb	2	8	5	26	–	0	–	0	–	0
been + verb	2	9	8	40	1	8	1	5	1	5
had + verb	1	4		3		3		2		2
three verb cluster with *be*		4								
three verb cluster with *have*		1								
Present	0.5	2	1	6		2	1	4	2	10
TOTAL N		364		524		736		388		607

[a] Includes *got* passives, modals with past morphology, and *do*-support.
[b] Includes *have*, *has*, and *'s* as well as *haven't*, *hasn't*.

accounts for a full 25% of present perfect contexts. Lone past participles represent 11%. All other variants represent less than 10%. We can now establish that the distinctive creole *been* in a preverbal, non-*have* deletion site, does not occur at all, nor does *ain't* + verb.

In sum, the Samaná data exhibit a system in which there was far more extensive alternation among competing forms than in contemporary Standard English. However, this profile is consistent with the historical record where a parallel set of forms existed in earlier stages. I suggested that preverbal *been* and *done* and the other "strange" forms in perfect contexts in Samaná were simply remnants of this earlier stage in the development of the present perfect in the history of the English language.

Perfect Have in Nova Scotia, Canada

By the early 1990s Shana Poplack and I had begun the African Nova Scotian project (Poplack and Tagliamonte 1991a) and naturally we were keen to know how the present perfect was faring in the sister communities in a Canadian context. We tabulated the overall distribution of forms in present perfect contexts in three Nova Scotian communities (North Preston, Guysborough Enclave, and Guysborough Village) and also Ottawa English, our control group for general Canadian English (Tagliamonte and Poplack 1995). The results are shown in Table 10.5.

A general observation is that the frequency and occurrence of the various nonstandard forms decrease from Samaná to Ottawa in direct relationship with the proximity of the varieties to mainstream norms (consistent with the findings for the *going to* future). Yet all the communities share the use of the preterite and *have* auxiliary for perfect meaning. Even in

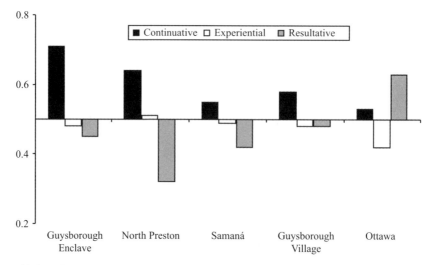

Figure 10.4   Hierarchy of constraints for semantic function across varieties.

Ottawa where auxiliary *have* occurs far more frequently than in any other community, the three main variants – *have* or *had*, preterite morphology, and lone past participle morphology – are productive. Perfect *have* has not spread to all contexts that meet the semantic meaning of the perfect. This, in turn, suggests that the category itself has not fully grammaticalized.

The next step is to find the linguistic patterns that might underlie these forms. The variable context is defined as the set of semantic-pragmatic meanings known to comprise the present perfect system. To facilitate cross-variety comparison, all the perfect forms have been grouped together (*have* + past participle, lone PP, *been, seen, done, gone*). Figure 10.4 displays a cross-variety comparison of these forms by semantic-pragmatic context.

Figure 10.4 shows that continuative contexts favor the perfect in all the communities. Recall that the simple past tense had originally covered all aspects of past time, including references which brought past time into relation with the present (Curme 1977: 358). As the preterite shifted in emphasis to mark explicitly past time there was a need for a distinct strategy to express a temporal relationship to present time (Curme 1977: 358). The continuative perfect, as in Example 10.29, is the semantic-pragmatic context that most closely matches this.

Example 10.29

    (a)   I'*ve been* here in this spot, on this hill now, for twenty years. (GYE/046)
    (b)   I'*ve had* a busy life. (GYV/102)

We argued that this demonstrated a specialization of the *have* perfect for this more circumscribed meaning. Experiential contexts neither favor nor disfavor *have*, except in Ottawa where this context favors the preterite. Resultatives demarcate the communities most dramatically – in Ottawa the perfect forms are favored with a factor weight of 0.63; other contexts favor the preterite. If Ottawa English can be taken as any indication of the general trend in mainstream varieties of English, then there appears to be a developing pattern across the semantic-pragmatic contexts of the perfect. Continuatives are in the lead, resultatives are neutral and experiential contexts are in flux. It may be the case that the more advanced pattern is for resultatives to take *have* while experientals lag behind.

One of the results that emerged from this study was that the constraint ranking for perfect *have* in Ottawa mirrors that reported in Trinidadian Creole (Winford 1993). Yet it contrasts with contemporary AAVE (Dayton 1996) where preverbal *done* has generalized to become the perfect marker in experiential and resultative, but not continuative, contexts. These comparisons are preliminary at best and without a full analysis of all the potential influencing linguistic factors remain speculative; however, it shows that different varieties may be following quite distinct pathways in the ongoing grammaticization of the present perfect. If so, then this variable may be the ideal diagnostic for disentangling the relationships among varieties.

Discussion and Conclusions

According to the historical record the present perfect has been developing out of an *earlier* more general system in which the preterite covered all areas of past temporal reference. In this process, the *have* perfect is carving out a small, highly circumscribed section of that system. We have found evidence for increasing use of the auxiliary *have* over the extant forms (the preterite and the verb stem). The pattern across varieties suggests that contact with mainstream (urban) varieties may be a major impetus behind this process, suggesting a change from above. Yet even in Ottawa there is still variability among the basic variants – *have*, the preterite, and the lone past participle – and these have been in competition from the earliest origins of the perfect. This means that the evolution of the present perfect is a long way from being complete in contemporary varieties of English.

The lone past participle does not appear to be spreading to functions beyond the well known perfect contexts. Examination of co-occurrence patterns of these forms (not shown) (see Tagliamonte and Poplack 1995) revealed that there are really only three lone past participles that occur with any degree of frequency – *seen*, *done*, and *been*. Of these, *seen* and *been* are virtually restricted to perfect contexts rather than extending beyond them. This suggests that the auxiliary deletion hypothesis is the most likely explanation for these forms. In contrast, *done* is found in perfect *and* preterite contexts; however, *done* behaves like this in many other varieties in North America and the United Kingdom as well. In this case, the explanation may be a simple case of regularization of preterite and past participle function analogically with other verbs such as *bring/brought/brought*, as has often been reported for varieties of English (Trudgill 1984: 22).

The principles of grammaticalization help to explain and situate these findings in time and space.

1. *The principle of layering*, whereby new forms are used in a functional domain and co-vary with older ones: according to Bybee *et al.* (1994: 8) it is typical of grammatical categories to reduce in size. The most straightforward explanation for the wealth of variants in conservative communities such Samaná and the Nova Scotian enclaves is that they represent an earlier stage in the development of the perfect tenses when the system had not yet stabilized. This explains why the perfect system in remote contexts is so much more elaborate than in mainstream communities. The communities are simply conservative with respect to linguistic change.

During the emergence of the present perfect as a tense/aspect category, periphrastic perfect constructions came to alternate with preterite forms for the same meaning. To date, the former have not completely ousted the latter from this domain. Samaná English captures this aspect of the diachrony of English quite accurately. A comparative sociolinguistic analysis with the African Nova Scotian communities makes this interpretation even more compelling since the retreat of older forms from the system can be viewed incrementally in across varieties.

2. *The principle of persistence*, whereby traces of the original lexical meanings of forms may be reflected in constraints on their grammatical distribution: this is observed in the statistically significant effect of continuative contexts which may have been the impetus for the development of perfect meaning out of the preterite.

3. *The principle of specialization*, whereby as grammaticalization proceeds, a smaller number of devices (out of a wider initial range) are used more generally and specialize for the relevant grammatical function, ousting the other alternatives and reducing their systemic and/or statistical distribution: this is obvious in Ottawa English where the *have* + past participle construction is the major expression of present perfect (even if it continues to compete with forms of the preterite). Nevertheless, *have* + past participle constructions and preterite forms continue to stand out as dominant expressions of present perfect in all the varieties.

In sum, *have* + verb, the preterite and *been, done*, and *seen* continue to share the same general semantic space after hundreds of years. Instead of leveling across the three semantic/pragmatic functions of the perfect, we observe ongoing specialization. Continuative contexts are the most favorable to the *have* variant; however, resultative contexts also favor the *have* auxiliary in mainstream Ottawa. Taken together, variation in the perfect across these varieties provides an in-depth view of a particular point in the development of the present perfect in English. Further points along this path can now be interpreted against this backdrop. Like the *going to* future, many linguistic patterns can be extrapolated from the historical record. These offer opportunities to track the grammaticalization process in remote locales (where earlier stages of gramamticalization may still be in evidence) and into the future. Studies of actively changing grammatical tense/aspect features such as this also underscore the interplay between ecological setting, linguistic variation, and language change.

Research on the perfect continues to provide important insights into several key issues in LVC: register differences (Miller 2000), origins (van Herk 2008), and L2 varieties of English (Davydova 2009; Siemund *et al.* 2010). But we still need more information from other varieties of English to flesh out the nature of this system.

Studying Tense/Aspect Variables

Tense/aspect variables are difficult to study for many reasons. They require extension and enhancement to the sociolinguistic methods elaborated by foundational work in the variationist tradition. First, the variants often do not mean exactly the same thing. How is the analyst to know which tokens should be included and which to leave aside? Second, non-overtly marked variants (i.e. zero forms) are characteristic of tense/aspect systems. How is the analyst to find something that is not there? Third, one's pre-existing assumptions about the data can have influence the nature of the analytic process. Let us consider each of these problems in turn.

I first encountered the problem of studying tense/aspect features in the analysis of variable past tense marking. Past tense is a linguistic variable involving verbs describing events that took place before speech time. The intriguing thing about past tense verbs is that in most varieties of English they are not categorically marked. Many past tense verbs are bare. Consider the narrative in Example 10.30 told in 1995 by a 23-year-old male born and raised in Canada. The story describes a childhood event that took place many years in the past.

Example 10.30   The Wasp

(a)   This one time <u>when I was young,</u>
(b)   we … well I <u>grew up</u> in the country right.
(c)   Everybody <u>had</u> BB guns, pellet guns
(d)   So we're out there eh
(e)   and my kid brother is climbing up the tree, right
(f)   So I'm a little scared eh
(g)   or I mean I'm trying to scare him.
(h)   So I'm lookin' at him,
(i)   and he's climbin' eh
(j)   So I'm young,
(k)   So I <u>aim</u> my gun eh,
(l)   and I <u>aim</u> about two feet over his head.
(m)   But I'm not accounting for over– over a large distance that the bullet's going to fall right.
(n)   So the kid he's about ten feet up in the tree eh.
(o)   <u>Aim</u> him up, wham! shoot,
(p)   All of a sudden "ptak!"
(q)   <u>Hit</u> him wham!
(r)   Kid <u>hits</u> the ground like a sack of potatoes.
(s)   I'm going "oh my God"!!
(t)   So I turn around
(u)   and I dash, right
(v)   Cause I don't know if I've killed him or what.
(w)   It's only a BB gun mind ya.
(x)   So anyways my mom runs out,
(y)   He's bawling eh,
(z)   and he has this red mark,
(aa)   and she thinks he got stung by a wasp.
(bb)   So I don't tell anybody eh
(cc)   Until like I <u>waited</u> until about oh ten years before I told anybody in my family that.
(dd)   Anyways just a little clip for ya.

NOTE   Notice the use of the quotative "go" with internal thought and encoded with present progressive. Given what we know about the quotative system more generally, what does this reveal about the Canadian system among young adults in 1995?

Narratives provide an excellent way of viewing tense/aspect features (see Tagliamonte and Poplack 1988). They provide a naturally bounded speech act where events are understood to have occurred prior to the moemnet of speaking. Narratives have recognized structures (Labov and Waletzky 1967) where different tense/aspect phenomena are known to occur. Notice that the entire narrative is told in the historical present. That are only four lines that have an overt past tense morpheme: the first three lines, a, b, and c, and line cc. This highlights another important attribute about tense/aspect features: they have patterns that go beyond the sentence.

TIP   To my knowledge variation in the past and historical present has never been studied outside the US (Johnstone 1987; Schiffrin 1981; Wolfson 1979, 1981), but see Levey (2006). I wonder if other varieties share the same patterns? I wonder to what extent this feature could be used as a diagnostic for ancestry?

Tense/aspect features are particularly slippery because depending on one's assumption the decisions one makes about how to extract, code, and circumscribe them will vary. The departure point for an analysis can be either one of the following:

- form as the baseline for analysis;
- function as the baseline for analysis.

In my earlier studies of the past tense in English the departure point for the analysis was the semantic function, the description of which can be found in any prescriptive grammar of English. I extracted every single clause with past reference in the data and then assessed the frequency and distribution of forms that occur in the same semantic space (Tagliamonte 1991; Tagliamonte and Poplack 1988). In other areas of the tense/aspect system (e.g. the perfect) some researchers will recommend one method; some will recommend another. The important thing is to keep track of whatever decisions you do make and record them in your methodology so that it can be repeated, improved upon, or compared across studies. For a detailed discussion of the delimitation and scope of the relevant contexts for variable (t,d) see Hackett (2008).

Finally, be cautious of what the literature says about tense/aspect features. Descriptions of creoles make it seem that bare verbs do not occur very often in English (but see Example 10.30). Descriptions of *have* deletion suggest that lone past participles are frequent and productive forms. In fact, a bare past participle is a rare item in English since the only contexts where one can be unambiguously identified are with strong verbs. Weak verbs, which have no distinction between preterite and past participle morphology, would appear as preterites in the event of *have* deletion, making them indistinguishable from the (simple) past tense.

One of the big problems one faces when examining tense/aspect variables is that the range of meanings the variants may embody are notoriously subjective, not only in English, but in many other languages as well. Take for example the nuances of future meaning: desire, intention, obligation, imminence, etc. There is no objective way to determine which of these may have been intended by the speaker, and there is every possibility that any one of them could be inferred by the analyst. To obviate this problem, analysts must find replicable measures to assess the uses of each variant in context. Fortunately, despite the diversity of nuances in meaning, there are typically other, more objective, ways to code the data.

Consider the case of deontic modality. Forms in this system include *must, have to*, and *have got to*, as in Example 10.31.

Example 10.31

(a) If you join the club, you *must* go to church. (MPT/020)
(b) They *have to* keep up with the Jones's now. (MPT/026)
(c) You *'ve got to* have a vice of some kind. (CMK/022)

The literature typically associates one form or another to a particular reading: *must* is thought to be strong, while the other forms are weak. This contrast has also been conceived as "core" vs. "periphery" (Coates 1983: 32). Most accounts group *have to* and *have got* to together, as toned down choices in contrast to *must*, distinguishing neither subtle meaning differences nor contrastive strength to the choice between them (Huddleston and Pullum 2002: 183). The main point of relevance here is that there are different meanings associated with each form. However, the variants *have to* and *have got to* represent the vast majority of uses in dialect data. This means that there is something more going on than a contrast (functional or otherwise) between *must* on the one hand, and *have to* grouped with *have got to* on the other. How is the analyst to code for different degrees of "strength" of the obligation/necessity reading?

A strong–weak distinction, either as contrastive or as a continuum, is virtually impossible to categorize impartially. To do so inevitably leads to circularity from the imposition of the analyst's own subjective interpretations. Fortunately, the encoding of grammatical person in English provides a reasonable facsimile. Coates (1983: 37), for example, notes that "It is generally true that examples with second person subjects are stronger than those with first person subjects, while examples with first person subjects are usually stronger than those with third person subjects." This means that we can posit grammatical person as a proxy to expose the relative strength of forms and categorize each context in our data according to this hierarchy, i.e. first person, second person, and third person subjects.

Exercises

Exercise 10.1   Identifying tense/aspect variables ————————

Question 1   Re-look at the Wasp narrative in Example 10.30. Are there any other suggestive tense/aspect phenomena of interest?

(a) _____

(b) _____

(c) _____

Exercise 10.2   Preamble: variable (habitual) past in York English ————

The expression of habitual past is an area of English grammar that has not been extensively studied. It has the interesting property of involving at least two overtly marked constructions,

Table 10.6   Three logistic regression analyses showing the results for discourse
position in habitual past contexts where all three forms are possible.

	Used to	Preterite	*Would*	Total Ns/Cell
Input	0.38	0.39	0.17	
Total N	675	629	288	1592
Position in sequence				
Unsequenced	0.55	0.48	0.47	318
First	0.55	0.50	0.40	253
Second	0.42	0.61	0.45	340
Middle	0.47	0.47	0.59	465
Last	0.49	0.48	0.53	216

Source: Tagliamonte and Lawrence 2000: 334, Table 2.

used to and *would*, as well as the preterite. Each of these forms is used in Example 10.32 to describe a situation that existed for a period of time but is no longer the case.

Example 10.32

(a)   We *used to go* the cinema and we*'d do* our shopping and then we*'d go* upstairs to the café and we*'d have* either beans on toast or toasted teacake, and then we*'d go* to the picture house below us and we *used to do* that. (YRK/001)

(b)   My father *used to* let us play on the beach in the morning and part of the afternoon, then he *would want* to take us for a walk you see … and we*'d go up*, climb up to the castle or something like that. (YRK/086)

Perhaps because none of these forms is overtly stigmatized and all are compatible with Standard English grammar, the potential interchangeability between them has not been the subject of explicit commentary in the literature. While some researchers list the preterite and *used to*, and sometimes *would*, as alternating forms (Quirk *et al.* 1972: 43), others do not mention the fact that there are actually three different constructions that embody the meaning of habitual past (Comrie 1976). Moreover, no attempt has been made to understand the use of the habitual past forms beyond the level of the clause.

Question 1   Given the data in Example 10.32a–b above, what observations can you make regarding the distribution of forms?

(a)   _____

(b)   _____

(c)   _____

Exercise 10.3   Interpreting tense/aspect variables   ——————

In 1997, Helen Lawrence and I conducted an analysis of variable (habitual) in York English (Tagliamonte and Lawrence 2000). Table 10.6 shows the results for discourse sequence of habitual contexts where all three forms were possible.

Question 1   Which form occurs most often?

Question 2   Do these results confirm, contrast, or offer fresh insights for the observations that were gleaned from the examples in Example 10.32? What evidence supports this interpretation?

Question 3   Is this pattern community-specific? Is it consistent with the historical record? The following examples come from the TEA. What do these examples in Example 10.33 suggest?

Example 10.33

(a)   I *used to* get so disgusted, 'cause like, I *would sit* across from him, right? And my parents *were* sitting across from each other and so I'*d have to* like, watch him eat. And it *was* so disgusting. (TOR/003)

(b)   There *used to be* separate doors for boys and girls in the public school, and we'*d march in*, in military style, there'*d be* music, somebody *playing* the piano and you'*d have to march in*, and we'*d line up* in our classes and go in order. (TOR/036)

Mini Quiz Answers

10.1   Q1: *c*
      Q2: *a*
      Q3: *d*
      Q4: *a*
      Q5: *d*
      Q6: *a*
      Q7: *b*
      Q8: *c*
      Q9: *b*
      Q10: *c*

Background reading

Studies of the future

Arnovick 1990; Berglund 1997; Bybee and Pagliuca 1987; Bybee, Pagliuca, and Perkins 1991; Close 1977; Curme 1913; Danchev and Kytö 1994; Fries 1925; Gagnon 1990; Haegeman 1981; Mair 1997b; Nehls 1988; Poplack and Turpin 1999; Royster and Steadman 1923/1968; Sankoff 1991; Sankoff and Wagner 2006; Torres-Cacoullos and Walker 2009a,b; Wales 1983.

Studies of the perfect

Bauer 1970; Brinton 1988; Comrie 1976; Fenn 1987; Jespersen 1924; Leech 1971; McCawley 1971; Mencken 1962; Menner 1926; Scur 1974; Vanneck 1955; Zandvoort 1932.

11

Other Variables

Changes in progress tell us much about the human beings who are engaged in them. They are surprising and at times difficult to understand. (Labov 2010: 375)

In this chapter, I will consider several linguistic variables that do not easily fit into any particular level of grammar, or which might be considered "unusual" for one reason or another.

This is a catchall group of stragglers that defy categorization. In some cases the variable is not easily defined. Consider the rising new interest in intensifiers. They represent a highly understudied area of the grammar – adverbs. The variation arises from the wide array of different adverbs that are used to intensify, e.g. *very* or *really* or *so* or some other variant. Is this a lexical variable or a morphological variable or a discourse-pragmatic variable? Other unusual studies arise when a researcher targets a subset of a linguistic system. Take, for example, variation in a particularly frequent verb, e.g. *come* vs. *came* (Tagliamonte 2001a), e.g. *sneaked* vs. *snuck* (Chambers 1998a; Hogg 1988), or a syntactic alternation, *give to me* vs. *give me it* (Bresnan and Hay 2008). What can you extrapolate from such an analysis, despite the limitation to a single lexical item? Consider too variation that arises in written data among the various new media. Acronyms, abbreviations, and other short forms have been in the news lately given their supposed rampant use in computer-mediated communication, e.g. *omg*, *lol*, and the like. What level of grammar is this? What type of variation? The issues that arise in the study of these variables are diverse, idiosyncratic, and often so novel that there is little in the literature to go by to devise a defensible methodology. How is the analysis to proceed? Because these variables are at the cutting edge of the field with implications for innovation, actuation, and embedding, we need to know how to deal with them effectively. Because they may not have been studied before, they offer us important new insights into the analysis of language variation and change.

When faced with the prospect of studying unusual features, how is one to proceed? What kinds of patterns do these features exhibit? What can they tell us about the relationship between language and society?

Variationist Sociolinguistics: Change, Observation, Interpretation, First Edition. Sali A. Tagliamonte.
© 2012 Sali A. Tagliamonte. Published 2012 by Blackwell Publishing Ltd.

Variable (come)

A common nonstandard features of English is the use of past reference *come*, as in Example 11.1 which alternates in many speakers with the standard form *came*, as in 11.1(b). This feature is so common that Chambers (1995: 240–241) classifies it as "ubiquitous" and "mainstream."

Example 11.1

(a) And I was coming along Skeldergate Bridge, and on the bike, and a car *come* straight in front of me. (YRK/007)

(b) When we first *came* into this house, this used be gardens. (YRK/007)

As we have discussed in earlier chapters, the verb *come* is one of the most frequent verbs in the English language. When it has been studied quantitatively, it has been found to make up between 10% and 20% of the total number of all strong verbs used in past reference contexts (e.g. Poplack and Tagliamonte 2001) (see Chapter 4). It exhibits extremely high levels of nonstandard usage compared to other verbs (e.g. Patrick 1991; Winford 1992). Because this verb is so frequent and so often variable it lends itself to quantitative study on its own.

Synchronic Perspective

In contemporary varieties of English variable (come) is widely attested. The Survey of English Dialects (SED), which was conducted in the 1950s, reports that although the standard form *came* was current for most of England, *come* was found all over the country as well, particularly in the east (Orton, Sanderson, and Widdowson 1978: 14). In North America, the Linguistic Atlas of New England and the Linguistic Atlas of the Middle and South Atlantic States shows past reference *come* occurring in all the communities that were surveyed. Atwood (1953: 9) reports its use by speakers in a variety of education brackets and by male as well as female speakers.

It is not difficult to find examples of past reference *come* in variationist studies from the 1960s onwards. Pick up any book that discusses dialects and you will find examples. Most studies explain the appearance of *come* for past reference as analogical leveling of the preterite and past participle to the same form – *came* in the preterite and *come* as a past participle become one form *come* for both (Christian *et al.* 1988: 108; Edwards and Weltens 1985: 110).

While this provides part of the explanation it is important to put *come* in context historically and socially. When someone uses *come* with past temporal reference how is it socially evaluated and why?

Historical Perspective

The historical literature indicates that the vowel of the morphological form *come* (and its equivalent earlier spellings) was used uniformly across the past paradigm in Old English and most of Middle English. The form *came* did not appear until the thirteenth or fourteenth century (Long 1944) and then only in northern varieties of Middle English.

Example 11.2

   (a) þer *come* to me to fair kniʒtes
   (b) And to þe cherche porche he *cam.* – c. 1300 (Sisam 1970: 6)

Example 11.3

   (a) With hem *com* mani champioun
   (b) þat he ne *kam* þider þe leyk to se – early thirteenth century (Dickens and Wilson 1969: 38–39)

According to the OED *came* did not entirely drive out *come* in the Midland and southern dialects of England until the fifteenth century. However, variation between two forms is readily found in the Helsinki Corpus as late as 1500–1570, as can be seen in Example 11.4.

Example 11.4

   (a) Sir, one the eving after the making of this letter, your servant Edmund Robyson *come* home.
   (b) So I wente with hym, and when we *came* downe, al the yarde was full of people. (Helsinki Corpus, c. 1500–1570)

Despite the long-term variability between *come* and *came*, late-twentieth-century studies claim that the use of past reference *come* is becoming increasingly infrequent, particularly among the younger generation (Christian *et al.* 1988; Tidholm 1979). The explanation given for this accelerated change is the effect of increasing literacy and education in the twentieth century, as well as social changes such as widespread urbanization. Studies of British dialects where past reference *come* was productive in the 1970s predicted that it would soon be obsolete (Tidholm 1979: 147).

Under the influence of strong standardizing external forces (pressure from above) it would be a reasonable hypothesis that *came* would win out over *come*. Yet, variability between the two forms persists in English, particularly in regional dialects. Thus, this area of the grammar, and the use of *come* and *came* in particular, may present a good reflection of the underlying currents of continuity and change in English, especially if it were possible to conduct a community-level study.

York English, c. 1997

All the uses of the verb *come* for past reference were extracted from the York English Corpus, providing 1016 tokens from 87 individuals. Each example was coded for a series of external and internal factors that could have an effect on the morphological form.

Distributional Analysis
Figure 11.1 shows the proportion of speakers using past reference *come* by age (line) as well as the proportion of *come* out of all tokens of past reference *come* or *came* by age (columns).

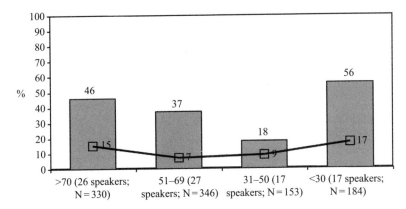

Figure 11.1 Use of past reference *come*.
Source: Tagliamonte 2001: 48, Figure 3.

Contrary to what might be expected, there is no stepwise change in apparent time toward the standard form. In fact, the youngest speakers are the most likely to use *come* (56%) followed closely by the oldest generation (46%) and there is a dip among the middle-aged speakers. This sociolinguistic pattern is consistent with age grading. Individuals in the working years of their lives produce the most standard language (see Chapter 3). How might we substantiate this interpretation?

Logistic Regression – Social Factors
We can predict that age graded linguistic features will be sensitive to education and occupation. Table 11.1 provides a logistic regression analysis of the external factors of sex, age, and education.

Table 11.1 reveals that three social factors exert statistically significant conditioning on variable (come). Age exerts the strongest effect with a range of 17, while education and sex contribute lesser effects with ranges of 13 and 10. The expected social correlates for age grading are present: men (0.56) and less educated speakers (0.54) favor the nonstandard form. The constraint hierarchy for age confirms the distributional result that the oldest and youngest members of the community favor the nonstandard form at 0.58 and 0.55 respectively while the middle-aged speakers disfavor it.

Of course we know that extralinguistic factors are highly interactive (Labov 1990). Moreover, age, sex, and education have previously been found to interact substantially in this community in particular (e.g. Tagliamonte 1998b). Using the variable rule program, the best way to understand these interactions is to alternate logistic regression analysis with cross-tabulation of factors (see Chapter 5). As an example, let us consider the intersection of age and sex, as in Figure 11.2.

The figure reveals a regular pattern of usage across generations in the way that would be predicted by principle 2: men use more *come* than women in all age groups. This pattern is regular across the population except for the oldest individuals. The oldest generation of men and women are using past reference *come* at near identical rates. This shows that variable (come) is not socially evaluated in the same way by all members of this community.

318

Other Variables

Table 11.1 Logistic regression analyses of the contribution of factors selected as significant to the probability of past reference *come*.

Corrected mean:	0.11	
Total N:	1016	

	Factor weight	Total N
Age		
>70	0.58	347
51–69	0.41	321
31–50	0.47	164
<30	0.55	184
Range	*17*	
Education		
Less educated	0.54	665
More educated	0.41	291
Range	*13*	
Sex		
Male	0.56	391
Female	0.46	625
Range	*10*	

Source: Tagliamonte 2001: 49, Table 1.

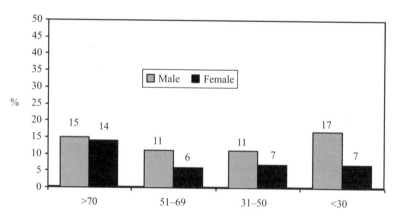

Figure 11.2 Distribution of past reference *come* by age and sex.

Explanation

The literature claims that past reference *come* would be obsolescent by the early twentieth century due to ongoing standardization of English and increasing education and literacy. Yet it is maintaining a foothold in the vernacular grammar of this northern British city. Moreover the youngest generation use past reference *come* just as much as the oldest generation, in fact more so. If this feature is obsolescing, this is an apparent contradiction. Why would this be the case?

One of the factors contributing to the survival of past temporal reference *come* is undoubtedly the extent of the verb's usage in the language (Strang 1970: 147). However, another factor contributing to its continuity may be the canonical form of the verb, [kʌm]. Research suggests that there is an ongoing trend for strong verbs with the phonetic shape /ʌ/ followed by a nasal and/or a velar consonant to gravitate toward the class of strong verbs that has the vowel /ʌ/ as its preterite form, e.g. *ring/rang/rung* → *ring/rung/rung* (Bybee 1983, 1988; Hogg 1988). Supportive to this interpretation is the fact that [ʌ] has been found to embody the idea of "pastness" in native speakers of English (Bybee 1983; Hogg 1988: 38). Under test conditions present-day speakers of English produce verbs with /ʌ/ far more than any other past tense form, suggesting that this particular form has a psychological reality for them (Bybee 1983: 254). Continuity of past reference *come*, which has this favored form, is consistent with the currents of this independent and ongoing drift within the strong verb system in English.

The different variants are also prime linguistic candidates for "the marking of a social differentiation" (Chambers 1995; Cheshire 1994: 188; Wolfram and Schilling-Estes 1998: 77). York is no different. Age, education, and male/female differences are significant factor groups in the variation between *come* and *came*. Thus, another important reason for the persistence of *come/came* variation is that it has become a sociolinguistic marker. However, sociolinguistic patterns must also be viewed in the context of shifting norms and practices at the community (see also Dubois and Horvath 1999). When the variation across age groups in the community is taken into account, we find that the older speakers in York do not exhibit the same social effects. The same general trend has been observed in contemporary US varieties (Atwood 1953). These supralocal patterns suggest that the contemporary social evaluation of preterite *come* is a relatively recent phenomenon resulting from colliding local dialects and Standard English over the last 200 years (Trudgill 1996: 422).

The endurance of preterite *come* is likely due to a convergence of factors, including the overall frequency of the verb in English, the favored status of its nonstandard canonical form, and the fact that it has developed social value. However, the robust variability that continues between the two forms, *come* and *came*, must also be seen as a result of the verb's distinctly layered history. Past reference *come* (including *com* and other orthographic variants) was the original form, remaining prevalent in written documents from midland and southern dialects of England until the sixteenth century while *came* is actually an interloper of much later pedigree. This suggests that *came* may not yet be a full participant in the past paradigm of all varieties of English. Moreover, it probably had not entirely stabilized in some of the spoken vernaculars of Britain that were transported to North America and elsewhere during the early colonization period in the late eighteenth century. Contemporary use of past reference *come* is the synchronic manifestation of this history. Next time you hear someone use past reference *come* think of the long journey that has led to the current situation.

NOTE   One morning in York my daughter Tara, aged 9, said something like this: *I brung it home from school.* Her father admonished her: "Tara, you don't say 'brung,' you say '*I brang it home from school*.'" There is apparently some confusion about the correct past participle across generations in my family.

Variable (Intensifiers)

A variable that has undergone tremendous study in recent years is the use of intensifiers, the type of adverb that adds a degree measure onto its referent, maximizing as in Example 11.5, or boosting as in Example 11.6.

Example 11.5

  Maximizers:
  (a) My mom's just like *absolutely* great. (TOR/008)
  (b) But during the week it was *absolutely* dead. (YRK/004)
  (c) I'm *completely* independent. (TOR/074)
  (d) I found the mental patients ah *extremely* interesting. (TOR/006)
  (e) I mean the chocolate making is *completely* different. (YRK/063)
  (f) It's all *entirely* different. (TOR/068)
  (g) He had a *perfectly* lovely name. (YRK/071)

Example 11.6

  Boosters:
  (a) I'm *really* lucky … (TOR/013)
  (b) That's *very* dangerous. (TOR/023)
  (c) She was *awful* tired. (TOR/002)
  (d) He had an *awful* big sheep– an awful lot of sheep. (YRK/066)
  (e) He's sarcastic but he's *dead* serious like. (TOR/020)
  (f) It's *so* funny he thinks he's *so* cool. (TOR/014)
  (g) Oh we were *blemmin'* terrified. (YRK/019)
  (h) That's *dead* naff. (YRK/034)
  (i) When I go up it was *right* slow and everything. (YRK/049)
  (j) Yeah it's *well* weird. (YRK/062)
  (k) Actually, It's *quite* bad … (TOR/004)
  (l) I'm *pretty* high-strung that way, like I'm usually pretty laid-back. (TOR/009)

Many scholars have studied intensifiers, identifying in them several key characteristics which make them an ideal choice for the study of linguistic variation change: (1) versatility and color (note the sheer number of different forms); (2) the capacity for rapid change; and (3) recycling of different forms. All of these characteristics lead to constant renewal as forms are continually replaced with newly coined expressions that can effectively express intensity. This means that in any given variety, at any point in time, the coexistence of different forms may be the result of older and newer layers in the process of change. Sociolinguistic forces may also be heavily implicated in the use of forms since any feature that changes rapidly will likely be sensitive to social evaluation.

Historical Perspective

Historically, competition, change, and recycling among intensifiers have been the norm since as early as the Old English period. Historical documents reveal that Old English *swipe*, as in Example 11.7a, gave way to *well*, as in Example 11.7b, which was replaced by *full*, as in Example 11.7c, and then *right*, as in Example 11.7d.

Example 11.7

(a) mayden *swiþe* fayrþer
     "maiden very fair" (Havelok 111, cited in Mustanoja 1960: 325)
(b) Seo leo, peah hio wel tam se, ...heo forȝit sona hire niwan taman.
     "The lioness, although she is very tame, ... she forgets soon her recent tameness."
     (c. 888, K. Ælfred Boeth. xxv, OED Vol. XII p. 285)
(c) *Ful* faire and fetisly
     "very fairly and prettily" Chaucer, CT A Prol. 119, 124 (cited in Mustanoja 1960: 319–320)
(d) (Laud), Ye diddyn hym vnder lok and sele / That he awey shuld not stele / But ye hym
     myssid *right* sone.
     "You put him under lock and seal, (so) that he away should not steal, but you him missed
     very recently." (c. 1450, Cursor Mundi 17413, OED Vol. VIII p. 675)

Sociolinguistic Perspective

The use of intensifiers has long had sociolinguistic correlates. Use of intensifiers generally is
associated with women. Moreover, women are accredited with leading in the use of new
intensifiers. Intensifiers are also associated with colloquial usage and nonstandard varieties.
Finally, the use of particular intensifiers is said to signal in-group membership, again subject
to changing norms.

Grammatical Change

The cycling and renewal of intensifiers reflects one of the general processes of
grammaticalization, namely "delexicalization" (Sinclair 1992; Partington 1993: 183).
Delexicalization is defined as "the reduction of the independent lexical content of a word, or
group of words, so that it comes to fulfill a particular function" (Partington 1993: 183).
Intensifiers typically start out as lexical items with semantic context. A prime example is *very*
which originally meant "true" or "real," as in Example 11.8a. However, this original sense
weakened over time so that the word is also used to convey emphasis, as in Example 11.8b.
Gradually the intensifer spread to a wider spectrum of contexts. Another step in this process
is said to occur when the word comes to be used with attributive adjectives, as in Example 11.8c.
Then, with frequent occurrences in this syntactic position, the word starts to develop into an
adverb (Mustanoja 1960: 326). The final stage is reached in examples, such as Example 11.8d,
where *very* is used with predicative adjectives to convey simple intensification and the
original lexical meaning of "truth" is gone.

Example 11.8

(a) The compyler here-of shuld translat *veray* so holy a story. (1485 OED Vol. XIS: 569, cited
     in Partington 1993: 181)
(b) For *verray* feere so wolde hir herte quake. (Chaucer, CT, Franklin's Tale, 860)
(c) He was a *verray* parfit gentil knyght. (Chaucer, CT, Prologue, 72)
(d) He was sike ... and was *verray* contrite and sorwful in his herte. (Trev. Hidg. VI 93) (all
     cited in Mustanoja 1960: 326)

An important concomitant of delexicalization is that collocation patterns change from narrow to broad patterns. The early phase of the development of an intensifier will typically be with one or a small set of adjectives, but as the form delexicalizes the intensifier will occur with an increasingly larger number of adjectives.

This scenario of variation and change presents an interesting area of study from a quantitative variationist perspective. First, the rapid rate of change means that the mechanisms of the delexicalization process may be sufficiently telescoped to tap the underlying mechanisms of change using the construct of apparent time. Further, because the development of intensifiers is particularly sensitive to social factors such as sex and group membership, extralinguistic distribution patterns may prove informative to the developmental process. The following testable hypotheses can be put forward (Ito and Tagliamonte 2003: 262):

1. Correlation of intensifiers with particular linguistic contexts can be related to their degree of delexicalization.
2. Correlation of intensifiers with social factors can be taken to tap into the social evaluation of the particular intensifier within the community.
3. Through the examination of (1) and (2), we may be able to track the interrelationship between linguistic and social factors in language change.

Circumscribing the Variable Context

The contexts where an intensifier occurs are very easy to find, but it is not so easy to find the contexts in which an intensifier did not occur, but could have. As it happens, the majority – some 80% – of all intensifiers in English occur with adjectival heads (Bäcklund 1973: 279). This natural distribution pattern in the language provides an excellent means to construct an accountable study of the intensifier system. Circumscribe the variable context to include all adjectives capable of being intensified whether they were modified by an intensifier or not.

Thus, in Example 11.9a the adjective *hard* is included but not with adverb *hard* as in Example 11.9b.

Example 11.9

(a)   But like, change is just *so* hard. (TOR/001)
(b)   They've worked Ø hard, those kids, you-know. (TOR/117)

Exclude contexts that do not permit an intensifier such as Example 11.10a, where the speaker talks about a kind of role, not a degree of color. Similarly, exclude Example 11.10b because the degree of newness is irrelevant.

Example 11.10

(a)   [5] Who was the um, who was the um, the actors in it? [032] John-K was in it. He was the red. Who was like, I guess, the communist-esque character. Ah Byron was the blue. (TOR/032)
(b)   My new job they like um, they don't tell me things, because I'm a temp. (TOR/012)

Attributive adjectives, as in Example 11.11, do not take *so*, at least only rarely. The odd one is heard from time to time. There is a single token in the TEA and I have heard my 7 year old use them, e.g. *There's so big waves!* (Dazzian, August 19, 2010). Attributive adjectives are included in the analysis, but only for the analysis of intensifiers that can appear there, e.g. *really, very, pretty*, etc.

Example 11.11

    (a)   He had a *very* jolly disposition. (TOR/035)
    (b)   She has like a *really* awesome job. (TOR/020)
    (c)   It's a *pretty* sweet set up. (TOR/008)

Mini Quiz 11.1

One time one of my students handed in a paper that reported on the use of intensifiers in the *Anne of Green Gables* series by Lucy Maud Montgomery. I was surprised to read that Anne used a very high frequency of the intensifier *so*, given that the books were written in the early 1900s. Was the heightened frequency of *so* a real result? Or could it have arisen from an error in circumscribing the variable context? An extract from the token file is shown below. Examine the contexts. Which tokens should be IN and which ones should be OUT (i.e. "don't count" cases)?

Anne of Green Gables 1908, Chapter 4
(a)   I've had so much experience
(b)   I think he's Ø lovely
(c)   He is so very sympathetic
(d)   I felt he was a Ø kindred spirit
(e)   I want to go out so much
(f)   It's so hard to keep from loving things
(g)   That was why I was so glad when I thought I was going to live here
(h)   I thought I'd have so many things to love and nothing to hinder me
(i)   But that Ø brief dream is over
(j)   Because it was so white

Sentence constructions that do not permit intensifier use (e.g. comparatives/superlatives and other constructions) as in Example 11.12a–b, were also excluded, as were constructions involving the lexical items *too* and *so* when their function was other than intensification, as in Example 11.12c–d.

Example 11.12

    (a)   And, so it's more fun. You can create your own, like, stuff. (TOR/004)
    (b)   My bed is the most comfortable bed in the whole entire planet. (TOR/005)
    (c)   He was so stealth we almost ran into him. (TOR/003)
    (d)   Wilson's too mature for that sort of thing. (TOR/013)

Finally, include affirmative contexts only. Negative contexts do not express the "higher" degree that we are interested in. Examples 11.13a–c do not mean the negative of the boosted meaning but a moderated one, e.g. a situation that is neither 'fun' nor 'boring', a moderately sized 'assignment' and an average performance, similar to the function of downtoners. Tokens such as Example 11.13d are included since the adjectival head is not immediately under the scope of negation.

Example 11.13

(a) It wasn't too fun. (TOR/023)
(b) Nah, well, that wasn't a real big assignment. (TOR/006)
(c) I heard he's not very good when it gets really complicated. (TOR/020)
(d) I don't know what's so controversial. (TOR/020)

What is the analyst to do with adjectives modified with downtoners, as in Example 11.14a–c? One possibility is to simply exclude them due to the focus on intensification. Another possibility is to include them with the non-intensified contexts.

Example 11.14

(a) And sometimes you get *sort of* dull ones. (TOR/035)
(b) The Greek community is still *fairly* strong in number. (TOR/093)
(c) I mean it's practical, so I'm *kind of* practical. (TOR/059)

NOTE   In all my studies of intensifiers, all the downtoners were extracted since they too are part of the variable context. However, due to the focus on intensifiers, these were never examined. The plan was to return to analyze the downtoners at some point, but so far we have not done that. Downtoning adverbs are not as frequent as intensifying adverbs. They represent only about 5% of modifiable adjectives. They would make an excellent study in their own right. What is the inventory of forms? Who uses them? Are they changing too? See Gries (2007) for a quantitative study of downtoners.

The variable context thus defined provides a consistent vantage point from which we can track the social evaluation and spread of individual intensifiers as well as ensuring that the analysis can be replicated elsewhere. This methodological approach to the study of intensifiers extends an assessment of the contexts in which a particular intensifier occurs, to understanding its distribution within the larger system of which it is a part (Labov 1972c: 127). It provides an accountable assessment of the frequency and patterning of intensifiers from an internal grammatical as well as an external sociolinguistic perspective.

York English, c. 1997

My first foray into the study of intensifiers began innocuously with a study of adverbs in York English (Tagliamonte and Ito 2002). Quite by accident we discovered that the use of *really* stood out (see Chapter 8). Not only was it overwhelmingly marked with the *-ly* suffix (instead of zero), it was highly frequent and further it was increasing rapidly in apparent time

Table 11.2 Frequency of intensifiers in York, UK, c. 1997 (N ≥ 10).

Lexical identity	%	N
very	38.3	364
really	30.2	287
so	10.1	96
absolutely	3.2	30
pretty	3.2	30
too	2.8	27
that	2.7	26
right	1.6	15
totally	1.4	13
completely	1.2	11
bloody	1.2	11
All other intensifiers	4.1	40
No intensification	76	3069
Total intensification	24	950/4019

Source: Ito and Tagliamonte 2003: 266, Table 4.

(Tagliamonte and Ito 2002: Figure 3). I speculated at the time that this was the result of a particular lexical choice, namely *really*, taking over in ongoing renewal of the intensifier system. To confirm this, however, an analysis had to be configured that would take into account all the intensifiers in the system. So began my studies of intensifiers.

Rika Ito and I analyzed the intensifier system in the York English Corpus (Ito and Tagliamonte 2003). Table 11.2 shows the overall distribution of forms.

Out of a total of 4019 intensifiable adjectives, 950 were intensified. This shows us that intensification generally is relatively rare. Of the intensified contexts, *very* and *really* represent the largest proportion. The high frequency of *very* was expected. According to the literature, *very* has been used as an intensifier in English since the fifteenth century (Mustanoja 1960: 327), and according to reports on American English from the early twentieth century (Fries 1940: 201) and American and British English from the 1960s (Bäcklund 1973: 290) *very* is still most frequent intensifier. However, the heightened rates of the intensifier *really* were not expected given the reports in the literature at the same time. The intensifier use of *really* is first attested in 1658, but it were not common until the early eighteenth century (Peters 1994). There was some indication of its use in southern British English (London) from the COLT corpus, a database of London teenage language from 1993 (Stenström 1999) and in American English (Labov 1985: 44). Finally, taking into account the full repertoire of intensifiers we discovered that intensifiers that had been attested from as early as Old English (e.g. *well*) were still part of the repertoire. Apparently, old intensifiers do not fade away, but may remain in the system indefinitely. This extraordinary continuity is consistent with research in the grammaticalization literature where the perpetuity of old forms and meanings have been traced back over a millennium and more (Bybee *et al.* 1994; 1991a; Traugott and Heine 1991b).

When we cross-tabulated the type of intensifier by speaker age, we discovered yet another facet to the intensifier system. This is shown in Figure 11.3.

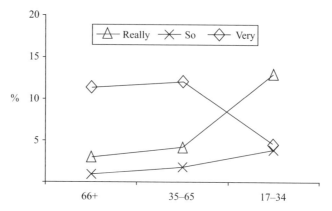

Figure 11.3 Distribution of major intensifiers in York in apparent time.
Source: Ito and Tagliamonte 2003: 267, Figure 2.

Figure 11.3 with a scale reduced to 20 (for illustration purposes) shows the trends for each of the individual intensifiers and their respective patterns. This perspective provides two important bits of information: (1) while intensification generally is increasing this is not uniform across intensifiers; and (2) although *really* and *very* compete for the most frequently used intensifiers, their relative contribution to the system is not consistent across generations.

The intensifier system is changing in terms of frequency and lexical preference. In this community two intensifiers in particular are used the majority of the time – *very* and *really*. However, this is changing rapidly amongst the current population: *really* in particular, but also *so*, is rising in frequency in the youngest speakers.

Mini Quiz 11.2

Q1 Ito and Tagliamonte (2003: 388) say they "discovered a tremendous generation gap in York English." Why? (Evaluate the trends in Figure 11.3.)

A logistic regression analysis of external factors is shown in Table 11.3.

The logistic regression analysis confirmed that women lead in the change from one intensifier to another. Among the middle-aged group where *really* is at the point of expansion, sex and education of the individual are statistically significant and females lead in the use of *really*. The effect of speaker sex, however, is not as straightforward as has been reported for intensifier use previously. Women do not just prefer to intensify and men not. The younger educated males are just as likely to use *really* as the women, while the less-educated men stand apart, with the lowest rates of intensification regardless of age (Ito and Tagliamonte 2003: 276, Figure 8). This is precisely the same pattern as has been found for phonological variables – the less educated men march in a different direction (Trudgill 1972b).

The York intensifier study also left many questions to be answered. Were the trends found in York particular to that community alone? Were they particular to the UK more generally? Would different communities have different "layers" of intensifiers? We suggested that

Table 11.3 Three logistic regression analyses of the contribution of factors to the probability of *really* in York English.

Input	Old 0.030			Middle 0.027			Young 0.124		
	FW	%	Ns/Cell	FW	%	Ns/Cell	FW	%	Ns/Cell
Syntactic function									
Predicative	[0.56]	4	541	[0.53]	5	731	0.54	15	943
Attributive	[0.45]	2	613	[0.47]	3	614	0.44	10	577
Range							*10*		
Education									
Secondary and beyond		n/a		0.60	3	429	0.55	15	1049
Up to secondary				0.44	3	732	0.40	8	471
Range				*16*			*15*		
Sex									
Female	[0.51]	3	804	0.66	6	732	[0.52]	14	880
Male	[0.48]	3	350	0.31	2	613	[0.48]	11	640
Range				*35*					

Source: Ito and Tagliamonte 2003: 274, Table 6.

systematic comparative studies in other varieties of English would be an ideal means to track the varying rates of grammatical change across dialects, as well as to tap into current trends in contemporary English.

> **NOTE**   There are many other fascinating nuances to intensifiers that were not part of the highly circumscribed area of the system I have studied so far. For example, what has happened to so-called "Generation-x *so*" as in *I'm so not impressed* that made inroads into English grammar in the late 1990s (see Tagliamonte 2008b: fn 17, 390–391)? To what extent are swear words used as intensifiers, how, and by whom? Another highly interesting question is how often and why do intensifiers recycle? For example, intensifier *well*, e.g. *That's well wicked*, was prominent in Middle English yet is currently reported among 10–30 year olds in the UK (see e.g. Ito and Tagliamonte 2003: n. 13, 278; Tagliamonte 2008b: 390). The story of intensifiers in contemporary varieties of English is not boring yet.

American English, c. 1990s, Television

The findings from the York intensifier study were provocative on a number of levels. About the same time, my children had just become old enough to appreciate one of the most popular comedies of the time – the television series *Friends* – and I noticed something strange going on. The *Friends* characters hardly ever used *very*; *really* was predominant; and curiously, *so*

Table 11.4 Frequency of intensifiers in *Friends*,
20 year olds, USA, c. 1990s.

Lexical identity	%	N
very	14.2	269
really	24.6	464
so	44.1	832
pretty	6.1	115
totally	2.8	53
All other intensifiers	8.1	153
No intensification	79	6785
Total intensification	22	1886/8611

Source: Tagliamonte and Roberts 2005: 287, Table 1.

was being used a lot. It was not long before I had embarked on a study of the intensifier system in the *Friends* data with one of my students, Christopher Roberts. Following the same methodological procedure laid out in the earlier study for circumscribing the variable context, Table 11.4 shows the overall distribution of forms.

Out of a total of 8611 intensifiable adjectives, 1886 were intensified, an overall rate of 22%, making the overall rate comparable to the York study, 24%.

The same three intensifiers were predominant – *very*, *really*, and *so*. However, the frequency of the major intensifiers in the system was radically different than in York. In the British data, *very* was the most popular intensifier whereas in the *Friends* data *so* was by far the front-runner, representing nearly 50% of all the intensifiers used.

Of course, the *Friends* data must be put in context. The individuals in the sample are American and comprise individuals in their 20s, while the York data is a variety of northern British English and the individuals in the sample are between 9 and 92. Given these parameters, we can posit a change from British to American English according to the age of the intensifiers. *Very* is the oldest, attested from the fifteenth century. In the *Friends* data it is present, but at a relatively low frequency. It is fading away. *Really*, which started to be used as an intensifier during the seventeenth century and is cited as the most common intensifier in British and American English, here appears more frequently than *very*. It is in its prime. *So*, on the other hand, is the most recently attested intensifier. In the *Friends* data it occurs more often than either *very* or *really*. We suggested that the *Friends* data may reflect the next phase in the changing intensifiers of English; *very* gave way to *really* which may be giving way to *so*.

Support for this interpretation is the fact that both the York English data (see Figure 11.3) (Ito and Tagliamonte 2003) and the new Toronto English data I had started working on by then (Tagliamonte 2003–2006) exhibited an acceleration of *so* among the youngest generation. A well-known aspect of linguistic change is Labov's Principle 4 (1990: 210–215; 2001a): "In change from below, women are most often the innovators." We also know from earlier linguistic observations that *really* and *so* are considered "nonstandard" in contrast to *very*. Taken along with the observation that women generally tend to use more intensification, we can predict that women will lead the use of intensifier *so*.

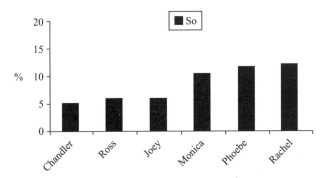

Figure 11.4 Distribution of intensifier *so* by sex in *Friends*.

If we consider the use of *so* in the *Friends* data according to sex of the speaker, as in Figure 11.4, we can see that the females use *so* far more frequently than the male characters – in fact, more than twice as often. Note too that separating the individuals instead of grouping them together affirms the coherence of each gender.

The analysis of the *Friends* data supported the hypothesis that *so* was an incoming intensifier. Further, we suggested that the television data appeared to be more innovative than in the general population, perhaps reflecting (and enhancing) changes already going on in the speech community.

The next question was to cross-check these findings with evidence from another speech community in North America. We turned to the Toronto English Corpus.

> **TIP**   I have heard William Labov say that linguistic variables have a way of grabbing you by the throat and never letting go. I agree. Be warned!

Toronto English, c. 2004

Table 11.5 shows the overall distribution of forms in Toronto English. Out of a total of 9859 intensifiable adjectives, 3525 were intensified, an overall rate of 36%, a rate that was somewhat higher than the other studies, York 24%, *Friends* 22%.

If we put this result in context, the Toronto data comprised individuals from 9 to 95 so the difference is understandable. Adolescents and pre-adolescents in particular are known for nonstandard linguistic behavior and for leading linguistic change.

> Adolescents are clearly significant bearers of change; their networks allow them to have wider contacts than younger children, and their desire for a distinct social identity means that they are willing to modify their speech. (Kerswill 1996a: 198)

Figure 11.5 shows the major intensifiers in apparent time. It exposes a telling sociolinguistic pattern. First, it confirms that these four main intensifiers are used by speakers of all ages in Toronto. However, there is a tremendous disproportion in the nature of the layering of forms. Consider the speakers 50 years of age and older: *very* is the most frequently used intensifier, but *very* declines rapidly among the under 40 year olds. In contrast, *really* increases steeply from oldest to youngest speakers, with a surge among the 20–29 year olds. While *so* is

Table 11.5 Frequency of intensifiers in Toronto,
c. 2003–2004 (N ≥ 10).

Lexical identity	%	N
really	13.0	1282
very	6.6	651
so	6.1	599
pretty	5.0	497
just	1.5	152
too	0.7	71
all	0.5	46
totally	0.4	42
completely	0.30	26
just really	0.2	20
just so	0.2	21
extremely	0.14	14
absolutely	0.10	10
Other intensifier	1.4	140
Ø intensification	64.2	6334
Total number		9905

Source: Tagliamonte 2008b: 368, Table 3.

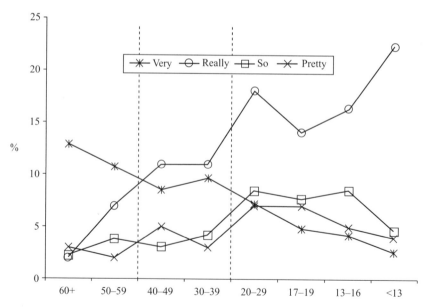

Figure 11.5 Distribution of major intensifiers in Toronto in apparent time.
Source: Tagliamonte 2008: 372, Figure 3.

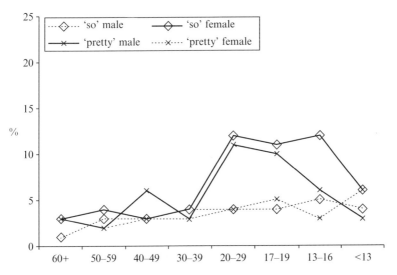

Figure 11.6 Distribution of *so* and *pretty* by sex of the speaker in apparent time, Toronto.
Source: Tagliamonte 2008: 384, Figure 7c.

a minor variant, it is most frequent among the 13–29 year olds and exhibits an incremental increase from the oldest generation to the 20 year olds and adolescents. The same pattern is found for *pretty*. Overall, these trends confirm that the intensifiers in this community are changing as quickly as in York. Notice how the community patterns naturally into three quite distinct intensifier systems: the 13–29 year olds have a common system which prefers *really*; the 20–29 year olds share a mixed system in which both *really* and *very* are dominant; and among the 50+ age group *very* is the favored intensifier.

Moreover, when we partition the data by speaker sex – a factor that we saw earlier has an important effect on intensifier use – we discover an interesting contrast among the youngest members of the speech community.

Figure 11.6 shows the use of the two incoming forms, *so* and *pretty*. The results corroborate the claims in the literature – the 16–29-year-old young women are leading the use of *so*. However, there is an equally dramatic trend among the young men; they are leading in the use of *pretty*. The unexpected result is: (1) the diametrically opposed behavior of the young people with respect to their choice of *so* or *pretty* and (2) the contrasting behavior of male and female speakers across the whole community with respect to the alternative forms. The male members of the Toronto speech community show virtually the same rate of *so* across the generations, whereas the female members of the Toronto speech community show virtually the same rate of *pretty* across the generations. Both young women and young men lead in the diffusion of incoming features but not the same ones!

Another important observation can be made with regard to Figures 11.5 and 11.6. Notice that the very youngest members of these data sets (the pre-adolescents) pattern more like the over 30 year olds than like the adolescents and 20 year olds. This confirms the view that children first pattern with their parents and only later integrate with and pattern with their peers (e.g. Kerswill 1996a; Kerswill and Williams 2000; Labov 2001a) (see Chapter 2).

Delexicalication process:
Lexical word
⇓
Used for occasional emphasis with particular adjectives
⇓
Used more frequently for emphasis
⇓
Used with a wider and wider range of words

The original lexical meaning is gradually lost

Figure 11.7   Delexicalization process.

NOTE   Lexically restricted intensifiers may also be present in a community without evidence of delexicalization. Can you think of a few of these in your local context? In Canada, the following may be heard, but so far show no evidence for generalization to other adjectives: *brand* new, *great* big, *dead* serious. Interestingly, *dead* has followed an entirely different route in some varieties of British English (see Macaulay 2007).

My goal was to document how the change from one intensifier to another was happening. According to the literature, new intensifiers arise through a process of grammaticalization via delexicalization. In this process the original meaning of the word is gradually lost as it evolves into a marker of intensification. Partington (1993: 183) argued that there is a direct correlation between delexicalization and the collocation of intensifiers with their referents. The more delexicalized an intensifier is, the more widely it collocates. Lorenz (2002: 144) echoes this observation by suggesting that the more delexicalized an intensifier becomes, "the more it will lose its lexical restrictions and increase in frequency." In other words, new intensifiers can be expected to collocate with a smaller set of lexical items whereas older, delexicalized intensifiers should occur across a wide range of adjectives.

We can conceive of delexicalization of intensifiers as evolving in a step-by-step fashion, as illustrated in Figure 11.7.

To test the status of each intensifier with respect to its collocational behavior, we examined the adjectives they intensified across generations. As a diagnostic for adjective type we used Dixon's (1977) research which divides adjectives into eight representative categories: dimension, physical property, human propensity, age, value, speech, position, and other. Figure 11.8 shows the pattern of the incoming form *so* by these adjective type across three age groups.

Figure 11.8 reveals a stepwise development: *so* is used in four adjectives types among the oldest generation, six among the middle aged, and eight among the youngest individuals. This pattern suggests that *so* first expanded before increasing in frequency amongst the youngest generation suggesting that the spread of an intensifier predates an overall increase in use, a finding consistent with its development in York (Ito and Tagliamonte 2003) and in *Friends* (Tagliamonte and Roberts 2005). Like grammaticalization more generally, where an increase in frequency is often associated with the development of grammatical status, these findings suggested that this tendency is actually a later part of the process (Bybee *et al.* 1994: 8).

The use of *so* in particular has also been linked to emotionally laden adjectives (e.g. Tagliamonte and Roberts 2005). This hypothesis can be tested by categorizing each of the adjectives in the data according to whether it encodes an emotion, as in Example 11.15,

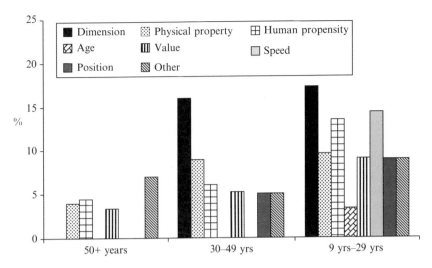

Figure 11.8 Distribution of *so* by adjective type across generations in Toronto.
Source: Tagliamonte 2008: 378, Figure 5b.

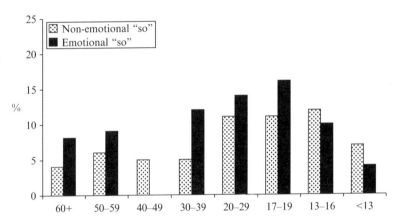

Figure 11.9 Distribution of *so* by emotional value of the adjective.
Source: Tagliamonte 2008: 381, Figure 6a.

as opposed to some physical attribute or other quality, as in Example 11.16. Figure 11.9 shows a test of this correlation.

Example 11.15

    (a)   I don't know; that's why I'm *so* <u>happy</u>. (TOR/001)
    (b)   'Cause she's *so* <u>funny</u>.. she's *so* <u>mean</u> … and *so* <u>evil</u>! (TOR/002)

Example 11.16

    (a)   I just thought it was like *so* <u>small</u>. (TOR/021)
    (b)   Like her belly's big and my belly's *so* <u>flat</u>. (TOR/017)

Table 11.6   Rough overview of intensifiers in the history of English.

Old English	Middle English				Early Modern English			Modern English	
	12th c	*13th c*	*14th c*	*15th c*	*16th c*	*17th c*	*18th c*	*19th c*	*20th c*
swiþe: ——————>									
well: ——————>									
full: (2nd to swiþe) 1250 ——————>									
			right: –>						
	very: ——————————————————————>								
		so ——————>							
		pretty ——————————————————>							
					really: ——————>				

Source: Ito and Tagliamonte, 2003: 260, Table 1.

Intensifier *so* has a consistent propensity for use with emotion-laden adjectives, suggesting an early stage of grammaticalization where usage is tied to a particular adjective or adjective cohort. Yet this tendency is reversed among the youngest speakers where this intensifier is most frequent. I argued that this is due to a more delexicalized state of *so* among this age group. Young people use it indiscriminately for any type of adjective.

The Toronto situation adds a number of new perspectives to the study of intensifiers and to the study of sociolinguistic variation. First, the same major intensifiers are undergoing dramatic change in Canada, just as in England, and in the United States. Are the shifting patterns in intensifier frequency the result of delexicalization or some other process? Despite stepwise developments in apparent time, the evidence from the linguistic factors we tested in Toronto does not unequivocally point to a diachronically rooted, *ongoing* delexicalization processes. Instead, *really*, *very*, and *pretty* are already delexicalized: they appear across a wide range of adjective types; they can appear with predicative adjectives; they are used across the speech community. Moreover, they've been around for hundreds of years. In the case of *so* there is evidence for ongoing lexical spread, early stage lexical associations (emotion), as well as very early evidence for extension into attributive position. Yet even *so* is not entirely new to the system. Table 11.6 displays an overview of the history of each intensifier, beginning with its earliest attestation date from the OED.

The oldest of the major current intensifiers is *very*; *pretty* has been around for 400 years; and *really* and *so* seem to have appeared at about the same time. This means that however remarkable the trajectories of contemporary waxing of forms (*really*), or waning of forms (*very*), and even the new trends (*so*), they are likely not the product of continuous grammatical change. Instead, it appears that intensifiers, once delexicalized – perhaps even partially delexicalized – can be left underdeveloped in the language or wane away yet remain available to be co-opted back into the active system. Note for example the break in the pattern for male use of *pretty* in Figure 11.6. Thus, what we are observing in Toronto are the rolling waves of intensifier recycling.

The idea is that renewal is critical to the use of intensifiers (Bolinger 1972; Peters 1994; Stoffel 1901). Bolinger, in particular, argued for conditions of "fevered invention," a process driven by speakers' desires to be original, demonstrate verbal skills, and to capture attention. It perhaps goes without saying then that intensifiers by their very nature cannot have staying power since their impact is only as good as their novelty. Overuse, diffused use, and long–time use will lead to a diminishment in the intensifier's ability to boost and intensify. Thus, waxing and waning of intensifiers is a requisite of the feature for the speech community. How long an intensifier lasts likely has as much to do with its sociolinguistic status as its success along the delexicalization path.

The results from Toronto corroborate this idea and suggest further that once a word has evolved to have an intensifier function it remains in the reservoir of forms that a language user may deploy to boost or maximize meaning from that point onwards, regardless of whether it actually becomes one of the favored forms or not. Whether the delexicalization process starts and stops and picks up again along with this perpetual recycling remains an empirical question. What is most curious of all, however, is exactly what it is that boosts a particular form to dominance at a given point in time and space. These are the questions that will be answered in years to come.

> **TIP**   What is the inventory of intensifiers used in your local community? How does your community fit in with York (England), *Friends* (US) and Toronto (Canada)? Are there older forms, newer forms? Who uses which ones? Make sure to disentangle age and sex when you conduct your investigations!

Summary

The intensifier studies from York and Toronto established a number of baselines for the quantitative study of intensifiers:

1. Intensifiers are grammatically layered in synchronic data and provide a particularly good window on linguistic variation and change.
2. Intensification generally has been increasing over the last 30 years.
3. The contemporary English intensifier system taps a recent, ongoing change in progress – the use of the intensifier *very* is the mark of being older, while a preference for *really* identifies a speaker as younger. However, intensifier *so* is on the rise.
4. Linguistic change in the intensifier system can be explained by delexicalization (a process of generalization).
5. The intensifier system tolerates considerable variation. Already delexicalized forms do not appear to die out entirely but remain in the system as low-frequency items over a long period of time.
6. Intensifiers seem to be able to recycle. Once dormant, they can rise again.

> **TIP**   Examination of intensifiers across a range of different situations may prove informative. Do you do sports? There is no better place to overhear intensifiers, e.g. *I'm feeling really good. This is starting to get really tough. Oh my God, I'm so sore. This is &*(&%$ awful!* etc. It would be interesting to hook up several individuals in a group or in pairs. Which intensifiers do they use under what conditions? When do expletives appear? Do the adjectives change over the course of a workout?

Language and the Internet

> The rude and busteous elements in uncultivated speech are being assimilated to form a
> re-invigorated form of speech (McKnight 1925: 16)

In 2001 David Crystal (2001: 48) proclaimed that the Internet was evolving a "new species of communication," complete with its own lexicon, orthography, grammar, and usage. All forms of Computer Mediated Communication (CMC) are heavily criticized for leading to a "breakdown in the English language," "the bastardization of language," even "the linguistic ruin of [the] generation" (Axtman 2002).

At about the same time my oldest daughter, Tara, became a teenager and I began to notice an intriguing fact about her behavior. She could type really fast. In fact, her typing speed and the sheer amount of time she spent typing on the computer was remarkable. Then, I realized what she was doing. She was "talking" to her friends using Instant Messaging (IM). I wondered what she was typing and what kind of new language might be evolving right under my nose.

It was not long before I got myself an IM account myself. But my kids would not talk to me! How was I ever going to study Internet language? Realistically, how can a middle-aged mom gain access to the natural informal discourse of a teenage speech community? Teenagers by their very nature want nothing to do with a parent peering over their shoulder or a sociolinguist snooping into their business. In order to study vernacular real-time IM I had to be very clever. First, I had to figure out what was going on with Internet language and IM.

Instant Messaging

IM is a form of computer-mediated communication that involves writing back and forth to an interlocutor in real time. In the early 2000s 80% of Canadian teens and 74% of American teens had used an IM program (Lenhart, Rainie, and Lewis 2001: 3; Randall 2002: 21). IM's popularity has sky-rocketed ever since, developing rapidly into systems that bridge computers and phones, and which integrate IM with other social-networking functions. These readily available new technologies are endemic to young people and involve written language. But what kind of language is in the writing? These new media have raised the concern of parents, teachers, psychologists, and grammarians because the grammar in the writing is thought to be like no written language has been before. This has led to an explosion of studies on the topic with more arising every day. Nearly all types of CMC have been subject to academic study, many of which appear in the dedicated *Journal of Computer-Mediated Communication*.[1] Others appear independently in journals from many fields, including linguistics, computer science, sociology, and psychology, many of them attesting to CMC's "funky" features (e.g. Palfreyman and Khalil 2003).

Baron's (2004) study is one of the earliest empirical studies of IM. This study is based on a corpus collected from American college students. Baron's (2004: 419) remarkable discovery was that IM was more conservative than is suggested by the press. A mere 0.3% of the words had typical IM abbreviations (e.g. *hrs*, *cuz*), less than 0.8% were acronyms (e.g. *lol*, *brb*), and 0.4% represented emoticons (smiley faces and the like) (Baron 2004: 411, 413). Furthermore, where lexical pairs could be contracted, as in "I'm" for "I am," Baron (2004: 413) found that 65% were shortened. The study concludes that IM conversations in this corpus "represent a blend of both spoken and written language conventions" (Baron 2004: 416). This is echoed in the concluding statements of Jones and Schieffelin (2009: 109):

The patterns of language use that we have documented in IM do not support the view that users are "simplifying" language to make communication easier or more efficient; in fact, users are less concerned with efficiency than with expressivity, seeking to make the language both look as well as 'sound' more like informal talk. To this end, they are mobilizing a collective creativity in accomplishing a specific style of communication.

The fact that IM diverges from written language at all raises alarm in teachers and parents. The common perception is that IM, particularly among adolescents, is close to laughable, filled with grammatical errors, incomprehensible words, and secret codes – by all counts an inferior mode of communication. Teachers often report that student assignments are littered with typical IM abbreviations and acronyms (Lee 2002). Though it is easy for teachers to pigeonhole CMC generally as the root of this problem, Baron (2003b: 88) offers an alternative explanation: "technology often enhances and reflects rather than precipitating linguistic and social change." What is happening in IM is simply mirroring the emergent tendency for all writing to become more speechlike. In other words, IM may actually be a bellwether in the evolution of the English language in general. If so, then IM and other CMC media offer the analyst a gold mine for the analysis of language variation and change.

Teen Language, c. 2004–2006

Between 2004 and 2006 Derek Denis and I embarked upon a study of IM among a large group of adolescents in Toronto. The data upon which this study is based was made possible by a unique project that was conducted at the University of Toronto, entitled *Teen Talk*. The Faculty of Arts and Science offers a mentorship program that encourages secondary school students to join university professors in their research projects.[2] From 2005 to 2006 I concocted a research project to seek out and study IM language called *Tween-Teen Talk in Toronto*. I set up a research project entitled *Teen Talk*. The project was specifically designed to tap IM communication among adolescents. Over the course of the three-year project two teams of teenagers (mentees) from secondary schools within the Toronto District School Board worked on this project. They became co-researchers and participant observers who engaged in fieldwork and data analysis of an immense corpus of IM language.

We constructed a 1.2 million word IM corpus from conversational histories – computerized records of the participants' IM interactions with friends. These massive text logs comprising literally thousands of individual conversations were donated to the project. An extraordinary facet of this IM data is that the vast majority of the material came from conversational histories that had been saved well before the study began.[3] Thus, this corpus is extraordinary among data sets in that it has had little to no effect on the observer's paradox (Labov 1972c: 209). This was a notable difference between this and any previous study of IM (Baron 2004: 404) at the time, making it an authentic picture of teen language and interactive CMC discourse from the early 2000s. All the conversations took place between individuals who were well known to each other, engaged in vibrant, interactive discourse. In total, the corpus comprises 71 teenagers between the ages of 15 and 20 in the years 2004–2006, 31 male and 40 female, all born and raised in Canada. This corpus could only have been created by the cooperation and generosity of the mentees and their friends who willingly and enthusiastically provided a wealth of data for study.

An example, taken verbatim from the corpus, is shown in Example 11.17.

Example 11.17

[2/14/2005 4:13:44 PM] [024] happy valentines day
[2/14/2005 4:19:11 PM] [3] happy valentines day!!
[2/14/2005 4:19:23 PM] [3] i had no school today
[2/14/2005 4:19:39 PM] [024] why?
[2/14/2005 4:19:42 PM] [024] because of weather
[2/14/2005 4:19:45 PM] [3] yeppp
[2/14/2005 4:20:00 PM] [3] i actually went but nobody was there so i just went home
[2/14/2005 4:20:24 PM] [024] *haha* thats so funny
[2/14/2005 4:20:30 PM] [024] i had school wish i didnt
[2/14/2005 4:20:34 PM] [024] haha but the school flooded
[2/14/2005 4:20:38 PM] [024] so i may not have it tomorrow
[2/14/2005 4:23:11 PM] [3] the school flooded?!
[2/14/2005 4:23:21 PM] [3] how? like the halls and everything?
[2/14/2005 4:23:27 PM] [024] yeah
[2/14/2005 4:23:36 PM] [024] so everyone was sent home early
[2/14/2005 4:24:38 PM] [3] omg hey so if they dont get cleaned up maybe you wont have school
     for a couple of days *lol*
[2/14/2005 4:24:46 PM] [024] i know!
[2/14/2005 4:24:50 PM] [024] *haha* that would be awesome
[2/14/2005 4:24:54 PM] [024] but probably wont happen
[2/14/2005 4:29:54 PM] [3] ah well at least you'll have tomorrow off ! so how's it going? new
     semester?
[2/14/2005 4:31:58 PM] [024] nope im not semestered
[2/14/2005 4:33:14 PM] [3] oh i see if i were you id be like crying *lol* im happy to have chem
     done with
[2/14/2005 4:33:51 PM] [024] yeah i bet
[2/14/2005 4:33:53 PM] [024] i hate it
[2/14/2005 4:34:47 PM] [3] im goin out now we'll catch up later! (K) xoxo ttyl!
[2/14/2005 4:36:49 PM] [024] kk bye bye xoxo
(CMC/3&024)

Notice that there are no capital letters; punctuation marks are rare; sentences are short and sometimes run into each other, e.g. *I had school wish I didnt*. There are reduplicated letters, e.g. *yeppp*, symbols, e.g. *(K)*, *xoxo*, and onomatopoeia, *haha*, *hehe*, and various nonstandard uses, e.g. *nope*, *goin*. Among the linguistics features of CMC generally and IM in particular, shortened forms are perhaps the most heavily referenced and criticized. While these phenomena have been in English from the earliest times; it is claimed that the vast majority have arisen in the twentieth century (Baum 1955).

Mini Quiz 11.3

Q1   Take another look at Example 11.17. Can you spot a morphological linguistic
     variable?
Q2   Can you spot a typographical variable?
Q3   Can you find a general extender?
Q4   Find at least one suggestive token.

Table 11.7 Distribution of characteristic IM forms among
Canadian teenagers, c. 2004–2006.

Feature	Total N	% of total n
haha *laughing*	16183	1.47%
lol *laugh out loud*	4506	0.41%
hehe *laughing*	2050	0.19%
omg *oh my God*	1261	0.11%
hmm *thinking*	1038	0.09%
brb *be right back*	390	0.04%
ttyl *talk to you later*	298	0.03%
btw *by the way*	249	0.02%
wtf *what the fuck*	218	0.02%
arg *frustration*	197	0.02%
hwk *homework*	99	0.01%
nvm *nevermind*	78	0.01%
gtg *got to go*	68	0.01%
np *no problem*	65	0.01%
lmao *laughing my ass off*	63	0.01%
nm *not much*	32	0.00%
TOTAL	26 795	2.44%

Source: Tagliamonte and Denis 2008:12, Table 3.

One of the characteristics of IM discourse is a wide range of short forms, including abbreviations, e.g. *chem*, single letter words, *u* "you," reduplications, *kk* "okay," initialisms, *omg*, and acronyms, *lol*.

> **NOTE** Acronyms once referred to abbreviations that are pronounced as words while initialisms were abbreviations comprising the first letters of a sequence of words; however, the term acronym has come to refer to all abbreviations made from initial letters, regardless of pronunciation (Harley 2004).

When we tabulated all the different short forms in the IM corpus we found 26 795 items. Table 11.7 presents a tabulation of the most numerous of these and their proportion of use (Tagliamonte and Denis 2008b).

Notice the thousands of uses of *haha* including its many variants, *hahaha, hah, ahahaha*, etc. The highest frequency acronym stereotypically associated with IM is *lol*. Yet the proportion of use of this form is well below *haha* at just over 4500 times. Next is *hehe* and its many variants, *hehehe, heh, eheheh*, etc., another laughter variant. The next acronym is *omg*, "oh my god" and then *hmm*, a fairly mundane form expressing contemplation. Thereafter the numbers decrease markedly and this is where we find many of the famed IM forms, such as *brb*, "be right back," *ttyl*, "talk to you later," and *wtf*, "what the fuck." The others vanish into nothing. The sheer infrequency of the so-called "characteristic IM forms" is dramatic when we look at the results through accountable proportional analysis. They represent a miniscule proportion of the total number of words in the discourse. All the forms combined represent only 2.4% of the corpus. This is remarkably consistent with Baron's (2004) findings for young adults in their early 20s in the early 2000s and a more recent study of college students' use of text messaging on cell phones (Baron and Ling 2003). It also jibes with the findings of Jones and Schieffelin (2009). The use of acronyms, short forms, and symbolic uses in IM is not nearly as prevalent the media have led us to believe.

Variable (Laughter)

The most infamous of all of the new CMC acronyms is *lol*, "laugh out loud," as in Example 11.18.

Example 11.18

(a) [8] yeah, she's telling a lot of people. [046] *lol* that's hilarious (CMC/8&046)
(b) [3] im never on the phone with jen
[025] *lol* oh yah
[025] ure always on the phone with her
[3] no im not i havent been on the phjone with her in … many days now
[025] *lol* y dont i believe u (CMC/3&025)

The use of *lol* is one of the more interesting features of IM from a sociolinguistic point of view because it is a natural linguistic variable, with at least two other variants, *hehe* and *haha*, as in Example 11.19 (see also above in Example 11.17).

Example 11.19

(a) [3] *hehe* anywhoo i want to go watch tv and eat more advent calender *lol* ill ttyl. [025] *lol* ok later (CMC/3&025)
(b) [3] *haha*
[3] i left *everything* at school
[027] *lol*, i dont blame ya!
[3] *hehe* anyway guess what i bought today a party sized pack of poppycock. *hahahahaha* (CMC/3&027)

The frequency of use of these laughter variants, 4506 instances in the IM corpus, provides an opportunity to examine their social distribution within this teenage speech community.

The OED refers to the forms *haha*, *hehe*, and *hoho* as "the ordinary representation of laughter", all of which have been in the English language from the earliest times, as in Example 11.20.

Example 11.20

(a) *Ha ha* and *he he* ӡetacniað hlehter on leden and on englisc. (c. 1000, Aelfric *Gram.* xlviii. (Z.) 279)
(b) *Haha* telaws be war for such a iape. (c. 1386, Chaucer, *Prologue to Prioress's Tale* in CT. 5 (Harl. MS.)
(c) How now! interiections? why then, some be of laughing, as *ha, ha, he.* (c. 1599, Shakespeare, *Much Ado* IV, i. 23)

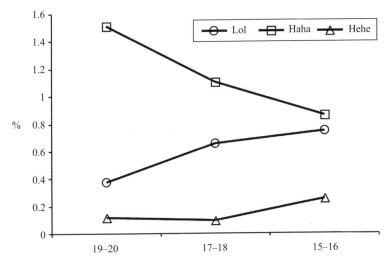

Figure 11.10   Distribution of laughter variants among adolescents in IM, c. 2004–2006.
Source: Tagliamonte and Denis 2008: 13, Figure 1.

Thus we can think of these as the "standard" variants and *lol* as the new, innovative, and nonstandard (at least *not adult*) variant. Further, since our corpus is comprised of a range of ages, it is possible to test for change in apparent time.

Figure 11.10 shows the distribution of the IM laughter variants, *lol, haha,* and *hehe* according to the age of the individuals.

The use of *lol* declines systematically according to age, with the younger individuals using it the most. In contrast, the more conservative form *haha* is the unmistakable preference of the oldest individuals. Since it is also the case that the older individuals have had the longest exposure to IM, we speculated that this trajectory is the result of incremental loss of the stylized form, i.e. *lol,* in favor of *haha.* This reveals that adolescents outgrow at least some of the IM forms. Thus, the use of *lol* provides a good contemporary example of age grading.

> **NOTE**   When I reported on these *lol* results to my children, the same daughter who had instigated my interest in IM language in the first place offered the following observation: "*I used to use lol when I was a kid.*" As it turns out, her intuition was exactly right.

There is evidence for further developments in the use of *lol.* The original meaning as an acronym for "laugh out loud" is often lost in its contemporary uses, as in Example 11.21.

Example 11.21

(a)   [025] drove fong home today?
      [3] yes… *lol*
      [025] shoulda let him walk
      [025] that lazy ass

[3] *lol* well the original plan was to drive him to yonge
q[3] then we were at yonge and he decided it was close enough so he told my mom to take
him all the way home :P
[3] *lol*
[3] i had nothing to do with it
[3] aw but he didnt have a jacket i feel bad
[3] *lol*
[025] *lol* good
[025] little girl needs to toughn up
[3] yes but its such a long walk
[3] *lol.*
[025] hees fine
[025] !!!!!!!
[3] *lol* brb
[025] ok (CMC/3&025)

Notice that *lol* does not have its original lexical meaning. Instead, it seems to be used in the flow of conversation as a signal of interlocutor involvement, just as one might say "mm-hm" in the course of speech. This is consistent with Baron's (2004: 416) comment that *lol* functions as a "phatic filler comparable to *okay, really,* or *yeah* in spoken discourse." It is testimony to the inbuilt nature of linguistic variation that a new-fangled register such as IM will still exhibit the standard underlying currents of grammatical change.

The continued use of *lol* in IM, SMS, email, and other forms of CMC offers sociolinguists an extraordinary opportunity to track this and other types of evolving grammatical systems.

Studying Unusual Variables

There are inevitable pitfalls for studying unusual variables. It could be the case that the feature of interest or the variety under investigation has not been studied before, such as the case of *lol* in IM. Although there may be many yet untapped dialects, varieties, and registers, this is rarely true of linguistic variables themselves. Inevitably, someone, somewhere has noticed the feature and has commented on it or written about it. My rule of thumb is to scour the literature for previous research. Do not simply browse the Internet; do something unprecedented – go to the library. Check for the form or forms of interest in the following sources:

- The OED
  - When was it first attested?
- Dialect dictionaries
  - Where is the form used geographically?
  - What register is it used in?
- Project Gutenburg
  - What authors use it?
  - How is it used?
- Relevant academic sources
- The Scholar's Portal, JSTOR
- Books in the library.

> **TIP** When you go to the library, head to the part of the stacks where the prescriptive grammars are kept. Start by browsing the table of contents and the indexes. A long time ago, in a library in Ottawa, I found an important quote in an old book written by a guy named Murray (see Chapter 8).

In the case of the variants of laughter in IM, who would have guessed that *ha ha* has been in the English language since 1100 or that three articles in *American Speech* document the rise of acronyms in American English through the twentieth century (Baum 1955; Cannon 1989; Harley 2004)? The detective component of Variationist Sociolinguistics comes to the fore in the analysis of unusual variables. The analyst must be persistent and wily in finding the right data in the first place, and both shrewd and inventive in figuring out how to study the variable.

> **TIP** The American Dialect Society has been publishing research about linguistic features in *American Speech* since 1925! If you can't find a linguistic variable anywhere else, this is the place to look.

Tips for Studying Unusual Variables

The challenges that arise in the study of unusual variables are dependent on the type of feature being examined. The main thing is to adhere to the basic principles of variationists' practice.

The study of intensifiers, for example, presented a methodological challenge for circumscribing the variable context. The intensifiers themselves are easy to find; however, finding the contexts in which they could have occurred but did not is much more demanding. However, once I discovered that the vast majority of intensifiers in English occur with adjectival heads (Bäcklund 1973: 279), it was a straightforward matter to restrict the analysis to adjectival heads capable of intensification.

Once completed, there are at least two advantages to having undertaken this practice. First, as with any study, it provides you with a database that can be used to ensure the comparability of all subsequent research. Second, it provides you with an inventory of intensifiable adjectives that can be used to streamline data extraction for another study. For example, in my 2009 study of IM features (Tagliamonte and Denis 2008b), we simply extracted from our IM corpus the top 20 adjectives that had previously been found in the study of intensifiers in the Toronto English Corpus (Tagliamonte 2008b). Although this meant we were missing innumerable low frequency adjectives, the database was substantial and the data extraction phase of the research was greatly simplified, efficient, and quick.

> **NOTE** The top 11 adjectives (with counts of over 200) in Toronto in the early 2000s are: *good* 1000, *big* 429, *nice* 376, *funny* 368, *different* 321, *cool* 277, *fun* 257, *great* 252, *bad* 244, *little* 242, *weird* 226.

The study of a single verb such as *come* or *give* might seem to be a simpler enterprise than studying the whole system of strong verbs or ditransitive verbs respectively. Consider the case of *come*. While one of the variants, the standard form *came*, is very easy to retrieve from a data set, it is quite an undertaking to find past reference *come*. (Note: I am not talking about grammatically tagged corpora, which would, of course, make this task a cinch!) For example, the oldest individual in the York English Corpus, Bobby Hamilton, aged 91 (c. 1997) has 10 tokens of *came* which can straightforwardly be extracted for analysis. However, each of the 17 contexts for *come* must be searched by hand to pick out the ones with past temporal reference, as in Example 11.22:

Example 11.22

Well when war *come* out they pulled me in. (YRK/076)

Multiplying this work by the 92 speakers in the corpus shows you that the time investment in extracting even a single verb from a moderately sized sociolinguistic (untagged) corpus is considerable. And what if after all that work you discover there is little or no variation? While preterite *come* was present with just enough frequency to analyze quantitatively in the York English Corpus, it is nearly obsolete in Toronto. A quick test of the oldest individual in the corpus, Bill Smart, aged 92 (c. 2004) revealed 10 tokens of *came* and 17 tokens of *come*, but not a single one of the *come* tokens had past temporal reference. Although it is possible that preterite *come* exists in the TEA, the investment involved to find out is perhaps not worth it!

Research Questions Arising

Variable (come), intensifiers and laughter each offer the analyst different perspectives on linguistic features that are unusual in one way or another, but which provide insights into language variation and change. Variable (come) is an obsolescent feature that can be used to study the history and perhaps the pace of change in varieties of English. Places where it is retained may be moving slower than other varieties of English or the variable may have been reinterpreted as a sociolinguistic marker. Variable intensifiers tap ongoing change in English in a way that no other variable can. They offer a unique opportunity to study innovation. Since increasing intensification seems to be a current trend and intensifiers by their very nature change more quickly than other areas of the grammar, we may be able to track the emergence and diffusion of the next layer of forms. Will *so* extend to attributive position soon? Internet language in general offers a unique new frontier for sociolinguistics. What will be the fate of *lol*? Is it destined to be a perpetual age-graded phenomenon or will it evolve into a new pragmatic marker? Will it (and other IM acronymns) enter the spoken language? If my teenagers are any indications, *lolls*, *omg*, and *jokes* are entering the spoken register already. More generally, what will be the fate of language on the Internet? Derek Denis and I have studied a compendium of linguistic features in our IM corpus (deontic modals, future temporal reference, quotatives); however, there are many more to explore. Any one of the many linguistic features that have been examined in this book could easily be studied on the Internet, in any one of the new media. Given the knowledge we have about these variables from the literature, we will be able to interpret what we find in new data sources in novel ways. For example, if the new media really do herald things to come, then we might expect that grammatical developments will be more advanced there. We might also expect the new media to host innovations first. Will linguistic variables that we know are sociolinguistic markers behave in the same way on the Internet? Will the principles of linguistic change prevail? Thinking about language on the Internet more specifically, it is important to capitalize on the new media for their potential for studying the most mysterious of sociolinguistic questions – how does a change begin? For example, over the last 10 years, adolescents have been interacting with their friends on computers, which means – possibly – that there are records of individuals in real time as they move from pre-adolescence to adolescence into early adulthood. Where once sociolinguistics had to rely on apparent time to track this development, perhaps there will be opportunities to find out how it actually happens. It would be worthwhile for other shrewd sociolinguists to figure out a way to do this. We need to know what's going on with different variables in different locations and in a broader range of data to track language variation and change into the future.

> **OBSERVATION**   Researchers predict that intensifiers by their very nature cannot have staying power since their impact is only as good as their novelty. If they're right, a new intensifier should emerge and begin diffusing soon. Watch for it!

Exercises

Preamble
Undoubtedly, the most important first step in any LVC analysis is to find a linguistic variable to study. I can recall the first time I did a variationist piece of work. I was challenged to find a linguistic variable and study it. Guess which one I ended up with? Variable (t,d). I was able to complete a competent piece of work, but my mentor was pretty ho-hum about it. From that time forward I have been determined to find the most interesting variables in the world. I am still working on that.

Exercise 11.1   Identifying unusual variables

The following examples come directly from the data file which Ito and Tagliamonte (2003) used to analyze the intensifier system in York, England.
  The data show the use of intensifiers with three adjectives, *bad*, *awful*, and *horrible*, by two speakers in the data set.

  Speaker A: female, aged 23
    so it's really bad
    i wanted to make him feel ø bad, you-know,
    what was really bad was you know
    oh it was just so bad. i was screaming my head off
    being ø awful.
    you-know, that ø awful feeling.

i-mean that must be ø awful.
it's ø awful.
it's ø horrible.
oh it was really horrible because
it was just ø horrible, thinking about it
this ø horrible sister, she like asked them, she said "oh
they were ø horrible.
  Speaker B: male, aged 85
    and it was a ø bad thing for the city, wasn't it?
    it was ø bad for the city as
    i don't consider this last one was very bad at all
    wouldn't be very bad or anything

    no one thought it ø awful
    it was a ø awful place to live
    the properties were ø awful, weren't they?
    it was ø awful.
    but it sounds ø awful nowadays.

Question 1 What is the overall distribution of intensification in these data?
Question 2 Which speaker intensifies the most?
Question 3 Which adjective – bad, awful, or horrible – is the most likely to be intensified?
Question 4 Is this the same across speakers?
Question 5 Which adjective, *bad, awful,* or *horrible*, has the most varied intensification?
Question 6 List two facts that distinguish these speakers.

(a) _____

(b) _____

Question 7 How do the results from this small sample of the data fit with the overall results reported in Ito and Tagliamonte about the changing intensifier system in English? List at least two major findings.

(a) _____

(b) _____

Question 8 Given your answers to the above questions and the results of Ito and Tagliamonte (2003), which of the intensifiers in the excerpt above may be in the process of innovating?

Exercise 11.2   Finding unusual (not boring!) variables ⎯⎯⎯⎯⎯⎯⎯⎯⎯

Here are two stories from a recording of the proprietor of Maple Station General Store and Post Office, W. Landon, born in the late 1800s. The first story is about the Ottawa train station and canal. The second is about the family cow.

Ottawa train station and canal
[1] So what was Ottawa like in those days, Papa? [3] Well, it was just the same as 'tis now. Yeah. Them] buildings is right there and the train pulled in there and there's a- a big hotel

right across' the street. And you see the- the train wa– it was all covered-in, the trains- the passenger-train went right inside, you see. And the- you could go up steps into the station, or you could walk through the tunnel into the- up to the hotel. … Well, you see it was all covered in, you see and the whole train went right inside. … And ah- and ah you see the tunnel went through to the hotel and the- if you went up steps you went up into the station. And you was up even with the street, you see … The trai– tracks was right up alongside of the canal, it was kind of all abutment in there, c– cement work, you see. And uh, there was one engineer there, Clough his name was- … And ah there was two kids come down on the ice. They was gonna, I guess, gonna skate on it or sleigh on it or something. And the ice wasn't hard enough and they both went through. He- he jumped out of the engine, went over and dove in and- and ah he got one of them, pull him up and threw him out on the ice, and went back for the other one. He couldn't find him. You see the water's runnin' there, I guess. But ah he come up and took a breath o' air and went back down and got the other one. And by that time there was people down there you see. He threw them out on the ice and- but he died. … I guess he had took in a lot of that cold water and had been in there too long, you see. … Well it was pretty near up to the railroad- you know, right full of water right up, you see. And they skate on there in the wintertime on that. … Oh, they drain it and skate on it, eh? Oh yeah.

The family cow

One winter I was coming back, there was a fella out at Tallyhoe Road with a cow. He had two cows and the feed was gettin' scarce. And he come out there. He owed me a billin' and- and turned it in and ah, turned it in on the billing, you see. Well, I just tied it to the horse's collar and brought it home and put it in the stable. That's that one we kept- we kept- 'cause she's only three years old. We kept her there for at least ten or fifteen years, you know. Oh yeah. Keep the calf in the barn, you see. In the summertime, she just roamed where she liked. And most of the time it would be down the railroad tracks. … And ah, you know, you took a chance of her getting killed on the railroad tracks. But ah, she didn't- she never walked on the track … No, she seemed to have ah- ah- just down long the side of the tracks. And the trains run past here all the time and everything. But you needed milk. So, the only way you could have fresh milk was to have a cow. And if she got killed, well, that was just too bad. You'd have to get another one. But she never got touched. Went up and down there all her life.

Question 1   How many suggestive tokens can you find? I found a dozen easily.
Question 2   What other features do you notice?
Question 3   How are these linguistic forms being used and what are their function(s)?

Mini Quiz Answers

11.1   **Q1:** *IN = b, c, d, f, g, i, j*
   OUT = a, e, h
   Note: c is a doubly intensified token; d and i are attributive adjectives which do not permit so, *but are IN because they permit* really *and* very.

11.2   **Q1:** *People over 35 use* **very**; *younger speakers under 35 use* **really**. *There actually is a generation gap!*

11.3   **Q1:** *-body vs. –one*
   Q2: *variable apostrophes, "thats" vs. "how's"*

Q3: *and everything*

Q4: *"had no" as opposed to "didn't have"; placement of "probably" in pre-aux. position as opposed to post-aux.; "i were" as opposed to "i was"; simple present as opposed to future in "im goin out now."*

Notes

1   http://jcmc.indiana.edu/ (accessed December 27, 2010, 2:49 pm).

2   Special thanks to Derek Denis and his IM buddies as well as my awesome mentees: Tamar Friedman, Milen Foto, Catherine Kierans, Anita Li, Vivian Li, Macy Siu, Helen Tsang.

3   Note that the MSN software allows users the option of saving the text record of their conversations. It was our luck that the mentees in our study had previously saved documents of this type on their computers when our project began. Many of them simply opted to donate these files to the project.

Background reading

Variable (come) and the strong verb system
Christian *et al.* 1988: 85–92; Eisikovits 1987; Feagin 1979: 322, 327; Hogg 1992: 154; Krygier 1994; Lass 1992: 131; Poplack and Tagliamonte 2001; Tagliamonte 2001a; Zettersten, 1969.

Intensifiers
Bauer and Bauer 2002; Bolinger 1972: 18; Ito and Tagliamonte 2003: Labov 1985; Lorenz 2002; Table 1; Méndez-Naya 2003; Mustanoja 1960: 319–327; Nevalainen and Rissanen 2002; Partington 1993; Peters 1994; Quirk *et al.* 1985: 590.

Instant messaging and Internet studies
Baron 2003a, 2004: 13; Cherny 1999; Ferrara, Hans, and Greg 1991; Hentschel 1998; Herring 1996a,b, 2001, 2003, 2004; Lenhart *et al.* 2001: 3; Palfreyman and Khalil 2003; Randall 2002: 21; Schiano *et al.* 2002; Thurlow 2002; Werry 1996; Yates 1996.

12

Sociolinguistic Explanations

I have come to see that much of the structured variation that exists in language can be ascribed to the social nature of its use, and to the plurality of functions that it serves. (Sankoff 1980b: 258)

This chapter considers the question: "Where did it all come from anyway?" The goal has been to find explanations for linguistic variation. Many variables and the constraints that operate on them reflect particular social meanings. Simultaneously, they may also store an imprint of the history of the language. Some variables change with the times, diverging from what has gone before and disappearing again as the next variant takes its place. Others endure for centuries. Still others lie dormant and unremarked until suddenly they are conscripted back into the grammar. Some variables are entirely new; some get remade. Why? Moreover, how can we spot which ones are which? While you ponder these questions, let me try to pull together the variables, the observations, and the interpretations that we have gone through in this book in a way that highlights the extraordinary nature of language variation and change, as well as the accumulating insights of many research findings in sociolinguistics.

I have now taken you from phonological variables, through morpho-syntactic variables to tense-aspect variables, to discourse-pragmatic variables, and even several relatively unusual variables. In each one I have told you what motivated the research, how it fit in with research that had gone before it, how the research was conducted, how the data were analyzed, and some interpretation of the findings. What have we discovered? To frame this question let's return to the questions that propelled Variationist Sociolinguistics from the beginning – the five problems in the study of linguistic change (Weinriech 1953/1968).

What Are the Constraints on Change?

We are fortunate in linguistics to have the signs of the system so prominently displayed in the record of our productions, both speech and writing. Uncovering the patterns of variation that lie in this mass of evidence is like a treasure hunt. The forms are visible, but it is only when

Variationist Sociolinguistics: Change, Observation, Interpretation, First Edition. Sali A. Tagliamonte.
© 2012 Sali A. Tagliamonte. Published 2012 by Blackwell Publishing Ltd.

you get right into the data and painstakingly analyze hundreds and sometimes thousands of tokens that the patterns are revealed. The constraints on change are the product of internal and external factors, from phonetics to pragmatics. While researchers once conceived of linguistic variables at one level of grammar as having constraints from that level, it is becoming more evident that every linguistic variable is impacted by multiple levels of grammar. Phonological variables are influenced by structure. Syntactic variables are influenced by phonetics. Phonetic variables have morphological constraints. Morphology is influenced by collocations and expressions. There is often little to distinguish the level of grammar of a linguistic variable despite my attempts at dividing them up into chapters in this book.

How Does Language Change?

Linguistic change happens everywhere but not at the same time, not in every era, and not in the same way in all places. Most of the grammar is intact at any given point in time. Which makes it all the more intriguing that variation happens in the first place. Yet when it does begin, the underlying processes are familiar. Words and systems change because of association, shared concepts that make one thing become like another, shared attributes that let the mind slip over the line (so to speak). The ambiguities of language are its stepping stones through time. As a change develops the original context will become (near) categorical. As it does, the change will spread to more extended, less favorable, environments. Depending on the nature of the change, the environments may remain constant or reorganize. Evidence of reweighting of constraints comes from minute shifts in the ranking and weighting of linguistic contexts over time and/or space. Sometimes constraints will remain constant across dialects and age levels, but the relative strength of factors can shift in the course of time or age. This may simply be a reflection of the rate of change or it may be the pathway of the change itself. Where historical linguists have centuries of perspective, contemporary sociolinguistics often only has a hundred years in apparent time. It is thus not surprising that the changes in sociolinguistics are more subtle. It is equally possible that original semantic associations will stay in place for centuries. Some expressions get left behind in islands or junkyards or hidey-holes beneath the radar. Innovations may come and go. Variants that lie dormant may rise again. For still unfathomable reasons, some forms entrench and change the face of the grammar.

> linguistic change in progress is heavily constrained by the physical environment in which it takes place, and by structural factors that limit the course of change. At the same time … the forces that motivate change, and are responsible for incrementation and transmission across generations are largely social in nature. (Labov 2001a: 498)

How Is a Change Embedded in Social and Linguistic Systems?

There is no black and white answer to this question. It depends on the ecology. The same linguistic variable in different situations will likely pattern in a completely different way. The pervasive influence of the local setting is visible in virtually every linguistic phenomenon, from variable (ing) (Labov 1989) to code-switching (Poplack 1987) to general extenders

(Tagliamonte and Denis 2010) to acronyms (Tagliamonte and Denis 2008b). We still need to conduct more extensive cross-variety comparisons to understand how the general mechanism of change may go off in a different direction, take a different route, choose a different pivot, take a different quotative. Where is the universal tendency and where is the local deviation? What does it take for *were* to regularize instead of *was*? What does it take for a tense marker to appear in third person singular whereas in most other languages third person singular is a default rather than a marked context? Why has *be like* taken the world by storm, but *be all* and *this is* are local products?

The geography in which the linguistic system evolves, the setting, and social situation of the speech community – its ecology – will impact on the state of development of the grammar in time and space (Mufwene 2001b). Varieties that have evolved in peripheral regions such as the Samaná peninsula in rural Dominican Republic or the fishing villages of Northern Ireland or the small islands of the east coast of the US – preserve obsolescent forms and patterns from earlier stages in the history of a change. They are the equivalent of linguistic woolly mammoths. They are diachrony in synchrony. In contrast, those communities that have evolved in situations with greater exposure to mainstream developments – like the great melting-pot cities of the United Kingdom, United States, Canada, New Zealand, and elsewhere – exhibit developments that can be interpreted as more fully advanced along the path of change. The burgeoning new adolescent varieties that are arising in large urban multicultural contexts in Europe appear to offer the ultimate in cutting-edge sociolinguistic fieldwork. Community differences and similarities at this grander scale will open new vistas for comparison and for putting sociolinguists back onto the streets. As communities develop in new global neighborhoods it will be exciting to discover the impact on structured variation of the speech community. Where there were regular layers by social class and style (as attention to speech) in New York City in 1966, what will the same array look like in 2011? Where once social organization and interaction took place in city blocks, country stores, and post offices, what are the relevant social networks now?

NOTE   Notice too the all-encompassing part that irony plays in language variation and change. Words and expressions are perpetually used to mean the opposite of what they seem to say, e.g. skinny friends are called "Fatty"; *sick* comes to mean "good"; old forms endure when they are *so not cool*, and new forms are proffered as stylistic invention when that *ain't necessarily* so! I wonder and marvel at the part humor plays in changing the way we speak and write and how this too may be part of the evolution of language.

Evaluation of a Change

How do members of a speech community evaluate a given change, and what is the effect of this evaluation on the change? These are accidents of history and settlement, of wars and treaties, of migration and immigration. We cannot know how a change actuates until we place a linguistic system in the context of where it came from, who speaks it, and what was going on before and during. Up to now, going backward has been difficult because the historical record is sparse and uneven and only certain registers survive, and so we have had to make the most of bad data. Today, technology, the new media, and the nature of society has made record-keeping commonplace, in fact over the top. There are untold possibilities for stalking a linguistic change from its inception into the upswing of the S-curve and in an ever-widening spectrum of registers and vernacular sources. The British Empire created colonies that underwent dialect leveling leaving a permanent record of the ebb and flow of social evaluation across vast new territories (Trudgill 1999) as well as evidence of deterministic change in the development of unique colonial varieties from the mix of dialects in the founders (Trudgill 2004). In some communities Word War II was "a watershed of linguistic behaviour" (Labov 2001a: 227). In others the rapid development of pidgins into creoles enabled the birth of a linguistic system to be recorded in several generations of speakers (Sankoff and Brown 1976; Sankoff and Laberge 1973). Wherever we can uncover the tracks of the past we will find in them patterns of language variation and change. The patterns, in turn, will reveal the story of the time and place.

> the existence of language change is among the most stubborn and difficult to assimilate when we try to come to grips with the nature of language in general as it is reflected in the history of a language (Labov 1994: 9)

I must say, however, that the more regions you consider in your research, the more difficult it is to arrive at a simple explanation. In York and Toronto where I have accumulated studies of many different linguistic variables, there are critical breakpoints in the apparent time continuum. There is a deep divide between the most elderly generation in York around people born between the World Wars (approximately 1930) (as with the complementizer study in Chapter 5), there is another turning point among the people born in the post-World War II era (c. 1945) (e.g. Tagliamonte and Smith 2006) and this latter trend is repeated in Toronto (e.g. Tagliamonte and D'Arcy 2007a). In contrast, in New Zealand where the ONZE project provides a historical record from 1850 to 2000, the accumulating findings reveal a significant shift at the beginning of the twentieth century (Bresnan and Hay 2008; Hay and Schreier 2004). Interestingly, both the York English Corpus and the ONZE materials exhibit reversals in the course of change for many linguistic variables. This can only implicate external social forces driving the language in an ever-evolving ebb and flow. As Variationist Sociolinguistics moves from the study of a single linguistic variable in a single community to broader cross-variety comparisons contrasting multiple variables and different types of linguistic features and in varying trajectories of change or stability, then we will be better placed to answer this still mysterious question of what actually propels a change forward (or backward) at a particular place and time.

In sum, the answer to the question of what explains linguistic variation and change is multiplex, inclusive, and encompasses a spectrum of human conditions. Consider the list from Wolfram and Schilling-Estes (2006):

Sociohistorical Explanation

- settlement
- migration routes
- geographical factors

- language contact
- economic ecology
- social stratification
- group reference
- personal identity.

Linguistic Explanation

- simplification
- maximization of contrast
- rule extension
- analogy
- the transparency principle
- grammaticalization
- pronunciation phenomena
- words and word meanings.

To these lists I think we would do well to add sociocultural factors, some new measures of social interaction, media type, media influence, and maybe others:

Cultural Explanation

- dialect leveling
- community typology
- type of change
- nature of the social network
- type of media
- media influence.

As LVC studies expand beyond local places to supralocal and global studies, it is becoming apparent that the process of change across the landscape implicates more than simply the leveling of regional dialects, but also the changing types of communities (see Britain 2002; Kerswill *et al.* 2008; 2009a,b; Britain 2002). Social networks cannot anymore be defined solely by space or time, but also by engagement with media (e.g. Stuart-Smith 2010) and technologically based networking of all kinds.

Statistical Modeling

The ability to model variation statistically is vital to understanding and explaining variation. This is why the LVC methodological toolkit is a pressing consideration. The frequency of variants is a useful starting point, but the contexts underlying variation provide the window into the variable grammar. Their relative strength provides yet another measure, especially when constraints are subtly shifting in time and space. For example, cross-variety parallels may tap into universal constraints on variation (e.g. variable (t,d)). Others reveal variation within universality. Recall that while the NP vs. pronoun contrast for variable (s) and (was) holds across dialects, the way it operates differs. In the case studies in this book, I have presented only one part or another of the analyses; however, in reality every little bit of evidence should be used together to arrive at an interpretation, especially if there are conflicting indications – and there usually are. In other words, the key to interpreting complex variable patterns is to make wise use of all the available evidence. The question is what evidence is available. Perhaps most crucially for future comparative research is to be able to assess the differences that emerge within the constraint ranking of factors.

These subtle differences in the operation of constraints disclose the omnipresent workings of the internal mechanisms of change. But we need to be certain which ones are relevant and which not. To do so will require more sensitive measures for the relative contributions of these effects within the composite of factors. Constraints and their weights vary from one variety to the next, from one context to the next, and between and among individuals limited only by the reality of our samples. At the same time, lexical items and collocation patterns, their frequency and distribution also need to be assessed. In broad studies of different types of change in varying ecologies we will also need to model the shifts from substrate to replica, from dialect to dialect, from place to place, from generation to generation, and from adult to child and to distinguish among them. When we find a reorganization of prevailing constraints, we must be able to distinguish the type of change – transmission vs. diffusion, leveling vs. divergence, change over time vs. lifespan change. There is tremendous add-on value to having many varieties, dialects, and data sets to study. Each new linguistic variable in every new variable context makes another contribution to the building repertoire of knowledge in the study of language variation and change. However, we are going to need a comprehensive toolkit to handle it all and, as ever, testing statistical models and methods will be part of the of LVC enterprise (Sankoff 1978a).

It doesn't always pay to be too fast in replying to important problems. (Labov, October 1, 1987)[1]

Traditional Explanations

The actuation problem is "the biggest mystery in diachrony. (Kroch 2003)

Traditional explanations of linguistic change focus on the causes of sound change. They were (1) the principle of least effort, (2) the principle of density, and (3) the principle of imitation (Labov 2001a:16); or, in more modern terms and put succinctly:

- everyone shortens, reduces, and eliminates anything that's not necessary;
- who you hang out with the most is who you sound like;
- you imitate who you admire.

Yet such processes do not always behave as one might predict, because they interact with each other. There is always give and take, and sometimes things are not always as they seem. Where features are being eliminated, others are gaining ground. Although Puerto Rican Spanish is eliminating redundancy from the surface structure of sentences through the phonological deletion of plural -*s*, it is simultaneously reorganizing its system of plural marking by retaining plural *–n* (Poplack 1980a: 385). This shows that languages accommodate phonological reduction processes by adjustments in other areas of the grammar. Where social networks can be "norm enforcement mechanisms" (Chambers 2003: 75), there will always be lames, oddballs, nerds, and weirdos who do not pattern with their group as well as insiders and leaders forging the way ahead (Chambers 1995: 93).

What about changes above the level of phonology? In the first 20 years of LVC research many people argued about whether LVC methods could be extended above the level of phonology. In the second 20 years a great deal of attention has been devoted to morpho-syntactic and discourse-pragmatic change, the realm of grammatical change. LVC has had much to offer in its ability to model the multiple factors that are involved when a lexical item begins the long journey to a grammatical morpheme. In the growing literature on grammaticalization processes a number of recurring patterns can be used to identify and measure the precise nature and extent of grammaticalization, specifically the strength and significance of multiple independent linguistic factors with the evolving grammatical morpheme (e.g. Poplack and Tagliamonte 1999b; Schwenter 1994b; Schwenter and Torres Cacoullos 2008; Tagliamonte 2000, 2001b, 2003, among others; Torres-Cacoullos 1999; Torres-Cacoullos and Walker 2009a,b). Such correlations are crucial to viewing the mechanism of diachronic grammaticalization in synchronic data (Traugott and Heine 1991a,b). With respect to the restructuring processes themselves, some researchers suggest that their origins may be found in discourse-level phenomena (Traugott 1982), particularly in pidgin and creole situations. Variation analyses have provided evidence to suggest that the grammatical functions of some markers may be the logical outgrowth of earlier, more facultative discourse-level phenomena (Sankoff 1977, 1980a, 1990). One of the questions that remains to be answered is whether grammatical change (i.e. grammaticalization) is any different from the general processes of linguistic change (e.g. analogy) (e.g. Joseph 2004; Joseph and Janda 2003a).

The Principle of Interaction

There must be a social force that activates the shift and drives the increment. (Labov 2001a: 463)

The findings of sociolinguistics can be considered a record of the shifting social, political, economic, and geographical history of human populations. In Europe, research has tracked a longitudinal shift away from older, stigmatized, often rural, vernacular forms into broader supralocal and national varieties (Labov 2001a: 230). In North America, the United Kingdom, and Canada changes are often led by women and the middle classes and resisted by men and the working classes. Yet the large cities of Europe, North America, and the Antipodes are changing. Migration of many different ethnicities into the urban centers is producing a population mix where a widely divergent set of immigrants outnumbers the locals. While such patterns have happened in the past, e.g. London in the fifteenth century, the impact of this new mix of peoples has already started to influence linguistic change where it has been studied (Cheshire and Fox 2009). The big city studies of early LVC research need to be expanded to represent the shifting composition of the social structure to include ethnicity, neighborhood, and other aspects of the social fabric. One of the problems with small ethnographic studies is whether their findings can be generalized and how they compare with the broader community of which they are a part. In Toronto we are beginning to conduct what we refer to as "small within large" studies which target smaller groups within the whole. For example, gay-lesbian-bisexual-queer populations (GLBQ), stutterers, ethnic neighborhoods, and any other subgroups of the Toronto speech community however defined. The small, circumscribed social network study can then be systematically and rigorously compared with its "twin" in the large, socially stratified TEA. Thus, while it may seem relatively ho-hum to discover in the early 2000s that less educated males in blue-collar jobs resist the innovations of middle class females – since that has been demonstrated ad nauseam in LVC research – it is entirely fresh and exciting to find that GLBQ youth in Toronto are way in the lead of linguistic change regardless of their biological sex (Tagliamonte and Uscher 2009). In this way, the behavior of the small group is not interpreted in isolation, but alongside the community as a whole.

Another tradition explanation is that language change does not arise from the media, but instead evolves in the context of "face-to-face interaction with peers" (Labov 2001a: 227). In the context of a veritable explosion of new media, can this be sustained? Modern teenagers are interacting with their peers in more complex social networks than ever before imagined. Even adults are interacting in ever more remarkable ways. When I sit down at my desk in the morning I may have had a conversation with several colleagues across diverse registers in countries around the world before my first conversation with someone in my department. New communication possibilities such as Skype are making face-to-face conversation possible regardless of location. Written media are expanding exponentially into multiplex registers – email, texting, instant messaging, Facebook, blogging – that mix spoken and written communication (e.g. Baron 2004, 2008; Jones and Schieffelin 2009; Tagliamonte and Denis 2008b). These new media break apart any traditional conceptions of interaction because none of them requires mobility. Moreover, the nature of the interactions is often unlike any that have previously existed. The social contacts of online worlds, games, and practices often involve interaction between people who do not actually know each other and perhaps do not share any other aspect of their lives. How will all these new forms of interaction influence the social-cultural landscape?

> **TIP**   I once attended a conference paper that studied a linguistic variable in a prominent magazine. It was a longitudinal study over real time. The data showed a dramatic break in the course of history, a veritable "about-face" in the use of one of the variants to another. The question was why. A world war? No. A sociocultural revolution? No. It was a change in editor! Watch out for these unexpected explanations for linguistic patterns.

Sociolinguistic Horizons

The outlook for sociolinguistics in the twenty-first century is as bright with promise as it was when it first began. Labov (1969) conceived of grammar as quantitative, heterogeneous, and uniquely social. Critiques condemned the idea that people had statistics in their heads and others dismissed performance (usage) as irrelevant. Some 40 years later grammars are purported to be probabilistic, gradient, usage-based, and require multilevel modeling techniques. These are the watchwords of a new wave of research and analysis.

Insights accumulate gradually, and only for those who can read the work of their predecessors with understanding. These kinds of theories grow slowly; they emerge from the dirt and debris of the everyday world, never entirely free of errors of measurement and other vulgar irregularities. They take shape, they grow strong and dependable to the extent that they keep their connection with that everyday world, and as long as they are cultivated by those who have the feel of it. Their beauty lies not in their simplicity or symmetry, but in their firm connection with reality. (Labov 1981: 305)

LVC is a secular discipline. It offers us the possibility of understanding human interactions like no other science can. It enables us to identify groups, practices, and types, to determine who is talking to whom and who is not. It can demonstrate how large communities are constructed, where allegiances lie, and how the channels of communications are operating, all without anyone ever directly telling us anything. The rest of the world should probably know this. Variationist Sociolinguistics has many practical applications. I recently spotted an advert in Toronto from an ongoing campaign to encourage students to use their student cards. The billboard read: *You've got it; use it!* I had to laugh. The target population doesn't even use that construction. Only old people in Toronto say *"you've got."* Are young people going to comply with the implicit plea from the company when the ad uses the language of their grandparents? I doubt it. If they had asked me I would have recommended: *You have it; use it!* The same type of counsel can be offered for TV, movies, advertising, marketing, teaching, learning, and any number of other areas of the public sector. If you want to reach an audience, LVC can tell you a lot about them, whoever they happen to be. In this new era, I believe that sociolinguistic theory and interpretation have the potential to grapple with and understand the complexities of our expanding global networks of communication. I believe that the field of LVC studies may be just mature enough to help start explaining what we find well enough to understand what might happen next. I believe that diachronic and synchronic approaches to linguistic variation and change can be reconciled. That is what LVC practitioners *do* – we are forever analyzing the present in terms of the past; the past in terms of the present; and when we are done, the future has become the present and we start over again.

Readers, I would like to end this book by specifically bringing you into the picture. The analyses and observations in this textbook are meant as inspiration for your creativity and for mapping out your own research. Contemplate your own particular background, personal history, and social circumstances – where you are in the world, where you are in your life, and who is sitting at your kitchen table. You may be sitting on a sociolinguistic gold mine. Choose the most promising vein, then let it take you wherever it will.

Sali
January 1, 2011

Note

1   From an essay posted at: http://linguistlist.org/studentportal/linguists/labov.cfm.

Appendix A

Corpora Cited

Corpus code	Name of community, Geographic location
BCK	Buckie, Northern Scotland
CDA	Storytelling corpus from undergraduate students in Ottawa, Canada, c. 1995
CLB	Culleybackey, Northern Ireland
CMC	Corpus of computer-mediated communication
CMK	Cumnock, Scotland
CT	*Canterbury Tales* (Chaucer)
DVN	Devon, southwest England
GYE	Guysborough Enclave, Nova Scotia
GYV	Guysborough Village, Nova Scotia
HEN	Henfield, Sussex, southern England
MPT	Maryport, northwest England
NI	Northern Ireland
NPR	North Preston, Nova Scotia
OED	Oxford English Dictionary
PVG	Portavogie, Northern Ireland
SAM	Samaná, Dominican Republic
SMT	Somerset, southwest England
TEA	Toronto English Archive
TIV	Tiverton, Devon, southwest England
TOR	Toronto, Canada
Trev.Higd	Legal Glossary in John Trevisa's ME Version of Higden's Polychronicon
UK	Storytelling corpus from undergraduate students in York, UK, c. 1996
WHL	Wheatley Hill, Durham, northeast England
YRK	York, northeast England

Variationist Sociolinguistics: Change, Observation, Interpretation, First Edition. Sali A. Tagliamonte.
© 2012 Sali A. Tagliamonte. Published 2012 by Blackwell Publishing Ltd.

Appendix B

Time Periods in the History of English

	Years	Sources cited
Old English		
I	–850	*Beowulf* (?)
I	850–950	
III	950–1050	*Aelfric*
IV	1050–1150	*Abelard* (1079–1142)
Middle English		
I	1150–1250	*Aquinas* (1225–1274)
II	1250–1350	*Cursor Mundi* (1325)
III	1350–1420	*Chaucer* (1343–1400)
IV	1420–1500	*Lydgate* (c. 1370–1451); *Malory* (c. 1405–1471)
Early Modern English		
I	1500–1570	*Shakespeare* (1564–1616); *Sidney* (1554–1586); *Spenser* (1552–1599)
II	1570–1640	*Donne* (1572–1631); *Marvell* (1621–1678); *Herbert* (1593–1633)
III	1640–1710	*Milton* (1608–1674); *Butler* (1612–1680)
Late Modern English		
I	1700s	*Swift* (1667–1745); *Pope* (1688–1744); *Johnson* (1709–1784); *Defoe* (c. 1659–1731); *Richardson* (1689–1761)
II	1800s	*Austen* (1775–1817); *Byron* (1788–1824) *Shelley* (1797–1851); *Dickens* (1812–1870; *Eliot* (1819–1880)
III	1900s	*Conrad* (1857–1924); *Joyce* (1882–1941); *Lawrence* (1885–1930); *Fitzgerald* (1896–1940); *Updike* (1932–2009); *Atwood* (1939–); *Rushdie* (1947–)
IV	2000s	*Time will tell …*

Variationist Sociolinguistics: Change, Observation, Interpretation, First Edition. Sali A. Tagliamonte.
© 2012 Sali A. Tagliamonte. Published 2012 by Blackwell Publishing Ltd.

References

Aaron, J.E. (2010) Pushing the envelope: Looking beyond the variable context. *Language Variation and Change* 22(1): 1–36.

Abbott, E.A. (1879) *A Shakespearian Grammar*. London: Macmillan.

Adger, D. and Smith, J. (2005) Variation and the minimalist program, in L. Cornips and K. Corrigan (eds), *Syntax and Variation: Reconciling the Biological and the Social*. Amsterdam and Philadelphia: John Benjamins, pp. 149–178.

Aijmer, K. (1985) What happens at the end of our utterances? – The use of utterance final tags introduced by "and" and "or," in O. Togeby (ed.), *Papers from the Eighth Scandinavian Conference of Linguistics*. Copenhagen: Institut for Philologie, pp. 366–389.

Aijmer, K. (2002) *English Discourse Particles, Evidence from a Corpus*. Amsterdam and Philadelphia: John Benjamins.

Alford, H. (1864) *A Plea for the Queen's English: Stray Notes on Speaking and Spelling*. London: Strahan.

Altmann, G.H., v. Buttlar, H., Rott, W. and Strauss, U. (1983) A law of change in language, in B. Brainerd (ed.), *Historical Linguistics*. Bochum: Studienverlag Dr. N. Brockmeyer, pp. 104–115.

Andersen, G. (2001) *Pragmatic Markers and Sociolinguistic Variation*. Amsterdam: John Benjamins.

Anttila, R. (1989) *Historical and Comparative Linguistics*. Amsterdam and New York: John Benjamins.

Anttila, R. (2003) Analogy: The warp and woof of cognition, in B.D. Joseph and R.D. Janda (eds), *The Handbook of Historical Linguistics*. Malden and Oxford: Blackwell.

Arends, J. (1995) The socio-historical background of creoles, in J. Arends, P. Muysken, and N. Smith (eds), *Pidgins and Creoles: An Introduction*. Amsterdam and Philadelphia, pp. 15–24.

Arnovick, L.K. (1990) *The Development of Future Constructions in English*. New York: Peter Lang.

Ash, S. (1982) *The Vocalization of /l/ in Philadelphia*. PhD dissertation, University of Pennsylvania.

Atwood, E.B. (1953) *A Survey of Verb Forms in the Eastern United States*. Ann Arbor: University of Michigan Press.

Axtman, K. (2002) "r u online?": the evolving lexicon of wired teens. December 12, 2002 edition. http://www.csmonitor.com/2005/0311/p01s02-ussc.html (accessed April 4, 2011).

Baayen, H. (2008) *Analyzing Linguistic Data: A Practical Introduction to Statistics*. Cambridge: Cambridge University Press.

Baayen, H. (2009) Exploring interactions involving numeric predictors. Presented at a Workshop on Using Statistical Tools to Explain Linguistic Variation. Convenor: Sali A. Tagliamonte. *New Ways of Analyzing Variation (NWAV) 38* Ottawa, Ontario, Canada. October 22–25, 2009.

Baayen, H., Davidson, D., and Bates, D. (2008) Mixed-effect modeling with crossed random effects for subjects and items. *Journal of Memory and Language* 59: 390–412.

Bäcklund, U. (ed.) (1973) *The Collocation of Adverbs of Degree in English*. Uppsala: Almqvist & Wiksell.

Bailey, C.J.N. (1973) *Variation and Linguistic Theory*. Washington, DC: Centre for Applied Linguistics.

Bailey, G. (1987) Are Black and White vernaculars diverging? *American Speech* 62(1): 32–40.

Bailey, G. (2002) Real and apparent time, in J.K. Chambers, P. Trudgill, and N. Schilling-Estes (eds), *The Handbook of Language Variation and Change*. Malden: Blackwell.

Bailey, G. and Maynor, N. (1985) The present tense of *be* in Southern Black Folk Speech. *American Speech* 60(3): 195–213.

Bailey, G. and Maynor, N. (1989) The divergence controversy. *American Speech* 64(1): 12–39.

Bailey, G., Maynor, N., and Cukor-Avila, P. (1989) Variation in subject–verb concord in Early Modern English. *Language Variation and Change* 1(3): 285–300.

Bailey, G., Maynor, N., and Cukor-Avila, P. (1991a) *The Emergence of Black English: Texts and Commentary*. Amsterdam and Philadelphia: John Benjamins.

Bailey, G., Wikle, T., Tillery, J., and Sand, L. (1991b) The apparent time construct. *Language Variation and Change* 3(3): 241–264.

Bailyn, B. (1986) *The Peopling of British North America: An Introduction*. New York: Alfred A. Knopf.

Bailyn, B. and DeWolfe, B. (1986) *Voyagers to the West: A Passage in the Peopling of America on the Eve of the Revolution*. New York: Alfred A. Knopf.

Baker, P. and Syea, A. (eds) (1996) *Changing Meanings, Changing Functions. Papers Relating to Grammaticalization in Contact Languages*. Westminster, UK: University of Westminster Press.

Barber, C.L. (1964) *Linguistic Change in Present-day English*. Edinburgh: Oliver & Boyd.

Baron, N.S. (2003a) Language of the Internet, in A. Farghali (ed.), *The Stanford Handbook for Language Engineers*. Stanford: CSLI Publications, pp. 1–63.

Baron, N.S. (2003b) Why email looks like speech: Proof-reading pedagogy and public face, in J. Atichison and D.M. Lewis (eds), *New Media Language*. London and New York: Routledge, pp. 85–94.

Baron, N.S. (2004) See you online: Gender issues in college student use of instant messaging. *Journal of Language and Social Psychology* 23(4): 397–423.

Baron, N.S. (2008) *Always on: Language in an Online and Mobile World*. Oxford/New York: Oxford University Press.

Baron, N.S. and Ling, R. (2003) IM and SMS: A linguistic comparison. *Fourth International Conference of the Association of Internet Researchers*. Toronto, October 16–19.

Bates, D. (2005a) Fitting linear mixed models in *R*. *R News* 5(1): 27–30.

Bates, D. (2005b) lme4: Linear mixed effects models using S4 classes, *R* package version 9.9975-7.

Bauer, G. (1970) The English "perfect" reconsidered. *Journal of Linguistics* 6(2): 189–198.

Bauer, L. and Bauer, W. (2002) Adjective boosters in the English of young New Zealanders. *Journal of English Linguistics* 30(3): 244–257.

Baugh, J. (1984) *Steady*: Progressive aspect in Black Vernacular English. *American Speech* 59(1): 3–12.

Baum, S.V. (1955) From "AWOL" to veep: The growth and specialization of the acronym. *American Speech* 30: 103–110.

Bayley, R.J. (1991) *Variation Theory and Second Language Learning: Linguistic and Social Constraints on Interlanguage Tense Marking*. PhD dissertation, Stanford University.

Bayley, R.J. (1994) Consonant cluster reduction in Tejana English. *Language Variation and Change* 6(2): 303–326.

Bayley, R.J. (2002) The quantitative paradigm, in J.K. Chambers, P. Trudgill and N. Schilling-Estes (eds), *The Handbook of Language Variation and Change*. Malden and Oxford: Blackwell, pp. 117–141.

Bayley, R.J. and Langman, J. (2004) Variation in the group and the individual: Evidence from second language acquisition. *International Review of Applied Linguistics in Language Teaching* 42(4): 303–317.

Bayley, R.J. and Pease-Alvarez, L. (1997) Null pronoun variation in Mexican-descent children's narrative discourse. *Language Variation and Change* 9(3): 349–371.

Bayley, R.J. and Regan, V. (2004) Introduction: The acquisition of sociolinguistic competence. *Journal of Sociolinguistics* 8(3): 323–492.

Bayley, R.J. and Young, R. (forthcoming) Varbrul: a special case of logistic regression, in R. Bayley and D. Preston (eds), *Linguistic Data Computation*. Amsterdam: John Benjamins.

Beal, J., Corrigan, K., and Moisl, H. (eds) (2007) *Using Unconventional Digital Language Corpora. Vol. 2: Diachronic Corpora*. Basingstoke, Hampshire: Palgrave Macmillan.

Beal, J., Corrigan, K., Smith, N., and Rayson, P. (2007) Writing the vernacular: Transcribing and tagging the Newcastle Electronic Corpus of Tyneside English. *Studies in Variation, Contacts and Change in English* 1 (http://www.helsinki.fi/varieng/journal/volumes/01/).

Berglund, Y. (1997) Future in present-day English: Corpus-based evidence on the rivalry of expressions. *ICAME Journal* 21: 7–19.

Biber, D., Johansson, S., Leech, G., *et al.* (1999) *Longman Grammar of Spoken and Written English*. Harlow: Longman.

Bickerton, D. (1975) *Dynamics of a Creole System*. New York: Cambridge University Press.

Bickerton, D. (1981) *Roots of Language*. Ann Arbor: Karoma.

Blake, R. (1997) Resolving the don't count cases in the quantitative analysis of the copula in African American Vernacular English. *Language Variation and Change* 9(1): 57–79.

Blake, R. and Josey, M. (2003) The /ay/ diphthong in a Martha's Vineyard community: What can we say 40 years later? *Language in Society* 32(4): 451–485.

Blondeau, H. (2001) Real-time changes in the paradigm of personal pronouns in Montreal French. *Journal of Sociolinguistics* 4(4): 453–474.

Bloomfield, L. (1933) *Language History*. New York: Holt, Rinehart & Winston.

Blyth, C., Jr., Recktenwald, S., and Wang, J. (1990) I'm like, "say what?!": A new quotative in American oral narrative. *American Speech* 65(3): 215–227.

Boberg, C. (2004) Real and apparent time in language change: Late adoption of changes in Montreal English. *American Speech* 79(3): 250–269.

Boberg, C. (2009) The emergence of a new phoneme: Foreign (a) in Canadian English. *Language Variation and Change* 21(3): 355–380.

Bolinger, D. (1972) *Degree Words*. The Hague, Paris: Mouton.

Börgars, K. and Chapman, C. (1998) Agreement and pro-drop in some dialects of English. *Linguistics* 36(1): 71–98.

Bourdieu, P. and Boltanski, L. (1975) Le fétichisme de la langue. *Actes de la Recherche en Sciences Sociales* 4: 2–32.

Breiman, L. (2001) Random forests. *Machine Learning* 45(1): 5–32.

Bresnan, J., Cueni, A., Hikitina, T., and Baayen, R.H. (2007) Predicting the dative alternation, in G. Boume, I. Krämer, and J. Zwarts (eds), *Cognitive Foundations of Interpretation*. Amsterdam: Royal Netherlands Academy of Science.

Bresnan, J. and Ford, M. (2010) Predicting syntax: Processing dative constructions in American and Australian varieties of English. *Language* 86(1): 168–213.

Bresnan, J. and Hay, J. (2008) Gradient grammar: an effect of animacy on the syntax of *give* in New Zealand and American English. *Lingua* 118(2): 245–259.

Brewer, J. (1974) *The Verb Be in Early Black English: A Study Based on the WPA Ex-slave Narratives*. PhD dissertation, University of North Carolina at Chapel Hill.

Brewer, J. (1979) Nonagreeing *am* and invariant *be* in Early Black English. *The SECOL Review* 3: 81–100.

Brewer, J. (1986) Durative marker or hypercorrection? The case of -s in the WPA Ex-Slave Narratives, in M.B. Montgomery and G. Bailey (eds), *Language Variety in the South. Perspectives in Black and White*. Alabama: University of Alabama, pp. 131–148.

Brink, L. and Lund, J. (1979) Social factors in the sound changes of modern Danish, in E. Fischer-Jørgensen, J. Rischel, and N. Thorsen (eds), *Proceedings of the 9th International Congress of Phonetic Sciences*. Copenhagen: University of Copenhagen, pp. 196–203.

Brinton, L.J. (1988) *The Development of English Aspectual Systems*. Cambridge: Cambridge University Press.

Brinton, L.J. (1996) *Pragmatic Markers in English*. Berlin: Mouton de Gruyter.

Britain, D. (2002) Diffusion, levelling, simplification and reallocation in past tense BE in the English Fens. *Journal of Sociolinguistics* 6(1): 16–43.

Brunner, K. (1963) *An outline of Middle English Grammar*. Oxford: Blackwell.

Bruyn, A. (1995) *Grammaticalization in Creoles: The Development of Determiners and Relative Clauses in Sranan*. Amsterdam: IFOTT.

Bucholtz, M. (1999) "Why be normal?": Language and identity practices in a community of nerd girls. *Language in Society* 28(2): 203–223.

Bucholtz, M. (2005) Identity and interation: A sociocultural linguistic approach. *Discourse Studies* 7(4–5): 585–614.

Buchstaller, I. (2001a) An alternative view of like: Its grammaticalisation in conversational American English and beyond. *Edinburgh Working Papers in Applied Linguistics* 11: 21–41.

Buchstaller, I. (2001b) "He goes and I'm like:" The new quotatives revisited. *NWAVE 30*, October 11–13, 2001. Raleigh, North Carolina, USA.

Buchstaller, I. (2002) He goes, and I'm like: The new quotatives revisited. *Internet Proceedings of the Postgraduate Conference, University of Edinburgh*. http://www.lel.ed.ac.uk/~pgc%20/archive/2002/proc02/buchstaller02.pdf.

Buchstaller, I. (2006) Social stereotypes, personality traints and regional percepton displaced: Attitudes towards the "new quotatives" in the UK. *Journal of Sociolinguistics* 10(3): 362–381.

Buchstaller, I. and D'Arcy, A. (2009) Localized globalization; A multi-local, multivarate investigation of quotative *be like*. *Journal of Sociolinguistics* 13(3): 291–331.

Budzhak-Jones, S. and Poplack, S. (1997) Two generations, two strategies: The fate of bare English-origin nouns in Ukrainian. *Journal of Sociolinguistics* 1(2): 225–258.

Bybee, J.L. (1983) Morphological classes as natural categories. *Language* 59: 251–270.

Bybee, J.L. (1988) Morphology as lexical organization, in M. Hammond and M. Noonan (eds), *Theoretical Morphology*. San Diego, CA: Aacademic Press.

Bybee, J.L. (2002) Word frequency and context of use in the lexical diffusion of phonetically conditioned sounds change. *Language Variation and Change* 14(3): 261–290.

Bybee, J.L. and Pagliuca, W. (1987) The evolution of future meaning, in A.G Ramat, O. Carruba, and G. Bernini (eds), *The Evolution of Future Meaning*. Papers from the 7th International Conference on Historical Linguistics: Amsterdam and Philadelphia, pp. 107–122.

Bybee, J.L., Pagliuca, W., and Perkins, R.D. (1991) Back to the future, in E.C. Traugott and B. Heine (eds), *Approaches to Grammaticalization*. Amsterdam and Philadelphia: John Benjamins. pp. 19–58.

Bybee, J.L., Perkins, R.D., and Pagliuca, W. (1994) *The Evolution of Grammar: Tense, Aspect, and Modality in the Languages of the World*. Chicago: University of Chicago Press.

Cameron, D. and Coates, J. (1988) Some problems in the sociolinguistic explanation of sex differences. *Women in their Speech Communities: New Perspectives on Language and Sex*. London: Longman, pp. 13–26.

Cameron, R. (1992) Ambiguous agreement, functional compensation and non-specific *tu* in the Spanish of San Juan, Puerto Rico, and Madrid, Spain. *Language Variation and Change* 5(3): 305–334.

Campbell, L. (1998) *Historical Linguistics*. Edinburgh: Edinburgh University Press.

Campbell, L. and Muntzel, M.C. (1989) The structural consequences of language death, in N.C. Dorian (ed.), *Investigating Obsolescence: Studies in Language Contraction and Death*. Cambridge: Cambridge University Press, pp. 181–196.

Campbell-Kibler, K. (2009) The nature of sociolinguistic perception. *Language Variation and Change* 21(1): 135–156.

Cannon, G. (1989) Abbreviations and acronymns in English word-formation. *American Speech* 64(1): 99–127.

Cedergren, H.J. (1973) *The Interplay of Social and Linguistic Factors in Panama.* PhD dissertation, Cornell University.

Cedergren, H.J. (1988) The spread of language change: Verifying inferences of linguistic diffusion, in P. Lowenberg (ed.), *Language Spread and Language Policy: Issues, Implications, and Case Studies.* Washington: Georgetown University Press, pp. 45–60.

Cedergren, H.J. and Sankoff, D. (1974) Variable rules: Performance as a statistical reflection of competence. *Language* 50(2): 333–355.

Chambers, J.K. (1991) Canada, in J. Cheshire (ed.), *English Around the World.* Cambridge: Cambridge University Press, pp. 89–107.

Chambers, J.K. (1995) *Sociolinguistic Theory: Linguistic Variation and Its Social Significance.* Oxford: Blackwell.

Chambers, J.K. (1998a) Social embedding of changes in progress. *Journal of English Linguistics* 26: 3–35.

Chambers, J.K. (1998b) TV makes people sound the same, in L. Bauer and P. Trudgill (eds), *Language Myths.* New York: Penguin, pp. 123–131.

Chambers, J.K. (2002a) Dynamics of dialect convergence. *Journal of Sociolinguistics* 6(1): 117–130.

Chambers, J.K. (2002b) Patterns of variation including change, in J.K. Chambers, P. Trudgill, and N. Schilling-Estes (eds), *The Handbook of Language Variation and Change.* Malden and Oxford: Blackwell, 349–372.

Chambers, J.K. (2003) *Sociolinguistic Theory: Linguistic Variation and Its Social Significance.* Malden and Oxford: Blackwell.

Chambers, J.K. (2004) "Canadian Dainty": The rise and decline of Briticisms in Canada, in R. Hickey (ed.), *The Legacy of Colonial English: Studies in Transported Dialects.* Cambridge: Cambridge University Press, pp. 224–241.

Chambers, J.K. and Trudgill, P. (1980) *Dialectology.* Cambridge: Cambridge University Press.

Cherny, L. (1999) *Conversation and Community: Chat in a Virtual World.* Stanford, CA, USA: CSLI Publications.

Cheshire, J. (1982) *Variation in an English Dialect: A Sociolinguistic Study.* Cambridge: Cambridge University Press.

Cheshire, J. (1994) Standardization and the English irregular verb, in D. Stein and I. Tieken-Boon von Ostade (eds), *Towards a Standard English, 1600–1800.* Berlin and New York: Mouton de Gruyter, pp. 15–133.

Cheshire, J. (1996) That jacksprat: An interactional perspective on English *that. Journal of Pragmatics* 25: 369–393.

Cheshire, J. (2002) Sex and gender in variationist research, in J.K. Chambers, P. Trudgill, and N. Schilling-Estes (eds), *The Handbook of Language Variation and Change.* Malden and Oxford: Blackwell, pp. 423–443.

Cheshire, J. (2003) Social dimensions of syntactic variation, in J. Cheshire and D. Britain (eds), *Social Dialectology: In Honour of Peter Trudgill.* Amsterdam and Philadelphia: John Benjamins, pp. 245–261.

Cheshire, J. (2005) Age and generation-specific use of language, in U. Ammon, N. Dittmar, J.J. Mattheier, and P. Trudgill (eds), *Sociolinguistics: An Introductory Handbook of the Science of Language and Society.* Berlin: Mouton de Gruyter, pp. 1552–1563.

Cheshire, J. (2007) Discourse variation, grammaticalisation and stuff like that. *Journal of Sociolinguistics* 11(2): 155–193.

Cheshire, J. and Fox, S. (2009) Was/were variation: A perspective from London. *Language Variation and Change* 21(1): 1–38.

Chomsky, N. (1986) *Knowledge of Language: Its Nature, Origin and Use.* New York: Praeger.

Christian, D., Wolfram, W., and Dube, N. (1988) *Variation and Change in Geographically Isolated Communities: Appalachian English and Ozark English.* Tuscaloosa, Alabama: American Dialect Society.

Clarke, S. (1997a) English verbal -*s* revisited: The evidence from Newfoundland. *American Speech* 72(3): 227–259.

Clarke, S. (1997b) On establishing historical relationships between New World and Old World varieties: Habitual aspect and Newfoundland Vernacular English, in E.W. Schneider (ed.), *Englishes around the World*. Amsterdam and Philadelphia: John Benjamins, pp. 277–293.

Clarke, S. (1997c) The search for origins: Habitual aspect and Newfoundland Vernacular English. *Journal of English Linguistics* 27(4): 328–340.

Clarke, S. (2010) Newfoundland and Labrador English, in D. Schreier, P. Trudgill, E.W. Schneider, and J.P. William (eds), *The Lesser Known Varieties of English: An Introduction*. Cambridge: Cambridge University Press.

Clarke, S., Elms, F., and Youssef, A. (1995) The third dialect of English: Some Canadian evidence. *Language Variation and Change* 7(2): 209–228.

Close, R.A. (1977) Some observations on the meaning and function of verb phrases having future reference, in W.-D. Bald and R. Ilson (eds), *Studies in English Usage: The Resources of a Present-day English Corpus of Linguistic Analysis*: Frankfurt A.M. and Berne: Peter Lang, pp. 125–156.

Coates, J. (1983) *The Semantics of the Modal Auxiliaries*. London: Croom Helm.

Cofer, T. (1975) Performance constraints on relative pronoun deletion. *Linguistics* 157: 13–32.

Collins, P.C. (2005) The modals and quasi-modals of obligation and necessity in Australian English and other Englishes. *English World-Wide* 26(3): 279–273.

Comrie, B. (1976) *Aspect: An Introduction to the Study of Verbal Aspect and Related Problems*. Cambridge: Cambridge University Press.

Conradie, C.J. (1987) Semantic change in modal auxiliaries as a result of speech act embedding, in M.B. Harris and P. Ramat (eds), *Historical Development of Auxiliaries*. Berlin: Mouton de Gruyter, pp. 171–189.

Cornips, L. and Corrigan, K. (eds) (2005) *Syntax and Variation: Reconciling the Biological and the Social*. Amsterdam/Philadelphia: John Benjamins.

Cornips, L. and Nortier, J. (2008) Losing grammatical gender in Dutch: The result of bilingual acquisition and/or an act of identity? *Journal of Bilingualism* 12(1 and 2): 105–120.

Corrigan, K.P. (2000) "What bees to be maun be": Aspects of deontic and epistemic modality in a Northern Dialect of Irish English. *English World-Wide* 21(2): 25–62.

Craigie, W.A., Aitken, A.J., Templeton, J.M., *et al.* (eds) (1937–) *Dictionary of the Older Scottish Tongue*. Chicago: University of Chicago Press.

Cravens, T.D. and Giannelli, L. (1995) Relative salience of gender and class in a situation of multiple competing norms. *Language Variation and Change* 7(2): 261–285.

Crystal, D. (1995) *The Cambridge Encyclopedia of the English Language*. Cambridge: Cambridge University Press.

Crystal, D. (2001) *Language and the Internet*. Cambridge: Cambridge University Press.

Cukor-Avila, P. (1995) *The Evolution of AAVE in a Rural Texas Community: An Ethnolinguistic Study*. PhD dissertation, University of Michigan.

Cukor-Avila, P. (1997) Change and stability in the use of verbal -*s* over time in AAVE, in E.W. Schneider (ed.), *Englishes around the World*. Amsterdam and Philadelphia: John Benjamins, pp. 295–306.

Cukor-Avila, P. (1999) Stativity and copula absence in AAVE: Grammatical constraints at the subcategorical level. *Journal of English Linguistics* 27(4): 341–355.

Cukor-Avila, P. (2002) *She say, She go, She be like:* Verbs of quotation over time in African American vernacular English. *American Speech* 77(1): 3–31.

Curme, G.O. (1913) Has English a future tense? *Journal of English and Germanic Philology* 12(4): 515–539.

Curme, G.O. (1931) *A Grammar of the English Language, III, Syntax*. Boston: DC: Heath.

Curme, G.O. (1977) *A Grammar of the English Language*. Essex, Connecticut: Verbatim.

Cutler, C.A. (1999) Yorkville Crossing: White teens, hip hop and African American English. *Journal of Sociolinguistics* 3(4): 428–442.

D'Arcy, A. (2004) Contextualizing St. John's Youth English within the Canadian quotative system. *Journal of English Linguistics* 32(4): 323–345.

D'Arcy, A. (2005a) *Like: Syntax and Development*. PhD dissertation, University of Toronto.

D'Arcy, A. (2005b) Tracking the development of discourse "like" in contemporary (Canadian) English. *Doctoral thesis proposal*. Toronto, Canada, March 16, 2005.

D'Arcy, A. (2006) Lexical replacement and the like(s). *American Speech* 81(4): 339–357.

D'Arcy, A. and Tagliamonte, S.A. (2008) Prestige, accommodation and the legacy of relative "who." *Language in Society* 39(2): 383–410.

Dailey-O'Cain, J. (2000) The distribution of and attitudes towards focuser *like* and quotative *like*. *Journal of Sociolinguistics* 4(1): 60–80.

Danchev, A. and Kytö, M. (1994) The construnction *be going to* + infinitive in Early Modern English, in D. Kastovsky (ed.), *Studies in Early Modern English*. Berlin: Mouton de Gruyter, pp. 59–77.

Davydova, J. (2009) *The Present Perfect: A Corpus-based Study of Variation across Non-native Englishes*. PhD dissertation, University of Hamburg.

Dayton, E. (1996) *Grammatical Categories of the Verb in African-American Vernacular English*. PhD, University of Pennsylvania.

Denison, D. (1993) *English Historical Syntax*. Harlow, Essex: Longman.

Dickens, B. and Wilson, R.M. (eds) (1969) *Early Middle English Texts*. Bowes & Bowes: Cambridge.

Diewald, G. (2002) A model for relevant types of contexts in grammaticalization, in I. Wischer and G. Diewald (eds), *New Reflections on Grammaticalization*. Amsterdam and Philadelphia: John Benjamins. 103–120.

Dines, E.R. (1980) Variation in discourse and stuff like that. *Language in Society* 9(1): 13–33.

Dion, N. and Poplack, S. (2007) Linguistic mythbusting: The role of the media in diffusing change. *New Ways of Analyzing Variation (NWAVE) 36*. University of Pennsylvania, Philadelphia, PA.

Dixon, R.M.W. (1977) Where have all the adjectives gone? *Studies in Language* 1(1): 19–80.

Docherty, G. and Foulkes, P. (1999) Newcastle and Derby: Instrumental phonetics and variationist studies, in G. Docherty and P. Foulkes (eds), *Urban Voices: Accent Studies in the British Isles*. London: Arnold, pp. 47–71.

Docherty, G. and Foulkes, P. (2000) Speaker, speech and knowledge of sounds, in N. Burton-Roberts, P. Carr, and G. Docherty (eds), *Phonological Knowledge: Conceptual and Empirical Issues*. Oxford: Oxford University Press. 103–129.

Docherty, G. and Foulkes, P. (2005) Glottal variants of /t/ in the Tyneside variety of English, in W.J. Hardcastle and J. Mackenzie Beck (eds), *A Figure of Speech: A Festschrift for John Laver*. Mahwah: Lawrence Erlbaum Associates, pp. 173–199.

Docherty, G., Foulkes, P., Dodd, B., and Milroy, L. (2002) *The Emergence of Structured Variation in the Speech of Tyneside Infants*. Newcastle: University of Newcastle.

Docherty, G., Foulkes, P., Milroy, J., *et al.* (1997) Descriptive adequacy in phonology: A variationist perspective. *Journal of Linguistics* 33(2): 275–310.

Dollinger, S. (2008) *New-Dialect Formation in Canada: Evidence from the English Modal Auxiliary System*. Amsterdam: John Benjamins.

Donner, M. (1991) Adverb form in Middle English. *English Studies* 72: 1–11.

Downes, W. (1984) *Language and Society*. London: Fontana Press.

Downes, W. (1998) *Language and Society*, 2nd edition. Cambridge: Cambridge University Press.

Drager, K. and Hay, J. (2010) A novice's guide to mixed effects modeling. Presented at the Statistical Tools Workshop. *NWAV 39*. San Antonio, Texas, November 3–6, 2010.

Dubois, S. (1992) Extension particles, etc. *Language Variation and Change* 4(2): 163–203.

Dubois, S. and Horvath, B.M. (1998) Let's tink about dat: Interdental fricatives in Cajun English. *Language Variation and Change* 10(3): 245–261.

Dubois, S. and Horvath, B.M. (1999) When the music changes, you change too: Gender and language change in Cajun English. *Language Variation and Change* 11(3): 287–314.

Dubois, S. and Horvath, B.M. (2007) Creoles and Cajuns: A portrait in Black and White. *American Speech* 78: 192–207.

Eckert, P. (1988) Adolescent social structure and the spread of linguistic change. *Language in Society* 17(2): 183–207.

Eckert, P. (1989) The whole woman: Sex and gender differences in variation. *Language Variation and Change* 1(3): 245–267.

Eckert, P. (1999) New generalizations and explanation in language and gender research. *Language in Society* 28(2): 185–202.

Eckert, P. (2000) *Language Variation as Social Practice*. Oxford and Malden: Blackwell.

Eckert, P. (2008) Variation and the indexical field. *Journal of Sociolinguistics* 12: 453–476.

Eckert, P. and Rickford, J.R. (2001) *Style and Sociolinguistic Variation*. Cambridge: Cambridge University Press.

Edwards, V. and Weltens, B. (1985) Research on non-standard dialects of British English: Progress and prospects, in W. Viereck (ed.), *Focus on England and Wales*. Amsterdam and Philadelphia: John Benjamins, pp. 97–139.

Eisikovits, E. (1987) Variation in the lexical verb in Inner-Sydney English. *Australian Journal of Linguistics* 7: 1–24.

El Salman, M. (2003) The use of the [q] variat in the Arabic Dialect of Itrat Haifa. *Anthropological Linguistics* 45(4): 413–425.

Ellegård, A. (1953) *The Auxiliary Do: The Establishment and Regulation of Its Use in English*. Stockholm: Almqvist & Wikwell.

Elsness, J. (1984) *That* or zero? A look at the choice of object clause connective in a corpus of American English. *English Studies* 65: 519–533.

Elsness, J. (1989) The English present perfect: Has it seen better days?, in L.E. Breivik, A. Hille, and S. Johansson (eds), *Essays on English Language in Honour of Bertil Sundby*. Oslo: Novus Forlag, pp. 95–106.

Elsness, J. (1997) *The Perfect and the Preterite in Contemporary and Earlier English*. Berlin: Mouton de Gruyter.

Emma, R.D. (1964) *Milton's Grammar*. The Hague: Mouton & Co.

Erker, D. and Guy, G. (2010) Exemplar theory and variable syntax: how lexical frequency conditions subject pronoun use in Spanish. *NWAV* 39, November 4–6. San Antonio, Texas.

Erman, B. (1995) Grammaticalization in progress; The case of *or something*, in I. Moen, H. Gram Simonsen, and H. Lødrup (eds), *Papers from the XVth Scandinavian Conference of Linguistics, Oslo, January 13–15, 1995*. Oslo, Norway: Department of Linguistics, University of Oslo, pp. 136–147.

Fabricius, A.H. (2002) Ongoing change in modern RP: Evidence for the disappearing stigma of t-glottaling. *English World-wide* 23(1): 115–136.

Facchinetti, R., Krug, M., and Palmer, F. (eds) (2003) *Modality in Contemporary English*. Berlin and New York: Mouton de Gruyter.

Fasold, R. (1969) Tense and the form *be* in Black English. *Language* 45(4): 763–776.

Fasold, R. (1971) Minding your z's and d's: Distinguishing syntactic and phonological variable rules. *Papers from the Seventh Regional Meeting, Chicago Linguistic Society*: Chicago, pp. 360–367.

Fasold, R. (1972) *Tense Marking in Black English: A Linguistic and Social Analysis*. Washington, DC: Center for Applied Linguistics.

Fasold, R. (1984) *The Sociolinguistics of Society*. Oxford: Blackwell.

Fasold, R. (1990) *Sociolinguistics of Language*. Cambridge, MA: Blackwell.

Fasold, R. (2004) Language change and variation in formal syntax, in D. Preston (ed.), *Needed Research in American Dialects*. Durham, N.C.: Duke University Press, pp. 223–247.

Feagin, C. (1979) *Variation and Change in Alabama English: A Sociolinguistic Study of the White Community*. Washington, DC: Georgetown University Press.

Feagin, C. (1991) Preverbal *done* in Southern States English, in P. Trudgill and J.K. Chambers (eds), *Preverbal Done in Southern States English*. Dialects of English: Studies in Grammatical Variation: London and New York, pp. 161–190.

Feagin, C. (1997) The African contribution to southern states English, in C. Bernstein, T. Nunnally, and R. Sabino (eds), *Language Variety in the South Revisited*. Tuscaloosa: University of Alabama Press, pp. 123–139.

Federal Writers' Project (1941) *Slave Narratives: A Folk History of Slavery in the United States from Interviews with Former Slaves*. Washington, DC: Federal Writers' Project.

Fenn, P. (1987) *A Semantic and Pragmatic Examination of the English Perfect*. Tübingen: Gunter Narr.

Ferrara, K. and Bell, B. (1995) Sociolinguistic variation and discourse function of constructed dialogue introducers: The case of be+like. *American Speech* 70(3): 265–289.

Ferrara, K., Brunner, H., and Whittemore, G. (1991) Interactive written discourse as an emergent register. *Written Communication* 8(1): 8–34.

Finegan, E. and Biber, D. (1995) *That* and zero complementisers in late Modern English, in B. Aarts and C. Meyer (eds), *The Verb in Contemporary English*. Cambridge: Cambridge University Press, pp. 241–257.

Finnegan, F.E. (1982) *Poverty and Prejudice: A Study of Irish Immigrants in York, 1840–75*. Cork: Cork University Press.

Fischer, D.H. (1989) *Albion's Seed: Four British Folkways in America*. New York and Oxford: Oxford University Press.

Fischer, O. and Rosenbach, A. (2000) Introduction, in O. Fischer, A. Rosenbach and D. Stein (eds), *Pathways of Change: Grammaticalization in English*. Amsterdam and Philadelphia: John Benjamins.

Fisher, J.L. (1958) Social influences on the choice of a linguistic variant. *Word* 14(1): 47–56.

Fought, C. (1999) A majority sound change in a minority community: /u/-fronting in Chicano English. *Journal of Sociolinguistics* 3(1): 5–23.

Fought, C. (2002) Ethnicity, in J.K. Chambers, P. Trudgill, and N. Schilling-Estes (eds), *The Handbook of Language Variation and Change*. Malden and Oxford: Blackwell.

Foulkes, P. (1998) English [r]-sandhi – a sociolinguistic perspective. *Leeds Working Papers in Linguistics and Phonetics* 6: 18–39.

Foulkes, P. (2006) Phonological variation: A global perspective, in B. Aarts and A. McMahon (eds), *Handbook of English Linguistics*. Oxford: Blackwell, pp. 625–669.

Foulkes, P. and Docherty, G. (eds) (1999) *Urban Voices*. London: Arnold.

Foulkes, P. and Docherty, G. (2000) Another chapter in the story of /r/: "labiodental" variants in British English. *Journal of Sociolinguistics* 4(1): 30–59.

Foulkes, P. and Docherty, G. (2006) The social life of phonetics and phonology. *Journal of Phonetics* 34(4): 409–438.

Foulkes, P., Docherty, G., and Watt, D. (1999) Tracking the emergence of structured variation; realisations of (t) by Newcastle children. *Leeds Working Papers in Linguistics*: 1–18.

Foulkes, P., Docherty, G., and Watt, D. (2005) Phonological variation in child-directed speech. *Language* 81(1): 177–206.

Fox, S. and Cheshire, J. (2009) A "youth" variety or long-term language change? An investigation of a multiracial vernacular. *New Ways of Analyzing Variation (NWAVE)*. University of Ottawa, Ottawa, Ontario, Canada, October 22–25, 2009.

Fridén, G. (1948) *Studies on the Tenses of the English Verb from Chaucer to Shakespeare with Special Reference to the Late Sixteenth Century*. Uppsala: Almqvist & Wiksells Boktryckeri AB.

Fries, C.C. (1925) The periphrastic future with "shall" and "will" in modern English. *Publications of the Modern Linguistic Association of America* 40: 963ff.

Fries, C.C. (1940) *American English Grammar*. New York: Appleton, Century, Crofts.

Gagnon, S. (1990) Future proche, futur éloigné: Problème terminologique et didactique. *Langues et Linguistique* 16: 253–258.

Gauchat, L. (1905) L'unité phonétique dans le patois d'une commune. *Aus romanischen sprachen und literaturen: Festschrift Heinrich Mort.* 175–232.

Gentner, D., Holyoak, K.J., and Kokinov, B.K. (eds) (2001) *The Analogical Mind: Perspectives from Cognitive Science.* Cambridge, MA: MIT Press.

Givón, T. (1990) *A Functional-Typological Introduction. Vol 2.* Amsterdam: John Benjamins.

Godfrey, E. and Tagliamonte, S.A. (1999) Another piece for the verbal *-s* story: Evidence from Devon in Southwest England. *Language Variation and Change* 11(1): 87–121.

Gold, E. (2005) Canadian *eh?*: A survey of contemporary use, in M.-O. Junker, M. McGinnis, and Y. Roberge (eds), *Proceedings of the 2004 Canadian Linguistics Association Annual Conference.*

Gordon, E., Campbell, L., Maclagan, M. *et al.* (2004) *New Zealand English: Its Origins and Evolution.* Cambridge: Cambridge University Press.

Gordon, E. and Hay, J. (2008) *New Zealand English.* Edinburgh: Edinburgh University Press.

Gordon, M. (2006) Interview with William Labov. *Journal of English Linguistics* 34(4): 332–351.

Greenough, J.B. and Kittredge, G.L. (1901) *Words and Their Ways in English Speech.* New York: Macmillan.

Gregersen, F., Maegaard, M., and Pharao, N. (2009) The long and short of (Æ)-variation in Danish – a panel study of short (Æ)-variants in Danish in real time. *Acta Linguistica Hafniensia* 41(1): 64–82.

Gries, S.T. (2009a) *Quantitative Corpus Linguistics with R: a Practical Introduction.* London and New York: Routledge, Taylor & Francis Group.

Gries, S.T. (2009b) *Statistics for Linguistics with R.* Berlin/New York: Mouton de Gruyter.

Gries, S.T. (2010) Useful statistics for corpus linguistics, in M. Almela (ed.), *New Horizons in Corpus Linguistics.* Frankfurt am Main: Peter Lang.

Gries, S.T. and David, C.V. (2007) This is *kind of/sort of* interesting: Variation in hedging in English, in P. Pahta, I. Taavitsainen, T. Nevalainen, and J. Tyrkköö (eds), *Towards Multimedia in Corpus Linguistics. Studies in Variation, Contacts and Change in English 2.* Helsinki: University of Helsinki.

Grondelaers, S., Speelman, D., Drieghe, D. *et al.* (2009) Introducing a new entity into discourse: Comprehension and production evidence for the status of Dutch er "there" as a higher-level expectancy monitor. *Acta Psychologica* 130: 153–160.

Guy, G.R. (1980) Variation in the group and the individual: The case of final stop deletion, in W. Labov (ed.), *Locating Language in Time and Space.* New York: Academic Press, pp. 1–36.

Guy, G.R. (1988) Advanced VARBRUL analysis, in K. Ferrara, B. Brown, K. Walters, and J. Baugh (eds), *Linguistic Change and Contact.* Austin, Texas: Department of Linguistics, University of Texas at Austin. 124–136.

Guy, G.R. (1991a) Contextual conditioning in variable lexical phonology. *Language Variation and Change* 3(2): 223–239.

Guy, G.R. (1991b) Explanation in variable phonology: An exponential model of morphological constraints. *Language Variation and Change* 3(1): 1–22.

Guy, G.R. (1993) The quantitative analysis of linguistic variation, in D. Preston (ed.), *American Dialect Research.* Amsterdam and Philadelphia: John Benjamins, pp. 223–249.

Guy, G.R. (1997) Competence, performance, and the generative grammar of variation, in F. Hinskens, R. Van Hout, and W.L. Wetzels (eds), *Variation, Change, and Phonological Theory.* Amsterdam and Philadelphia: John Benjamins, pp. 125–143.

Guy, G.R. and Boberg, C. (1997) Inherent variability and the Obligatory Contour Principle. *Language Variation and Change* 9(2): 149–164.

Guy, G.R. and Boyd, S. (1990) The development of a morphological class. *Language Variation and Change* 2(1): 1–18.

Hacket, S. (2008) Counting and coding the past: Circumscribing the variable context in quantitative analyses of past inflection. *Language Variation and Change* 20(1): 127–153.

Haegeman, L. (1981) *The Use of Will and the Expression of Futurity in Present-day British English. Part 1: Future Time Expression in a Corpus of Standard British English*. DPhil. dissertation, University College, London.

Haegeman, L. and Guéron, J. (1999) *English Grammar: A Generative Perspective*. Oxford: Blackwell.

Harley, H. (2004) Why is it the CIA but not the NASA? *American Speech* 79(4): 368–399.

Harris, A. and Campbell, L. (1995) *Historical Syntax in Cross-linguistic Perspective*. Cambridge: Cambridge University Press.

Harris, J. (1984) Syntactic variation and dialect divergence. *Journal of Linguistics* 20(2): 303–327.

Harris, J. (1986) Expanding the superstrate: Habitual aspect markers in Atlantic Englishes. *English World-Wide* 7(2): 171–199.

Hawkins, J. (1994) *A Performance Theory of Order and Constituency*. Cambridge: Cambridge University Press.

Hay, J. (2006a) Modelling sociophonetic variation. *Journal of Phonetics* 34(4): 405–408.

Hay, J. (2006b) Spoken syntax: The phonetics of giving a hand in New Zealand English. *The Linguistic Review* 23(3): 321–349.

Hay, J. (2011) Statistical analysis, in M. Di Paolo and M. Yaeger-Dror (eds), *Sociophonetics: A Student Handbook*. London and New York: Routledge.

Hay, J., Nolan, A., and Drager, K. (2006) From fush to feesh: Exemplar priming in speech perception. *The Linguistic Review* 23(3): 351–379.

Hay, J. and Schreier, D. (2004) Reversing the trajectory of language change; Subject-verb agreement with *be* in New Zealand English. *Language Variation and Change* 16(3): 209–235.

Hazen, K. (2002) Identity and language variation in a rural community. *Language* 78(2): 240–257.

Hedevind, B. (1967) *The Dialect of Dentdale in the West Riding of Yorkshire*. Stockholm: Almquist & Wiksell.

Heine, B. (1993) *Auxiliaries: Cognitive Forces and Grammaticalization*. Oxford: Oxford University Press.

Heine, B., Claudi, U., and Hünnemeyer, F. (1991) *Grammaticalization: A Conceptual Framework*. Chicago: The University of Chicago Press.

Henry, A. (1995) *Belfast English and Standard English: Dialect Variation and Parameter Setting*. New York and Oxford: Oxford University Press.

Henry, A. (1998) Parameter setting within a socially realistic linguistics. *Language in Society* 27(1): 1–21.

Hentschel, E. (1998) Communication on IRC. *Linguistik Online*. 1/98. http://www.linguistik-online. de/ (accessed April 4, 2011).

Hermann, M.E. (1929) Lautveränderungen in der individualsprache einer Mundart. *Nachrichten der gesellschaft der wissenschaften zu Göttingen, Philosophisch-historische Klasse* 11: 195–214.

Herring, S.C. (ed.) (1996a) *Computer-mediated Communication*. Amsterdam and Philadephia: John Benjamins.

Herring, S.C. (1996b) Introduction, in S.C. Herring (ed.), *Computer-Mediated Communication*. Amsterdam and Philadelphia: John Benjamins, pp. 1–28.

Herring, S.C. (2001) Computer-mediated discourse, in D. Schiffrin, D. Tannen, and H. Hamilton (eds), *The Handbook of Discourse Analysis*. Oxford: Blackwell, pp. 612–634.

Herring, S.C. (2003) Gender and power in on-line communication, in J. Holmes and M. Meyerhoff (eds), *The Handbook of Language and Gender*. Malden: Blackwell, pp. 202–228.

Herring, S.C. (2004) Slouching toward the ordinary: Current trends in computer-mediated communication. 6(1): 26–36.

Hickey, R. (ed.) (2004) *Legacies of Colonial English: Studies in Transported Dialects*. Cambridge: Cambridge University Press.

Hock, H.H. (1986) *Principles of Historical Linguistics*. Amsterdam: Mouton de Gruyter.

Hock, H.H. (1991) *Principles of Historical Linguistics*. Berlin and New York: Mouton de Gruyter.

Hock, H.H. and Joseph, B.D. (1996) *Language History, Language Change, Language Relationship: An Introduction to Historical and Comparative Linguistics*. Berlin and New York: Mouton de Gruyter.

Hoenigswald, H.M. (1960) *Language Change and Linguistic Reconstruction*. Chicago: University of Chicago Press.

Hogg, R.M. (1988) "Snuck": The development of irregular preterite forms, in G. Nixon and J. Honey (eds), *An Historic Tongue: Studies in English Linguistics in Memory of Barbara Strang*. London: Routledge, pp. 31–40.

Hogg, R.M. (1992) Phonology and morphology, in R.M. Hogg (ed.), *Cambridge History of the English Language: Volume 1: The Beginnings to 1066*. Cambridge: Cambridge University Press, pp. 67–164.

Holm, J. (1975/1984) Variability of the copula in Black English and its creole kin. *American Speech* 59(4): 291–309.

Holmes, J. (1992) *An Introduction to Sociolinguistics*. London and New York: Longman.

Holmes, J. (2001) *An introduction to Sociolinguistics*. London and New York: Longman.

Hopkins, T. (1994) Variation in the use of the auxiliary verb *da* in contemporary Gullah, in M. Montgomery (ed.), *The Crucible of Carolina*. Athens, Georgia: University of Georgia Press, pp. 60–86.

Hopper, P.J. (1991) On some principles of grammaticization, in E.C. Traugott and B. Heine (eds), *Approaches to Grammaticalization, Volume 1: Focus on Theoretical and Methodological Issues*. Amsterdam and Philadelphia: John Benjamins, pp. 17–35.

Hopper, P.J. and Traugott, E.C. (1993) *Grammaticalization*. Cambridge: Cambridge University Press.

Horvath, B.M. (1985) *Variation in Australian English*. Cambridge: Cambridge University Press.

Horvath, B.M. and Horvath, R.J. (2003) A closer look at the constraint hierarchy: Order, contrast, and geographical scale. *Language Variation and Change* 15(2): 143–170.

Houston, A. (1985) *Continuity and Change in English Morphology: The Variable (ing)*. PhD dissertation, University of Pennsylvania.

Huddleston, R. and Pullum, G.K. (2002) *The Cambridge Grammar of the English Language*. Cambridge: Cambridge University Press.

Hughes, A. and Trudgill, P. (1987) *English Accents and Dialects*. London: Edward Arnold.

Hundt, M. and Mair, C. (1999) "Agile" and "uptight" genres: The corpus-based approach to language change in progress. *International Journal of Corpus Linguistics* 4(2): 221–242.

Ito, R. and Tagliamonte, S.A. (2003) *Well weird, right dodgy, very strange, really cool:* Layering and recycling in English intensifiers. *Language in Society* 32(2): 257–279.

Jaeger, T.F. (2005) Optional that indicates production difficulty: Evidence from disfluencies. *Proceedings of DiSS'05, Disfluency in Spontaneous Speech Workshop*. Aix-en-Provence, France, September 10–12, 2005, pp. 103–109.

Jaeger, T.F. (2008) Categorical Data Analysis: Away from ANOVAs (transformation or not) and towards Logit Mixed Models. *Journal of Memory and Language, Special issue on Emerging Data Analysis* 59: 434–446.

Jaeger, T.F. (2010) Redundancy and reduction: Speakers manage syntactic information density. *Cognitive Psychology* 61(1): 23–62.

Jankowski, B.L. (2004) A transatlantic perspective of variation and change in English deontic modality. *Toronto Working Papers in Linguistics* 23: 85–114.

Jensen, T.J. (2009) Generic variation? Development in use of generic pronouns in late 20th century spoken Danish. *Acta Linguistica Hafniensia* 41(1): 83–115.

Jeremiah, M.A. (1977) *The Linguistic Relatedness of Black English and Antiguan Creole: Evidence from the Eighteenth and Nineteenth Centuries*. PhD dissertation, Brown University.

Jespersen, O.H. (1924) *The Philosophy of Grammar*. London: George Allen & Unwin.

Jespersen, O.H. (1940) *A Modern English Grammar on Historical Principles: Part V: Syntax*. London: George Allen & Unwin.

Jespersen, O.H. (1961a) *A Modern English Grammar on Historical Principles: Part I: Sounds and Spellings*. London and Copenhagen: George Allen & Unwin/Ejnar Munksgaard.

Jespersen, O.H. (1961b) *A Modern English Grammar on Historical Principles: Part VI: Morphology*. London: Bradford & Dickens. 14–23.

Jespersen, O.H. (1964) *Essentials of English Grammar*. Alabama: University of Alabama Press.

Johnson, D.E. (2009) Getting off the GoldVarb standard: Introducing Rbrul for mixed effects variable rule analysis. *Language and Linguistics Compass* 3(1): 359–383.

Johnson, D.E. (2010) Rbrul manual. http://www.danielezrajohnson.com/Rbrul.R.

Johnstone, B. (1987) "He says ... so I said": Verb tense alternation and narrative depictions of authority in American English. *Linguistics* 25: 33–52.

Johnstone, B. (1990) Variation in discourse: Midwestern narrative style. *American Speech* 65(3): 195–214.

Jones, G.M. and Schieffelin, B.B. (2009) Enquoting voices, accomplishing talk: Uses of *be* + *like* in Instant Messaging. *Language and Communication* 29(1): 77–113.

Jones, M. and Tagliamonte, S.A. (2004) From Somerset to Samaná: pre-verbal *did* in the voyage of English. *Language Variation and Change* 16(2): 93–126.

José, B. (2007) Appalachian English in southern Indiana: The evidence from verbal -s. *Language Variation and Change* 19: 249–280.

Joseph, B. (2001) Is there such a thing as grammaticalization? *Language Sciences* 23(2): 163–186.

Joseph, B. (2004) Rescuing traditional (historical) linguistics from grammaticalization theory, in O. Fischer, M. Norde, and H. Perridon (eds), *Up and Down the Cline: The Nature of Grammaticalization*. Amsterdam and Philadelphia: John Benjamins, pp. 45–69.

Joseph, B.D. and Janda, R.D. (2003a) On language, change, and language change – or, of history, linguistics, and historical linguistics, in B.D. Joseph and R.D. Janda (eds), *The Handbook of Historical Linguistics*. Malden and Oxford: Blackwell, pp. 3–180.

Joseph, B.D. and Janda, R.D. (2003b) *The Handbook of Historical Linguistics*. Malden and Oxford: Blackwell.

Kemenade, A. van (1997) V2 and embedded topicalization in Old and Middle English, in A. Kemenade and N. Vincent (eds), *Parameters of Morphosyntactic Change*. Cambridge: Cambridge University Press.

Kerswill, P. (1994) *Dialects Converging: Rural Speech in Urban Norway*. Oxford: Clarendon Press.

Kerswill, P. (1995) Children, adolescents and language change, in P. Kerswill, R. Ingham, Y. Huang and L. Shockey (eds), *Reading Working Paper in Linguistics*. Reading: Department of Linguistic Science, University of Reading, pp. 68–90.

Kerswill, P. (1996a) Children, adolescents, and language change. *Language Variation and Change* 8(2): 177–202.

Kerswill, P. (1996b) Milton Keynes and dialect levelling in south-eastern British English, in L. Graddol and S. Swann (eds), *English: History, Diversity and Change*. London: Routledge.

Kerswill, P. (2003) Dialect levelling and geographical diffusion in British English, in D. Britain and J. Cheshire (eds), *Social Dialectology: In Honour of Peter Trudgill*. Amsterdam and Philadelphia: John Benjamins.

Kerswill, P. (2009a) Community type, dialect contact and change. *LSA Summer Institute 2009*. Berkeley, California, USA.

Kerswill, P. (2009b) Endogeny, exogeny, ideology and community typology: modelling linguistic innovation, levelling and conservatism in a monolingual Old World society. *UK-LVC 7*. Newcastle, England, September 1–3, 2009.

Kerswill, P., Torgersen, Eivind N., and Fox, S. (2008) Reversing "drift": Innovation and diffusion in the London diphthong system. *Language Variation and Change* 20(3): 451–491.

Kerswill, P. and Williams, A. (2000) Creating a new town koine: Children and language change in Milton Keynes. *Language in Society* 29(1): 65–115.

Koerner, K. (1991) Toward a history of modern sociolinguistics. *American Speech* 66(1): 57–70.

Kotsinas, U.-B. (2001) Pidginization, creolization, and creoloids in Stockholm, in N. Smith and T. Veenstra (eds), *Creolization and Contact*. Amsterdam: John Benjamins.

Kroch, A.S. (1978) Toward a theory of social dialect variation. *Language in Society* 7(1): 17–36.

Kroch, A.S. (1989) Reflexes of grammar in patterns of language change. *Language Variation and Change* 1(3): 199–244.

Kroch, A.S. (2003) Syntactic change, in M. Baltin and C. Collins (eds), *The Handbook of Contemporary Syntactic Theory*. Malden and Oxford: Blackwell.

Kroch, A.S. and Taylor, A. (1997) Verb movement in Old and Middle English: Dialect variation and language contact, in A. van Kemenade and N. Vincent (eds), *Parameters of Morphosyntactic Change*. Cambridge: Cambridge University Press. 297–325.

Krug, M. (1998) *Gotta* – the tenth central modal in English? Social, stylistic and regional variation in the British National Corpus as evidence of ongoing grammaticalization, in H. Lindquist, S. Klintborg, M. Levin, and M. Estling (eds), *The Major Varieties of English*. Växjö: Växjö University, pp. 177–191.

Krug, M. (2000) *Emerging English Modals: A Corpus-based Study of Grammaticalization*. Berlin and New York: Mouton de Gruyter.

Krygier, M. (1994) *The Disintegration of the English Strong Verb System*. Frankfurt: Lang.

Kurath, H. (1928) The origin of the dialectal differences in spoken American English. *Modern Philology* 25: 385–395.

Kurath, H. (1939) *Handbook of the Linguistic Geography of New England*. Providence, RI: Brown University.

Kurath, H. (1949) *A Word Geography of the Eastern United States*. Ann Arbor: University of Michigan Press.

Kurath, H. (1964) British sources of selected features of American pronunciation: Problems and methods, in D. Abercrombie, D.B. Fry, P. MacCarthy, *et al.* (eds), *In Honour of Daniel Jones: Papers Contributed on the Occasion of His Eightieth Birthday 12 September 1961*. London: Longmans, pp. 146–155.

Kurylowicz, J. (1965) The evolution of grammatical categories. *Diogenes* 51: 55–71.

Labov, W. (1963) The social motivation of a sound change. *Word* 19: 273–309.

Labov, W. (1966) *The Social Stratification of English in New York City*. Washington, DC: Center for Applied Linguistics.

Labov, W. (1969) Contraction, deletion, and inherent variability of the English copula. *Language* 45(4): 715–762.

Labov, W. (1970) The study of language in its social context. *Studium Generale* 23(1): 30–87.

Labov, W. (1971) Some principles of linguistic methodology. *Language in Society* 1(1): 97–120.

Labov, W. (1972a) *Language in the Inner City*. Philadelphia: University of Pennsylvania Press.

Labov, W. (1972b) Negative attraction and negative concord in English grammar. *Language* 48: 773–818.

Labov, W. (1972c) *Sociolinguistic Patterns*. Philadelphia: University of Pennsylvania Press.

Labov, W. (ed.) (1980a) *Locating Language in Time and Space*. New York: Academic Press.

Labov, W. (1980b) The social origins of sound change, in W. Labov (ed.), *Locating Language in Time and Space*. New York: Academic Press, pp. 251–265.

Labov, W. (1981) Resolving the neogrammarian controversy. *Language* 57(2): 267–308.

Labov, W. (1982) Building on empirical foundations, in W.P. Lehmann and Y. Malkiel (eds), *Perspectives on Historical Linguistics*. Amsterdam and Philadelphia: John Benjamins, pp. 17–92.

Labov, W. (1985) Intensity, in D. Schiffrin (ed.), *Meaning, Form and Use in Context: Linguistic Applications*. Washington, D: Georgetown University Press, pp. 43–70.

Labov, W. (1989) The child as linguistic historian. *Language Variation and Change* 1(1): 85–97.

Labov, W. (1990) The intersection of sex and social class in the course of linguistic change. *Language Variation and Change* 2(2): 205–254.

Labov, W. (1991) The three dialects of English, in P. Eckert (ed.), *New Ways of Analyzing Sound Change*. New York: Academic Press, pp. 1–44.

Labov, W. (1994) *Principles of Linguistic Change: Volume 1: Internal Factors*. Cambridge and Oxford: Blackwell.

Labov, W. (1997) Resyllabification, in F. Hinskens, R. Van Hout, and W.L. Wetzels (eds), *Variation, Change, and Phonological Theory*. Amsterdam and Philadelphia: John Benjamins, pp. 145–179.

Labov, W. (2001a) *Principles of Linguistic Change: Volume 2: Social Factors*. Malden and Oxford: Blackwell.

Labov, W. (2001b) The anatomy of style-shifting, in P. Eckert and J.R. Rickford (eds), *Style and Sociolinguistic Variation*. Cambridge: Cambridge University Press, pp. 85–108.

Labov, W. (2007) Transmission and diffusion. *Language* 83(2): 344–387.

Labov, W. (2010) *Principles of Linguistic Change: Volume 3: Cognitive and Cultural Factors*. Malden and Oxford: Wiley-Blackwell.

Labov, W., Cohen, P., Robins, C., and Lewis, J. (1968) A study of the non-standard English of Negro and Puerto Rican speakers in New York City. Philadelphia: U.S. Regional Survey.

Labov, W. and Waletzky, J. (1967) Narrative analysis: Oral versions of personal experience, in J. Helm (ed.), *Essays on the Verbal and Visual Arts*. Seattle: University of Washington Press, pp. 12–44.

Labov, W., Yaeger, M., and Steiner, R. (1972) A quantitative study of sound change in progress. Philadelphia: U.S. Regional Survey.

Lass, R. (1992) Phonology and morphology, in N. Blake (ed.), *The Cambridge History of the English Language*. Cambridge: Cambridge University Press, pp. 23–154.

Lavandera, B.R. (1978) Where does the sociolinguistic variable stop? *Language in Society* 7(2): 171–183.

Lawson, E. and Stuart-Smith, J. (1999) A sociophonetic investigation of the 'Scottish' consonants (/x/ and /w/) in the speech of Glaswegian children. *Proceedings of the 14th International Congress of Phonetic Sciences*, pp. 2641–2544.

Le Page, R.B. and Tabouret-Keller, A. (1985) *Acts of Identity: Creole-based Approaches to Language and Ethnicity*. Cambridge: Cambridge University Press.

Lee, J. (2002) Nu shortcuts in school R 2 much 4 teachers. *The New York Times*, September 19, 2002.

Leech, G.N. (1971) *Meaning and the English Verb*. London: Longman.

Leech, G.N. (1987) *Meaning and the English Verb*. New York: Longman.

Leech, G.N. (2003) Modality on the move: The English modal auxiliaries 1961–1992, in R. Facchinette, M. Krug, and F. Palmer (eds), *Modality in Contemporary English*. Berlin and New York: Mouton de Gruyter. 223–240.

Leech, G.N. and Svartvik, J. (1975) *A Communicative Grammar of English*. London: Longman.

Leeds, W. (1974) *Herefordshire Speech: The South-west Midland Dialect as Spoken in Herefordshire and Its Environs*. Upton Crews: M. Spurway.

Lehmann, W. (1973) *Historical Linguistics*. New York: Holt, Rinehart & Winston.

Lenhart, A., Rainie, L., and Lewis, O. (2001) Teenage life online: The rise of the instant-message generation and the internet's impact on friendships and family relationships. Pew Internet and American Life Project.

Levey, S. (2007) *The Next Generation: Aspects of Grammatical Variation in the Speech of Some London Preadolescents*. Unpublished PhD dissertation. Queen Mary, University of London.

Liddle, R. (1999) A comparative study of the dual-form adverb lexemes *quick* and *slow*. Växjö, Sweden: Växjö University.

Lightfoot, D. (1979) *Principles of Diachronic Syntax*. Cambridge: Cambridge University Press.

Long, M.M. (1944) *The English Strong Verb from Chaucer to Caxton*. Menasha, Wisconsin: George Banta.

Lopez Couso, M.J. (1996) A look at *that/zero* variation in restoration English, in D. Britton (ed.), *English Historical Linguistics 1994: Papers from the 8th International Conference on English Historical Linguistics*. Amsterdam: John Benjamins.

Lorenz, G. (2002) Really worthwhile or not really significant? A corpus-based approach to the delexicalization and grammaticalization of intensifiers in Modern English, in I. Wischer and G. Diewald (eds), *New Reflections on Grammaticalization*. Amsterdam/Philadelphia: John Benjamins, pp. 144–161.

Lowth, R. (1762/1775) *A Short Introduction to English Grammar*. London: Printed by J. Hughs for A. Millar and J. Dodsley.

Lowth, R. (1762/1967) *A Short Introduction to English Grammar*. Menston, England: Scolar Press.

Macaulay, R. (1995) The adverbs of authority. *English World-Wide* 16(1): 37–60.

Macaulay, R. (2007) Pure grammaticalization: The development of a teenage intensifier. *Language Variation and Change* 18(2): 267–283.

Macaulay, R. and Trevelyan, G.D. (1977) *Language, Social Class and Education: A Glasgow Study*. Edinburgh: Edinburgh University Press.

McCafferty, K. (2003) The northern subject rule in Ulster: How Scots, how English? *Language Variation and Change* 15(1): 105–139.

McCafferty, K. (2004) "[T]under storms is verry dangese in this countrey they come in less than a minnits notice ….": The Northern Subject Rule in Southern Irish English. *English World-Wide* 25(1): 51–79.

McCawley, J.D. (1971) Tense and time reference in English, in C.J. Fillmore and D.T. Langendoen (eds), *Studies in Linguistic Semantics*. New York: Holt, Rinehart and Winston, pp. 97–113.

McDavid, R.I., Jr (1969) Dialects: British and American standard and nonstandard, in A.A. Hill (ed.), *Linguistics Today*. New York: Basic Books, pp. 79–88.

McDavid, R.I., Jr (1977) Evidence, in D.L. Shores and C.P. Hines (eds), *Evidence*. Papers in Language Variation. SAMLA-ADS Collection: University of Alabama, pp. 125–132.

McDavid, R.I., Jr (1985) Dialect areas of the Atlantic seaboard, in P. Benes (ed.), *American Speech: 1600 to the Present*. Boston: Boston University, pp. 15–26.

McDavid, R.I., Jr and Davis, L.M. (1972) The dialects of Negro Americans, in M.E. Smith (ed.), *The Dialects of Negro Americans*. Studies in Linguistics in Honor of George L. Trager: The Hague, pp. 303–312.

McKnight, G.H. (1925) Conservatism in American Speech. *American Speech* 1(1): 1–17.

Mair, C. (1997a) Parallel corpora: A real-time approach to the study of language change in progress, in M. Ljung (ed.), *Corpus-based Studies in English: Papers from the Seventeenth International Conference on English Language Research on Computerized Corpora (ICAME 17)*. Amsterdam: Rodopi, pp. 195–209.

Mair, C. (1997b) The spread of the *going-to*-future in written English: A corpus-based investigation into language change in progress, in R. Hickey and S. Puppel (eds), *Language History and Linguistic Modelling*. Berlin: Mouton de Gruyter, pp. 1537–1543.

Mallinson, C. and Wolfram, W. (2002) Dialect accomodation in a bi-ethnic mountain enclave community: more evidence on the development of African American English. *Language in Society* 31(4): 743–775.

Martinet, A. (1952) Function, structure and sound change. *Word* 8(1): 1–32.

Mathis, T. and Yule, G. (1994) Zero quotatives. *Discourse Processes* 18: 63–76.

Matthews, W. (1938) *Cockney Past and Present: A Short History of the Dialect of London*. London: Routledge.

Meechan, M. and Foley, M. (1994) On resolving disagreement: Linguistic theory and variation – There's bridges. *Language Variation and Change* 6(1): 63–85.

Mees, I. (1987) Glottal stops as a prestigious feature of Cardiff English. *English World-Wide* 8: 25–39.

Meillet, A. (1912) *Linguistique historique et linguistique générale*. Paris: Champion.

Meillet, A. (1967) *The Comparative Method in Historical Linguistics*. Paris: Librairie Honoré Champion.

Mencken, H.L. (1961) *The American Language: Supplement II*. New York: Alfred A. Knopf.

Mencken, H.L. (1962) *The American Language*. New York: Alfred A. Knopf.

Méndez-Naya, B. (2003) Intensifiers and grammaticalization: The case of swipe. *English Studies* 84(4): 372–391.

Menner, R.J. (1926) Verbs of the vulgate in their historical relations. *American Speech* 1(4): 230–240.

Meyerhoff, M. (1997) Engendering identities: Pronoun selection as an indicator of salient intergroup identities. *University of Pennsylvania Working Papers in Linguistics* 4(1): 23–38.

Meyerhoff, M. (2009) Replication, transfer, and calquing: Using variation as a tool in the study of language contact. *Language Variation and Change* 21(2): 297–317.

Meyerhoff, M. and Walker, J.A. (2007) The persistence of variation in individual grammars: Copula absence in "urban sojourners" and their stay-at-home peers, Bequia (St Vincent and the Grenadines). *Journal of Sociolinguistics* 11(3): 346–366.

Miller, J. (2000) The perfect in spoken and written English. *Transactions of the Philological Society* 98(2): 323–352.

Milroy, J. (1981) *Regional Accents of English: Belfast*. Belfast: Blackstaff Press.

Milroy, J. (1984) The history of English in the British Isles, in P. Trudgill (ed.), *The History of English in the British Isles*. Cambridge: Cambridge University Press, pp. 5–31.

Milroy, J. (1992) *Linguistic Variation and Change*. Oxford: Blackwell.

Milroy, J. and Milroy, L. (1985) *Authority in Language: Investigating Language Prescription and Standardisation*. London and New York: Routledge & Kegan Paul.

Milroy, J., Milroy, L., and Hartley, S. (1994a) Local and supra-local change in British English: The case of glottalisation. *English World-Wide* 15(1): 1–32.

Milroy, J., Milroy, L., Hartley, S., and Walshaw, D. (1994b) Glottal stops and Tyneside glottalization: Competing patterns of variation and change in British English. *Language Variation and Change* 6(3): 327–357.

Milroy, L. (1980) *Language and Social Networks*. Baltimore: University Park Press.

Milroy, L. (1987) *Observing and Analysing Natural Language*. Oxford: Blackwell.

Milroy, L. and Gordon, M. (2003) *Sociolinguistics: Method and Interpretation*. Malden and Oxford: Blackwell.

Mohanan, K.P. (1986) *The Theory of Lexical Phonology*. Dordrecht: Reidel.

Montgomery, M.B. (1989) Exploring the roots of Appalachian English. *English World-Wide* 10(2): 227–278.

Montgomery, M.B. (1997) Making transatlantic connections between varieties of English. *Journal of English Linguistics* 25(2): 122–141.

Montgomery, M.B. (2001) British and Irish antecedents, in J. Algeo (ed.), *The Cambridge History of the English Language: Volume VI: English in North America*. Cambridge: Cambridge University Press, pp. 86–151.

Montgomery, M.B. and Chapman, C. (1992) The pace of change in Appalachian English, in M. Rissanen, O. Ihalainen, T. Nevalainen, and I. Taavitsainen (eds), *History of Englishes: New methods and Interpretations in Historical Linguistics*. Berlin: Mouton de Gruyter, pp. 624–639.

Montgomery, M.B. and Fuller, J.M. (1996) What was verbal -*s* in 19th-century African American English?, in E.W. Schneider (ed.), *Focus on the USA*. Amsterdam and Philadelphia: John Benjamins, pp. 211–230.

Montgomery, M.B., Fuller, J.M., and DeMarse, S. (1993) "The black men has wives and sweet harts [and third person plural -*s*] jest like the white men": Evidence for verbal -*s* from written documents on 19th-century African American speech. *Language Variation and Change* 5(3): 335–357.

Mufwene, S.S. (1984) Observations on time reference in Jamaican and Guyanese creoles. *English World-Wide* 4(2): 199–229.

Mufwene, S.S. (1994) Theoretical linguistics and variation analysis: Strange bedfellows?, in K. Beals, J. Denton, R. Knippen, *et al.* (eds), *Papers from the Parasession on Language Variation and Linguistic Theory*. Chicago: Chicago Linguistics Society, pp. 202–217.

Mufwene, S.S. (1996a) Creolization and grammaticization: What creolistics could contribute to research on grammaticization, in P. Baker and A. Syea (eds), *Grammaticalization and Creoles*. Westminster: University of Westminster Press, pp. 5–28.

Mufwene, S.S. (1996b) The founder principle in creole genesis. *Diachronica* 13(1): 83–134.

Mufwene, S.S. (1998) The structure of the noun phrase in African-American vernacular English, in S.S. Mufwene, J.R. Rickford, G. Bailey, and J. Baugh (eds), *African-American English: Structure, History and Use*. London and New York: Routledge, pp. 69–81.

Mufwene, S.S. (2000) Some sociohistorical inferences about the development of African-American English, in S. Poplack (ed.), *The English History of African American English*. Oxford & Malden: Blackwell, pp. 233–263.

Mufwene, S.S. (2001a) African-American English, in J. Algeo (ed.), *The Cambridge History of the English Language*. Cambridge: Cambridge University Press, pp. 291–324.

Mufwene, S.S. (2001b) *The Ecology of Language Evolution*. Cambridge: Cambridge University Press.

Mufwene, S.S., Rickford, J.R., Bailey, G., and Baugh, J. (eds) (1998) *African-American English: Structure, History and Use*. London: Routledge.

Murray, J.A.H. (1873) *The Dialect of the Southern Counties of Scotland: Its Pronunciation, Grammar and Historical Relations*. London: Philological Society.

Mustanoja, T.F. (1960) *A Middle English syntax*. Helsinki: Société Néophilologique.

Myhill, J. (1988) The rise of *be* as an aspect marker in Black English Vernacular. *American Speech* 63(4): 304–325.

Myhill, J. (1995) Change and continuity in the functions of the American English modals. *Linguistics* 33: 157–211.

Myhill, J. and Harris, W.A. (1986) The use of verbal *-s* inflection in BEV, in D. Sankoff (ed.), *Diversity and Diachrony*. Amsterdam and Philadelphia: John Benjamins, pp. 25–32.

Nahar Al-Ali, M. and Mahmoud Arafa, H.I. (2010) An experimental sociolinguistic study of language variation in Jordanian Arabic. *Buckingham Journal of Language and Linguistics* 3: 207–230.

Nahkola, K. and Saanilahti, M. (2004) Mapping language changes in real time: A panel study on Finnish. *Language Variation and Change* 16(1): 75–92.

Nehls, D. (1988) Modality and the expression of future time in English. *International Review of Applied Linguistics* 26(4): 295–307.

Neu, H. (1980) Ranking of constraints on /t,d/ deletion in American English: A statistical analysis, in W. Labov. (ed.), *Locating Language in Time and Space*. New York: Academic Press, pp. 37–54.

Nevalainen, T. (1994a) Aspects of adverbial change in Early Modern English, in D. Kastovisky (ed.), *Studies in Early Modern English*. Berlin and New York: Mouton de Gruyter, pp. 243–259.

Nevalainen, T. (1994b) Diachronic issues in English adverb derivation, in U. Fries, G. Tottie, and P. Schneider (eds), *Creating and Using English Language Corpora: Papers from the Fourteenth International Conference on English Language on Computerized Corpora, Zürich 1993*. Amsterdam and Atlanta: Rodopi B.V., pp. 139–147.

Nevalainen, T. (1997) The processes of adverb derivation in Late Middle and Early Modern English, in M. Rissanen, M. Kytö, and K. Heikkonen (eds), *Grammaticalization at Work: Studies of Long Term Developments in English*. Berlin and New York: Mouton de Gruyter, pp. 145–189.

Nevalainen, T. and Raumolin-Brunberg, H. (1996) Sociolinguistics and language history: Studies based on the corpus of Early English correspondence. *Language and Computers: Studies in Practical Linguistics*. Amsterdam and Atlanta: Rodopi, p. 213.

Nevalainen, T. and Raumolin-Brunberg, H. (2003) *Historical Sociolinguistics: Language Change in Tudor and Stuart England*. Harlow, Essex: Pearson Education.

Nevalainen, T., Raumolin-Brunberg, H., and Trudgill, P. (2001) Chapters in the social history of East Anglian English: The case of the third-person singular, in J. Fisiak and P. Trudgill (eds), *East Anglian English*. Cambridge: Boydell & Brewer, pp. 187–204.

Nevalainen, T. and Rissanen, M. (2002) Fairly pretty or pretty fair? On the development and grammaticalization of English downtoners. *Language Sciences* 24: 359–380.

Nokkonen, S. (2006) The semantic variation of NEED TO in four recent British English corpora. *International Journal of Corpus Linguistics* 11(1): 29–71.

Nordberg, B. (1975) Contemporary social variation as a stage in a long-term phonological change, in K.-H. Dahlstedt (ed.), *The Nordic Languages and Modern Linguistics*. Stockholm: Almqvist & Wiksell, pp. 587–608.

Nordberg, B. and Sundgren, E. (1998) On observing real-time language change: A Swedish case study. FUMS Report No. 190 Uppsala: Enhenten för Sociolingvistik, Institutionen för Nordiska Språk vid Uppsala Universitet.

Norrby, C. and Winter, J. (2001) Affiliation in adolescents' use of discourse extenders. *Proceedings of the Australian Linguistic Society*.

Noseworthy, R.G. (1972) Verb usage in Grand Bank. *Regional language studies Newfoundland* 4: 19–24.

Nurmi, A. (1999) *A Social History of Periphrastic Do*. Mémoires de la Société Néophilologique de Helsinki LVI.

Ochs, E. (1992) Indexing gender, in A. Duranti and C. Goodwin (eds), *Rethinking Context: Language as an Interactional Phenomenon*. Cambridge: Cambridge University Press, pp. 335–358.

Onions, C.T. (ed.) (1966) *The Oxford Dictionary of English Etymology*. Oxford: Oxford University Press.

Opdahl, L. (2000a) *LY or Zero Suffix?: A Study in Variation of Dual-form Adverbs in Present-day English*. Volume 1. Frankfurt am Main: Peter Lang.

Opdahl, L. (2000b) *LY or Zero Suffix?: A Study in Variation of Dual-form Adverbs in Present-day English*. Volume 2. Frankfurt am Main: Peter Lang.

Orton, H. (1962) *Survey of English Dialects, Introduction*. Leeds: E.J. Arnold.

Orton, H., Sanderson, S., and Widdowson, J. (1978) *The Linguistic Atlas of England*. London: Croom Helm.

Otheguy, R., Zentella, A.C., and Livert, D. (2007) Language and dialect contact in Spanish in New York: Toward the formation of a speech community. *Language* 83(4): 770–802.

Overstreet, M. (1999) *Whales, Candlelight, and Stuff like that: General Extenders in English Discourse*. New York: Oxford University Press.

Overstreet, M. and Yule, G. (1997) On being inexplicit and stuff in contemporary American English. *Journal of English Linguistics* 25(3): 250–258.

Oxford English Dictionary (OED) (1989) *Oxford English Dictionary*, 2nd edition. Oxford: Oxford University Press.

Palander, M. (2005) Changes in an idiolect from childhood to middle age. *Paper presented at Methods in Dialectology 12*, August 1–5, 2005, Moncton, New Brunswick, Canada.

Palfreyman, D. and al Khalil, M. (2003) "A funky language for teenzz to use": Representing Gulf Arabic in instant messaging. *Journal of Computer-Mediated Communication* 9(1).

Palmer, F.R. (1979) *Modality and the English Modals*. New York: Longman Group.

Paolillo, J. (2002) *Analyzing Linguistic Variation: Statistical Models and Methods*. Stanford, CA: CSLI Publications.

Paolillo, J. (2009) Model vs. software in variation analysis. Presented at a Workshop on Using Statistical Tools to Explain Linguistic Variation. Convenor: S.A. Tagliamonte. *New Ways of Analyzing Variation (NWAV) 38* Ottawa, Ontario, Canada. October 22–25, 2009.

Pargman, S. (2000) Gullah *duh* and periphrastic *do* in English dialects: Another look at the evidence. *Gullah: A Linguistic Legacy of Africans in America – A Conference on the 50th Anniversary of Africanisms in the Gullah Dialect*. Howard University, Washington DC, USA.

Partington, A. (1993) Corpus evidence of language change: The case of intensifiers, in M. Baker, G. Francis, and E. Tognini-bonelli (eds), *Text and Technology: In Honour of John Sinclair*. Amsterdam and Philadelphia: John Benjamins, pp. 177–192.

Partridge, A.C. (1969) *Tudor to Augustan English: A Study in Syntax and Style from Caxton to Johnson*. London: André Deutsch.

Patrick, P.L. (1991) Creoles at the intersection of variable processes: *t-,d*-deletion and past-marking in the Jamaican mesolect. *Language Variation and Change* 3(2): 171–189.

Patrick, P.L. (1999) *Urban Jamaican Creole: Variation in the Mesolect*. Amsterdam and Philadelphia: John Benjamins.

Paunenen, H. (1996) Language change in apparent time and in real time. *Samspel and Variation: Sprakliga studier tillägnade Bengt Nordberg pa 60-ardsdagen*. Uppsala: Uppsala Universitet, Institut för Nordiska Sprak, pp. 375–386.

Payne, A.C. (1980) Factors controlling the acquisition of the Philadelphia dialect by out-of-state children, in W. Labov (ed.), *Locating Language in Time and Space*. New York: Academic Press, pp. 143–178.

Peters, H. (1994) Degree adverbs in early modern English, in D. Kastovsky (ed.), *Studies in Early Modern English*. Berlin and New York: Walter de Gruyter, pp. 269–288.

Petyt, K.M. (1985) *Dialect and Accent in Industrial West Yorkshire*. Amsterdam and Philadelphia: John Bejamins.

Pichler, H. (2009) The functional and social reality of discourse variants in a northern English dialect: *I don't know* and *I don't think* compared. *Intercultural Pragmatics* 6(4): 561–596.

Pierrehumbert, J. (2001) Exemplar dynamics: Word frequency, lenition and contrast, in J. Bybee and P. Hopper (eds), *Frequency and the Emergence of Linguistic Structure*. Amsterdam and Philadelphia: John Benjamins, pp. 137–157.

Pierrehumbert, J. (2002) Word-specific phonetics. *Laboratory Phonology* 7: 101–139.

Pierrehumbert, J. (2003) Probabilistic phonology: Discrimination and robustness, in R. Bod, J. Hay, and S. Jannedy (eds), *Probabilistic Linguistics*. Malden, MA: MIT Press, pp. 97–138.

Pierrehumbert, J. (2006) The next toolkit. *Journal of Phonetics* 34: 516–530.

Pietsch, L. (2005) *Variable Grammars: Verbal Agreement in Northern Dialects of English*. Tübingen: Niemeyer.

Pinheiro, J.C. and Bates, D. (2000) *Mixed-effects Models in S and S-PLUS*. New York: Springer.

Pintzuk, S. (1993) Verb seconding in Old English: Verb movement to Infl. *Linguistic Review* 10: 5–35.

Pintzuk, S. (1995) Variation and change in Old English clause structure. *Language Variation and Change* 7(2): 229–260.

Pintzuk, S. (2003) Variationist approaches to syntactic change, in B.D. Joseph and R.D. Janda (eds), *Handbook of Historical Linguistics*. Malden and Oxford: Blackwell, pp. 509–528.

Pintzuk, S. and Kroch, A. (1989) The rightward movement of complements and adjuncts in the Old English of *Beowulf. Language Variation and Change* 1: 115–143.

Pintzuk, S. and Taylor, A. (2006) The loss of OV order in the History of English, in A. van Kemenade and B. Los (eds), *Blackwell Handbook of the History of English*. Oxford and Malden: Blackwell.

Pitts, W. (1981) Beyond hypercorrection: The use of emphatic *-z* in BEV. *Chicago Linguistic Society* 17: 303–310.

Pitts, W. (1986) Contrastive use of verbal *-z* in slave narratives, in D. Sankoff (ed.), *Diversity and Diachrony*. Amsterdam and Philadelphia: John Benjamins, pp. 73–82.

Podesva, R. (2007) Phonation as a stylistic variable: The use of falsetto in constructing a persona. *Journal of Sociolinguistics* 11: 478–504.

Pooley, R.C. (1933) *Real* and *sure* as adverbs. *American Speech* 8(1): 60–62.

Pope, J., Meyerhoff, M., and Ladd, D.R. (2007) Forty years of language change on Martha's Vineyard. *Language* 83: 615–627.

Poplack, S. (1979) Sobre la elisión y la ambigüedad en el español puertorriqueño: el caso de la (n) verbal. *Boletín de la academia puertorriqueña de la lengua española* 7(2): 129–143.

Poplack, S. (1980a) Deletion and disambiguation in Puerto Rican Spanish. *Language* 56(2): 371–385.

Poplack, S. (1980b) The notion of the plural in Puerto Rican Spanish: Competing constraints on (s) deletion, in W. Labov (ed.), *Locating Language in Time and Space*. New York: Academic Press, pp. 55–67.

Poplack, S. (1981) Mortal phonemes as plural morphemes, in D. Sankoff and H.J. Cedergren (eds), *Mortal Phonemes as Plural Morphemes*. Variation Omnibus: Edmonton, pp. 59–71.

Poplack, S. (1987) Contrasting patterns of code-switching in two communities, in E. Wande, J. Anward, B. Nordberg, *et al.* (eds), *Aspects of Bilingualism: Proceedings from the Fourth Nordic Symposium on Bilingualism, 1984*. Uppsala, pp. 51–76.

Poplack, S. (1989) The care and handling of a megacorpus: The Ottawa-Hull French Project, in R. Fasold and D. Schiffrin (eds), *Language Change and Variation*. Amsterdam and Philadelphia: John Benjamins, pp. 411–444.

Poplack, S. (1992) The inherent variability of the French subjunctive, in C. Lauefer and T.A. Morgan (eds), *Theoretical Studies in Romance Linguistics*. Amsterdam and Philadelphia: John Benjamins, pp. 235–263.

Poplack, S. (ed.) (2000) *The English History of African American English*. Malden: Blackwell.

Poplack, S. (2007) Introduction, in J. Beal, K. Corrigan, and H. Moisel (eds), *Using Unconventional Digital Language Corpora: Volume 1: Synchronic Corpora*. Basingstoke, Hampshire: Palgrave Macmillan.

Poplack, S. and Meechan, M. (1995) Patterns of language mixture: Nominal structure in Wolof-French and Fongbe-French bilingual discourse, in L. Milroy and P. Muysken (eds), *One Speaker, Two Languages*. Cambridge: Cambridge University Press, pp. 199–232.

Poplack, S. and Meechan, M. (eds) (1998a) *Instant Loans, Easy Conditions: The Productivity of Bilingual Borrowing; Special Issue, International Journal of Bilingualism*. London: Kingston Press.

Poplack, S. and Meechan, M. (1998b) Introduction: How languages fit together in codemixing. Instant loans, easy conditions: The productivity of bilingual borrowing; Special Issue. *Journal of Bilingualism* 2(2): 127–138.

Poplack, S. and Sankoff, D. (1987) The Philadelphia story in the Spanish Caribbean. *American Speech* 62(4): 291–314.

Poplack, S. and Tagliamonte, S.A. (1989a) There's no tense like the present: Verbal -*s* inflection in early Black English. *Language Variation and Change* 1(1): 47–84.

Poplack, S. and Tagliamonte, S.A. (1989b) There's no tense like the present: Verbal -*s* inflection in early Black English [reprint]. *York Papers in Linguistics* 13: 237–278.

Poplack, S. and Tagliamonte, S.A. (1991a) African American English in the diaspora: Evidence from old-line Nova Scotians. *Language Variation and Change* 3(3): 301–339.

Poplack, S. and Tagliamonte, S.A. (1991b) There's no tense like the present: Verbal -*s* inflection in early Black English, in G. Bailey, N. Maynor, and P. Cukor-Avila (eds), *The Emergence of Black English: Text and Commentary*. Amsterdam and Philadelphia: John Benjamins, pp. 275–324.

Poplack, S. and Tagliamonte, S.A. (1999a) Nothing in context: Variation, grammaticisation and past time marking in Nigerian Pidgin English, in J.C. Conde-Silvestre and J.M. Hernandez-Campoy (eds), *Cuadernos de Filologia 8, Inglesea: Variation and Linguistic Change in English: Diachronic and Synchronic Studies*. Secretariado de Publiaciones e Intercambia Cientifico, Universidad de Murcia, pp. 193–217.

Poplack, S. and Tagliamonte, S.A. (1999b) The grammaticalization of *going to* in (African American) English. *Language Variation and Change* 11(3): 315–342.

Poplack, S. and Tagliamonte, S.A. (2001) *African American English in the Diaspora: Tense and Aspect*. Malden: Blackwell.

Poplack, S. and Tagliamonte, S.A. (2004) Back to the present: verbal -*s* in the (African American) English diaspora, in R. Hickey (ed.), *Legacies of Colonial English*. Cambridge: Cambridge University Press, pp. 203–223.

Poplack, S. and Tagliamonte, S.A. (2005) Back to the present: Verbal -s in the (African American) diaspora, in R. Hickey (ed.), *Transported Dialects: The Legacies of Non-standard Colonial English*. Cambridge: Cambridge University Press, pp. 203–223.

Poplack, S. and Turpin, D. (1999) Does the FUTUR have a future in (Canadian) French? *Probus* 11: 133–164.

Poutsma, H. (1926 [1904]) *A Grammar of Late Modern English*. Groningen: P. Noordhoff.

Preston, D. (1985) The Li'l Abner syndrome: written representations of speech. *American Speech* 60(4): 328–336.

Pulgram, E. (1968) A socio-linguistic view of innovation: -*ly* and -*wise*. *Word* 24: 380–391.

Quirk, R., Greenbaum, S., Leech, G., and Svartvik, J. (1972) *A Grammar of Contemporary English*. New York: Harcourt Brace Jovanovich.

Quirk, R., Greenbaum, S., Leech, G., and Svartvik, J. (1985) *A Comprehensive Grammar of the English Language*. New York: Longman.

Ramisch, H. (1989) *The Variation of English in Guernsey/Channel Islands*. Frankfurt am Main: Verlag Peter Lang.

Rand, D. and Sankoff, D. (1990) GoldVarb: A variable rule application for the Macintosh. Montreal, Canada: Centre de recherches mathématiques, Université de Montréal.

Randall, N. (2002) *Lingo Online: A Report of the Language of the Keyboard Generation.* University of Waterloo, pp. 1–45.

Raumolin-Brunberg, H. (2005) Language change in adulthood: Historical letters as evidence. *European Journal of English Studies* 9(1): 37–51.

Raumolin-Brunberg, H. (2009) Lifespan changes in the language of three early modern gentlemen, in M. Nevala, A. Nurmi, and M. Palander-Collin (eds), *The Language of Daily Life in England (1450–1800).* Amsterdam and Philadelphia: John Benjamins, pp. 165–196.

Raymond, W.D., Dautricourt, R., and Hume, E. (2006) Word-internal /t,d/ deletion in spontaneous speech: Modeling the effects of extra-linguistic, lexical and phonological factors. *Language Variation and Change* 18(1): 55–97.

Rice, J. (1765) *An Introduction to the Art of Reading with Energy and Propriety.* London: J. & R. Tonson.

Rice, W. (1927) Go slow-Proceed slowly. *American Speech* September: 489–491.

Rickford, J.R. (1977) The question of prior creolization of Black English, in A. Valdman (ed.), *The Question of Prior Creolization of Black English.* Pidgin and Creole Linguistics: Bloomington, pp. 190–221.

Rickford, J.R. (1986a) Some principles for the study of Black and White speech in the south, in M.B. Montgomery and G. Bailey (eds), *Language Variety in the South.* Alabama: University of Alabama Press, pp. 38–62.

Rickford, J.R. (1986b) Social contact and linguistic diffusion: Hiberno-English and new world Black English. *Language* 62(2): 245–289.

Rickford, J.R. (1987) *Dimensions of a Creole Continuum: History, Texts, and Linguistic Analysis of Guyanese Creole.* Stanford, CA: Stanford University Press.

Rickford, J.R. (1990a) *Grammatical Variation and Divergence in Vernacular Black English.* The Hague: Mouton.

Rickford, J.R. (1990b) Number delimitation in Gullah: A response to Mufwene. *American Speech* 65(2): 148–163.

Rickford, J.R. (1991) Contemporary source of comparison as a critical window on the Afro-American linguistic past, in W.F. Edwards and D. Winford (eds), *Verb Phrase Patterns in Black English and Creole.* Detroit: Wayne State University Press, pp. 302–323.

Rickford, J.R. (1996) Copula Variability in Jamaican Creole and African American Vernacular English: A reanalysis of DeCamp's texts, in J. Baugh, C. Faegin, G. Guy, and D. Schiffrin (eds), *A Festschrift for William Labov.* Amsterdam and Philadelphia: John Benjamins.

Rickford, J.R. (1997) Unequal partnership: Sociolinguistics and the African American speech community. *Language in Society* 26(2): 161–197.

Rickford, J.R. (1998) The creole origins of African-American vernacular English: Evidence from copula absence, in S. Mufwene, J.R. Rickford, G. Bailey, and J. Baugh (eds), *African-American English: Structure, History, and Use.* London: Routledge, pp. 154–200.

Rickford, J.R. (1999) *African American Vernacular English.* Malden and Oxford: Blackwell.

Rickford, J.R. and Blake, R. (1990) Copula contraction and absence in Barbadian English, Samaná English and Vernacular Black English, in K. Hall, J.-P. Koenig, M. Meacham, *et al.* (eds), *Copula Contraction and Absence in Barbadian English, Samaná English and Vernacular Black English.* Proceedings of the Sixteenth Annual Meeting of the Berkeley Linguistic Society, Berkeley, pp. 257–268.

Rickford, J.R., Wasow, T., Zwicky, A., and Buschtaller, I. (2007) Intensive and quotative *all*: Something old; something new. *American Speech* 82(1): 3–31.

Rissanen, M. (1985) Periphrastic *do* in affirmative statements in Early American English. *Journal of English Linguistics* 18(2): 163–183.

Rissanen, M. (1991) On the history of *that*/zero as object clause links in English, in K. Aijmer and B. Altenberg (eds), *English Corpus Linguistics: Studies in Honour of Jan Svartvik.* London and New York: Longman, pp. 272–289.

Rissanen, M. (1999) *Syntax,* in R. Lass (ed.), *The Cambridge History of the English Language. Volume 3. 1476–1776.* Cambridge: Cambridge University Press.

Roberts, P.A. (1976) Hypercorrection as systematic variation. *The Society for Caribbean Linguistics*, August 1976. Guyana.

Robertson, S. (1954) *The Development of Modern English, Revised by Frederic G. Cassidy*. Englewood Cliffs, N.J.: Prentice-Hall.

Robson, B. (1975) Jenepher revisited: adult language change, in R.W. Fasold and R.W. Shuy (eds), *Analyzing Variation in Language: Papers from the Second Colloquium on New Ways of Analysing Variation*. Washington, DC: Georgetown University Press, pp. 283–290.

Rohdenburg, G. (1998) Clausal complementation and cognitive complexity in English, in F.-W. Neumann and S. Schülting (eds), *Anglistentag Erfurt*. Trier: Wissenschaftlicher Verlag, pp. 101–112.

Romaine, S. (1984) On the problem of syntactic variation and pragmatic meaning in sociolinguistic theory. *Folia Linguistica* 18: 409–439.

Romaine, S. (1994) *Language in Society*. Oxford: Oxford University Press.

Romaine, S. and Lange, D. (1991) The use of *like* as a marker of reported speech and thought: A case of grammaticalization in progress. *American Speech* 66(3): 227–279.

Ross, C.N. (1984) Adverbial change: Implications for a theory of lexical change, in D. Testen, V. Mishra, and J. Drogo (eds), *Papers from the Parasession on Lexical Semantics*. Chicago: Chicago Linguistic Society, pp. 243–249.

Rousseau, P. and Sankoff, D. (1978a) Advances in variable rule methodology, in D. Sankoff (ed.), *Linguistic Variation: Models and Methods*. New York: Academic Press, pp. 57–69.

Rousseau, P. and Sankoff, D. (1978b) A solution to the problem of grouping speakers, in D. Sankoff (ed.), *Linguistic Variation: Models and Methods*. New York: Academic Press, pp. 97–117.

Roy, Joseph (submitted) Extending variable rule analysis: Equivalence constraints and statistical significance in variationist sociolinguistics. *Cahiers Linguistiques d'Ottawa*.

Royster, J.F. and Steadman, J.M. (1923/1968) The "going-to" future. *Manly Anniversary Studies in Languages and Literature*. Freeport, NY: Books for Libraries Press, pp. 394–403.

Sankoff, D. (ed.) (1978a) *Linguistic Variation: Models and Methods*. New York: Academic Press.

Sankoff, D. (1978b) Probability and linguistic variation. *Synthèse* 37: 217–238.

Sankoff, D. (1988a) Sociolinguistics and syntactic variation, in F.J. Newmeyer (ed.), *Linguistics: The Cambridge Survey*. Cambridge: Cambridge University Press, pp. 140–161.

Sankoff, D. (1988b) Problems of representativeness, in U. Ammon, N. Dittmar and K.J. Mattheier (eds), *Sociolinguistics: An International Handbook of the Science of Language and Society*. Berlin: Walter de Gruyter, pp. 899–903.

Sankoff, D. (1988c) Variable rules, in U. Ammon, N. Dittmar, and K.J. Mattheier (eds), *Sociolinguistics: An International Handbook of the Science of Language and Society Vol. 2*. Berlin: Walter de Gruyter, pp. 984–997.

Sankoff, D. and Laberge, S. (1978) The linguistic market and the statistical explanation of variability, in D. Sankoff (ed.), *The Linguistic Market and the Statistical Explanation of Variability*. Linguistic Variation: Models and Methods: New York, pp. 239–250.

Sankoff, D. and Labov, W. (1979) On the uses of variable rules. *Language in Society* 8(2): 189–222.

Sankoff, D. and Rousseau, P. (1979) Categorical contexts and variable rules, in S. Jacobson (ed.), *Papers from the Scandinavian Symposium on Syntactic Variation, Stockholm, May 18–19, 1979*. Stockholm: Almqvist & Wiksell, pp. 7–22.

Sankoff, D., Tagliamonte, S.A., and Smith, E. (2005) Goldvarb X. Department of Linguistics, University of Toronto, Toronto, Canada. http://individual.utoronto.ca/tagliamonte/Goldvarb/GV_index.htm.

Sankoff, D. and Thibault, P. (1981) Weak complementarity: Tense and aspect in Montreal French, in B.B. Johns and D.R. Strong (eds), *Syntactic Change*. Ann Arbor: University of Michigan Press, pp. 205–216.

Sankoff, G. (1973) Above and beyond phonology in variable rules, in C.-J.N. Bailey and R.W. Shuy (eds), *New Ways of Analyzing Variation in English*. Washington, DC: Georgetown University Press, pp. 44–62.

Sankoff, G. (1974) A quantitative paradigm for the study of communicative competence, in R. Bauman and J. Sherzer (eds), *Explorations in the Ethnography of Speaking*. Cambridge: Cambridge University Press, pp. 18–49.

Sankoff, G. (1977) Creolization and syntactic change in new Guinea Tok Pisin, in M. Sanches and M. Blount (eds), *Sociocultural Dimensions of Language Change*. New York: Academic Press, pp. 119–130.

Sankoff, G. (1979) The genesis of a language, in K.C. Hill (ed.), *The Genesis of a Language*. Ann Arbor, MI: Karoma, pp. 23–47.

Sankoff, G. (1980a) The origins of syntax in discourse: A case study of Tok Pisin relatives, in G. Sankoff (ed.), *The Social Life of Language*. Philadelphia: University of Pennsylvania Press, pp. 211–255.

Sankoff, G. (ed.) (1980b) *The Social Life of Language*. Philadelphia: University of Pennsylvania Press.

Sankoff, G. (1990) The grammaticalization of tense and aspect in Tok Pisin and Sranan. *Language Variation and Change* 2(3): 295–312.

Sankoff, G. (1991) Using the future to explain the past, in F. Byrne and T. Huebner (eds), *Using the Future to Explain the Past*. Development and Structures of Creole Languages: Amsterdam and Philadelphia. 61–74.

Sankoff, G. (2004) Adolescents, young adults and the critical period: two case studies from "Seven Up," in C. Fought (ed.), *Sociolinguistic Variation: Critical Reflections*. Oxford and New York: Oxford University Press, pp. 121–139.

Sankoff, G. (2005) Cross-sectional and longitudinal studies in sociolinguistics, in U. Ammon, N. Dittmar, K.J. Mattheier, and P. Trudgill (eds), *International Handbook of the Science of Language and Society*. Berlin: Mouton de Gruyter, pp. 1003–1013.

Sankoff, G. (2006) Apparent time and real time. *Elsevier Encyclopedia of Language and Linguistics*. Amsterdam: Elsevier, pp. 110–116.

Sankoff, G. and Blondeau, H. (2007) Language change across the lifespan: /r/ in Montreal French. *Language* 83(3): 560–588.

Sankoff, G., Blondeau, H., and Charity, A. (2001) Individual roles in a real-time change: Montreal (r→R) 1947–1995, in R. van Hout and H. van de Velde (eds), *R-atics: Sociolinguistic, Phonetic and Phonological Characteristics of /r/*. Brussels, Belgium: Université Libre de Bruxelles, Institute des Langues Vivantes et de Phonétique, pp. 141–157.

Sankoff, G. and Brown, P. (1976) The origins of syntax in discourse. *Language* 52(3): 631–666.

Sankoff, G. and Cedergren, H. (1973) Some results of a sociolinguistic study of Montreal French, in R. Darnell (ed.), *Linguistic Diversity in Canadian Society*. Edmonton: Linguistic Research, pp. 61–87.

Sankoff, G. and Laberge, S. (1973) On the acquisition of native speakers by a language. *Kivung* 6(1): 32–47.

Santa Ana, O.A. (1996) Sonority and syllable structure in Chicano English. *Language Variation and Change* 8(1): 63–90.

Santorini, B. (1993) The rate of phrase structure change in the history of Yiddish. *Language Variation and Change* 5(3): 257–283.

Sapir, E. (1921) *Language: An Introduction to the Study of Speech*. New York: Harcourt, Brace.

Scherre, M. and Naro, A. (1991) Marking in discourse: "Birds of a feather." *Language Variation and Change* 3(1): 23–32.

Scherre, M. and Naro, A. (1992) The serial effect on internal and external variables. *Language Variation and Change* 4(1): 1–13.

Schiano, D.J., Chen, C.P., Ginsberg, J., *et al.* (2002) Teen use of messaging media. *Proceedings of ACM Conference on Human Factors in Computing Systems*, pp. 594–595.

Schibsbye, K. (1965) *A Modern English Grammar*. London: Oxford University Press.

Schiffrin, D. (1981) Tense variation in narrative. *Language* 57(1): 45–62.

Schilling-Estes, N. and Wolfram, W. (1994) Convergent explanation and alternative regularization patterns: *Were/weren't* leveling in a vernacular English variety. *Language Variation and Change* 6(3): 273–302.

Schneider, E.W. (1983) The origin of verbal *-s* in Black English. *American Speech* 58(2): 99–113.

Schneider, E.W. (1989) *American Earlier Black English.* Tuscaloosa, AL: The University of Alabama Press.

Schneider, E.W. (2004) The English dialect heritage of the southern United States, in R. Hickey (ed.), *Transported Dialects: The Legacy of Non-standard Colonial English.* Cambridge: Cambridge University Press.

Schreier, D. (2002) Past *be* in Tristan da Cunha: The rise and fall of categoricality in language change. *American Speech* 77(1): 70–99.

Schwenter, S. (1994a) "Hot news" and the grammaticalization of perfects. *Linguistics* 6: 995–1028.

Schwenter, S. (1994b) The grammaticalization of an anterior in progress: Evidence from a peninsular Spanish dialect. *Studies in Language* 18(1): 71–111.

Schwenter, S. and Torres Cacoullos, R. (2008) Defaults and indeterminacy in temporal grammatialization: The "perfect" road to perfective. *Language Variation and Change* 20(1): 1–39.

Scur, G.S. (1974) On the typology of some peculiarities of the perfect in the English of Tristan da Cunha. *Orbis* 23(2): 392–396.

Shepherd, S.C. (1983) From deontic to epistemic: An analysis of modals in the history of English, creoles, and language acquisition, in A. Ahlqvist (ed.), *Papers from the Fifth International Conference on Historical Linguistics.* Amsterdam: John Benjamins, pp. 316–323.

Shnukal, A. (1978) *A Sociolingusitic Study of Australian English: Phonological and Syntactic Variation in Cessnock, NSW.* Georgetown.

Shopen, T. (1978) Research on variable (ING) in Canberra. *Talanya* 5: 42–52.

Siemund, P., Davydova, J., Hilbert, M., and Pietsch, L. (2010) Comparing varieties of English: Problems and perspectives, in P. Siemund (ed.), *Linguistic Universals and Language Variation.* Berlin/New York: Mouton de Gruyter.

Sigley, R. (2003) The importance of interaction effects. *Language Variation and Change* 15(2): 227–253.

Silverstein, M. (1976) Shifters, linguistic categories and cultural description, in K.H. Basso and H.A. Selby (eds), *Meaning in Anthropology.* Albuquerque: University of Mexico Press, pp. 11–55.

Silverstein, M. (1979) Language structure and linguistic ideology, in P.R. Cyne, W.F. Hanks and C.L. Hofbauer (eds), *The Elements: A Parasession on Linguisic Units and Levels.* Chicago: Chicago Linguistic Society, pp. 193–247.

Silverstein, M. (1985) Language and the culture of gender; at the intersection of structure, usage and ideology, in R.M. and R.J. Parmentier (eds), *Semiotic Mediation: Sociocultural and Psychological Perspectives.* Orlando, FL: Academic Press, pp. 219–259.

Silverstein, M. (2003) Indexical order and the dialectics of sociolinguistic life. *Language and Communication* 23(2): 193–229.

Sinclair, J. (1992) Trust the text: the implications are daunting, in M. Davies and L. Ravelli (eds), *Advances in Systemic Linguistics: Recent Theory and Practice.* London: Pinter, pp. 5–19.

Singler, J.V. (1991) Copula variation in Liberian Settler English and American Black English, in W.F. Edwards and D. Winford (eds), *Verb Phrase Patterns in Black English and Creole.* Detroit: Wayne State University Press, pp. 129–164.

Singler, J.V. (1997) On the genesis, evolution, and diversity of African American English: Evidence from verbal *-s* in the Liberian Settler English of Sinoe. *Society for Pidgin and Creole Linguistics.* London, UK.

Singler, J.V. (2001) Why you can't do a Varbrul study of quotatives and what such a study can show us. *University of Pennsylvania Working Papers in Linguistics* 7: 257–278.

Sisam, K. (ed.) (1970) *Fourteenth Century Verse and Prose.* Oxford: Clarendon Press.

Smith, J. (2001) *Ye o na hear that kind o' things*: Negative *do* in Buckie. *English World-Wide* 21(2): 231–259.

Smith, J., Durham, M., and Fortune, L. (2007) Community, caregiver and child in the acquisition of variation in a Scottish dialect. *Language Variation and Change* 19(1): 63–99.

Smith, J., Durham, M., and Fortune, L. (2009) Universal and dialect-specific pathways of acquisition: Caregivers, children, and t/d deletion. *Language Variation and Change* 21(1): 69–95.

Smith, J. and Tagliamonte, S.A. (1998) *"We* were *all thegither ... I think we* was *all thegither"*: *was* regularization in Buckie English. *World Englishes* 17(2): 105–126.

Stein, D. (1990) *The Semantics of Syntactic Change*. Berlin and New York: Mouton de Gruyter.

Stein, D. (1991) Semantic aspects of syntactic change, in D. Kastovsky (ed.), *Historical English Syntax*. Berlin: Mouton de Gruyter, pp. 355–366.

Stenström, A.-B. (1999) He was really gormless – She's bloody crap: Girls, boys and intensifiers, in H. Hasselgård and S. Okesfjell (eds), *Out of Corpora: Studies in Honour of Stig Johansson*. Amsterdam and Atlanta: Rodopi, pp. 69–78.

Stenström, A.-B., Andersen, G., and Hasund, I.K. (2002) *Trends in Teenage Talk: Corpus Compilation, Analysis and Findings*. Amsterdam: John Benjamins.

Stoffel, C. (1901) *Intensives and Down-toners*. Heiderberg: Carl Winter's Universitätsbunchhandlung.

Storms, G. (1966) That-clauses in Modern English. *English Studies* 47: 249–270.

Strang, B.M.H. (1970) *A History of English*. London: Methuen & Co.

Stuart-Smith, J. (1999a) Glasgow: accent and voice quality, in P. Foulkes and G. Docherty (eds), *Glasgow: Accent and Voice Quality*. Urban Voices: London.

Stuart-Smith, J. (1999b) Glottals past and present: a study of T-glottaling in Glaswegian. *Leeds Studies in English* 30: 181–204.

Stuart-Smith, J. (2010) Television is also a factor in language change: Evidence from an urban dialect. University of Glasgow, Glasgow, Scotland. Manuscript.

Stubbe, M. and Holmes, J. (1995) You know, eh and other "exasperating expressions": an analysis of social and stylistic variation in the use of pragmatic devices in a sample of New Zealand English. *Language and Communication* 15: 63–88.

Sundgren, E. (2009) The varying influence of social and linguistic factors on language stability and change: The case of Eskilstuna. *Language Variation and Change* 21(1): 97–133.

Tagliamonte, S.A. (1991) *A Matter of Time: Past Temporal Reference Verbal Structures in Samaná English and the Ex-slave Recordings*. PhD dissertation, University of Ottawa.

Tagliamonte, S.A. (1996) Has it ever been PERFECT? Uncovering the grammar of early Black English. *York Papers in Linguistics* 17: 351–396.

Tagliamonte, S.A. (1996–1998) Roots of identity: Variation and grammaticization in contemporary British English. Economic and Social Sciences Research Council (ESRC) of Great Britain. Reference #R000221842.

Tagliamonte, S.A. (1997) Obsolescence in the English Perfect? Evidence from Samaná English. *American Speech* 72(1): 33–68.

Tagliamonte, S.A. (1998a) Modelling an emergent grammar: Past temporal reference in St Kitts Creole in the 1780s, in P. Baker, A. Bruyn, and N. Shrimpton (eds), *St Kitts and the Atlantic Creoles: The Texts of Samuel Augustus Mathews in Perspective*. Westminster: University of Westminster Press, pp. 201–236.

Tagliamonte, S.A. (1998b) *Was/were* variation across the generations: View from the city of York. *Language Variation and Change* 10(2): 153–191.

Tagliamonte, S.A. (1999–2001) Grammatical variation and change in British English: Perspectives from York. Economic and Social Sciences Research Council (ESRC) of Great Britain. Research Grant R000238287.

Tagliamonte, S.A. (2000) The grammaticalization of the PRESENT PERFECT in English: Tracks of change and continuity in a linguistic enclave, in O. Fischer, A. Rosenbach, and D. Stein (eds), *Pathways of Change – Grammaticalization in English*. Berlin: Mouton de Gruyter, pp. 329–354.

Tagliamonte, S.A. (2000–2001) Vernacular roots: A database of British dialects. Research Grant B/RG/ AN 6093/APN11081. Arts and Humanities Research Board of the United Kingdom (AHRB).

Tagliamonte, S.A. (2001a) *Come/came* variation in English dialects. *American Speech* 76(1): 42–61.

Tagliamonte, S.A. (2001b) "Have to, gotta, must": Grammaticalisation, variation, and specialisation. Paper presented at corpus research on grammaticalization in English. Växjö, Sweden, April 21, 2001.

Tagliamonte, S.A. (2001–2003) Back to the roots: The legacy of British dialects. Research Grant. Economic and Social Research Council of the United Kingdom (ESRC) #R000239097.

Tagliamonte, S.A. (2002) Comparative sociolinguistics, in J.K. Chambers, P. Trudgill, and N. Schilling-Estes (eds), *Handbook of Language Variation and Change*. Malden and Oxford: Blackwell, pp. 729–763.

Tagliamonte, S.A. (2003) "Every place has a different toll": Determinants of grammatical variation in cross-variety perspective, in G. Rhodenberg and B. Mondorf (eds), *Determinants of Grammatical Variation in English*. Berlin and New York: Mouton de Gruyter, pp. 531–554.

Tagliamonte, S.A. (2003–2006) Linguistic changes in Canada entering the 21st century. Research Grant. Social Sciences and Humanities Research Council of Canada (SSHRC) #410-2003-0005.

Tagliamonte, S.A. (2004a) *Have to, gotta, must*: Grammaticalization, variation and specialization in English deontic modality, in H. Lindquist and C. Mair (eds), *Corpus Research on Grammaticalization in English*. Amsterdam: John Benjamins, pp. 37–55.

Tagliamonte, S.A. (2004b) Someth[in]'s go[ing] on!: Variable *ing* at ground zero, in B.-L. Gunnarsson, L. Bergström, G. Eklund, *et al.* (eds), *Language Variation in Europe: Papers from the Second International Conference on Language Variation in Europe, ICLAVE 2*. Uppsala, Sweden: Dept. of Scandinavian Languages, Uppsala University, June 12–14, 2003.

Tagliamonte, S.A. (2005) *So* who? *Like* how? *Just* what? Discourse markers in the conversations of young Canadians. *Journal of Pragmatics, Special Issue, Guest Editors, A.B. Stenström and K. Aijmer*, 37(11): 1896–1915.

Tagliamonte, S.A. (2006a) *Analysing Sociolinguistic Variation*. Cambridge: Cambridge University Press.

Tagliamonte, S.A. (2006b) "So cool, right?": Canadian English entering the 21st century. *Canadian English in a Global Context. Theme Issue of Canadian Journal of Linguistics* 51(2/3): 309–331.

Tagliamonte, S.A. (2006c) Sometimes there's universals; sometimes there aren't: A comparative sociolinguistic perspective on "default singulars." Presented at World Englishes: Vernacular Universals vs. Contact-Induced Change: An International Symposium. University of Joensuu Research Station, Mekrijärvi, Finland. September 1–3, 2006.

Tagliamonte, S.A. (2007) Quantitative analysis, in R. Bayley and L. Ceil (eds), *Sociolinguistic Variation: Theory, Methods, and Applications, Dedicated to Walt Wolfram*. Cambridge: Cambridge University Press.

Tagliamonte, S. A. (2008a) From adolescence to adulthood: A panel study of "Clara." *Symposium on Linguistic Variation Across the Lifespan*, Columbus, Ohio, USA, May 2–3, 2008.

Tagliamonte, S.A. (2008b) *So* different and *pretty* cool! Recycling intensifiers in Canadian English. *Special issue of English Language and Linguistics, Intensifiers, Guest Editor Belén Mendez-Naya* 12(2): 361–394.

Tagliamonte, S.A. (2009) *Be like*: the new quotative of English, in N. Coupland and A. Jaworski (eds), *The New Sociolinguistics Reader*. New York: Palgrave/Macmillan, pp. 75–91.

Tagliamonte, S.A. (2010–2013) Transmission and diffusion in Canadian English. Standard Research Grant #410-101-129. Social Sciences and Humanities Research Council of Canada (SSHRCC).

Tagliamonte, S.A. (forthcoming) *Roots of English: Exploring the History of Dialects*. Cambridge: Cambridge University Press.

Tagliamonte, S.A. and Baayen, R.H. (forthcoming) Models, forests and trees of York English: *Was/were* variation as a case study for statistical practice. *Language Variation and Change*.

Tagliamonte, S.A. and D'Arcy, A. (2004a) *He's like; She's like*: The quotative system in Canadian youth. *Journal of Sociolinguistics* 8(4): 493–514.

Tagliamonte, S.A. and D'Arcy, A. (2004b) Mom *said*, and my daughter*'s like:* Tracking the quotative system through the generations. *New Ways of Analyzing Variation (NWAV)* 33. Ann Arbor, MI.

Tagliamonte, S.A. and D'Arcy, A. (2005) When people say, " I was like": The quotative system in Canadian youth. *Pennsylvania Working Papers in Linguistics 10(2): Selected Papers from NWAV 32*. Philadelphia: University of Pennsylvania Press.

Tagliamonte, S.A. and D'Arcy, A. (2007a) Frequency and variation in the community grammar: Tracking a new change through the generations. *Language Variation and Change* 19(2): 1–19.

Tagliamonte, S.A. and D'Arcy, A. (2007b) The modals of obligation/necessity in Canadian perspective. *English World-Wide* 28(1): 47–87.

Tagliamonte, S.A. and D'Arcy, A. (2009) Peaks beyond phonology: Adolescence, incrementation, and language change. *Language* 85(1): 58–108.

Tagliamonte, S.A. and Denis, D. (2008a) From community to community: Transmission and diffusion in Canadian English. *NWAV 37 (New Ways of Analyzing Variation)*. Houston, Texas, November 6–9, 2008.

Tagliamonte, S.A. and Denis, D. (2008b) Linguistic ruin? LOL! Instant messaging, teen language and linguistic change. *American Speech* 83(1): 3–34.

Tagliamonte, S.A. and Denis, D. (2010) The *stuff* of change: General extenders in Toronto, Canada. *Journal of English Linguistics* 38(4): 335–368.

Tagliamonte, S.A. and Hudson, R. (1999) Be like et al. beyond America: The quotative system in British and Canadian youth. *Journal of Sociolinguistics* 3(2): 147–172.

Tagliamonte, S.A. and Ito, R. (2002) Think *really* different: Continuity and specialization in the English adverbs. *Journal of Sociolinguistics* 6(2): 236–266.

Tagliamonte, S.A. and Lawrence, H. (2000) "I used to dance, but I don't dance now": The HABITUAL PAST in contemporary English. *Journal of English Linguistics* 28(4): 324–353.

Tagliamonte, S.A. and Poplack, S. (1988) How Black English *past* got to the present: Evidence from Samaná. *Language in Society* 17(4): 513–533.

Tagliamonte, S.A. and Poplack, S. (1993) The zero-marked verb: Testing the creole hypothesis. *Journal of Pidgin and Creole Languages* 8(2): 171–206.

Tagliamonte, S.A. and Poplack, S. (1995) Obsolescence in the English perfect: Evidence from the perfect in African Nova Scotian English. *American Dialect Society*. Chicago, Illinois, December 1995.

Tagliamonte, S.A., Poplack, S., and Eze, E. (1997) Pluralization patterns in Nigerian Pidgin English. *Journal of Pidgin and Creole Languages* 12(1): 103–129.

Tagliamonte, S.A. and Roberts, C. (2005) So cool, so weird, so innovative! The use of intensifiers in the television series "Friends." *American Speech* 80(3): 280–300.

Tagliamonte, S.A. and Smith, J. (2000) Old *was*; new ecology: Viewing English through the sociolinguistic filter, in S. Poplack (ed.), *The English History of African American English*. Oxford and Malden: Blackwell, pp. 141–171.

Tagliamonte, S.A. and Smith, J. (2005) No momentary fancy! The zero "complementizer" in English dialects. *English Language and Linguistics* 9(2): 1–21.

Tagliamonte, S.A. and Smith, J. (2006) Layering, change and a twist of fate: Deontic modality in dialects of English. *Diachronica* 23(2): 341–380.

Tagliamonte, S.A., Smith, J., and Lawrence, H. (2005) No taming the vernacular! Insights from the relatives in northern Britain. *Language Variation and Change* 17(2): 75–112.

Tagliamonte, S.A. and Temple, R. (2005) New perspectives on an ol' variable: (t,d) in British English. *Language Variation and Change* 17(3): 281–302.

Tagliamonte, S.A. and Uscher, D. (2009) Queer youth in the speech community: A comparative analysis of variation and change. *New Ways of Analysing Variation [NWAV]*. Ottawa, Canada.

Taglicht, J. (1970) The genesis of the conventional rules of "shall" and "will." *English Studies* 51(3): 193–213.

Taylor, A. (1994) The change from SOV to SVO in Ancient Greek. *Language Variation and Change* 6(1): 1–37.

Team, R Development Core (2007) *R: A Language and Environment for Statistical Computing*. Vienna, Austria: R Foundation for Statistical Computing. http://www.R-project.org.

Thibault, P. (1986) Grammaticalisation des pronoms de la troisième personne en français parlé à Montréal, in D. Sankoff (ed.), *Grammaticalisation des Pronoms de la Troisième Personne en Français Parlé à Montréal*. Diversity and Diachrony: Amsterdam and Philadelphia, pp. 301–310.

Thibault, P. (1991) Semantic overlaps of French modal expressions. *Language Variation and Change* 3(2): 191–222.

Thibault, P. and Daveluy, M. (1989) Quelques traces du passage du temps dans le parler des Montréalais. *Language Variation and Change* 1(1): 19–45.

Thompson, S. and Mulac, A. (1991a) The discourse conditions for the use of the complementizer *that* in conversational English. *Journal of Pragmatics* 15: 237–251.

Thompson, S. and Mulac, A. (1991b) A quantitative perspective on the grammaticization of epistemic parentheticals in English, in E.C. Traugott and B. Heine (eds), *Approaches to Grammaticalization*. Amsterdam and Philadelphia: John Benjamins, pp. 313–329.

Thorndike, E.L. (1943) Derivation ratios. *Language* 19: 27–37.

Thurlow, C. (2002) Generation Txt? Exposing the sociolinguistics of young people's text-messaging. *Discourse Analysis Online*. http://extra.shu.ac.uk/daol/index.html (accessed April 4, 2011).

Tidholm, H. (1979) *The Dialect of Egton in North Yorkshire*. Goteborgn: Bokmaskine.

Timberlake, A. (1977) Reanalysis and actualization in syntactic change, in C. Li (ed.), *Mechanisms of Syntactic Change*. Austin, TX: University of Texas, pp. 141–177.

Torbet, B. (2001) Tracing Native American language history through consonant cluster reduction: The case of Lumbee English. *American Speech* 76(4): 361–387.

Torres, L. (1989) Mood selection among New York Puerto Ricans. *International Journal of the Sociology of Language* 79: 67–77.

Torres-Cacoullos, R. (1999) Variation and grammaticalization in progressives: Spanish *-ndo* constructions. *Studies in Language* 23(1): 25–59.

Torres-Cacoullos, R. (2003) Bare English-origin nouns in Spanish: Rates, constraints, and discourse functions. *Language Variation and Change* 15(2): 289–328.

Torres-Cacoullos, R. and Walker, J.A. (2009a) On the persistence of grammar in discourse formulas: a variationist study of *that*. *Linguistics* 47(1): 1–43.

Torres-Cacoullos, R. and Walker, J.A. (2009b) The present of the English Future: Grammatical variation and collocations in discourse. *Language* 85(2): 321–354.

Tottie, G. and Harvie, D. (2000) It's all relative: Relativization strategies in early African American English, in S. Poplack (ed.), *The English History of African American English*. Oxford and Malden: Blackwell, pp. 198–230.

Traugott, E.C. (1972) *A History of English Syntax: A Transformational Approach to the History of English Sentence Structures*. New York: Holt, Rinehart & Winston.

Traugott, E.C. (1982) From propositional to textual to expressive meanings: Some semantic-pragmatic aspects of grammaticalization, in W.P. Lehmann and Y. Malkiel (eds), *From Propositional to Textual to Expressive Meanings: Some Semantic-Pragmatic Aspects of Grammaticalization*. Perspectives in Historical Linguistics: Amsterdam and Philadelphia, pp. 245–271.

Traugott, E.C. (1989) From less to more situated in language, in S. Adamson, V. Law, N. Vincent, and S. Wright (eds), *Papers from the Fifth International Conference on English Historical Linguistics*. Amsterdam and Philadelphia: John Benjamins, pp. 497–518.

Traugott, E.C. (1999) Why *must* is not *moot*. *Fourteenth International Conference on Historical Linguistics*. Vancouver, British Columbia.

Traugott, E.C. (2010) The persistence of linguistic contexts over time: Implications for corpus research. *ICAME*. Plenary Address, Giessen, Germany, 26–30 May 2010.

Traugott, E.C. and Dasher, R.B. (2002) *Regularity in Semantic Change*. Cambridge: Cambridge University Press.

Traugott, E.C. and Heine, B. (1991a) *Approaches to Grammaticalization, Vol. I*. Amsterdam and Philadelphia: John Benjamins.

Traugott, E.C. and Heine, B. (1991b) *Approaches to Grammaticalization, Vol. II*. Amsterdam and Philadelphia: John Benjamins.

Trudgill, P.J. (1972a) Linguistic change and diffusion. *Language in Society* 3(2): 229–252.

Trudgill, P.J. (1972b) Sex, covert prestige, and linguistic change in urban British English. *Language in Society* 1(2): 179–195.

Trudgill, P.J. (1974a) Linguistic change and diffusion: Description and explanation in sociolinguistic dialect geography. *Language in Society* 3: 215–246.

Trudgill, P.J. (1974b) *The Social Differentiation of English in Norwich*. Cambridge: University of Cambridge Press.

Trudgill, P.J. (ed.) (1978) *Sociolinguistic Patterns in British English*. London: Edward Arnold.

Trudgill, P.J. (1983) *On Dialect: Social and Geographical Perspectives*. Oxford: Basil Blackwell.

Trudgill, P.J. (1984) *Language in the British Isles*. Cambridge: Cambridge University Press.

Trudgill, P.J. (1986) *Dialects in Contact*. Oxford: Blackwell.

Trudgill, P.J. (1988) Norwich revisited: Recent linguistic changes in an English urban dialect. *English World-Wide* 9: 33–49.

Trudgill, P.J. (1990) *The Dialects of England*. Oxford: Blackwell.

Trudgill, P.J. (1996) Language contact and inherent variability: The absence of hypercorrection in East Anglian present-tense verb forms, in J. Klemola, M. Kytö, and M. Rissanen (eds), *Speech Past and Present*. Frankfurt: Peter Lang, pp. 412–425.

Trudgill, P.J. (1998) Third-person singular zero: AAVE, East Anglian dialects, and Spanish persecution in the Low Countries. *Linguistica Historica* 18(1–2): 139–148.

Trudgill, P.J. (1999) New-dialect formation and dedialectalisation: embryonic and vestigal variants. *Journal of English Linguistics* 27(4): 319–327.

Trudgill, P.J. (2000) *Sociolinguistics: An Introduction to Language in Society*. London: Penguin.

Trudgill, P.J. (2003) *The Norfolk Dialect*. Cromer, England: Poppyland Publishing.

Trudgill, P.J. (2004) *New-dialect Formation: The Inevitability of Colonial Englishes*. Oxford: Oxford University Press.

Underhill, R. (1988) Like is like, focus. *American Speech* 63(3): 234–246.

van de Velde, H. and van Hout, R. (1998) Dangerous aggregations. A case study of Dutch (n) deletion, in C. Paradis *et al.* (eds), *Papers in Sociolinguistics*. Québec: Nuits Blanches, pp. 137–147.

Van Draat, P. F. (1910) *Rhythm in English Prose*. Heidelberg: Carl Winter's Universitätsbuchhandlung.

van Gelderen, E. (2004) *Grammaticalization as Economy*. Amsterdam and Philadelphia: John Benjamins.

van Herk, G. (2008) The present perfect in early African American correspondence. *English World-Wide* 29(1): 45–69.

van Herk, G. and Walker, J. (2000) "Since my last, things has Takeing quite an other aspect": Verbal *-s* in Early Liberian Settler English. *American Dialect Society Annual Meeting*. Chicago.

van Herk, G. and Walker, J.A. (2005) S marks the spot? Regional variation and early African American correspondence. *Language Variation and Change* 17(1): 113–131.

Vanneck, G. (1955) The colloquial preterite in Modern American English. *Word* 14: 237–242.

Viereck, W. (1988) Invariant *be* in an unnoticed source of American Early Black English. *American Speech* 63(4): 291–303.

Visser, F.T. (1966) *An Historical Syntax of the English Language: Part Two: Syntactical Units with One Verb (continued)*. Leiden, the Netherlands: E.J. Brill.

Visser, F.T. (1963–1973) *An Historical Syntax of the English Language*. Leiden: E.J. Brill.

Visser, F.T. (1970) *An Historical Syntax of the English Language*. Leiden: E.J. Brill.

Wagner, S. (2007) Unstressed periphrastic *do* – from Southwest England to Newfoundland? *English World-Wide* 28(3): 249–278.

Wagner, S. Evans and Sankoff, G. (forthcoming) Age grading in the Montréal French inflected future. *Language Variation and Change* 23(3).

Waksler, R. (2001) A new *all* in conversation. *American Speech* 76(2): 128–138.

Wald, B. and Shopen, T. (1981) A researcher's guide to the sociolinguistic variable (ING), in T. Shopen and J.M. Williams (eds), *Style and Variables in English*. Cambridge, MA: Winthrop, pp. 219–249.

Wales, M.L. (1983) The semantic distribution of "aller + infinitive" and the future tense in spoken French. *General Linguistics* 23(1): 19–28.

Walker, J.A. (2000) Rephrasing the copula: Contracted and zero copula in Early African American English, in S. Poplack (ed.), *The English History of African American English*. Oxford and Malden: Blackwell, pp. 35–72.

Walker, J.A. (2010) *Variation in Linguistic Systems*. London and New York: Routledge.

Walker, J.A. and Hoffman, M. (2010) Ethnolects and the city: Ethnic orientation and linguistic variation in Toronto English. *Language Variation and Change* 22(1): 37–67.

Wardaugh, R. (2002) *An Introduction to Sociolinguistics*. Malden and Oxford: Blackwell.

Warner, A. (1993) *English Auxiliaries: Structure and History*. Cambridge: Cambridge University Press.

Warner, A. (2004) What Drove Do?, in J.K. Christian, S. Shorobin, and J. Smith (eds), *New Perspectives on English Historical Linguistics*. Amsterdam and Philadelphia: John Benjamins, pp. 229–242.

Warner, A. (2005) Why *Do* Dove: Evidenced for register variation in Early Modern English Negatives. *Language Variation and Change* 17: 257–280.

Warner, A. (2007) Parameters of variation between verb–subject and subject–verb order in Late Middle English. *English Language and Linguistics* 11(1): 81–111.

Waters, C. (2011) *Social and Linguistic Correlates of Adverb Variability in English*. Department of Linguistics, University of Toronto. PhD dissertation.

Watt, D. (2002) "I don't speak with a Geordie accent, I speak, like, the Northern accent": Contact-induced levelling in the Tynesdie vowel system. *Journal of Sociolinguistics* 6(1): 22–63.

Weiner, J. and Labov, W. (1983) Constraints on the agentless passive. *Journal of Linguistics* 19(1): 29–58.

Weinreich, U. (1953/1968) *Languages in Contact*. The Hague: Mouton.

Weinreich, U., Labov, W., and Herzog, M. (1968) Empirical foundations for a theory of language change, in W.P. Lehmann and Y. Malkiel (eds), *Directions for Historical Linguistics*. Austin: University of Texas Press, pp. 95–188.

Wells, J.C. (1982) *Accents of English*. Cambridge: Cambridge University Press.

Werry, C.C. (1996) Linguistic and interactional features of internet relay chat, in S.C. Herring (ed.), *Computer-Mediated Communication*. Amsterdam and Philadelphia: John Benjamins, pp. 47–63.

Wilson, A. (2005) Modal verbs in written Indian English: A quantitative and comparative analysis of the Kolhapur corpus using correspondence analysis. *ICAME Journal* 29: 151–170.

Winford, D. (1992) Back to the past: The BEV/Creole connection revisited. *Language Variation and Change* 4: 311–357.

Winford, D. (1993) Variability in the use of perfect *have* in Trinidadian English: A problem of categorial and semantic mismatch. *Language Variation and Change* 5(2): 141–188.

Winford, D. (1997) On the origins of African American Vernacular English – A creolist perspective. Part I: Sociohistorical background. *Diachronica* 14(2): 305–344.

Winford, D. (1998) On the origins of African American Vernacular English – A creolist perspective. Part 2: Linguistic features. *Diachronica* 15(1): 99–154.

Winter, J. (2002) Discourse quotatives in Australian English: adolescents performing voices. *Australian Journal of Linguistics* 22(1): 5–21.

Winter, J. and Norrby, C. (2000) "Set marking tags" and stuff, in J. Henderson (ed.), *Proceedings of the 1999 Conference of the Australian Linguistic Society*.

Wolfram, W. (1969) *A Sociolinguistic Description of Detroit Negro Speech*. Washington, DC: Center for Applied Linguistics.

Wolfram, W. (1971) Black-White speech differences revisited, in W. Wolfram and N.S. Clarke (eds), *Black-White Speech Relationships*: Washington, DC: Center for Applied Linguistics, pp. 139–161.

Wolfram, W. (1974) The relationship of White Southern speech to Vernacular Black English. *Language* 50(3): 498–527.

Wolfram, W. (1993) Identifying and interpreting variables, in D. Preston (ed.), *American Dialect Research*. Amsterdam and Philadelphia: John Benjamins, pp. 193–221.

Wolfram, W. (1999) Principles of donor dialect attribution. *Methods X*. Memorial University of Newfoundland, St John's, Newfoundland, Canada.

Wolfram, W. (2000) Issues in reconstructing earlier African-American English. *World Englishes* 19(1): 39–58.

Wolfram, W. and Beckett, D. (2000) The role of the individual and the group in earlier African American English. *American Speech* 75: 3–33.

Wolfram, W. and Fasold, R. (1974) *The Study of Social Dialects in American English*. Englewood Cliffs, NJ: Prentice-Hall.

Wolfram, W. and Schilling-Estes, N. (1995) Moribund dialects and the endangerment canon: The case of the Ocracoke Brogue. *Language* 71(4): 696–721.

Wolfram, W. and Schilling-Estes, N. (1998) *American English*. Malden and Oxford: Blackwell.

Wolfram, W. and Schilling-Estes, N. (2004) Remnant dialects in the coastal United States, in R. Hickey (ed.), *Legacies of Colonial English: A Study of Transported Dialects*. Cambridge: Cambridge University Press.

Wolfram, W. and Schilling-Estes, N. (2006) *American English*, 2nd edn. Malden and Oxford: Blackwell.

Wolfram, W. and Sellers, J. (1999) Ethnolinguistic marking of past *be* in Lumbee vernacular English. *Journal of English Linguistics* 27: 94–114.

Wolfram, W. and Thomas, E. (2002) *The Development of African American English: Evidence from an Isolated Community*. Malden: Blackwell.

Wolfram, W., Thomas, E., and Green, E. (1997) Reconsidering the development of AAVE: Insights from isolated African American speakers. *NWAVE 26*. Québec City, Canada.

Wolfson, N. (1979) The conversational historical present alternation. *Language* 55(1): 168–182.

Wolfson, N. (1981) Tense-switching in narrative. *Language and Style* 14(3): 226–231.

Wright, J. (1898–1905) *The English Dialect Grammar*. Oxford: Clarendon Press.

Wright, L. (2001) Third-person singular present-tense *-s, -th* and zero, 1575–1648. *American Speech* 77(2): 242–263.

Wright, L. (2002) Third person plural present tense markers in London prisoners' depositions, 1562–1623. *American Speech* 77(2): 242–263.

Wright, L. (2004) The language of transported Londoners: third-person-singular present-tense markers in depositions from Virginia and the Bermudas, 1607–1625, in R. Hickey (ed.), *Legacies of Colonial English: Studies in Transported Dialects*. Cambridge: Cambridge University Press, pp. 158–171.

Wyld, H.C. (1927) *A Short History of English*. London: John Murray.

Yates, S.J. (1996) Oral and written linguistic aspects of computer conferencing: A corpus based study, in S.C. Herring (ed.), *Computer-Mediated Communication*. Amsterdam and Philadelphia: John Benjamins, pp. 29–46.

Young, R. and Bayley, R. (1996) VARBRUL analysis for second language acquisition research, in R. Bayley and D.R. Preston (eds), *Second Language Acquisition and Linguistic Variation*. Amsterdam: John Benjamins, pp. 253–306.

Youssef, V. (1993) Marking solidarity across the Trinidad speech community: the use of *an ting* in medical counselling to break down power differentials. *Discourse and Society* 4(3): 291–306.

Zandvoort, R.W. (1932) On the perfect of experience. *English Studies* 14(1): 11–20.

Zandvoort, R.W. (1969) *A Handbook of English Grammar*. London: Longmans, Green & Co.

Zettersten, A. (1969) *The English of Tristan da Cunha*. Lund: Gleerup.

Zhang, Q. (2005) A Chinese yuppie in Beijing: Phonological variation and the construction of a new professional identity. *Language in Society* 34 (431–466).

Subject Index

The general index is followed on p. 400 by an index of linguistic variables.

Variationist Sociolinguistics: Change, Observation, Interpretation, First Edition. Sali A. Tagliamonte.
© 2012 Sali A. Tagliamonte. Published 2012 by Blackwell Publishing Ltd.

Index of Linguistic Variables

Variationist Sociolinguistics: Change, Observation, Interpretation, First Edition. Sali A. Tagliamonte.
© 2012 Sali A. Tagliamonte. Published 2012 by Blackwell Publishing Ltd.

Index compiled by Michael A. Ritter